A BIBLIOGRAPHY FOR
ADLERIAN PSYCHOLOGY

A BIBLIOGRAPHY FOR ADLERIAN PSYCHOLOGY

HAROLD H. MOSAK
Alfred Adler Institute of Chicago

and

BIRDIE MOSAK

HEMISPHERE PUBLISHING
CORPORATION
Washington, D.C.

A HALSTED PRESS BOOK
JOHN WILEY & SONS
New York London Sydney Toronto

Hemisphere Publishing Corporation
1025 Vermont Ave., N.W., Washington, D.C. 20005

Distributed solely by Halsted Press, a Division of John Wiley & Sons, Inc., New York.

Library of Congress Cataloging in Publication Data

Mosak, Harold H.
    A bibliography for Adlerian psychology.

    1. Psychoanalysis—Bibliography.   2. Adler,
Alfred, 1870–1937—Bibliography. I. Mosak, Birdie,
joint author. II. Title. [DNLM: 1. Psychiatry—
Bibliography. 2. Psychological theory—Bibliography.
ZWM100 M894b]
Z7204.P8M67   016.6168'917   74-26938
ISBN 0-470-61852-3

Printed in the United States of America

TO
RUDOLF DREIKURS
and
ERWIN O. KRAUSZ
our friends and teachers
Mitmenschen

CONTENTS

FOREWORD

By ROBERT L. POWERS, PRESIDENT
By ROBERT L. POWERS, PRESIDENT
AMERICAN SOCIETY OF ADLERIAN PSYCHOLOGY

During many years in which he has been actively working both as a practicing clinician and as a lecturer and teacher, Harold Mosak has also been engaged in searching the literature for references to Alfred Adler and to Adler's Individual Psychology. With the continuing assistance of his wife, Birdie, these references were painstakingly filed, cross-indexed, and finally collected into a remarkable research tool, namely this bibliography.

One of the tests of any scientific theory is whether and to what extent it has served as a stimulus to further thought, study, and research. For many years, popular wisdom in the social sciences assumed that Adler's theories of personality, psychopathology, and psychotherapy had failed this test. This assumption was probably based on a cultural bias during a time in which an understanding of human behavior was being sought in reductionist explanations of behavior. Couched in the language of causal determinism, such explanations were supported by analogies drawn largely from the nineteenth century's fascination with the discovery of steam mechanics and its practical applications. Pressures, drives, and forces were hypothesized to account for all human thought, feelings, and aspiration.

The present work assures us that Adler's Individual Psychology has, in fact, passed the test of fostering further study. There have been, and there continue to be, many who, following Adler, have been pursuing a better understanding of human being in human terms. It is as if they have been acknowledging that the strictures forbidding anthropomorphism in animal studies and in the physical sciences were valid beyond the reach of their usual applications. Converting these strictures, they have assumed, means that mechanomorphism and zoomorphism were equally illicit in efforts designed to account for the uniquely human behaviors of human beings. Adler recognized the human striving toward the goals of individual success and social harmony as the subjective experience of an overall evolutionary development. This has enabled him and his followers to consider human cognitive processes as the work of a psychic organ fitting human beings for survival and for the continuing struggle toward a better adaptation. Standing in contrast to theories which reduce the cognitive function to the task of rationalizing more elementary processes as a kind of epi-phenomenon, this approach encourages respect for the human reality and, further, encourages those who would foster the development of self-respect and mutual respect in every area of our common human tasks.

There is no way to estimate or to anticipate the value which this bibliography may have to future scholarship. Its cost can be computed more precisely. Since scholarly apparatus has limited commercial value, and since the publication of such a book as this is an extremely costly undertaking, the American Society of Adlerian Psychology has entered into a cooperative arrangement with the authors and the publisher to make its appearance possible. As the current president of that Society, it pleases me on behalf of all our members to salute a past president, Harold Mosak, and his most valued colleague and collaborator, Birdie Mosak, for the work they have done in creating this bibliography, and for the gift they have given of themselves thereby, in dedication to the future of Individual Psychology and of the human community.

By BERNARD H. SHULMAN, PRESIDENT
INTERNATIONAL ASSOCIATION OF INDIVIDUAL PSYCHOLOGY

The rapid expansion of interest in Individual Psychology, the school of thought founded by Alfred Adler, is not surprising to those who have been watching the developing trends in psychiatry, psychology, and education for the past two decades. For many years the publications of Adlerians were overlooked or considered too simplistic and fit only for popular consumption. With increasing interest in an interpersonal, teleologic, social field, and holistic orientation, the insights and statements of Individual Psychologists suddenly assumed a new importance. In one publication after another, Adler was being "rediscovered." Instead of being classified merely as a deviant disciple of Freud, Adler was now recognized as the founder of a sophisticated theory of psychology. Adlerian personality theory, psychodynamics, psychotherapy, pedagogy, group methods, and community mental health became fields of their own as Adlerians continued to expand the horizons of their discipline. Always practice-oriented, Adlerians filled their literature with case reports and descriptions of technique. Research came later, when research methods finally began to catch up with Adlerian theory.

Until the Ansbachers reached the psychologists with their writings; until Dreikurs reached teachers, parents, and counselors with his demonstrations and his books, Adlerian literature was often neglected by others. An unfortunate result was that this literature was often unknown even to Adlerians. It was disheartening to see therapists claiming to develop new techniques and new theories without even knowing that Adlerians had already passed that way many years earlier. That is one reason this current volume is so sorely needed. In addition, however, there has been no previous extensive bibliography for the constantly growing group of students and scholars of Individual Psychology. That lack is now corrected. This volume is as near to a complete bibliography as is possible.

Harold and Birdie Mosak have assembled and indexed this collection of nearly 10,000 entries with loving care. The work itself is a milestone in Adlerian writings. The amount of labor involved in such a process is huge. The utility of the compendium is immeasurable. It will be useful to scholars and students of Individual Psychology for all the years to come. For their patient labor and endurance, the authors deserve the thanks of all Individual Psychologists: those who will use the work now and those who will do so in days to come.

PREFACE

The nearly 10,000 entries contained in this volume represent six years of work—searching out references, filing, typing, copyediting, and proofreading. We addressed ourselves to the task because with the increasing interest in Adlerian psychology, many graduate students and researchers wrote us requesting assistance in locating references in their areas of interest. It soon became apparent that the problem was not one of location, but that the inquirers were unaware of the vast, rich Adlerian literature which dates to the beginning of the century.

While initially we embarked on a search whose goal (a fine Adlerian concept) was the compilation of a bibliography *of* Adlerian psychology, we shifted our direction in mid-course to collecting a bibliography *for* Adlerians. One purpose (another fine Adlerian term) was to place Adlerian psychology in context. The researcher in, or student of, Early Recollections, say, would do well to read Freud's "Screen Memories." Second, we felt that the student or researcher might be interested in comparing and contrasting other viewpoints with those of Adlerian psychology. Third, it became obvious that portions of the non-Adlerian literature parelleled that produced by Adlerians, tested, and in many instances confirmed Adlerian hypotheses. Often this occurred without awareness on the part of the writers of the Adlerian antecedents of their investigations. For these reasons we have included (1) Adlerian references by Adlerian writers, (2) references to topics of Adlerian interest written by non-Adlerians, and (3) writings by Adlerians on non-Adlerian topics. Whether the labels, Adlerian and non-Adlerian, are always appropriate is susceptible to question and debate. We have, for example, included the writings of such Adlerians as Viktor Frankl, Fritz Künkel, and Erwin Wexberg, who subsequently moved away from Adlerian psychology. Similarly, we have listed the writings of such writers as Albert Ellis and Wilhelm Stekel, who were originally non-Adlerians but later in their careers accepted membership in their respective national Adlerian societies.

While the bulk of the work was done by the authors, many others checked references and did some of the typing. To each for his or her contribution goes our heartfelt gratitude for lightening our burden. We especially thank Dr. Rosa Abraira, Ms. Juliet Cavadas (Greece), Ms. Susan Feldman, Dr. Eva Ferguson, Dr. Robin Gushurst, Ms. Habavli (Israel), Dr. Richard Kopp, Dr. Carol LeFevre, Ms. Aronette Lopin, Ms. Rosemary Moran, Mr. Ira Moscowitz, Dr. Shirley Plessner, Mr. Paul Rom (England), Dr. Herbert Schaffer (France), Ms. Gail Shandler, Ms. Blanche Stein, Ms. Janet Terner, and Ms. Harriet Weichman, for demonstrating their social interest through their contributions to this effort. Last, we thank our children, Derin, Lisa, and Neal, for the hours spent at libraries, for typing, for alphabetizing, and above all for their patient understanding of their parents through the long period when it sometimes appeared to all of us that we had undertaken an interminable task.

We are especially grateful to the American Society of Adlerian Psychology for its moral support and to individual members of that Society for their financial support of this undertaking. The issuance of this volume was possible only through their concrete demonstration of social interest. Although the list of contributors is too large to print, we wish to acknowledge specifically the contributions of Dr. Joseph Meiers, a long-time friend of both the Mosaks and Adlerian psychology, and of Dr. William Statton in memory of his wife, Vicki Stoltz Statton, whose recent death deprived both the Mosaks and the Society of a warm friend and coworker.

While every effort has been exerted to ensure the completeness and accuracy of each entry, in a few instances it was not possible to secure completeness. This was especially true with some foreign journals and books that were not available to us. In a task of this magnitude, the inevitability of error at every stage of collection, typing, and printing exists. We would appreciate your calling these errors to our attention. One last word, however. As S. O. Lesser cautions in a review of another bibliography, ". . . it is as ill advised to be critical of bibliographers as it is to make disparaging comments about den mothers, scoutmasters and workers for community improvement. Discourage them from their tasks and they may turn from their socially useful activities to ones they enjoy more."

Harold H. Mosak
Birdie Mosak

HOW TO USE THIS BIBLIOGRAPHY

1. All entries are listed alphabetically by author.
2. Where multiple authorship exists, the article is listed under each author. This permits a complete listing for each author under his or her name heading, sparing the reader the necessity of looking for references to a single author in different places in the volume.
3. Most Adlerian journals are listed by acronym. A list of these acronyms follows.

   AJIP   American Journal of Individual Psychology
   BISFPA   Bulletin d'Information, Société Française de Psychologie Adlérienne
   BSFPA   Bulletin, Société Française de Psychologie Adlérienne
   IJIP   International Journal of Individual Psychology
   IP   Individual Psychologist
   IPB   Individual Psychology Bulletin
   IPMP   Individual Psychology Medical Pamphlets
   IPN   Individual Psychology News
   IPNL   Individual Psychology Newsletter
   IPP   Individual Psychology Pamphlets
   IZIP   Internationale Zeitschrift für Individualpsychologie
   JIP   Journal of Individual Psychology
   MNWIP   Mededelingenblad von de Nederlandse Werkgemeenschap voor Individual-psychologie
   OSIPNL   Oregon Society of Individual Psychology Newsletter
   ZIP   Zeitschrift für Individualpsychologie

4. Where the reference to a chapter in a book appears, if the book itself is also listed, the complete reference for the book appears only under the citation for the book.
5. With respect to a review of a book or article, if the book or article is also listed, the complete reference for the book or article appears only under its citation.
6. Translations appear in alphabetical order under their translated titles.
7. Titles referred to in the index are signified by letter of the alphabet and by number within the alphabetical listing. In cases of multiple authorship, reference is made only to the first alphabetical listing.

A BIBLIOGRAPHY FOR
ADLERIAN PSYCHOLOGY

A

1 **A.** Review of H. von Hattenberg, Die Typik der neurotischen Krise. *Der Nervenarzt*, [   ], 1(12), [   ]. In *IZIP*, 1929, 7(1), 68–69.

2 **A. B.** Zum problem der Selbstblockade durch männlichen Protest. *IZIP*, 1925, 3(6), 298–307.

3 **Abe, K.** The significance of birth order and age difference between siblings as observed in drawings of pre-kindergarten children. *Folia psychiat. neurol. Japoniat.*, 1964, 17, 315–325 (with K. Tsiji & H. Suzuki).

4 **Abelson, R. P.** & others (Eds.). *Theories of cognitive consistency: A sourcebook.* Chicago: Rand McNally, 1968.

5 **Abernathy, Ethel M.** Further data on personality and family position. *J. Psychol.*, 1940, 10, 303–307.

6 **Abramovitz, Christine V.** Birth order, sensitivity to socialization and student activism. *J. couns. Psychol.*, 1971, 18, 184–185 (with S. I. Abramovitz).

7 **Abramovitz, S. I.** Birth order, sensitivity to socialization and student activism. *J. couns. Psychol.*, 1971, 18, 184–185 (with Christine V. Abramovitz).

8 **Abt, L. E.** (Ed.). *Acting out: Theoretical and clinical aspects.* New York: Grune & Stratton, 1965 (with S. L. Weissman).

9 ———— (Ed.). *Progress in clinical psychology.* New York: Grune & Stratton, 1956 (with D. Brower).

10 ———— (Ed.). *Progress in clinical psychology.* New York: Grune & Stratton, 1963 (with B. F. Reiss).

11 **Acker, Mary.** The Obscure Figures Test: An instrument for measuring "cognitive innovation". *Percep. mot. Skills*, 1965, 21, 815–821.

12 **Ackerknecht, E. A.** Review of H. F. Ellenberger, *The discovery of the unconscious.* In *JIP*, 1971, 27(2), 216–220.

13 **Ackerknecht, Lucy.** Adlerian marathons. *IPNL*, 1972, 21(1), 5–7.

14 ————. Le coin du rire. *IPNL*, 1968, 18(7–8, Whole No. 204–205). P. 57.

15 ————. Involvement as leitmotif of a psychotherapeutic practice. *IP*, 1972, 9(1), 8–12.

16 ————. *"Life-meanings" of future teachers: A value study.* New York: Phil. Libr., 1964.

17 **Ackerknecht, Lucy.** Marathon, Adlerian style. *JIP*, 1971, 27(2), 176–180.

18 ————. Marathons als Beitrag zur individualpsychologischer Behandlung. *Prakt. Psychol.*, 1972, 26(7–8), 183–187.

19 ————. Portrait. *IPNL*, 1971, 20(6), 111.

20 ————. Roleplaying of embarrassing situations. *Grp. Psychother.*, 1967, 20, 39–42.

21 ————. Die Rolle der Eltern in der Erziehungsberatung. *Schule u. Psychol.*, 1968, 10, 289–295.

22 ————. Some political predictions of an early anthropologist. *Amer. Anthropol.*, 1950, 52(2), 287–291.

23 ————. Wilhelm Muehlman, Geschichte der Anthropologie. *Arch. Int. Hist. Sci.*, 1950, 3(13), 986–990.

24 **Ackerman, N. W.** Interpersonal disturbances in the family. *Psychiat.*, 1954, 17, 359–368.

25 ————. *Psychodynamics of family life.* New York: Basic Books, 1958.

26 **Ackerson, L.** Inferiority attitudes and their correlations among children examined in a behavior clinic. *J. genet. Psychol.*, 1943, 62, 85–96.

27 **Adams, P. L.** Puberty as a biosocial turning point. *Psychosom.*, 1969, 10, 343–349.

28 **Adams, S. T.** Birth order, family size and extra-sensory perception. *Brit. J. soc. clin. Psychol.*, 1966, 5, 150–152 (with C. E. Green & M. E. Eastman).

29 **Adams, Suzanne.** *The shaping of personality: Text and readings for a social learning view.* Englewood Cliffs, N. J.: Prentice-Hall, 1967 (with Georgia Babledalis).

30 **Adesso, V. J.** What do you want to be when you grow up? *Child & Fam.*, 1966, 5, 29–31 (with D. N. Lombardi).

31 **Adler, Alexandra.** Adler, A. In *Collier's Encyclopedia.* Vol. 1. New York: Crowell-Collier, 1962.

32 ————. Adler, Alfred. In *International encyclopedia of the social sciences.* New York: Crowell, 1968. Pp. 57–61.

33 ————. Alfred Adler's viewpoint in child guidance. In E. Harms (Ed.), *Handbook of child guidance.* Pp. 707–722. Also in P. L. Harriman (Ed.), *Encyclopedia of psychology.*

34 ————. Aus dem Grenzgebiet von Neurose und Psychose. *IZIP*, 1935, 13(3), 141–146.

35 ————. Autobiographical glimpses (II). *IPNL*, 1966, 16(11–12, Whole No. 184–185). P. 42.

36 **Adler, Alexandra.** Beitrag zur Lehre vom Phantomgliede. *Monatschr. Psychiat. Neurol.*, 1930, 76, 80–86 (with H. Hoff).

37 ———. Chronische Quecksilbervergiftung, auf medikamentöser Grundlage, bei einem Syphilophoben. *Wien. klin. Wchnschr.*, 1929, 42, 1666–1668.

38 ———. Clinical results with Elsberg's Olfactory Test. *Arch. Neurol. Psychiat.*, 1939, 40, 147–150.

39 ———. The concept of compensation and over-compensation in Alfred Adler's and Kurt Goldstein's theories. *JIP*, 1959, 15, 79–82.

40 ———. Concerning the border-line between neurosis and psychosis. *IJIP*, 1935, 1(4), 34–39.

41 ———. Course and outcome of visual agnosia. *J. nerv. ment. Dis.*, 1950, 111, 41–51.

42 ———. Diagnosis and treatment of borderline psychoses. *Med. Circle Bull.*, 1959, 6, 10–11.

43 ———. Different stages in the development of mental diffculties. *IPN*, 1941, 1(4), 1–3.

44 ———. Disintegration and restoration of optic recognition in visual agnosia. *Arch. Neurol. Psychiat.*, 1944, 51, 243–259.

45 ———. Emil Froeschels (1884–1972). *JIP*, 1972, 28, 112–113.

46 ———. Equine encephalomyelitis in man. *Amer. J. Pathol.*, 1941, 27, 407–410.

47 ———. Erziehungsberatung and child guidance (with E. Papanek). In V. E. Frankl, et al. (Eds.), *Handbuch der Neurosenlehre und Psychotherapie*. Pp. 569–583.

48 ———. Die extrapyramidalen Syndrome: Das Resultat einer Interferenz zwischen dem "alten" und "neuen" motorischen System. In H. Urban (Ed.), *Festschrift.* Innsbruck: , 1949. Pp. 43–54.

49 ———. Folie à deux in identical twins treated with electroshock therapy. *J. nerv. ment. Dis.*, 1946, 103, 181–186 (with W. W. Magruder).

50 ———. Foreword to A. Nikelly (Ed.), *Techniques for behavior change.* P. ix.

51 ———. Gehäuftes Auftreten von Polyneuritiden unter dem Bild der Landry'schen Paralyse. *Deutsche med. Wchnschr.*, 1929, 55, 1880–1882 (with H. Hoff).

52 ———. Goals, procedures and achievements in clinic psychotherapy. *J. Mt. Sinai Hosp.*, 1951, 18, 221–227 (with S. R. Lehrman, M. Schatner & F. Spiegel).

53 **Adler, Alexandra.** Group therapy and Individual Psychology. *Exp. Med. Surg.*, 1962, 20, 5–9.

54 ———. *Guiding human misfits.* New York: Phil. Libr., 1938, 1948; New York: Macmillan, 1938, 1950; London: Faber & Faber, 1948; Bristol, U.K.: Western Printing Services, 1948.

55 ———. Hans Hoff (1897–1969). *JIP*, 1969, 25, 262.

56 ———. Historical review. *AJIP*, 1952, 10, 80–82.

57 ———. Individualpsychologie. In V. E. Frankl et al. (Eds.), *Handbuch der Neurosenlehre und Psychotherapie*. Pp. 221–268.

58 ———. Individual Psychology: Adlerian school. In P. L. Harriman (Ed.), *Encyclopedia of psychology*. Pp. 262–269.

59 ———. The Individual Psychology of the alcoholic patient. *J. crim. Psychopathol.*, 1941, 3, 74–77.

60 ———. Influence of early experiences upon the formation of the personality. *Nerv. Child,* 1947, 6, 318–320; *IZIP*, 1948, 17(2), 57–60.

61 ———. Influence of the social level on psychiatric symptomatology of childhood difficulties. *Proc. Inst. Child Res. Clin. Woods Schs.*, 1945, 12, 35–45.

62 ———. Introduction to S. Hegeler, *Peter and Caroline: A child asks about childbirth and sex.*

63 ———. Introduction to L. Way, *Adler's place in psychology.*

64 ———. Malariabehandlung einer schwangern Paralytikerin. *Deutsche med. Wchnschr.*, 1931, 57, 2018–2019 (with H. Hartmann).

65 ———. Melanin pigment in the brain of the gorilla. *J. comp. Neurol.*, 1942, 76, 501–507.

66 ———. Melanin pigment in the central nervous system of vertebrates. *J. comp. Neurol.*, 1939, 70, 315–329.

67 ———. Mental symptoms following head injury. *Arch Neurol. Psychiat.*, 1945, 53, 34–43.

68 ———. Metrazol reaction in patients with arterial hypertension. *Amer. J. Psychiat.*, 1939, 96, 699.

69 ———. Modern drug treatment and psychotherapy. *JIP*, 1957, 13, 146–149. Also reprinted as a portion of "Problems in psychotherapy" in K. A. Adler & Danica Deutsch (Eds.), *Essays in Individual Psychology.* Pp. 177–179.

70 **Adler, Alexandra.** Nagelveränderung bei Thalliumvergiftung. *Dermat. Z.*, 1932, 63, 259-261.

71 ———. Die neuen Heilmittel in der Psychotherapie. In Int. Verein Indivpsy., *Alfred Adler zum gedenken*. Pp. 11-15.

72 ———. Neuropsychiatric complications in the victims of the Boston Coconut Grove disaster. *J. Amer. Med. Assn.*, 1943, 123, 1098-1101.

73 ———. Neuroses in children. *Proc. Rudolf Virchow Med. Soc. N. Y.*, 1948, 6, 13-16.

74 ———. New ways? *IPB*, 1942, 2(4), 77.

75 ———. Obituary [Asya Kadis]. *IPNL*, 1971, 20(3), 45.

76 ———. Office treatment of the chronic schizophrenic. In P. H. Hoch & J. Zubin (Eds.), *Psychopathology of schizophrenia*. Pp. 366-371.

77 ———. One hundred cases of a condition diagnosed as acute encephalitis. *Arch. Neurol. Psychiat.*, 1940, 44, 541-567.

78 ———. The only child. In A. Adler & assoc., *Guiding the child*. Pp. 195-209.

79 ———. Our way. *IPN*, 1941, 1(8-9), 2.

80 ———. Pällidares Syndrom mit H/perkinesen und Zwangsgedenken als Folgezustand nach Nitrobenzolvergiftung. *Z. gesam. Neurol. Psychiat.*, 1934, 150, 341-345.

81 ———. Portrait. *IPNL*, 1970, 19(4), 80; 1971, 20(6), 111, 112; *Miami Herald*, Apr. 18, 1971.

82 ———. Post-traumatic neuroses in war and peace. *IPB*, 1944-45, 4, 75-78.

83 ———. Prefatory note to Sidonie Reiss, *Mental readjustment*. P. 12.

84 ———. Present-day Adlerian psychiatric practice. *JIP*, 1971, 27(2), 153-159.

85 ———. Problems in psychotherapy. *AJIP*, 1956, 12, 12-24. Also in K. A. Adler & Danica Deutsch (Eds.), *Essays in Individual Psychology*. Pp. 177-199.

86 ———. Problems regarding our knowledge of hysteria in childhood. *Nerv. Child*, 1953, 10, 211-213.

87 ———. Professor Dr. Emil Froeschels (1884-1972). *IPNL*, 1972, 21(4), 66-68.

88 ———. The psychology of repeated accidents in industry. *Amer. J. Psychiat.*, 1941, 98, 99-101.

89 ———. Psychotherapy, its present and future. *Amer. J. Psychother.*, 1962, 16, 307-310.

90 ———. Recollections of my father. *Amer. J. Psychiat.*, 1970, 127, 771-772.

91 **Adler, Alexandra.** Review of Theresa Benedek, *Psychosexual functions in women*. New York: Ronald Press, 1952. In *Amer. J. Psychiat.*, 1954, 110, 875-876.

92 ———. Review of E. Glover, *Freud or Jung*. New York: Norton, 1950. In *Amer. J. Psychiat.*, 1952, 10, 714.

93 ———. Review of A. R. Mahrer, *The goals of psychotherapy*. In *Amer. J. Psychiat.*, 1968, 125, 409-410.

94 ———. Review of P. Schilder, *Contributions to developmental neuropsychiatry*. New York: Int. Univer. Press, 1964. In *Amer. J. Neuropsychiat.*, 1966, 122, 1072.

95 ———. Review of F. Weidenreich, *Rasse und Körperbau*. Berlin: J. Springer, 1927. In *IZIP*, 1927, 5(4), 319.

96 ———. Die Senkungsgeschwindkeit der roten Blutkörpchen bei der Malariabehandlung der Paralyse. *Z. gesam. Neurol. Psychiat.*, 1928, 117, 793-800.

97 ———. Sibyl Mandell (1896-1968). *JIP*, 1969, 25, 138.

98 ———. Some psychiatric aspects of female offenders in the Women's House of Detention. *J. soc. Ther.*, 1955, 1, 199-202.

99 ———. Die Störung des Wasserhaushalter während der Morphiumentziehung und deren therapeutische Beeinflussing durch Euphyllin. *Klin. Wchnschr.*, 1930, 9, 2011-2015.

100 ———. Technik der Erziehungsberatung. *IZIP*, 1929, 7(3), 196-202.

101 ———. Technique of educational guidance. In A. Adler & assoc., *Guiding the child*. Pp. 102-118.

102 ———. Two different types of post-traumatic neuroses. *Amer. J. Psychiat.*, 1945, 102, 237-240.

103 ———. Über die Bedingtheit der Häufung gewerblicher Unfälle. *Arch. Gewerbpath. Gewerbhyg.*, 1931, 2, 359-384 (with E. Brezina & J. Wastl).

104 ———. Über eine eigenartig Reaktion auf Meskalin bei einer Kranken mit doppelseitigen Herden in der Sehsphare. *Jb. Psychiat. Neurol.*, 1936, 53, 13-34 (with O. Potzl).

105 ———. Unsuccessful sex adjustment in marriage. *J. Contracep.*, 1939, 4, 232.

106 ———. Vascular architecture of the lesions of multiple sclerosis. *Arch. Neurol. Psychiat.*, 1937, 38, 1-15.

107 ———. Weitere Beitrag zur Therapie der Abstinenzbeschwerden bei Morphiumentzug. *Jb. Psychiat. Neurol*, 1931, 48, 105-111.

108 **Adler, Alexandra.** The work of Paul Schilder. *Bull. N.Y. Acad. Med.,* 1965 (2nd series), 41, 841–853.

109 ———. *Youth in danger becomes a danger: A symposium on juvenile delinquency.* New York: Indiv. Psychol. Assn., 1956 (with J. Dumpson, H. Epstein & E. Papanek).

110 ———. Zur Lokalisation des Konvergenzzentrums und der Kerne der glatten Augenmuskeln. *Z. gesam. Neurol. Psychiat.,* 1933, 145, 185–207.

111 ———. Zur Topik der corticalen Geschmackssphare. *Z. gesam. Neurol. Psychiat.,* 1935, 152, 25–34.

112 ———. Zur Topik des Verlaufes der Geschmacksinnfasern und anderer afferenter Bahnen in Thalamus. *Z. gesam. Neurol. Psychiat.,* 1933, 145, 208–222.

113 **Adler, Alfred.** Advances in Individual Psychology. *ZIP,* 1923, 2(1), 1–7; 1923, 2(3), 10–12.

114 ———. Advantages and disadvantages of the inferiority feeling. In H. L. Ansbacher & Rowena R. Ansbacher (Eds.), *Superiority and social interest.* Pp. 50–58.

115 ———. Der Aggresionstrieb in Leben und in der Neurose. *Fortschr. Med.,* 1908, 26, 577–584. Also in A. Adler & C. Furtmüller (Eds.), *Heilen und Bilden* (1914). Pp. 23–32; (1928). Pp. 31–41.

116 ———. Das Alexius-Lied. *IZIP,* 1932, 10(6), 473–476.

117 ———. Alfred Adler über Amerika: Geltungsstreben in Amerika. *IZIP,* 1927, 5, 225–228.

118 ———. *Al-Hayat Al-Nafsiyah* (The science of living). Translated by M. A. Badran & A. M. Abd Al-Khaliq. Cairo: Lajnat al-Talif wa al-Tarjamah wa al-Nashr, 1944.

119 ———. *Die andere seite: Eine massenpsychologische Studie über die Schuld des Volkes.* Wien: Leopold Heidrich, 1919.

120 ———. *Anthropinio Characteres.* Translated by N. Vocos. Athens: Atlas, 1958.

121 ———. *Anthropognosia* (Understanding human nature). Translated by G. Palaiologos. Athens: Petros Dimitrakos, 1934, 1948; Athens: Mlougoumane, 1971.

122 ———. The anti-social personality. In *Sex, personality and the Establishment.* Pp. 25–34.

123 ———. Are Americans neurotic? *Forum,* 1936, 95, 44–45.

124 ———. Der Arzt als Erzieher. *Ärztl. Standeszeitung* (Wien), 1904, 3(13), 4–6;

1904, 3(14), 3–4; 1904, 3(15), 4–5. Also in A. Adler & C. Furtmüller (Eds.), *Heilen und Bilden* (1914). Pp. 1–10; (1928). Pp. 16–23.

125 **Adler, Alfred.** Der Aufbau der Neurose. *IZIP,* 1932, 10, 321–328.

126 ———. *Die Aufgabe der Jugend in unserer Zeit.* Berlin: Laubsche, 1927.

127 ———. [Autobiographical notes]. In Phyllis Bottome, *Alfred Adler: A biography.* Pp. 9–12. Reprinted as "How I chose my career". *IPB,* 1947, 6, 9–11.

128 ———. Beitrag zur Lehre vom Widerstand. *Zbl. Psychoanal.,* 1911, 1, 214–219. Also in *Praxis und Theorie.* Pp. 100–105.

129 ———. Beiträge zur Lehre von der organischen Grundlage der Psychoneurosen. *Osterreich. Ärzte-Zeitung,* 1912, 9(23), 1–12.

130 ———. Berufseignung und Berufsmeigung. *Jugend und Beruf,* 1926, 1, 89–93.

131 ———. Besuch bei Dr. Alfred Adler (Interview with A. Ernst). *Neues Wiener Tagblatt,* July 1, 1928. Pp. 5–6.

132 ———. Bibliography. In H. L. Ansbacher & Rowena Ansbacher (Eds.), *The Individual Psychology of Alfred Adler.* Pp. 465–470.

133 ———. Bibliography. In H. L. Ansbacher & Rowena Ansbacher (Eds.), *Superiority and social interest.* Pp. 397–417.

134 ———. Bolschewismus und Seelenkunde. *Int. Rundsch.* (Zurich), 1918, 4, 597–600.

135 ———. Brief comments on reason, intelligence, and feeblemindedness. In H. L. Ansbacher & Rowena Ansbacher (Eds.), *Superiority and social interest.* Pp. 41–49.

136 ———. *El caracter neurotico.* Mexico: Ed. "Latino Americana", n.d.

137 ———. A case from guidance practice. In A. Adler & Assoc., *Guiding the child.* Pp. 127–147.

138 ———. Case interpretation. *IPB,* 1941, 2(1), 1–9. Reprinted as "Two grade-school girls" in H. L. Ansbacher & Rowena Ansbacher (Eds.), *Superiority and social interest.* Pp. 143–158.

139 ———. *The case of Miss R: The interpretation of a life story.* Translated by Eleanore & F. Jensen. New York: Greenberg, 1929; London: Allen & Unwin, 1929.

140 ———. The case of Mrs. A: The diagnosis of a life style. *IPP,* 1931, No. 1. Also in H. L. Ansbacher & Rowena Ansbacher (Eds.), *Superiority and social interest.* Pp.

159-190. Also Chicago: Alfred Adler Inst., 1969.

141 **Adler, Alfred.** The cause and prevention of neuroses. *J. abnorm. soc. Psychol.*, 1928, 23, 4-11.

142 ———. The cause and prevention of neurosis. *IZIP*, 1927, 5, 245-252. Reprinted as "The cause and prevention of neuroses". *J. ment. Sci.*, 1927, 73, 1-8; *J. abnorm. soc. Psychol.*, 1928, 23, 4-11. Also in *Sex, personality and the Establishment*. Pp. 13-22.

143 ———. Character and talent. *Harper's Mag.*, 1927, 155, 64-72.

144 ———. Characteristics of the first, second and third child. *Children*, 1928, 3, 14 & 52.

145 ———. Choice of neuroses and training in a dream. *ZIP*, 1924, 2(5), 5-8.

146 ———. *A ciencia de natureza humana* [Understanding human nature]. Translated by G. Rangel & A. Teixeira. Sao Paulo, Brazil: Edit. National, 1945.

147 ———. *A ciencia de viver.* Translated by T. N. Neto. Rio de Janeiro: José Olympio, 1943, 1956.

148 ———. Clinic for sick marriages. [Interview with Helena H. Smith]. *Delineator*, 1929, 115, 12, 56 & 59.

149 ———. *La compensation psychique de l'état d'inferiorité des organes* suivi de *Le problème de l'homosexualité.* Translated by H. Schaffer. Paris: Payot, 1956.

150 ———. Complex compulsion as part of personality and neurosis. In H. L. Ansbacher & Rowena Ansbacher (Eds.), *Superiority and social interest.* Pp. 71-80.

151 ———. Compulsion neurosis. In *The practice and theory of Individual Psychology.* Pp. 197-207.

152 ———. Compulsion neurosis. *IJIP*, 1936, 2(4), 3-22. Reprinted as "The compulsion to be big". In S. J. Beck & H. B. Molish (Eds.), *Reflexes to intelligence: A reader in clinical psychology.* Pp. 79-90. Also in H. L. Ansbacher & Rowena Ansbacher (Eds.), *Superiority and social interest.* Pp. 112-138.

153 ———. The compulsion to be big. In S. J. Beck & H. B. Molish (Eds.), *Reflexes to intelligence: A reader in clinical psychology.* Pp. 79-90. Reprint of "Compulsion neurosis". *IJIP*, 1936, 2(4), 3-22. Also in H. L. Ansbacher & Rowena Ansbacher (Eds.), *Superiority and social interest.* Pp. 112-138.

154 **Adler, Alfred.** The concept of resistance during treatment. In *The practice and theory of Individual Psychology.* Pp. 144-152.

155 ———. *Connaissance de l'homme: Étude de caractérologie individuelle.* Translated by J. Marty. Paris: Payot, 1949.

156 ———. *Conocimiento del hombre.* Translated by U. Bark. Madrid: Espasa-Calpe, 1931; Buenos Aires: , 1947.

157 ———. *Conoscenza dell' uomo.* Milan: Arnoldo Mondadori, 1954.

158 ———. Contribución a la comprensión de la resistencia en el tratamiento. In *Practica y teoría de la Psicologia del Individuo.*

159 ———. Contribución a la teoría de la alucination. In *Practica y teoría de la Psicología del Individuo.*

160 ———. Contributions to the theory of hallucination. In *The practice and theory of Individual Psychology.* Pp. 51-58.

161 ———. The criminal pattern of life. *Police J.* (New York), 1930, 17 (Mar.), 8-11, 22-23; 1930, 17 (Apr.), 5-7, 24; 1930, 17 (July), 5. Reprinted as "The anti-social personality" in *Sex, personality and the Establishment.*

162 ———. The criminal personality and its cure. *IPP*, 1932, No. 5. Pp. 46-59. Also appeared as "The individual criminal and his cure: An address".

163 ——— (Ed.). *Curar y educar.*   (with C. Furtmüller).

164 ———. Danton, Marat, Robespierre: Eine Charakterstudie. *Arbeiter-Zeitung* (Wien), December 25, 1923. Pp. 17-18.

165 ———. The death problem in neurosis. In H. L. Ansbacher & Rowena Ansbacher (Eds.), *Superiority and social interest.* Pp. 239-247.

166 ———. Demoralized children. In *The practice and theory of Individual Psychology.* Pp. 339-350.

167 ———. El dialecto de los órganos. In A. Adler & C. Furtmüller (Eds.), *Curar y educar.*

168 ———. The differences between Individual Psychology and psychoanalysis. In H. L. Ansbacher & Rowena Ansbacher (Eds.), *Superiority and social interest.* Pp. 205-218.

169 ———. Diskussionsbemerkungen zum Vortrage des Prof. Max Adler. *IZIP*, 1925, 3, 221-223.

170 ———. Disposición a la neurosis. In A. Adler & C. Furtmüller (Eds.), *Curar y educar.*

171 Adler, Alfred. La disposición neurótica. In A. Adler & C. Furtmüller (Eds.), *Curar y educar.*

172 ———. Die Disposition zur Neurose. *Jb. psychoanal. psychpathol. Forsch.,* 1909, 1.

173 ———. A doctor remakes education. *Survey Graphic,* 1927, 58, 490–495.

174 ———. Dostoevsky. In *The practice and theory of Individual Psychology.* Pp. 280–290.

175 ———. Dostoievsky. In *Práctica y teoría de la Psicología del Individuo.*

176 ———. Dostojewski. In *Praxis und Theorie.* Pp. 195–202.

177 ———. Dreams and dream interpretation. In *The practice and theory of Individual Psychology.* Pp. 214–226.

178 ———. Drei Beiträge zum Problem des Schülerselbstmord (with D. E. Oppenheim & K. Molitor). In A. Adler & C. Furtmüller (Eds.), *Heilen und Bilden* (1914). Pp. 341–373; (1928) Same with F. Künkel instead of K. Molitor. Pp. 206–227.

179 ———. Drei Psycho-Analysen von Zahleneinfällen und obsedierenden Zahlen. *Psychiat.-neurol. Wchnschr.,* 1905, 7, 263–266.

180 ———. The drive for superiority. In H. Greenwald (Ed.), *Great cases in psychoanalysis.* Pp. 175–186; Also in H. Greenwald (Ed.), *Active psychotherapy.* Pp. 27–35.

181 ———. La educación desde el punto vista de Psícología del Individuo. In *Practica y teoría de la Psícología del Individuo.*

182 ———. *The education of children.* Translated by Eleanore & F. Jensen. London: Allen & Unwin, 1930, 1935, 1947, 1957; New York: Greenberg, 1930; Chicago: Gateway, 1970.

183 ———. *Los educación de los ninos.* Buenos Aires: I. Luzuriaga de Lamana-Losada, 1960.

184 ———. Die Ehe als Aufgabe. In H. Keyserling (Ed.), *Buch der Ehe.* Also in *Bereitschaft,* 1926, 6(7); *IZIP,* 1926, 4, 22–24.

185 ———. Ehe und Kind. In J. Spier (Ed.), *Die Schule der Ehe.* Pp. 348–385.

186 ———. Ein Beitrag zum Distanzproblem. *IZIP,* 1926, 4, 141–143.

187 ———. Ein Beitrag zur Psychologie der ärztlicher Berufswahl. In A. Adler & C. Furtmüller (Eds.), *Heilen und Bilden* (1914). Pp. 336–340; (1928). Pp. 341–344.

188 ———. Das Eindringen sozialer Triebkräfte in die Medizin. *Ärztl. Standeszeitung* (Wien), 1902, 1(1), 1–3.

189 Adler, Alfred. Ein erlogener Traum: Beitrag zum Mechanismus der Lüge in der Neurose. *Zbl. Psychoanal.,* 1910, 1, 103–108.

190 ———. Ein Fall von Enuresis diurna: Stenographische Aufnahme einer Erziehungsberatung. *IZIP,* 1930, 8(5), 471–478.

191 ———. Ein Fall von Karzinomangst. *Gemeinschaft* (Berlin), 1926, 1(5).

192 ———. Ein Fall von Melancholie. *IZIP,* 1924, 3(3), 103–105.

193 ———. Eine Beratung: Stenographische Aufnahme. *IZIP,* 1929, 7(3), 207–214.

194 ———. Eine häufige Wurzel des Sadismus. *IZIP,* 1924, 3(2), 49–50.

195 ———. Emotions, sex and experimentation. In *Sex, personality and the Establishment.* Pp. 39–56.

196 ———. Entwicklung des Kindes. In A. Adler & C. Furtmüller (Eds.), *Heilen und Bilden* (1914). Pp. 33–40; (1928). Pp. 42–48.

197 ———. Enuresis. In M. Kahane (Ed.), *Medizinische Handlexikon prak. Ärzte.* Pp. 321–322.

198 ———. Erklärung. *Zbl. Psychoanal.,* 1911, 1, 433.

199 ———. Erörterungen zum Paragraph 144. *IZIP,* 1925, 3(6), 338–340.

200 ———. Erotisches Training und erotischer Rückzug. In M. Marcuse (Ed.), *Verhandlung I. Int. Kongr. Sex. Forschung, Berlin, 1926.*

201 ———. Erste Kindheitserrinerungen. *IZIP,* 1933, 11, 81–90. Also in *Der Sinn des Lebens.* Ch. 10.

202 ———. Erwiderung [am A. Maeder]. *Zbl. Psychoanal.,* 1913, 3, 564–567.

203 ———. Die Erziehung zum Mut. *IZIP,* 1927, 5, 324–326.

204 ———. Erziehungsberatungsstellen. In A. Adler, C. Furtmüller & E. Wexberg (Eds.), *Heilen und Bilden* (1922). Pp. 119–121; (1928). Pp. 142–144.

205 ———. Failures of personalities. *IPN,* 1941, 1(8–9), 2–8.

206 ———. The fear of woman. Translated by Laura Hutton. *IPP,* 1932, No. 3. Pp. 11–13. Reprinted as part of "Emotions, sex and experimentation" in *Sex, personality and the Establishment.* Pp. 39–56.

207 ———. The feeling of inferiority and the striving for recognition. *IZIP,* 1927, 5(1), 12–19; *Proc. Royal Soc. Med.,* 1927, 20, 1881–1886. Also in *Understanding human*

nature. Ch. 5. Also in C. L. Stacey & M. F. De Martino (Eds.), *Understanding human motivation.* Pp. 466–473.

208 Adler, Alfred. Feelings and emotions from the standpoint of Individual Psychology. In M. L. Reymert (Ed.), *Feelings and emotions: The Wittenberg symposium.* Pp. 316–321. Reprinted as part of "Emotions, sex and experimentation" in *Sex, personality and the Establishment.* Pp. 39–56.

209 ———. First comes mother, next comes father. [Interview with Lola J. Simpson]. *Good Housekeeping,* Nov. 1930. Pp. 36–37.

210 ———. Fondamenti e progressi della "Psicologia Individuale". *Arch. gen. Neurol. Psicol. Psicoanal.,* 1925, 6, 227–238.

211 ———. Foreword to K. A. Adler & Danica Deutsch (Eds.), *Essays in Individual Psychology.* P. xiii. Reprint of Foreword to R. Dreikurs, *Fundamentals of Adlerian Psychology.* P. vii.

212 ———. Foreword to R. Dreikurs, *An introduction to Individual Psychology.* P. vii. Reprinted as Foreword to K. A. Adler & Danica Deutsch (Eds.), *Essays in Individual Psychology.* P. xiii.

213 ———. Die Formen der seelischen Aktivität: Ein Beitrag zur individualpsychologischen Charakterkunde. *Ned. Tijdschr. Psychol.,* 1933, 1, 229–235. Also in *IZIP,* 1934, 12(1), 1–5.

214 ———. The forms of psychological activity. In H. L. Ansbacher & Rowena Ansbacher (Eds.), *Superiority and social interest.* Pp. 59–65.

215 ———. Fortschritte der Individualpsychologie. *IZIP,* 1923, 2(1), 1–7; 1923, 2(3), 10–12. Also in *Brit. J. med. Psychol.,* 1924, 4, 12–21.

216 ———. Fortune-telling and prophecy. *JIP,* 1965, 21, 41–43.

217 ———. Foundations for Individual Psychology. *Pädagog. Heute,* 1969, 3–4.

218 ———. Die Frau als Erzieherin. *Arch. Frauenkunde.* (Würzburg), 1916, 2(3), 342–349.

219 ———. The fundamental views of Individual Psychology. *IJIP,* 1935, 1(1), 5–8.

220 ———. Fundamentals of Individual Psychology. *JIP,* 1970, 26, 36–49.

221 ———. Die Funktion der Mutter. *Gemeinschaft* (Berlin), 1926, 1(4).

222 ———. Die Gefahren der Isolierung. *Zbl. Vormundschaftsw.,* 1923, 15(3), 53.

223 Adler, Alfred. Geleitwort. *Indiv. Gemeinschaft* (München), 1926, No. 1. Pp. ix–xi.

224 ———. Geleitwort. In *Über den nervösen Charakter.*

225 ———. *Gesundheitsbuch für das Schneidergewerbe.* Berlin: C. Heymanns, 1898.

226 ———. Die Grundbegriffe der Individualpsychologie. In F. Giese (Ed.), *Handwörterbuch der Arbeitswissenschaft.* Vol. 1. Halle: Marhold Verlag, 1930. Pp. 2428–2437.

227 ———. *Guiando al nino.* Translated by J. Bernstein. Buenos Aires: , 1947.

228 ——— and assoc. *Guiding the child* [on the principles of Individual Psychology]. Translated by B. Ginzburg. London: Allen & Unwin, 1930, 1938, 1949. New York: Greenberg, 1930.

229 ——— (Ed.). *Heilen und Bilden. Ärztlichpädagogisch Arbeiten des Vereins für Individualpsychologie.* München: Reinhardt, 1914 (with C. Furtmüller).

230 ——— (Ed.). *Heilen und Bilden: Ein Buch der Erziehungskunst für Ärzte und Pädagogen.* München: Bergmann, 1928 (with C. Furtmüller & E. Wexberg).

231 ——— (Ed.). *Heilen und Bilden:* Grundlagen der Erziehungskunst für Ärzte und Pädagogen.* München: Bergmann, 1922 (with C. Furtmüller & E. Wexberg).

232 ———. El hermafrodismos psiquico. In A. Adler & C. Furtmüller (Eds.), *Curar y educar.*

233 ——— et al. Het Moelijke Kind [The difficult child]. Translated by P. Dijkema. Antwerpen: Wreld Bibliotheek, 1956.

234 ———. The homosexual problem. *Urol. cutan. Rev., Tech. Suppl.* (St. Louis), Oct., 1914; *Alienist & Neurol.,* 1917, 38, 268–287.

235 ———. La homosexualidad. In *Práctica y teoría de la Psicología del Individuo.*

236 ———. Homosexualität. In A. Bethe *et al.* (Eds.), *Handbuch norm. path. Physiologie.* Pp. 881–886.

237 ———. Homosexuality. In *The practice and theory of Individual Psychology.* Pp. 184–196.

238 ———. How the child selects his symptoms. *IPB,* 1946, 5, 67–78.

239 ———. How I chose my career. *IPB,* 1947, 6, 9–11. Also in Phyllis Bottome, *Alfred Adler: A biography.* Pp. 9–12.

240 **Adler, Alfred.** Hygiene der Geschlechtslebens. *Ärztl. Standeszeitung* (Wien), 1904, 3(18), 1-3; 1904, 3(19), 1-3.

241 ———. Les idées fondamentales de la Psychologie Individuelle. *Rev. Psychol. concréte*, 1929, 1, 89-101.

242 ———. *Index of Individual Psychology* [A collection of Adlerian writings containing 6 volumes including: A. Adler, *The pattern of life, Problems of neurosis*, and *What life should mean to you;* E. Wexberg, *Individual Psychology;* and W. B. Wolfe, *How to be happy though human*]. New York: T. O. Warfield, 1922; New York: Dodd, Mead, 1926. Also an index on general topics, child behavior, development, education, etc. (with E. Wexberg & W. B. Wolfe).

243 ———. Individual and social disorganization. *Amer. J. Sociol.*, 1937, 42, 773-780. Also in *Sex, personality and the Establishment.* Pp. 50-66.

244 ———. *The individual criminal and his cure: An address.* New York: Natl. Comm. on Prisons & Prison Labor, 1930. Reprinted as "The criminal personality and its cure". *IPP*, 1930, No. 5. Pp. 46-59; Palo Alto, Cal.: San Francisco Bay Area Soc. for Adlerian Psychol., 1972.

245 ———. Individualpsychologie. In E. Saupe (Ed.), *Einführung in die neuere Psychologie.* Pp. 399-407.

246 ———. Die Individualpsychologie. *Scientia,* 1926, 39, 409-418.

247 ———. Die Individualpsychologie als Weg zur Menschenkenntnis und Sichtsterkenntnis. In J. Neumann (Ed.), *Du und der Alltag.* Pp. 211-236.

248 ———. Die Individualpsychologie, ihre Voraussetzungen und Ergebnisse. *Scientia,* 1914, 16, 74-87. Also in *Praxis und Theorie.* Pp. 1-10.

249 ———. Die Individualpsychologie in der Neurosenlehre. *IZIP*, 1929, 7(1), 81-88. Also in *Deutsch. med. Wchnschr.*, 1929, 55, 213-215.

250 ———. *Individualpsychologie in der Schule: Vorlesungen für Lehrer und Erzieher.* Leipzig: Hirzel, 1929.

251 ———. Individualpsychologie und Psychoanalyse. I. Individualpsychologie. *Schweiz. Erziehungs-Rundsch.*, 1931, 4(4), 59-61. II. Die Unterschiede zwischen Individualpsychologie und Psychoanalyse. *Schweiz. Erziehungs-Rundsch.*, 1931, 4(5), 89-93.

252 **Adler, Alfred.** Individualpsychologie und Weltanschauung. *IZIP*, 1923, 2(2), 30-31.

253 ———. Individualpsychologie und Weltanschauung. *IZIP*, 1924, 3, 132-133.

254 ———. Individualpsychologie und Wissenschaft. *IZIP*, 1927, 5, 401-408.

255 ———. Individual-Psychological conclusions on sleep disturbances. In *The practice and theory of Individual Psychology.* Pp. 172-183.

256 ———. Individual-Psychological education. In *The practice and theory of Individual Psychology.* Pp. 317-326.

257 ———. Individual-Psychological remarks on Alfred Berger's *Hofrat Eysenhardt.* In *The practice and theory of Individual Psychology.* Pp. 263-279.

258 ———. Individual-Psychological treatment of neuroses. In *The practice and theory of Individual Psychology.* Pp. 32-50. Also in R. W. Marks (Ed.), *Great ideas in psychology.* New York: Bantam Books, 1966. Pp. 151-168.

259 ———. Individualpsychologische Behandlung der Neurosen. In D. Sarason (Ed.), *Jahreskurse für ärztliche Fortbildung.* Pp. 39-51. Also in *Praxis und Theorie.* Pp. 22-35.

260 ———. Individualpsychologische Bemerkungen zu Alfred Berger's *Hofrat Eysenhardt. Z. psychol. med. Psychother.*, 1913, 5, 77-89. Also in *Praxis und Theorie.* Pp. 183-194.

261 ———. Individualpsychologische Ergebnisse bezüglich Schaft-störungen. *Fortschr. Med.*, 1913, 31, 925-933. Also in *Praxis und Theorie.* Pp. 119-126. Parts reprinted in A. Adler & C. Furtmüller (Eds.), *Heilen und Bilden.* Pp. 336-340.

262 ———. Individualpsychologische Skizze einer Zwangsneurose. *IZIP*, 1926, 4, 253-256.

263 ———. Die Individualpsychologischen Erziehungsberatungsstellen in Wien. *IZIP*, 1929, 7, 161-170.

264 ———. Individual Psychology. *Brit. J. med. Psychol.*, 1924, 4, 12-21.

265 ———. Individual Psychology. *J. abnorm. soc. Psychol.*, 1927, 22, 116-122; *Psyche*, 1927, 28, 46-63. Also in *Sex, personality and the Establishment.* Pp. 3-10.

266 ———. Individual Psychology. In C. Murchison (Ed.), *Psychologies of 1930.* Pp. 395-405. Also *Repr. Series Soc. Sci.,*

Indianapolis: Bobbs-Merrill, n.d. Also in G. Lindzey & C. S. Hall (Eds.), *Theories of personality: Primary sources and research.* Pp. 97–104.

267 Adler, Alfred. *Individual Psychology.* 2nd ed. London: Kegan Paul, Trench, Trubner, 1927.

268 ———. Individual Psychology: A new way to the understanding of human nature. *Psyche*, 1927, No. 28. Pp. 46–63.

269 ———. Individual Psychology and experimental psychology. *Charac. & Pers.*, 1933, 1, 265–267. Reprinted as part of "Emotions, sex and experimentation" in *Sex, personality and the Establishment.* Pp. 39–56.

270 ———. Individual Psychology and sexual difficulties. (I). *IPP*, 1932, No. 3 (with R. Dreikurs, E. Wexberg, Adele Hervat, J. C. Young, F. G. Crookshank, Mary C. Luff & others).

271 ———. Individual Psychology and sexual difficulties. (II). *IPP*, 1936, No. 13 (with F. G. Crookshank).

272 ———. Individual Psychology and social problems. (I). *IPMP*, 1932, No. 5 (with W. B. Wolfe, C. L. C. Burns, and J. C. Young).

273 ———. Individual Psychology, its assumptions and its results. In *The practice and theory of Individual Psychology.* Pp. 1–15. Also in H. M. Ruitenbeek (Ed.), *Varieties of personality theory.* Pp. 65–79.

274 ———. The Individual Psychology of prostitution. In *The practice and theory of Individual Psychology.* Pp. 327–338.

275 ———. Die Individuelle Psychologie der Prostitution. In *Praxis und Theorie.* Pp. 228–236.

276 ——— (Ed.). *Individuum und Gemeinschaft.* München: Bergmann, 1926–27. (Includes J. Neumann, Die Gefühle und das Ich, 1926; A. Neuer, Mut und Entmutigung; Die Prinzipen der Psychologie Alfred Adlers, 1926; O. Kaus, Die Traume in Dostojewskis "Raskalnikoff", 1926; Elisabeth Bellott, Individualpsychologie und Schule, 1926; Sofie Lazarsfeld, Die Ehe von Heute und Morgen, 1927; and F. Wilken, Die nervöse Erkrankung als sinnvolle Erscheinung unseres gegenwartigen Kulturzeitraumes: Eine Untersuchung über die Störung des heutigen Soziallebens, 1927) (with O. Kaus & L. Seif).

277 Adler, Alfred. Infancia abandanada. In *Práctica y teoría de la Psícología del Individuo.*

278 ———. Insomnia neurótico. In *Práctica y teoría de la Psícología del Individuo.*

279 ———. Inschriften der menschlichen Seele. *Bereitschaft*, 1925, 6(2).

280 ———. *The intelligent mother's guide to child behavior.* New York: T. O. Warfield, 1932.

281 ———. Introduction to M. Maltz, *New faces—new futures: Rebuilding character with plastic surgery.* New York: R. R. Smith, 1936.

282 ———. Ist der Fortschritt der Menschheit möglich? Wahrscheinlich? Unmöglich? Sicher? *IZIP*, 1937, 15(1), 1–4.

283 ———. Kinderpsychologie und Neurosenforschung. *Z. Pathopsychol.*, 1914–19, 3, 35–52.

284 ———. Kindliches Seelenleben und Gemeinsinn. *Ann. Natur-Kulturphil.*, 1914, 13, 38–45.

285 ———. Der Komplexzwang als Teil der Persönlichkeit und Neurose. *IZIP*, 1935, 13(1), 1–6.

286 ———. Körperliche Auswirkungen seelischer Störungen. *IZIP*, 1934, 12(2), 65–71.

287 ———. Die kriminelle Persönlichkeit und ihre Heilung. *IZIP*, 1931, 9(5), 321–329.

288 ———. Kritische Erwägungen über den Sinn des Lebens. In *Der Leuchter: Weltanschauung und Lebensgestaltung.* Vol. 5. Darmstadt: Reichl, 1924. Pp. 343–350. Also in *IZIP*, 1924, 3(2), 93–96.

289 ———. Kulturelle Einschränkung in der Erziehung der Frau zur Aktivität. *IZIP*, 1924, 2(6), 39.

290 ———. Kurze Bemerkungen über Vernunft, Intelligenz und Schwachsinn. *IZIP*, 1928, 6, 267–272.

291 ———. Lebenslüge und Verantwortlichkeit in der Neurose und Psychose: Ein Beitrag zur Melancholiefrage. *ZIP*, 1914, 1, 44–53. Also in *Praxis und Theorie.* Pp. 164–170.

292 ———. Lebererkrankungen. In M. Kahane (Ed.), *Med. Handlex. praktiz. Ärzte.* Vienna: Urban and Schwarzenberg, 1908. Pp. 578–580.

293 ———. Lecture to the Medical Society of Individual Psychology, London, May 17, 1934. *IPP*, 1934, No. 13, Pp. 11–24.

294 ———. *Levensproblemen.* [Problems of living]. Translated by P. H. Ronge. Utrecht: Bijleveld, 1937.

295 **Adler, Alfred.** Liebesbeziehungen und deren Störungen. In Sofie Lazarsfeld (Ed.), *Richtige Lebensführung.*

296 ———. Life-lie and responsibility in neurosis and psychosis. In *The practice and theory of Individual Psychology.* Pp. 235-245.

297 ———. *Livets Mening* [The meaning of life]. Stockholm: Bokfolaget Naturoog Kultur, 1934.

298 ———. Love is a recent invention. *Esquire,* May, 1936. Pp. 56, 128; *JIP,* 1972, 27(2), 144-152.

299 ———. Manipulation or education? *IPNL,* 1971, 20(5), 87-88. Excerpted from E. Jahn & A. Adler, *Religion and Individual Psychology.*

300 ———. The masculine attitude in female neurotics. In *The practice and theory of Individual Psychology.* Pp. 109-143.

301 ———. Mass psychology. *IJIP,* 1937, 3(2), 111-120.

302 ———. The meaning of life. *Lancet,* 1931, 220, 223-228. Also in *IPP,* 1932, No. 5. Pp. 9-22.

303 ———. Mekoro ve-hitpatchuto shel regesh hanchitut v'totsayotov [The origins and development of the inferiority feeling and its consequences]. In *Kovets Individual-Psychologie.* Pp. 34-49.

304 ———. Melancholia and paranoia. In *The practice and theory of Individual Psychology.* Pp. 246-262.

305 ———. Melancholie und Paranoia: Individualpsychologische Ergebnisse aus den Untersuchungen der Psychosen. In *Praxis und Theorie.* Pp. 171-182.

306 ———. Melancolía y paranoia. In *Práctica y teoría de la Psicología del Individuo.*

307 ———. *Menneskekundstab* [Understanding human nature]. Translated by O. Gelsted. Copenhagen-Oslo: Martins Førlog, 1930.

308 ———. *Menschenkenntnis.* Leipzig: Hirzel, 1927; Zurich: Rascher, 1947, 1954; : Fischer, 1966, 1972.

309 ———. *Mensenkennis* [Understanding human nature]. Translated by P. van Schilfgaarde. Utrecht: Bijleveld, 1932, 1949.

310 ———. Mitoch ha-praktika be-hadracha [From guidance practice]. In *Kovets Individual-Psychologie.* Pp. 93-103.

311 ———. Mitteilungen aus Erziehungsberatungsstellen. *IZIP,* 1925, 3, 201-203.

312 **Adler, Alfred.** Moeilijke Kinderen [Difficult children]. In O. Rühle & Alice Rühle (Eds.), *Moeilijke Kinderen.* 3rd ed. Amsterdam: Wereldbibliotheek, 1935. Pp. 16-26.

313 ———. *Mondaiji No Shinri Taji Takahashi.* Tokyo: Toko Shoin, 1960.

314 ———. Myelodysplasia (organ inferiority). In *The practice and theory of Individual Psychology.* Pp. 307-316.

315 ———. Myelodysplasie oder Organminderwertigkeit. *Wien. med. Wchnschr.,* 1909, No. 45. Pp. 2631-2636. Also in *Praxis und Theorie.* Pp. 214-220.

316 ———. Der nervöse Charakter. *Soz. Monatschr.,* 1913, 19. Also in Alfred Adler & C. Furtmüller (Eds.), *Heilen und Bilden* (1914). Pp. 140-150; (1928). Pp. 130-138.

317 ———. Der nervöse Charakter. *Z. angew. Psychol. Beih.,* 1931, 17(59), 1-14.

318 ———. Nervöse Schlafflosigkeit. *IZIP,* 1914, 1, 65-72. Also in *Praxis und Theorie.* Pp. 113-118.

319 ———. Nervöser Hungerstreik. In *Praxis und Theorie.* Pp. 147-148.

320 ———. Nervous disturbances of sleep. *ZIP,* 1914, 1, 65-72.

321 ———. Nervous insomnia. In *The practice and theory of Individual Psychology.* Pp. 163-171.

322 ———. Neue Leitsätze zur Praxis der Individualpsychologie. In *Praxis und Theorie.* Pp. 16-21.

323 ———. Die neuen Gesichtspunkte in der Frage der Kriegsneurose. *Med. Klin.,* 1918, 14, 66-70. Also in *Praxis und Theorie.* Pp. 203-213.

324 ———. Neuropsychologische Bemerkungen zu Freiherr Alfred von Berger's "Hofrat Eysenhardt". *Ver. f. freie psychoanal. Forsch.,* 1913, 5(2), 77-89.

325 ———. Neurose und Lüge. *IZIP,* 1926, 4, 173-174.

326 ———. Neurose und Verbrechen. *IZIP,* 1924-25, 3, 1-11.

327 ———. Neurosenwandel und Training in Traum. *IZIP,* 1924, 2(5), 5-8.

328 ———. La neurosis compulsiva. In *Práctica y teoría de la Psicología del Individuo.*

329 ———. Neurosis and crime. *ZIP,* 1924, 3(1), 1-11.

330 ———. *The neurotic constitution.* Translated by B. Glueck & J. E. Lind. New York: Moffatt, Yard, 1917; London: Kegan Paul, 1921; New York: Dodd, Mead, 1926.

331 **Adler, Alfred.** Neurotic hunger-strike. In *The practice and theory of Individual Psychology*, Pp. 212-213.

332 ———. The neurotic's picture of the world. *IZIP*, 1936, 2(3), 3-13. Also in H. L. Ansbacher & Rowena Ansbacher (Eds.), *Superiority and social interest*. Pp. 96-111.

333 ———. Neurotisches Rollenspiel. *IZIP*, 1928, 6(6), 427-432.

334 ———. Neurotisches Weltbild. *IZIP*, 1936, 14(3), 129-137.

335 ———. *Les névroses: Commentaires, observations et presentations de cas.* Translated by Odette Chabas. Paris: Aubier, 1969.

336 ———. New leading principles for the practice of Individual-Psychology. In *The practice and theory of Individual Psychology*, Pp. 23-31. Also in R. W. Marks (Ed.), *Great ideas in psychology*. New York: Bantam Books, 1966. Pp. 143-150.

337 ———. New view-points on war neuroses. In *The practice and theory of Individual Psychology*. Pp. 291-306.

338 ———. Nierenkrankungen. In M. Kahane (Ed.), *Med. Handlex. praktiz. Ärzte*. Pp. 698-704.

339 ———. Nochmals—die Einheit der Neurosen. *IZIP*, 1930, 8(2), 201-216.

340 ———. Note to a clergyman. *JIP*, 1966, 22, 234.

341 ———. On capital punishment (From *Social interest*. P. 105). *IPNL*, 1956, 5(8), Whole No. 60). P. 3.

342 ———. On the effect of education. *Pädagog. Heute*, 1969, 3-4.

343 ———. On the function of the compulsion-conception as a means of intensifying the individuality-feeling. In *The practice and theory of Individual Psychology*. Pp. 208-211.

344 ———. On the interpretation of dreams. *IJIP*, 1936, 2(1), 3-16.

345 ———. On leadership. *JIP*, 1958, 14, 127.

346 ———. On Mussolini [Interview with G. Seldes]. *New York World*, Dec. 26, 1926. P. 3E.

347 ———. On the origin of the striving for superiority and social interest. In H. L. Ansbacher & Rowena Ansbacher (Eds.), *Superiority and social interest*. Pp. 29-40.

348 ———. On the role of the unconscious in neurosis. In *The practice and theory of Individual Psychology*. Pp. 227-234.

349 **Adler, Alfred.** [On suicide]. In P. Friedman, *On suicide: With particular reference to suicide among young students.* (Discussions of the Vienna Psychoanalytic Society, 1910). Pp. 109-121.

350 ———. On teaching courage. *Survey Graphic*, 1928, 61, 241-242.

351 ———. Organdialekt. In A. Adler & C. Furtmüller (Eds.), *Heilen und Bilden*, (1914). Pp. 130-139; (1928). Pp. 122-129.

352 ———. Das organische Substrat der Psychoneurosen: Zur Ätiologie der Neurosen und Psychosen. *Z. ges. Neurol. Psychiat.*, 1912, 13, 481-491. *J. Psychol. u. Neurol.*, (Leipzig), 1913, 20, 130-139. Also in *Praxis und Theorie*. Pp. 168-176.

353 ———. The pattern of life: Case histories of American children. Edited by W. B. Wolfe. New York: Cosmopolitan, 1930; London: Kegan Paul, Trench, Trubner, 1931.

354 ———. Per l'educazione del genitore. *Psiche*, 1914, 3, 368-382.

355 ———. Persönlichkeit als geschlossene Einheit. *IZIP*, 1932, 10, 81-88.

356 ———. Physical manifestations of psychic disturbances. *IPB*, 1944, 4, 3-8. Also in H. L. Ansbacher & Rowena Ansbacher (Eds.), *Superiority and social interest*. Pp. 224-232.

357 ———. Portrait. *IPB*, 1944, 3, 104; *IPNL*, 1967, 18(7-8, Whole No. 192-193). P. 51; *IPNL*, 1970, 19(4), 61; *William Alanson White Inst. Nwsltr.*, Fall, 1970; *ADAM: Int. Rev.* (London), 1970, 35(340-342); *JIP*, 1957, 13, facing p. 111; *JIP*, 1970, 26, Frontispiece; *Amer. J. Psychother.*, 1950, 4, facing p. 223; *IZIP*, 1937, 15(3-4), Frontispiece; *IZIP*, 1930, 8(1), Frontispiece; *IPNL*, 1972, 21(6), 109; *N. Y. Times Mag.*, Feb. 28, 1971. Cover. Also in P. Rom, Note on Alfred Adler; In H. L. Ansbacher & Rowena Ansbacher (Eds.), *The Individual Psychology of Alfred Adler*. In Anon., *Kovets Individual-Psykhologie.* In H. L. Ansbacher & Rowena Ansbacher (Eds.), *Superiority and social interest*, Frontispiece. In J. Gunther, *Freud's Schüler und Widersacher.* In L. Seif & L. Zilahi, *Selbsterziehung des Charakters.* In J. Rattner, *Alfred Adler in Selbstzeugnissen und Bilddokumenten.* In P. H. Ronge, In memoriam Alfred Adler. In H. Schaffer, *Un chercheur et ses idées.*

358 **Adler, Alfred.** La posición masculina en neuró-
ticos femeninos. In *Práctica y teoría de la
Psícología del Individuo.*

359 ———. Position in the family constellation influences life-style. *IJIP*, 1937, 3(3),
211–227.

360 ———. *Poznavanje Coveka* [Understanding
human nature]. Translated by V. Drovinskovic
& M. Djieric. Beograd: Kosmos, 1934, 1958.

361 ———. *Práctica y teoría de la Psícología
del Individuo.*

362 ———. The practice and theory of Individual Psychology. In T. Shipley (Ed.), *Classics
in psychology.* Pp. 687–714.

363 ———. *The practice and theory of Individ-
ual Psychology.* Translated by P. Radin.
London: Kegan Paul, 1924, 1925, 1929;
New York: Harcourt, Brace, 1927; London:
Kegan Paul, Trench, Trubner, 1946; New
York: Humanities Press, 1951; Paterson,
N. J.: Littlefield, Adams, 1963. Paper.

364 ———. [*The practice and theory of Individual Psychology*]. Beograd: Geza-Don.
A. D., 1937.

365 ———. Prassi e teoria della Psicologia Individuale [*Practice and theory of Individual Psychology*]. Rome: Astrolabio, 1949;
Rome: Newton Compton Italiana, 1970.

366 ———. *Pratique et theorie de la Psychologie Individuelle Comparée.* Translated by
H. Schaffer. Paris: Payot, 1961.

367 ———. *Praxis und Theorie der Individualpsychologie: Vorträge zur Einführung in
die Psychotherapie für Aerzte, Psychologen,
und Lehrer.* Munich: Bergmann, 1920,
1924, 1930; Darmstadt, Germany: Wissenschaftl. Buchgesellschaft, 1965.

368 ———. A preface by Adler. *IPNL*, 18(9–
10, Whole No. 206–207). P. 88.

369 ———. Preface to R. Dreikurs, *Fundamentals of Adlerian psychology.*

370 ———. Preface to the English translation
of *Praxis und Theorie der Individualpsychologie. IZIP*, 1924, 2(3), 53–54.

371 ———. Preface to H. F. Wolf, *Strategie
der männliche Annäherung.*

372 ———. The prevention of delinquency.
IJIP, 1935, 1(3), 3–13.

373 ———. Prevention of neurosis. *IJIP*,
1935, 1(4), 3–12.

374 ———. *The problem child: The life style
of the difficult child as analyzed in specific
cases.* Translated by G. Daniels. New York:
Capricorn Books, 1963.

375 **Adler, Alfred.** El problem de la distancia. In
*Práctica y teoría de la Psícología del Indi-
viduo.*

376 ———. Das Problem der "Distanz": Über
einen Grundcharakter der Neurose und Psychose. *ZIP*, 1914, 1, 8–16. Also in *Praxis
und Theorie.* Pp. 70–75.

377 ———. *Das Problem der Homosexualität.*
München: Reinhardt, 1917; Leipzig: Hirzel,
1930.

378 ———. The problem of distance. In *The
practice and theory of Individual Psychology.* Pp. 100–108.

379 ———. *El problema del homosexualismo y
otros problemas sexuales.* Barcelona: Apollo
Ed., 1936; Santiago de Chile: Cultura Ed., 1937.

380 ———. *Problems of neurosis: A book of
case-histories.* Edited by P. Mairet. Preface
by F. G. Crookshank. London: Kegan Paul,
Trench, Trubner, 1929; New York: Cosmopolitan, 1930; New York: Harper Torchbooks, 1964. Paper.

381 ———. Progress in Individual Psychology.
Brit. J. med. Psychol., 1924, 4, 22–31.

382 ———. The progress of mankind. *JIP*,
1957, 13, 9–13. Also in K. A. Adler &
Danica Deutsch (Eds.), *Essays in Individual
Psychology.* Pp. 3–8. Also in H. L. Ansbacher & Rowena Ansbacher (Eds.), *Superiority and social interest.* Pp. 23–28.

383 ———. La Psícología del Individuo y la
prostitución. In *Práctica y teoría de la
Psícología del Individuo.*

384 ———. *La Psicologia Individual en la escuela.* Translated by J. Salas. Madrid: Rev.
de Pedag., 1936; Buenos Aires: Edit.
Losada, 1941.

385 ———. The psychic treatment of trigemi-
nal neuralgia. In *The practice and theory
of Individual Psychology.* Pp. 78–99.

386 ———. Psychical hermaphroditism and the
masculine protest—The cardinal problem of
nervous diseases. In *The practice and theory of Individual Psychology.* Pp. 16–22.

387 ———. Die psychische Behandlung der
Trigeminusneuralgie. *Zbl. Psychoanal.*,
1910, 1, 10–29. Also in *Praxis und Theorie.* Pp. 54–69.

388 ———. Psychische Einstellungen der
Frau zum Sexualleben. In A. Bethe *et
al.*, (Eds.), *Handb. norm. path. Physiol.*
Vol. 14. Pp. 802–807. Also in A. Adler,
Das Problem der Homosexualität. Pp.
89–97.

389 **Adler, Alfred.** Der psychische Hermaphroditismus im Leben und in der Neurose. *Fortschr. Med.*, 1910, 28, 486–493. Also in A. Adler & C. Furtmüller (Eds.), *Heilen und Bilden* (1914). Pp. 74–83; (1928). Pp. 76–83.

390 ———. Psychischer Hermaphroditismus und männlicher Protest: Ein Kernproblem der nervösen Erkrankungen. In *Praxis und Theorie.* Pp. 11–15.

391 ———. Psychische Kausalität. *IZIP*, 1924, 2(6), 38.

392 ———. *Psychologia Individualit b'vet Sefer Hartzaot l'Morim ul' Mekhankhim* [Individual Psychology in the school.   ]. Jerusalem: Ever   , 1944.

393 ———. *La psychologie de l'enfant difficile: Technique de la Psychologie Individuelle Comparée.* Translated by H. Schaffer. Paris: Payot, 1952.

394 ———. La Psychologie Individuelle dans la pédagogie moderne. *L'Avenir soc.* (Brussels), 1929, 1, 25–26.

395 ———. La Psychologie Individuelle, son importance au point de vue du traitement de la nervosité, de l'éducation et de la vue conception générale du monde. *Scientia, Suppl.*, 1926, 39, 115–123.

396 ———. *De psychologie van het individueele op school en in het gezin* [Individual Psychology in the school]. Translated by P. van Schilfgaarde. Utrecht: Bijleveld, 1933.

397 ———. Psychologie der Macht. In F. Kobler (Ed.), *Gewalt und Gewaltlosigkeit: Handbuch des aktiven Pazifismus.* Zürich: Rotapfel-Verlag, 1928. Pp. 41–46.

398 ———. Psychologie und Medizin. *Wien med. Wchnschr.*, 1928, 78, 697–700.

399 ———. *Psycholgja Indywidualna* [Individual Psychology]. Krakow: Gebethner i Wolff, 1934.

400 ———. *The psychology of the difficult child.* New York: Capricorn Books, 1960.

401 ———. The psychology of power. *JIP*, 1966, 22, 166–172. Also in H. J. Vetter & B. D. Smith, (Eds.), *Personality theory: A source book.*

402 ———. Psychosexuelle Haltung des Mannes. In A. Bethe *et al.*, (Eds.), *Handb. norm. path. Physiol.* Vol. 14. Pp. 808–812. Also in A. Adler, *Das Problem der Homosexualität.* Pp. 98–106.

403 **Adler, Alfred.** Pubertätserscheinungen. In A. Bethe *et al.*, (Eds.), *Handb. norm. path. Physiol.* Vol. 14. Pp. 842–844. Also in A. Adler, *Das Problem der Homosexualität.* Pp. 85–89.

404 ———. Rauschgift. *Fortschr. Med.*, 1931, 49, 535–540, 571–575. Also in *IZIP*, 1932, 10, 1–19.

405 ———. Religion and Individual Psychology. In H. L. Ansbacher & Rowena Ansbacher (Eds.), *Superiority and social interest.* Pp. 271–308.

406 ———. *Religion et Psychologie Individuelle Comparée* (with E. Jahn) suivi *La nevrose obsessionnelle, Complement à l'étude de la nevrose obsessionnelle* et *Les enfants difficile.* Translated by H. Schaffer. Paris: Payot, 1958.

407 ———. Religion und Individualpsychologie. In E. Jahn & A. Adler, *Religion und Individual psychologie: Eine prinzipelle Auseinandersetzung über Menschenführung.* Vienna: Rolf Passer, 1933.

408 ———. Report of lecture by Dr. Alfred Adler to the Medical Society of I. P. at 11 Chandos Street, W. *IPMP*, 1934, No. 13. Pp. 13–24.

409 ———. **Review of** [Anon.], *Hinter Schloss und Riegel.* **Munich:** Langen, 1910. In *Zbl. Psychoanal.*, 1910, 1, 112–113.

410 ———. Review of W. Astrow (Ed.), Petersburger Träume: Eine unbekannte Erzählung von Dostojewsky. *Neue Freie Press*, Ostersnumer. 1914. In *ZIP*, 1914, 1, 63–64.

411 ———. Review of T. Becker, Zur Diagnose paranoischer Zustände. *Münchn. med. Wiss.*, 1914, No. 12. In *ZIP*, 1914, 1(2), 62–63.

412 ———. Review of W. B. Cannon, *The wisdom of the body.* New York: Norton, 1932. In *IZIP*, 1933, 11(2), 154.

413 ———. Review of P. Engelen, Suggestionsfaktoren bei der Freudschen Psychoanalyse. *Deutsche med. Wchnschr.*, 1914. No. 19. In *ZIP*, 1914, 1, 92–93.

414 ———. Review of C. G. Jung, Über Konflikte der kindlichen Seele. *Jb. Psychoanal. psychopath. Forsch.*, 1910, 2. In *Zbl. Psychoanal.*, 1910, 1, 122–123.

415 ———. Review of E. V. Koehler, Warum denken Wir im Wachen in Worten im Traume in Bildern? *Psychiat. neurol. Wchnschr.*, 1914, No. 46. In *ZIP*, 1914, 1, 142.

416 **Adler, Alfred.** Review of J. Langermann, *Der Erziehungsstaat.* Berlin: Mathilde Zimmer-Haus, 1910. In *Zbl. Psychoanal.*, 1911, 1, 258–259.

417 ————. Review of S. Meyer, Organische und geistige Entwicklung. *Deutsche med. Wchnschr.*, 1914, No. 19. In *ZIP*, 1914, 1, 142.

418 ————. Review of F. Nadastiny, *Untermenschen oder Narren?* Wien: Konegen, 1910. In *Zbl. Psychoanal.*, 1910, 1, 113.

419 ————. Review of K. Pelmann, *Psychische Grenzzustände.* Bonn: Cohen, 1910. In *Zbl. Psychoanal.*, 1910, 1, 78–79.

420 ————. Review of P. Schuster, *Drei Vorträge aus dem Gebiete der Unfall-Neurologie.* Leipzig: Georg Thieme, 1910. In *Zbl. Psychoanal.*, 1910, 1, 122.

421 ————. Review of H. Sperber, *Todesgedanke und Lebensgestaltung.* Wien: M. Perles, 1930. In *IZIP*, 1930, 8(6), 591–592.

422 ————. Review of W. Stekel, *Nervöse Angstzustände und ihre Behandlung.* Vienna: Urban & Schwarzenberg, 1912. In *Sex. Probl.*, 1913, 9(1), 62–64.

423 ————. Review of E. Wulffen, *Der Sexualverbrecher.* Berlin: Langenscheidt, 1910. In *Zbl. Psychoanal.*, 1910, 1, 118–119.

424 ————. Die Rolle der Sexualität in der Neurose. In A. Adler & C. Furtmüller (Eds.), *Heilen und Bilden,* (1914). Pp. 94–103.

425 ————. Die Rolle des Unbewussten in der Neurose. *Zbl. Psychoanal.*, 1913, 3, 169–174. Also in *Praxis und Theorie.* Pp. 158–163.

426 ————. Sadismus, Masochismus und andere Perversionen. In A. Bethe *et al.*, (Eds.), *Handb. norm. path. Physiol.* Vol. 14. Pp. 887–894. Also in A. Adler, *Das Problem der Homosexualität.* Pp. 67–78.

427 ————. Salvaging mankind by psychology. [Interview with E. Bagger]. N. Y. Times, Sept. 20, 1925. P. 12. Also in *IZIP*, 1925, 3(6), 332–335.

428 ————. Schlusswort. In A. Adler & C. Furtmüller (Eds.), *Heilen und Bilden* (1914). P. 399; (1928). P. 355.

429 ————. A schoolgirl's exaggeration of her own importance. *IJIP,* 1937, 3(1), 3–12.

430 ————. Schwererziehbare Kinder. In. O. & Alice Rühle (Eds.), *Schwererziehbare Kinder: Eine Schriftenfolge.* Dresden: Am Andern Ufer, 1926.

431 **Adler, Alfred.** Schwereziehbare Kinder und nervöse Erwachsene. *IZIP*, 1924, 3, 145–146.

432 ————. *The science of living.* Preface by P. Mairet. New York: Greenberg, 1929; Garden City, N. Y.: Garden City Publ. Co., 1929; London: Allen & Unwin, 1930, 1952; Cleveland: World Publ. Co., 1943; New York: Doubleday Anchor Books, 1969 (with introduction by H. L. Ansbacher).

433 ————. Selbstmord. *IZIP*, 1937, 15(2), 49–52.

434 ————. *Le sens de la vie.* Translated by H. Schaffer. Paris: Payot, 1950.

435 ————. *Sens Zycia.* Krakow: Gebethner i Wolff, n.d.

436 ————. *El sentido de la vida.* Translated by O. Brachfeld. Barcelona: Louis Miracle, 1935, 1949.

437 ————. Separate the Quins: It must be done for their own good. *Hearst's Int.—Cosmopol.,* March, 1936, 89–90.

438 ————. *Sex, personality and the Establishment.* Edited by G. H. LaPorte. New York: Editor, 1970.

439 ————. The sexual function. *IPB*, 1944–45, 4, 99–101. Also in H. L. Ansbacher & Rowena Ansbacher (Eds.), *Superiority and social interest.* Pp. 219–223.

440 ————. Sexualneurasthenie. In A. Bethe *et al.*, (Eds.), *Handb. norm. path. Physiol.* Vol. 14. Pp. 895–899. Also in A. Adler, *Das problem der Homosexualität.* Pp. 78–84.

441 ————. Sexual perversions. Translated by M. Marcus. *IPP*, 1932, No. 3. Reprinted as part of "Emotions, sex and experimentation" in *Sex, personality and the Establishment.* Pp. 39–56.

442 ————. Sexual perversions. *IPP*, 1934, No. 13. Pp. 25–36.

443 ————. Das sexuelle Problem in der Erziehung. *Neue Gesellschaft,* (Berlin) 1905, 1, 360–362.

444 ————. Sifilofobia. In *Práctica y teoría de la Psicología del Individuo.*

445 ————. Significance of early recollections. *IJIP,* 1937, 3(4), 283–287. Also in E. L. Hartley, H. G. Birch, & Ruth E. Hartley (Eds.), *Outside readings in psychology.* Pp. 361–365.

446 ————. Der Sinn des Lebens. *IZIP*, 1931, 9 (3), 161–171.

447 **Adler, Alfred.** *Der Sinn des Lebens.* Wien-Leipzig: Passer, 1933; München: Bergmann, 1932.

448 ———. Sitzungbericht des Vereins für Individualpsychologie, March 7, 1914. *ZIP,* 1914, 1, 96.

449 ———. Sitzungbericht des Vereins für Individualpsychologie, March 21, 1914. *ZIP,* 1914, 1, 143.

450 ———. Sleeplessness. *IPB,* 1944, 3, 60–64. Also in H. L. Ansbacher & Rowena Ansbacher (Eds.), *Superiority and social interest.* Pp. 233–238.

451 ———. *Social interest: A challenge to mankind.* Translated by J. Linton & R. Vaughan. London: Kegan Paul, 1929; New York: Cosmopolitan, 1930; London: Faber & Faber, 1938, 1940, 1945; New York: Putnam, 1939; London: Plymouth, Trend, 1945; New York: Capricorn Books, 1964. Paper.

452 ———. Something about myself. *Childhood & Charac.,* 1930, 7(7), 6–8.

453 ———. Soziale Einflüss in der Kinderstube. *Pädag. Arch.* (Leipzig), 1914, 56, 473–487.

454 ———. Staatshilfe oder Selbsthilfe? *Ärztl. Standeszeitung* (Wien), 1903, 2(21), 1–3; 1903, 2(22), 1–2.

455 ———. Stadt und Land. *Ärztl. Standeszeitung* (Wien), 1903, 2(18), 1–3; 1903, 2(19), 1–2; 1903, 2(20), 1–2.

456 ———. Die Strafe in der Erziehung. *Arbeiter-Zeitung,* Wien, June 14, 1924. P. 12.

457 ———. The structure and prevention of delinquency. In H. L. Ansbacher & Rowena Ansbacher (Eds.), *Superiority and social interest.* Pp. 253–268.

458 ———. The structure of neuroses. *IJIP,* 1935, 1(2), 3–12. Also in H. L. Ansbacher & Rowena Ansbacher (Eds.), *Superiority and social interest.* Pp. 83–95.

459 ———. The structure of neurosis. *Lancet,* 1931, 220, 136–137.

460 ———. *Studie über Minderwertigkeit von Organen.* Wien: Urban & Schwarzenberg, 1907; München: Bergmann, 1927; Darmstadt, Germany: Wissenschaftl. Buchgesellschaft, 1965.

461 ———. The study of child psychology and neurosis. In *The practice and theory of Individual Psychology.* Pp. 59–77.

462 ———. *Study of organ inferiority and its psychical compensation: A contribution to clinical medicine.* Translated by S. E. Jelliffe. New York: Moffat-Yard, 1907; New York: Nerv. Ment. Dis. Publ. Co., 1917.

463 **Adler, Alfred.** El sueno y su interpretacion. In *Práctica y teoría de la Psícología del Individuo.*

464 ———. Suicide. *JIP,* 1958, 14, 57–61. Also in H. L. Ansbacher & Rowena Ansbacher (Eds.), *Superiority and social interest.* Pp. 248–252.

465 ———. *Superioridad e interés social: Una coleccion de sus ultimos escritos.* Translated by Maria Martinez Penaloza. Mexico City: Fondo de Cultura Economica, 1968.

466 ———. El sustrato orgánico de las psiconeurosis. In *Práctica y teoría de la Psícología del Individuo.*

467 ———. Symptomwahl. *IZIP,* 1936, 14(2), 65–80.

468 ———. Symptomwahl beim Kinde. *Kinderärztl. Praxis,* 1931, 2, 398–409.

469 ———. *Synkritiki atomiki psychologia kai psychotherapeia. O nevrikos charaktir* [The neurotic constitution]. Translated by G. D. Konstantinidi. Athens: Gobosti, 1938.

470 ———. Syphilophobia. In *The practice and theory of Individual Psychology.* Pp. 153–162.

471 ———. Syphilidophobie: Ein Beitrag zur Bedeutung der Hypochondrie in der Dynamik der Neurose. *Zbl. Psychoanal.,* 1911, 1, 400–406. Also in *Praxis und Theorie.* Pp. 106–112.

472 ———. Die Systematik der Individualpsychologie. *IZIP,* 1932, 10, 241–244.

473 ———. *Die Technik der Individualpsychologie: I. Die Kunst, eine Lebens und Krankengeschichte zu lesen.* München: Bergmann, 1928.

474 ———. *Die Technik der Individualpsychologie: II. Die Seele des schwererziehbaren Schulkindes.* München: Bergmann, 1930.

475 ———. Technique of treatment. In H. L. Ansbacher & Rowena Ansbacher (Eds.), *Superiority and social interest.* Pp. 191–201.

476 ———. *Le tempérament nerveux: Elements d'une Psychologie Individuelle et applications à la psychothérapie.* Translated by [ ] Roussel. Paris: Payot, 1926, 1948.

477 ———. *Il temperamento nervoso* [The neurotic character]. Rome: Astrolabio, 1950; Rome: Newton Compton Italiana, 1971.

478 ———. Las tendencias agresivas en la vida y en la neurosis. In A. Adler & C. Furtmüller (Eds.), *Curar y educar.*

479 **Adler, Alfred.** Terquedad y obediencia. In A. Adler & C. Furtmüller (Eds.), *Curar y educar.*

480 ———. Die Theorie der Organminderwertigkeit und ihre Bedeutung für Philosophie und Psychologie. *Univ. Wien Phil. Gesellschaft Wiss. Beil.*, 1908, 21, 11–26. Also in A. Adler & C. Furtmüller (Eds.), *Heilen und Bilden* (1914). Pp. 11–22; (1928). Pp. 24–32.

481 ———. Das Todesproblem in der Neurose. *IZIP*, 1936, 14(1), 1–6.

482 ———. Die Tragfähigkeit der menschlichen Seele. *IZIP*, 1923, 2(2), 42.

483 ———. Training? *IZIP*, 1924, 2(6), 39.

484 ———. Transformation of neuroses and training in the dream. *IZIP*, 1924, 2(5), 5–8.

485 ———. Tratamento psíquico de la neuralgia del trigémino. In *Práctica y teoría de la Psicología del Individuo.*

486 ———. Trátase del "Consejero áulico Eysenhardt" de Alfred von Berger. In *Práctica y teoría de la Psicología del Individuo.*

487 ———. Traum und Traumdeutung. *Zbl. Psychoanal.*, 1913, 3, 574–583. Also in A. Adler & C. Furtmüller (Eds.), *Heilen und Bilden*, Pp. 149–157.

488 ———. Trick and neurosis. *IJIP*, 1936, 2 (2), 3–10.

489 ———. Trick und Neurose. *IZIP*, 1931, 9(6), 417–423.

490 ———. Trotz und Gehorsam. *Monatschr. Pädag. Schulpol.*, 1910, 2, 321–328. Also in A. Adler & C. Furtmüller (Eds.), *Heilen und Bilden* (1914). Pp. 84–93; (1928). Pp. 84–91.

491 ———. Tsorekh-hachibah shel Hayeled [The child's need for affection]. In Anon., *Kovets Individual-Psykhologie.* Pp. 88–92.

492 ———. Two grade-school girls. In H. L. Ansbacher & Rowena Ansbacher (Eds.), *Superiority and social interest.* Pp. 143–158. Also appears as "Case interpretation", *IPB*, 1941, 2(1), 1–9.

493 ———. Two letters to a patient. *JIP*, 1966, 22, 112–115.

494 ———. Typology of meeting life problems. In H. L. Ansbacher & Rowena Ansbacher (Eds.), *Superiority and social interest.* Pp. 66–70.

495 ———. Über das materielle Substrat psychischen Vorgänge. *Psychiat. neurol. Wchnschr.*, 1910, 11, 369–370.

496 **Adler, Alfred.** Über das Wesen und die Entstehung des Charakters. *IZIP*, 1935, 13(1), 29–30.

497 ———. Über den nervösen Charakter. *Arch. f. Krim. Anthropol. u. Kriminalistik*, 1912, 49, 173.

498 ———. *Über den nervösen Charakter.* Wiesbaden: Bergmann, 1912; München: Bergmann, 1922, 1926, 1928.

499 ———. *Über den Selbstmord, inbesondere den Schülerselbstmord. Diskuss. Wien. psychoanal. Ver.* Wiesbaden: Bergmann, 1910. Pp. 44–50. Also in A. Adler & C. Furtmüller (Eds.), *Heilen und Bilden.* Pp. 356–363.

500 ———. Über den Ursprung des Strebens nach Überlegenheit und des Gemeinschaftsgefühls. *Mitteilungsbl. Indivpsy.*, 1933, 2(7), 1.

501 ———. Über die Homosexualität. In *Praxis und Theorie.* Pp. 127–135.

502 ———. Über die Unschädlichmachung der sogenannten "geisteskranken" Verbrecher. *Monatschr. Krim.-Psychol. u. Strafrechtsref.*, 1925, 16, 191–193.

503 ———. Über die Vererbung von Krankheiten. *Kampf* (Wien), 1908, 1(9), 425–430. Also in A. Adler & C. Furtmüller (Eds.), *Heilen und Bilden.* (1914). Pp. 41–49; (1928). Pp. 49–55.

504 ———. Über individualpsychologische Erziehung. In *Praxis und Theorie.* Pp. 221–227

505 ———. Über Kritzeleien. *IZIP*, 1934, 12(4), 201–203.

506 ———. Über männliche Einstellung bei weiblichen Neurotikern. III. Versuch der Umkehrung als männlicher Protest. *Zbl. Psychoanal.*, 1911, 1, 174–178. Also in *Praxis und Theorie.* Pp. 80–99.

507 ———. Über Neurose und Begabung. *IZIP*, 1925, 3, 346.

508 ———. Über neurotische Disposition: Zugleich ein Beitrag zur Aetiologie und zur Frage der Neurosenwahl. *Jb. psychoanal., psychopath. Forsch.*, 1909, 1, 526–545. Als in A. Adler & C. Furtmüller (Eds.), *Heilen und Bilden.* (1914). Pp. 54–73; (1928). Pp. 59–75.

509 ———. Über Weltanschauung. *IZIP*, 1924, 2(6), 38.

510 ———. Übertreibung der eigenen Wichtigkeit. *IZIP*, 1929, 7(4), 245–252. Also in *Die Technique der Individualpsychologie.* Vol. II. Ch. 1.

511 **Adler, Alfred.** *Understanding human nature.*
Translated by W. B. Wolfe. London: Unwin,
1918; New York: Greenberg, 1927, 1946;
New York: World Publ. Co., 1927, 1941;
New York: Garden City Publ. Co., 1927;
Philadelphia: Chilton, 1927; London: Allen
& Unwin, 1928, 1954; New York: Perma-
books, 1949. Paper; Greenwich, Conn.:
Premier Books, 1957. Paper.

512 ———. [Understanding human nature].
Translated into Japanese by H. Yamashita.
Tokyo: Nippon Kyobunsha, 1957.

513 ———. Unerziehbarkeit des Kindes oder Un-
belehrkeit der Theorie? Bemerkungen zum
Falle Hug. *Arbeiter-Zeitung* (Wien), Mar. 5,
1925. P. 6.

514 ———. Unspoiling the spoiled child. *Parents
Mag.,* May, 1929. Pp. 72–73.

515 ———. El valor: Su importancia en la educacion del nino. *Nueva Era,* 1927, 8, 115–
116.

516 ———. "Verdrängung" und "männlicher
Protest": Ihre Rolle und Bedeutung für
die neurotische Dynamik. In A. Adler &
C. Furtmüller (Eds.), *Heilen und Bilden*
(1914). Pp. 103–114.

517 ———. Verwahrloste Kinder. In *Praxis und
Theorie.* Pp. 237–244.

518 ———. Vor-und Nachteile des Minderwertigkeitsgefühls. *Pädag. Warte,* 1933, 40, 15–
19.

519 ———. Die Vorbeugung der Delinquenz.
IZIP, 1935, 13(4), 197–206.

520 ———. Vorrede. In R. Dreikurs, *Einführung in die Individualpsychologie.*

521 ———. Vorrede. In E. Wexberg (Ed.),
Handbuch der Individualpsychologie. Vol.
1. Pp. v–vi.

522 ———. Vorrede. In H. F. Wolf, *Strategie
der männlichen Annäherung.* Wien: Ilos
Verlag, 1926.

523 ——— Vorwort des Herausgebers. *Schr.
Ver. freie psychoanal. Forsch.,* 1912, No. 7.
Pp. v–vii.

524 ——— Was ist wirklich eine Neurose? *IZIP,*
1933, 11, 177–184. Also in *Der Sinn des
Lebens.* Ch. 10.

525 ———. Was kann die Individualpsychologie zur mathematischen "Begabung" sagen?
IZIP, 1933, 11, 42–43.

526 ———. Weiteres zur individualpsychologischen Traumtheorie. *IZIP,* 1927, 5(4), 241–245.

527 ———. Weiteres zur Zwangsneurose. *IZIP,*
1936, 14(4), 193–196.

528 **Adler, Alfred.** What is neurosis? *IJIP,* 1935,
1(1), 9–17.

529 ———. *What life should mean to you.*
Edited by A. Porter. Boston: Little, Brown,
1931; New York: Blue Ribbon Books, 1931;
New York: Grosset & Dunlap, 1931, 1944;
London: Allen & Unwin, 1931, 1952; New
York: Capricorn Books, 1958, 1960. Paper;
London: Unwin Books, 1962. Paper.

530 ———. Wide, wide world. [Interview with
Lola J. Simpson]. *Good Housekeeping,*
October, 1931. Pp. 40–41.

531 ———. Witwenverbrennung und Witwen-
neurose. *IZIP,* 1928, 6(1), 23–25.

532 ———. Wo soll der Kampf gegen die Verwahrlosung einsetzen? *Soc. Praxis* (Vienna),
1921. In A. Adler, C. Furtmüller & E. Wexberg (Eds.), *Heilen und Bilden* (1922). Pp.
116–118; (1928). Pp. 139–141.

533 ———. Das Zärtlichkeitsbedürfnis des
Kindes. *Monatschr. Pädag. Schulpol.,* 1908,
1, 7–9. Also in A. Adler & C. Fürtmuller
(Eds.), *Heilen und Bilden* (1914). Pp. 50–
53; (1928). Pp. 56–58.

534 ———. *Der zin fun leben* [The meaning of
life]. Translated into Yiddish by B. Bodluck
& R. Lichstein. Wilno, Poland: 1938.

535 ———. *De zin van het leven* [The meaning
of life]. Translated into Dutch by P. H.
Ronge. Utrecht: Bijleveld, 1935, 1963.

536 ———. *Znajomosc czlowieka* [Understand-
ing human nature]. Lodz, Poland: Jaiol-
kowski, 1948.

537 ———. Zum Leib-Seele Problem. *IZIP,*
1933, 11, 337–345. Also in *Der Sinn des
Lebens.* Ch. 4.

538 ———. Zum Thema sexuelle Perversionen.
IZIP, 1932, 10, 401–409.

539 ———. Zum Verständnis einiger psycho-
pathischer Konstitutionen. *Psychiat.-
Neurol. Wchnschr.,* 1927, 29, 256.

540 ———. Zur Aetiologie, Diagnostik und
Therapie der Nephrolithiasis. *Wien klin.
Wchnschr.,* 1907, 20, 1534–1539.

541 ———. Zur Erziehung der Eltern. In A.
Adler & C. Furtmüller (Eds.), *Heilen und
Bilden* (1914), Pp. 113–129; (1928). Pp.
110–121. Reprint of "Zur Erziehung der
Erzieher".

542 ———. Zur Erziehung der Erzieher. *Monatschr. Pädag. Schulpol.,* 1912, 8. Reprinted as "Zur Erziehung der Eltern". In
A. Adler & C. Furtmüller (Eds.), *Heilen
und Bilden* (1914). Pp. 113–129.

543 **Adler, Alfred.** Zur Funktion der Zwangsvorstellung als eines Mittels zur Erhöhung des Persönlichkeitgefühls. In *Praxis und Theorie.* Pp. 144–146.

544 ———. Zur Kinderpsychologie und Neurosenforschung. *Wien. klin. Wchnschr.,* 1914, 27, 511–516. Also in *Praxis und Theorie.* Pp. 41–53.

545 ———. Zur Kritik der Freudschen Sexualtheorie der Nervösität. In A. Adler & C. Furtmüller (Eds.), *Heilen und Bilden* (1914). Pp. 94–114; (1928). Pp. 92–109.

546 ———. Zur Rolle des Unbewussten in der Neurose. *Zbl. Psychoanal.,* 1913, 3, 169–174. Also in *Praxis und Theorie.* Pp. 158–163.

547 ———. Zur Sitophobie. *ZIP,* 1914, 1(1), 27–28. Reprinted as "Nervoser Hungerstreik" in *Praxis und Theorie.* Pp. 147–148.

548 ———. Zur Theorie der Haluzination. In *Praxis und Theorie.* Pp. 36–40.

549 ———. Zusammenhänge zwischen Neurose und Witz. *IZIP,* 1927, 5(2), 94–96.

550 ———. Zwangsneurose. *IZIP,* 1931, 9, 1–16.

551 ———. Die Zwangsneurose. In *Praxis und Theorie.* Pp. 136–143.

552 ———. Zwei Träume einer Prostitutieren. *Z. Sexualwiss.,* 1908, 1, 103–106.

553 **Adler, A.*** *The education of the individual.* New York: Phil. Libr., 1958; New York: Greenwood Press, 1958.

554 ———. Yvain, der Löwenritter. *IZIP,* 1935, 13(3), 185–189.

555 ———. Zur Psychologie des primitiven Menschen. *IZIP,* 1936, 14(4), 209–220.

556 **Adler, C. A.** The anti-Babel: An attempt to clarify some controversial points in "guidance". *Prog. Educ.,* 1939, 16, 568–573.

557 ———. The first interview (Three approproaches to guidance). *IPB,* 1943, 3, 71–80.

558 ———. The nature of character. *IJIP,* 1935, 1(3), 59–70.

559 ———. Review of Caroline Zachry, *Emotion and conduct in adolescence.* New York: Appleton, 1940. In *IPN,* 1940, 1(2), 3–4.

560 ———. Richard III—his significance as a study in criminal life style. *IJIP,* 1936, 2(3), 55–60.

561 **Adler, K. A.** Adlerian view of the present-day scene. *JIP,* 1970, 26(2), 113–121.

562 ———. Adler's Individual Psychology. In B. B. Wolman (Ed.), *Psychoanalytic*

techniques: A handbook for the practicing psychoanalyst.* Pp. 299–337.

563 **Adler, K. A.** Depression in the light of Individual Psychology. *JIP,* 1961, 17, 56–67. Also in H. D. Werner (Ed.), *New understandings of human behavior.* Pp. 127–134.

564 ——— (Ed.). *Essays in Individual Psychology: Contemporary application of Alfred Adler's theories.* New York: Grove Press, 1959 (with Danica Deutsch).

565 ———. Foreword. In A. Adler, *The problem child.* Pp. vii–viii.

566 ———. Individual Psychologist. *MD,* 1970, 14(2), 185–190 (with F. Marti-Ibanez).

567 ———. Introduction to A. Adler, *The problem child.* Pp. iv–vi.

568 ———. The life style. *OSIPNL,* 1972, 13(3), 13–14.

569 ———. Life style, gender role, and the sympton of homosexuality. *JIP,* 1967, 23, 67–78. Also in W. S. Sahakian (Ed.), *Psychopathology today.* Pp. 511–518.

570 ———. Life style in schizophrenia. *JIP,* 1958, 14, 68–72. Also in K. A. Adler & Danica Deutsch (Eds.), *Essays in Individual Psychology.* Pp. 45–55.

571 ———. A new look at law and order. In W. L. Pew (Ed.), *The war between the generations.* Pp. 1–5.

572 ———. Non-Freudian techniques. In B. B. Wolman (Ed.), *Psychoanalytic techniques: A handbook for the practicing psychoanalyst.*

573 ———. Point de vue adlérienne à propos de la situation actuelle. *BSFPA,* 1971, No. 11. Pp. 1–10.

574 ———. Portrait. *IPNL,* 1970, 19(4), 62.

575 ———. Power in Adlerian theory. In J. H. Masserman (Ed.), *Science and psychoanalysis.* Vol. 20. *The dynamics of power.* Pp. 53–63.

576 ———. The present-day scene. *IPNL,* 1971, 20(2), 21–22. Excerpt from *JIP,* 1970, 26, 113–121.

577 ———. The relevance of Adler's psychology to present-day theory. *Amer. J. Psychiat.,* 1970, 127, 773–776.

578 ———. Review of W. Bonime, *The clinical use of dreams.* In *JIP,* 1963, 19, 233–234.

579 ———. Structure of a nervous breakdown. *Treatm. Monogr. analyt. Psychother.,* (Jamaica Ctr. Psychother., N. Y.), 1968, No. 2. Pp. 2–3.

*This Alfred Adler is a distant relative of Alfred Adler.

580 **Adler, K. A.** Student unrest and race relations. *Treatm. Monogr. analyt. Psychother.*, (Jamaica Ctr. Psychoter., N.Y.), 1971, No. 3. Pp. 7–11.

581 ———. Techniques that shorten psychotherapy. *JIP*, 1972, 28(2), 155–168.

582 **Adler, M.** Erkenntniskritische Bemerkungen zur Individualpsychologie. *IZIP*, 1925, 3(5), 209–221.

583 **Adler, Raissa.** Boris Pasternak (1890–1960). *IPNL*, 1960, 10(11–12, Whole No. 112–114). P. 43.

584 ———. The future progress of Individual Psychology. *IPB*, 1942, 2(3), 54.

585 ———. Kindererziehung in der Sowjetunion. *IZIP*, 1931, 9(4), 297–309.

586 ———. Portrait. *IPNL*, 1970, 19(4), 61.

587 ———. Review of S. Gurewitch & F. Grosser, *Probleme des Geschlechtslebens*. Charkow: Staatsverlag der Ukraine, 1930. In *IZIP*, 1931, 9(2), 157.

588 ———. Review of S. Gurewitch & A. Salewski, *Der Alkoholismus*. Moscow: Staatsverlag, 1930 and G. Klatt, *Die Alkoholfrage*. In *IZIP*, 1932, 10(2), 154–155.

589 ———. Review of L. Pantelejew, *Die Uhr*. Berlin: Verlag der Jugendinternationale, 1930. In *IZIP*, 1932, 10(4), 320.

590 ———. Review of F. Torberg, *Der Schüler Gerber hat absolviert*. Berlin: Paul Zsolnay, 1930. In *IZIP*, 1930, 8(6), 596–597.

591 ———. Review of H. von Braken, *Die Progelstrafe*. In *IZIP*, 1926, 4(3), 166.

592 ———. Sollen die Frauen sich dem Studium der Medizin zuwenden? *Dokumente der Frauen* (Wien), 1899, Juli-Dez., 289–293.

593 **Adler, Tanya.** Portrait. *IPNL*, 1970, 19(4), 62.

594 **Adler, Valentina.** Bemerkungen über die soziologischen Grundlagen des "männlichen Protest". *IZIP*, 1925, 3(6), 307–310.

595 ———. Portrait. In J. Rattner, *Alfred Adler in Selbstzeugnissen und Bilddokumenten*.

596 ———. Review of F. Giese (Ed.), *Handworterbuch der Arbeitswissenschaft*. Halle: Carl Marhold [ ]. In *IZIP*, 1929, 7(1), 73–74.

597 **Aichinger, Berta.** Review of K. E. Baumgärtel, *Die Gedichte des Knaben*. Heilbronn um Neckar: Erich Kunter, [ ]. In *IZIP*, 1927, 5(2), 159.

598 **Aiginger, J.** Affektkrisen und psychotherapeutisches Verhalten. *IZIP*, 1947, 16(2), 56–65.

599 **Albrecht, H.** Diskussionsbemerkungen zum Vorträge des Prof. Max Adler. *IZIP*, 1925, 3(5), 223–227.

600 ———. Review of A. Herzberg, *Zur Psychologie der Philosophie und der Philosophen*. Leipzig: F. Meiner, 1926. In *IZIP*, 1926, 4(4), 246.

601 **Albrecht, W.** Review of V. Neubauer, *Der Weg zur Persönlichkeit*. Innsbruck: Tyrolia, 1947. In *IZIP*, 1950, 19(3), 143.

602 ———. Review of J. Wyrsch, *Psychopathologie und Verbrechen*. Innsbruck: Tyrolia, 1949. In *IZIP*, 1950, 19(2), 93–94.

603 **Alcock, Gudrun.** Clearing house for problems of children. *Chicago Sun-Times*, March 5, 1953.

604 ———. Guiding troubled children back to happiness [about Harold Mosak]. *Chicago Sunday Tribune*, June 17, 1951.

605 ———. Strangers saved my marriage. *McCall*, Jan., 1955.

606 **Alexander, C. N., Jr.** Ordinal position and social mobility. *Sociom.*, 1968, 31, 285–293.

607 ———. Ordinal position and sociometric status. *Sociom.*, 1966, 29, 41–51.

608 **Alexander, F. G.** *The history of psychiatry: An evaluation of psychiatric thought and practice from prehistoric times to the present*. New York: Harper & Row, 1966; New York: Mentor, 1966. Paper (with S. T. Selesnick).

609 ———. *Psychoanalytic pioneers: A history of psychoanalysis as seen through the lives and works of its most eminent teachers*. New York: Basic Books, 1966.

610 [**Alexander-Kounina, Irina**]. Memories of Alfred Adler. *IPNL*, 1972, 21(2), 21–22; 1972, 21(3), 43–44.

611 **The Alfred Adler Consultation Center.** Second Annual Report. *IPB*, 1950, 8, 169–171.

612 ———. Third annual report. *IPB*, 1951, 9, 176–178.

613 **Algad, R.** Translator of R. Dreikurs, *Nisooin Ha-etgar*.

614 **al Khaliq, A. M. Abd.**, Translator, with M. A. Badran, of A. Adler, *Al-Hayat Al Nafsiyah*.

615 **Alkaly, A.** Translator of A. Adler, *Psichologia Individualit bevais hasefer*.

616 **Allen, C.** *Les découvertes modernes de la psychiatrie*. Paris: Payot, 1951.

617 ———. *Modern discoveries in medical psychology*. New York: Macmillan, 1937; London: Pan Books, 1965. Paper.

618 **Allen, C. E.** Birth order and reaction to threat: A comparison of self-evaluation and anxiety reduction motives. *Diss Abstr.*, 1967, 27, 3510; Unpubl. Ph.D. Diss., Univ. Connecticut, 1966.

619 **Allen, G. Margery.** The Adlerian interpretation of compulsion. In K. A. Adler & Danica Deutsch (Eds.), *Essays in Individual Psychology.* Pp. 55–58.

620 **Allen, M. Harriet.** The Adlerian approach to counseling. *J. Rehab.*, 1968, 34(5), 11–13.

621 **Allen, T. W.** Adlerian interview strategies for behavior change. *Couns. Psychologist,* 1971, 3(1), 40–48.

622 ———. Commentaries. In V. Calia & R. Corsini (Eds.), *Critical incidents in counseling.*

623 ———. *Dimensions of effective counseling: Cognitive flexibility and psychological openness in counselor selection.* Columbus, Ohio: Merrill, 1968 (with J. M. Whiteley).

624 ———. Discussion of D. Blocher, What counseling can offer clients: Implications for research on selection. In J. Whiteley (Ed.), *Research problems in counseling.* Pp. 21–28.

625 ———. Effectiveness of counselor trainees as a function of psychological openness. *J. couns. Psychol.*, 1967, 14, 35–40.

626 ———. Empathy as a crucial variable in the counseling relationship. Unpubl. qualifying paper, Harvard Univ., 1964.

627 ———. The evaluation of a program of special classes for "disruptive children" in an urban school system. *Comm. ment. Hlth.*, 1970, Summer.

628 ———. The Individual Psychology of Alfred Adler: An item of history and a promise of revolution. *Couns. Psychologist,* 1971, 3(1), 3–24.

629 ———. A life style. *Couns. Psychologist,* 1971, 3(1), 25–29.

630 ———. A premature truce: The deradicalization of client-centered therapy. *Couns. Psychologist,* 1969, 1(2), 28–35.

631 ———. Purpose is alive and well and living in the empty organism. *Couns. Psychologist,* 1969, 1(4), 72–80.

632 ———. Task group report (with J. Krumboltz, F. Robinson, W. Cottle, J. Cody, D. Homra & J. Ray). In J. Whiteley (Ed.), *Research problems in counseling.* Pp. 219–237.

633 ———. "Willingness to Accept Limitations" Scale: Further cross-validation and item analysis. *JIP*, 1969, 25, 52–55.

634 **Allen, V. L.** Ordinal position and conformity: A role-theory analysis. *Sociom.*, 1970, 33, 371–381 (with B. W. Bragg).

635 **Allensmith, Beverly.** Parental discipline and children's aggression in two social classes. Ph.D. Diss., Univ. Michigan, 1954.

636 **Allers, R.** Arbeit, Ermüdung, Ruhe. In *Soziale Physiologie und Pathologie.*

637 ———. Bibliography. In M. v. Gruber, *Fortpflanzung, Vererbung, Rassenhygiene.* München: J. F. Lehmann, 1911.

638 ———. Charakter als Ausdruck. In E. Utitz (Ed.), *Jahrbuch der Charakterologie.* Berlin: Pan Verlag, 1924.

639 ———. *Difficulties in life.* Cork, Ireland: Mercier, 1939. Also published as *Self improvement.* New York: Benziger, 1939.

640 ———. Ein Fall von Pavor nocturnus. *IZIP,* 1924, 2(6), 26–27.

641 ———. *Existentialism and psychiatry.* Springfield, Ill.: C. C. Thomas, 1961.

642 ———. Gemeinschaft als Idee und Erlebnis. *IZIP,* 1923, 2(1), 7–10.

643 ———. *Heilerziehung bei Abwegigkeit des Charakters.* Köln: Benziger, 1926.

644 ———. *The new psychologies.* London: Sheed & Ward, 1932.

645 ———. *Psychologie des Geschlechtslebens.* München: E. Reinhardt, 1912, 1922.

646 ———. *The psychology of character.* London: Sheed & Ward, 1931; New York: Sheed & Ward, 1943.

647 ———. *Self improvement.* New York: Benziger, 1939. Also published as *Difficulties in life.* Cork, Ireland: Mercier, 1939.

648 ——— (Ed.). *Soziale Physiologie und Pathologie.* Berlin: J. Springer, 1927.

649 ———. *The successful error: A critical study of Freudian psychoanalysis.* New York: Sheed & Ward, 1940.

650 ———. Über die Verwertung umbemerkter eindrücke bei Assoziationen. *Z. gesam. Neurol. Psychol.*, 1924, 89, 1398. (with H. Teler).

651 ———. *Über Psychoanalyse.* Berlin: S. Karger, 1922.

652 ———. *Das Werden der sittlichen Person.* Freiburg: Herder, 1929.

653 **Allman, T. S.** Birth order categories as predictors of select personality characteristics. *Psychol. Rep.*, 1968, 22, 857–860 (with W. F. White).

654 **Allport, G. W.** *Becoming: Basic considerations for a psychology of personality.* New Haven, Conn.: Yale Univ. Press, 1955, 1960. Paper.

655 Allport, G. W. The ego in contemporary psychology. *Psychol. Rev.*, 1943, 50, 451–468. Also in *Personality and social encounter: Selected essays.* Boston: Beacon Press, 1960. Pp. 71–93.

656 ———. The general and the unique in psychological science. *J. Pers.*, 1962, 30, 405–422.

657 ———. *Pattern and growth of personality.* New York: Holt, Rinehart & Winston, 1961.

658 ———. The study of the undivided personality. *J. abnorm. soc. Psychol.*, 1924–25, 19, 132–141.

659 Allred, G. H. *Mission for Mother: Guiding the child.* Salt Lake City: Bookcraft, 1968.

660 Alm, H. Ansprache an Alfred Adler bei der Abschiedsfeier an Siljankolan, Schweden am 29 Juni, 1934. *IZIP*, 1934, 12(3), 193–194.

661 Alper, Thelma S. Memory for socially-relevant material. *J. abnorm. soc. Psychol.*, 1952, 47, 25–37 (with S. Korchin).

662 Altus, W. D. Birth order and academic primogeniture. *J. Pers. soc. Psychol.*, 1965, 2, 877–882.

663 ———. Birth order and choice of college major. *Proc. 75th Ann. Conv. Amer. Psychol. Assn.*, 1967, 2, 287–288.

664 ———. Birth order and its sequelae. *Science*, 1966, 151, 44–49.

665 ———. Birth order and mean score on a ten-item aptitude test. *Psychol. Rep.*, 1965, 16, 956.

666 ———. Birth order and the Omnibus Personality Inventory, Form C. *Proc. 74th Ann. Conv. Amer. Psychol. Assn.*, 1966, 1, 279–280.

667 ———. Birth order and scholastic aptitude. *J. consult. Psychol.*, 1965, 29, 202–205.

668 ———. The first born as a conservative: Adler revisited. *Amer. Psychologist*, 1963, 18, 356 (Abstract).

669 ———. Marriage and order of birth. *Proc. 78th Ann. Conv. Amer. Psychol. Assn.*, 1970, 5, 361–362 (Abstract).

670 ———. Sex role dissatisfaction, birth order, and parental favoritism. *Proc. 79th Ann. Conv. Amer. Psychol. Assn.*, 1971, 6, 161–162 (Abstract).

671 American Society of Adlerian Psychology. Annual conference, May 31, 1968—June 2, 1968. *IP*, 1968, 5(2), 61.

672 ———. By-laws. *AJIP*, 1952, 10, 92–96.

673 American Society of Adlerian Psychology. Program of the Sixth Annual Meeting. *JIP*, 1957, 13, 103–106.

674 ———. Seventh Annual Conference, Los Angeles, California, May 17–18, 1958. *JIP*, 1958, 14, 84–85.

675 Amery, Jean. Seelenkunde im Kreuzfeuer der Kritik [Review of M. Sperber, *Alfred Adler oder das Elend der Psychologie*]. *Merkur*, 1970, 10, 978–984.

676 Ames, Louise B. The sense of self of nursery school children as manifested by their verbal behavior. *J. genet. Psychol.*, 1952, 81, 193–232.

677 Ames, V. M. Mead and Husserl on the self. *Phil. phenomenol. Res.*, 1955, 15, 320–331.

678 Amoroso, A. J. Social comparison and ordinal position. *J. Pers. soc. Psychol.*, 1965, 2, 101–104 (with A. J. Arrowood).

679 Amsel, A. Review of O. H. Mowrer, *Learning theory and behavior.* In *Contemp. Psychol.*, 1961, 6, 33–36.

680 Anderson, Camilla M. The self-image: A theory of dynamics of behavior. *Ment. Hyg., N. Y.*, 1952, 36, 227–244.

681 Anderson, Gladys L. Review of K. A. Adler & Danica Deutsch (Eds.), *Essays in Individual Psychology.* In *Int. J. Grp. Psychother.*, 1961, 11, 481–482.

682 Anderson, H. Alfred Adler's Individual Psychology and pastoral care. *Past. Psychol.*, 1970, 21(207), 15–26.

683 ———. Individual Psychology and pastoral psychology: Some common concerns. *JIP*, 1971, 27(1), 25–35.

684 Anderson, I. The reading of projected books with special reference to rate and visual fatigue. *J. educ. Res.*, 1948, 41(6), 453–460 (with C. W. Meredith).

685 Anderson, W. Sibling relationship and mental deficiency diagnosis as reflected in Wechsler test patterns. *J. ment. Defic.*, 1966, 71, 406–410 (with O. Spreen).

686 Andics, Margit. Tolkühnheit und Prädestinationsvorstellung. *IZIP*, 1935, 13(3), 158–161.

687 Andreas-Salomé, Lou. *The Freud Journal.* Translated by S. A. Leavy. New York: Basic Books, 1964.

688 Angel, C. *Existence.* New York: Basic Books, 1958 (with R. May, & H. F. Ellenberger).

689 Angelino, H. R. The effects of ego-involvement on learning. *Proc. Okla. Acad.*

Sci., 1952, 33, 285-288 (with C. L. Shedd).

690 **Angers, W. P.** Achievement motivation: An Adlerian approach. *Psychol. Rec.*, 1960, 10, 179-186.

691 ———. An Adlerian approach to the dangers of evaluative labeling. *Voc. Guid. Quart.*, 1958, 7, 26-30.

692 ———. The boy who grew up. *Past. Life*, 1959, 7, 32-37.

693 ———. The case of Benny: An Adlerian approach. *Cath. Educ.*, 1961, 31, 379-381, 384, 389.

694 ———. The challenge of Individual Psychology for Catholic psychologists. *Amer. Cath. Psychol. Assn. Nwsltr. Suppl.*, 1958, 36, 1-2.

695 ———. Clarifications toward the rapprochement between religion and psychology. *JIP*, 1960, 16, 73-76.

696 ———. Familial ordinal position in relation to guidance and counseling. *J. educ. Res.*, 1963, 57, 116-124.

697 ———. First memories of drug addicts. *IP*, 1967, 5, 7-13 (with D. N. Lombardi).

698 ———. Individual Psychology and Catholics. *Homilet. past. Psychol.*, 1958, 58, 1057-1059.

699 ———. Job counseling of the epileptic. *J. Psychol.*, 1960, 49, 123-132.

700 ———. Parental counseling in psychological services. *J. soc. Ther.*, 1959, 5, 289-306.

701 ———. Parents and the challenge of children. *The Life of the Spirit* (London), 1960, 15(168), 34-40.

702 ———. The priest and the psychologist. *The Priest*, 1960, 16, 773-776.

703 ———. Psychological services: An adjunct to pastoral counseling. *Past. Psychol.*, 1966, 17, 49-54.

704 ———. The psychological significance of Adlerian concepts in counseling. *Voc. Guid. Quart.*, 1960, 9, 139-143.

705 ———. Psychotherapy with the epileptic. In G. N. Wright, F. A. Gibbs, & Shirley M. Linde (Eds.), *Total rehabilitation of epileptics—Gateway to employment*. Pp. 129-133.

706 ———. The spiritual life and Individual Psychology. *Spirit. Life* (Milwaukee), 1961, 7, 243-247.

707 ———. The use of Adlerian principles in understanding employee maldevelopment. *IP*, 1964, 2(2), 6-10.

708 **Angyal, A.** *Neurosis and treatment: A holistic theory.* New York: Wiley, 1965.

709 **Anonymous.** Abstracts of papers presented at the Eighth Annual Conference of the American Society of Adlerian Psychology, 2nd May, 1959. *IPNL*, 1959, 9(11, Whole No. 100). Pp. 41-44; 1959, 9(12, Whole No. 101). P. 48; 1959, 10(1, Whole No. 102-103). P. 6.

710 ———. Adler and aggression. *The Listener* (London), April 23, 1970.

711 ———. Adler son assails "encounter fads". *Med. Trib.*, Sept. 7, 1970.

712 ———. Adler's psychology behind recital. *Daily Telegraph* (London), Apr. 25, 1969.

713 ———. Afterthoughts [on anorexia nervosa]. *IPMP*, 1931, No. 2. Pp. 57-63.

714 ———. Alfred Adler [Obituary]. *IZIP*, 1937, 15(2). Foreword.

715 ———. Alfred Adler—Centenary of his birth. *Amer. J. Psychother.*, 1970, 24(1), 183-185.

716 ———. [Alfred Adler Centennial]. *J. Otto Rank Assn.*, 1970, 5(2), 108-109.

717 ———. Alfred Adler Centennial. *William Alanson White Inst., N. Y., Nwsltr.*, Fall, 1970.

718 ———. Alfred Adler Centennial, 1870-1970: Conclusion. *JIP*, 1971, 27(1), 81-84.

719 ———. Alfred Adler dead; Viennese psychologist. *Chicago Tribune*, May 28, 1937.

720 ———. Alfred Adler extolled as followers open centennial. *Psychiat. News*, 1970, 5(3), 30.

721 ———. Alfred Adler honored today on centennial of birth. *Corvallis Gazette Times*, Feb. 7, 1970.

722 ———. Alfred Adler in the Great Soviet Encyclopedia. *JIP*, 1972, 26(2), 183-185.

723 ———. Alfred Adler: In memoriam. *IJIP*, 1937, 3(2), 109-110.

724 ———. Alfred Adler presented as "humanistic psychologist". *Roche Rept: Frontiers Psychiat.*, 1971, 1(7), 3.

725 ———. Alfred Adler, psychologist, dies in Scotland. *World J. Trib.*, May 28, 1937.

726 ———. Alfred Adler, psychologist, dies in street. *New York Times*, May 28, 1937.

727 ———. Alfred Adler, zum hundertsten Geburtstag. *Neue Züricher Zeit.*, Feb. 9, 1970.

728 ———. Allen Ross McClelland (1917-1971). *JIP*, 1972, 28, 114.

729 ———. The anatomy of Angst. *Time Mag.*, Mar. 31, 1961.

730 **Anonymous.** Anniversary Individual Psychology. *MD*, Feb., 1970.

731 ———. Aus der Schule geplaudert (von einem Lehrer). In Sofie Lazarsfeld (Ed.), *Richtige Lebensführung.*

732 ———. Authors (Kenneth B. Clark). *Psychol. Today*, 1967, 1(5), 7.

733 ———. Authors (Rollo May). *Psychol. Today*, 1968, 1(9), 6.

734 ———. Authors (O. H. Mowrer). *Psychol. Today*, 1967, 1(5), 7.

735 ———. The basic needs of children. *IPB*, 1950, 8, 49–72.

736 ———. Bericht über den I. internationalen Kongress für Individualpsychologie in München, 1922 Dezember. *IZIP*, 1923, 2 (2), 30–45.

737 ———. Bericht über den zweiten internationalen Kongress für Individualpsychologie. *IZIP*,1925, 3(6), 240–346; 1926 4(2), 101-103.

738 ———. Bericht über eine Tagung der Internationalen Vereines für Individualpsychologie. *IZIP*, 1924, 2(6), 36–39.

739 ———. Carl Furtmüller [Obituary]. *IZIP*, 1951, 20(1), 47–48.

740 ———. The challenge of social equality [A review]. *Futurist*, 1972, 6(4), 155–156.

741 ———. Child's play. *Chicago Daily News*, Jan. 9-10, 1972.

742 ———. The coming Ninth International Congress. *IPNL*, 1962, 13(1-2, Whole No. 138-139). P. 8.

743 ———. Community child guidance center, Morgantown, W. Va., *OSIPNL*, 1969, 10(5), insert.

744 ———. Le Congrès Centenaire. *BISFPA*, 1970, No. 8, Pp. 31–35.

745 ———. Delinquency and psychology. *IPP*, 1939, No. 21. Pp. 55–56.

746 ———. Dr. Alfred Adler: 1870–1937. *Amer. J. Psychother.*, 1950, 4, 223.

747 ———. Dr. Alfred Adler, psychologist, dies. *New York Times*, May 28, 1937.

748 ———. Dr. Angers and the world of psychology and religion. *U. S. Cath.*, Feb., 1965. Pp. 43–48.

749 ———. Dr. Grete Querfeld [Obituary]. *IZIP*, 1929, 7(2), III.

750 ———. Draft for discussion: Constitution of the International Association of I. P. *IPNL*, 1951, No. 1. Pp. 2–3.

751 ———. Das dritte Internationale Kongress für Individualpsychologie. *IZIP*, 1926, 4(6), 386–388.

752 **Anonymous.** Edmond R. Schlesinger (1893–1968). *JIP*, 1968, 24, 218–219.

753 ———. Edmund Schletter, 1891–1964. *JIP*, 1965, 21(1), 112.

754 ———. Edward W. Sinnott (1889–1968). *JIP*, 1968, 24, 125.

755 ———. Eighth Annual Conference and Banquet of the American Society of Adlerian Psychology. *IPNL*, 1959, 9(8, Whole No. 96-97). Pp. 27–28.

756 ———. Entwurf eines individualpsychologischen Fragebogen. *IZIP*, 1923, 2(2), 1–3.

757 ———. Ernstes und Heiteres zur Kritik der Individualpsychologie. *IZIP*, 1927, 5(5), 388–389.

758 ———. Esquisse d'un questionnaire basé sur la Psychologie Individuelle. *IZIP*, 1923, 2(2), 6–8.

759 ———. Events at De Pietersberg. *IPNL*, 1957, 8(1-3, Whole No. 77-79). P. 1.

760 ———. Ferdinand Ray (1905–1972). *JIP*, 1972, 28, 113.

761 ———. Fortschritte in der modernen Psychologie. *IZIP*, 1931, 9(2), 145–150.

762 ———. Die Frau in der jüdischen Religion. *IZIP*, 1925, 3(6), 335–337.

763 ———. *Fünfzig Jahre Volksheim: Eine Festschrift zum 24. Februar 1951.* Wien: Volksheim, Ludo-Hartmann-Platz 7, 1951.

764 ———. General centennial events. *JIP*, 1972, 26(2), 168–170.

765 ———. George A. Kelly, 1905–1967. *JIP*, 1967, 23, 138.

766 ———. Group therapy for schizophrenics: Reports by 4 psychoanalysts. *Frontiers clin. Psychiat.*, 1967, 4(16), 1–2 & 8.

767 ———. Highlights: 18th Annual Convention of the American Society of Adlerian Psychology and 11th Congress of the International Association of Individual Psychology, New York City, July 1-5, 1970. *Sandoz Psychiat. Spectator*, 1970, 6(11), 1–18.

768 ———. I. P. training the world over. *IPNL*, 1957, 8(1-3, Whole No. 77-79). P. 9.

769 ———. The individual and the world as seen in existential psychiatry [about Antonia Wenkart]. *Frontiers clin. Psychiat.*, 1968, 5(10), 6 & 8.

770 ———. An Individual Psychological questionnaire. *IZIP*, 1923, 2(2), 3-6.

771 ———. Individualpsychologische Gedankengänge bei alten und neuen Autoren.

IZIP, 1926, 4(2), 95-99; 1926, 4(3), 157-161.

772 **Anonymous.** Individualpsychologische Gedankengänge in Vergangenheit und Gegenwart. *IZIP*, 1926, 4(6), 383-386; 1927, 5(1), 74-76; 1927, 5(2), 150-153; 1927, 5(3), 305-308; 1927, 5(4), 390.

773 ———. Individual Psychology and its philosophical implications. *IPMP*, 1932, No. 5. Pp. 44-45.

774 ———. Individual Psychology as ethical belief: Recognition by a Selective Service Board. *JIP*, 1971, 27(1), 44-45.

775 ———. The Individual Psychology of Alfred Adler. *Inscape* (S. Ill. Univ.), 1971 (Fall), 7-10.

776 ———. Individual Psychological Who's Who. *IPN*, 1940, 1(1), 6-8; 1940, 1(2), 6-7.

777 ———. In memoriam [Grete Jeenel-Sternberg]. *AJIP*, 1956, 12, 183.

778 ———. In memoriam Leonhard Deutsch. *IPNL*, 1952, No. 17. Pp. 1-2.

779 ———. International Congress, Vienna, 1960. *IPNL*, 1959, 9(6-7, Whole No. 94-95). P. 21.

780 ———. International Congress of Individual Psychology, Vienna, 28th August-September, 1960. *IPNL*, 1959, 10(1, Whole No. 102-103). P. 1.

781 ———. [Interviews with Alexandra Adler and K. A. Adler.] *Frontiers clin. Psychiat.*, 1970, 7(10), 1-2 & 11.

782 ———. Johannes Neumann, 1897-1964. *JIP*, 1964, 20(2), 247-248.

783 ———. Kinderheitserinnerungen einer ehemals Nervösen. In A. Adler & C. Furtmüller (Eds.), *Heilen und Bilden* (1914). Pp. 380-389.

784 ———. *Kovets Individual-Psikhologi* [Collected papers on Individual Psychology]. Tel Aviv: Urim Press, 1952.

785 ———. "Krankheit als geistiger Antrieb." From *J. Amer. Med. Assn.*, Nov. 10, 1934. In *IZIP*, 1935, 13(4), 215-217.

786 ———. The lectures delivered at the IAAP Congress [Oosterbeck, Holland, August 12-18, 1957]. *IPNL*, 1957, 8(1-3, Whole No. 77-79). Pp. 1-3.

787 ———. Literature of Individual Psychology. *IJIP*, 1935, 1(1), 126; 1935, 1(2), 125; 1935, 1(3), 132; 1935, 1(4), 133.

788 ———. Marcel Proust as data for psychology. *IZIP*, 1929, 7(1), 57-59.

789 **Anonymous.** The memorial meeting of New York [5th anniversary of Adler's death]. *IPB*, 1942, 2(4), 78.

790 ———. Mental hospital dedicates building to Alfred Adler. *JIP*, 1961, 17, 248-249.

791 ———. A new chapter on Adler. *JIP*, 1970, 26(2), 178-182.

792 ———. 1910 "symposium" on suicide not chaired by Dr. Freud. *Frontiers clin. Psychiat.*, 1969, 6(10), 1-2.

793 ———. Obituary [E. Arnstein]. *IPNL*, 1959, 9(12, Whole No. 101). Pp. 45-46.

794 ———. Obituary [M. Bajor]. *IPNL*, 1958, 8(6-7, Whole No. 82-83). P. 22.

795 ———. Obituary [Rudolf Dreikurs]. *Amer. J. Psychother.*, 1972, 26(3), 472.

796 ———. Obituary [Emil Froeschels]. *Amer. J. Psychother.*, 1972, 26(3), 471-472.

797 ———. Obituary [Rosel Frohnknecht]. *IPNL*, 1958, 8(10-12, Whole No. 86-88). P. 43; *JIP*, 1958, 14, 200.

798 ———. Obituary [E. Gutheil]. *JIP*, 1959, 15, 255.

799 ———. Obituary [Hilde Kramer]. *IPNL*, 1958, 8(8-9, Whole No. 84-85). P. 33.

800 ———. Obituary [Erwin O. Krausz]. *JIP*, 1968, 24, 217-218.

801 ———. Obituary [Margaret Levine]. *IP*, 1967, 5, 36; *JIP*, 1967, 23, 262.

802 ———. Obituary [Margarete Minor]. *IZIP*, 1927, 5(3), xxxv.

803 ———. Obituary [M. Moore]. *IPNL*, 1958, 8(6-7, Whole No. 82-83). P. 22.

804 ———. Obituary [E. M. Nash]. *IPNL*, 1958, 8(6-7, Whole No. 82-83). P. 22.

805 ———. Obituary [Otto P. Radl]. *IP*, 1965, 3(1), 9.

806 ———. Obituary [Luna Reich]. *IP*, 1967, 5, 36; *JIP*, 1967, 23, 262.

807 ———. Obituary [Susanne Rolo]. *IPNL*, 1961, 11(9-10, Whole No. 125-126). P. 46.

808 ———. Obituary [Edmond R. Schlesinger]. *JIP*, 1968, 24, 218-219.

809 ———. Obituary [E. Schmidt]. *IPNL*, 1958, 8(6-7, Whole No. 82-83). P. 22.

810 ———. Obituary [Regine Seidler]. *IP*, 1967, 4(2), 70.

811 ———. Obituary [Elisabeth Sorge-Boehmke] *JIP*, 1960, 16, 115.

812 ———. Obituary [Clara Thompson]. *JIP*, 1959, 15, 137.

813 ———. Obituary [S. von Maday]. *IPNL*, 1959, 9(12, Whole No. 101). Pp. 45-46; *JIP*, 1959, 15, 137.

814 **Anonymous.** Obituary [E. Wexberg]. *IPNL,* 1958, 8(6–7, Whole No. 82–83). P. 22.

815 ———. Otto Peter Radl, 1902–1965. *JIP,* 1965, 21(2), 234–235.

816 ———. Our coming Congress, 1960. *IPNL,* 1959, 9(8, Whole No. 96–97). Pp. 27–28.

817 ———. Our institutes. *IPNL,* 1961, 11(7–8, Whole No. 121–122). P. 27.

818 ———. Our International Congress in Holland. *IPNL,* 1957, 7(10–12, Whole No. 74–76). Pp. 37–38.

819 ———. Our international summer school. *IPNL,* 1955, 5(1–2, Whole No. 53–54). Pp. 1–2.

820 ———. Our Ninth International Congress, Paris, Aug. 30 to Sept. 2, 1963. *IPNL,* 1963, 13(9–10, Whole No. 146–147). Pp. 39–40.

821 ———. Our 9th International Congress. *IPNL,* 1963, 13(11–12, Whole No. 148–149). Pp. 41–43.

822 ———. Our Tenth International Congress: Salzburg, 1966. *IPNL,* 1966, 17(1–2, Whole No. 186–187). Pp. 1–2.

823 ———. Paul Klemperer, 1887–1964. *JIP,* 1964, 20(1), 124.

824 ———. Physical findings in psychoneurosis. *IPMP,* 1932, No. 4. Pp. 67–69.

825 ———. Pitirim A. Sorokin (1889–1968). *JIP,* 1968, 24, 125–126.

826 ———. The private intelligence of bank robbers: Two self accounts. *JIP,* 1962, 18, 77–88.

827 ———. Problems created by value conflicts demand understanding. *Frontiers clin. Psychiat.,* 1969, 6(6), 5, 8.

828 ———. Proceedings: American Society of Adlerian Psychology. *JIP,* 1965, 21, 204–205.

829 ———. Proceedings of the Eighth International Congress of Individual Psychology. *JIP,* 1961, 17, 212–221.

830 ———. Proceedings of the 11th International Congress of Individual Psychology combined with the 18th Annual Convention of the American Society of Adlerian Psychology. *JIP,* 1970, 26(2), 217–227.

831 ———. Proceedings of the 15th Annual Conference of the American Society of Adlerian Psychology. *JIP,* 1967, 23, 236.

832 ———. Proceedings of the Ninth International Congress of Individual Psychology. *JIP,* 1964, 20, 219–227.

833 **Anonymous.** Proceedings of sessions at American Psychiatric Association, Association for Humanistic Psychology and American Psychological Association. *JIP,* 1970, 26(2), 161–167.

834 ———. Proceedings of the 19th annual meeting of the American Society of Adlerian Psychology. *JIP,* 1971, 27(2), 208–212.

835 ———. Proceedings of the 16th Annual Conference of the American Society of Adlerian Psychology. *JIP,* 1968, 24, 193–194.

836 ———. Proceedings, 12th Annual Conference of the American Society of Adlerian Psychology, New York, May 31–June 2, 1963. *IP,* 1963, 1(2), 18–24.

837 ———. Program of the Tenth Annual Conference of the American Society of Adlerian Psychology. *JIP,* 1961, 17, 224–225.

838 ———. Psychoanalysis diagnosed as thriving but in transition. *Frontiers clin. Psychiat.,* 1967, 4(6), 1–2 & 8 & 11.

839 ———. Psychologist Adler is dead. *Chicago Herald & Examiner,* May 28, 1937.

840 ———. The psychology of chess [About K. A. Adler]. *Time,* Sept. 4, 1972. P. 45.

841 ———. Psychology professors rate psychological theorists. *JIP,* 1962, 18, 204.

842 ———. Raissa Adler. *JIP,* 1962, 18, 180–181.

843 ———. Report from Rio de Janeiro. *IPN,* 1940, 1(1), 5.

844 ———. Report of annual dinner [of Medical Society of Individual Psychology, January 14, 1937]. *IPP,* No. 17. Pp. 60–62.

845 ———. Reports about memorial meetings on the occasion of the 20th anniversary of Adler's death. *IPNL,* 1957, 7(10–12, Whole No. 74–76). Pp. 38–40.

846 ———. Review of A. Adler, *The Individual Psychology of Alfred Adler.* In *The Times* (London) *Lit. Suppl.,* Nov. 21, 1958, 665–666.

847 ———. Review of Phyllis Bottome, *Alfred Adler: Apostle of freedom.* In *Time,* June 30, 1958.

848 ———. Review of M. Hirschfeld, *Aus dem Jahrbuch für Sexuelle Zwischenstufen,* 1923. In *IZIP,* 1924, 2(3), 62.

849 ———. Review of H. E. Timerding, *Das Problem der Ledigen Frau.* Bonn: A. Marcus & E. Weber, 1925. In *IZIP,* 1925, 3(6), 346–348.

850 **Anonymous.** Rudolf Allers, 1883-1963. *JIP*, 1965, 21(1), 112.

851 ———. Rudolf Dreikurs bibliography: 1925-1967. *JIP*, 1967, 23, 158-166.

852 ———. Ruth L. Munroe, 1903-1963. *JIP*, 1964, 20(1), 124-125.

853 ———. Das Seminar für Massenpsychologie vom Oktober 1923 bis Jänner 1924. *IZIP*, 1924, 2(4), 30-31.

854 ———. Sitzungsberichte des Vereins für Individualpsychologie. *ZIP*, 1914, 1(1), 28-32; 1914, 1(3), 95-96; 1914, 1(4-5), 142-144.

855 ———. The Sixth International Congress. *IPNL*, 1954, No. 39-40. Pp. 1-2.

856 ———. A strong voice in Germany [about W. Metzger]. *JIP*, 1964, 20(1), 123-124.

857 ———. Summer congresses. *IPNL*, 1967, 18(1-2, Whole No. 198-199). Pp. 1-4.

858 ———. Teaching I. P. in many countries. *IPNL*, 1960, 11 (1-2, Whole No. 115-116). Pp. 3-4.

859 ———. The 10th International Congress of Individual Psychology. *IPNL*, 1965, 16(1-3, Whole No. 174-176). P. 12.

860 ———. Themes of our International Congresses. *IPNL*, 1964, 15(1-2, Whole No. 162-163). P. 1.

861 ———. Therapeutic, antitherapeutic factors in group process evaluated [about Helene Papanek]. *Frontiers clin. Psychiat.*, 1969, 6(13), 8 & 11.

862 ———. Die Todesnachricht in der Welt öffentlichkeit [obituaries for Alfred Adler]. *IZIP*, 1937, 15(3-4), 171-198.

863 ———. The 20th anniversary of the death of Alfred Adler (1870-1937). *JIP*, 1957, 13, 111.

864 ———. Über den Selbstmord: Inbesondere den Schülerselbstmord. *Diskussionen des Wiener psychoanalytischen Vereins.* Vol. 1. Wiesbaden: Bergmann, 1910.

865 ———. Various international congresses in Europe. Summer, 1964. *IPNL*, 1964, 15(1-2, Whole No. 162-163). Pp. 1-3.

866 ———. Vortragsreise Alfred Adlers in Amerika. *IZIP*, 1927, 5, xix-xx.

867 ———. We love you, Mr. Tarbox. *Life*, Apr. 24, 1970. Pp. 76-78.

868 ———. Wien gedenkt des Schöpfers der Individualpsychologie. *Neues Oesterreich*, May 26, 1956.

869 ———. Youth grievances valid, Adlerian [K. A. Adler] argues. *Psychiat. News*, 1970, 5(11), 1, 8.

870 **Anonymous.** Zum 100. Geburtstag von Alfred Adler. *Tages-Anzeiger* (Zürich), Feb. 10, 1970.

871 **Ansbacher, H. L.** Abstract of H. H. Mosak, Early recollections as a projective technique. In *IPNL*, 1958, 9(1-2, Whole No. 89-90). P. 8.

872 ———. Adler and Binswanger on schizophrenia. *JIP*, 1960, 16, 77-80 (with W. Van Dusen).

873 ———. Adler and religion. *IPNL*, 1972, 21(6), 101-103.

874 ———. Adler and the 1910 Vienna symposium on suicide: A special review. *JIP*, 1968, 24, 181-190.

875 ———. Adler and the Vienna Suicide Symposium. *Contemp. Psychol.*, 1969, 14, 258-259.

876 ———. Adler on the college textbook level. *IPNL*, 1957, 8(4-5, Whole No. 80-81). Pp. 13-14.

877 ———. An Adler quotation on religion. *IPNL*, 1957, 6(6-7, Whole No. 70-71). Pp. 23.

878 ———. The Adlerian alternative. *Playboy*, Sept., 1970.

879 ———. An Adlerian case or a character by Sartre? *JIP*, 1965, 21, 32-40 (with P. Rom).

880 ———. Adlerian concepts of schizophrenia: Symposium at the Second International Congress for Psychiatry [Zurich, Sept. 6, 1957]. *JIP*, 1958, 14, 73-78.

881 ———. Adlerian psychology: The tradition of brief psychotherapy. *JIP*, 1972, 28(2), 137-151.

882 ———. "Adler's brilliance" coming into its own. [Review of E. Becker, *The birth and death of meaning*]. In *IPNL*, 1962, 13(3-4, Whole No. 140-141). P. 1.

883 ———. Adler's importance—statistically derived. *IPNL*, 1958, 8(10-12, Whole No. 86-88). Pp. 40-41.

884 ———. Adler's place today in the psychology of memory. *J. Pers.*, 1946, 15, 197-207; *IPB*, 1947, 6, 32-40; *IZIP*, 1947, 16, 97-111.

885 ———. Adler's "striving for power", in in relation to Nietzsche. *JIP*, 1972, 28, 12-24.

886 ———. Adler's theory of Individual Psychology. In L. Gorlow & W. Katkovsky (Eds.), *Readings in the psychology of adjustment.* Pp. 135-148.

887 Ansbacher, H. L. Again: Causality and finality. *IPNL*, 1967, 18(3-4, Whole No. 200-201). Pp. 18-19.

888 ———. Alfred Adler. In *Encycl. Brittanica.*

889 ———. Alfred Adler. In *Encycl. Judaica.* Jerusalem: Israel Program for Scientific Translations; New York: Macmillan, 1971. P. 271.

890 ———. Alfred Adler. In *Lexikon der Pädagogik.* Freiberg i. Br.: Verlag Herder, 1970. P. 8.

891 ———. Alfred Adler: A historical perspective. *Amer. J. Psychiat.*, 1970, 127(6), 777-782.

892 ———. Alfred Adler and G. Stanley Hall: Correspondence and general relationship. *J. Hist. behav. Sci.*, 1971, 7, 337-352.

893 ———. Alfred Adler and Ortega y Gasset. Editorial comment. *JIP*, 1971, 27(2), 133.

894 ———. Alfred Adler and humanistic psychology. *J. humanist. Psychol.*, 1971, 11(1), 53-63.

895 ———. Alfred Adler—antidote to pessimism. *Bull. Univ. Vermont*, July, 1956.

896 ———. Alfred Adler: 1870-1937. *Sociom.*, 1937, 1, 259-261 (with Rowena R. Ansbacher).

897 ———. Alfred Adler, Individual Psychology & Marilyn Monroe. *Psychol. Today*, 1970, 3(10), 42-44, 66.

898 ———. Alfred Adler in the *Great Soviet Encyclopedia. JIP*, 1970, 26, 183-185.

899 ——— (Ed.). *Alfred Adler's Individualpsychologie.* Munich: Reinhardt, 1972 (with Rowena Ansbacher).

900 ———. Alfred Adler's place in psychology today. *IZIP*, 1947, 16(3), 97-100.

901 ———. The "alienation syndrome" and Adler's concept of "distance". *J. consult. Psychol.*, 1956, 20, 483-484.

902 ———. "Anomie", the sociologist's conception of "lack of social interest". *IPNL*, 1956, 5(11-12, Whole No. 63-64). Pp. 3-5; *JIP*, 1959, 15, 212-214.

903 ———. Another confirmation of the increasing recognition of Adler. *IPNL*, 1967, 17(11-12, Whole No. 196-197). P. 88.

904 ———. An attack on psychological reductionism [Review of A. Montagu, *The biosocial nature of man*]. In *IPNL*, 1957, 6 (6-7, Whole No. 70-71). Pp. 22-23.

905 ———. Attendant-patient commonality as a psychotherapeutic factor. *JIP*, 1962, 18, 157-167 (with W. N. Deane).

906 Ansbacher, H. L. Attitudes of German prisoners of war: A study of the dynamics of National-Socialistic fellowship. *Psychol. Monogr.*, 1948, 62(1).

907 ———. Biography and portrait. *Psychol. Today*, 1970, 3(9), 78.

908 ———. Bleibendes und Vergängliches aus der deutschen Wehrmacht-psychologie. *Mitt. Berufsverb. Deutscher Psychologen*, 1949, 3(11), 3-9.

909 ———. Can Blacky blacken testing? *Amer. Psychologist*, 1959, 14, 654.

910 ———. Causality and indeterminism according to Alfred Adler and some current American personality theories. *IPB*, 1951, 9, 96-107. Also in K. A. Adler & Danica Deutsch (Eds.), *Essays in Individual Psychology*. Pp. 27-40.

911 ———. Causality and/or finality. *IPNL*, 1967, 18(1-2, Whole No. 198-199). P. 10.

912 ———. Le coin du rire. *IPNL*, 1961, 12(1-2, Whole No. 127-128). P. 8.

913 ———. The concept of social interest. *JIP*, 1968, 24, 131-149.

914 ———. Curtailment of military psychology in Germany. *Science*, 1942, 98, 218-219.

915 ———. The desire to be a man. *IPNL*, 1958, 8(6-7, Whole No. 82-83). P. 21.

916 ———. Discussion of P. Rom, The beginnings of training for the end. *Voices*, 1969, 5(1), 41-42.

917 ———. Distortion in the perception of real movement. *J. exp. Psychol.*, 1944, 34, 1-23.

918 ———. Editor of and introduction to A. Adler, *The science of living*. Pp. vii-xxii.

919 ———. Editorial introduction to C. Furtmüller, Alfred Adler: A biographical essay. In H. L. Ansbacher & Rowena R. Ansbacher (Eds.), *Superiority and social interest*. Pp. 311-329.

920 ———. Ego psychology and Alfred Adler. *Soc. Casework*, 1964, 45(5), 269-270. Also in H. D. Werner (Ed.), *New understandings of human behavior*. Pp. 165-168.

921 ———. Expansion and exploration. *JIP*, 1958, 14, 103-104.

922 ———. Experimental confirmation of the relationship between inferiority feelings and the depreciation tendency (Review of Katherine T. Omwake, The relationship between acceptance of self and acceptance of others shown by three personality inventories). *J. consult. Psychol.*, 1954, 18,

443–446. In *IPNL*, 1955, 4(6–7, Whole No. 46–47). Pp. 2–3.

923 **Ansbacher, H. L.** Fetishism: An Adlerian interpretation. *Psychiat. Quart.*, 1958, 32, 384–387.

924 ———. Foreword. *JIP*, 1972, 28(2), 121–122.

925 ———. Freudian authoritarianism. *IPNL*, 1958, 9(1–2, Whole No. 89–90). Pp. 2–3.

926 ———. A Freudian behaviorist reconsiders his view on Adler. *IPNL*, 1957, 6(6–7, Whole No. 70–71). P. 19.

927 ———. Freud's death instinct re-interpreted. *IPNL*, 1955–56, 5(5–7, Whole No. 57–59). Pp. 1–2.

928 ———. The future progress of Individual Psychology. *IPB*, 1942, 2(3), 53–54.

929 ———. The Gasierowski bibliography of military psychology. *Psychol. Bull.*, 1941, 38, 505–508.

930 ———. Gemeinschaftsgefuehl. *IPNL*, 1966, 16(11–12, Whole No. 184–185). P. 43; 1966, 17(3–4, Whole No. 189–190). Pp. 13–15.

931 ———. German industrial psychology in the fifth year of war. *Psychol. Bull.*, 1944, 41, 605–614.

932 ———. German military psychology. *Psychol. Bull.*, 1941, 38, 370–392.

933 ———. *German naval psychology* (NavPers 18080). Washington: Bur. Nav. Personnel; Princeton, N. J.: Coll. Entrance Exam. Bd., 1948.

934 ———. German war evaluation of children. *Sch. & Soc.*, 1941, 54, 470.

935 ———. The goal of psychotherapy. *IPNL*, 1956, 6(1–2, Whole No. 65–66). P. 1.

936 ———. The Goodenough Draw-A-Man Test and primary mental abilities. *J. consult. Psychol.*, 1952, 16, 172–180.

937 ———. Group differences in size estimation. *Psychometrika*, 1945, 10, 37–56 (with K. Mather).

938 ———. History of an anecdote used by Adler. *JIP*, 1966, 22, 237–238.

939 ———. The history of the leaderless group discussion technique. *Psychol. Bull.*, 1951, 48, 383–391.

940 ———. I. P. bibliographies. *IPNL*, 1955, 4(6–7, Whole No. 46–47). P. 6.

941 ———. The increasing recognition of Adler. In H. L. Ansbacher & Rowena R. Ansbacher (Eds.), *Superiority and social interest.* Pp. 3–19.

942 **Ansbacher, H. L.** An independent rediscovery of the principles of Individual Psychology. *IPNL*, 1956, 6(3–4, Whole No. 67–69). Pp. 9–11.

943 ———. Indexing the Psychological Index. *Psychol. Bull.*, 1939, 36, 477–487 (with A. T. Poffenberger, H. C. Brown, R. G. Wetmore, & S. C. Miller).

944 ———. Individual Psychology. In *Int. Encycl. Soc. Sci.* Vol. 7. New York: Crowell, Collier, & Macmillan, 1968. Pp. 213–218 (with Rowena R. Ansbacher).

945 ———. Individual Psychology. In B. B. Wolman & E. Nagel (Eds.), *Scientific psychology: Principles and approaches.* New York: Basic Books, 1965. Pp. 340–364.

946 ———. Individual Psychology in Germany. *IPB*, 1949, 7, 30–32 (with A. Bornemann).

947 ——— (Ed.). *The Individual Psychology of Alfred Adler.* New York: Basic Books, 1956, 1958; London: Allen & Unwin, 1956, 1958; New York: Harper Torchbooks, 1964. Paper (with Rowena R. Ansbacher).

948 ———. In honor of Rudolf Dreikurs on his 70th birthday. *JIP*, 1967, 23, 143.

949 ———. In memoriam of Martin Luther King, Jr., 1929–1968. *IPNL*, 1968, 18(7–8, Whole No. 204–205). Pp. 51–52.

950 ———. In praise of *Essays in Individual Psychology. IPNL*, 1960, 11(3–4, Whole No. 117–118). P. 12.

951 ———. Introduction to A. Adler, *Problems of neurosis.* Pp. ix–xxvi.

952 ———. Introduction to A. Adler, *The science of living.* Pp. vii–xxii.

953 ———. Introduction to the papers by Adler, Sinnott, and Cantril. *JIP*, 1957, 13, 6–8.

954 ———. J. L. Moreno's "Transference, countertransference and tele" in relation to certain formulations by Alfred Adler. *Grp. Psychother.*, 1955, 8, 179–180.

955 ———. Johannsen's terminology applied to Adler's theory of personality. *IJIP*, 1935, 1(1), 63–66.

956 ———. Lack of social interest on the road. *IPNL*, 1969, 19(1), 8.

957 ———. Lasting and passing aspects of German military psychology. *Sociom.*, 1949, 12, 301–312.

958 ———. Lee Harvey Oswald: An Adlerian interpretation. *Psychoanal. Rev.*, 1966, 53, 379–390; *JIP*, 1967, 23, 24–36.

Condensed in *OSIPNL*, 1967, 8(3), 9–11 (with Rowena R. Ansbacher, D. Shiverick, & Kathleen Shiverick).

959 **Ansbacher, H. L.** Lee Harvey Oswald in Freudian, Adlerian, and Jungian views. *JIP*, 1967, 23, 19.

960 ———. [Letter]. *Amer. J. Psychother.*, 1971, 25(1), 165–166.

961 ———. Life style: A historical and systematic review. *JIP*, 1967, 23, 191–212.

962 ———. Love and violence in the view of Adler. *Humanitas*, 1966, 2, 109–127.

963 ———. A method for evaluating suicidal threats. Reported by F. C. Thorne in *Clinical judgment: A study of clinical error.* Pp. 139–140.

964 ———. Murray's and Simoneit's (German military) methods of personality study. *J. abnorm. soc. Psychol.*, 1941, 36, 589–592.

965 ———. "Neo-Freudian" or "Neo-Adlerian"? *AJIP*, 1952, 10, 87–88; *Amer. Psychologist*, 1953, 8, 165–166.

966 ———. A new chapter on Adler. *JIP*, 1970, 26, 178–182.

967 ———. A note concerning Baumgarten-Tramer's "German psychologists and recent events". *J. abnorm. soc. Psychol.*, 1951, 46, 604.

968 ———. Note on the psychology of proper names. *IPB*, 1947, 6, 142–143.

969 ———. Number judgment of postage stamps: A contribution to the psychology of social norms. *J. Psychol.*, 1938, 5, 347–350.

970 ———. On the efficacy of Adlerian psychology. *IPNL*, 1962, 12(11–12, Whole No. 136–137). P. 46.

971 ———. On the origin of holism. *JIP*, 1961, 17, 142–148.

972 ———. On the permanence of college learning. *J. educ. Psychol.*, 1940, 31, 622–624.

973 ———. On the position of Adler in current psychotherapy. *IPNL*, 1962, 12 (11–12, Whole No. 136–137). Pp. 43–44.

974 ———. Perception of number as affected by the monetary value of the objects. *Arch. Psychol.*, No. 215.

975 ———. Personality and achievement in mathematics. *JIP*, 1960, 16, 84–87 (with R. I. Keimowitz).

976 ———. The place of the Journal of Individual Psychology in psychological literature. *IPNL*, 1962, 12(11–12, Whole No. 136–137). Pp. 48–49.

977 **Ansbacher, H. L.** Portrait. *IPNL*, 1971, 20 (6), 110.

978 ———. Postage stamps as indicators of a government's character. *Stamps*, 1947, 61, 334–336.

979 ———. Present-day Soviet psychology and Individual Psychology. *IPNL*, 1956, 5(8, Whole No. 60). Pp. 1–2.

980 ———. The problem of interpreting attitude survey data: A case study of the attitude of Russian workers in wartime Germany. *Publ. Opin. Quart.*, 1950, 11, 126–138.

981 ———. Psychoanalytic acceptance of early childhood recollections as a method. *IPNL*, 1956, 6(1–2, Whole No. 65–66). P. 2.

982 ——— (Ed.). *La Psicologia Individual de Alfred Adler: Presentación sistemática de una selección de sus escritos.* Translated by Nuria Cortada de Kohan. Buenos Aires: Troquel, 1959 (with Rowena R. Ansbacher).

983 ——— (Ed.). *Psychological Index: Abstract references of volumes 1–35, 1894–1928.* 2 vols. New York & Evanston, Ill.: Works Proj. Admin., Amer. Psychol. Assn., & Northwestern Univ., 1940–41.

984 ———. Die Psychologie Alfred Adlers, ihre Entwicklung und Bedeutung. *Fortschr. Med.*, 1957, 75, 675–677.

985 ———. Die Psychologie Alfred Adlers: Ihre Entwicklung und Bedeutung. In N. Petrilowitsch (Ed.), *Die Sinnfrage in der Psychotherapie.* Pp. 162–174.

986 ———. Psychology in Germany, 1956. *Tech. Rep. ONRL-95-96.*

987 ———. Purcell's "Memory and psychological security" and Adlerian theory. *J. abnorm. soc. Psychol.*, 1953, 48, 596–597.

988 ———. Reaction of two young American psychologists on becoming aware of Adler. *IPNL*, 1961, 11(9–10, Whole No. 125–126). Pp. 50–51.

989 ———. Recent trends in the Nordic doctrine. *J. Psychol.*, 1936, 2, 151–159 (under pseudonym of A. Baker).

990 ———. The rediscovery of Alfred Adler in the United States. *Schule u. Psychol.* (München), Dec., 1970.

991 ———. Reduced father identification in parental discord and in mental disturbance. *JIP*, 1964, 20, 165–166.

992 ———. Rehabilitation of chronic schizophrenic patients for social living. *JIP*, 1960, 16, 189–196.

993 Ansbacher, H. L. The relativity of trauma—even in animals. *IPNL*, 1957, 6(6-7, Whole No. 70-71). Pp. 21-22.

994 ———. Religion and Individual Psychology. Introduction. *JIP*, 1971, 27(1), 3-9.

995 ———. Review of L. Ackerson, Inferiority attitudes and their correlations among children examined in a behavior clinic. In *IPB*, 1943, 3, 55-56.

996 ———. Review of A. Adler, *La compensation psychique de l'état d'infériorité des organes* suivi de *Le problème de l'homosexualité.* In *JIP*, 1958, 14, 191-192.

997 ———. Review of A. Adler, *Understanding human nature.* In *JIP*, 1957, 13, 201.

998 ———. Review of A. Adler & E. Jahn, *Religion et Psychologie Individuelle Comparée;* suivi de *La névrose obsessionnelle* et *Les enfants difficile.* In *JIP*, 1959, 15, 132.

999 ———. Review of G. W. Allport, *Pattern and growth in personality.* In *JIP*, 1962, 18, 90-91.

1000 ———. Review of G. W. Allport, *Personality and social encounter.* In *JIP*, 1961, 17, 114-115.

1001 ———. Review of Lou Andreas-Salomé, *The Freud Journal.* In *JIP*, 1965, 21, 93-94.

1002 ———. Review of H. Baruk, *Hebraic civilization and the science of man.* London: World Fed. Ment. Hlth., 1961. In *JIP*, 1965, 21, 221.

1003 ———. Review of J. Bierer, Psychotherapy in mental hospital practice; being the preliminary report of a full-time therapist in a public mental hospital. In *IPN*, 1941, 1(5), 3.

1004 ———. Review of H. Bonner, *On being mindful of man.* In *JIP*, 1966, 22, 243-244.

1005 ———. Review of J. Braunthal, *In search of the millenium.* London: Gellanez, 1945. In *J. abnorm. soc. Psychol.*, 1947, 42, 146-148.

1006 ———. Review of J. C. Coleman, *Personality dynamics and effective behavior.* Chicago: Scott, Foresman, 1960. In *JIP*, 1961, 17, 233.

1007 ———. Review of Agnes M. Conklin, Failures of highly intelligent pupils: A study of their behavior by means of the control group. *Teach. Coll. Contrib. Educ.*, 1940, No. 792. In *IPN*, 1940, 1(3), 3.

1008 Ansbacher, H. L. Review of M. Curti, *Human nature in American historical thought.* Columbia, Mo.: Univ. Missouri Press, 1968. In *JIP*, 1970, 26, 233-234.

1009 ———. Review of L. Jimenez de Asua, Psicoanalisis delito y pena. *Arqu. med. leg. Ident.*, 1939, 9, 407-433. In *IPN*, 1941, 1(5), 4.

1010 ———. Review of M. Erdelyi & F. Grossman, *Dictionary of terms and expressions of industrial psychology ("Psychotechnics").* New York: Pitman, 1939. In *Amer. J. Psychol.*, 1941, 54, 626-627.

1011 ———. Review of J. Forgione, El sentimento de inferioridad en los ninos. *Bol. Educ.* (Argentina), 1940, No. 22. Pp. 25-38.

1012 ———. Review of E. Fromm, *Marx's concept of man.* New York: Frederick Ungar, 1961. In *JIP*, 1961, 17, 227-229.

1013 ———. Review of C. S. Hall & G. Lindzey, *Theories of personality.* In *Contemp. Psychol.*, 1957, 2, 201-202.

1014 ———. Review of R. A. Harper, *Psychoanalysis and psychotherapy: 36 systems.* In *JIP*, 1960, 16, 214.

1015 ———. Review of D. L. Hart, *Der tiefenpsychologische Begriff der Kompensation.* In *JIP*, 1958, 14, 191.

1016 ———. Review of E. L. Hartley & G. D. Wiebe, *Casebook in social processes.* New York: Crowell, 1960. In *JIP*, 1960, 16, 106-107.

1017 ———. Review of Mabel Hirschka, Psychopathological disorders in the mother. *J. nerv. ment. Dis.*, 1941, 7, 76-83. In *IPB*, 1942, 2(2), 24.

1018 ———. Review of R. Inoguchi, T. Nakajima, & R. Pineau, *The divine wind: Japan's Kamikaze force in World War II.* Annapolis, Md.: U. S. Nav. Inst., 1958. In *JIP*, 1959, 15, 244-245.

1019 ———. Review of H. Kammaer, *Alfred Adler's Leer tot 1914.* In *JIP*, 1960, 16, 218.

1020 ———. Review of S. Kusane, A sketch of the nervous temperament. *Jap. J. Psychol.*, 1940, 15, 331-341. In *IPN*, 1941, 1(5), 3-4.

1021 ———. Review of R. W. Leeper & P. Madison, *Toward understanding human personalities.* New York: Appleton-Century-Crofts, 1959. In *JIP*, 1961, 17, 232-233.

1022 ———. Review of L. H. Levy, *Psychological interpretation.* New York: Holt, Rinehart &

Winston, 1963. In *JIP*, 1963, 19, 232–233.

1023 **Ansbacher, H. L.** Review of E. G. Lion, H. M. Jambon, H. G. Corrigan, & K. P. Bradway, *An experiment in the treatment of promiscuous girls.* San Francisco: Dept. Publ. Hlth., 1945. In *IPB*, 1946, 5, 124–125.

1024 ———. Review of E. Lossart, Les sentimentos de inferioridad. In *IPB*, 1941, 2(1), 20.

1025 ———. Review of A. R. Mahrer (Ed.), *The goals of psychotherapy.* In *JIP*, 1967, 23, 246–247.

1026 ———. Review of F. W. Matson, *The broken image.* In *JIP*, 1968, 24, 99.

1027 ———. Review of W. McCord & Jean McCord, *Psychopathy and delinquency.* In *JIP*, 1958, 14, 86–88.

1028 ———. Review of C. E. Moustakas (Ed.), *The self: Explorations in personal growth.* In *Humanist*, 1957, 17, 252–253.

1029 ———. Review of D. Mueller-Hegemann, *Psychotherapie: Ein Leitfaden für Ärzte und Studierende.* Berlin: VEB Verlag Volk u. Gesundheit, 1961. In *JIP*, 1962, 18, 197–198.

1030 ———. Review of H. Nunberg & E. Federn (Eds.), *Minutes of the Vienna Psychoanalytic Society.* Vol. 1. 1906–1908. In *JIP*, 1963, 19, 90–91.

1031 ———. Review of H. Nunberg & E. Federn (Eds.), *Minutes of the Vienna Psychoanalytic Society.* Vol. 2. 1908–1910. In *JIP*, 1968, 24, 197–198.

1032 ———. Review of J. Nuttin, *Psychoanalysis and personality.* In *JIP*, 1963, 19, 95–97.

1033 ———. Review of Hertha Orgler, *Alfred Adler, der Mann und sein Werk* and Phyllis Bottome, *Alfred Adler: Apostle of freedom.* In *JIP*, 1957, 13, 199–200.

1034 ———. Review of Hertha Orgler, *Alfred Adler, the man and his work* (Paper). In *JIP*, 1966, 22, 251.

1035 ———. Review of L. Phillips, *Human adaptation and failure.* New York: Academic Press, 1968. In *JIP*, 1969, 25, 238.

1036 ———. Review of P. H. Ronge, *Psychoanalysis and Individual Psychology.* In *IPB*, 1942, 2(2), 24.

1037 ———. Review of L. Salzman, *The obsessive personality.* New York: Science House, 1968. In *JIP*, 1968, 24, 200–201.

1038 **Ansbacher, H. L.** Review of E. G. Schachtel, *Metamorphosis.* New York: Basic Books, 1959. In *JIP*, 1959, 15, 235–236.

1039 ———. Review of F. C. S. Schiller, *Humanistic pragmatism.* New York: Free Press, 1966. In *JIP*, 1968, 24, 103–104.

1040 ———. Review of L. Seif (Ed.), *Wege der Erziehungshilfe.* In *IPN*, 1941, 1(5), 3.

1041 ———. Review of E. J. Shoben, Jr., Toward a concept of the normal personality. In *IPNL*, 1957, 7(10–12, Whole No. 74–76). Pp. 41–43.

1042 ———. Review of E. Simmel (Ed.), *Antisemitism: A social disease.* New York: Int. Univer. Press, 1946. In *J. abnorm. soc. Psychol.*, 1947, 42, 484–488.

1043 ———. Review of *Soviet psychology: A symposium.* New York: Phil. Libr., 1961. In *JIP*, 1961, 17, 229–230.

1044 ———. Review of N. D. Sundberg & Leona Tyler, *Clinical psychology.* New York: Appleton-Century-Crofts, 1962. In *JIP*, 1963, 19, 93–94.

1045 ———. Review of P. Swartz, *The study of behavior.* Princeton: N. J.: Van Nostrand, 1963. In *JIP*, 1963, 19, 238–239.

1046 ———. Review of T. S. Szasz, *The myth of mental illness.* In *JIP*, 1961, 17, 234–235.

1047 ———. Review of B. Szekely, *El psicoanalisis: Theoria y aplicación.* Buenos Aires: Colegio Libre Estudies Superiores, 1940. In *IPB*, 1941, 2(1), 20.

1048 ———. Review of F. C. Thorne, *Personality: A clinical eclectic viewpoint.* Brandon, Vt.: J. Clin. Psychol., 1961. In *JIP*, 1962, 18, 91–92.

1049 ———. Review of L. Way, *Alfred Adler: An introduction to his psychology.* In *JIP*, 1957, 13, 201–202.

1050 ———. Review of J. M. Wepman & R. W. Heine (Eds.), *Concepts of personality.* In *JIP*, 1963, 19, 236–237.

1051 ———. Review of R. W. White (Ed.), *The study of lives.* New York: Atherton Press, 1963. In *JIP*, 1963, 19, 237–238.

1052 ———. Review of K. Winetrout, *F. C. S. Schiller and the dimensions of pragmatism.* Columbus, Ohio: Ohio St. Univ. Press, 1967. In *JIP*, 1968, 24, 104–105.

1053 ———. Review of R. B. Winn (Ed.), *Psychotherapy in the Soviet Union.* New York: Phil. Libr., 1961. In *JIP*, 1962, 18, 94–95.

1054 **Ansbacher, H. L.** Review of B. B. Wolman, *Contemporary theories and systems in psychology.* In *JIP*, 1961, 17, 226–227.

1055 ———. Review of B. B. Wolman (Ed.), *Handbook of clinical psychology.* New York: McGraw-Hill, 1965. In *JIP*, 1966, 22, 131–132.

1056 ———. Rudolf Hildebrand: A forerunner of Alfred Adler. *JIP*, 1962, 18, 12–17.

1057 ———. Selecting the Nazi officer. *Infantry J.*, 1941, 49(Nov.), 44–48 (with K. R. Nichols).

1058 ———. Sensus Privatus versus Sensus Communis. *JIP*, 1965, 21, 48–50.

1059 ———. The significance of the socio-economic status of the patients of Freud and Adler. *Amer. J. Psychother.*, 1959, 13, 376–382.

1060 ———. Social interest, an Adlerian rationale for the Rorschach human movement response. *J. proj. Tech.*, 1956, 20, 363–365. Also in K. A. Adler & Danica Deutsch (Eds.), *Essays in Individual Psychology.* Pp. 41–45.

1061 ———. Social interest and performance on the Goodenough Draw-A-Man Test. *JIP*, 1965, 21, 178–186 (with Patricia A. Stone).

1062 ———. Stamps in experimental psychology. *Amer. Philatelist*, 1938, 51, 536–587.

1063 ———. The structure of Individual Psychology. In B. B. Wolman (Ed.), *Scientific psychology.* Pp. 340–364.

1064 ———. Suicide: Adlerian point of view. In N. L. Farberow & E. S. Schneidman (Eds.), *The cry for help.* Pp. 204–219.

1065 ———. Suicide as communication: Adler's concept and current applications. *JIP*, 1969, 25, 174–180; *Humanitas*, 1970, 6(1), 5–13.

1066 ——— (Ed.). *Superioridad e interés social: Una collección de sus escritos.* Translated by Maria Martinez Peñaloza. Mexico: Fondo de Cultura Economica, 1968 (with Rowena R. Ansbacher).

1067 ——— (Ed.). *Superiority and social interest.* Evanston, Ill.: Northwestern Univ. Press, 1964, 1970; London: Routledge & Kegan Paul, 1965; New York: Viking Press, 1972. Paper (with Rowena R. Ansbacher).

1068 ———. Testing, management and reactions of foreign workers in Germany during World War II. *Amer. Psychologist*, 1950, 5, 38–49.

1069 **Ansbacher, H. L.** Training devices for Individual Psychology. *IPNL*, 1960, 10(5–6, Whole No. 107). P. 21.

1070 ———. A training unit in individual testing at the undergraduate level. *Amer. Psychologist*, 1957, 12, 151–153.

1071 ———. Utilization of creativity in Adlerian psychotherapy. *JIP*, 1971, 27(2), 160–166.

1072 ———. Die Wandlung der Adlerschen Individualpsychologie. *Psychol. Rundsch.*, 1961, 12, 264–267.

1073 ———. Was Adler a disciple of Freud? A reply. *JIP*, 1962, 18, 126–135.

1074 ———. What's in a dream? (Discussion on case fragment). *Voices*, 1966, 2(4), 38–39.

1075 ———. Whose masculine protest? *Contemp. Psychol.*, 1960, 5, 28–29.

1076 ———. Die Wiederentdeckung Alfred Adlers in den Vereinigten Staaten. *Schule u. Psychol.*, 1970, 17(12), 355–366 (with Rowena R. Ansbacher).

1077 **Ansbacher, Rowena R.** Alfred Adler: 1870–1937. *Sociom.*, 1937, 1, 259–261 (with H. L. Ansbacher).

1078 ———. Berichte über Linkhändigkeit. *IZIP*, 1932, 10(6), 410–414.

1079 ———. "Contemporary psychotherapists examine themselves"—a special review. *JIP*, 1957, 13, 94–102.

1080 ———. Danica Deutsch at eighty. *JIP*, 1970, 26(2), 213–216.

1081 ———. Definition der Neurose. *IZIP*, 1933, 11(3), 161–176.

1082 ———. First workshop on training Adlerian counselors. *IP*, 1970, 8(2), 41–48.

1083 ———. Individual Psychology. In *Int. J. Encycl. Soc. Sci.*, Vol. 7. New York: Crowell, Collier & Macmillan, 1968. Pp. 213–218 (with H. L. Ansbacher).

1084 ——— (Ed.). *The Individual Psychology of Alfred Adler* (with H. L. Ansbacher). New York: Basic Books, 1956, 1958; London: Allen & Unwin, 1956, 1958; New York: Harper Torchbooks, 1964. Paper.

1085 ———. Lee Harvey Oswald: An Adlerian interpretation. *Psychoanal. Rev.*, 1966, 53, 379–390. Also in *JIP*, 1967, 23, 24–36 (with H. L. Ansbacher, D. Shiverick & Kathleen Shiverick). Condensed in *OSIPNL*, 1967, 8(3), 9–11.

1086 ——— (Ed.). *La Psychologia individual de Alfred Adler: Presentación sistemática de una selección de sus escritos.*

Translated by Nuria Cortado de Kohan. Buenos Aires: Troquel, 1959 (with H. L. Ansbacher).

1087 **Ansbacher, Rowena R.** Reality therapy and Individual Psychology in the classroom: A special review. *JIP*, 1969, 25, 106–111.

1088 ———. Review of F. Alexander, S. Einstein & M. Grotjahn (Eds.), *Psychoanalytic pioneers.* In *JIP*, 1967, 23, 245–246.

1089 ———. Review of T. W. Allen (Ed.), Individual Psychology: The legacy of Alfred Adler. *Couns. Psychologist*, 1971, 3(1), 3–72. In *JIP*, 1972, 28, 90–91.

1090 ———. Review of G. H. Allred. *Mission for Mother.* In *JIP*, 1972, 28, 99–100.

1091 ———. Review of Virginia Axline, *DIBS: In search of self.* Boston: Houghton Mifflin, 1964. In *JIP*, 1966, 22, 137–138.

1092 ———. Review of Marguerite and W. Beecher, *The Mark of Cain.* In *JIP*, 1971, 27(1), 111–112.

1093 ———. Review of P. A. Bertocci & R. M. Millard, *Personality and the good.* New York: David McKay, 1963. In *JIP*, 1964, 20, 103–105.

1094 ———. Review of J. Bierer & R. I. Evans, *Innovations in social psychiatry.* In *JIP*, 1970, 26, 86–88.

1095 ———. Review of M. Boss, *Psychoanalysis and Daseinanalysis.* New York: Basic Books, 1963. In *JIP*, 1963, 19, 234–236.

1096 ———. Review of J. F. T. Bugental (Ed.), *Challenges of humanistic psychology.* New York: McGraw-Hill, 1967. In *JIP*, 1969, 25, 115–118.

1097 ———. Review of J. F. T. Bugental, *The search for authenticity.* New York: Holt, Rinehart & Winston, 1965. In *JIP*, 1966, 22, 244–245.

1098 ———. Review of C. H. Campbell, *Induced delusions: The psychopathy of Freudism.* Chicago: Regent House, 1957. In *JIP*, 1959, 15, 243.

1099 ———. Review of H. Cantril, *The human dimension.* New Brunswick, N. J.: Rutgers Univ. Press, 1967. In *JIP*, 1967, 23, 243–244.

1100 ———. Review of H. Cantril & C. H. Bumstead, *Reflections on the human venture.* New York: New York Univ. Press, 1960. In *JIP*, 1960, 16, 97–98.

1101 ———. Review of R. R. Carkhuff, *Helping and human relations.* New York: Holt, Rinehart & Winston, 1969. In *JIP*, 1970, 26, 90–91.

1102 **Ansbacher, Rowena R.** Review of R. A. Chittick, G. W. Brooks, F. S. Irons & W. N. Deane, *The Vermont Story: Rehabilitation of chronic schizophrenic patients.* Washington, D. C.: Off. Voc. Rehab., 1962. In *JIP*, 1962, 18, 196–197.

1103 ———. Review of Dorothy R. Disher, *Workbook for students of adolescent adjustment.* In *JIP*, 1960, 16, 220–221.

1104 ———. Review of R. Dreikurs, *Psychology in the classroom.* In *JIP*, 1957, 13, 197–199.

1105 ———. Review of R. Dreikurs, R. Corsini, R. Lowe, & M. Sonstegard (Eds.), *Adlerian family counseling.* In *JIP*, 1960, 16, 93–94.

1106 ———. Review of R. Dreikurs & Vicki Soltz, *Children: The challenge.* In *JIP*, 1964, 20, 111–112.

1107 ———. Review of A. Ellis, *The art and science of love.* In *JIP*, 1960, 16, 221–222.

1108 ———. Review of A. Ellis, *Reason and emotion in psychotherapy.* In *JIP*, 1963, 19, 94–95.

1109 ———. Review of Joen Fagan & Irma L. Shepherd (Eds.), *Gestalt therapy now: Theory, techniques, applications.* Palo Alto: Science & Behavior Books, 1970. In *JIP*, 1972, 28, 93–95.

1110 ———. Review of V. E. Frankl, *From death-camp to existentialism.* In *JIP*, 1959, 15, 236–237.

1111 ———. Review of Lucy Freeman & H. Greenwald, *Emotional maturity in love and marriage.* New York: Harper, 1961 and A. Ellis & R. A. Harper, *Creative marriage.* In *JIP*, 1961, 17, 237–238.

1112 ———. Review of M. Freud, *Sigmund Freud: Man and father.* New York: Vanguard Press, 1958. In *JIP*, 1958, 14, 196–197.

1113 ———. Review of S. Freud, *Psychoanalysis and faith: The letters of Sigmund Freud and Oskar Pfister.* New York: Basic Books, 1963. In *JIP*, 1964, 20, 235–237.

1114 ———. Review of E. Fromm, *Sigmund Freud's mission.* New York: Harper, 1959. In *JIP*, 1960, 16, 103.

1115 ———. Review of H. Ginott, *Between parent and child.* New York: Macmillan, 1965. In *JIP*, 1968, 24, 202–204.

1116 Ansbacher, Rowena, R. Review of H. G. Ginott, *Teacher and child.* New York: Macmillan, 1972. In *JIP*, 1972, 28, 98–99.

1117 ———. Review of W. Glasser, *Reality therapy.* In *JIP*, 1965, 21, 208–209.

1118 ———. Review of H. Greenwald, *The call girl.* New York: Ballantine Books, 1958. In *JIP*, 1958, 14, 192–193.

1119 ———. Review of I. D. Harris, *The promised seed.* In *JIP*, 1966, 22, 136.

1120 ———. Review of J. Haley (Ed.), *Changing families: A family therapy reader.* In *JIP*, 1972, 28, 95–97.

1121 ———. Review of A. B. Hollingshead & F. C. Redlich, *Social class and mental illness.* New York: Wiley, 1958. In *JIP*, 1958, 14, 195–196.

1122 ———. Review of R. R. Koegler & N. Q. Brill, *Treatment of psychiatric outpatients.* New York: Appleton-Century-Crofts, 1967. In *JIP*, 1970, 26, 93.

1123 ———. Review of L. Krasner & L. Ullman (Eds.), *Research in behavior modification.* New York: Holt, Rinehart & Winston, 1965. In *JIP*, 1967, 23, 117.

1124 ———. Review of M. D. Kushner, *Freud—A man obsessed.* Philadelphia: Dorrance, 1967. In *JIP*, 1970, 26, 93–94.

1125 ———. Review of R. La Piere, *The Freudian ethic.* New York: Duell, Sloan & Pearce, 1959. In *JIP*, 1960, 16, 103–104.

1126 ———. Review of A. H. Maslow, *Eupsychian management.* Homewood, Ill.: R. D. Irwin & Dorsey Press, 1965. In *JIP*, 1966, 22, 130–131.

1127 ———. Review of A. H. Maslow, *Toward a psychology of being.* In *JIP*, 1962, 18, 188–190.

1128 ———. Review of R. May, *Love and will.* In *JIP*, 1970, 26, 230–233.

1129 ———. Review of R. May, *Psychology and the human dilemma.* Princeton, N. J. Van Nostrand, 1967. In *JIP*, 1968, 24, 107–108.

1130 ———. Review of R. A. McClelland, *The errant dawn.* In *JIP*, 1969, 25, 241–242.

1131 ———. Review of W. McCord & Joan McCord, *Origins of alcoholism.* Stanford, Cal.: Stanford Univ. Press, 1960. In *JIP*, 1961, 17, 123–124.

1132 ———. Review of R. W. McIntire, *For love of children: Behavioral psychology for patients.* Del Mar, Cal.: CRM Books, 1970. In *JIP*, 1971, 27 (1), 109–111.

1133 Ansbacher, Rowena R. Review of J. L. Moreno, *The first book on group psychotherapy.* Beacon, N. Y.: Beacon House, 1957. In *JIP*, 1958, 14, 92–93.

1134 ———. Review of O. H. Mowrer, *The crisis in psychiatry and religion.* In *JIP*, 1961, 17, 235–236.

1135 ———. Review of O. H. Mowrer, *The new group therapy.* In *JIP*, 1964, 20, 234–235.

1136 ———. Review of Edith G. Neisser, *The eldest child.* In *JIP*, 1960, 16, 219.

1137 ———. Review of Genevieve Painter, *Teach your baby.* In *JIP*, 1971, 27(2), 228–229.

1138 ———. Review of F. S. Perls, *Gestalt therapy verbatim.* Lafayette, Cal.: Real People Press, 1969. In *JIP*, 1970, 26, 88–90.

1139 ———. Review of E. L. Phillips, D. N. Wiener, & N. G. Haring, *Discipline, achievement and mental health.* Englewood Cliffs, N. J.: Prentice-Hall, 1960. In *JIP*, 1960, 16, 220.

1140 ———. Review of Marie Beynon Ray, *The importance of feeling inferior.* In *JIP*, 1958, 14, 95–96.

1141 ———. Review of W. G. Schutz, *Joy.* New York: Grove Press, 1967. In *JIP*, 1968, 24, 108–109.

1142 ———. Review of J. P. Scott, *Aggression.* Chicago: Univ. Chicago Press, 1958. In *JIP*, 1959, 15, 246.

1143 ———. Review of Vicki Soltz, *Study group leader's manual.* In *JIP*, 1968, 24, 109.

1144 ———. Review of S. W. Standal & R. J. Corsini, *Critical incidents in psychotherapy.* In *JIP*, 1959, 15, 238–239.

1145 ———. Review of F. C. Thorne, *Clinical judgment.* Brandon, Vt.: J. Clin. Psychol., 1961. In *JIP*, 1961, 17, 121–122.

1146 ———. Review of F. C. Thorne, *Tutorial counseling: How to be psychologically healthy.* Brandon, Vt.: Clin. Psychol. Publ. Co., 1965. In *JIP*, 1966, 22, 133–134.

1147 ———. Review of A. van Kaam, *Existential foundations of psychology.* Pittsburgh: Duquesne Univ. Press, 1966. In *JIP*, 1967, 23, 242–243.

1148 ———. Review of Rita Vuyk, *Das Kind in der Zweikinderfamilie.* In *JIP*, 1960, 16, 219.

1149 ———. Review of C. Wenar, *Personality development: From infancy to adulthood.* Boston: Houghton Mifflin, 1971. In *JIP*, 1971, 27(2), 220–225.

A BIBLIOGRAPHY FOR ADLERIAN PSYCHOLOGY

1150 **Ansbacher, Rowena R.** Review of R. W. White, *Lives in progress.* New York: Holt, Rinehart & Winston, 1966. In *JIP*, 1968, 24, 105-107.

1151 ———. Review of Blanche C. Weill, *Through children's eyes; true stories out of the practice of a consultant psychologist.* In *IPN*, 1941, 1(7), 2-3.

1152 ———. Review of L. L. Whyte, *The unconscious before Freud.* New York: Basic Books, 1960. In *JIP*, 1961, 17, 115-117.

1153 ———. Sane Ben Franklin: An Adlerian view of his autobiography. *JIP*, 1971, 27(2), 189-207 (with J. McLaughlin).

1154 ———. *A study of the infant's feeding reactions during the first six months of life.* New York: Arch. Psychol., 1930, No. 116.

1155 ———. Sullivan's interpersonal psychiatry and Adler's Individual Psychology: A special review. *JIP*, 1971, 27(1), 85-98.

1156 ——— (Ed.). *Superioridad y interés social: Una colección de sus últimos escritos.* Translated by Maria Martinez Penaloza. Mexico: Fonde de Cultura Economica, 1968 (with H. L. Ansbacher).

1157 ——— (Ed.). *Superiority and social interest.* Evanston, Ill.: Northwestern Univ. Press, 1964; London: Routledge & Kegan Paul, 1965 (with H. L. Ansbacher).

1158 ———. Die Wiederentdeckung Alfred Adlers in den Vereinigten Staaten. In *Schule u. Psychologie*, 1970, 17(12), 355-366 (with H. L. Ansbacher).

1159 **Antman, J.** The father in parent-child counseling. *Jewish soc. serv. Quart.*, 1954, 30, 301-306.

1160 **Appelt, A.** Fortschritte der Stottererbehandlung. In A. Adler & C. Furtmüller (Eds.), *Heilen und Bilden* (1914). Pp. 226-245; (1928). Pp. 228-248.

1161 ———. *Die heilpädagogische Beeinflussung sprachgestörter Kinder in den Sonderschulen Deutschlands.* Berlin: A. Hoffmann, 1930.

1162 ———. Review of K. C. Rothe, *Das Stottern, die Assoziative Aphasie und ihre heilpädagogische Behandlung.* In *IZIP*, 1926, 4(3), 166-167.

1163 ———. Sprachstörungen. In E. Wexberg (Ed.), *Handbuch der Individualpsychologie.* Pp. 532-534.

1164 ———. *Stammering and its permanent cure: A treatise on Individual Psychology.* London: Methuen, 1911, 1929.

1165 ———. *Das Stotternde Kind.*   1926.

1166 **Appelt, A.** *Die wirkliche Ursache des Stotterns und seine dauernde Heilung.* Berlin: A. Hoffmann, 1931.

1167 ———. Zur Behandlung des Stotterns. *IZIP*, 1924, 2(4), 1-6.

1168 ———. Zur therapie des Stotterns. *IZIP*, 1930, 8(1), 125-132.

1169 **Arbeitsgemeinschaft der Internationalen Vereinigung für Individualpsychologie.** *Alfred Adler zum Gedenken.* Wien: Selbstverlag des Verein für Individualpsychologie, 1957.

1170 **Arcinega, M.** Not budgeted for a guidance counselor? You can still offer a guidance program. *Elementary principals service: Operational briefing.* Croft Educational Service, Inc., 1970 (with O. C. Christensen).

1171 **Arlitt, Ada.** *Psychology of infancy and early childhood.* New York: McGraw-Hill, 1930.

1172 **Arlow, J. A.** Finger painting in the psychotherapy of children. *Amer. J. Orthopsychiat.*, 1946, 16, 134-146 (with Asya Kadis)

1173 **Armstrong, C. P.** Delinquency and primogeniture. *Psychol. Clin.*, 1933, 22, 48-52.

1174 **Arnold, A.** Review of Phyllis Bottome, *Alfred Adler: A biography.* In *IPN*, 1940, 1(2), 3.

1175 **Arnold, Magda B.** *Emotion and personality.* 2 vols. New York: Columbia Univ. Press, 1960.

1176 **Arnold, M. R.** Let 'em fight: How to raise kids and stay sane [about R. Dreikurs]. *Nat. Observer*, 1972, 2(1).

1177 **Arnold, Nita.** An Adlerian evaluation of methods and techniques in psychotherapy of adults. *AJIP*, 1954, 11, 34-46.

1178 ———. A call for loyalty. *IPB*, 1942, 2(4), 66.

1179 ———. What is an Adlerian? *IPB*, 1951, 9, 143-145.

1180 ———. Who is neurotic? *IJIP*, 1937, 3(3), 243-253.

1181 **Arnstein, E. E.** Early childhood memories as a projective test in vocational guidance (Summary). *IPNL*, 1957, 6(8-9, Whole No. 72-73). Pp. 35-36.

1182 ———. Ha-individual psihologia v'ha-psihotehnika (Individual Psychology and psychotechnics). *Hahinukh*, 1950-52, 24, 266-277.

1183 **Aronov, B. M.** Use of co-therapists in group psychotherapy. *J. consult. Psychol.*, 1952, 16, 76-80 (with W. H. Lundin).

1184 **Arrowood, A. J.** Social comparison and ordinal position. *J. Pers. soc. Psychol.*, 1965, 2, 101–104 (with D. M. Amoroso).

1185 **Arthur, Grace.** The relation of I. Q. to position in family. *J. educ. Psychol.*, 1926, 17, 541–550.

1186 **Asch, S. E.** *Social psychology.* New York: Prentice-Hall, 1952.

1187 **Ascher, E. A.** Review of *Fortschritte der Neurologie, Psychiatrie und ihre Grenzgebiete*, 1929, 1(1). In *IZIP*, 1930, 8(2), 271–272.

1188 **Asnaourow, F.** Las defensas psiquicas su mecanismo y aplicacion en la vida. *Rev. Criminol.* (Buenos Aires), 1926.

1189 ———. Erziehung zur Grausamkeit. In A. Adler & C. Furtmüller (Eds.), *Heilen und Bilden* (1914). Pp. 246–251.

1190 ———. Fortschritte der Psychologie. *Nosotros* (Buenos Aires), 1922, 152.

1191 ———. Las ideas maniáticas y su papel en la vida humana. *Revis. Criminol, Psiquiat. y med. Legal* (Buenos Aires), 1922, 9, 276–291.

1192 ———. Sadismus und Masochismus in Kultur und Erziehung. *Schr. Ver. freie psychoanal. Forsch.*, 1913, No. 4.

1193 ———. *Sadismus und Masochismus in der Weltgeschichte.* München: Ernst Reinhardt, 1929.

1194 ———. Über onirische Überkompensation. *IZIP*, 1929, 7(6), 469–471.

1195 ———. Über strenge Erziehung. In A. Adler & C. Furtmüller (Eds.), *Heilen und Bilden* (1914). Pp. 252–261.

1196 **Atkins, Frances.** The social meaning of the Oedipus myth. *JIP*, 1966, 22, 173–184. Also in H. D. Werner (Ed.), *New understandings of human behavior.* Pp. 246–260.

1197 **Atkinson, G. C.** Perceptual defense, dissimulation, and response styles. *J. consult. Psychol.*, 1964, 28, 529–535 (with P. G. Liberty, Jr. & C. E. Lunneborg).

1198 **Atkinson, J.** Achievement motive and test anxiety conceived as motive to approach success and motive to avoid failure. *J. abnorm. soc. Psychol.*, 1960, 60, 52–63 (with G. H. Litwin).

1199 ———. Motivational determinants of risk-taking behavior. *Psychol. Rev.*, 1957, 64, 359–373.

1200 ———. Performance as a function of motive strength and expectancy of goal attainment. *J. abnorm. soc. Psychol.*, 1956, 53, 361–367 (with W. R. Reitman).

1201 **Atkinson, J.** *A theory of achievement motivation.* New York: Wiley, 1966 (with N. T. Feather).

1202 **Aubry, W. E.** Family counseling in a children's center. *Marr. Fam. Counselors Quart.*, 1972, 7(3), 9–15.

1203 **Auer, Elizabeth.** The case history of Anne. In K. A. Adler & Danica Deutsch (Eds.), *Essays in Individual Psychology.* Pp. 297–311.

1204 ———. Review of O. Strunk, Jr., *Readings in the psychology of religion.* New York: Abingdon Press, 1959. In *JIP*, 1960, 16, 102.

1205 **Auerbach, H.** Einwände die Individualpsychology: Zur Lehre von den Neurosen. *IZIP*, 1933, 11(3), 248–253.

1206 **August, W–E.** Translator of Genevieve Painter, *Baby-Schule.*

1207 **Ausdenmoore, R.** Color preferences in chromatic H-T-P drawings. *Ohio Res. Quart.*, 1967, 1, 48–52 (with V. J. Bieliauskas).

1208 **Austin, R.** Simenon's "Maigret" and Adler. *ADAM: Int. Rev.* (London), 1970, 35 (340–342), 45–50.

1209 **Ausubel, D. P.** Perceived parent attitudes as determinants of ego structure. *Child Developm.*, 1955, 25, 173–183 (with E. E. Balthazar, I. Rosenthal, L. S. Blackman, S. N. Schpoont, & J. Welkowitz).

1210 **Ayrault, Evelyn W.** *Take one step.* Garden City, N. Y.: Doubleday, 1963.

1211 ———. *You can raise your handicapped child.* New York: Putnam, 1964.

B

1 **B.** Review of K. Vorländer, *Von Macchiavelli bis Lenin.* Leipzig: Quelle & Meyer, 1926. In *IZIP*, 1928, 6(3), 265.

2 **Babledalis, Georgia.** *The shaping of personality: Text and readings for a social learning view.* Englewood Cliffs, N. J.: Prentice-Hall, 1967.

3 **Baca, J. A.** Translator of D. Dinkmeyer & R. Dreikurs, *Como estimular al nino.*

4 **Bader, Helene.** Ein verzärteltes Kind. *IZIP*, 1929, 7(4), 309–311.

5 ———. Das Geschwister des schwererziehbare Kindes. *IZIP*, 1930, 8(5), 499–502 (with Victoria Fritz).

6 Bader, Helene. Glimpses of the life-style in dreams, fantasies and play of children. *IJIP*, 1936, 2(1), 84–90.

7 ———. Kinderspiel und Aufsatz als Ausdrucksformen der kindlichen Leitlinie. *IZIP*, 1928, 6(4), 334.

8 ———. Die Lebensstil des Kindes in Erzählung, Traum und Spiel. *IZIP*, 1932, 10 (3), 224–229.

9 ———. Review of F. Kanitz, *Kämpfer der Zukunft*. Wien: Jungbrunnen, 1929. In *IZIP*, 1929, 7(1), 152.

10 ———. Review of *Schweiz. Erziehungsrundsch*. In *IZIP*, 1931, 9(5), 415–416.

11 ———. Verzärtelung und Schwachisinn. *IZIP*, 1928, 6(5), 409–411.

12 Badran, M. A. Translator, with A. M. Abd. Al-Khaliq, of A. Adler, *Al-Hayat Al-Nafsiyah*.

13 Baehr, Melanie. *Work Interest Test*. Education-Industry Service, Univ. Chicago, 1957 (with R. Burns & R. J. Corsini).

14 Baer, M. Acceptance of self, parents and people in patients and normals. *J. clin. Psychol.*, 1956, 12, 327–332 (with M. Zuckerman & I. Monashkin).

15 Bagger, E. Inferiority sense to be our chief enemy. *New York Times*, Sept., 20, 1925.

16 ———. Salvaging mankind by psychology [Interview with A. Adler]. *New York Times*, Sept. 20, 1925. P. 12. Also in *IZIP*, 1925, 3(6), 332–335.

17 Bailey, Jane. On the positive side, examples. *OSIPNL*, 1962, 3(2), 5.

18 ———. On the positive side, jobs for children. *OSIPNL*, 1963, 4(5), 9–10.

19 Baker, A. Pseudonym of H. L. Ansbacher.

20 Baker, Elizabeth. The child guidance center at Abraham Lincoln Centre. *IPB*, 1942, 2 (3), 41–45.

21 ———. Review of R. Dreikurs, The importance of camp life. In *IPN*, 1941, 1(7), 3–4.

22 ———. Selected problems and suggested treatment. *IPN*, 1941, 1(6), 2–5.

23 Baker, H. J. A study of juvenile theft. *J. educ. Res.*, 1929, 20, 81–87 (with F. J. Decker & A. S. Hall).

24 Baker, R. R. Action therapy intervention in human interaction training. *Nwsltr. Res. Psychol.*, 1972, 14(4), 23–25 (with W. E. O'Connell, P. G. Hanson & R. Ermalinski).

25 Baldie, A. Post-war planning: A view of the future of the Society. *IPP*, 1943, No. 23. Pp. 17–21.

26 Baldrian, R. Können ist Macht. *IZIP*, 1933, 12(5), 396–398.

27 Baldwin, A. L. Patterns of parent behavior. *Psychol. Monogr.*, 1945, 58, No. 3 (Whole No. 268) (with Joan Kallhorn & Fay Breese).

28 Balester, R. The self concept and juvenile delinquency. Unpubl. Doctor's Diss., Vanderbilt Univ., 1956.

29 Balls, Josephine. *The child is always right: A challenge to parents and other adults.* London: Longmans, 1947, 1950 (with J. Hemming).

30 Balogh, Sara C. *The counseling relationship: A casebook.* Chicago: Sci. Res. Assoc., 1961 (with A. Buchheimer).

31 Balthazar, E. E. Perceived parent attitudes as determinants of ego structure. *Child Developm.*, 1955, 25, 173–183 (with D. P. Ausubel, I. Rosenthal, L. S. Blackman, S. N. Schpoont & J. Welkowitz).

32 Bancroche, F. Review of R. Allers, *The new psychologies*. In *IPMP*, 1933, No. 9. Pp. 56–58.

33 Barbach, J. Compensation and the crime of pigeon dropping. *J. clin. Psychol.*, 1952, 8, 92–94.

34 Barbara D. A. Some aspects of stuttering in the light of Adlerian psychology. *JIP*, 1957, 13, 188–193.

35 Barber, J. D. Classifying and predicting presidential styles: Two "weak" presidents. *J. soc. Issues*, 1968, 24(3), 51–80.

36 Barber, T. X. Hypnosis as a perceptual cognitive restructuring. I. Analysis of concepts. *J. clin. exp. Hypn.*, 1957, 5, 147–166.

37 Barger, B. Attitudinal structures of older and younger siblings. *JIP*, 1964, 20, 59–68.

38 Barilari, M. J. *Contribución a la medicina psiquica*. Buenos Aires: Frascoli & Bindi, 1934.

39 ———. Reflexions sobre psicoterapia. *El Dia Medico*, 1932, 6.

40 ———. Self-review of *Contribución a la medicina psiquica*. In *IZIP*, 1935, 13 (3), 192–193.

41 Bark, U. Translator of A. Adler, *Conocimiento del hombre*.

42 Barker, C. The approach to the patient. *IPP*, 1943, No. 23. Pp. 33–43.

43 Barnes, Hazel E. Adler and Sartre: Comment. *JIP*, 1965, 21, 201.

44 Barrett, D. M. Memory in relation to hedonic tone. *Arch. Psychol., N.Y.*, 1938, No. 223. Pp. 61.

45 **Barry, H.** Birth order of recovered and non-recovered schizophrenics. *Arch. gen. Psychiat.*, 1963, 9, 224–228 (with A. Farina & N. Garmezy).

46 **Barry, H., Jr.** Sex differences in birth order of alcoholics. *Brit. J. Psychiat.*, 1971, 119, 657–661 (with H. Barry, III and H. T. Blane).

47 **Barry, H., III.** Sex differences in birth order of alcoholics. *Brit. J. Psychiat.*, 1971, 119, 657–661 (with H. Barry, Jr. and H. T. Blane).

48 **Bartelme, K.** Attitudes of San Quentin prisoners. *J. correct. Psychol.*, 1952, 4, 43–46 (with R. J. Corsini).

49 ———. Penology and the attitude of prisoners. *Brit. J. Delinqu.*, 1953, 4, 55–58 (with R. J. Corsini).

50 **Barten, H. H.** Comments: Health oriented psychotherapy, *JIP*, 1972, 28(2), 152–153.

51 **Bartholow, R. G.** How to hold a family council. *OSIPNL*, 1969, 10(2), 9–11.

52 ———. Review of H. D. Werner (Ed.), *New understandings of human behavior.* In *JIP*, 1971, 27(1), 102–103.

53 **Bartlett, E. W.** Childrearing practices, birth order, and the development of achievement-related motives. *Psychol. Rep.*, 1966, 19, 1201–1216 (with C. P. Smith).

54 **Bartlett, F. C.** *Remembering: A study in experimental and social psychology.* New York: Macmillan, 1932; London: Cambridge Univ. Press, 1932.

55 **Bathelt, K.** Individualpsychologie und Soziologie. *IZIP*, 1933, 12(5), 394–395.

56 ———. Review of F. Sternberg, *Der Niedergang des deutschen Kapitalismus.* In *IZIP*, 1934, 12(3), 195.

57 **Bathory, M.** (Ed.) *School counseling: Perspectives and procedures.* Itasca, Ill.: F. E. Peacock, 1968 (with H. Peters).

58 **Batt, C. E.** Mexican character: An Adlerian interpretation. *JIP*, 1969, 25, 183–201.

59 **Battle, Esther S.** Children's feelings of personal control as related to social class and ethnic group. *J. Pers.*, 1963, 31, 482–490 (with J. B. Rotter).

60 **Bauer, J.** Review of J. B. Schairer, *Ehenot und Eherat.* Gütersloh: Bertelsmann, 1931. In *IZIP*, 1931, 9(5), 411–412.

61 **Bauer, Mary L.** Sibling sex distribution and psychiatric status. *Psychol. Rep.*, 1966, 18, 365–366 (with H. J. Ehrlich).

62 **Bauermeister, H.** Die Begabungsfrage in der bildenden Kunst. *IZIP*, 1929, 7(2), 108–111.

63 ———. Zum Problem der hässlichen Frau. *IZIP*, 1929, 7(6), 436–442.

64 **Baumgaertel, K.** (Ed.). *Aspekte in der Arbeit mit schwierigen Kindern.* Wien: Verlag f. Jugend u. Volk, n.d.

65 ———. Die Jugend Stendhals. *IZIP*, 1949, 18(3), 130–133.

66 ——— (Ed.). *Lexikon der Erziehung.* Wien: Ulstein, 1956 (with F. Friedmann).

67 ———. Portrait. *IPNL*, 1970, 19(4), 79: 1971, 20(6), 112.

68 ———. Review of E. Fenz, *Von den menschlichen Beziehungen.* Wien: Luckmann, 1948, 17(4), 187.

69 **Baxter, J. C.** Father identification as a function of mother-father relationship. *JIP*, 1964, 20, 167–171 (with D. L. Horton & R. E. Wiley).

70 ———. Parental complementarity and parental conflict. *JIP*, 1965, 21, 149–153.

71 **Bayer, A. E.** Birth order and college attendance. *J. Marr. & Fam.*, 1966, 480–484.

72 **Baynes, H. G.** The parent-child relation. *IPMP*, 1937, No. 17 (with S. Crown, S. H. Lubner, A. C. Court, M. Marcus, & F. G. Crookshank).

73 ———. The psychological background of the parent-child relation. *IPMP*, No. 17. Pp. 7–29.

74 **Beacher, A. I.** Psychoanalytic treatment of a sociopath in a group situation. *Amer. J. Psychother.*, 1962, 16, 278–288.

75 ———. Psychosomatic illness: An Adlerian concept. *Psychosom.*, 1960, 1, 1–5.

76 **Beaglehole, E.** A note on cultural compensation. *J. abnorm. soc. Psychol.*, 1938, 33, 121–123.

77 **Beattie, N. R.** Foreword to 2nd edition of Hertha Orgler, *Alfred Adler, the man and his work.*

78 ———. Parents in a modern world. *Marr. Guid.*, 1956.

79 ———. The position of the child in the family and its significance. *Nursery J.*, Oct.-Nov., 1956.

80 ———. Psychosomatic medicine. *Pharmaceu. J.*, 1950, 10, 8–9.

81 ———. Review of Hertha Orgler, *Alfred Adler: The man and his work.* In *J. Royal Inst. Publ. Hlth. & Hyg.*, 1963, 26, 285.

82 **Beauchamp, G.** The effects of expectation, experience and social class on group productivity. *Res. Educ.*, July, 1971, 1-9 (with L. Sperry).

83 **Beck, O.** Jugendliche nach der Strafhaft. *IZIP*, 1928, 6(2), 100-107.

84 ———. Ursache und therapie bei verwahrlosten Jugendlichen. *IZIP*, 1931, 9(5), 396-402.

85 **Beck, S. J.** (Ed.). *Reflexes to intelligence: A reader in clinical psychology.* Glencoe, Ill.: Free Press, 1959 (with H. B. Molish).

86 **Becker, E.** Adler and the modern world: A special review. *JIP*, 1963, 19, 83-89.

87 ———. Anthropological notes on the concept of aggression. *Psychiat.*, 1962, 25, 328-338.

88 ———. *The birth and death of meaning: A perspective in psychiatry and anthropology.* New York: The Free Press of Glencoe, 1962.

89 ———. Toward a comprehensive theory of depression: A cross-disciplinary appraisal of objects, games and meaning. *J. nerv. ment. Dis.*, 1962, 135, 26-35.

90 **Becker, G.** Affiliate perception and the arousal of the participation-affiliation motive. *Percep. mot. Skills*, 1967, 24, 991-997.

91 ———. Birth order and subject recruitment. *J. soc. Psychol.*, 1965, 65, 63-66 (with T. C. Brock).

92 ———. Visual acuity, birth order, achievement vs. affiliation and other Edwards Personal Preference Schedule scores. *J. psychosom. Res.*, 1965, 9, 277-283.

93 **Becker, S. W.** Conformity as a function of birth order, payoff, and type of group pressure. *J. abnorm. soc. Psychol.*, 1964, 69, 318-323 (with M. J. Lerner & J. Carroll).

94 ———. Ordinal position and conformity. *J. abnorm. soc. Psychol.*, 1962, 65, 129-131 (with Jean Carroll).

95 **Beckh-Widmanstetter, H. A.** Zur Geschichte der Individualpsychologie: Julius Wagner-Jauregg über Alfred Adler. *Unsere Heimat* (Wien), 1965, 36 (10-12), 182-188.

96 **Beecher, Marguerite.** *Besser leben ohne Neid und Eifersucht.* Translated by Helga Kunzel. Genf: Ramon F. Keller, 1972 (with W. Beecher).

97 ———. *Beyond success and failure: Ways to self-reliance and maturity.* New York: Julian Press, 1966 (with W. Beecher).

98 **Beecher, Marguerite.** Building social awareness in school. *IJIP*, 1937, 3(1), 88-99; 1937, 3(2), 179-197 (with W. Beecher).

99 ———. Causality versus indeterminism. *IPB*, 1951, 9, 118-121 (with W. Beecher).

100 ———. *The mark of Cain: An anatomy of jealousy.* New York: Harper & Row, 1971 (with W. Beecher).

101 ———. *Parents on the run.* New York: Julian Press, 1955; New York: Agora Books, 1966. Paper (with W. Beecher).

102 ———. Remedial reading. *IPB*, 1949, 7, 99-118 (with W. Beecher).

103 ———. Re-structuring mistaken family relationships. *JIP*, 1957, 13, 176-181 (with W. Beecher).

104 ———. Two hundred cases in retrospect. *AJIP*, 1954, 11, 9-22. Also in K. A. Adler & Danica Deutsch (Eds.), *Essays in Individual Psychology.* Pp. 312-321.

105 ———. What makes an Adlerian? *IPB*, 1951, 9, 146-148 (with W. Beecher).

106 **Beecher, W.** Are you feared or respected? *Forbes Mag.*, Dec. 1, 1942.

107 ———. *Besser leben ohne Neid und Eifersucht.* Translated by Helga Kunzel. Genf: Ramon F. Keller, 1972 (with Marguerite Beecher).

108 ———. *Beyond success and failure: Ways to self-reliance and maturity.* New York: Julian Press, 1966 (with Marguerite Beecher).

109 ———. Building social awareness in school. *IJIP*, 1937, 3(1), 88-99; 1937, 3(2), 179-197 (with Marguerite Beecher).

110 ———. Causality versus indeterminism. *IPB*, 1951, 9, 118-121 (with Marguerite Beecher).

111 ———. Classroom discipline. *IPB*, 1943, 3, 64-71.

112 ———. The common sense of sex education. *IPB*, 1941, 2(1), 10-21; 1949, 7, 12-14.

113 ———. Cooperation: What does it mean? *Gen. semant. Bull.*, 1957, No. 20-21.

114 ———. Cooperation: What is it? *OSIPNL*, 1965, 5(4), 14.

115 ———. Democracy. *IPB*, 1942, 2(4), 63-66.

116 ———. Discover your powers of self-reliance. *Management Inform.*, Nov. 3, 1969.

117 **Beecher, W.** Every stick has two ends. *IPB*, 1946, 5, 84–86.

118 ——. Guilt feelings: Masters of our fate, or our servants. *IPB*, 1950, 8, 22–31. Also in K. A. Adler & Danica Deutsch (Eds.), *Essays in Individual Psychology*. Pp. 59–70.

119 ——. Hints for executives. *Forbes Mag.*, Sept. 15, 1942.

120 ——. How are "problem" children made? *IPB*, 1942, 2(2), 21–24.

121 ——. Industrial relations in the light of Individual Psychology. *AJIP*, 1954, 11, 123–130.

122 ——. Language habits. *Clearing House*, 1942, 16, 272–274.

123 ——. *The mark of Cain: An anatomy of jealousy*. New York: Harper & Row, 1971 (with Marguerite Beecher).

124 ——. The meaning of theories. *IPB*, 1942, 2(3), 46–49.

125 ——. The myth of "the unconscious". *IPB*, 1950, 8, 99–110.

126 ——. A new approach to remedial instruction. *AJIP*, 1952, 10, 4–19.

127 ——. "None so deaf as . . . " *IPB*, 1943, 3(1), 1–5.

128 ——. Oblique hostility. *IPB*, 1949, 7, 51–74.

129 ——. Observations about alcoholics. *IPB*, 1947, 6, 71–73.

130 ——. *Parents on the run*. New York: Julian Press, 1955; New York: Agora Books, 1966. Paper (with Marguerite Beecher).

131 ——. A psychologist looks at Clearing House's case histories. *Clearing House*, 1942, 17, 80–82.

132 ——. Psychoneurotics: Why our schools have not helped them. *Clearing House*, 1946, 20, 519–521.

133 ——. Remedial reading. *IPB*, 1949, 7, 99–118 (with Marguerite Beecher).

134 ——. Re-structuring mistaken family relationships. *IPB*, 1957, 13, 176–181 (with Marguerite Beecher).

135 ——. Thoughts on creativity. *News-Bull., Artists Guild of Chicago*, June, 1959.

136 ——. The truth about remedial reading. *Clearing House*, 1943, 17, 271–274.

137 ——. The unrecognized purpose. *IJIP*, 1937, 3(3), 228–232.

138 ——. What is work and what is play? *Clearing House*, 1942, 16, 396–397.

139 **Beecher, W.** What makes an Adlerian? *IPB*, 1951, 9, 146–148 (with Marguerite Beecher).

140 ——. What to use instead of moral indignation. *Clearing House*, 1941, 16, 195–197.

141 ——. You are a creator. *IPNL*, 1972, 21 (2), 40.

142 **Beechley, R. M.** Emotional disturbances in children with peculiar given names. *J. genet. Psychol.*, 1954, 85, 337–339 (with A. Ellis).

143 **Beil, Ada.** "Ein Liebender des Lebens sein." *IZIP*, 1926, 4(6), 371–375.

144 ——. Erkenntnis und psychische Dynamik. *IZIP*, 1927, 5(1), 62–73.

145 ——. Inhalt und Wandel der Idee der Mütterlichkeit. In A. Adler, L. Seif, & O. Kaus (Eds.), *Individuum und Gemeinschaft*.

146 ——. *Die Kultur die Frau: Eine Lebenssymphonie des XX Jahrhunderts*. Berlin: Kultur u. Wissenschaft, 1930.

147 ——. Mütterlichkeit. *IZIP*, 1925, 3(6), 323–327.

148 ——. Review of Erna Meyer, *Der neue Haushalt*. Stuttgart: Franksche Verlagshandlung, 1926. In *IZIP*, 1927, 5(2), 160.

149 ——. Review of O. & Alice Rühle, *Schwererziehbare Kinder*. In *IZIP*, 1926, 4(4), 245.

150 ——. Das Schöpfertum der Frau. In A. Adler, L. Sief & O. Kaus (Eds.), *Individuum und Gemeinschaft*.

151 ——. *Das trotzige Kind*. Dresden: Verlag am Andern Ufer, 1926.

152 ——. *Die unbekannte Männerseele*. Leipzig: S. Hirzel, 1927.

153 ——. Zur Psychologie von Welt-und-Lebensanschauung. In E. Wexberg (Ed.), *Handbuch der Individualpsychologie*.

154 **Beke, E.** Über mathematischen Begabung. *IZIP*, 1933, 11(1), 33–41.

155 **Bell, J. E.** *Family group therapy* (Publ. Hlth. Monogr. No. 64). Washington, D. C.: U. S. Govt. Printing Office, 1961.

156 **Bell, R. L.** Small group dialogue and discussion: An approach to police-community relationships. *J. crim. Law, Criminol., Police Sci.*, 1969, 60, 242–246 (with S. E. Cleveland, P. G. Hanson & W. E. O'Connell).

157 **Bell, W.** Anomie, social isolation and the class structure. *Sociom.*, 1957, 22, 105–116.

158 Bell, W. Social choice, life styles, and the suburban residence. In W. Dobriner (Ed.), *The suburban community*. New York: Putnam, 1958. Pp. 225–242.

159 Bellak, L. (Ed.). *Handbook of community psychiatry and community mental health*. New York: Grune & Stratton, 1964.

160 Bellerose, D. Behavior problems of children. Master's essay, Smith Coll. Soc. Work, 1927.

161 Bellott, Elisabeth. *Individualpsychologie und Schule*. München: J. F. Bergmann, 1926.

162 ———. Individualpsychologie und Schule. In A. Adler, L. Seif, & O. Kaus (Eds.), *Individuum und Gemeinschaft*.

163 ———. Review of H. Würtz, *Das Seelenleben des Krüppels*. Leipzig: L. Voss, 1921. In *IZIP*, 1926, 4(3), 163.

164 ———. Das verwahrloste Mädchen. *IZIP*, 1928, 6(2), 130–141.

165 Bellsmith, Ethel B. A group therapy service in a psychiatric hospital: The place of social service in the program. *Psychiat. Quart. Suppl.*, Part 2, 1949, 23, 332–344 (with O. Pelzman).

166 Bender, I. E. Ascendance-submission in relation to certain other factors in personality. *J. abnorm. soc. Psychol.*, 1928, 23, 137–143.

167 Benjamin, H. Transsexualism and transvestitism: A symposium. *Amer. J. Psychother.*, 1954, 8, 219–230 (with E. A. Gutheil & R. V. Sherwin).

168 Benjamins, J. Changes in performance in relation to influences upon self-conceptualization. *J. abnorm. soc. Psychol.*, 1952, 45, 473–480.

169 Bennet, E. A. The significance of dreams. *IPP*, 1939, No. 21. Pp. 9–22.

170 Ben-Nahum, A. Translator of R. Dreikurs, *Ha-adom v'hashivuyon*.

171 ———. Translator of R. Dreikurs, *Shivuyon: Ha-etgar*.

172 Benoist, J–M. The timeliness of Adler. *ADAM: Int. Rev.* (London), 1970, 35(340–342), 42–45.

173 Berardinelli, W. *Tratado de biotipilogia*. Rio de Janeiro: Rodrigues, 1942.

174 Berelson, B. *The people's choice*. New York: Duell, Sloan & Pearce, 1944 (with P. Lazarsfeld & Hazel Gaudet).

175 Berg, I. *et al.* Birth order and family size of approved school boys. *Brit. J. Psychiat.*, 1967, 113, 793–800.

176 Berger, E. M. Antithetical thinking in personality problems. *JIP*, 1964, 20, 32–37.

177 ———. The relation between expressed acceptance of self and expressed acceptance of others. *J. abnorm. soc. Psychol.*, 1952, 47, 778–782.

178 Berger, M. (Ed.). *Group psychotherapy and group function*. New York: Basic Books, 1963 (with M. Rosenbaum).

179 Berger, N. Individual Psychology as an aid to the medical specialist. *IJIP*, 1935, 1(4), 82–86.

180 Bergler, E. Diagnosis and prognosis in psychotherapy versus prediction, "guesses" and hunches. *J. clin. Psychopathol.*, 1947, 8, 771–784.

181 Berlyne, D. E. The present status of research on exploratory and related behavior. *JIP*, 1958, 14, 121–126.

182 Berman, H. H. Order of birth in manic-depressive reactions. *Psychiat. Quart.*, 1933, 7, 430–435.

183 Berman, L. A. The projective interpretation of early recollections. Unpubl. Ph.D. Diss., Univ. Michigan, 1957.

184 Bermond, J. R. Review of Alexandra Adler, *Guiding human misfits*. In *IPN*, 1940, 1(3), 1–2.

185 Bermond, Jane. Review of E. Wexberg, *Problems of adolescence*. In *IPN*, 1941, 1(4), 3–4.

186 Berner, P. *Die Zeit und ihre Neurose*. Wien: UNESCO-Schrif-tenreche, 1957 (with H. Hoff & E. Ringel).

187 Bernstein, J. Individualpsychologische Darstellung eines nervösen Symptoms. *Zbl. Psycho-anal. Psychother.*, 1914, 4, 7–8.

188 ———. Translator of A. Adler & others, *Guiando al nino*.

189 Bernstein, R. Wechsler-Bellevue patterns of female delinquents. *J. clin. Psychol.*, 1953, 9, 176–179 (with R. J. Corsini).

190 Berruezo, J. J. *Complejo de inferioridad*. Buenos Aires: Guillermo Kraft, 1950.

191 ———. Escuela dinamico-integral, psicologia de Adler y educación. *Primera Conf. de Hyg. Ment.*, La Plata, Oct., 1949.

192 Bertocci, P. A. *Personality and the good: Psychological and ethical perspectives*. New York: David McKay, 1963 (with R. M. Millard).

193 ———. The psychological self, the ego and personality. *Psychol. Rev.*, 1945, 52, 91–99.

194 **Berzon, Betty.** The therapeutic event in group psychotherapy: A study of subjective reports by group members. *JIP*, 1963, 19, 204–212 (with C. Pious & R. E. Farson).

195 **Bethe, A.** *et al.* (Eds.). *Handbuch norm. path. Physiologie.* Vol. 14(1). Berlin: Springer, 1926.

196 **Bevan, W.** *Contemporary approaches to psychology.* Princeton, N. J.: Van Nostrand, 1967 (with H. Helson).

197 **Bevan-Brown, C. M.** Anorexia nervosa. *IPP*, 1931, No. 2 (with J. C. Young, W. Langdon-Brown, F. G. Crookshank & G. Gordon).

198 ———. Individual Psychology: Theory and practice. *IPMP*, 1936, No. 15 (with G. E. S. Ward & F. G. Crookshank).

199 ———. Individual Psychology and practice (II). *IPMP*, 1934, No. 12 (with F. G. Layton, O. H. Woodcock, & F. Margery Edwards).

200 ———. Psychological schools: A plea for correlation. *IPMP*, 1936, No. 15. Pp. 9–42.

201 ———. The relationship between psychology and general medicine. *IPMP*, 1934, No. 12.

202 **Bevan-Brown, F. V.** Awareness and the neuroses of declining years. *IPMP*,   , No. 14 (with Mary Ferguson, O. H. Woodcock, & J. C. Young).

203 **Bey, E. H.** *Ferdi Ruhiyat.* Nesreden: Konya, 1933.

204 **Bialer, I.** Conceptualization of success and failure in mentally retarded and normal children. *J. Pers.*, 1961, 29, 303–320.

205 **Bichlmann, P. G.** Diskussionsbemerkungen zum Vortrage des Prof. Max Adler. *IZIP*, 1925, 3(5), 227–228.

206 **Biddle, Virginia.** Revolt of the parents. *Mirror Mag.*, Dec. 18, 1955.

207 **Bieliauskas, V. J.** Angst, Furcht, Erfurcht. *Im Ausland*, 1948, 20, 7.

208 ———. Aspects psychologiques de la masculinité et de la femininité. In P. J. Braceland *et al* (Eds.), *Marriage et Celibat*. Pp. 117–134.

209 ———. Aspects psychologiques des rélations pastoral avec les groups. In L. Beirnaert *et al*, (Eds.), *La rélation pastorale*. Paris: Les Editions du Cerf, 1969. Pp. 13–24.

210 ———. Atmintis [Memory]. *Lithuanian Encycl.* Vol. 1. So. Boston, Mass: Kapecius, 1953. Pp. 357–358.

211 **Bieliauskas, V. J.** The attitude of industrial employers toward hiring of former state mental hospital patients. *J. clin. Psychol.*, 1960, 16, 256–259 (with H. E. Wolfe).

212 ———. Behaviorizmus. *Lithuanian Encycl.* Vol. II. So. Boston, Mass.: Kapecius, 1954. Pp. 340–341.

213 ———. Choice behavior and freedom. *Bull. Albertus Magnus Guild*, 1966, 14, 1–7.

214 ———. Color preference in chromatic H-T-P drawings. *Ohio Res. Quart.*, 1967, 1, 48–52 (with R. Ausdenmoore).

215 ———. *Community relations training program for police supervisers.* Xavier Univ., Dept. Psychol., 1969.

216 ———. Darbe eksperimentas [Continuous addition technique]. *Lithuanian Encycl.* Vol. IV. So. Boston, Mass.: Kapecius, 1954. Pp. 317–318.

217 ———. Darbe Psichologija [Psychology of work]. *Lithuanian Encycl.* Vol. IV. So. Boston, Mass.: Kapecius, 1954. Pp. 325–326.

218 ———. Die Denkform der Frau. Ph.D. Diss., Univ. Tübingen, 1943.

219 ———. Developmental trends in children's H-T-P drawings of a person. *Virginia J. Sci.*, 1954, 4, 323 (with L. W. Pennington, Jr.).

220 ———. Differences in performance on the chromatic vs. achromatic H-T-P drawings. *J. clin. Psychol.*, 1960, 16, 334–335 (with A. R. Heffron).

221 ———. Ebbinghaus. *Lithuanian Encycl.* Vol. V. So. Boston, Mass.: Kapecius, 1955. P. 323.

222 ———. The effect of formal art training upon the quantitative scores on the H-T-P. *J. clin. Psychol.*, 1959, 15, 57–59 (with R. B. Bristow).

223 ———. An evaluation of the organic signs in the H-T-P drawings. *J. clin. Psychol.*, 1958, 14, 50–54 (with Sandra L. Kirkham).

224 ———. Familie und Auswanderung. *Im Ausland*, 1948, 9, 1–2.

225 ———. Four negativistic phases in man's life. *Virginia J. Sci.*, 1952, 4, 350.

226 ———. *H-T-P bibliography.* Beverly Hills, Calif.: Western Psychol. Services, 1957.

227 ———. *The House-Tree-Person (H-T-P) Research Review.* 2nd ed. Beverly Hills, Calif.: Western Psychol. Services, 1965.

228 ———. An investigation of the validity of the H-T-P as an intelligence test for children. *J. clin. Psychol.*, 1961, 17, 178–180 (with J. F. Moens).

229 Bieliauskas, V. J. Ipretis [Habit]. *Lith-uanian Encycl.* Vol. IX. So. Boston, Mass.: Kapecius, 1956. Pp. 48–49.

230 ———. Jaunuelie vystymasis tarp dvieju kulturu [Adolescent development in between two cultures]. *Laiskai Lietuviams,* 1966, 1, 1–7.

231 ———. Jausmas [Feeling·and emotion]. *Lithuanian Encycl.* Vol. IX. So. Boston, Mass.: Kapecius, 1956. Pp. 357–358.

232 ———. Kaltes Jausmas [Guilt feeling]. *Lith-uanian Encycl.* Vol. X. So. Boston, Mass.: Kapecius, 1957. Pp. 353–355.

233 ———. Keturies revoliucijes zmogaus gyvenime [Four revolutions in men's life]. *Laikas,* 1950, 19, 2; 1950, 20, 2.

234 ———. Kontreliuejama laisve [Controlled freedom]. *Musu Vytis,* 1959, 2–3, 97–105.

235 ———. Masculinity, femininity, and conjugal love. *Relig. & Hlth.,* 1971, 10(1), 37–48.

236 ———. Mase Kryzkeleje [Mass at the crossroads]. *Aidai,* 1945, 8, 1–5.

237 ———. Die Masse am Scheideweg [The mass before a decision]. *Scholar,* 1946, 1, 1–10.

238 ———. Meile seimeje [Love in marriage]. *Laiskai Lietuviams,* 1965, 16, 190–191.

239 ———. Nauju keliu beieskant [Seeking for new ways]. *Aidai,* 1945, 9, 1–4.

240 ———. Neostriatal and hippocampal functions in the behavior variability of the chick. *J. genet. Psychol.,* 1967, 110, 59–69 (with A. J. Pantle).

241 ———. The obviousness of two masculinity-femininity tests. *J. consult. clin. Psychol.,* 1968, 32, 314–318 (with L. M. Lanskey & S. B. Miranda).

242 ———. Performance of paranoid schizophrenics and passive-aggressives on two masculinity-femininity tests. *Psychol. Rep.,* 1972, 31, 251–254 (with R. P. Butler).

243 ———. The problem of shading in H-T-P drawings. Its internal consistency and relation to personality characteristics. *J. gen. Psychol.,* 1963, 72, 295–300 (with W. J. Clarke).

244 ———. Profil psychologique contemporain des pretres et des religieux. *Le Supplement,* 1970, 93, 257–264.

245 ———. Psychoanalysis and existential philosophy. In R. W. Russell *et al.* (Eds.), *Frontiers of psychology.* Chicago: Scott, Foresman, 1965. Pp. 17–24.

246 Bieliauskas, V. J. Recent advances in the psychology of masculinity and femininity. *J. Psychol.,* 1965, 60, 255–263.

247 ———. A report on police community relations training program for police supervisors in Cincinnati, Ohio. Cincinnati: Xavier Univ., 1969.

248 ———. Review of E. L. Cowen, E. A. Gardner, & M. Zax (Eds.), *Emergent approaches to mental health problems.* In *JIP,* 1969, 25, 237–238.

249 ———. Science, philosophy, and psychology. In F. L. Ruch, *Psychology and life.* Chicago: Scott, Foresman, 1963. Pp. 575–579.

250 ———. Scorer's reliability in the quantitative scoring of the H-T-P technique. *J. clin. Psychol.,* 1956, 4, 366–369.

251 ———. Der Seelenbegriff in der Psychologie der Gegenwart. In A. Däumling (Ed.), *Seelenleben und Menschenbild.* Pp. 27–41.

252 ———. Sexual identification in children's drawings of the human figure. *J. clin. Psychol.,* 1960, 16, 42–44.

253 ———. Shifting of the guilt feeling in the process of psychotherapy. In J. L. Moreno (Ed.), *Handbook of group psychotherapy.* New York: Phil. Libr., 1966. Pp. 265–269.

254 ———. Short-term psychotherapy with college students: Prevention and cure. *Confinia Psychiat.,* 1968, 11, 18–33.

255 ———. Tautes kulturinese varzybose [Nations in the cultural competition]. *Aidai,* 1946, 3, 35–36.

256 ———. Training program in interpersonal relations for police officers. *Nwsltr., Div. 13, Amer. Psychol. Assn.,* 1970, 24(1), 16–18.

257 ———. Theory and method in H-T-P research. *Virginia J. Sci.,* 1954, 4, 321–322.

258 ———. Über die Entwicklung und die Wesenzuege der Litauischen Kunst. *Im Ausland,* 1948, 6, 4.

259 ———. The use of continuous addition technique in psychological diagnosis. *Virginia J. Sci.,* 1953, 4, 278–279.

260 ———. Zmogaus dvasia moderniesies psichologijes svieseje [Human mind in the light of modern psychology]. *Laiskai Lietuviams,* 1960, 9(8–9), 230–235, 262–266.

261 ———. Zmogaus siu dienu problematikoje [Human contemporary problems]. München: Aidai, 1945.

262 ———. Zur Psychologie der Baltischen Völker. *Im Ausland,* 1948, 16, 7.

263 **Bierer, Aliska.** Portrait. *IPNL*, 1970, 19(4), 79.

264 **Bierer, I.** Psychosomatic approach to gynaecology and obstetrics. *AJIP*, 1956, 12, 99–105.

265 **Bierer, J.** An attempt to induce suffering from catatonia to active and voluntary movements. *J. ment. Sci.*, 1940, 86, 287–293.

266 ———. Child guidance clinic. *Brit. med. J.*, 1954, 2, 362.

267 ———. Clubs de thérapie sociale. *Hyg. ment.*, 1954, No. 3. Pp. 75–84.

268 ———. Critical analysis of some concepts in present day group psychotherapy. *Acta Psychother.* (Basel), 1959, 7(2–3), 110–118.

269 ———. The day hospital. *Soc. Welf.*, 1955, 9(8), 173–180.

270 ———. The day hospital. *Howard J.*, 1952, 7, 3.

271 ———. *The day hospital, an experiment in social psychiatry and syntho-analytic psychotherapy.* London: H. K. Lewis, 1951.

272 ———. The day hospital: Therapy is guided democracy. *Ment. Hosp.*, 1962, 13, 246–252.

273 ———. Day hospitals—further developments. *Int. J. soc. Psychiat.*, 1961, 7(2), 148–151.

274 ———. Day hospitals and community care. *Comprehen. Psychiat.*, 1963, 4(6).

275 ———. Day hospitals and community psychiatry. *Comprehen. Psychiat.*, 1963, 4(6).

276 ———. Editorial. *Int. J. soc. Psychiat.*, 1961, 7(2), 85–86.

277 ———. Eine Revolution in der Psychiatrie Grosbritanniens. *Das Deutsche Gesundheitswesen*, 1960, 15(13), 645–650.

278 ———. An experiment with a psychiatric night hospital. *Proc. Royal Soc. Med.*, 1960, 53(11), 930–932 (with I. Browne).

279 ———. Group psychotherapy. *Brit. med. J.*, 1942, 1(Part I), 214–217.

280 ———. *Innovations in social psychiatry.* London: Avenue Publ. Co., 1969 (with R. I. Evans).

281 ———. Introduction to the second volume. *Int. J. soc. Psychiat.*, 1956, 2(1), 5–11.

282 ———. Las investigationes experimentales psicoterapia. *Dia Med.* (Buenos Aires), 1951, 23(72), 3278–3280.

283 ———. The Marlborough experiment. In L. Bellak (Ed.), *Handbook of community psychiatry and community mental health.* Ch. 11.

284 **Bierer, J.** Marlborough Night Hospital. Treatment with L. S. D. and group therapy (1). *Nurs. Times*, 1961, 57(19), 594–596; (2). *Nurs. Times*, 1961, 57(20), 637–639 (with J. Buckman).

285 ——— et al. A memorandum on therapeutic social clubs in psychiatry. *Brit. med. J.*, 1944, 2, 861.

286 ———. Mental health services in Greater London. *Lancet*, 1959, 2, 737.

287 ———. Mental hospitals. *Hosp. J., Amer. Psychiat. Assn.*, Apr., 1962. Pp. 203–207; May, 1962. Pp. 246–252.

288 ———. Modern social and group therapy. In N. G. Harris (Ed.), *Modern trends in psychological medicine.* London: Butterworth, 1948. New York: Hoeber, 1948. Pp. 289–309.

289 ———. A new form of group psychotherapy. *Ment. Hlth.* (London), 1944, 5, 23–26; Also in *Proc. Royal Soc. Med.*, 1944, 37, 208–209.

290 ———. Past, present, and future. *Int. J. soc. Psychiat.*, 1960, 6(3–4), 165–173.

291 ———. Preliminary report on the foundation of an International Association of Adlerian (Individual) Psychology. *IPNL*, 1954, No. 38. Pp. 2–6 (with A. Müller & V. Louis).

292 ———. Prolonged sneezing. *Psychosom. Med.*, 1951, 13(1), 56–58 (with N. Murray).

293 ———. Psychiatric day hospitals in theory and practice. *Harefuah*, 1961, 69(12), 383–387.

294 ———. Psychiatrische Tageskliniken in Theorie und Praxis. *Psychiat. Neurol. u. med. Psychol.* (Leipzig), 1960, 12(6), 201–208.

295 ———. Psychotherapy in mental hospital practice; being the preliminary report of full-time psychotherapist in a public mental hospital. *J. ment. Sci.*, 1940, 86, 928–952.

296 ———. The recording of psychotherapeutic sessions. *Lancet*, 1948, 1(254), 957–958 (with R. S. Olsen).

297 ———. Review of H. L. & Rowena Ansbacher (Eds.), *The Individual Psychology of Alfred Adler.* In *Int. J. soc. Psychiat.*, 1956, 2(1), 74.

298 ———. Review of D. Stafford-Clark, *Psychiatry today.* London: Penguin

Books, [   ]. In *Int. J. soc. Psychiat.*, 1956, 2(1), 73-74.

299 **Bierer, J.** Review of M. Valentine, *An introduction to psychiatry*. Edinburgh: E. & S. Livingstone, 1955. In *Int. J. soc. Psychiat.*, 1955, 1(3), 74-75.

300 ———. A self-governed patients' social club in a public mental hospital. *J. ment. Sci.*, 1941, 87, 419-426 (with F. P. Haldane).

301 ———. *Some experiments in social and clinical psychiatry in Great Britain*. Osaka: Memorial Res. Monogr., 1960. Pp. 21-62.

302 ———. The specific contribution of Individual Psychology to the treatment of schizophrenia. *JIP*, 1958, 14, 74 (Abstract).

303 ———. Stilbestrol in out-patient treatment of sexual offenders. *Brit. med. J.*, 1950, 1, 935-939 (with G. A. van Someren).

304 ———. Theory and practice of psychiatric day hospitals. *Lancet*, Nov. 21, 1959. Pp. 901-902.

305 ———. The therapeutic community hostel. *Int. J. soc. Psychiat.*, 1961, 7(1), 5-9.

306 ——— (Ed.). *Therapeutic social clubs*. London: H. K. Lewis, 1948.

307 ———. Die therapeutischen social Clubs. *Z. Psychother. u. med. Psychol.* (Stuttgart), 1955, 5(2), 58-64.

308 ———. Thérapies collectives. *Psyché* (Paris), 1950, 5(47), 633-639.

309 ———. Thomas A. C. Rennie [Obituary]. *Int. J. soc. Psychiat.*, 1956, 2(1), 4.

310 ———. Transference in the light of Adlerian theory and its developments. *Acta psychother. psychosom. Orthopaedagog.*, 1954, 2(3-4), 250-266.

311 ———. Über ein und beidhandige Arbeit am Ergographen. *Arbeitsphysiol.*, 1935, 8, 490-501.

312 ———. The validity of psychiatric diagnostics. *Int. J. soc. Psychiat.*, 1955, 1(1), 22-30.

313 ———. Vision, dream or misconception (A proposal for a new educational system). *Int. J. soc. Psychiat.*, 1958, 4(3), 165-170.

314 **Biermann, G.** (Ed.). *Handbuch der Kinderpsychotherapie*. München: Ernst Reinhardt, 1969.

315 **Binswanger, L.** *Grundformen und Erkenntnis menschlichen Daseins*. Zurich: Niehans, 1942.

316 **Birch, D.** *Motivation: A study of action*. Belmont, Calif.: Brooks-Cole, 1966 (with J. Veroff).

317 **Birch, H. G.** (Ed.). *Outside readings in psychology*. New York: Crowell, 1950 (with E. L. Hartley & Ruth E. Hartley).

318 **Birmingham, F. A.** Review of W. & Marguerite Beecher, *Parents on the run*. In *Esquire*, Oct. 1956. Also in *OSIPNL*, 1964, 4(4), 12-13.

319 **Birnbaum, E. Ann.** Competitive fighting between mice with different hereditary backgrounds. *J. genet. Psychol.*, 1954, 85, 271-280 (with E. Frederickson).

320 **Birnbaum, F.** Alfred Adler: In memoriam. *IZIP*, 1937, 15(3-4), 97-127.

321 ———. Anlage und Umwelt. *IZIP*, 1948, 17(1), 20-24.

322 ———. Applying Individual Psychology in school. *IJIP*, 1935, 1(3), 109-119.

323 ———. Die Bedeutung Alfred Adlers für die Gegenwart. *IZIP*, 1947, 16, 13-28.

324 ———. Begabung und Erziehung. In A. Adler & C. Furtmüller (Eds.), *Heilen und Bilden* (1928). Pp. 185-205.

325 ———. Das Begabungsproblem. In E. Wexberg (Ed.), *Handbuch der Individualpsychologie*. Pp. 83-113.

326 ———. Beispiel und Selbstbeispiel. *IZIP*, 1950, 20(2), 66-79.

327 ———. Der Denkakt im Lichte der Individualpsychologie. *IZIP*, 1923, 2(2), 17-20.

328 ———. Development of character. *IJIP*, 1935, 1(1), 67-75.

329 ———. Erziehungstechnik. In Sofie Lazarsfeld (Ed.), *Technik der Erziehung*.

330 ———. Der "Fallmut". *IZIP*, 1948, 17(1), 31-33.

331 ———. Formen des Minderwertigkeitsgefühls. *IZIP*, 1948, 17(2), 60-71.

332 ———. Frankl's existential psychology from the viewpoint of Individual Psychology. *JIP*, 1961, 17, 162-166.

333 ———. Gibt es eine Konvergenz der tiefenpsychologischen Lehrmeinungen? *IZIP*, 1948, 17(4), 156-171.

334 ———. Grundsätzliches zur Umerziehung. *IZIP*, 1949, 18(1), 15-32; 18(2), 75-96.

335 ———. Hilfe und Selbsthilfe. *IZIP*, 1950, 19(4), 178-180.

336 ———. The importance of Alfred Adler for the present. *IPB*, 1948, 6, 164-176.

337 ———. Individualpsychologie, Wissenschaft und Leben. *IZIP*, 1937, 15(2), 66-72.

338 ———. The Individual Psychological Experimental School in Vienna. *IJIP*, 1935, 1(2), 118-124.

339 **Birnbaum, F.** Die individualpsychologische Versuchschule in Wien. *IZIP*, 1932, 10(3), 176–183.

340 ———. Inferno-Purgatorio-Paradiso. *IZIP*, 1948, 17(3), 97–108.

341 ———. Lebensführung. *IZIP*, 1930, 8(1), 9–17.

342 ———. Das Lust-Unlustprinzip in der Erziehung. *IZIP*, 1951, 20(1), 27–34.

343 ———. Mahnung, Warnung, Drohung. *IZIP*, 1949, 18(4), 173–176.

344 ———. Die pädagogische Atmosphäre. *IZIP*, 1950, 19(1), 9–20.

345 ———. Portrait. *IPB*, 1947, 6. Facing p. 155.

346 ———. Die praktischen Auswirkungen der Individualpsychologie in der Schule. *IZIP*, 1931, 9(3), 171–182.

347 ———. Das prälogische Denken und sein Aufstieg zum Logischen vom Standpunkte der Individualpsychologie. *IZIP*, 1924, 2(5), 23–26.

348 ———. Die Psychologie Alfred Adlers. *IZIP*, 1950, 19(2), 56–70.

349 ———. Review of A. Adler, *Individualpsychologie in der Schule*. In *IZIP*, 1931, 9(1), 61–62.

350 ———. Review of A. Adler, *Die Technik der Individualpsychologie. II. Die Seele des schwererziehbaren Kind*. In *IZIP*, 1931, 9(1), 61.

351 ———. Review of R. Allers & J. Teler, Über die Verwertung unbemerkter eindrücke bei Assoziationen. In *IZIP*, 1926, 4(6), 395–396.

352 ———. Review of Annalies Argelander & Ilse Weitsch, *Aus den Seelenleben verwahrloster Mädchen auf Grund ihrer Tagebuchaufzeichnungen*. Jena: Gustav Fischer, 1933. In *IZIP*, 1935, 13(3), 190.

353 ———. Review of Elisabeth Bellott, *Individualpsychologie und Schule*. In *IZIP*, 1927, 5(4), 317.

354 ———. Review of G. Bichlmair, *Religion und seelische Gesundheit*. Wien: Mayer, [ ]. In *IZIP*, 1932, 10(3), 232.

355 ———. Review of F. Brentano, *Kategorienlehre*. Leipzig: Felix Meiner, 1933. In *IZIP*, 1935, 13(2), 127–128.

356 ———. Review of A. Bruckner, *Das Problem der Schulerbeurteilung*. Langensalza: Hermann Beyer & Söhne, 1931. In *IZIP*, 1933, 11(2), 155–156.

357 **Birnbaum, F.** Review of Charlotte Bühler, *Drei Generationen im Jugendtagebuch*. Jena: Gustav Fischer, 1934. In *IZIP*, 1935, 13(2), 125–126.

358 ———. Review of Charlotte Bühler, *Der menschliche Lebenslauf als psychologisches Problem*. Leipzig: S. Hirzel, 1933. In *IZIP*, 1933, 11(2), 155–156.

359 ———. Review of W. Buttner, *Der gotische Mensch*. Hannover: Hellwingsche Buchhandlung. In *IZIP*, 1934, 12(1), 57.

360 ———. Review of J. Castiello, *Geistesformung*. Berlin: Ferdinand Däumler, 1934. In *IZIP*, 1936, 14(2), 118–119.

361 ———. Review of P. Dahlke, *Der Buddhismus*. Leipzig: E. Reinicke, 1926. In *IZIP*, 1928, 6(3), 260.

362 ———. Review of J. Donat, *Über Psychoanalyse und Individualpsychologie*. In *IZIP*, 1934, 12(4), 258–260.

363 ———. Review of H. Driesch, *Grundprobleme der Psychologie*. Leipzig: Emanuel Reinicke, 1929. In *IZIP*, 1931, 9(1), 66–67.

364 ———. Review of H. Ellis, *Der Tanz des Lebens*. Leipzig: F. Meiner, 1928. In *IZIP*, 1931, 9(4), 319–320.

365 ———. Review of O. Epstein, *Erziehung und Wirklichkeit*. Potsdam: Müller & I. Kiepenhauer. In *IZIP*, 1934, 12(1), 57.

366 ———. Review of *Festschrift zu William Sterns 60. Geburtstag*. Leipzig: J. A. Barth, 1931. In *IZIP*, 1932, 10(1), 74–75.

367 ———. Review of A. Fuchs, *Erziehungsklassen (E-Klassen) für schwererziehbare Kinder der Volksschule*. Halle: Carl Marhold, 1930. In *IZIP*, 1932, 10(5), 395–396.

368 ———. Review of Jenny Gertz, *Wie Wir Zusammenwuchsen*. Hamburg: Author. In *IZIP*, 1925, 3(3), 138–139.

369 ———. Review of W. Hansen, *Beiträge zur pädagogischen Psychologie*. Münster: Münster-Verlag. In *IZIP*, 1935, 13(1), 58–59.

370 ———. Review of R. Hauser, *Lehrbuch der Psychologie*. In *IZIP*, 1934, 12(1), 52–53.

371 ———. Review of R. Heller, *Das Wesen der Schönheit*. Leipzig: Braumüller, 1936. In *IZIP*, 1937, 15(2), 93.

372 ———. Review of Hildegard Hetzer, *Die symbolische Darstellung in der frühen Kindheit*. Wien: Deutscher Verlag f. Jugend u. Volk, 1926. In *IZIP*, 1934, 12(2), 127.

373 **Birnbaum, F.** Review of Hildegard Hetzer, *Das volksstümliche Kinderspiel.* Wien: Deutscher Verlag f. Jugend u. Volk, 1927. In *IZIP*, 1934, 12(2), 127–128.

374 ———. Review of H. F. Hoffmann, *Die Schichttheorie.* Stuttgart: Ferdinand Enke, 1935. In *IZIP*, 1936, 14(4), 242.

375 ———. Review of O. Janssen, *Das erlebende Ich und sein Dasein.* Berlin: Walter de Gruyter, 1932. In *IZIP*, 1933, 11(2), 155.

376 ———. Review of Maria Kaczynska, *Succes scolaire et intelligence.* Neuchatel: Ed. Delachaux & Niestlé, [   ]. In *IZIP*, 1935, 13(3), 193.

377 ———. Review of S. Kaweran, *Der Bund entschiedener Schulreformer.* In *IZIP*, 1925, 3(1), 44–45.

378 ———. Review of B. Kern, *Wirkungsformen der Übung.* Münster: Helios, 1930. In *IZIP*, 1930, 8(6), 592.

379 ———. Review of *Der kleine Brockhaus.* In *IZIP*, 1926, 4(1), 46.

380 ———. Review of O. Klemm (Ed.), *Psychologie des Gemeinschaftslebens.* Jena: Gustav Fischer, 1935. In *IZIP*, 1936, 14(2), 120–121.

381 ———. Review of S. Krauss, *Der seelische Konflikt.* Stuttgart: Ferdinand Enke, 1933. In *IZIP*, 1936, 14(4), 241–242.

382 ———. Review of O. Kroh, *Die Psychologie des Grundschulkindes in ihrer Beziehung zur kindlichen Gesamtentwicklung.* Langensalza: Hermann Beyer & Söhne, 1931. In *IZIP*, 1933, 11(1), 80.

383 ———. Review of A. Kronfeld, *Perspektiven der Seelenheilkunde.* In *IZIP*, 1931, 9(2), 150–151.

384 ———. Review of F. Krueger, *Psychologie des Gemeinschaftslebens.* Jena: Gustav Fischer, 1934. In *IZIP*, 1936, 14(2), 119–120.

385 ———. Review of O. Krull, *Die Geissel der Kindheit.* In *IZIP*, 1926, 4(1), 44–45.

386 ———. Review of H. Künkel, *Der furchtlose Mensch.* Jena: Eugen Diederichs, 1930. In *IZIP*, 1931, 9(1), 80.

387 ———. Review of R. Kynast, *Problemgeschichte der Pädagogik.* Berlin: Junker & Dünnhaupt, 1932. In *IZIP*, 1937, 15(2), 89–90.

388 ———. Review of W. Lange-Eichbaum, *Das Genieproblem.* München: Ernst Reinhardt, 1931. In *IZIP*, 1932, 10(6), 431.

389 **Birnbaum, F.** Review of M. Levy-Suhl, *Die seelischen Heilmethoden des Arztes.* Stuttgart: Ferdinand Enke, 1930. In *IZIP*, 1931, 9(1), 65–66.

390 ———. Review of R. Matthaei, *Das Gestaltproblem.* München: J. F. Bergmann, 1929. In *IZIP*, 1931, 9(1), 66.

391 ———. Review of A. Messer, *Einführung in die Psychologie und die psychologischen Richtungen der Gegenwart.* In *IZIP*, 1934, 12(1), 56–57.

392 ———. Review of *Pädagogischer Führung 85, Jahr.* Wien: Verlag f. Jugend u. Volk, 1935. In *IZIP*, 1935, 13(2), 126–127.

393 ———. Review of O. Rühle, *Grundfragen der Erziehung.* In *IZIP*, 1924, 2(3), 60–61.

394 ———. Review of O. Rühle, *Die Sozialisierung der Frau.* In *IZIP*, 1924, 2(4), 34–35.

395 ———. Review of O. & Alice Rühle, *Blätter für sozialistische Erziehung.* In *IZIP*, 1926, 4(1), 45.

396 ———. Review of M. Scherer, *Die Lehre von der Gestalt.* Berlin: Walter de Gruyter, 1931. In *IZIP*, 1932, 10(4), 314–315.

397 ———. Review of G. Schliebe, *Reifejahre im Internat.* Leipzig: Julius Klinckhardt, 1922. In *IZIP*, 1936, 14(4), 240.

398 ———. Review of K. Schmeing, *Ideal und Gegenideal.* Leipzig: Joh. Ambrosius Barth, 1935. In *IZIP*, 1937, 15(2), 90–91.

399 ———. Review of N. Seelhammer, *Die Individualpsychologie Alfred Adlers.* In *IZIP*, 1935, 13(1), 57–58.

400 ———. Review of G. Simon, *Die Auseinandersetzung des Christentums mit ausserchristlichen Mystik.* Gütersloh: C. Bertelsmann, 1930. In *IZIP*, 1933, 11(1), 79–80.

401 ———. Review of M. Solms, *Bau und Gliederung der Menschengruppen.* Karlsruhe: G. Braun, 1929. In *IZIP*, 1931, 9(5), 414.

402 ———. Review of O. Spann, *Erkenne dich Selbst.* Jena: Gustav Fischer. In *IZIP*, 1936, 14(2), 121.

403 ———. Review of E. Steinbüchel, *Das Grundproblem der Hegelschen Philosophie.* Bonn: Peter Hansteins, 1933. In *IZIP*, 1934, 12(1), 57–58.

404 ———. Review of Clara & W. Stern, *Dauerphantasien im vierten Lebenjahr.* Leipzig: Joh. Ambrosius Barth, 1931. In *IZIP*, 1932, 10(1), 80.

405 ———. Review of E. Stern, *Das Problem der innern Wandlung.* In *IZIP*, 1930, 8(6), 592–593.

406 **Birnbaum, F.** Review of W. Stern, *Person-alistik der Erinnerung.* Leipzig: Joh. Ambrosius Barth, 1931. In *IZIP*, 1932, 10(1), 80.

407 ———. Review of W. Stern, *Studien zur Personenwissenschaft.* Leipzig: Quelle & Meyer, 1930. In *IZIP*, 1932, 10(3), 240; 1933, 11(1), 79.

408 ———. Review of G. Stiehler, *Person und Masse.* Leipzig: Felix Meiner, 1929. In *IZIP*, 1935, 13(2), 125.

409 ———. Review of G. Storrung, *Methoden der Psychologie des Gefühlslebens.* Berlin: Urban & Schwarzenberg, 1931. In *IZIP*, 1934, 12(1), 58-59.

410 ———. Review of H. Stürmer, *Der Ablauf der nervösen Energie.* Stuttgart: Hugo Matthaes, 1929. In *IZIP*, 1930, 8(6), 593.

411 ———. Review of P. O. Tacke, *Der Sprachunterricht muss umkehren.* In *IZIP*, 1926, 4(1), 46.

412 ———. Review of G. Tscharmann, *Der Weg der Intellektuellen.* Wien: Verlag f. Literatur u. Politik, 1924. In *IZIP*, 1924, 3(3), 138.

413 ———. Review of Olga von Koenig-Fachsenfeld, *Wanderungen des Traumproblems von der Romantik bis zur Gegenwart.* Stuttgart: Ferdinand Enke, 1935. In *IZIP*, 1936, 14(4), 240-241.

414 ———. Review of *Das werdende Zeitalter.* In *IZIP*, 1924, 2(4), 33-34.

415 ———. Review of H. Winkler, *Der Trotz.* München: Ernst Reinhardt, 1929. In *IZIP*, 1931, 9(1), 69-70.

416 ———. Review of T. Ziehen, *Erkenntnistheorie.* Jena: Gustav Fischer, 1934. In *IZIP*, 1935, 13(2), 124.

417 ———. The school and educational guidance (with O. Spiel). In A. Adler & assoc., *Guiding the child.* Pp. 66-83.

418 ———. Schule und Erziehungsberatung. *IZIP*, 1929, 7(3), 184-190 (with O. Spiel).

419 ———. *Die seelischen Gefahren des Kindes: Ein individualpsychologischer Wegweiser zur Verhuetung der Schwererziehbarkeit.* Leipzig: Hirzel, 1931.

420 ———. Der Sinn der Welt. *IZIP*, 1948, 17 (1), 51-56.

421 ———. Some principles to be observed in a healthy conduct of life. *IJIP*, 1936, 2(3), 46-54.

422 ———. Technik der Erziehung. In Sofie Lazarsfeld (Ed.), *Technik der Erziehung.*

423 **Birnbaum, F.** Über Begabung. *IZIP*, 1927, 5(5), 362-378.

424 ———. Über Belehrung. *IZIP*, 1949, 18(3), 134-137.

425 ———. Über den Strukturwandel der Persönlichkeit. *IZIP*, 1951, 20(4), 145-159.

426 ———. Die Umerziehung als Problem. In Int. Verein Indivpsy., *Alfred Adler zum Gedenken.* Pp. 16-31.

427 ———. Umerziehung als Verführung zur Lebenskunst. *IZIP*, 1948, 17(1), 34-42.

428 ———. Umerziehung in der Schule. *IZIP*, 1934, 2(1), 33-37.

429 ———. Unseren Toten. *IZIP*, 1947, 16(1), 5-13.

430 ———. *Versuch einer Systematisierung der Erziehungsmittel.* Wien: Verlag f. Jugend u. Volk, 1950.

431 ———. Viktor E. Frankls Existentialpsychologie individualpsychologisch gesehen. *IZIP*, 1947, 16, 145-152.

432 ———. Vom Vorsatz zur Haltung. *IZIP*, 1951, 20(3), 138-141.

433 ———. Vor- und Nachwort zu O. Spiel: Unsere Klassengemeinde arbeitet. *IZIP*, 1947, 16, 83, 91-93.

434 ———. Was ist ein Erziehungsmittel? *IZIP*, 1950, 19(3), 129-135.

435 ———. Was ist Mut? *IZIP*, 1948, 17(1), 14-19.

436 ———. Wertpädagogik und Individualpsychologie. *IZIP*, 1935, 13(3), 161-166; 1948, 17(1), 25-31.

437 ———. Wie individualpsychologische Artikel richtig zu lesen wären. *IZIP*, 1934, 12(4), 232-233.

438 ———. Zum Toleranzproblem. *IZIP*, 1948, 17(1), 46-50.

439 ———. Zur Individualpsychologie primitiver Geisteshaltungen. *IZIP*, 1948, 17(1), 42-46.

440 **Birnbaum, Maria.** Hoffnungslose Eltern. *IZIP*, 1924, 2(3), 46-49.

441 ———. Die Repetenten. *IZIP*, 1927, 5(4), 283.

442 **Birnbaum, O.** Review of I. Caruso, *Tiefenpsychologie und Daseinswert.* Wien: Herder, 1948. In *IZIP*, 1949, 18, 45-46.

443 **Birstein, J.** Individualpsychologische Darstellung eines nervösen Symptom. *Zbl. Psychoanal. Psychother.*, 1914, 4, 364-372.

444 **Bischof, L. J.** Humanitarianism, common sense, hope [Tribute to Alfred Adler on his 100th birthday]. *JIP*, 1970, 26(1), 10.

445 **Bischof, L. J.** *Interpreting personality theories.* New York: Harper & Row, 1964.

446 ———. Review of A. Adler, *Problems of neurosis.* In *JIP*, 1965, 21, 91–92.

447 **Bitter, W.** *Angst und Schuld in theologischer und psychotherapeutischer Sicht, ein Tagungsbericht.* 2nd ed. Stuttgart: Ernst Klett, 1950.

448 ———. *Krisis und Zukunft der Frau.* Stuttgart: Ernst Klett.

449 **Blackman, L. S.** Perceived parent attitudes as determinants of ego structure. *Child Developm.*, 1955, 25, 173–183 (with D. P. Ausubel, E. E. Balthazar, I. Rosenthal, S. N. Shpoont, & J. Welkowitz).

450 **Blair, D.** Group psychotherapy of war neuroses. *Lancet*, 1943, 1, 204–205.

451 **Blake, R. R.** *Role-playing in business and industry.* New York: Free Press of Glencoe, 1961 (with R. J. Corsini & M. E. Shaw).

452 **Blanchard, Phyllis.** The status of psychoanalysis with general psychology. *IZIP*, 1924, 2(4), 17–18.

453 **Blane, H. T.** Sex differences in birth order of alcoholics. *Brit. J. Psychiat.*, 1971, 119, 657–661 (with H. Barry III & H. Barry, Jr.).

454 **Blanton, S.** *Diary of my analysis with Sigmund Freud.* New York: Hawthorn Books, 1971.

455 **Blau, A.** *The master hand.* New York: Amer. Orthopsychiat. Assn. Monogr., 1946, No. 5.

456 **Bledsoe, J. C.** Self concepts of children and their intelligence, achievement, interests, and anxiety. *JIP*, 1964, 20, 55–58.

457 **Bliss, W. D.** Birth order of creative writers. *JIP*, 1970, 26(2), 200–202.

458 **Block, E.** Romantiker und Klassiker. *IZIP*, 1929, 7(1), 27–36.

459 **Block, J.** Personality characteristics associated with fathers' attitudes toward childrearing. *Child Developm.*, 1955, 26, 41–48.

460 **Blocklinger, Nancy.** The reeducation of a pampered prince. *IP*, 1969, 6(2), 29–33 (with Jean H. Cripps & Ann Tuites).

461 **Blonsky, P. P.** Das einzige Kind in seinem ersten Schuljahr. *Z. päd. Psychol.*, 1930, 31, 84–97.

462 ———. Problem of earliest childhood memory and its significance. *Arch. gesam. Psychol.*, 1929, 1, 369–390.

463 **Bluekirchen, J.** Aus dem Entwicklungang eines Zwillingspaares. *IZIP*, 1932, 10(3), 207–216.

464 **Bluekirchen, J.** Concerning the development of twins. *IJIP*, 1935, 1(4), 73–81.

465 **Blum, A. H.** Children's cognitive style and response modification. *J. genet. Psychol.*, 1967, 110, 95–103 (with D. M. Broverman).

466 **Blum, Klara.** Review of A. T. Wegner, *Moni oder die Welt von unten.* Stuttgart: Deutsche Verlaganstalt, [   ]. In *IZIP*, 1929, 7(4), 323–324.

467 **Blum, U.** Generations and layers of society in Israel. *AJIP*, 1956, 12, 128–135.

468 ———. Im ha-kovets ha-Individual Psikhologie [The anthology of Individual Psychology]. In *Kovets Individual-Psikhologie.* Pp. 143–146.

469 **Blumenthal, E.** Die Bedeutung des Altersunterschieds von Zwillingen. Unpubl. Diss., Inst. f. Angewandte Psychol., Zürich, 1966.

470 ———. Review of R. Dreikurs, *Grundbegriffe der Individualpsychologie.* In *JIP*, 1971, 27(2), 225–226.

471 ———. Translator of R. Dreikurs, *Die Ehe: Eine Herausforderung.*

472 ———. Translator of R. Dreikurs, *Psychologie im Klassenzimmer.*

473 ———. Translator of R. Dreikurs & Vicki Soltz, *Kinder fordern uns heraus.*

474 ———. *Wege zur inneren Freiheit—Praxis und Theorie der Selbsterziehung.* München: Rex, 1972.

475 **Bodluck, B.** Translator, with R. Lichtstern, of A. Adler, *Der zin fun leben.*

476 **Bogardus, E. S.** Social distance in poetry. *Sociol. soc. Res.*, 1951, 36, 40–47.

477 **Bohannon, E. W.** The only child in a family. *Ped. Sem.*, 1898, 5, 475–496.

478 **Bohne, G.** Individualpsychologische Beurteilung krimineller Persönlichkeiten. *IZIP*, 1931, 9(5), 330–344.

479 **Boisen, A. T.** *The exploration of the inner world.* New York: Harper, 1962.

480 ———. Personality changes and upheavals arising out of the sense of personal failure. *Amer. J. Psychiat.*, 1926, 5, 531–551.

481 **Bonime, W.** *The clinical use of dreams.* New York: Basic Books, 1962.

482 ———. The psychodynamics of neurotic depression. In S. Arieti (Ed.), *American Handbook of Psychiatry.* Vol. 3. New York: Basic Books, 1966. Pp. 239–255.

483 **Bonner, H.** Idealization and mental health. *JIP*, 1962, 18, 136–146.

484 Bonner, H. *On being mindful of man: Essay toward a proactive psychology.* Boston: Houghton Mifflin, 1965.

485 ———. Review of A. Adler, *The science of living.* In *JIP*, 1969, 25, 233–234.

486 Bonsall, M. R. *What I like to do: An inventory of children's interests.* Chicago: Sci. Res. Assoc., 1954 (with C. E. Meyers & L. P. Thorpe).

487 Bopp, L. *Allgemeine Heilpädagogik in systematischer Grundlegung und mit erziehungspraktischer Einstellung.* Freiburg: Herder, 1930.

488 Borgatta, E. (Ed.). *Handbook of personality theory.* Chicago: Rand McNally, 1968 (with W. Lambert).

489 ———. *The Picture Test.* Educational Service Publications, 1968 (with R. J. Corsini).

490 ———. *Quick Word Test* (6 forms). World Book Co., 1960 (with R. J. Corsini).

491 ———. *Quick Word Test.* Junior Ed. World Book Co., 1968 (with R. J. Corsini).

492 ———. The Quick Word Test and the WAIS. *Psychol. Rep.*, 1960, 6, 201 (with R. J. Corsini).

493 Borge, G. F. Birth order and the obsessive-compulsive character. *Arch. gen. Psychiat.*, 1967, 17, 751–754 (with L. Kayton).

494 Bornemann, A. Individual Psychology in Germany. *IPB*, 1949, 7, 30–32 (with H. L. Ansbacher).

495 Bornemann, E. Die Erste Internationale Sommerschule der Arbeitsgemeinschaft für Individualpsychologie. *Psychol. Rundsch.*, July, 1956. Pp. 249–250.

496 ———. *Erziehungsberatung: Ein Weg zur Überwindung der Erziehungsnot.* München: Reinhardt, 1963.

497 Boroson, W. First born—fortune's favorite. *N. Y. Times Mag.*, Dec. 13, 1970. Pp. 87, 92, 97, 99.

498 Bosley, Florida. Portrait. *St. Louis Post Dispatch*, July 27, 1971.

499 Boshier, R. Attitudes toward self and one's proper names. *JIP*, 1968, 24, 63–66.

500 ———. Self-regarding attitudes: A bibliography. Wellington, New Zealand: Author.

501 Boss, M. *The analysis of dreams.* New York: Phil. Libr., 1958.

502 ———. *The dream and its interpretation.* London: Rider, 1957.

503 Bosshard, H. M. Review of J. Black, *You can't win.* New York: A. L. Burt, 1925. In *IZIP*, 1931, 9(1), 78–79.

504 Bosshard, H. M. Review of H. S. Sullivan, Socio-psychiatric research. *Amer. J. Psychiat.*, 1931, 10, 977–991. In *IZIP*, 1931, 9(5), 411.

505 ———. Die Träume des Herrn P. *IZIP*, 1936, 14(3), 166–176.

506 Bostrom, J. A. Psychotherapy as reorientation and readjustment (with A. G. Nikelly). In A. G. Nikelly (Ed.), *Techniques for behavior change.* Pp. 103–107.

507 Boszormenyi-Nagy, I. Family treatment of schizophrenia: A symposium. *Fam. Proc.*, 1962, 1, 101–140 (with H. Hildreth, C. Midelfort, J. Franco, and A. Friedman).

508 Bottome, Phyllis. *Against whom?* London: Faber & Faber, 1954, 1957.

509 ———. *Alfred Adler.* Translated by O. Brachfeld. Barcelona: Ed. Miracle, 1951.

510 ———. *Alfred Adler: A portrait from life.* New York: Vanguard Press, 1957.

511 ———. *Alfred Adler: Apostle of freedom.* London: Faber & Faber, 1939, 1946, 1957; New York: Putnam, 1939.

512 ———. *Best short stories of Phyllis Bottome.* Chosen with a preface by Daphne du Maurier. London: Faber & Faber, 1963.

513 ———. *The challenge.* London: Faber & Faber, 1952.

514 ———. *Danger signal.* Boston: Little, Brown, 1939. Also titled *Murder in the bud.* London: Faber & Faber, 1940.

515 ———. *The devil's due.* New York: Grosset & Dunlap, 1933.

516 ———. *Eldorado Jane.* London: Faber & Faber, 1956. Also titled *Jane.* New York: Vanguard, 1957.

517 ———. Frau Dr. Adler (Mrs. Raissa Adler). *JIP*, 1962, 18, 182–183.

518 ———. *From the life: Character studies.* London: Faber & Faber, 1944.

519 ———. *The goal.* New York: Vanguard, 1962.

520 ———. *Heart of a child.* New York: G. P. Putnam's Sons, 1940, London: Faber & Faber, 1958.

521 ———. How to apply sincerity to democracy. *IPB*, 1943, 3, 31–37.

522 ———. How to get anywhere: Psychological approach to Everest. *IPNL*, 1954, No. 34–35. Pp. 1–3.

523 ———. Individual Psychology in America. *IPNL*, 1940, 1(2), 1–3.

524 ———. The IPNL loses two more eminent and faithful friends [Lydia

Sicher & Raissa Adler], *IPNL*, 1962, 11 (7–8, Whole No. 132–133). Pp. 25–27.

525 **Bottome, Phyllis**. *Innocence and experience*. Boston, Mass.: Houghton Mifflin, 1934.

526 ———. *Jane*. New York: Vanguard, 1957. Also titled *Eldorado Jane*. London: Faber & Faber, 1956.

527 ———. *Life line*. Boston: Little, Brown, 1946.

528 ———. Limits to a human being—if any. *IJIP*, 1936, 2(4), 32–36.

529 ———. *London pride*. Boston: Little, Brown, 1941.

530 ———. Love—A stranglehold. *IJIP*, 1937, 3(2), 198–201.

531 ———. Main relationships. *IJIP*, 1936, 2(1), 55–61.

532 ———. *Masks and faces*. Boston: Little, Brown, 1940.

533 ———. *The mortal storm*. New York: Blue Ribbon Books, 1939.

534 ———. *Murder in the bud*. London: Faber & Faber, 1940. Also titled *Danger Signal*. Boston: Little, Brown, 1939.

535 ———. *Neurosis and genius*. IPNL, 1954, No. 36–37. Pp. 7–8; 1954, No. 39–40. Pp. 4–8.

536 ———. [Obituary for Raissa Adler]. *IPNL*, 1962, 12(9–10, Whole No. 134–135). Pp. 34–36.

537 ———. [Obituary for Lydia Sicher]. *IPNL*, 1962, 11(7–8, Whole No. 132–133). Pp. 26–27.

538 ———. *Old wine*. New York: Frederick A. Stokes, 1937.

539 ———. Portrait. *N. Y. Times*, Aug. 24, 1963; *IPNL*, 1970, 19(4), 79; *IPNL*, 1972, 21(6), 111.

540 ———. Reflections on Ernest Jones' biography of Freud. *JIP*, 1958, 14, 79–83.

541 ———. Review of M. Sperber, *The Achilles heel*. In *JIP*, 1960, 16, 217–218.

542 ———. *Search for a soul*. London: Faber & Faber, 1947; New York: Harcourt Brace, 1948.

543 ———. *Walls of glass*. London: Faber & Faber, 1958.

544 ———. *Within the cup*. London: Faber & Faber, 1943.

545 **Bovet, P.** Preface to Madelaine Ganz, *The psychology of Alfred Adler*. Pp. xi–xv.

546 **Bowman, Garda.** Adlerian concepts and problems of aging. In K. A. Adler & Danica

Deutsch (Eds.), *Essays in Individual Psychology*. Pp. 70–75.

547 **Bowman, L.** Opening remarks [Proceedings of the Inaugural Meeting of the American Society of Adlerian Psychology, New York. May 16, 1952]. *AJIP*, 1952, 10, 78–79.

548 **Braceland, F. J.** Psychiatry in a world still more troubled. *J. Natl. Assn. Priv. Psychiat. Hosp.*, 1971, 3(1), 5–12.

549 **Braceland, P. J.** *et al.* (Eds.). *Marriage et Celibat*. Paris: Editions du Cerf, 1965.

550 **Brachfeld, O.** Alfred Adler, Der Sexualpsychologe. *Z. sex. Wissensch. Sexualpolitik*, 1936.

551 ———. André Gides Werdegang. *IZIP*, 1930, 8(4), 376–388.

552 ———. Angel Sancho Rivero's individual-psychologische Epostheorie. *IZIP*, 1934, 12(3), 166–169.

553 ———. Bolivar, pedagogo moderno. *Revista de la Soc. Bolivariana de Venezuela*, 1951, 11, 31–

554 ———. Changes and resistance to change in the field of human relations. In *Research into factors influencing human relations*. Report of the Int. Conf., Berg en Dal, Nijmegen, Netherlands, Sept. 3–15, 1956. Hilversum, Neth.: Uitgeverij Paul Brand, 1956. Pp. 31–38.

555 ———. Christopher Marlowe als Vorläufer der Individualpsychologie. *IZIP*, 1928, 6(1), 63–66.

556 ———. Chronophobia as a nervous symptom. *Revista Med. de Barcelona*, 1932, ; *Revista Balear. de Med.*, 1933.

557 ———. *Como interpretar los suenos?* Barcelona: Jose Janes, 1949.

558 ———. *Los complejos de inferioridad de la mujer*. Barcelona: Condal, 1949.

559 ———. Die Deutung eines Traumes in Rousseau's "Nouvelle Héloise". *IZIP*, 1928, 6(5), 374–377.

560 ———. *La educacion por si mismo*. 2nd ed. Barcelona: Ed. Victoria, 1946.

561 ———. Editor of F. Künkel, *Introduccion a la caracterologia*.

562 ———. *El examen de la inteligencia en los ninos*. Gerona-Madrid: Dalmáu Carles, 1936.

563 ———. Individualpsychologie und positivistische Soziologie. *IZIP*, 1934, 12(1), 44–46.

564 ———. Individual Psychology in the learning of languages. *IJIP*, 1936, 2(1), 77–83.

565 **Brachfeld, O.** *Inferiority feelings in the individual and the group.* London: Routledge & Kegan Paul, 1951; New York: Grune & Stratton, 1951.

566 ———. Introduction to A. Adler, *El problema del homosexualismo y otros problemas sexuales.*

567 ———. Is woman less intelligent than man? *IPB,* 1946, 5, 87–88.

568 ———. Der Kampf der Beschlechter und der "Mannliche Protest". In W. Bitter (Ed.), *Krisis und Zukunft der Frau.*

569 ———. Krankheit als geistiger Antrieb. *IZIP,* 1935, 13(4), 215–217.

570 ———. M. Ernest Seillière et l'"Individualpsychologie" adlérienne. *IZIP,* 1929, 7(5), 344–350.

571 ———. *Minderwerdskomplekser.* Copenhague: H. Hirschprung's Førlag, 1949.

572 ———. *Minderwertigkeitsgefühle.* Stuttgart: Ernst Klett, 1953.

573 ———. *Un nou teòtic del géni: Alfred Adler.* Barcelona: La Revista, 1930.

574 ———. Ortega y Gasset über Alfred Adler und über die Individualpsychologie. *IZIP,* 1931, 9(2), 139–140.

575 ———. Poul Bjerre und die Psychosynthese. *Psychologe* (Berne), 1963, 15, 283–286.

576 ———. Portrait, *IPNL,* 1971, 20(6), 111.

577 ———. La psicologia adleriana y la sociologia. *Revista Int. de Sociol.* (Madrid), 1948, 6,

578 ———. La responsibilité morale et la psychologie adlérienne. *Psyché* (Paris), 1951, 6, 554–573.

579 ———. Review of R. Allendy, *Les rêves et leur interprétation psychoanalytique.* Paris: [   ], 1930. In *IZIP,* 1930, 8(6), 595.

580 ———. Review of [   ] Anaies, De la seccion de orientacion profesional de la escuela del trabajo. 1928–30, 1–3. In *IZIP,* 1932, 10(1), 74.

581 ———. Review of *L'année psychologique.* Paris: Alcan, 1930. In *IZIP,* 1931, 9(6), 482.

582 ———. Review of J. Bab, *Das Theater im Lichte der Soziologie.* Leipzig: C. L. Hirschfeld, 1931. In *IZIP,* 1931, 9(5), 414–415.

583 ———. Review of N. Braunshausen, *Le bilinguisme et les méthodes d'enseignement des langues étrangères.* In *IZIP,* 1934, 12(4), 258.

584 **Brachfeld, O.** Review of A. Burns, *Colour prejudice with particular reference to the relationship between whites and negroes.* London: Allen & Unwin, 1948. In *Revista Int. de Sociol.* (Madrid), 1949, Nos. 26–27.

585 ———. Review of A. Chlerisebairque, *Orientacion profesional.* Barcelona: Editorial Labor, 1934. In *IZIP,* 1934, 12(4), 258.

586 ———. Review of A. Comte, *Aufruf an die Konservativen* & R. T. Mendes, *Die katholisch-feudale Herrschaft* & E. Lippman, *Was ist Positivismus?* In *IZIP,* 1931, 9(2), 154.

587 ———. Review of A. de Rochetal, *La caractère par le prenom.* Paris: [   ], 1929. In *IZIP,* 1930, 8(6), 593–594.

588 ———. Review of T. D. Eliot, *Psychiatrische Soziologie und soziologische Psychiatrie.* In *IZIP,* 1932, 10(1), 73.

589 ———. Review of I. Fülöp, *Egységes alkotrendszer.* Budapest: Author, 1932. In *IZIP,* 1932, 10(3), 235–236.

590 ———. Review of Madelaine Ganz, *La psychologie d'Alfred Adler et le développement de l'enfant.* In *IZIP,* 1936, 14(4), 238–239.

591 ———. Review of J–C. Grière, *Vers la sociologie constructive.* Paris: Marcel Scheur, 1930. In *IZIP,* 1930, 8(6), 595.

592 ———. Review of E. Gutheil, *Alibido und Impotenz. Z. Sexualwissensch.,* 1930, 17(6), 348–355. In *IZIP,* 1931, 9(2), 154.

593 ———. Review of P. Harkai-Schiller, *A lélektani kategóriák rendszerének kialakulása.* Budapest: Diss, 1930. In *IZIP,* 1931, 9(6), 482.

594 ———. Review of P. Heintz, *Soziale Vorurteile.* Köln: Verlag f. Politik u. Wirtsch., 1957. In *Int. J. soc. Psychiat.,* 1959, 5(2), 156–157.

595 ———. Review of A. Hesnard, *Psychologie homosexuelle.* Paris: [   ], 1930. In *IZIP,* 1930, 8(6), 594–595.

596 ———. Review of R. König & Margaret Tønnesman (Eds.), *Probleme der Medizin-Soziologie.* Köln: Westdeutscher Verlag, 1958. In *Int. J. soc. Psychiat.,* 1959, 5(2), 155.

597 ———. Review of I. Kulcsar, *Beveztis az individuál-pszichologiaba.* In *IZIP,* 1932, 10, 155–160.

598 ———. Review of H. Lantz, *People of Coal Town.* New York: Columbia Univ.

Press, 1958. In *Int. J. soc. Psychiat.*, 1959, 4(4), 316–317.

599 **Brachfeld, O.** Review of M. Mignard, *L'unité psychique et les troubles mentaux.* Paris: [   ], 1928. In *IZIP*, 1931, 9(2), 153.

600 ———. Review of E. Mira, *El Psico-analisi.* Barcelona: Monografies Mediques, 1926; *Estado actual del concepto de las esquizo-frénas.* Barcelona: Monografies Mediques, 1927; and *Estado actual del concepto de las psiconeurosis.* Barcelona: Monografies Mediques, 1924. In *IZIP*, 1932, 10(1), 74.

601 ———. Review of W. Muschg, *Psychoana-lyse und Literaturwissenschaft.* Berlin: Junker & Dünnhaupt, 1930. In *IZIP*, 1931, 9(6), 482.

602 ———. Review of S. S. Myers, *Attitudes to minority groups.* In *Revist. Int. de Sociol.* (Madrid), 1949, Nos. 26–27.

603 ———. Review of *Revista de psicologia i pedagogia.* In *IZIP*, 1934, 12(4), 257–258.

604 ———. Review of E. Santovenia, *Estudios, biografias y ensayos.* Habaña: Ucar, Garcia, 1957. In *Int. J. soc. Psychiat.*, 1959, 4(4), 309.

605 ———. Review of E. Seillière, *Psychoan-alyse ou psychologie imperialiste Allemande.* Paris: [   ], 1928, In *IZIP*, 1929,

606 ———. Review of G. Sutter, *Mystik und Erotik.* Heidelberg: K. Winter, 1929. In *IZIP*, 1931, 9(5), 415.

607 ———. Review of B. Székely, *A gyer-mekevek szekszualitása.* Budapest: Pantheon, 1935. In *IZIP*, 1936, 14(2), 121–122.

608 ———. Review of B. Székely, *A te gyreked. . .* Budapest: Pantheon, 1934. In *IZIP*, 1934, 12(4), 257.

609 ———. *Selbsterziehung des Charakters.* Leipzig: [   ] 1930.

610 ———. *Les sentiments d'inferiorité.* Geneva: Editions du Mont Blanc, 1945.

611 ———. *Los sentimientos de inferioridad.* Barcelona: Luis Miracle, 1944, 1959.

612 ———. *Sexual difficulties. IJIP*, 1936, 2(3), 61–72.

613 ———. *Sexuelle Lebensschwierigkeiten. IZIP*, 1930, 8(1), 142–151.

614 ———. Translator of A. Adler, *El sentido de la vida.*

615 ———. Translator of R. Allers, *Sexual-pädagogik.*

616 ———. Translator of Phyllis Bottome, *Al-fred Adler.*

617 **Brachfeld, O.** Über die Furcht vor der Frau, in Sage, Märchen und Literatur. *IZIP*, 1928, 6(6), 442–456.

618 ———. Les vétos catégoriques. In [   ], *Culture Humaine.* Paris: [   ], 1948.

619 ———. Zur Individualpsychologie des Sprach-enerlernens. *IZIP*, 1932, 10(3), 201–207.

620 ———. Zwei Beiträge zur Individualpsy-chologie. *IZIP*, 1935, 13(4), 213–215.

621 **Brachyahu, M.** Ein streitsüchtiges Mädchen. *IZIP*, 1930, 8(2), 268–270.

622 **Bragg, B. W. E.** Academic primogeniture and sex-role contrast of the second born. *JIP*, 1970, 26(2), 196–199.

623 **Braginsky, Dorothea.** The relationship of birth order to self-evaluation, anxiety re-duction, and susceptibility to emotional contagion. *Psychol. Monogr.*, 1965, 79, (Whole No. 603). Pp. 1–24 (with K. Ring & C. E. Lipinski).

624 **Braisted, S. B.** Reciprocal assessment of life style and the achievement of educational goals in the urban community college. *The New Jersey Comm. Coll.*, Fall, 1971.

625 **Branan, Karen.** ". . . Don't feel like being bad anymore" or "Discipline, a search for something better". *Scholas. Teacher*, May, 1972. Pp. 4–7.

626 **Brandhuber-Etschfeld, F.** Die Individual-psychologie Alfred Adlers und der Uni-versalismus Othmar Spanns. *IZIP*, 1929, 7(5), 367–369.

627 ———. Verbrechen und Neurose. *IZIP*, 1932, 10(5), 362–368.

628 **Brandon, B.** Could you use free time? *OSIPNL*, 1972, 12(5), 13–17.

629 ———. Problem prevention: Applied de-mocracy. *OSIPNL*, 1972, 13(3), 7–9.

630 ———. Problem solving. *OSIPNL*, 1971, 12(2), 11–12.

631 **Brandon, R. A.** Early recollections re-lated to anxiety and introversion-extrover-sion. *J. consult. Psychol.*, 1967, 31, 107.

632 **Brandt, W.** Psychische Hygiene im Lichte Individualpsychologie. *Aerz. Prax.*, 1958, 10(12),

633 **Branham, V.** (Ed.). *Encyclopedia of crimi-nology.* New York: Phil. Libr., 1949 (with S. B. Kutash).

634 **Branthover, Gertrude.** Individual Psychology class for seniors. *OSIPNL*, 1966, 7(4), 8–9.

635 **Branton, H.** Die Grenzen der Methodik. *IZIP*, 1950, 19(4), 174–177 (with Renée Leistner).

636 Brauchle, A. *Psychoanalyse und Individual-psychologie.* Leipzig: Reclam, 1930, 1963.

637 ———. *Von der Macht des Unbewussten.* Stuttgart: Reclam, 1949.

638 Bräuer, A. Rembrandt, vom Standpunkt der Individualpsychologie ausgesehen. *IZIP*, 1935, 13(4), 245–256.

639 Braverman-Kanjuk, Sara. *Ketzad l'horot— Kriah l'yaldei olim.* Tel Aviv: Urim la-Morim, 1956.

640 Breddels-Munnik, H. De mogelijkheden in de ergotherapie tot he behandelen van perceptiestoornissen. *MNWIP*, 1971, 20(3).

641 Breese, Fay. Patterns of parent behavior. *Psychol. Monogr.*, 1945, 58, No. 3 (Whole No. 268) (with A. L. Baldwin & Joan Kallhorn).

642 Brekstad, A. Factors influencing the reliability of anamnestic recall. *Child Developm.*, 1966, 37, 603–612.

643 Brennan, J. F. Autoeroticism or social feeling as basis of human development. *JIP*, 1969, 25, 3–18.

644 ———. Friendship: The Adlerian mode of existence. *JIP*, 1966, 22, 43–48.

645 ———. Review of A. Schutz, *The phenomenology of the social world.* In *JIP*, 1970, 26, 234–235.

646 ———. Self-understanding and social feeling. *JIP*, 1967, 23, 53–57.

647 ———. Upright posture as the foundation of Individual Psychology: A comparative analysis of Adler and Straus. *JIP*, 1968, 24, 25–32.

648 Bressler, D. M. Masochism in terms of Adlerian psychology. *AJIP*, 1956, 12, 123–127.

649 Brewer, Deanna. *Group guidance: A source book for teachers.* Houston: Harris County Dept. Educ., 1970.

650 ———. *Problem solving in group guidance: Communication and decision making.* Houston: Harris County Dept. Educ., 1971.

651 ———. The value of role reversal in psychodrama and action therapy. *Handbook int. Sociom.*, 1971, 6, 98–104 (with W. E. O'Connell).

652 Brezina, E. Über die Bedingheit der Häufung gewerblicher Unfälle. *Arch. Gewerbpathol. u. Gewerbhyg.*, 1931, 2, 359–384 (with Alexandra Adler & J. Wastl).

653 Brind, Anna. Remembering Alfred Adler. *OSIPNL*, 1964, 5(1), 11–12.

654 Brind, Anna. The therapeutic hour and the rest of the week. *Grp. Psychother.*, 1964, 17, 139–142 (with N. Brind).

655 Brind, B. Child guidance as a community service. *IPB*, 1942, 2(3), 52.

656 Brind, N. The therapeutic hour and the rest of the week. *Grp. Psychother.*, 1964, 17, 139–142 (with Anna Brind).

657 Briner, Dorothy. Portrait. *St. Louis Post-Dispatch*, July 27, 1971.

658 Bristow, R. B. The effect of formal art training upon the quantitative scores on the H-T-P. *J. clin. Psychol.*, 1959, 15, 57–59 (with V. J. Bieliauskas).

659 Brock, T. C. Birth order and subject recruitment. *J. soc. Psychol.*, 1965, 65, 63–66 (with G. Becker).

660 Brodlie, J. F. Review of J. S. Roucek (Ed.), *Programmed teaching: A symposium on automation in teaching.* New York: Phil. Libr., 1965. In *IP*, 1966, 3(2), 22.

661 Brodsky, Mimi. Problem child [A poem]. *OSIPNL*, 1966, 6(4), 16.

662 Brodsky, P. *Adolescence.* New York: Libra Publ., 1966.

663 ———. *Children's songs.* Elgin, Ill.: Cook Publ. House, 1966.

664 ———. Confused [A poem]. *IPNL*, 1964, 15(1-2, Whole No. 162-163). P. 3.

665 ———. Dependence-interdependence. *IP*, 1963, 1(2), 13–17.

666 ———. The diagnostic importance of early recollections. *Amer. J. Psychother.*, 1952, 6, 484–493.

667 ———. The educational work of the private teacher. In A. Adler & assoc., *Guiding the child.* Pp. 247–268.

668 ———. Erziehungsarbeit des Privatlehrers. *IZIP*, 1929, 7(3), 239–243.

669 ———. Eva S. Olman (1889-1969). *JIP*, 1969, 25, 262–263.

670 ———. Gemeinschaftsgefuehl. *IPNL*, 1966, 16(11-12, Whole No. 184-185). P. 43.

671 ———. It's yours [A poem]. *IPNL*, 1965, 15(12, Whole No. 173). P. 45.

672 ———. Der Lehrer und die Gemeinschaft. *IZIP*, 1948, 17(2), 72–77.

673 ———. Lydia Sicher (1890-1962). *JIP*, 1962, 18, 184–186.

674 ———. The maladjusted child. *IP*, 1967, 4(2), 62–64.

675 ———. Margaret Kearney (1901-1967). *JIP*, 1968, 24, 125.

676 **Brodsky, P.** Mental health prophylaxis. In A. Nikelly (Ed.), *Techniques for behavior change.* Pp. 211–216.

677 ———. *Music round the clock.* , 1955.

678 ———. Poem for the living. *IPNL*, 1963, 13(5–6, Whole No. 142–143). P. 22.

679 ———. Problems of adolescence: An Adlerian view. In *Adolescence*, 1968, 3, 9–22.

680 ———. Psychologie des Nachhilfeunterrichtes. *IZIP*, 1935, 13(2), 88–104.

681 ———. Religious [A poem]. *IPNL*, 1965, 15(3–4, Whole No. 164–165). P. 9.

682 ———. The rocking chair [A poem]. *IPNL*, 1964, 14(10–12, Whole No. 159–161). P. 41.

683 ———. Talk to [A poem]. *IPNL*, 1964, 15 (3–4, Whole No. 164–165). P. 9.

684 ———. *Together we sing.* Chicago: Follett, 1955.

685 ———. Tutoring a problem child. *IJIP*, 1936, 2(4), 91–106.

686 ———. Zur individualpsychologischen Beeinflussbarkeit der Epilepsie. *IZIP*, 1933, 12(5), 369–377.

687 **Brody Oller, Olga.** Medical practice and psychotherapy. *IPB*, 1947, 6, 19–21. Also in K. A. Adler & Danica Deutsch (Eds.), *Essays in Individual Psychology.* Pp. 231–235.

688 ———. Understanding and management of psychosomatic problems in children. *AJIP*, 1954, 10, 175–181.

689 **Brody, S.** *Patterns of mothering: Maternal influence during infancy.* New York: Int. Univer. Press, 1956.

690 **Bromberg, W.** *The nature of psychotherapy.* New York: Grune & Stratton, 1962.

691 **Brome, V.** *Freud and his early circle.* New York: William Morrow, 1967.

692 **Brook, A.** Schülerbesprechung bei den kleinsten. *IZIP*, 1936, 14(4), 220–227.

693 **Brookes, R. H.** The anatomy of anomie. *Polit. Sci.*, 1951, 3, 44–51.

694 **Brooks, G. W.** Rehabilitation of chronic schizophrenic patients for social living. *JIP*, 1960, 16, 189–196 (with W. N. Deane & H. L. Ansbacher).

695 ———. Review of G. W. Albee, *Mental health manpower trends.* New York: Basic Books, 1959. In *JIP*, 1959, 15, 243–244.

696 **Brooks, Mabelle.** A camp climate for personality growth. *IPB*, 1946, 5, 60–61.

697 ———. Can the teacher help? *IPB*, 1944–45, 4, 93–94.

698 **Brooks, Mabelle.** The cultivation of responsibility and self-discipline. In A. Nikelly (Ed.), *Techniques for behavior change.* Pp. 191–196.

699 ———. Training the child for self-discipline. *IPB*, 1949, 7, 75–86.

700 **Broser, O.** Mehr Psychologie—eine Voraussetzung für den Weltfrieden. *IZIP*, 1947, 16 (4), 168–182.

701 **Brouilhet, C. A.** Individual Psychology. *IP*, 1970, 7(1), 1–2; *Rev. Psychother. Psychol. Appliquée*, 1929, 38(1).

702 **Broverman, D. M.** Ability to automatize and automatization cognitive style: A validation study. *Percep. mot. Skills*, 1966, 23, 419–437 (with Inge Broverman & E. L. Klaiber).

703 ———. Children's cognitive style and response modification. *J. genet. Psychol.*, 1967, 110, 95–103 (with A. H. Blum).

704 ———. Generality and behavioral correlates of cognitive styles. *J. consult. Psychol.*, 1964, 28, 487–500.

705 **Broverman, Inge.** Ability to automatize and automatization cognitive style: A validation study. *Percep. mot. Skills*, 1966, 23, 419–437 (with D. M. Broverman & E. L. Klaiber).

706 **Brower, D.** (Ed.). *Progress in clinical psychology.* New York: Grune and Stratton, 1956 (with L. E. Abt).

707 **Brown, C.** *Manchild in the promised land.* New York: Macmillan, 1965.

708 **Brown, D. G.** Masculinity-femininity development in children. *J. consult. Psychol.*, 1957, 21, 197–202.

709 ———. Sex-role development in a changing culture. *Psychol. Bull.*, 1958, 55, 232–242.

710 **Brown, E.** Measurement of existential mental health: Further exploration. *JIP*, 1968, 24, 71–73 (with H. Smith).

711 **Brown, J. A. C.** *Freud and the post-Freudians.* Baltimore: Penguin Books, 1961.

712 **Brown, W. L.** Anorexia nervosa. *IPMP*, 1931, No. 2. Pp. 11–17.

713 ———. Unrecognized weakness and compensatory learning. *Amer. J. Psychol.*, 1957, 70, 126–127.

714 **Browne, I. W.** An experiment with a psychiatric night hospital. *Proc. Royal Soc. Med.*, 1960, 53(11), 930–932 (with J. Bierer).

715 **Brownfain, J. J.** Stability of the self-concept as a dimension of personality. *J. abnorm. soc. Psychol.*, 1952, 47, 597–606.

716 **Bruck, A.** Adlerian philosophy. *IPB*, 1947, 6, 80–87.

717 ———. The concept of the "unconscious". *IPB*, 1950, 8, 81–98.

718 ———. Do we need the concept of "guilt feelings?" *IPB*, 1950, 8, 44–48.

719 ———. Enlightening children. *AJIP*, 1956, 12, 157–170.

720 ———. The teaching of social philosophy in primary schools. *IPB*, 1943, 3, 81–91.

721 ———. "Tests" or "themes". *IPB*, 1943, 3(1), 20–26.

722 ———. Unity of personality shown in class themes written by a schoolboy. *IPB*, 1946, 5, 53–59.

723 ———. What does life mean to us? *IPB*, 1942, 2(3), 50–52.

724 **Bruck, M. A.** See Bruck, A.

725 **Bruner, J. S.** The perception of people (with R. Tagiuri). In G. Lindzey (Ed.), *Handbook of social psychology*. Vol. 2. Cambridge, Mass.: Addison-Wesley, 1954. Pp. 634–654.

726 ———. Personal values as selective factors in perception. *J. abnorm. soc. Psychol.*, 1948, 42, 142–154 (with E. McGinnies & L. Postman).

727 ———. Value and need as organizing factors in perception. *J. abnorm. soc. Psychol.*, 1947, 42, 33–44 (with C. C. Goodman).

728 **Buber, M.** *I and thou.* New York: Scribner, 1937; Edinburgh: R. R. Clark, 1937; New York: Charles Scribner's Sons, 1958. Paper.

729 **Bucaria, Jeanene.** Role playing. *OSIPNL*, 1966, 7(2), 6.

730 **Buchheimer. A.** *The counseling relationship: A casebook.* Chicago: Science Research Assoc., 1961 (with Sara C. Balogh).

731 ———. From group to "gemeinschaft". In K. A. Adler & Danica Deutsch (Eds.), *Essays in Individual Psychology*. Pp. 242–247.

732 **Buchner, L.** Neurotischer Mystizismus. *IZIP*, 1923, 2(1), 31–33.

733 **Bucking, M.** Ein verzärteltes Kind. *IZIP*, 1929, 7(4), 311–313.

734 **Buckle, D.** *Child guidance centers.* Geneva: World Hlth Org., 1960 (with S. Lebovic).

735 **Buckman, J.** Marlborough Night Hospital. Treatment with L. S. D. and group therapy. 1. *Nurs. Times*, 1961, 57(19), 594–596; 2. *Nurs. Times*, 1961, 57(20), 637–639 (with J. Bierer).

736 **Budd, W. C.** Is free will necessary? *Amer. Psychologist*, 1960, 15, 217–218.

737 **Buelow, F.** Die Berufswahl. *Koel. Z. Soziol.*, 1953, 5, 166–190.

738 **Bugental, J. F. T.** Investigation into self concept: II. Stability of reported self identifications. *J. clin. Psychol.*, 1955, 11, 41–46 (with Evelyn C. Gunning).

739 ———. *The search for authenticity: An existential-analytic approach to psychotherapy.* New York: Holt, Rinehart & Winston, 1965.

740 **Bühler, Charlotte.** Review of R. A. Spitz & W. G. Cobliner, *The first year of life.* New York: Int. Univer. Press, 1964. In *JIP*, 1967, 23, 118–119.

741 **Bullard, Eva.** Characteristics of the referred child. *OSIPNL*, 1964, 4(4), 13–14.

742 ———. The counseling center of Wesley Methodist Church of Minn. *OSIPNL*, 1967, 8(5), 67.

743 ———. Emas in Ponape. *OSIPNL*, 1970, 11(1), 7–8.

744 ———. Fun ideas for mothers and teachers. *OSIPNL*, 1966, 7(2), 6–7.

745 ———. Homework for study groups? *OSIPNL*, 1965, 6(5), 8–9.

746 ———. News. *IP*, 1966, 4(1), 29–32.

747 ———. Newsletter. *IP*, 1966, 3(2), 18–21; 1967, 4(2), 67–72; 1967, 5(1), 32–36; 1968, 5(2), 65–68.

748 ———. Portrait. *IPNL*, 1971, 20(6), 112.

749 ———. Review of A. Adler, *The problem child*. In *OSIPNL*, 1963, 4(1), 9–10.

750 ———. Review of A. Adler, *Problems of neurosis*. In *OSIPNL*, 1965, 5(3), 15.

751 ———. Review of G. H. Allred, *Mission for mothers*. In *OSIPNL*, 1970, 11(2), 8–9.

752 ———. Review of S. Blanton & A. Gordon, *Now or never*. Englewood Cliffs, N. J.: Prentice-Hall, 1960. In *OSIPNL*, 1963, 4(2), 8.

753 ———. Review of C. Brown, *Manchild in the promised land*. In *OSIPNL*, 1970, 11(1), 13.

754 ———. Review of D. Dinkmeyer & R. Dreikurs, *Encouraging children to learn*. In *OSIPNL*, 1963, 3(5), 9.

755 ———. Review of R. Dreikurs & L. Grey, *Parents' guide to child discipline*. In *OSIPNL*, 1970, 11(1), 13.

756 ———. Review of R. Dreikurs & Vicki Soltz, *Children: The challenge*. In *OSIPNL.*, 1964, 4(5), 9.

757 ———. Review of T. Grubbe, The challenge of kindergarten. In *OSIPNL*, 1965, 5(5), 15–16.

758 **Bullard, Eva.** Review of Marion Hilliard, *A woman doctor looks at love and life.* Garden City, N. Y.: Doubleday, 1957. In *OSIPNL*, 1964, 4(3), 8.

759 ———. Review of W. H. Missildine, *Your inner child of the past.* New York: Simon & Schuster, 1963. In *OSIPNL*, 1965, 5(50), 16.

760 ———. Review of T. Poffenberger, *The family council.* Corvallis, Ore.: Oregon St. Univ., 1953. In *OSIPNL*, 1964, 4(3), 9.

761 ———. Review of Lisa A. Richette, *The throwaway children,* Philadelphia: Lippincott. In *OSIPNL*, 1969, 10(2), 9.

762 ———. Toy phone for Jr. *OSIPNL*, 1964, 5(3), 11.

763 **Bullard, M.** Adlerian history and a modern problem (History of the organization). *OSIPNL*, 1965, 6(4), 2-4.

764 ———. Alexandra Adler. *OSIPNL*, 1971, 12(5), 10-11.

765 ———. An anthropological approach to youth group discussion. *OSIPNL*, 1969, 10(3), 6-8.

766 ———. An approach to a technique in vocational guidance. Unpubl. master's thesis, Oregon St. Univ., 1949.

767 ———. Attitude and child training. *OSIPNL*, 1966, 7(1), 11.

768 ———. Bernice Grunwald—master discussion leader. *OSIPNL*, 1964, 4(3), 13.

769 ———. Champions. *OSIPNL*, 1967, 8(5), 11-12.

770 ———. Development of the Adlerian movement in Oregon. *OSIPNL*, 1971, 12(5), 3-6.

771 ———. Dr. Dreikurs at A. P. G. A. in Las Vegas. *OSIPNL*, 1969, 9(5), 6-7.

772 ———. The durability of Alfred Adler. *OSIPNL*, 1969, 10(5), 1-4.

773 ———. Fresh topics for a series, from D. Cruickshank. *OSIPNL*, 1972, 13(3), 7 (with Mary Ann Smith).

774 ———. Genesis of the life style. *OSIPNL*, 1969, 19(2), 2-4.

775 ———. Goal recognition. *OSIPNL*, 1969, 19(5), 17-18.

776 ———. *Goal recognition outline.* Corvallis, Ore.: Author, 1961. Mimeo.

777 ———. Group discussion in a classroom—3rd & 4th gr. *OSIPNL*, 1965, 6(2), 8-9.

778 ———. Group personality influences leadership methods. *OSIPNL*, 1965, 5(3), 8-10.

779 **Bullard, M.** High adventure for little David, & St. Moritz in the backyard. *OSIPNL*, 1971, 12(4), 9-10.

780 ———. The human side of the International Congress. *OSIPNL*, 1969, 10(6), 3-4.

781 ———. Individual Psychology in sr. high school; Individual Psychology in homemaking class. *OSIPNL*, 1964, 5(5), 4-6.

782 ———. *Inferiority feelings and their effects.* Corvallis, Ore.: Author, 1961. Mimeo.

783 ———. In Memoriam—Rudolf Dreikurs. *OSIPNL*, 1972, 13(1), 1-2.

784 ———. IP pays off [about John Platt]. *OSIPNL*, 1967, 7(4), 11.

785 ———. Leadership as related to two extremes of group personality. *IPNL*, 1965, 15(9-10, Whole No. 170-172). Pp. 35-36.

786 ———. Life style analysis. *OSIPNL*, 1972, 13(4), 1-2.

787 ———. Mutual respect as an operational procedure. *OSIPNL*, 1969, 10(3), 9-11.

788 ———. NEA filmstrip experience. *OSIPNL*, 1965, 6(1), 8.

789 ———. A new parent training program comes to Oregon. *OSIPNL*, 1969, 9(4), 9-11.

790 ———. The Norris Haring approach to educating children with behavior problems. *OSIPNL*, 1965, 6(1), 9-10.

791 ———. On the positive side, examples. *OSIPNL*, 1963, 4(4), 8-9.

792 ———. Oregon discovers the man. *IP*, 1967, 4(2), 45-46.

793 ———. *An orientation sheet for Individual Psychology.* Corvallis, Ore.: Author, 1959.

794 ———. Outline using *Children: The challenge,* Parent study groups. *OSIPNL*, 1969, 10(1), insert (with Nancy Pearcy).

795 ———. Portrait. *IPNL*, 1971, 20(6), 112.

796 ———. Program enthusiasm. *OSIPNL*, 1972, 13(3), 4-6.

797 ———. Promotion of study groups. *OSIPNL*, 1968, 9(3), 9-10.

798 ———. Public school Adlerian counseling program. *OSIPNL*, 1963, 4(5).

799 ———. Report on the behavior problems class. *OSIPNL*, 1965, 6(2), 13-14.

800 ———. Review of H. L. & Rowena Ansbacher (Eds.), *Superiority and social interest.* In *OSIPNL*, 1965, 5(3), 13-14.

801 ———. Review of R. J. Corsini, *Methods of group psychotherapy.* In *OSIPNL*, 1963, 3(3), 5.

802 **Bullard, M.** Review of R. J. Corsini & D. D. Howard, *Critical incidents in teaching.* In *OSIPNL*, 1964, 4(5), 10–11.

803 ———. Review of J. H. Peck, *All about men.* New York: Permabooks, 1958. In *OSIPNL*, 1963, 3(4), 7.

804 ———. Review of H. & Elizabeth Swift, *Running a happy family.* New York: John Day, 1960. In *OSIPNL*, 1964, 4(3), 8.

805 ———. Review of W. Toman, *Family constellation.* In *OSIPNL*, 1963, 3(4), 8.

806 ———. The Smope. *OSIPNL*, 1963, 4(2), 11–12.

807 ———. Sydney Roth—Adlerian. *OSIPNL*, 1963, 4(1), 12–13.

808 ———. Who's Who in Individual Psychology—Alfred Adler. *OSIPNL*, 1966, 7(3), 13–16.

809 ———. Who's Who in Individual Psychology: Heinz L. Ansbacher. *OSIPNL*, 1965, 6(1), 14.

810 ———. Who's Who in Individual Psychology: Paul Brodsky. *OSIPNL*, 1966, 7(4), 5.

811 ———. Who's Who in Individual Psychology—Ray Lowe and Oscar Christiansen. *OSIPNL*, 1966, 7(5), 4–5.

812 ———. Who's Who in Individual Psychology—Oskar Spiel. *OSIPNL*, 1966, 7(2), 9.

813 **Bullough, Bonnie.** Birth order and achievement in eighteenth century Scotland. *JIP*, 1971, 27(1), 80 (with V. L. Bullough, Martha Voight, & Lucy Kluckhohn).

814 **Bullough, V. L.** Birth order and achievement in eighteenth century Scotland. *JIP*, 1971, 27(1), 80 (with Bonnie Bullough, Martha Voight, & Lucy Kluckhohn).

815 **Burchard, E. M. L.** Mystical and scientific aspects of the psychoanalytic theories of Freud, Adler and Jung. *Amer. J. Psychother.*, 1960, 14, 289–307.

816 **Burla-Adar, E.** Translator of R. Dreikurs, *Yeladim: Ha-etgar.*

817 **Burnell, G. M.** Earliest memories and ego functions. *Arch. gen. Psychiat.*, 1964, 11, 556–567 (with G. F. Solomon).

818 **Burnham, R. W.** Case studies of identical twins. *J. genet. Psychol.*, 1940, 56, 323–351.

819 **Burns, C. L. C.** Individual Psychology and Catholic belief. *IPMP*, 1932, No. 5. Pp. 30–43.

820 ———. Individual Psychology and social problems (I). *IPMP*, 1932, No. 5 (with A. Adler, W. B. Wolfe, & J. C. Young).

821 **Burns, R.** Work Interest Test. Education-Industry Service, Univ. Chicago, 1957 (with M. Baehr & R. J. Corsini).

822 **Burrows, Muriel.** Portrait. *IPNL*, 1970, 19(4), 79.

823 **Burt, C.** Foreword to J. Hemming, *Teaching of social studies in secondary schools.*

824 **Burt F.** William Somerset Maugham: An Adlerian interpretation. *JIP*, 1970, 26, 64–82.

825 **Busemann, A.** Die Familie als Erlebnismiliew des Kindes. *Z. Kinderforsch.*, 1928, 36, 17–82.

826 **Butler, F. O.** Birth primacy and idiopathic epilepsy. *Bull. Los Angeles Neurol. Soc.*, 1948, 13, 176–178 (with J. M. Nielsen).

827 **Butler, J. M.** Changes in the relation between self-concepts and ideal concepts consequent upon client-centered counseling (with G. B. Haigh). In C. R. Rogers & R. F. Dymond (Eds.), *Psychotherapy and personality change.* Chicago: Univ. Chicago Press, 1954.

828 ———. The interaction of client and therapist. *J. abnorm. soc. Psychol.*, 1952, 47, 366–378.

829 ———. Self-ideal congruence in psychotherapy. *Psychother.*, 1968, 5(1), 13–17.

830 **Butler, R. A.** Exploratory and related behavior: A new trend in animal research. *JIP*, 1958, 14, 111–120.

831 **Butler, R. N.** The life review: An interpretation of reminiscence in the aged. *Psychiat.* 1963, 26, 65–76.

832 **Butler, R. P.** Performance of paranoid schizophrenics and passive-aggressives on two masculinity-femininity tests. *Psychol. Rep.*, 1972, 31, 251–254 (with V. J. Bieliauskas).

833 **Butler, S.** How to create an inferiority complex. *IPNL*, 1953, No. 23–24. P. 1.

834 **Butts, Linda.** What happened to the trauma *OSIPNL*, 1971, 12(3), 10–11.

835 **Buytendijk, F. J. J.** The function of the parts within the structure of the whole: The excitability of the nerves. *JIP*, 1959, 15, 73–78.

836 **Byrne, Anne.** Graffiti therapy. *Perspec. psychiat. Care*, 1972, 10(1), 34–36 (with D. Peven & B. Shulman).

837 **Byrne, D.** (Ed.). *Current research in psychology: A book of readings.* New York: Wiley, 1971 (with H. C. Lindgren & F. Lindgren).

838 **Byrne, D.** *An introduction to personality: A research approach.* Englewood Cliffs, N. J.: Prentice-Hall, 1966.

C

1 **Caldwell, C. E.** *Developmental counseling and guidance: A comprehensive school approach.* New York: McGraw-Hill, 1970 (with D. Dinkmeyer).

2 **Calia, V.** *Critical incidents in school counseling.* Englewood Cliffs, N. J.: Prentice-Hall, 1970 (with R. J. Corsini).

3 **Calvin, A. D.** Adjustment and the discrepancy between self concept and inferred self. *J. consult. Psychol.,* 1953, 17, 39–44 (with W. H. Holtzman).

4 **Cameron, K.** Foreword to Hertha Orgler, *Alfred Adler: The man and his work.* Pp. v–vi.

5 **Cammaer, H.** *Alfred Adler's Leer tot 1914: De Evolutie von zijn Theorie over het "Levensplan".* Louvain, Belgium: Catholic Univ., 1958. Paper.

6 **Camp, W. L.** Early recollections: Reflections of the present. *J. couns. Psychol.,* 1970, 17, 510–515 (with D. M. Verger).

7 **Campbell, A. A.** A study of the personality adjustments of only and intermediate children. *J. genet. Psychol.,* 1933, 43, 197–206.

8 **Canfield, J. V.** (Ed.). *Purpose in nature.* Englewood Cliffs, N. J.: Prentice-Hall, 1966.

9 **Cantor, A. J.** (Ed.). *Psychosomatic aspects of surgery.* New York: Grune & Stratton, 1956 (with A. N. Foxe).

10 **Cantril, H.** The concept of transaction in psychology and neurology. *JIP,* 1963, 19, 3–16 (with W. K. Livingston).

11 ———. Effective democratic leadership: A psychological interpretation. *JIP,* 1958, 14, 128–138.

12 ———. Gordon W. Allport (1897–1967). *JIP,* 1968, 24, 97–98.

13 ———. The human design. *JIP,* 1964, 20, 129–136.

14 ———. The nature of faith. *JIP,* 1957, 13, 24–37.

15 ———. Self-anchoring scaling: A measure of individual's unique reality worlds. *JIP,* 1960, 16, 158–173 (with F. P. Kilpatrick).

16 **Capra, P. E.** Birth order as a selective factor among volunteer subjects. *J. abnorm. soc. Psychol.,* 1962, 64, 302 (with H. E. Dittes).

17 **Caprio, F. S.** A study of some psychological reactions during pre-pubescence to the idea of death. *Psychiat. Quart.,* 1950, 24, 495–505.

18 **Carkhuff, R. R.** Lay mental health counseling: Prospects and problems. *JIP,* 1968, 24, 88–93.

19 ———. Review of F. C. Thorne, *Integrative psychology.* Brandon, Vt.: Clin. Psychol. Publ. Co., 1967. In *JIP,* 1969, 25, 114–115.

20 **Carle, Irmgard L.** Group dynamics as applied to the use of music with schizophrenic adolescents. *J. contemp. Psychother.,* 1971, 3(2), 111–116.

21 ———. Music at Hillside Hospital. *Music J.,* 1970, 28(9A), 20–21, 47–48.

22 ———. Orff-Schulwerk: A vitalizing tool in music therapy programs. *Musart,* 1971, 23(3), 10–11, 28–31.

23 **Carmichael, L.** *Manual of child psychology.* New York: Wiley, 1946.

24 **Carnois, A.** *Le drame de l'inferiorité chez l'enfant.* Lyon: Vitte, 1958.

25 **Carossa, H.** Life-style interpretation of a mad king. *IPNL,* 1958, 9(1–2, Whole No. 89–90). P. 4.

26 **Carrigan, W. F.** Sex and birth order differences in conformity as a function of need affiliation arousal. *J. Pers. soc. Psychol.,* 1966, 3, 479–483 (with J. W. Julian).

27 **Carroll, J.** Conformity as a function of birth order, payoff, and type of group pressure. *J. abnorm. soc. Psychol.,* 1964, 69, 318–323 (with S. W. Becker & M. J. Lerner).

28 ———. Ordinal position and conformity. *J. abnorm. soc. Psychol.,* 1962, 65, 129–131 (with S. W. Becker).

29 **Cartwright, D.** (Ed.). *Studies in social power.* Ann Arbor, Mich.: Univ. Michigan, 1959.

30 **Caruso, I.** Zur Psychologie der Morphiumsucht. *IZIP,* 1947, 16(4), 152–168.

31 **Casler, L.** *Maternal deprivation: A critical review of the literature.* Yellow Springs, Ohio: Antioch Press, Soc. Res. Child Developm., 1961.

32 **Cason, H.** The learning and retention of pleasant and unpleasant activities. *Arch. Psychol.* (New York), 1932, No. 134. Pp. 96.

33 Cass, L. K. An investigation of some important variables in the parent-child relationship. Unpubl. Ph.D. Diss., Ohio St. Univ., 1950–51.

34 Cassel, Pearl. Discipline without tears. Toronto: Alfred Adler Inst., 1972 (with R. Dreikurs).

35 Cassell, R. N. Level of aspiration and sociometric distance. Sociom., 1952, 15, 318–325 (with R. C. Saugsted).

36 Castaneda, A. Anxiety in children, school achievement, and intelligence. Child Developm., 1956, 27, 379–382 (with B. R. McCandless).

37 Catlin, Nancy. Children's fears by race, sex, sibling position, grade level, and socioeconomic level. Unpubl. Ph.D. Diss., Florida St. Univ., 1972.

38 Cau, J. Freud s'est trompé. Tonus, avril, 1971.

39 Caudill, W. Sibling ranks and style of life among Japanese psychiatric patients. Folia Psychiat. Neurol. Jap., 1963, Suppl. 7.

40 Cava, Esther L. Identification and the adolescent boy's perception of his father. J. abnorm. soc. Psychol., 1952, 47, 855–856 (with H. L. Raush).

41 Cavadas, Juliet. Editor and translator of R. Dreikurs, Eclogi Dreikurs.

42 ———. Translator of R. Dreikurs, I psikhologia stin.

43 ———. Translator of R. Dreikurs, To pedi.

44 Cecetka, J. Individual Psychology.

45 Cesarec, A. Psihoanalisa i Individualna Psihologija. Zagreb: Kajizara Merkantile, 1932.

46 Chabas, Odette. La doctrine psychologique d'Alfred Adler et le respect de soi. Actes du Vème Congr. médico-social protestant, Montpélier, 30 avril-2 mai 1954, 1954, 29(2), 124–128.

47 ———. L'homme et son prochain selon la doctrine d'Alfred Adler. Proc. VIIIème Congr. des Soc. de Phil. de Langue Française, Toulouse, Sept. 6-9, 1956. Pp. 269–272.

48 ———. Intervention adlérienne. In [ ], Notion de structure et structure de la connaissance. Paris: Ed. Albin Michel, 1957.

49 ———. Liberté et valeur selon la doctrine d'Alfred Adler. Actes du XIIème Congr. Int. de Phil. Florence: Sansoni, 1961. Pp. 89–94.

50 Chabas, Odette. Portrait. IPNL, 1970, 19(4), 80.

51 ———. Quelques aspects adlériens de la santé mentale. Hyg. Ment., 1962, 5(1), 236–244. Also in Chroniques de Police, 1964, 12, No. 66. Pp. 31–40.

52 ———. Translator of A. Adler, Les névroses: Commentaires, observations, présentations de cas.

53 Chambliss, E. J. Change: A result, not a target. Texas Outlook, July, 1970 (with L. J. Lambert & J. W. Tidrow).

54 Champney, H. The variables of parent behavior. J. abnorm. soc. Psychol., 1941, 36, 525–542.

55 Chance, E. The father's perception of his first child. Unpubl. Ph.D. Diss., Stanford Univ., 1953.

56 Chantigny, J. G. Parent Practices Research Scale. Iowa City: St. Univ. Iowa, 1956 (with L. L. Lovell & B. R. McCandless).

57 Chaplin, J. P. Commentary on three Oswald interpretations. JIP, 1967, 23, 48–52.

58 ———. The presidential assassins: A confirmation of Adlerian theory. JIP, 1970, 26(2), 205–212.

59 ———. Review of D. H. Ford & H. B. Urban, Systems of psychotherapy. In JIP, 1964, 20, 105–107.

60 ———. Review of B. F. Skinner, Contingencies of reinforcement: A theoretical analysis. New York: Appleton-Century-Crofts, 1969. In JIP, 1970, 26, 83–84.

61 ———. Review of L. von Bertalanffy, Robots, men and minds: Psychology in the modern world. New York: Braziller, 1967. In JIP, 1968, 24, 195–196.

62 ———. Systems and theories of psychology. 2nd ed. New York: Holt, Rinehart, & Winston, 1968 (with T. S. Krawiec).

63 Chapman, J. E. Future expectation, social orientation, simple language. [Tribute to Alfred Adler on his 100th birthday]. JIP, 1970, 26(2), 10-11.

64 Chase, S. Utilization of childhood memories in psychoanalytic therapy. J. child Psychiat., 1951, 2, 189–193.

65 Chassé, J. V. A nervous child. IJIP, 1935, 1(2), 86–95.

66 ———. Über Heilpädagogik. IZIP, 1926, 4(6), 354–363.

67 Chein, I. The genetic factor in ahistorical psychology. J. gen. Psychol., 1947, 36, 151-172.

68 **Chenery, Janet.** *Wolfie.* New York: Harper & Row, 1969.

69 **Chernoff, M.** Parents and teachers: Friends or enemies? *Educ.*, 1970, 91, 147–154 (with R. Dreikurs).

70 **Chess, S.** Utilization of childhood memories in psychoanalytic therapy. *J. child Psychiat.*, 1951, 2, 187–193.

71 **Chiappo, L. H.** The noetic-perceptive configuration test and impairment of the abstract attitude. *JIP*, 1959, 15, 93–99.

72 **Child, I.** The relation between measures of infantile amnesia and of neuroticism. *J. abnorm. soc. Psychol.*, 1940, 35, 453–456.

73 **Chodorkoff, B.** Adjustment and the discrepancy between the perceived and ideal self. *J. clin. Psychol.*, 1954, 10, 266–268.

74 ———. Self-perception, perceptual defense, and adjustment. *J. abnorm. soc. Psychol.*, 1954, 49, 508–512.

75 **Choisy, Maryse.** Freud, Jung et Adler. *Psyché*, 1950, 5, 450–463.

76 **Cholden, L.** Observations on psychotherapy of schizophrenia. In Frieda Fromm-Reichman & J. L. Moreno (Eds.), *Progress in psychotherapy.* New York: Grune & Stratton, 1956.

77 **Chopra, S. L.** Family size and sibling position as related to intelligence test scores and academic achievement. *J. soc. Psychol.*, 1968, 70, 133–137.

78 **Chotlos, J. W.** Obsessive and hysterical syndromes in the light of existential considerations. *J. exist. Psychol.*, 1960, 1, 315–329 (with M. H. Miller).

79 **Christensen, A. H.** A quantitative study of personality dynamics in stuttering and non-stuttering siblings. *Speech Monogr.*, 1952, 19, 187–188.

80 **Christensen, O. C.** Family counseling: An Adlerian orientation. *Proc. Symp. Fam. Couns. & Ther.*, Coll. Educ., Univ. Georgia, 1971. Pp. 15–36.

81 ———. Family education: A model for consultation. *Elem. Sch. Guid. Couns.*, 1972, 7(2), 121–129.

82 ———. A model for counseling. *Elem. Sch. Guid. Couns.*, 1969, 4(1), 12–19.

83 ———. Not budgeted for a guidance counselor? You can still offer a guidance program. In *Elementary principals service: Operational briefing.* Croft Educ. Service, 1970 (with M. Arcinega).

84 **Christensen, O. C.** The protection racket and other crimes against youth. *Old Oregon*, July, 1964. Pp. 12–15.

85 ———. The students' crusade against authority. In W. L. Pew (Ed.), *The war between the generations.*

86 ———. Understanding the needs of today's youth. *4-H Leader Forum*, Mar., 1970. Pp. 1–14.

87 ———. The uncontrollable nature of control groups. *J. couns. Psychol.*, 1968, 15, 63–67 (with M. L. LeMay).

88 ———. Review of D. C. Dinkmeyer, *Child development.* In *JIP*, 1966, 22, 135.

89 **Chusmir, Janet.** Like father, like daughter [about Alexandra Adler]. *Miami Herald*, Apr. 18, 1971.

90 **Cialix, R.** La formation des maitres. *BISFPA*, 1970, No. 7. Pp. 22–25.

91 **Cizon, F.** *Men in jail.* Chicago: Loyola Univ., 1965 (with C. O'Reilly, J. Flanagan & S. Pflanczer).

92 **Claparède, E.** *Le sentiment d'infériorité chez l'enfant.* Geneva: Cahiers de Pédagogie Expérimentale et de Psychologie de l'Enfant, 1934.

93 **Clark, K. B.** *Dark ghetto.* Foreword by G. Myrdal. New York: Harper, 1965; New York: Harper Torchbooks, 1967.

94 ———. The development of consciousness of self and the emergence of racial identification in Negro pre-school children. *J. soc. Psychol.*, 1939, 10, 591–599 (with Mamie Clark).

95 ———. *Effect of prejudice and discrimination on personality development.* Fact finding report, Midcentury White House Conference on Children and Youth. Washington, D. C.: Children's Bureau, Federal Security Agency, 1950. Mimeo.

96 ———. Emotional factors in racial identification and preference in Negro children. *J. Negro Educ.*, 1950, 19, 341–350 (with Mamie Clark).

97 ———. Explosion in the ghetto. *Psychol. Today*, 1967, 1(5), 30–38, 62–64.

98 ———. Implications of Adlerian theory for an understanding of civil rights problems and action. *JIP*, 1967, 23, 181–190. Also in H. J. Vetter & B. D. Smith (Eds.), *Personality theory: A source book.* New York: Appleton-Century-Crofts, 1971.

99 ———. Job training: A need for seriousness. *Wall St. J.*, Sept. 25, 1969.

100 Clark, K. B. (Ed.). *The Negro American.* Foreword by L. B. Johnson. Boston: Houghton Mifflin, 1966; Boston: Beacon, 1966. Paper (with T. Parsons).

101 ———. The pathos of power: A psychological perspective. *Amer. Psychologist,* 1971, 26(12), 1047–1057.

102 ———. *Prejudice and your child.* 2nd ed. Boston: Beacon Press, 1963.

103 ———. Problems of power and social change: Toward a relevant social psychology. *J. soc. Issues,* 1965, 21(3), 4–20.

104 ———. Psychology and social responsibility. *APA Monitor,* 1971, 2(1), 2.

105 ———. Racial identification and preference in Negro children (with Mamie Clark). In T. M. Newcomb & E. L. Hartley (Eds.), *Readings in social psychology.* New York: Holt, 1947. Pp. 169–178.

106 ———. Segregation as a factor in racial identification of Negro pre-school children. *J. exp. Educ.,* 1939, 8, 161–163 (with Mamie Clark).

107 ———. Skin color as a factor in racial identification of Negro pre-school children. *J. soc. Psychol.,* 1940, 11, 159–169 (with Mamie Clark).

108 Clark, Mamie. The development of consciousness of self and the emergence of racial identification in Negro pre-school children. *J. soc. Psychol.,* 1939, 10, 591–599 (with K. B. Clark).

109 ———. Emotional factors in racial identification and preference in Negro children. *J. Negro Educ.,* 1950, 19, 341–350 (with K. B. Clark).

110 ———. Racial identification and preference in Negro children (with K. B. Clark). In T. M. Newcomb & E. L. Hartley (Eds.), *Readings in social psychology.* New York: Holt, 1947. Pp. 169–178.

111 ———. Segregation as a factor in racial identification of Negro pre-school children. *J. exp. Educ.,* 1939, 8, 161–163 (with K. B. Clark).

112 ———. Skin color as a factor in racial identification of Negro pre-school children. *J. soc. Psychol.,* 1940, 11, 159–169 (with K. B. Clark).

113 Clarke, A. C. Preferences of male or female children: Traditional or affectional. *Marr. Fam. Living,* 1954, 16, 128–130 (with S. Dinitz & R. R. Dynes).

114 Clarke, W. J. The problem of shading in H-T-P drawings: Its internal consis-

tency and relation to personality characteristics. *J. gen. Psychol.,* 1963, 72, 295–300 (with V. J. Bieliauskas).

115 Cleland, C. C. Birth order, sex, and achievement gain of institutionalized retardates. *Psychol. Rep.,* 1966, 19, 327–330 (with W. F. Patton).

116 Clemont, M. A. Review of Genevieve Painter, *Teach your baby.* In *IP,* 1972, 9(1), 30–31.

117 ———. Review of N. & Margaret Rau, *"My dear ones".* Englewood Cliffs, N. J.: Prentice-Hall, 1971. In *IP,* 1972, 9(1), 33–34.

118 Cline, V. B. Accuracy of interpersonal perception—a general trait? *J. abnorm. soc. Psychol.,* 1960, 60, 1–7 (with J. M. Richard

119 Coan, R. W. Contemporary ratings of psychological theorists. *Psychol. Rec.,* 1962, 12, 315–322 (with S. W. Zagona).

120 ———. Dimensions of psychological theory. *Amer. Psychologist,* 1968, 23, 715–722.

121 Cobb, S. Birth order among medical students. *J. Amer. Med. Assn.,* 1966, 195, 312–313 (with J. R. French, Jr.).

122 Cochran, J. R. *Guidance: An introduction—selected readings.* Charles E. Merrill Pub. Co., 1972 (with H. Peters).

123 Cody, J. Task group report (with T. W. Allen, J. Krumboltz, F. Robinson, W. Cottle, D. Homra, & J. Ray). In J. Whiteley (Ed.), *Research problems in counseling.* Columbus, Ohio: Charles E. Merrill, 1968. Pp. 219–237.

124 Coelho, G. V. A guide to literature on friendship: A selectively annotated bibliography. *Psychol. Nwsltr.,* 1959, 10, 365–394.

125 Coffey, H. S. Interpersonal diagnosis: Some problems of methodology and validation. *J. abnorm. soc. Psychol.,* 1955, 50, 110–124 (with T. Leary).

126 Cohen, F. Psychological characteristics of the second child as compared with the first. *Indian J. Psychol.,* 1951, 26, 79–84.

127 Cohen, L. D. Level-of-aspiration behavior and feelings of adequacy and self-acceptance *J. abnorm. soc. Psychol.,* 1954, 49, 84–86.

128 Cohn, Edith. Einführung in die Technik der Kinderanalyse. *IZIP,* 1927, 5(5), 351–356.

129 Cohn, Rosalyn. Day treatment center and school: Seven years experience. *Amer. J. Orthopsychiat.,* 1965, 15(1), 160–169

(with Ruth Ronall, Ruth la Viete & Renee Reens).

130 Cohn, Ruth C. Now there is only ONE Mother Earth: Asya L. Kadis—1902-1971. *Amer. Acad. Psychotherapists*, 1971, 15(2-3), 26.

131 Colby, K. M. On the disagreement between Freud and Adler. *Amer. Imago*, 1951, 8, 229-238. Excerpts printed in H. L. Ansbacher & Rowena Ansbacher (Eds.), *The Individual Psychology of Alfred Adler.* Pp. 69-74.

132 Cole, D. L. The influence of experimentally induced inadequacy feelings upon the appreciation of humor. *J. soc. Psychol.*, 1964, 64, 113-117.

133 Cole, Estelle M. Eine psychologische Betrachtung der Urticaria. *IZIP*, 1929, 7(1), 2-6.

134 Cole, L. E. *Human behavior: Psychology as bio-social science.* Yonkers-on-Hudson, N. Y.: World Book Co., 1953.

135 Colegrove, F. W. Individual memories. *Amer. J. Psychol.*, 1899, 10, 228-255.

136 Coleman, J. C. Specificity of attitudes toward paternal and non-parental authority figures. *JIP*, 1961, 17, 96-101 (with B. H. Marsten).

137 Coleman, R. P. *Workingman's wife: Her personality, world and life style.* Dobbs Ferry, N. Y.: Oceana Publications, 1959 (with G. Handel & L. Rainwater).

138 Collier, R. M. A figure-ground model replacing the conscious-unconscious dichotomy. *JIP*, 1964, 20, 3-16.

139 ———. A holistic-organismic theory of consciousness. *JIP*, 1963, 19, 17-26.

140 ———. Independence: An overlooked implication of the open system concept. *JIP*, 1962, 18, 103-113.

141 ———. Review of A. Gurwitsch, *The field of consciousness.* Pittsburgh: Duquesne Univ. Press, 1964. In *JIP*, 1964, 20(2), 228-229.

142 ———. Review of S. S. Tompkins, *Affect, imagery, consciousness.* New York: Springer, 1962-63. In *JIP*, 1964, 20(2), 229-230.

143 ———. The role of affect in behavior: A holistic-organismic approach. *JIP*, 1966, 22, 3-32.

144 ———. The self concept in context of a holistic-organismic theory of consciousness. *JIP*, 1965, 21, 3-17.

145 Collins, L. G. Family structure and pain reactivity. *J. clin. Psychol.*, 1966, 22, 33 (with L. A. Stone).

146 Combs, A. W. *Individual behavior.* New York: Harper, 1949, 1959 (with D. Snygg).

147 ———. Intelligence from a perceptual point of view. *J. abnorm. soc. Psychol.*, 1952, 47, 662-673.

148 ———. A phenomenological approach to adjustment theory. *J. abnorm. soc. Psychol.*, 1949, 44, 29-35.

149 ———. Self-acceptance and adjustment. *J. consult. Psychol.*, 1952, 16, 89-91 (with C. Taylor).

150 ———. The self, its derivative terms, and research. *JIP*, 1957, 13, 134-145 (with D. W. Soper). Also in A. E. Kuenzli (Ed.), *The phenomenological problem.* Pp. 31-48.

151 Commins, W. D. The complementarity of personality needs in friendship choice. *J. abnorm. soc. Psychol.*, 1960, 61, 292-294 (with Mary St. Anne Reilly & E. C. Steffic).

152 Commoss, Harriet H. Some characteristics related to social isolation of second grade children. *J. educ. Psychol.*, 1962, 53, 38-42.

153 Community Child Guidance Centers. A report. *IPB*, 1950, 8, 162-166.

154 Conn, Doris. Calendar. *IPB*, 1941, 2(1), 1-2.

155 Connors, C. K. Birth order and need for affiliation. *J. Pers.*, 1963, 31, 408-416.

156 Coopersmith, S. *The antecedents of self-esteem.* San Francisco: W. H. Freeman, 1967.

157 ———. A method for determining types of self-esteem. *J. abnorm. soc. Psychol.*, 1959, 59, 87-94.

158 ———. Studies in self-esteem. *Scientific Amer.*, 1968, 218(2), 96-106.

159 Coppock, H. Inter-trial responses as "rehearsal". *Amer. J. Psychol.*, 1947, 60, 608-616 (with O. H. Mowrer).

160 Cornelison, Alice R. The prediction of family interaction from a battery of projective techniques. *J. proj. Tech.*, 1957, 21, 199-208 (with Dorothy T. Sohler, J. D. Holzberg, S. Fleck, Eleanor Kay, & T. Lidz).

161 Cornett, S. Unpleasantness of early memories and maladjustment of children. *J. Pers.*, 1952, 20, 315-321 (with F. A. Pattie).

162 Corrigan, D. The contributions of a psychiatric nurse on a medical service. *Perspec. psychiat. Care*, 1966, 4(2), 22-37 (with

B. H. Shulman, Jean Hudnut, & Zoe Pfouts).

163 **Corsini, R. J.** The ABC's of psychological testing. *Personnel Ideas*, 1959, 1-7.

164 ———. Adler and group therapy. *IPNL*, 1958, 8(8-9, Whole No. 84-85). P. 29.

165 ———. *Adlerian family counseling.* Eugene, Ore.: Univ. Oregon Press, 1959 (with R. Dreikurs, M. Sonstegard, & R. Lowe).

166 ———. Appearance and criminology. *Amer. J. Sociol.*, 1959, 45, 49-51.

167 ———. Attitudes of San Quentin prisoners. *J. correc. Psychol.*, 1952, 4, 43-46 (with K. Bartelme).

168 ———. The behind-the-back technique in group psychotherapy. *Grp. Psychother.*, 1953, 6, 102-109.

169 ———. Bernreuter patterns of prison inmates. *J. clin. Psychol.*, 1946, 2, 283-285.

170 ———. Bibliography of group psychotherapy. *Grp. Psychother. Monogr.*, 1957, No. 29.

171 ———. The blind men and the elephant. *ETC*, 1955, 12, 245-247.

172 ———. Clinical psychology in correctional institutions. In D. Brower & L. E. Abt (Eds.), *Progress in clinical psychology.* Vol. II. Pp. 260-265.

173 ———. Counseling and psychotherapy. In E. Borgatta & W. Lambert (Eds.), *Handbook of personality theory.* Chicago: Rand McNally, 1968.

174 ———. Criminal and correctional psychology. In F. L. Marcuse (Ed.), *Areas of psychology.* New York: Harper, 1954. Pp. 148-179.

175 ———. Criminal conversion. *J. clin. Psychopath.*, 1945, 7, 139-146.

176 ———. Criminal psychology. In V. Branham & S. B. Kutash (Eds.), *Encyclopedia of criminology.* New York: Phil. Libr., 1949.

177 ———. *Critical incidents in psychotherapy.* Englewood Cliffs, N. J.: Prentice-Hall, 1959 (with S. W. Standal).

178 ———. *Critical incidents in school counseling.* New York: Prentice-Hall, 1970 (with V. Calia).

179 ———. *Critical incidents in teaching.* Englewood Cliffs, N. J.: Prentice-Hall, 1964 (with D. D. Howard).

180 ———. A cross validation of Davidson's Rorschach Adjustment Scale. *J. consult. Psychol.*, 1954, 18, 277-279.

181 **Corsini, R. J.** The dilemma of prisons. *Guardian*, 1966, 2, 1-2.

182 ———. Education and therapy. *J. correc. Educ.*, 1952, 4, 24-26.

183 ———. The elbow and feet technique. *IP*, 1970, 7(2), 47-52.

184 ———. *The family council.* Chicago: Family Educ. Assn., 1970 (with Kleona Rigney).

185 ———. Fields of psychology. *Amer. Psychologist*, 1951, 6, 177-179.

186 ———. Freud, Rogers and Moreno. *Grp. Psychother.*, 1956, 9, 274-281.

187 ———. Functions of the prison psychologist. *J. consult. Psychol.*, 1945, 9, 101-104. Also in R. I. Watson (Ed.), *The clinical method in psychology.* New York: Harper, 1949.

188 ———. Grades: Some new ideas. Selected articles for elementary school principals. *Nat. Educ. Assn.*, 1968, 137-142 (with D. Dinkmeyer).

189 ———. Group psychotherapy. In A. Nikelly (Ed.), *Techniques for behavior change.* Pp. 111-115.

190 ———. Group psychotherapy. Annual review of the year's literature. In E. A. Spiegel (Ed.), *Progress in neurology and psychiatry.* 1955, Vol. X (with J. W. Klapman); 1956, Vol. XI (with J. W. Klapman); 1957, Vol. XII (with J. W. Klapman); 1958, Vol. XIII (with J. W. Klapman); 1959, Vol. XIV (with J. W. Klapman); 1960, Vol. XV (with R. Daniels & R. McFarland).

191 ———. Group psychotherapy in correctional rehabilitation. *Brit. J. Delin.*, 1964, 15, 272-278.

192 ———. Group psychotherapy in the Midwest. *Grp. Psychother.*, 1955, 8, 316-320.

193 ———. Group psychotherapy with a hostile group. *Grp. Psychother.*, 1954, 9, 184-185.

194 ———. Historic background of group psychotherapy: A critique. *Grp. Psychother.*, 1955, 8, 213-219.

195 ———. How to improve CP. *Contemp. Psychol.*, 1961, 6, 30.

196 ———. The IDEAS technique in conference leadership. *Grp. Psychother.*, 1959, 12, 175-178.

197 ———. The Immediate Test. *J. clin. Psychol.*, 1951, 7, 127-130.

198 **Corsini, R. J.** *Immediate Test.* Beverly Hills, Cal.: Sheridan Supply Co., 1951.

199 ———. Immediate therapy. *Grp. Psychother.*, 1952, 4, 322–330.

200 ———. Immediate therapy in groups. In G. M. Gazda (Ed.), *Innovations to group psychotherapy.* Pp. 15–41.

201 ———. In memoriam: Rosemary Lippitt (1911–1958). *Grp. Psychother.*, 1958, 11, 86.

202 ———. Intelligence and aging. *J. genet. Psychol.*, 1953, 83, 249–264 (with K. K. Fassett).

203 ———. Issues in encounter groups: Comments on Coulson's article. *Couns. Psychologist*, 1970, 2(2), 28–34.

204 ———. Let's invent a first-aid kit for marriage problems. *Consultant*, 1967, 7, 40.

205 ———. Logic and the scientific method reconsidered. *Worm Runner's Dig.*, 1971, 13(2), 111–112.

206 ———. The marriage conference. *Marr. Couns. Quart.*, 1970, 5(4), 21–29.

207 ———. The meaning of Adlerian family counseling. In R. Dreikurs, R. J. Corsini, R. Lowe, & M. Sonstegard (Eds.), *Adlerian family counseling.* Pp. 1–6.

208 ———. Mechanisms of group psychotherapy. *J. abnorm. soc. Psychol.*, 1955, 51, 406–411 (with Bina Rosenberg). Also in M. Rosenbaum & M. Berger (Eds.), *Group psychotherapy and group approaches.* Pp. 340–351.

209 ———. The method of psychodrama in prison. *Grp. Psychother.*, 1951, 3, 321–326.

210 ———. *Methods of group psychotherapy.* New York: McGraw-Hill, 1957; Chicago: William James Press, 1964.

211 ———. Moreno's theory of interpersonal therapy. *Grp. Psychother.*, 1955, 8, 73–78.

212 ———. Multiple predictors of marital happiness. *Marr. Fam. Living.* 1956, 17, 240–242.

213 ———. A new compensation system for counselors. *Concept*, 1959,   (with R. E. Limbrecht).

214 ———. A new method for the administration of individual intelligence tests. *J. appl. Psychol.*, 1945, 29, 37–40.

215 ———. Nondirective vocational guidance of prison inmates. *J. clin. Psychol.*, 1947, 3, 96–100.

216 **Corsini, R. J.** *Non-verbal reasoning.* Educational-Industry Service, Univ. Chicago, 1961.

217 ———. A note towards an experimental penology. *Prison World*, 1945, 7, 5 and *passim.*

218 ———. On the theory of change resulting from group therapy. *Grp. Psychother.*, 1951, 4, 179–180.

219 ———. Penology and the attitude of prisoners. *Brit. J. Delin.*, 1953, 4, 55–58 (with K. Bartelme).

220 ———. *The Picture Test.* Educational Service Publications, 1969 (with E. F. Borgatta).

221 ———. The pin prick method of secret balloting. *J. appl. Psychol.*, 1948, 32, 641.

222 ———. Pitfalls in do-it-yourself testing. *Personnel Ideas*, 1959,   , 1–5.

223 ———. Portrait. *IPNL*, 1972, 21(6), 112; In "Let's invent a first-aid kit for marriage problems". P. 40.

224 ———. Pruritis ani. *Voices*, 1965, 1(1), 103–104.

225 ———. Psychodrama with a psychopath. *Grp. Psychother.*, 1951, 4, 33–39.

226 ———. Psychodramatic treatment of a pedophile. *Grp. Psychother.*, 1951, 4, 166–171.

227 ———. Psychological services in prisons. In V. Branham & S. B. Kutash (Eds.), *Encyclopedia of criminology.* New York: Phil. Libr., 1949.

228 ———. Psychology in prison. *Amer. Psychologist*, 1954, 9, 184–185 (with G. Miller).

229 ———. *Quick Word Test* (6 forms). World Book Co., 1960 (with E. F. Borgatta).

230 ———. *Quick Word Test.* Junior Ed. World Book Co., 1968 (with E. F. Borgatta).

231 ———. The Quick Word Test and the WAIS. *Psychol. Rep.*, 1960, 6, 201 (with E. F. Borgatta).

232 ———. Retesting prison inmates for intelligence. *J. correc. Educ.*, 1951, 3, 20–23.

233 ———. Review of K. A. Adler & Danica Deutsch (Eds.), *Essays in Individual Psychology.* In *JIP*, 1960, 16, 92–93.

234 ———. Review of L. J. Bischof, *Interpreting personality theories.* In *JIP*, 1964, 20, 232–233.

235 ———. The role of theory in integrating correctional treatment. *Univ.*

Hawaii, Proc. Inst. Youth Correc. Programs, 1965, 1, 53–57.

236 **Corsini, R. J.** *Roleplaying in business and industry.* Glencoe, Ill.: Free Press, 1961 (with M. E. Shaw & R. R. Blake).

237 ———. Role-playing: Its use in industry. *Adv. Management,* 1960.

238 ———. *Roleplaying in psychotherapy.* Chicago: Aldine, 1966.

239 ———. The roleplaying technique in business and industry. Univ. Chicago Industrial Rel. Ctr. occasional paper, 1957.

240 ———. Rudolf Dreikurs: A consensual appreciation. *JIP,* 1967, 23, 167–180.

241 ———. Season of birth and mental ability of prison inmates. *J. soc. Psychol.,* 1946, 23, 65–72.

242 ———. Semantics of intellectual classification. *J. consult. Psychol.,* 1951, 15, 487–491.

243 ———. The separation capacity of the Rorschach. *J. consult. Psychol.,* 1955, 19, 194–196 (with W. Severson, T. Tunney, & H. Uehling).

244 ———. Social perception of one other self. *J. soc. Psychol.,* 1961, 53, 235–242 (with R. H. Oakes).

245 ———. *The Standard Adjective Q-Sort.* Chicago: Psychometric Affiliates, 1956.

246 ———. A standard recording and reporting system for smoking withdrawal research. *Amer. J. Pub. Hlth.,* 1972, 62, 159–163.

247 ———. A study of certain attitudes of prison inmates. *J. crim. Law & Criminol.,* 1946, 37, 132–140.

248 ———. A time and motion study of handscoring the Minnesota Multiphasic Personality Inventory. *J. consult. Psychol.,* 1949, 13, 62–63.

249 ———. Towards a definition of group psychotherapy. *Ment. Hyg.,* 1955, 37, 647–656.

250 ———. Training through roleplaying. *Concept,* 1960, (with D. D. Howard).

251 ———. 20 years of group psychotherapy. *Amer. J. Psychiat.,* 1954, 110, 567–575 (with R. Dreikurs). Also in R. Dreikurs, *Group psychotherapy and group approaches.* Pp. 21–33.

252 **Cortada de Kohan, Nuria.** Translator of H. Ansbacher & Rowena Ansbacher (Eds.), *La Psicologia Individual de Alfred Adler: Presentacion de una selección de sus escritos.*

253 **Cottle, W.** Task group report (with T. W. Allen, J. Cody, J. Krumboltz, F. Robinson, D. Homra, & J. Ray). In J. Whiteley (Ed.), *Research problems in counseling.* Pp. 219–237.

254 **Couch, A.** Yea-sayers and nay-sayers: Agreeing response set as a personality variable. *J. abnorm. soc. Psychol.,* 1960, 60, 151–174 (with K. Deniston).

255 **Court, A. C.** Psychotherapy in general practice. *IPMP,* 1937, No. 17. Pp. 39–42.

256 ———. The parent-child relation. *IPMP,* 1937, No. 17 (with H. G. Baynes, S. Crown, S. H. Lubner, M. Marcus, & F. G. Crookshank).

257 **Covert, C.** Death attitudes and humor appreciation among medical students. *Existent. Psychiat.,* 1967, 6(24), 433–442 (with W. E. O'Connell).

258 **Cowen, E. L.** The negative self-concept as a personality measure. *J. consult. Psychol.,* 1954, 18, 138–142.

259 **Cowen, J.** Program note [Fourth Annual Conf. on Brief Psychotherapy]. *IPNL,* 1972, 21(1), 38.

260 **Cowgill, Sallie.** Wit, humor and defensiveness. *Nwsltr. Res. Psychol.,* 1970, 12, 32–33 (with W. E. O'Connell).

261 **Crandall, J. W.** The diagnostic uses of the early spouse memory in marriage counseling. *Marr. Fam. Counselors Quart.,* 1971, 6(3), 31–41.

262 ———. The early spouse memory as a diagnostic aid in marriage counseling. *J. contemp. Psychother.,* 1971, 3(2), 82–88.

263 **Cranford, I.** Review of L. W. Dodd, *The golden complex.* In *IZIP,* 1928, 6(1), 78–79.

264 ———. Review of Abbé Le Maitre, *Science and religion.* In *IZIP,* 1933, 11(2), 156–157.

265 **Crawford, Susan.** Application of Adlerian principles in kindergarten. *OSIPNL,* 1966, 7(2), 7.

266 ———. Planning for the first day of kindergarten. *OSIPNL,* 1967, 8(1), 8–9.

267 ———. Preparing parents for child's kindergarten entry. *OSIPNL,* 1967, 8(2), 4–6.

268 ———. Study groups for parents of children in kindergarten. *OSIPNL,* 1968, 9(3), 4–5.

269 **Credner, Lene.** Co-editor of L. Seif, *Wege die Erziehungshilfe.*

270 **Credner, Lene.** Neurose als Flucht von Verantwortung. *IZIP*, 1933, 11(3), 207–215.

271 ———. Neurosis as retreat from responsibility. *IJIP*, 1935, 1(3), 33–43.

272 ———. Phobia as an expedient. *IJIP*, 1935, 1(2), 34–39.

273 ———. Phobie als Mittel. *IZIP*, 1931, 9(2), 117–122.

274 ———. Review of H. Reichardt, *Die Früherinnerung als Tragerin kindlicher Selbstbeobachtungen in der ersten Lebensjahren.* Halle: Karl Marhold, 1926. In *IZIP*, 1927, 5(3), 235.

275 ———. Safeguards. *IJIP*, 1936, 2(3), 95–102.

276 ———. Sicherungen. *IZIP*, 1930, 8(1), 87–92.

277 ———. Über den Traum. *Het Kind*, 1923.

278 ———. Verwahrlosung. In E. Wexberg (Ed.), *Handbuch der Individualpsychologie.* Pp. 209–234.

279 ———. Zwei Fälle von Kindermisshandlung. *IZIP*, 1928, 6(2), 155–163.

280 **Cresta, M.** Review of Eugeni D'Ors, *La formule biologique de la logique. Arch. Neurol.*, 1910. In *ZIP*, 1914, 1(3), 92.

281 ———. Review of A. Kind & E. Fuchst, *Die Weiberschaft in der Geschichte der Menschheit.* München: A. Langen, 1913. In *ZIP*, 1913, 1(1), 27.

282 **Crichton-Miller, H.** Discipline and leadership. *IPP*, 1940, No. 22. Pp. 31–39.

283 ———. Early infancy, puberty, and adolescence. *IPMP*, 1937, No. 18 (with Joyce Partridge, T. A. Ross & F. G. Crookshank).

284 ———. Puberty and adolescence. *IPP*, 1937, No. 18. Pp. 28–32.

285 **Cripps, Jean H.** The reeducation of a pampered prince. *IP*, 1969, 6(2), 29–33 (with Ann Tuites & Nancy Blockinger).

286 **Croake, J. W.** The anxious child. *SDEA J.*, Sept., 1966, 32–34 (with K. Joy).

287 ———. Attitudes toward authority figures. *Coll. Student Survey*, 1970, 4, 60–62 (with F. Knox).

288 ———. Attitudes toward premarital behavior as a function of behavioral commitment. *Coll. Student J.*, 1972, 6.

289 ———. Attitudes toward premarital sexual behavior. In G. Neubeck, *Human sexual behavior.* Pp. 125–131.

290 **Croake, J. W.** College student attitudes toward premarital sexual behavior. *Youth Culture and Counter Culture*, SECFR, Greensboro, N. C., 1972.

291 ———. Common fears. *Florida Pupil Personnel Quart.*, 1971, 3(3), 2–4 (with F. Knox).

292 ———. Community experience with the 1969 attack on sex education. *Fam. Coordinator*, 1970, 19(1), 104–110.

293 ———. Dissonance theory and fear retention. *Psychol.*, Aug., 1969, 19–23.

294 ———. The family life educator of the future. *Fam. Coordinator*, 1971, 20(4), 315–325.

295 ———. Fears of adolescence. *J. Adolesc.*, 1967, 7(8), 459–469.

296 ———. Fears of children. In R. Smart & Mollie Smart (Eds.), *Readings in child development and relationships.*

297 ———. Fears of children. *Hum. Developm.*, 1969, 12(4), 239–247.

298 ———. Fears of Nebraska children. *Guid. Bull.*, Mar., 1968, 7–11.

299 ———. Fears of South Dakota children. *South Dakota Educ. J.*, Nov.–Dec., 1968, 28–31.

300 ———. Group counseling. *Psychol. in the Schools*, 1970, 7(1), 32–36.

301 ———. Group marriage counseling: A review and proposal. *Marr. Couns. Quart.*, Winter, 1971, 42–47 (with B. E. James).

302 ———. How far are students ready to go? *Sexol.*, May, 1970, 49–52 (with B. E. James).

303 ———. Isometrics in the elementary classroom. *Instructor*, Aug.–Sept., 1966, 128–132.

304 ———. Latent learning. *Wash.–Ore. Psychol. Assn.*, Spring, 1963.

305 ———. Non-reinforced learning: A critical review. *Interamer. J. Psychol.*, Winter, 1972, 17–32.

306 ———. Reasons for college attendance. *Coll. Student Survey*, 1967, 1(1), 32–34.

307 ———. A reinvestigation of fear retention and dissonance. *Psychol.*, 1971, 8(1) (with F. Knox).

308 ———. Restitution for destruction: Family council involvement. *IP*, 1971, 9(1), 4–7.

309 ———. Review of R. Dreikurs, *Social equality.* In *JIP*, 1971, 27(2), 226–228.

310 **Croake, J. W.** A second look at adolescent fears. *Adolesc.*, 1971, 6(23), 279–284 (with F. Knox).

311 ———. Training children to live in a democracy. *Florida Educ. J.*, 1971, 49(1), 23–27.

312 ———. TV and the development of the getting personality. *Alfred Adler Inst. of Minnesota*, Nov.–Dec., 1972.

313 ———. Unrewarded exploration and maze learning. *Psychol. Rep.*, 1971, 29, 1335–1340.

314 ———. Upward Bound at the University of South Dakota. *Dakota Bull.*, Summer, 1967, 3-6.

315 ———. Value orientation of college students. *Coll. Student Survey*, 1967, 1(4), 28–29.

316 ———. Whatever happened to the parlor? *J. Home Econ.*, 1972, 64(4), 22–28.

317 **Crocker, Dorothy.** Music therapy with psychotic children. *Mus. Ther.*, 1955, 5, 62–73 (with R. Dreikurs). Also in R. Dreikurs, *Child guidance and education.* Pp. 50–58.

318 **Cronbach, L. J.** Further evidence on response sets and test designs. *Educ. psychol. Measmt.*, 1950, 10, 3–31.

319 ———. Response sets and test validity. *J. educ. Psychol.*, 1946, 6, 616–623.

320 **Crook, G. H.** Memory of infantile life—Scrap of personal experience. *J. abnorm. soc. Psychol.*, 1925, 20, 90–91.

321 **Crook, M. N.** A quantitative investigation of early memories. *J. soc. Psychol.*, 1931, 2, 252–255 (with L. Harden).

322 **Crookshank, F. G.** Anorexia nervosa. *IPP*, 1931, No. 2 (with W. Langdon-Brown, J. C. Young, G. Gordon & C. M. Bevan-Brown).

323 ———. Anorexia nervosa. *IPP*, 1931, No. 2. Pp. 19–40.

324 ———. *Diagnosis and spiritual healing.* London: Kegan Paul, Trench, Trubner, 1927.

325 ———. Early infancy, puberty and adolescence. *IPMP*. 1937, No. 18 (with Joyce Partridge, H. Crichton-Miller, & T. A. Ross).

326 ———. *Epidemiological essays.* New York: Macmillan, 1930.

327 ———. *Essays and clinical studies.* London: H. K. Lewis, 1911.

328 ———. The family, society, and education. *IPP*, 1938, No. 20. Pp. 54–68.

329 **Crookshank, F. G.** *Flatulence and shock.* London: H. K. Lewis, 1912.

330 ———. Foreword to A. Adler, *The case of Mrs. A.* Pp. 7–12.

331 ———. The history and basis of Individual Psychology. *IPP*, 1936, No. 15. Pp. 60–72.

332 ———. Humanizing medicine. *IJIP*, 1937, 3(4), 288–302.

333 ———. The importance of a theory of signs and a critique of language in the study of medicine. In C. K. Ogden & I. A. Richards (Eds.), *The meaning of meaning.* London: Routledge & Kegan Paul, 1956. Pp. 337–355.

334 ———. *Individual diagnosis.* London: Kegan Paul, Trench, Trubner, 1930, 1950.

335 ———. Individualpsychologie. *IZIP*, 1930, 8(3), 335–353.

336 ———. Individualpsychologie und allgemeine Medizin. Translated by Trudi Seif. *IZIP*, 1932, 10(1), 35–52.

337 ———. *Individual Psychology and general medicine.* Cambridge, England: King's Parade, 1930.

338 ———. Individual Psychology and ill-health. *IPMP*, 1933, No. 9. Pp. 46–55.

339 ———. Individual Psychology, medicine, and the bases of science. *IPMP*, 1932, No. 3a.

340 ———. Individual Psychology and Nietzsche. *IPMP*, 1933, No. 10. Pp. 7–76.

341 ———. Individual Psychology and psychosomatic disorders. *IPMP*, 1932, No. 4 (with W. Langdon-Brown, O. H. Woodcock, J. C. Young, S. V. Pearson, M. B. Ray, & M. Robb).

342 ———. Individual Psychology and psychosomatic disorders (II). *IPP*, 1933, No. 9 (with J. S. Fairbairn, W. M. Eccles, M. Marcus & Mary B. Ferguson).

343 ———. Individual Psychology and sex. *IPMP*, 1934, No. 13. Pp. 37–54.

344 ———. Individual Psychology and the sexual demand. *IPP*, 1939, No. 21. Pp. 39–54.

345 ———. Individual Psychology and sexual difficulties (I). *IPP*, 1932, No. 3 (with A. Adler, R. Dreikurs, E. Wexberg, [Adele] Hervat, J. C. Young, Mary C. Luff and others).

346 ———. Individual Psychology and sexual difficulties (II). *IPP*, 1934, No. 13 (with A. Adler).

347 Crookshank, F. G. Individual Psychology: Theory and practice. *IPMP*, 1936, No. 15 (with S. M. Bevan-Brown & G. E. S. Ward).

348 ———. *Individual sexual problems.* London: Kegan Paul, Trench, Trubner, 1931, 1932.

349 ——— (Ed.). *Influenza.* London: Heinemann, 1922.

350 ———. Inter-relation of physical and psychical. *IJIP*, 1937, 3(2), 121–127.

351 ———. Introduction to A. Adler, *Problems of neurosis.*

352 ———. Introduction to E. Wexberg, *Individual Psychology and sex.*

353 ———. *Migraine: And other common neuroses.* London: Kegan Paul, Trench, Trubner, 1926.

354 ———. *Mongol in our midst: A story of man and his three faces.* New York: Dutton, 1927; London: Kegan Paul, Trench, Trubner, 1931.

355 ———. The neurotic character. *IPP*, 1937, No. 18. Pp. 49–60.

356 ———. Organ inferiorities. *IPP*, 1936, No. 16. Pp. 44–56.

357 ———. The parent-child relation. *IPMP*, 1937, No. 17 (with H. G. Baynes, S. Crown, S. H. Lubner, A. C. Court, & M. Marcus).

358 ———. Personality, character, life style and the demands of life. *IPP*, 1937, No. 17. Pp. 47–59.

359 ———. Physical findings in psychoneuroses. *IPMP*, 1932, No. 4. Pp. 67–68.

360 ———. Place of psychology in the medical curriculum. *IPMP*, 1936, No. 16 (with W. Langdon-Brown, R. G. M. Ladell, & F. Gray).

361 ———. Prefatory essay to A. Adler, *Problems of neurosis.* Pp. vii–xxxvii.

362 ———. The relation of history and philosophy to medicine. In C. G. Cumston, *An introduction to the history of medicine.* New York: Knopf, 1926.

363 ———. Review of E. Wexberg, *Individual Psychology and sex.* In *IPMP*, 1932, No. 3. Pp. 67–70.

364 ———. The treatment of sexual incompetence by the methods of Individual Psychology. *IPMP*, 1932, No. 3. Pp. 29–49 (with J. C. Young).

365 Crown, B. M. Construct validity of the Ebner-Shaw test of reconciliation. *JIP*, 1968, 24, 177–180 (with D. O'Donovan).

366 Crown, S. The parent-child relation. *IPMP*, 1937, No. 17 (with H. G. Baynes, S. H. Lubner, A. C. Court, M. Marcus, & F. G. Crookshank).

367 ———. Psychotherapy in general practice. *IPP*, 1937, No. 17. Pp. 29–34.

368 Crowne, D. P. Self-acceptance and self-evaluative behavior: A critique of methodology. *Psychol. Bull.*, 1961, 58, 104–121 (with M. W. Stephens).

369 ———. Review of S. Schachter, *The psychology of affiliation.* In *JIP*, 1962, 18, 92–94.

370 Crowther, H. *The oblique equalizer.* New York: Vantage Press, 1965.

371 Crumbaugh, J. C. The case for Frankl's "will to meaning". *J. exis. Psychol.*, 1963, 4, 43–48 (with L. T. Maholick).

372 ———. Cross-validation of purpose-in-life test based on Frankl's concepts. *JIP*, 1968, 24, 74–81.

373 ———. An experimental study in existentialism: The psychometric approach to Frankl's concept of *noogenic* neurosis. *J. clin. Psychol.*, 1964, 20, 200–207 (with L. T. Maholick).

374 Cruze, W. W. *Educational psychology.* New York: Ronald Press, 1942.

375 Curtius, F. Organminderwertigkeit und Erbenlage. *Klin. Wchnschr.*, 1932, 5, 177–180.

376 Cushna, B. First born and last born children in a child development clinic. *JIP*, 1964, 20, 179–182 (with M. Greene & B. C. F. Snyder).

377 Cutts, Norma. *The only child.* New York: Putnam, 1954 (with N. Moseley).

378 Czaczkes, W. Review of A. Brauchle, *Hypnose und Autosuggestion.* Leipzig: Reclam, 1929. In *IZIP*, 1930, 8(2), 274.

D

1 Daack, Georgia. Portrait. *IPNL*, 1971, 20(6), 112.

2 Dahlberg, G. Do parents want boys or girls? *Acta Genet.*, 1948, 1, 163–167.

3 Dailey, C. A. The experimental study of clinical guessing. *JIP*, 1966, 22, 65–79.

4 ———. Natural history and phenomenology. *JIP*, 1960, 16, 36–44.

5 **Daleiden, G.** Review of E. L. Phillips, D. N. Wiener, & N. G. Haring, *A teacher's guide to wholesome action.* Englewood Cliffs, N. J.: Prentice-Hall, 1960. In *OSIPNL*, 1964, 5(2), 10.

6 **Dameron, L.** Mother-child interaction in the development of self-restraint. *J. genet. Psychol.*, 1955, 86, 289–308.

7 **Dana, R. H.** From therapists anonymous to therapeutic community. *JIP*, 1963, 19, 185–190.

8 ———. Psychopathology: A developmental interpretation. *JIP*, 1965, 21, 58–65.

9 **Daniels, G.** Translator of A. Adler, *The problem child.*

10 ———. Group psychotherapy (with R. J. Corsini & R. McFarland). In E. A. Spiegel (Ed.), *Progress in neurology and psychiatry.* New York: Grune & Stratton, 1960, Vol. 15. Pp. 526–534.

11 **Danshen, D. G.** An introduction to K. S. U. students. Unpubl. report. Kansas St. Univ., Student Counseling Ctr., Sept., 1964.

12 **Darmstadter, H. J.** The superior attitude and rigidity of ideas. *Arch. Neurol. Psychiat.*, 1949, 61, 621–643.

13 **Das, J. P.** Differential learning and forgetting as a function of the social frame of reference. *J. abnorm. soc. Psychol.*, 1960, 61, 82–86 (with R. N. Kanurgo).

14 **Datta, L. E.** Birth order and early scientific attainment. *Percep. mot. Skills*, 1967, 24, 157–158.

15 **Dauber, Devorah.** Portrait. *IPNL*, 1970, 19(4), 79.

16 **Dauber, M.** Translator of R. Dreikurs, *Psichologia ba-kitah.*

17 **Däumling, A.** Psychologische Leitbild-theorien. *Psychol. Rundsch.*, 1960, 11, 92–108.

18 ——— (Ed.). *Seelenleben und Menschenbild.* München: Barth, 1958.

19 **Davidson, K. S.** Differences between mothers' and fathers' ratings of low-anxious and high-anxious children. *Child Developm.*, 1958, 29, 155–160 (with S. B. Sarason, F. F. Lightfall, R. R. Waite, & I. Sarnoff).

20 **Davis, Alice.** Wird der Lebensstil eines Menschen von der Umgebung bestimmt? *IZIP*, 1934, 12(2), 123–125.

21 **Davis [   ].** Review of H. N. Bosshard, *Our attitude toward mental patients.* In *IZIP*, 1932, 10(6), 479.

22 **Davis [   ].** Review of R. Dodge and E. Kahn, *The craving for superiority.* In *IZIP*, 1932, 10(3), 232.

23 ———. Review of F. Krüger, *Die Aufgaben der Psychologie an den deutschen Hochschulen.* Jena: Gustav Fischer, 1932. In *IZIP*, 1932, 10(6), 479.

24 ———. Review of P. H. Ronge, *Über Kausalität und Finalität in der Psychologie.* In *IZIP*, 1932, 10(6), 478–479.

25 **Davis, D. R.** The effect of one experience upon the recall of another. *Quart. J. exp. Psychol.*, 1950, 2, 43–52 (with D. Sinha).

26 **Davis, K. A.** Value consensus and need complementarity in mate selection. *Amer. sociol. Rev.*, 1962, 27, 295–303 (with A. Kerckhoff).

27 **Davis, W. A.** *Father of the man.* Boston: Houghton Mifflin, 1947 (with R. J. Havighurst).

28 **Davol, S. H.** The role of anomie as a psychological concept. *JIP*, 1959, 15, 215–225 (with G. Reimanis).

29 **Dean, D. A.** The relation of ordinal positions to personality in young children. Unpubl. master's thesis, St. Univ. Iowa, 1947.

30 **Deane, W. N.** Attendant-patient commonality as a psychotherapeutic factor. *JIP*, 1962, 18, 157–167 (with H. L. Ansbacher).

31 ———. On talking with the deluded schizophrenic patient in social therapy. *JIP*, 1963, 19, 191–203.

32 ———. Rehabilitation of chronic schizophrenic patients for social living. *JIP*, 1960, 16, 189–196 (with G. W. Brooks & H. L. Ansbacher).

33 ———. Review of A. Adler, *Understanding human nature.* In *JIP*, 1965, 21(2), 221–222.

34 ———. Review of J. W. Bockoven, *Moral treatment in American psychiatry.* New York: Springer, 1963. In *JIP*, 1963, 19, 239–240.

35 **de Buda, A.** Portrait. *IPNL*, 1970, 19(4), 79.

36 **De Busscher, J.** Alfred Adler and psychotherapy. *IP*, 1967, 4(2), 35–40.

37 **Dechene, H. C.** *Geschwisterkonstellation und psychische Fehlentwicklung.* München: J. A. Barth, 1967.

38 **Decker, F. J.** A study of juvenile theft. *J. educ. Res.*, 1929, 20, 81–87 (with H. J. Baker & A. S. Hill).

39 **Decurtius, F.** Hinrichsens Beziehungen zur Individualpsychologie. *Allgem. Z. Psychiat. psychisch-gerichtliche Med.*, 1931, 95.

40 **de Koningh, H. L.** De schichtentheorie met Betrekking tot de Bouw van de menselijke Personlijkherd. *MNWIP*, 1971, 21(1),

41 **Delhez, J. A.** Portrait. *IPNL*, 1970, 19(4), 80.

42 **De Lint, J. E. E.** Alcoholism, birth order and socializing agents. *J. abnorm. soc. Psychol.*, 1964, 69, 457–458.

43 ———. Note on birth order and intelligence test performance. *J. Psychol.*, 1967, 66, 15–17.

44 **Dellaert, R.** L'énurésie: Syndrome psychiatrique. *Acta neurol. psychiat. Belgique*, 1950, 50, 26–39.

45 **De Martino, M. F.** (Ed.). *Understanding human motivation.* Cleveland: Howard Allen, 1958 (with C. L. Stacey).

46 **Dember, W. N.** Birth order and need affiliation. *Amer. Psychologist*, 1963, 18, 356 (Abstract).

47 **Dembo, Tamara.** Das Ärger als dynamisches Problem. *Psychol. Forsch.*, 1931, 15, 1–44.

48 **Demos, R.** Lying to oneself. *J. Phil.*, 1960, 57, 588–595.

49 **Denenberg, V. H.** (Ed.). *Readings in the development of behavior.* Stamford, Conn.: Sinauer, 1972.

50 **Denig, F.** Review of H. C. Dechene, *Geschwisterkonstellation und psychische Fehlentwicklung.* In *JIP*, 1969, 25, 113–114.

51 **Deniston, K.** Yea-sayers and nay-sayers: Agreeing response set as a personality variable. *J. abnorm. soc. Psychol.*, 1960, 60, 151–174 (with A. Couch).

52 **Dennerline, June.** Test für moralische Meinung. *IZIP*, 1928, 6(5), 347–349 (with Marie Rasey).

53 **Dennis, N.** Alfred Adler and the style of life. *Encounter*, [   ], 35(2), 5–11.

54 ———. *Cards of identity.* London: Weidenfeld, 1950; London: Penguin, 1960. Paper.

55 ———. Doomed to a smokeless agony. *Life*, Nov. 17, 1958.

56 ———. Man with a will. *Time*, June 30, 1958.

57 ———. "Papa Freud". A review of E. L. Freud (Ed.), *Letters of Sigmund Freud, 1873–1939.* London: Hogarth, 1960. In *London Sunday Telegraph*, June 18, 1961.

58 **Dennis, N.** Review of A. Storr, *Human aggression.* In *London Sunday Telegraph*, June 30, 1968.

59 ———. Treasury of eccentricities. *Life*, Dec. 2, 1957.

60 **Depelchin, R.** *De Opvattingen van Alfred Adler over de Droom.* Louvain, Belgium: Catholic Univ., 1963.

61 **De Porte, Elizabeth.** Suicide in twins and only children. *Amer. J. hum. Genet.*, 1949, 1, 113–126 (with F. J. Kallman, J. De Porte & Lissy Feingold).

62 **De Porte, J.** Suicide in twins and only children. *Amer. J. hum. Genet.*, 1949, 1, 113–126 (with F. J. Kallman, Elizabeth De Porte & Lissy Feingold).

63 **Derbolowsky, U.** (Ed.). *Die Wirklichkeit und das Böse.* Hamburg: Hans Christian Verlag, 1970 (with E. Stephan).

64 **Derognat, Denise.** Caractère et environnement. *BSFPA*, 1972, No. 14. Pp. 19–29.

65 ———. Dysgraphie comme expression d'une personnalité decouragée. *BISFPA*, 1970 (avril), No. 7. Pp. 15–18.

66 ———. L'homme, être social. *BSFPA*, 1971, No. 9. Pp. 25–29; 1971, No. 10. Pp. 24–27.

67 ———. Perspectives adlériennes en rééducation psychomotrice. *Thérapie psychomotrice*, 1970, No. 8. Pp. 1–38. Also *BSFPA*, 1972, No. 12. Pp. 12–20.

68 **De Rosis, Helen A.** Supervision of first-year psychiatric residents. *Psychiat. Quart.*, 1970, 44, 435–442.

69 **de Saussure, R.** Les sentiments d'inferiorité. *Ann. Médico-psychologiques*, [   ], 15,

70 **de Souza, D.** Quelques aspects de la délinquance juvénile. *BSFPA*, 1972, No. 12. Pp. 5–11.

71 **Deutsch, Danica.** Activité des groupes Adleriens à l'étranger. *Bull. du Centre de Psychol. Adlérienne*, 1950, No. 1. Pp. 10–11.

72 ———. Alfred Adler and Margaret Mead: A juxtaposition. *JIP*, 1966, 22, 228–233.

73 ———. Alfred Adler Mental Hygiene Clinic, 1966-1968 report. *JIP*, 1969, 25, 133–135.

74 ———. Alfred Adler's theory of compensation applied to current studies on sidedness. *IPB*, 1947, 6, 27–31 (with Asya Kadis).

75 **Deutsch, Danica.** A case of transvestism. *Amer. J. Psychother.*, 1954, 8, 239-242.

76 ———. A case of transvestitism. *Case Rep. clin. Psychol.*, 1956, 3(3-4), 109-179. Also in K. A. Adler & Danica Deutsch (Eds.), *Essays in Individual Psychology*. Pp. 328-329.

77 ———. Coercion in the nursery school. *Nerv. Child*, 1946, 5, 244-246 (with Sylvia Fischer).

78 ———. Didactic group discussion with mothers in a child guidance setting. *Grp. Psychother.*, 1958, 1, 52-56. Also in K. A. Adler & Danica Deutsch (Eds.), *Essays in Individual Psychology*. Pp. 247-255.

79 ———. Eighth annual report of the Alfred Adler Consultation Center and Mental Hygiene Clinic. *AJIP*, 1956, 12, 180-182.

80 ———. Eleventh annual report of the Alfred Adler Consultation Center and Mental Hygiene Clinic. *JIP*, 1959, 15, 233-234.

81 ———. Erwin O. Krausz (1887-1968). *JIP*, 1968, 24, 217-218.

82 ——— (Ed.). *Essays in Individual Psychology: Contemporary applications of Alfred Adler's theories*. New York: Grove Press, 1959 (with K. A. Adler).

83 ———. Extracts from the tenth annual report of the Alfred Adler Consultation Center and Mental Hygiene Clinic. In K. A. Adler & Danica Deutsch (Eds.), *Essays in Individual Psychology*. Pp. 457-460.

84 ———. Family therapy and family life style. *JIP*, 1967, 23, 217-223.

85 ———. Fourteenth annual report of the Alfred Adler Mental Hygiene Clinic, New York. *JIP*, 1962, 18, 187.

86 ———. Group therapy with married couples. The birth pangs of a new family life style in marriage. *IP*, 1967, 4(2), 56-62.

87 ———. An instance of Adlerian psychotherapy. *Case Rep. clin. Psychol.*, 1956, 3(3-4), 113-120.

88 ———. A multiple approach to child guidance. *JIP*, 1957, 13, 171-175.

89 ———. Ninth annual report of the Alfred Adler Consultation Center and Mental Hygiene Clinic. *JIP*, 1957, 13, 194-196.

90 ———. [Obituary for E. Froeschels]. *IPNL*, 1972, 21(4), 68.

91 **Deutsch, Danica.** Portrait. *IPNL*, 1970, 19(4), 79; 1971, 20(6), 111.

92 ———. Review of *Aspects of family mental health in Europe*. Geneva: World Hlth. Org., 1965. In *JIP*, 1967, 23, 122-123.

93 ———. Review of Evelyn West Ayrault, *You can raise your handicapped child*. In *JIP*, 1966, 22, 138-139.

94 ———. Review of D. Carnegie, *How to stop worrying and start living*. New York: Simon & Schuster, 1948. In *IPB*, 1949, 7, 95-96.

95 ———. Review of R. May, *The art of counseling*. New York: Abingdon Press, n.d. In *JIP*, 1960, 16, 108.

96 ———. Review of K. Menninger, M. Mayman, & P. Pruyser, *The vital balance*. New York: Viking Press, 1963. In *JIP*, 1965, 21(1), 96-97.

97 ———. Review of A. S. Neill, *Summerhill*. New York: Hart, 1960. In *JIP*, 1962, 18, 194-196.

98 ———. Review of J. Rattner, *Psychologie und Psychopathologie des Liebeslebens*. In *JIP*, 1967, 23, 247-248.

99 ———. Review of L. Steiner, *Where do people take their troubles?* and *A practical guide for troubled people*. In *AJIP*, 1954, 11, 91.

100 ———. Review of *Summerhill: For and against*. In *JIP*, 1970, 26, 235-236.

101 ———. Review of W. F. Vaughan, *The lure of superiority* and *Personal and social adjustment*. In *AJIP*, 1954, 11, 93-94.

102 ———. Sixteenth-seventeenth annual report, Alfred Adler Mental Hygiene Clinic, New York. *JIP*, 1965, 21, 206-207.

103 ———. A step toward successful marriage. *AJIP*, 1956, 12, 78-83.

104 ———. Tenth annual report of the Alfred Adler Mental Hygiene Clinic. *JIP*, 1958, 14, 185-187.

105 ———. Thirteenth annual report of the Alfred Adler Mental Hygiene Clinic, New York. *JIP*, 1961, 17, 222-223.

106 ———. Twelfth annual report of the Alfred Adler Consultation Center and Mental Hygiene Clinic. *JIP*, 1960, 16, 208-209.

107 ———. Two "psychosomatic" case histories. *AJIP*, 1954, 10, 186-189.

108 **Deutsch, L.** Die Erziehungsaufgabe des Klavierunterrichts. *IZIP*, 1929, 7(1), 47-50.

109 **Deutsch, L.** From causality to creative freedom. *IPB*, 1951, 9, 133-142.

110 ———. *Guided sight reading.* New York: Crown, 1950; Chicago, Nelson Hall, 1959; Chicago: Alfred Adler Inst., n.d. Paper.

111 ———. *Individualpsychologie im Musik-unterricht: Ein Beitrag zur Grundlegung musikalischer Gemeinkultur.* Leipzig: Steingräber, 1931.

112 ———. Individual Psychology and pedagogy. *IPB*, 1947, 6, 48-50.

113 ———. *Klavierspiel.* Leipzig: Steingräber, 1929.

114 ———. Kritische Betrachtungen. *IZIP*, 1948, 17(2), 84-91.

115 ———. Menschenkenntnis und Naturwis-senschaft. *IZIP*, 1950, 19(1), 20-25.

116 ———. Portrait. *IPNL*, 1970, 19(4), 61.

117 ———. Review of P. Lecomte du Noüy, *Human destiny.* New York: Longmans, Green, 1947. In *IPB*, 1949, 7, 94-95.

118 ———. Review of E. Froeschels, *The human race.* In *IPB*, 1949, 7, 33.

119 ———. Review of L. R. Hubbard, *Dianetics.* New York: Hermitage House, 1950. In *IPB*, 1951, 9, 38-39; *IZIP*, 1951, 20(2), 92-93.

120 ———. Review of P. Mullahy, *Oedipus, myth and complex.* In *IPB*, 1951, 9, 174.

121 ———. Review of F. J. Sheen, *Lift up your heart.* New York: McGraw-Hill, 1950. In *IPB*, 1951, 9, 37-38.

122 ———. Self-review of *Klavierspiel.* In *IZIP*, 1930, 8(6), 599-600.

123 ———. Talent or training? *IPB*, 1944-45, 4, 79-84.

124 ———. *A treasury of the world's finest folk song.* Rev. ed. New York: Crown, 1967.

125 ———. Von Kausalität zu Schöpferischer Freiheit. *IZIP*, 1951, 20(4), 165-174.

126 ———. Woman's role: An Adlerian view. *JIP*, 1970, 26(2), 122-123.

127 **Deutsch, M.** Cooperation and trust: Some theoretical notes. In M. R. Jones (Ed.), *Nebraska symposium on motivation, 1962.* Lincoln, Nebr.: Univ. Nebraska Press, 1962. Pp. 275-319.

128 ———. A theory of cooperation and com-petition. *Hum. Rel.,* 1949, 2, 129-151.

129 **de Vries, Sophie.** Some basic princi-ples of Adlerian psychology. *IPB*, 1951, 9, 149-151.

130 **Dewey, Edith.** Family atmosphere. In A. Nikelly (Ed.), *Techniques for behavior change.* Pp. 41-47.

131 ———. Family climate. In *The vital years—From birth to seven.* Toronto: Ontario Fed. Home & Sch. Assns., 1969.

132 ———. Understanding ourselves, topics for advanced study group. *OSIPNL*, 1968, 9(2), 6 (with M. Dewey).

133 **Dewey, J.** *Individualism old and new.* New York: Capricorn Books, 1962.

134 ———. Individualität in der Gegenwart. *IZIP*, 1930, 8(6), 567-576.

135 ———. Individuality in our day. In *Indi-vidualism old and new.* New York: Capri-corn Books, 1962. Ch. 8.

136 **Dewey, M.** Understanding ourselves, topics for advanced study group. *OSIPNL*, 1968, 9(2), 6 (with Edith Dewey).

137 **Dexter, Emily S.** Three items related to personality: Popularity, nicknames, and homesickness. *J. soc. Psychol.,* 1949, 30, 155-158.

138 **De Wit, G. A.** *Symbolism of masculinity and femininity.* New York: Springer, 1963.

139 **Dey, M.** An attempt to analyse the effect of non-competitive co-acting group. *Indian J. Psychol.,* 1949, 49, 86-95.

140 **Diab, L. N.** Authoritarian ideology and attitudes on parent-child relationships. *J. abnorm. soc. Psychol.,* 1955, 51, 13-16 (with S. L. Kates).

141 ———. Cross-cultural study of some cor-relates of birth order. *Psychol. Rep.,* 1968, 22, 1137-1142 (with E. T. Prothro).

142 **Dickerson, R. E.** *How character develops.* New York: Scribner, 1940 (with F. Künkel).

143 **Dickinson, Emily.** The goal. *IZIP*, 1928, 6(5), 386.

144 **Dickey, Brenda A.** Attitudes toward sex roles and feelings of adequacy in homo-sexual males. *J. consult. Psychol.,* 1961, 25, 116-122.

145 **Dicks, H. V.** Analysis under hypnotics. *IPP*, 1943, No. 23. Pp. 43-58.

146 **Dietz, P.** A case of extreme discourage-ment. *IJIP*, 1936, 2(4), 66-74.

147 ———. Ein extremer Fall von Entmutig-ungsneurose. *IZIP*, 1928, 6(4), 313-320.

148 **Dijkema, P.** Translator of A. Adler *et al., Het Moelijke Kindern.*

149 **Diller, L.** Conscious and unconscious self-attitudes after success and failure. *J. Pers.,* 1954, 23, 1-12.

150 **Dimond, R. E.** Ordinal position of birth and self-disclosure in high school students. *Psychol. Rep.*, 1968, 21, 829–833 (with D. C. Munz).

151 **Dinitz, S.** Decision-making in a mental hospital: Real, perceived, ideal. *Amer. sociol. Rev.*, 1959, 24, 822–829 (with M. Lefton & B. Pasamanick).

152 ———. Preferences of male or female children: Traditional or affectional. *Marr. Fam. Living*, 1954, 16, 128–130 (with R. R. Dynes & A. C. Clarke).

153 **Dinkmeyer, D.** The "C" group: Integrating knowledge and experience to change behavior: An Adlerian approach to consultation. *Couns. Psychologist*, 1971, 3(1), 63–72.

154 ———. *Child development: The emerging self.* Englewood Cliffs, N. J.: Prentice-Hall, 1965.

155 ———. Child development research and the elementary school teacher. In W. Foster & [   ] Jacobs (Eds.), *Problems of the beginning elementary school teacher.*

156 ———. *Como estimular al niño: El proceso del estimulo.* Translated by J. A. Baca. Valencia: Alcoy, 1960 (with R. Dreikurs).

157 ———. Conceptual foundations of counseling: Adlerian theory and practice. *Sch. Counselor*, 1964, 11(3), 174–178. Also in *OSIPNL*, 1964, 5(2).

158 ———. The consultant in elementary school guidance. In H. Peters, A. Riccio, & J. Quaranta (Eds.), *Guidance in the elementary school.* Pp. 281–286.

159 ———. Contributions of teleoanalytic theory and techniques to school counseling. *Pers. Guid. J.*, 1968, 46, 898–902.

160 ———. Counseling theory and practice in the elementary school. In J. Hansen (Ed.), *APGA Reprint Series Two*, 1971.

161 ———. The counselor as consultant to the teacher. In R. Dreikurs (Ed.), *Education, guidance, psychodynamics.* Pp. 6–11.

162 ———. *Developmental counseling and guidance: A comprehensive approach.* New York: McGraw-Hill, 1970 (with E. Caldwell).

163 ———. Developmental counseling in the elementary school. In H. Peters & M. Bathory (Eds.), *School counseling: Perspectives and procedures.* Pp. 105–111.

164 ———. *Encorajando crianças a apprender* [Encouraging children to learn]. Translated by Terezinha Eboli & Yedda Salles. Sao Paolo, Brazil: Edicoes Melhoramentos, 1972 (with R. Dreikurs).

165 **Dinkmeyer, D.** *Encouraging children to learn: The encouragement process.* Englewood Cliffs, N. J.: Prentice-Hall, 1963 (with R. Dreikurs).

166 ———. *Ermutigung als Lernhilfe.* Stuttgart: Ernst Klett, 1970 (with R. Dreikurs).

167 ———. Grades: Some new ideas. Selected articles for elementary school principals. *Nat. Educ. Assn.*, 1968, 137–142 (with R. J. Corsini).

168 ———. *Group counseling theory and practice.* Itasca, Ill.: Peacock Press, 1971 (with J. J. Muro).

169 ———. Group counseling theory and techniques. In J. R. Cochran & H. J. Peters (Eds.), *Guidance: An introduction.* Also in *Sch. Counselor*, 1969, 17(2), 148–152.

170 ——— (Ed.). *Guidance and counseling in the elementary school: Readings in theory and practice.* New York: Holt, Rinehart & Winston, 1968.

171 ———. Guidance and instruction: Complementary for the educative process. *Elem. Sch. Guid. Couns.*, 1969, 3(4), 260–268 (with Karen Owens).

172 ———. Guidance for every child. *New Era*, 1969, 50(6), 143–147.

173 ———. Humanizing the educational process through guidance procedures. *Lutheran Educ.*, 1970, 105(5), 237–242.

174 ———. The process of encouragement (with A. G. Nikelly). In A. Nikelly (Ed.), *Techniques for behavior change.* Pp. 97–101.

175 ———. The school age child. In *Childcraft*, 1964. Pp. 342–345.

176 ———. The teacher as counselor: Therapeutic approaches to understanding self and others. *Childhood Educ.*, 1970, 46, 314–317.

177 ———. Theory and principles of group counseling in the elementary school. In J. Muro & S. Freeman (Eds.), *Readings in group counseling.* Pp. 36–40.

178 **Di Peri, J.** Heroin and God. *Cath. Psychol. Rec.*, 1965, 3(1), 35–38 (with D. N. Lombardi).

179 **Disher, Dorothy R.** Improvement without fundamental change. In K. A. Adler & Danica Deutsch (Eds.), *Essays in Individual Psychology.* Pp. 340–343.

180 **Disher, Dorothy R.** (Ed.). *Workbook for students of adolescent adjustment.* Ann Arbor, Mich.: Edwards Bros., 1959.

181 **Dodd, L. W.** The golden complex. *IZIP,* 1928, 6, 55-62.

182 ———. *The golden complex: A defense of inferiority.* New York: John Day, 1927.

183 **Dodge, R.** *The craving for superiority.* New Haven: Yale Univ. Press, 1931 (with E. Kahn).

184 **Doerries, L. E.** Purpose in life and social participation. *JIP,* 1970, 26, 50-53.

185 **Does, R. B.** Review of R. R. Carkhuff, *Helping and human relations.* Vol. 2. *Practice and research.* New York: Holt, Rinehart & Winston, 1969. In *JIP,* 1971, 27(1), 108-109.

186 **Dohrenwend, B. P.** Stress situations, birth order and psychological symptoms. *J. abnorm. Psychol.,* 1966, 71, 215-223 (with Barbara S. Dohrenwend).

187 **Dohrenwend, Barbara S.** Factors interacting with birth order in self-selection among volunteer subjects. *J. soc. Psychol.,* 1967, 72, 125-128 (with S. Feldstein, Joyce Plosky, & Gertrude R. Schmeidler).

188 ———. Stress situations, birth order and psychological symptoms. *J. abnorm. Psychol.,* 1966, 71, 215-223 (with B. P. Dohrenwend).

189 **Dollard, J.** A method of measuring tension in written documents. *J. abnorm. soc. Psychol.,* 1947, 42, 3-32 (with O. H. Mowrer).

190 **Donat, J.** *Über Psychoanalyse und Individualpsychologie.* Innsbruck: Felix Rauch, 1932.

191 **Dopff, C. F.** La importancia de l'auto-estimació. *Rev. Psicol. Pedag.* (Barcelona), 1933, 1.

192 **Dormandy, Clara.** The voice: Its rises and falls. *IPNL,* 1970, 19(6), 109-111.

193 **Dornbush, S. M.** A test of interactionalist hypotheses of self-conception. *Amer. J. Sociol.,* 1956, 61, 399-403 (with S. F. Miyamoto).

194 **Dosek, M.** Portrait. *IPNL,* 1971, 20(6), 110.

195 **Doyle, J. F.** The effect of cognitive style on the ability to attain concepts and to perceive embedded figures. *Diss. Abstr.,* 1966, 27(3A), 668-669. Unpubl. Ed. D. Diss., Univ. Florida, 1965.

196 **Dreikurs, R.** *The ABC's of guiding the child.* Chicago: North Side Unit, Comm. Child Guid. Ctrs., 1964. Paper. Also in Prine Areas, B. C. Primary Teachers Assn., 1972, 15(1), (with Margaret Goldman).

197 **Dreikurs, R.** Adlerian analysis of interaction. *Grp. Psychother.,* 1955, 8, 298-307. Also in *Group psychotherapy and group approaches.* Pp. 70-77.

198 ———. Adlerian analysis of interaction. In K. A. Adler & Danica Deutsch (Eds.), *Essays in Individual Psychology.* Pp. 75-87.

199 ———. The Adlerian approach. *Ann. Psychother.,* 1961, 2(2), 40-43.

200 ———. *The Adlerian approach in the changing scope of psychiatry: Collected papers on psychodynamics and counseling.* Chicago: Author, 1955. Mimeo.

201 ———. The Adlerian approach to psychodynamics. In M. I. Stein (Ed.), *Contemporary psychotherapies.* Pp. 60-79.

202 ———. The Adlerian approach to therapy. In M. I. Stein (Ed.), *Contemporary psychotherapies.* Pp. 80-94.

203 ——— (Ed.). *Adlerian family counseling.* Eugene, Ore.: Univ. Oregon Press, 1959 (with R. Lowe, M. Sonstegard, & R. J. Corsini). Paper.

204 ———. The Adlerian or teleoanalytic group counseling approach. In G. M. Gazda (Ed.), *Basic approaches to group psychotherapy and group counseling.* Pp. 197-232 (with M. Sonstegard).

205 ———. Adlerian psychology. In H. M. Ruitenbeek (Ed.), *Group therapy today: Styles, methods, and techniques.* Pp. 37-48.

206 ———. Adlerian psychotherapy. In Frieda Fromm-Reichman & J. L. Moreno (Eds.), *Progress in psychotherapy.* Pp. 111-118. Also in *Psychodynamics, psychotherapy, and counseling.* Pp. 63-72.

207 ———. Adleriana. *IPN,* 1940, 1(3), 5.

208 ———. Adler's contribution to contemporary psychology. *IP,* 1968, 5(3), 15-21.

209 ———. Adler's contribution to Individual Psychology. 1969, 3, 4-9.

210 ———. Adler's contribution to medicine, psychology, and education. *AJIP,* 1953, 10, 83-86.

211 ———. *Adult-child relations: A workshop on group discussion with adolescents.* Eugene, Ore.: Univ. Oregon Press, 1961.

Mimeo; Chicago: Alfred Adler Inst., 1967.

212 **Dreikurs, R.** *Alfred Adlers Individual-psychologie.* Translated by P. Ronge & A. C. Pabbruwe. Rotterdam: J. M. Bredee's, 1934.

213 ———. Alte und neue Erziehungsmethoden. *Die Nachlese,* June 4, 1965.

214 ———. Am I an Adlerian? *IP,* 1972, 9(2), 35-37.

215 ———. Die Anfänge der Gruppenpsychotherapie in Wien. *Wien. med. Wchnschr.,* 1958, 108, 845-848.

216 ———. Aphorism. *Voices,* 1965, 1(1), 24.

217 ———. Are psychological schools of thought outdated? *JIP,* 1960, 16, 3-10.

218 ———. Die aufgabe der modernen Geisteskrankenfürsorge. *Oesterr. Bl. Krankenpfl.,* 1926, 2, 52-58.

219 ———. Basic principles in dealing with children. In R. Dreikurs, R. J. Corsini, R. N. Lowe & M. A. Sonstegard (Eds.), *Adlerian family counseling.* Eugene, Ore.: Univ. Oregon Press, 1959. Pp. 23-32.

220 ———. Die Bedeutung der Sport -und Kampfspiele. *Volkssport,* 1930, 2(2), 1-3.

221 ———. Die Bedeutung des Gemeinschaftsgefühles für die moralische Erziehung. *Résumés du Congres Cracovicie,* 1934, 25-28.

222 ———. Die Bedeutung des Gruppenunterrichts. In E. Meyer (Ed.), *Didaktische Studien.* Pp. 95-103.

223 ——— (Ed.). Bibliography of Individual Psychology. *IPB,* 1947, 6(1-2), 89-99.

224 ———. Can we find peace in the war between the generations? In W. L. Pew (Ed.), *War between the generations.* Pp. 33-43.

225 ———. Can you be sure the disease is functional? *Consultant* (Smith Kline & French Labs.), August, 1962.

226 ———. A case of functional disturbance of the digestive system. *IJIP,* 1935, 1(1), 57-62. Also in *Psychodynamics, psychotherapy and counseling.* Pp. 55-62.

227 ———. Causality versus indeterminism. *IPB,* 1951, 9, 108-117.

228 ———. Certain factors effective in psychotherapy. *IJIP,* 1936, 2(1), 39-54.

229 ———. *The challenge of child training—A parent's guide.* New York: Hawthorn Books, 1972. Paper.

230 ———. *The challenge of marriage.* New York: Duell, Sloan and Pearce, 1946.

231 **Dreikurs, R.** *The challenge of parenthood.* New York: Duell, Sloan and Pearce, 1948, 1958.

232 ———. The changing scope of psychiatry. *Chicago Med. Sch. Quart.,* 1942, 3(2), 7-9, 25-27; *Med. Dig.* (Bombay), 1964, 32, 333-353.

233 ———. *Character education and spiritual values in an anxious age.* Boston: Beacon Press, 1952. Also *Alfred Adler Inst. Monog No. 1.* Chicago: Alfred Adler Inst., 1971.

234 ———. *Child guidance and education: Collected papers.* Eugene, Ore.: Univ. Oregon Press, 1957. Mimeo.

235 ———. A child with compulsive neurosis. *IPB,* 1947, 6, 134-141. Also in *Child guidance and education.* Pp. 29-32.

236 ———. *Children: The challenge.* New York Duell, Sloan and Pearce, 1964 (with Vicki Soltz).

237 ———. The choice of a mate. *IJIP,* 1935, 1(4), 99-112.

238 ———. Clinical child guidance. *Ment. Hlth. Bull.,* 1944, 22(4), 1-4.

239 ———. Clinical interpretation of music therapy. *Music Ther.,* 1954, 4, 79-84.

240 ———. *Collected papers on music therapy.* Chicago: Author, n.d. Mimeo.

241 ———. Comments on "Code of ethics of group psychotherapists". *Grp. Psychother.,* 1957, 10, 226-229.

242 ———. [Comments on six incidents]. In V. Calia and R. J. Corsini (Eds.), *Critical incidents in school counseling.*

243 ———. [Comments on twelve incidents]. In S. W. Standal and R. J. Corsini (Eds.), *Critical incidents in psychotherapy.*

244 ———. Communication within the family. *Cent. States Speech J.,* 1959, 11(1), 11-19. Also in *Psychodynamics, therapy and counseling.* Pp. 189-204. Also in *Group psychotherapy and group approaches.* Pp. 84-94.

245 ———. *Como estimular al niño: El proceso del estimulo.* Translated by J. A. Baca. Valencia: Alcoy, 1960 (with D. Dinkmeyer).

246 ———. *Como lograr la disciplina en el niño y en el adolescente.* Buenos Aires: Paidos, 1972 (with L. Grey).

247 ———. A comparison of client-centered and Adlerian psychotherapy. *Couns. Ctr. Discussion Papers,* 1960, 6, No.

A BIBLIOGRAPHY FOR ADLERIAN PSYCHOLOGY

8 (with J. M. Shlien & H. H. Mosak).

248 **Dreikurs, R.** Conflict solving. *Alberta Counselor,* 1972, 2(4), 13–22.

249 ————. The confusion of sex. *Chicago Med. Sch. Quart.,* 1946, 7(2), 11–14, 32–34.

250 ————. The contribution of group psychotherapy to psychiatry. *Grp. Psychother.* 1956, 9, 115–125.

251 ————. Coping with the child's problems in the classroom. In M. G. Gottsegen & Gloria Gottsegen (Eds.), *Professional school psychology.* Pp. 162–176.

252 ————. *Coping with children's misbehavior.* New York: Hawthorn Press, 1972.

253 ————. Counseling a boy. *JIP,* 1972, 28(2), 223–231.

254 ————. Counseling for family adjustment. *IPB,* 1949, 7, 119–137. Also in *Psychodynamics, psychotherapy and counseling.* Pp. 241–262.

255 ————. Counseling the adolescent. In J. A. Peterson and Neysa M. Peterson (Eds.), *Study guide.*

256 ————. *The courage to be imperfect.* In Various, *Articles of supplementary reading for parents.* Pp. 17–25.

257 ————. The cultural implications of group psychotherapy. *Z. diagnost. Psychol. Persönlichkeitsforsch.* (Berne), 1957, 5, 186–197. Also in *Group psychotherapy and group approaches.* Pp. 53–63.

258 ————. The cultural implications of reward and punishment. *Int. J. soc. Psychiat.,* 1958, 4, 171–178.

259 ————. *Cultural upheaval and modern family life.* Chicago: Comm. Child Guid. Ctrs., 1950.

260 ————. The current dilemma in psychotherapy. *J. Existent. Psychiat.,* 1960, 1, 187–206.

261 ————. *Le défi de l'enfant.* Translated by Yvé Leschallier de l'Isle. Paris: Laffont, 1972.

262 ————. The delinquent in the community. *IP,* 1971, 3, 7–14.

263 ————. *Demokrati og opdragelse. En vejledning for foraeldre.* [A parent's guide to child discipline]. Translated by Nina Lautrup-Larsen. Copenhagen: Hans Reitzels Forlag, 1971 (with L. Grey).

264 ————. Determinants of changing attitudes of marital partners toward each other. In S. Rosenbaum & I. Alger (Eds.), *The marriage relationship: Psychoanalytic perspectives.* Pp. 83–102.

265 **Dreikurs, R.** The developing self in human potentialities. In H. A. Otto (Ed.), *Human potentialities.* Pp. 80–92.

266 ————. The development of the child's potential. In H. A. Otto (Ed.), *Explorations in human potentialities.* Pp. 223–239.

267 ————. The development of Individual Psychology in Brazil. *IPB,* 1946, 5, 91–93.

268 ————. Dialog in der Familie. In H. J. Schultz (Ed.), *Kontexte.* Vol. 5. Pp. 51–57.

269 ————. Differential diagnosis. In W. S. Kroger (Ed.), *Psychosomatic obstetrics, gynecology, and endocrinology.* Pp. 455–459.

270 ————. *Discipline without tears.* Toronto: Alfred Adler Inst., 1972 (with Pearl Cassel).

271 ————. Do teachers understand children? *Sch. and Soc.,* 1959, 87, 88–90. Also in D. Dinkmeyer (Ed.), *Guidance and counseling in the elementary school.* Pp. 180–183.

272 ————. Dreikurs sayings. *IP,* 1972, 9(2), 38–45.

273 ————. *Dynamics of classroom behavior.* Chicago: Author, 1969.

274 ————. *Dynamics of classroom behavior: A teacher's guide to accompany twelve 30-minute in-service lessons, Vermont Educational Television, WETK.* Lincoln, Neb.: Great Plains Natl. ITV Libr., Univ. Neb., 1969.

275 ————. The dynamics of music therapy. *Music Ther.,* 1953, 3, 15–23.

276 ————. The dynamics of music therapy. In Mariana Bing (Ed.), *Music therapy.*

277 ————. Early experiments in social psychiatry. *Int. J. soc. Psychiat.,* 1961, 7, 141–147.

278 ————. Early experiments with group psychotherapy. *Amer. J. Psychother.,* 1959, 13, 882–891. Also in *Group psychotherapy and group approaches.* Pp. 1–9. Also in H. M. Ruitenbeek (Ed.), *Group therapy today.* Pp. 18–27.

279 ————. *Eclogi Dreikurs.* Edited and translated by Juliet Cavadas. Athens: Kedros, 1970.

280 ————. Editorial. *IPB,* 1950, 8, 3.

281 ————. Editorial. *AJIP,* 1956, 12, 177–179.

282 **Dreikurs, R.** Editorial note. *IPB*, 1951, 9, 94–95.

283 ———. Education at the crossroads. *IP*, 1972, 9(2), 56–62.

284 ———. L'éducation des parents et le travail de groupe. *Congr. Int. de Santé Ment.*, Paris, Sept., 1961; *Inform. Socials*, 1961, No. 12. Pp. 32–33.

285 ———. Education for self-governance: A survey of four experimental groups. *Humanist*, 1965, 25(1), 8–12.

286 ———. (Ed.). *Education, guidance, psychodynamics*. Chicago: Alfred Adler Inst., 1966.

287 ———. The educational implications of the "four freedoms". *IPB*, 1942, 2(4), 69–71.

288 ———. The educational revolution or a new deal for youth. *Tantalus*, 1965, 2(1), 1–2.

289 ———. Effect of time limits: A comparison of client-centered and Adlerian psychotherapy. *Amer. Psychologist*, 1960, 15, 415 (with J. M. Shlien & H. H. Mosak). Abstract.

290 ———. Effect of time limits: A comparison of two psychotherapies. *J. couns. Psychol.*, 1962, 9, 31–34.

291 ———. *Die Ehe: Eine Herausforderung.* Translated by E. A. Blumenthal. Stuttgart: Klett, 1968.

292 ———. Ein Fall von Platzangst. *IZIP*, 1934, 12, 92–96.

293 ———. *Einführung in die Individualpsychologie.* Leipzig: Hirzel, 1933.

294 ———. Einige Probleme der Epileptilerfürsorge. *Wien. klin. Wchnschr.*, 1926, 39, 602–605.

295 ———. Einige wirksame Faktoren in der Psychotherapie. *IZIP*, 1932, 10(3), 161–176.

296 ———. Emotional predisposition to reading difficulties. *Arch. Pediat.*, 1954, 71, 339–353. Also in *Child guidance and education.* Pp. 19–28.

297 ———. *Encorajando crianças a apprender* [Encouraging children to learn]. Translated by Terezinha Eboli & Yedda Salles. Sao Paolo, Brazil: Edicoes Melhoramentos, 1972.

298 ———. *Encouraging children to learn: The encouragement process.* Englewood Cliffs, N. J.: Prentice-Hall, 1963 (with D. Dinkmeyer).

299 **Dreikurs, R.** Die Entwicklung der psychischen Hygiene in Wien, unter besonder Berücksichtigung der Alkoholiker und Psychopathen -(Selbstmorder-) Fürsorge. *Allg. Z. Psychiat.*, 1928, 88, 469–489.

300 ———. Epilogue. In A. Nikelly (Ed.), *Techniques for behavior change.* Pp. 217–219.

301 ———. *Equality: The challenge of our times.* Chicago: Author, 1961. Mimeo.

302 ———Equality: The life-style of tomorrow. *Futurist*, 1972, 6(4), 153–155.

303 ———. *Ermutigung als Lernhilfe.* Translated by Rosemarie Hagen. Stuttgart: Ernst Klett, 1970 (with D. Dinkmeyer).

304———. Die Erziehungsberatung in Wien. *Sozialärztl. Rundsch.*, 1934, 9(1),

305 ———. Family counseling. *JIP*, 1972, 28(2), 207–222.

306 ———. Family group therapy in the Chicago Community Child Guidance Centers. *Ment. Hyg.* (N. Y.), 1951, 35, 291–301. Also in *Child guidance and education.* Pp. 85–91.

307 ———. Ferdinand Birnbaum, a biographical sketch. *IPB*, 1948, 6, 157–161.

308 ———. Die Finalität im menschlichen Seelenleben. *Action et Pensée*, 1935, 11, 73–79, 100-110.

309 ———. Foreword. In Genevieve Painter, *Teach your baby.* Pp. 7–9.

310 ———. Foreword. In Genevieve Painter, *Baby-Schule.*

311 ———. The four goals of the disturbed child. *Sauvegarde de l'enfance* (Paris), 1951, 12, 104–114. Also in *Child guidance and education.* Pp. 8–13.

312 ———. The four goals of the maladjusted child. *Nerv. Child*, 1947, 6, 321–328. Also in *Child guidance and education.* Pp. 1–7.

313 ———. Four steps in problem solving. *OSIPNL*, 1970, 11(2), 11; *OSIPNL*, 1971, 12(2), 13.

314 ———. Der frauensport im Altertum. *Volkssport*, 1930, 2(3),

315 ———. Freud and Adler. *Guide psychiat. psychol. Lit.*, 1956, 2(8–9), 8–9.

316 ———. Frigidity. *IPMP*, 1932, No. 3. Pp. 13–18.

317 ———. Frigidity. In W. S. Kroger (Ed.), *Psychosomatic obstetrics, gynecology and endocrinology.* Pp. 415–417.

318 ———. The function of emotions. *Christian Regis.*, 1951, 130(3), 11–14, 24. Also in

Psychodynamics, psychotherapy, and counseling. Pp. 205–218.

319 **Dreikurs, R.** The function of scientific religion. United Secularists of America, Milwaukee, Wis., Aug. 6, 1949.

320 ———. Fundamental principles of child guidance. In R. Dreikurs, R. J. Corsini, R. N. Lowe, & M. A. Sonstegard (Eds.), *Adlerian family counseling.* Pp. 17–21.

321 ———. *Fundamentals of Adlerian psychology.* London: Kegan Paul, 1935; New York: Greenberg, 1950; Chicago: Alfred Adler Inst., 1950. Paper; Jamaica: Knox Educ. Services, 1958. Paper.

322 ———. Der gegenwärtige Stand der psychischen Hygiene in Wien. *Volksgesundh. Z. soz. Hyg.,* 1929, 3, 211–221.

323 ———. General review [of group psychotherapy]. *First Int. Cong. Psychiat.,* Paris, 1950. Vol. 5. Paris: Hermann, 1952. Pp. 223–239.

324 ———. Goals in psychotherapy. *Amer. J. Psychoanal.,* 1956, 16, 18–23. Also in *Psychodynamics, psychotherapy and counseling.* Pp. 103–112.

325 ———. Goals of psychotherapy. In A. R. Mahrer (Ed.), *Goals in psychotherapy.* Pp. 221–237.

326 ———. Die "Grenzen" der Leistungsfähigkeit. *Lebenserfolg,* 1933, 29, 80–87.

327 ———. Group dynamics in the classroom. *Proc. Thirteenth Cong. Int. Assn. Appl. Psychol.* Rome: Tip. Ferri, 1958. Also in *Group psychotherapy and group approaches.* Pp. 127–142.

328 ———. *Group psychotherapy and group approaches: Collected papers.* Chicago: Alfred Adler Inst., 1960. Paper.

329 ———. Group psychotherapy and the third revolution in psychiatry. *Int. J. soc. Psychiat.,* 1955, 1(3), 23–32. Also in *Group psychotherapy and group approaches.* Pp. 34–45.

330 ———. Group psychotherapy from the point of view of Adlerian psychology. *Int. J. Grp. Psychother.,* 1957, 7, 363–375. Also in *Group psychotherapy and group approaches.* Pp. 95–105. Also in M. Rosenbaum & M. Berger (Eds.), *Group psychotherapy and group function.* Pp. 168–179. Also in H. M. Ruitenbeek (Ed.), *Group therapy today.* Pp. 37–48.

331 ———. Group psychotherapy: General review. *First Int. Cong. Psychiat. (1950).*

Paris: Hermann, 1952. Pp. 223–237. Also in *Group psychotherapy and group approaches.* Pp. 10–20.

332 **Dreikurs, R.** *Grundbegriffe der Individualpsychologie.* Stuttgart: Ernst Klett, 1969.

333 ———. Guiding, teaching and demonstrating: An Adlerian autobiography. *JIP,* 1967, 23, 145–157.

334 ———. Guilt feelings as an excuse. *IPB,* 1950, 8, 12–21. Also in *Psychodynamics, psychotherapy and counseling.* Pp. 229–240.

335 ———. *Ha-adom v'hashvuyon.* Tel Aviv: Ha-agudah l'kidum yachsei enosh, n.d.

336 ———. *Happy children: The challenge for parents.* London: Souvenir Press, 1970 (with Vicki Soltz).

337 ———. Hesitant therapists. *Voices,* 1967, 3(4), 17.

338 ———. *Het Huwelijk een Uitdaging.* Utrecht: Bijleveld, 1961.

339 ———. *Hoe voed ik mijn kind op?* Translated by P. H. Ronge. Utrecht: Bijleveld, 1936, 1948.

340 ———. The holistic approach: Two points of a line. In *Education, guidance, psychodynamics.* Pp. 19–24.

341 ———. How does humor effect our lives? *Northwestern Rev. Stand,* 1951, 17(10).

342 ———. How equal can we get? *Torch,* Jan., 1953.

343 ———. How the psychiatrist can assist the attorney in rehabilitating broken marriages. In N. C. Kohut (Ed.), *Therapeutic family law.* Pp. 207–218.

344 ———. *The human element in urban renewal.* Tel Aviv: Urban Renewal Authority Ministry of Housing, 1970.

345 ———. *Human patterns in a changing society.* Jerusalem: Civil Service Comm., 1970.

346 ———. Humanism—a philosophy for daily living. *Humanist,* 1950, 10, 25, 73–74, 121–122.

347 ———. A humanistic view of sex. *Humanist,* 1959, 19, 84–92.

348 ———. *I bambini una sfida.* Translated by Isola Gentile. Milan: Ferro Edizione, 1969.

349 ———. The immediate purpose of children's misbehavior, its recognition and correction. *IZIP,* 1950, 19(2), 70–87.

350 ———. The impact of equality. *Humanist,* 1964, 24, 143–146.

351 ———. The impact of the group for music therapy and music educa-

tion. *Music Ther.*, 1959, 9, 93–106.

352 **Dreikurs, R.** The importance of group life. *Camping Mag.*, 1940, 12(8–9); 1941, 13(1). Also in *Child guidance and education.* Pp. 33–42.

353 ———. In memoriam Alfred Adler. *Psychother. Prax.*, 1937, 3, 208–209.

354 ———. In memoriam—Alfred Adler. *IPB*, 1942, 2(4), 76–77.

355 ———. Individual psychological anecdote. *IPB*, 1943, 3, 96.

356 ———. Individualisierung und Sozialisierung im Unterricht. In E. Meyer, *Didaktische Studien.* Pp. 95–103.

357 ———. The Individual Psychological approach. In B. B. Wolman (Ed.), *Handbook of child psychoanalysis.* Pp. 415–459.

358 ———. Die Individualpsychologie Alfred Adlers. In E. Stern (Ed.), *Die Psychotherapie in der Gegenwart.* Pp. 68–88.

359 ———. Die Individualpsychologie des praktischen Arztes. *Med. Klin.*, 1934, 30, 10–11.

360 ———. Die Individualpsychologie und ihre Kritiker. *IZIP*, 1933, 11, 103–107.

361 ———. *I psikhologia stin* [Psychology in the classroom]. Translated by Juliet Cavadas. Athens: Kedros, 1968.

362 ———. IP anecdote. *IPB*, 1943, 3, 54.

363 ———. IP anecdotes. *IPN*, 1941, 1(7), 5; 1941, 1(10), 4.

364 ———. Individual Psychology. In A. A. Roback (Ed.), *Present-day psychology.* Pp. 711–731.

365 ———. Individual Psychology: The Adlerian point of view. In J. M. Wepman & R. W. Heine (Eds.), *Concepts of personality.* Pp. 234–256.

366 ———. Individual Psychology: The Adlerian point of view. In S. R. Maddi (Ed.), *Perspectives on personality.* Pp. 260–272.

367 ———. Individual Psychology and sexual difficulties (I). *IPMP*, 1932, No. 3 (with A. Adler, E. Wexberg, [Adele] Hervat, J. C. Young, F. G. Crookshank, Mary C. Luff, & others).

368 ———. The influence of Individual Psychology on the international scene. *IP*, 1970, 7(2), 29–37.

369 ———. The international picture of Individual Psychology. *IPB*, 1951, 9, 1–3.

370 ———. The interpersonal relationship in hypnosis: Some fallacies in current

thinking about hypnosis. *Psychiat.*, 1962, 25, 219–226.

371 **Dreikurs, R.** An interview with Rudolf Dreikurs. *Couns. Psychologist*, 1971, 3(1), 49–54.

372 ———. Introduction to Alexandra Adler et al., *Youth in danger becomes a danger.*

373 ———. Introduction to A. Adler, *The education of children* (Gateway edition).

374 ———. An introduction to Individual Psychology. *IJIP*, 1937, 3(4), 320–349.

375 ———. *An introduction to Individual Psychology.* Translated by Edna G. Fannin. London: Kegan Paul, Trench, Trubner, 1935.

376 ———. Irvin Neufeld, M. D. (1903–1969): Orthopedist and Individual Psychologist. *JIP*, 1969, 25, 226–230.

377 ———. *Itsuv ha-ofi v'hakniyat orchim b'iday shel charada.* Tel Aviv: Alfred Adler Inst., n.d.

378 ———. The Jewish family. *New Currents*, 1944, 2(4), 28–31.

379 ———. Karl Nowotny, 1895–1965. *JIP*, 1965, 21(2), 234.

380 ———. *Kinder fordern uns heraus: Wie erziehen wir sie zeitgemäss?* Translated by E. Blumenthal. Stuttgart: Ernst Klett, 1966 (with Vicki Soltz).

381 ———. Kinderpsychotherapie durch Erziehungsberatung. In G. Biermann (Ed.), *Handbuch der Kinderpsychotherapie.* Vol. 1. Pp. 95–107.

382 ———. Koffein und vegetatives Nervensystem. *Deutsche Z. Nervenheilk.*, 1928, 107, 184–190.

383 ———. Koffein und vegetatives System. *Wien. klin. Wchnschr.*, 1927, 40(5), 156–160.

384 ———. The last ten years. *IPB*, 1947, 6, 1–3.

385 ———. Learning to live together in a democracy. *Canad. Counselor*, 1969, 3, 4–9.

386 ———. The life tasks. III. The fifth life task. *IP*, 1967, 5, 16–22 (with H. H. Mosak).

387 ———. *Lineamenti della psicologia di Adler.* Translated by G. Falzoni. Italy: La Nuova Italia, 1968.

388 ———. Living together in a family. *Fam. Life*, 1962, 122, 1–5.

389 ———. *Logical consequences: A new approach to discipline.* New York: Meredith, 1968 (with L. Grey).

390 **Dreikurs, R.** Madua zekukim hahorim beyamenu l'hadrachah? *Urim la-horim,* Jan., 1962.

391 ———. *Maintaining sanity in the classroom: Illustrated teaching techniques.* New York: Harper & Row, 1971 (with Bernice Grunwald & Floy Pepper).

392 ———. *Manual of child guidance.* Chicago: Chicago Med. Sch., 1945, 1947; Ann Arbor, Mich: Edward Bros., 1946.

393 ———. *Manual for life style assessment: Part I.* Minneapolis: Hennepin County Court Services, May, 1971 (with Miriam L. Pew, W. L. Pew, & Vicki Soltz Statton).

394 ———. Margaret Goldman (1920-1972). *JIP,* 1972, 28, 113.

395 ———. The meaning of dreams. *Chicago Med. Sch. Quart.,* 1944, 5(3), 4-7. Also in *Psychodynamics, psychotherapy, and counseling.* Pp. 219-228.

396 ———. Minor psychotherapy: A practical psychology for physicians. *Trans. Acad. Psychosom. Med.,* 1958, 5, 253-260. Also in *Psychodynamics, psychotherapy, and counseling.* Pp. 263-278.

397 ———. Models of man. *Humanist,* 1965, 25, 259-260.

398 ———. *Motivating children to learn.* Burlington, Vt.: Univ. Vermont, 1971 (with Bronia Grunwald).

399 ———. Musiktherapie mit psychotischen Kindern. In H. R. Teirich (Ed.), *Musik in der Medizin.* Pp. 68-76.

400 ———. Music therapy. In Nichola J. Long, W. C. Morse, & Ruth G. Neuman (Eds.), *Conflict in the classroom: the education of emotionally disturbed children.* Belmont, Calif.: Wadsworth, 1965. Pp. 199-202.

401 ———. Music therapy with psychotic children. *Music Ther.,* 1955, 5, 62-73. Also in *Child guidance and education.* Pp. 50-58 (with Dorothy Crocker).

402 ———. Music therapy with psychotic children. *Psychiat. Quart.,* 1960, 34, 722-734.

403 ———. Musiktherapie mit psychotischen Kindern. In G. Biermann (Ed.), *Handbuch der Kinderpsychotherapie.* Vol. 1. Pp. 499-507.

404 ———. *Das nervöse Symptom.* Wien & Leipzig: Moritz Perles, 1932.

405 ———. Neurose: Um desafio à medicina. *Rev. Brasil. Med.,* 1946, 3, 557-562.

406 **Dreikurs, R.** Neurosis, a challenge to medicine. *Chicago Med. Sch. Quart.,* 1943, 4, No. 2. Also in *Psychodynamics, psychotherapy, and counseling.* Pp. 21-28.

407 ———. Never underestimate the power of children. *Intel. Dig.,* 1972, 11(10), 54-56 (with Bronia Grunwald & Floy Pepper).

408 ———. A new Adlerian contribution to education. *AJIP,* 1956, 12, 69.

409 ———. *Nisooin: Ha-etgar* [*The challenge of marriage*]. Translated by R. Algad. Tel Aviv: Joshua Chachik, n.d.

410 ———. On knowing oneself. *IJIP,* 1937, 3(1), 13-23.

411 ———. *Organic or functional disorder: A diagnostic aid.* North Chicago, Ill.: Abbott Labs, 1958. Pp. 8-9.

412 ———. Organizing distribution of knowledge. *IPB,* 1942, 2(2), 38-39.

413 ———. Orientacao da crianco: I. A situation dos pais. *Rev. Brasil. de Med.,* 1946, 3(5), 363-372; II. 458-467.

414 ———. Os novos designios da psiquiatria. *Rev. Brasil. Med.,* 1946, 3, 647-649.

415 ———. Our child guidance clinics in Chicago. *IPB,* 1943, 3(1), 14-19. Also in *Child guidance and education.* Pp. 80-84.

416 ———. *A parent's guide to child discipline* [A new, revised edition of *Logical consequences*]. New York: Hawthorn Books, 1970 (with L. Grey).

417 ———. Parents and teachers: Friends or enemies? *Educ.,* 1970, 91, 147-154 (with M. Chernoff).

418 ———. Patient-therapist relationship in multiple psychotherapy. I. Its advantages to the therapist. *Psychiat. Quart.,* 1952, 26, 219-227. Also in *Group psychotherapy and group approaches.* Pp. 114-120 (with B. H. Shulman & H. H. Mosak).

419 ———. Patient-therapist relationship in multiple psychotherapy. II. Its advantages for the patient. *Psychiat. Quart.,* 1952, 26, 590-596. Also in *Group psychotherapy and group approaches.* Pp. 121-126 (with H. H. Mosak & B. H. Shulman).

420 ———. Portrait. *JIP,* 1967, 23, facing p. 141; *IPNL,* 1970, 19(4), 62; In "Ten premises for a humanist philosophy of life"; *IPNL,* 1972, 21(6), 110, 112; In K. Stokes, Mommy's mad; In Equality: The life-style of tomorrow. P. 154.

421 ———. The potential of the White House Conference on Children and Youth.

Nat. Comm. Children & Youth Reporter. 1970, 1, 1-2.

422 Dreikurs, R. The present position of Individual Psychology. *IPB*, 1941, 2(1), 13-17.

423 ———. *Prevention and correction of juvenile delinquency.* St. Louis: Metropolitan Youth Commission of St. Louis, 1961. Paper; Chicago: Alfred Adler Inst., 1962.

424 ———. The problem of neurasthenia. *IJIP*, 1936, 2(3), 14-34. Also in *Psychodynamics, psychotherapy, and counseling.* Pp. 25-54.

425 ———. The programme of humanism. In *Proc. First Int. Cong. Humanism Ethic. Culture.* Utrecht: Human Verband, 1953.

426 ———. *Psicologia do casamento.* Translated by O. Rocha & Maria A. Perestrello. Rio de Janeiro: Editors Civilizaçao Brazileira, 1949.

427 ———. *Psicologia in classe. (Psychology in the classroom.)* Translated by Corinna Ranchitti. Firenze: Editrice Universitario, 1961.

428 ———. *Psikhologia ba-kitah* [*Psychology in the classroom*]. Translated by M. Dauber. Tel Aviv: Otser Ha-moreh, 1962.

429 ———. Psychiatric concepts of music therapy for children. *Music Ther.*, 1954, 4, 81-84. Also in *Child guidance and education.* Pp. 47-49.

430 ———. Psychiatric considerations of music therapy. *Music Ther.*, 1957, 7, 31-36.

431 ———. Psychische Hygiene, ihre Bedeutung und ihre Methoden. *Arbeiterschutz*, 1928, 24.

432 ———. Psychodynamic diagnosis in psychiatry. *Amer. J. Psychiat.*, 1963, 119, 1045-1048. Also in *Psychodynamics, psychotherapy, and counseling.* Pp. 95-102.

433 ———. The psychodynamics of disability—a group therapy approach. *Amer. Arch. Rehab. Ther.*, 1954, 2(2), 4-8. Also in *Group Psychotherapy and group approaches.* Pp. 64-69.

434 ———. *Psychodynamics, psychotherapy, and counseling: Collected papers.* Jamaica, W. I.: Knox Educ. Serv., 1958. Mimeo; Eugene, Ore.: Univ. Oregon Press, 1963. Mimeo; Chicago: Alfred Adler Inst., 1955, 1967. Paper.

435 ———. The psychological approach in the classroom. *Amer. Teacher*, 1955, 39(4), 9-12. Also in *Child guidance and education.* Pp. 14-18.

436 Dreikurs, R. Psychological differentiation of psychopathological disorders. *IPB*, 1944-45, 4, 35-48. Also in *Psychodynamics, psychotherapy and counseling.* Pp. 5-24.

437 ———. Psychological goal disclosure. *OSIPNL*, 1972, 13(5), 7.

438 ———. The psychological interview in medicine. *AJIP*, 1954, 10, 99-122; *Indian J. Psychol.*, 1963, 5, 59-71; 1963, 5(3), 134-139. Also in *Psychodynamics, psychotherapy, and counseling.* Pp. 125-153.

439 ———. The psychological and philosophical significance of rhythm. *Bull. Natl. Assn. Music Ther.*, 1957, 6, 7-8, 10-11.

440 ———. The psychological and philosophical significance of rhythm. *Bull. Natl. Assn. Music Teachers*, 1961, 10(4), 8-17.

441 ———. The psychological uncertainty principle. *Topic. Probl. Psychother.*, 1963, 4, 23-31.

442 ———. *La psychologie Adlérienne.* Paris: Bloud & Gay, 1971.

443 ———. *Psychologie im Klassenzimmer.* Translated by E. Blumenthal. Stuttgart: Ernst Klett, 1967.

444 ———. *Psychology in the classroom.* New York: Harper, 1957, 1968. London: Staples Press, 1958; New York: Harper & Row, 1968. Paper.

445 ———. Psychotherapie de groupe. *Bull. Centre Psychol. Adlérienne*, 1950, 2, 3-14.

446 ———. Psychotherapie—Überwindung falscher gesellschaftlicher Normen. In U. Derbolowsky & E. Stephan (Eds.), *Die Wirklichkeit und das Böse.* Pp. 247-257.

447 ———. Psychotherapy as correction of faulty social values. *JIP*, 1957, 13, 150-158. Also in *Psychodynamics, psychotherapy and counseling.* Pp. 113-124.

448 ———. Psychotherapy through child guidance. *Nerv. Child*, 1949, 8, 311-328. Also in *Child guidance and education.* Pp. 64-79.

449 ———. *Psykologi i klassvaereket: En håndbog for laerere.* [Psychology in the classroom]. Translated by J. Nielsen. Copenhagen: Hans Reitzel Forlag, 1969.

450 ———. Raising children in a democracy. *Humanist*, 1958, 18, 77-83.

451 ———. Rationale in counseling. In *Delta workshop on counseling minority youth.* Portland, Ore.: Oregon St. Syst. Higher Educ., 1961.

452 Dreikurs, R. Rationale of group counseling (with M. Sonstegard). In D. Dinkmeyer (Ed.), *Guidance and counseling in the elementary school.* Pp. 278–287.

453 ———. A record of family counseling sessions. In R. Dreikurs, R. Corsini, R. Lowe & M. Sonstegard (Eds.), *Adlerian family counseling.* Pp. 109–152.

454 ———. The realization of equality in the home. *IP*, 1972, 9(2), 46–55.

455 ———. Regine Seidler, 1895–1967. *JIP*, 1967, 23, 137.

456 ———. A reliable differential diagnosis of psychological or somatic disturbances. *Int. Rec. Med.*, 1958, 171, 238–242. Also in *Psychodynamics, psychotherapy, and counseling.* Pp. 153–162.

457 ———. The religion of democracy. *Humanist*, 1955, 15, 210–215, 266–273.

458 ———. The religion of the future. In A. E. Kuenzli (Ed.), *Reconstruction in religion.* Pp. 3–20.

459 ———. Religion without the supernatural. *Progress. World*, 1950, 9, 388–395.

460 ———. Réponse. *C. R. First Int. Cong. Psychiat. Paris, 1950.* Vol. 5. Paris: Hermann, 1952. Pp. 301–302.

461 ———. Review of Ethel M. Abernathy, Further data on personality and family position. *J. Psychol.*, 1940, 10, 303–307. In *IPN*, 1941, 1(10), 6.

462 ———. Review of A. Adler, *Das Problem der Homosexualität.* In *IZIP*, 1931, 9(1), 62–63.

463 ———. Review of C. A. Adler, The anti-Babel: An attempt to clarify some controversial points in "guidance". In *IPN*, 1940, 1(3), 2–3.

464 ———. Review of Rose H. Alschuler & La Berta W. Hattwick, *Painting and personality: A study of young children.* In *Coll. Art J.*, 1948, 8, 155–157.

465 ———. Review of *Bull. Menninger Clin.*, 1943, 7(5–6). In *IPB*, 1943, 3, 92–96.

466 ———. Review of L. E. Cole & W. F. Bruce, *Educational psychology.* Yonkers, N. Y.: World Book Co., 1958. In *JIP*, 1959, 15, 241–242.

467 ———. Review of L. Fischer, *Ghandi & Stalin.* New York: Harper, 1947.

468 ———. Review of S. Freud, *The origins of psychoanalysis: Letters, drafts and notes to Wilhelm Fliess, 1887–1902.* In *Science*, 1954, 120, No. 3116.

469 Dreikurs, R. Review of G. Klatt, *Psychologie des Alkoholismus.* In *IZIP*, 1932, 10(2), 153–154.

470 ———. Review of J. Neumann, *Der nervöse Charakter und seine Heilung.* In *JIP*, 1960, 16, 94–96.

471 ———. Review of N. E. Shoobs & G. Goldberg, *Corrective treatment for unadjusted children.* In *IPB*, 1942, 2(4), 73–75.

472 ———. Review of T. S. Szasz, *The ethics of psychoanalysis.* In *Humanist*, 1965, 25, 274.

473 ———. Review of E. Wexberg, *Einführung in die Psychologie des Geschlechtslebens.* In *IZIP*, 1931, 9(1), 63.

474 ———. Die Rolle die Gruppe in der Erziehung. In E. Meyer (Ed.), *Sozialerziehung und Gruppenunterricht, international gesehen.* Pp. 16–35.

475 ———. The scientific revolution. *Humanist*, 1966, 26, 8–13.

476 ———. The scientific revolution. In C. E. Smith & O. G. Mink (Eds.), *Foundations of guidance and counseling.* Pp. 59–68.

477 ———. *Seelische Impotenz.* Leipzig: Hirzel, 1933.

478 ———. *La sfida al matrimonio.* Translated by G. Manelli. Firenze: Casa Editrice Nerbini, n.d.

479 ———. *Shivuyon: Ha-etgar* [The challenge of equality]. Translated by A. Ben-Nahum. Tel Aviv: Joshua Chachik, n.d.

480 ———. Significance of 4 goals. *OSIPNL*, 1963, 4(5), 12–13.

481 ———. *A significão dos sonhos. Rev. Brasil. Med.*, 1946, 3, 895–898.

482 ———. *Social equality: The challenge of today.* Chicago: Henry Regnery, 1971.

483 ———. *Social interest: The basis of normalcy. Couns. Psychologist*, 1969, 1(2), 45–48.

484 ———. The socio-psychological dynamics to disability: A review of the Adlerian concept. *J. soc. Issues*, 1948, 4, 39–54. Also in *Psychodynamics, psychotherapy, and counseling.* Pp. 167–188.

485 ———. Die soziale Fürsorge in der Psychiatrie. *Jb. Psychiat. Neurol.*, 1925, 44, 247–266.

486 ———. *Soziale Gleichwertigkeit, die Forderung unserer Zeit.* Stuttgart: Ernst Klett, 1972.

487 ———. Soziale Not und Spitalaufenthalt. *Oesterr. Bl. Krankenpfl.*, 1931, 7(4-5), 49-54.

488 **Dreikurs, R.** A specific approach to practicum supervision. *Counselor Educ. Supervis.*, 1966, 6, 18–25 (with M. Sonstegard).

489 ———. *Student guidebook for "Understanding your children": 26 television sessions.* Edited by J. A. & Neysa M. Peterson. Burlington, Vt.: Univ. Vt. Educ. TV, 1969.

490 ———. The tasks of life. I. Adler's three tasks. *IP*, 1966, 4(1), 18–22 (with H. H. Mosak).

491 ———. The tasks of life. II. The fourth life task. *IP*, 1967, 4(2), 51–56 (with H. H. Mosak).

492 ———. The technique of psychotherapy. *Chicago Med. Sch. Quart.*, 1944, 5(1), 4–8, 35; 5(2), 7–10. Also in *Psychodynamics, psychotherapy, and counseling.* Pp. 73–94.

493 ———. Techniques and dynamics of multiple psychotherapy. *Psychiat. Quart.*, 1950, 24, 788–799. Also in *Group psychotherapy and group approaches.* Pp. 106–113.

494 ———. Technology of conflict resolution. *JIP*, 1972, 28(2), 203–206.

495 ———. Técnica psicoterápica. I. *Rev. Brasil. Med.*, 1946, 3, 706–710; II. 820–824.

496 ———. Tele and inter-personal therapy: Appraisal of Moreno's concept from the Adlerian point of view. *Grp. Psychother.*, 1955, 8, 185–191. Also in *Group psychotherapy and group approaches.* Pp. 78–83.

497 ———. *The teleoanalytic approach to group counseling.* Chicago: Alfred Adler Inst., 1967 (with M. Sonstegard).

498 ———. Ten premises for a humanist philosophy of life. *Humanist*, 1949, 1, 19.

499 ———. *To pedi* [Children: The challenge]. Translated by Juliet Cavadas. Athens: Tachijdromos, 1964.

500 ———. The training of organic symptoms. *Arch. First Inter-Amer. Cong. Med.*, Rio de Janeiro, 1946.

501 ———. Toward a technology of human relationship. *JIP*, 1972, 28(2), 127–136.

502 ———. Twenty years of group psychotherapy. *Amer. J. Psychiat.*, 1954, 110, 567–575. Also in *Group psychotherapy and group approaches.* Pp. 21–33 (with R. J. Corsini).

503 ———. Über Coffetylin. *Wien. klin. Wchnschr.*, 1927, 40(2), 67 (with E. Mattauschek).

504 **Dreikurs, R.** Über den gegenwartigen Stand und die Probleme der Geisteskrankenfürsorge in Wien. *Wien. klin. Wchnschr.*, 1926, 39, 869–872.

505 ———. Über die Kombination von Schlafmitteln mit Koffein. *Wien. klin. Wchnschr.*, 1925, 49, (with O. Sperling).

506 ———. Über Liebeswahl. *IZIP*, 1932, 10, 339–353.

507 ———. Über psychische Hygiene. *Z. soz. Hyg. Volksgesundh.*, 1927, 1(11).

508 ———. Über Rauschsucht und ihre individualpsychologische Behandlung. *Biol. Heilkunst*, 1932, 13(36).

509 ———. Über die Verschlimmerung von alten Neurosen bei Kriegsbeschädigten aus sozialen Gründen (soziale Verschlimmerung). *Z. ges. Neurol. Psychiat.*, 1929, 119, 679–700 (with E. Mattauschek).

510 ———. *Understanding the child: A manual for teachers.* Chicago: Alfred Adler Inst., 1951. Mimeo.

511 ———. Understanding the exceptional child. *Music Ther.*, 1951, 1, 41–46. Also in *Child guidance and education.* Pp. 43–46.

512 ———. The unique social climate experienced in group psychotherapy. *Grp. Psychother.*, 1951, 3, 292–299. Also in *Group psychotherapy and group approaches.* Pp. 46–52.

513 ———. Die unrichtige Wahl in der Liebe. *Lebenserfolg*, 1933, 29, 257–262.

514 ———. *Úvod do Individuální Psychologie* [Fundamentals of Individual Psychology]. Prague: Unie a. s. v. Praze, 1937.

515 ———. Value of Funkenstein test in predicting psychosurgery. *Dis. nerv. Syst.*, 1957, 18(4), 134–138 (with J. D. Freund).

516 ———. Von der Geisteskrankenfürsorge über die soziale Psychiatrie zur psychischen Hygiene. *Allg. Z. Psychiat.*, 1928, 88, 567–573.

517 ———. The war between generations: Juvenile delinquency stumps the experts. *Humanist*, 1961, 21, 15–24.

518 ———. The war between the generations. *Brit. J. soc. Psychiat.*, 1970, 4(1), 31–39.

519 ———. Was ist in Wirklichkeit die Neurose? *IZIP*, 1933, 11(3), 193–201.

520 ———. Was soll mit unseren epileptischen Kindern geschehen? *Z. Heilpädag.*, 1926, 18(2).

521 **Dreikurs, R.** What is psychotherapy? *Ann. Psychother.*, 1959, No. 1. Pp. 16–22.

522 ———. The White House Conference on Children and Youth, 1960; a critique: Triumph of institutionalism. *Humanist,* 1960, 20, 281–287.

523 ———. The White House Conference on Children and Youth—Another triumph of institutionalism? *Humanist,* 1970, 30, 6–7.

524 ———. Woher stammen die Konflikte in der Liebe? *Lebenserfolg,* 1933, 29, 118–121, 154–156.

525 ———. *Yeladim: Ha-etgar* [Children: The challenge]. Translated by E. Burla-Adar. Tel Aviv: Izreel Publ. House, 1966.

526 ———. *Your child and discipline: A briefing for parents.* Washington, D. C.: Natl. Educ. Assn., 1964; *NEA J.,* 1965, 54, 32–47 (with Vicki Soltz).

527 ———. Znaczenie uczucia spolecznego dia moralnego wychowania [The importance of communal feeling for moral education]. In P. Zbiorowa (Ed.), *Sily Moralne: Wspolne Wszystkim Ludziom, Ich zrodla I Roswoj Przez Wychowanie.* Krakow: Sklad Glowny, 1934. Pp. 221–230.

528 ———. Zum Problem der Neurasthenie. *IZIP,* 1931, 9(1), 16–25.

529 ———. Zur Frage der Selbsterkenntnis. *IZIP,* 1930, 8(4), 361–369.

530 ———. Zur Frage der Selbstmordprophylaxe. *Allg. Z. Psychiat.,* 1930, 93, 98–114.

531 ———. Zur Kasuistik der funktionellen Magen-Darmstörungen. *IZIP,* 1934, 12(1), 11–15.

532 ———. Zwischen Verwöhnung und Strenge. In R. Hörl (Ed.), *Kinder in ihrer Welt— Kinder in unserer Welt.* Pp. 48–70.

533 **Dreikurs, Sadie G.** Art therapy for psychiatric patients. *Perspec. psychiat. Care,* 1969, 7(3), 134–143 (with B. Shulman).

534 ———. Portrait. *IPNL,* 1972, 21(6), 110, 112.

535 ———. Psychological techniques applied in a group situation—an experiment in group work. *IPB,* 1944–45, 4, 110–125.

536 ———. "Rita": An experiment in the psychological approach in group work. *IPB,* 1944–45, 4, 26–28.

537 **Dresden, M.** Lebensplan und Persönlichkeit. *IZIP,* 1949, 18(3), 121–127.

538 **Drew, Janet.** Selectivity in memory of personally significant material. *J. gen. Psychol.,* 1961, 65, 25–32 (with D. K. Kamano).

539 **Dreyer, A. S.** Aspiration behavior as influenced by expectation and group comparison. *Hum. Relat.,* 1954, 7, 175–190.

540 **Dreyfus, E. A.** Existential-humanism in Adlerian psychotherapy (with A. G. Nikelly). In A. G. Nikelly (Ed.), *Techniques for behavior change.* Pp. 13–20.

541 ———. Humanness: A therapeutic variable. *Pers. Guid. J.,* 1967, 45, 573–578.

542 ———. Humanness and psychotherapy: A confirmation. *JIP,* 1968, 24, 82–85.

543 ———. On being human. *J. Existent.,* 1964, 17, 67–76 (with B. Mackler).

544 **Dreyfus, Madeleine.** L'association départmentale favorise la réussité de nos enfants. *L'École de Région Parisienne,* 1953, No. 31 (with A. Hauser).

545 ———. Ce qu'est pour la femme l'homme d'aujourd'hui. *Le group familial,* May, 1966.

546 ———. Compte-rendu d'une consultation psycho-pédagogique donnée selon la technique d'Alfred Adler. *L'École des Parents* (Paris), 1953, No. 2. Pp. 39–41 (with A. Hauser).

547 ———. L'enfant Lambin. *Brochure de l'École des Parents* (Paris), 1957, 17.

548 ———. Position de la psychologie adlérienne en face des enfants caractèriels. *Les Cahiers de l'Enfance inadaptée,* 1955, 6(1), 1–9.

549 ———. Les punitions chez l'école des parents et des éducateurs. *L'École des Parents* (Paris), 1950.

550 ———. Translator of S. H. Foulkes, Asya Kadis, J. D. Krasner, & C. Winick, *Guide du psychothérapeute de groupe.*

551 ———. Translator of Hertha Orgler, *Alfred Adler et son oeuvre.*

552 ———. Un cas de jumeaux séparés à la naissance. *Rev. Psychée,* 1953, No. 84–85.

553 **Drovinskovic, V.** Translator of A. Adler, *Poznaunje Coveka.*

554 **Dry, Avis.** Origins of psychology. *Ment. Hlth.,* Spring, 1970. Pp. 45–57.

555 **Dubsky, Lola.** Review of T. Dreiser, *Eine amerikanische Tragödie.* Berlin: P. Zsolnay, 1927. In *IZIP,* 1928, 6(3), 262–263.

556 ———. Review of K. Esselbrugge, Struktur des Humors bei Gottfried Keller. *Jb. Charakterologie f. 1929.* Berlin: Pan-Verlag, 1929. In *IZIP,* 1930, 8(3), 360.

557 ———. Review of H. Hesse, *Der Steppenwolf.* Berlin: S. Fischer, 1927. In *IZIP,* 1930, 8(2), 279.

558 **Dubsky, Lola.** Review of E. M. Remarque, *Im Westen nichts neues.* Berlin: Propyläen, 1929. In *IZIP*, 1929, 7(4), 320-321.

559 ———. Review of Hedwig Schulhof, *Ein Buch vom Leben und Gelebtwerden.* In *IZIP*, 1933, 11(2), 156.

560 ———. Review of H. G. Wells, *Die Geschichte eines grossen Schulmeisters.* Wien: P. Zsolnay, 1928. In *IZIP*, 1928, 6(5), 421-422.

561 **Dück, J.** Betätigungstrieb und Nervosität. In A. Adler & C. Furtmüller (Eds.), *Heilen und Bilden* (1914). Pp. 151-168.

562 ———. Review of M. Hirsch (Ed.), *Arch. Frauenkunde und Eugenik.* In *ZIP*, 1914, 1(2), 61-62.

563 **Dudman, Helga.** The difficult shift away from autocracy. *Jerusalem Post,* Dec., 29, 1972.

564 **Dukes, C.** *Adler's contribution to the study of organ inferiorities. IPMP,* 1938, No. 19. Pp. 33-38.

565 **Dukes, Ethel.** Childhood and the infectious quality of neurosis. *IPP,* 1939, No. 21. Pp. 34-39.

566 ———. The psychological effects of war on the family and its individual members. *Amer. J. Orthopsychiat.,* 1946, 16, 64-73.

567 **Dudycha, G. J.** Adolescents' memories of preschool experiences. *J. genet. Psychol.,* 1933, 42, 468-480 (with M. M. Dudycha).

568 ———. Childhood memories, a review of the literature. *Psychol. Bull.,* 1941, 38, 668-682 (with M. M. Dudycha).

569 ———. Some factors and characteristics in childhood memories. *Child Devlopm.,* 1933, 4, 265-278 (with M. M. Dudycha).

570 **Dudycha, M. M.** Adolescents' memories of preschool experiences. *J. genet. Psychol.,* 1933, 42, 468-480 (with G. J. Dudycha).

571 ———. Childhood memories, a review of the literature. *Psychol. Bull.,* 1941, 38, 668-682 (with G. J. Dudycha).

572 ———. Some factors and characteristics in childhood memories. *Child Developm.,* 1933, 4, 265-278 (with G. J. Dudycha).

573 **Du Maurier, Daphne** (Ed.). *Best short stories of Phyllis Bottome.* London: Faber & Faber, 1963.

574 **Dumpson, J.** *Youth in danger becomes a danger: A symposium on juvenile delinquency.* New York: Indiv. Psychol. Assn., 1956 (with Alexandra Adler, H. Epstein, & E. Papanek).

575 **Dunham, F.** Birth order and spatial-perceptual ability: Negative note. *Percep. mot. Skills,* 1969, 28, 301-302 (with C. M. Culver).

576 **Dunn, R. E.** Empathy, self-esteem and birth order. *J. abnorm. soc. Psychol.,* 1963, 66, 532-540 (with E. Stotland).

577 ———. Identification, "oppositeness", authoritarianism, self-esteem and birth order. *Psychol. Monogr.,* 1962, 76 (9, Whole No. 528) (with E. Stotland).

578 **Dutschewitch, C.** *Nervosnija Tschowek* [The nervous person]. Sofia: Author.

579 **Dutta, S.** Retention of affective material: Frame of reference or intensity? *J. Pers. soc. Psychol.,* 1966, 4, 27-35.

580 **Dyck, A. J.** Questions for the global conscience. *Psychol. Today,* 1968, 2(4), 38-42.

581 **Dynes, R. R.** Preferences of male or female children: Traditional or affectional. *Marr. Fam. Living,* 1954, 16, 128-130 (with S. Dinitz & A. C. Clarke).

E

1 **E.** Review of O. Kauders, *Keimdrüse, Sexualität und Zentralnervensystem.* Berlin: S. Karger, 1927. In *IZIP*, 1928, 6(1), 74.

2 **E. B.** Review of R. A. Spitz, *Die Entstehung der ersten Objektbeziehungen.* Stuttgart: Ernst Klett, 1957. In *IPNL*, 1958, 9(1-2, Whole No. 89-90). P. 6.

3 **E. F.** Review of R. Allers, *Psychologie des Geschlechtslebens.* In *IZIP*, 1923, 2(2), 45-46.

4 ———. Review of G. Hoffenstein, *Das Problem des Unbewussten.* Stuttgart: J. Püttman, 1923. In *IZIP*, 1924, 2(3), 56-57.

5 **E. S. S.** Review of *Brit. J. Psychol.,* 1921. In *IZIP*, 1924, 2(3), 61-62.

6 ———. Review of W. Brown, *Talks on psychotherapy.* In *IZIP*, 1924, 2(3), 61.

7 **Eastlack, Katherine.** The Wesley Family Health Center: A study in behavior and attitude changes. Unpubl. thesis, Univ. Minnesota, 1970.

8 **Eastman, M. E.** Birth order, family size and extra-sensory perception. *Brit. J. soc. clin. Psychol.,* 1966, 5, 150-152 (with C. E. Green & S. T. Adams).

9 **Ebner, J-M.** L'analyse du comportement de Raskolnikov (Dostoievski). *BSFPA*, 1972, No. 14. Pp. 35–43.

10 ———. La coopération, problème vital de notre époque. *BSFPA*, 1972, No. 12. Pp. 21-23.

11 **Ebner, Marie Thérèse.** Problèmes actuels de la femme. *BSFPA*, 1971, No. 9. Pp. 20-24.

12 **Eboli, Terezinha.** Translator, with Yedda Salles, of D. Dinkmeyer & R. Dreikurs, *Encorojandos crianças a apprender.*

13 **Eccles, W. M. I. P.** and psychosomatic disorders (II.). *IPP*, 1933, No. 9 (with J. S. Fairbairn, M. Marcus, Mary B. Ferguson, & F. G. Crookshank).

14 ———. The psychological surroundings of the surgical patient. *IPP*, 1933, No. 9. Pp. 25-37.

15 **Edinger, F.** Bemerkungen über Takt, Höflichkeit, Güte und soziale Betätigung. *IZIP*, 1931, 9(2), 136-137.

16 ———. Review of M. Vaerting, *Die Macht der Massen*. Berlin: M. Pfeiffer, 1928. In *IZIP*, 1929, 7(5), 479.

17 **Edwards, A. L.** Political frames of reference as a factor influencing recognition. *J. abnorm. soc. Psychol.*, 1941, 36, 24-50.

18 ———. The retention of affective experiences: A criticism and restatement of the problem. *Psychol. Rev.*, 1942, 49, 43-53.

19 **Edwards, F. Margery.** Impressions of China under war conditions. *IPP*, 1940, No. 22. Pp. 40-48.

20 ———. Individual Psychology and practice (II). *IPMP*, 1934, No. 12 (with C. H. Bevan-Brown, F. G. Layton, & C. H. Woodcock).

21 ———. The psychological approach to gynecological problems. *IPMP*, 1933-34, No. 9. Pp. 51-52.

22 ———. The psychological approach to gynecological problems. *IPMP*, 1934, No. 12.

23 **Edwards, W.** The theory of decision making. *Psychol. Bull.*, 1954, 51, 380-417.

24 **Eglash, A.** Creative restitution, a correctional technique and a theory. *JIP*, 1959, 15, 226-232 (with E. Papanek).

25 ———. The dilemma of fear as a motivating force. *Psychol. Rev.*, 1952, 59, 376-379.

26 ———. Review of H. A. Bloch & A. Niederhoffer, *The gang*. New York: Phil. Libr., 1958. In *JIP*, 1959, 15, 247-248.

27 **Ehrenstein, A.** Das Martyrium des Edgar Allan Poe. *IZIP*, 1930, 8(4), 389-400.

28 ———. Nationaljudentum. *IZIP*, 1927, 5 (3), 198-206.

29 ———. Die Verblendung. *IZIP*, 1924, 2(4), 15-17.

30 **Ehrenstein, Maude.** Dr. Alfred Adler (1870-1970). *Morley Mag.* (London), 1970, 75, 60 (with Toni Towns).

31 **Ehrenwald, J.** (Ed.). *From medicine man to Freud*. New York: Dell, 1956. Pp. 345-359.

32 **Ehrlich, J. J.** Sibling sex distribution and psychiatric status. *Psychol. Rep.*, 1966, 18, 365-366 (with Mary L. Bauer).

33 **Eiloart, A.** Translator of E. Wexberg, *Individual psychological treatment.*

34 **Ein Grosser Mann.** Ratschläge für den Berater. *IZIP*, 1929, 7(3), 202-203.

35 **Einstein, S.** (Ed.). *Psychoanalytic pioneers: A history of psychoanalysis through the lives and the works of its most eminent teachers*. New York: Basic Books, 1966 (with F. Alexander & M. Grotjahn).

36 **Eisen, J.** Review of D. Karagueuzian, *Blow it up*. Boston: Gambit, 1971. In *Psychol. Today*, 1971, 5(5), 16, 20.

37 **Eisenberg, P.** Expressive movements related to feelings of dominance. *Arch. Psychol.*, 1937, No. 211.

38 **Eisenbud, Ruth-Jean.** Factors influencing the repudiation of femininity. Unpubl. Ph.D. Diss., Radcliffe Coll., 1952.

39 **Eisenman, R.** Birth order, aesthetic preference, and volunteering for an electric shock experiment. *Psychonom. Sci.*, 1965, 3, 151-152.

40 ———. Birth order and artistic creativity. *JIP*, 1964, 20, 183-185.

41 ———. Birth order and MMPI patterns. *JIP*, 1966, 22, 208-211 (with R. E. Taylor).

42 ———. Birth order and sex differences in aesthetic preference for complexity-simplicity. *J. gen. Psychol.*, 1967, 77, 121-126.

43 ———. Birth order, anxiety, and verbalization in group psychotherapy. *J. consult. Psychol.*, 1966, 30, 521-526.

44 ———. Birth order and sex differences in future time perspective. *Developm. Psychol.*, 1969, 1, 70 (with J. J. Platt).

45 ———. Complexity-simplicity: II. Birth order and sex differences. *Psychonom. Sci.*, 1967, 8, 171-172.

46 Eisenman, R. Generality of creativity on two tasks. *JIP*, 1969, 25, 48-51 (with Diane Jones).

47 ———. Sex and birth order, and future expectations of occupational status and salary. *JIP*, 1968, 24, 170-173 (with J. J. Platt & D. D. Moskalski).

48 ———. Usefulness of the concepts of inferiority feeling and life style with schizophrenics. *JIP*, 1965, 21, 171-177.

49 Eisenstein, V. Psychodynamic significance of the first conscious memory. *Bull. Menninger Clin.*, 1951, 15, 213-220 (with R. Ryerson).

50 Ekenberg, M. Review of D. Katz & Rosa Katz, *Gespräche mit Kindern.* In *IZIP*, 1929, 7(1), 153.

51 Ekman, G. The four effects of cooperation. *J. soc. Psychol.*, 1955, 41, 149-162.

52 Elam, H. Action of dicyclopropyl ketoxine in clinical tetanus. *Federat. Proceed.*, 1958, 17, 405 (with R. K. Richards, L. Blockus, & M. Perlstein).

53 ———. Aneurysma of the great vein of Galen complicated by chronic subdural abscess. *West African med. J.*, 1967, 16(4), 109-113 (with E. L. Odeku & O. Ransone-Kuti).

54 ———. Cooperation between African and Afro-American, cultural highlights: A possible approach. *J. Natl. Med. Assn.*, 1969, 61, 30-35.

55 ———. Discordant congenital hydrocephalus—Identical twins. *Ghana med. J.*, 1966, 5, 20-24 (with L. Odeku).

56 ———. Electromyographic patterns in cerebral palsy. *Amer. J. phys. Med. Rehab.*, 1958, 37, 302-326 (with M. Perlstein & M. Turner).

57 ———. Electromyographic studies in tetanus with special reference to the effect of drugs. *Arch phys. Med.*, 1958, 39, 283-289 (with M. Perlstein).

58 ———. Electromyographic studies of neuromuscular disorders in children. *Arch. phys. Med.*, 1961, 42, 447-457 (with M. Perlstein & M. Turner).

59 ———. Lead encephalopathy in children. *New England J. Med.*, 1961, 264, 1027-1031 (with J. Greengard, W. Rowley, & M. Perlstein).

60 ———. Malignant cultural deprivation, its evolution. *Pediat.*, 1969, 44, 319-326.

61 Elam, H. Panoramic view of the children's neurology service. University Hospital, Ibadan, Nigeria. *Developm. Med. & Child Neurol.*, 1967, 9, 784-790.

62 ———. The potential use of Individual Psychology in clinical pediatrics. *JIP*, 1970, 26, 224.

63 ———. Psychosocial development of African children. *J. Natl. Med. Assn.*, 1968, 60, 104-109.

64 ———. The treatment of tetanus in Cook County Hospital. *J. Amer. Med. Assn.*, 1960, 173, 1536-1541.

65 ———. Use of strychnine in hypotonia. *Arch. phys. Med.*, 1963, 44, 195-203 (with M. Perlstein & J. Fudeman).

66 Eliot, T. D. Psychiatrische Soziologie und soziologische Psychiatrie. *Kölner Vierteljahrschr.*, 1930, 1, 82 ff.

67 Elkisch, Ilse. A case of "organ dialect". In K. A. Adler & Danica Deutsch (Eds.), *Essays in Individual Psychology.* Pp. 344-347.

68 ———. Review of Margarete Kaiser, *Die Liebe als Kunst.* Berlin: Ibis Verlag, [   ]. In *IZIP*, 1932, 10(4), 319.

69 Ellenberger, H. F. *The discovery of the unconscious.* New York: Basic Books, 1970; London: Allen Lane, 1970.

70 ———. *Existence.* New York: Basic Books, 1958 (with R. May & C. Angel).

71 ———. Hans Beckh-Widmanstetter (1888-1970). *JIP*, 1971, 27(1), 123-124.

72 ———. Superiority and social interest: A review. *JIP*, 1965, 21, 82-84.

73 Ellenbogen, R. Creativity, conformity, and rebellion. In K. A. Adler & Danica Deutsch (Eds.), *Essays in Individual Psychology.* Pp. 87-99.

74 ———. Relation of children's speech usage to age and to sex, as a function of precision requirements in performance: An investigation of formulations by Piaget, Vigotsky and Goldstein. Unpubl. Ph.D. Diss., New York Univ., 1955; *Diss. Abstr.*, 1955, 15, 1447-1448.

75 Ellis, A. Adultery: Pros and cons. *Independent*, 1956, No. 61. P. 4.

76 ———. Adultery reconsidered. *Independent*, 1957, No. 67. P. 4.

77 ———. Adventures with sex censorship. *Independent*, No. 62. P. 4; 1957, No. 63. P. 4.

78 ———. *The American Academy of Psychotherapists.* New York: American Academy of Psychotherapists, 1964.

79 Ellis, A. *The American sexual tragedy.* New York: Twayne, 1954; New York: Lyle Stuart, 1960, 1962.

80 ———. The anatomy of a private practitioner. *Nwsltr., Div. Consult. Psychol., Amer. Psychol. Assn.,* July, 1962. Pp. 26–28.

81 ———. Another look at sexual abnormality. *Independent,* 1956, No. 55. P. 6.

82 ———. An answer to some objections to rational emotive psychotherapy. *Psychother.,* 1965, 2, 108–111. New York: Inst. Rat. Living, 1965.

83 ———. The application of scientific principles to scientific publications. *Sci. Monthly,* 1948, 66, 427–430.

84 ———. Applications of clinical psychology to sexual disorders. In D. Brower & L. A. Abt (Eds.), *Progress in clinical psychology.* Vol. 1. Pp. 467–480.

85 ———. Are homosexuals really creative? *Sexol.,* 1962, 29, 88–93.

86 ———. Are homosexuals necessarily neurotic? *One,* 1955, 3(4), 8–12. Also in D. W. Cory (Ed.), *Homosexuality: A cross-cultural approach.* New York: Julian Press, 1956.

87 ———. Are suburban wives af-fair game? *New York Mirror Mag.,* July 20, 1958. Pp. 4–5.

88 ———. Are we secretly afraid of being touched? *Pageant,* 1969, 24(10), 132–137.

89 ———. *The art and science of love.* New York: Lyle Stuart, 1960; New York: Dell Books, 1965; New York: Bantam Books, 1969.

90 ———. Art and sex. In A. Ellis & A. Abarbanel (Eds.), *The encyclopedia of sexual behavior.* Pp. 161–179.

91 ———. *Art of erotic seduction.* New York: Lyle Stuart, 1967; New York: Ace Books, 1968 (with R. O. Conway).

92 ———. Articles of interest to marriage and family life educators and counselors. *Marr. Fam. Living,* 1950, 12, 106–110 (with C. Groves, M. W. Brown, & H. D. Lamson).

93 ———. The attitude of psychologists toward psychological meetings. *Amer. Psychologist,* 1948, 3, 511–512.

94 ———. The authentic man. *Humanist,* 1970, 30(1), 19–26 (with Joan Baez, J. Campbell, & P. Goodman).

95 ———. Banned program: The sexual revolution in America. *Mademoiselle,* 1963 (Oct.), 112–113, 158–164 (with D. Susskind, A. L. Kinsolving, Maxine Davis, R. Ginzburg, H. Hefner, & M. Lerner).

96 Ellis, A. The Blacky Test used with a psychoanalytic patient. *J. clin. Psychol.,* 1953, 9, 167–172.

97 ———. Books on marriage. *Voices,* 1966, 2(3), 83–85.

98 ———. A brief for sex honesty. *Real Life Guide,* 1960, 3(4), 31–38.

99 ———. Brief report for effective psychotherapeutic technique: Showing the patient that he is not a worthless individual. *Voices,* 1966, 1(2), 74–77; New York: Inst. Rat. Living, 1966.

100 ———. The case against religion. *Mensa Bull.,* 1970, No. 38. Pp. 5–6; New York: Inst. Rat. Living, 1971.

101 ———. The case against religion: A psychotherapist's view. *Independent,* 1962, No. 126. Pp. 4–5. Also in B. N. Ard (Ed.), *Counseling and psychotherapy.* Palo Alto, Cal.: Science & Behavior Books, 1966. Pp. 270–282.

102 ———. A case for polygamy. *Nugget,* 1960, 5(1), 19, 24, 26. Reprinted as A plea for polygamy. *Eros,* 1962, 1(1), 22–23.

103 ———. *The case for sexual liberty.* Tucson: Seymour Press, 1965.

104 ———. Case histories: Fact and fiction. *Contemp. Psychol.,* 1958, 3, 318–319.

105 ———. Case presentation and critical comments. In S. W. Standal & R. J. Corsini (Eds.), *Critical incidents in psychotherapy.* Pp. 88–91 & *passim.*

106 ———. The case study as a research method. *Rev. educ. Res.,* 1945, 15, 352–359 (with P. M. Symonds).

107 ———. Characteristics of convicted sex offenders. *J. soc. Psychol.,* 1954, 40, 3–15 (with Ruth R. Doorbar & Robert Johnston III).

108 ———. Classified bibliography of articles, books, and pamphlets on sex, love, marriage and family relations published during 1950. *Marr. Fam. Living,* 1951, 13, 71–86. (with Ruth R. Doorbar).

109 ———. Classified bibliography of articles, books, and pamphlets on sex, love, marriage and family relations published during 1951. *Marr. Fam. Living,* 1952, 14, 154–176 (with Ruth R. Doorbar).

110 ———. Classified bibliography of articles, books, and pamphlets on sex, love, marriage and family relations published during 1952. *Marr. Fam. Living,* 1953, 15, 156–175 (with Ruth R. Doorbar).

111 **Ellis, A.** A cognitive approach to behavior therapy. *Int. J. Psychiat.*, 1969, 8, 896–900.

112 ———. The cognitive element in experiential and relationship psychotherapy. *Exis. Psychiat.*, 1970, 7(28), 35–52.

113 ———. Coincidences. *Interim: The Mensa J.*, 1964, No. 67. P. 12.

114 ———. Coitus. In A. Ellis & A. Abarbanel (Eds.), *The encyclopedia of sexual behavior.* Pp. 284–292.

115 ———. A comparison of child guidance clinic patients coming from large, medium and small families. *J. genet. Psychol.*, 1951, 79, 131–144 (with R. M. Beechley).

116 ———. A comparison of matched groups of mongoloid and non-mongoloid children. *Amer. J. ment. Defic.*, 1950, 54, 464–468 (with R. M. Beechley).

117 ———. Comparison of Negro and white children seen at a child guidance clinic. *Psychiat. Quart. Suppl.*, 1950, 24, 93–101 (with R. M. Beechley).

118 ———. A comparison of the use of direct and indirect phrasing in personality questionnaires. *Psychol. Monogr.*, 1947, 61, No. 3. Pp. 1–41.

119 ———. Constitutional factors in homosexuality: A reexamination of the evidence. In H. Beigel (Ed.), *Advances in sex research.* New York: Hoeber, 1963. Pp. 161–186.

120 ———. Continuing personal growth of the psychotherapist. A rational emotive view. *J. humanist. Psychol.*, 1966, 6, 156–169.

121 ———. The contribution of psychotherapy to school psychology. *Sch. Psychol. Dig.*, 1972, 1(2), 6–9.

122 ———. Correspondence relating to "marriage counseling with couples indicating sexual incompatibility." *Marr. Fam. Living*, 1953, 15, 250–254.

123 ———. *Creative marriage.* New York: Lyle Stuart, 1961 (with R. A. Harper).

124 ———. A critical evaluation of marriage counseling. *Marr. Fam. Living*, 1956, 18, 65–71.

125 ———. A critique of Adolph DiLoreto's comparative psychotherapy. In A. O. DiLoreto, *Comparative psychotherapy, an experimental analysis.* Chicago: Aldine-Atherton, 1971. Pp. 213–221.

126 ———. Critique of "The homosexual in our society." *Mattachine Rev.*, 1959, 5(6), 24–28.

127 **Ellis, A.** A critique of systematic theoretical foundations in clinical psychology. *J. clin. Psychol.*, 1952, 8, 11–15.

128 ———. A critique of the theoretical contributions of nondirective therapy. *J. clin. Psychol.*, 1948, 4, 248–255.

129 ———. Deviation, an ever-increasing social problem. In J. Fairchild, *Personality problems and psychological frontiers.* New York: Sheridan House, 1957. Pp. 138–151.

130 ———. Diane David on sex. *Realist*, 1963, No. 42. Pp. 11–12, 16.

131 ———. Discussion of Heinlein's comment on "The validity of personality questionnaires." *Psychol. Bull.*, 1947, 44, 83–86.

132 ———. Discussion of Mrs. Bernard's comments on research methods. *Amer. sociol. Rev.*, 1948, 13, 218–219.

133 ———. Discussion of prediction data for marriage counseling. *Marr. Fam. Living*, 1950, 12, 56–57. Also in C. E. Vincent (Ed.), *Readings in marriage counseling.* New York: Crowell, 1956.

134 ———. Discussion of "Premarital sexual behavior" by Walter Stokes and David R. Mace. *Marr. Fam. Living*, 1953, 15, 53–59. Also in C. E. Vincent (Ed.), *Readings in marriage counseling.* New York: Crowell, 1956.

135 ———. Dr. Albert Ellis answers the 17 most asked questions about sex. *Pageant*, 1971, 26(⁻), 46–58. (with M. Cohen).

136 ———. Dr. Albert Ellis on fantasies during intercourse. *Liaison*, 1963, 1(12), 1–6.

137 ———. Dr. Ellis answers the charges of Dr. Levin. *Curr. med. Dig.*, 1964, 31, 518–522.

138 ———. Does morality require religious sanctions? *Controversy*, 1959, 1(2), 16–19.

139 ———. Effectiveness of psychotherapy with individuals who have severe homosexual problems. *J. consult. Psychol.*, 1956, 20, 191–195.

140 ———. Ellis on Kinsey, Part I. *Penthouse*, 1970, 2(4), 115–121; Part II. *Penthouse*, 1971, 2(5), 71–73.

141 ———. The emerging counselor. *Canad. Counsellor*, 1970, 4(2), 99–105.

142 ———. Emotional disturbance and its treatment in a nutshell. *Canad. Counsellor*, 1971, 5(3), 168–171; New York: Inst. Rat. Living, 1971.

143 ———. Emotional disturbances in children with peculiar given names. *J. genet.*

Psychol., 1954, 85, 337-339 (with R. M. Beechley).

144 **Ellis, A.** Emotional problems of the young adult. In Forest Hospital Foundation, *The young adult.* Des Plaines, Ill.: Forest Hosp. Foundation, 1969. Pp. 83-102. Also in *Rat. Living,* 1971, 5(2), 2-11.

145 ——— (Ed.). *The encyclopedia of sexual behavior.* New York: Hawthorn Books, 1961, 1967. New York: Ace Books, 1969 (with A. Abarbanel).

146 ———. *The essence of rational psychotherapy: A comprehensive approach to treatment.* New York: Inst. Adv. Study Rational Psychother., 1969; New York: Inst. Rat. Living, 1970.

147 ———. The essence of sexual morality. *Issue: Sex Ethics,* 1964, 2(1), 20-24; New York: Inst. Rat. Living, 1965.

148 ———. Evolving standards for practicing psychologists. In M. H. Krout (Ed.), *Psychology, psychiatry and the public interest.* Minneapolis: Univ. Minnesota Press, 1956. Pp. 186-200.

149 ———. An experiment in the rating of essay-type examination questions. *Educ. psychol. Msmt.,* 1950, 10, 707-711.

150 ———. Female sexual response and marital relations. *Soc. Probs.,* 1954, 1, 152-155.

151 ———. 15 ways to get more out of sex. *Sexol.,* 1968, 35, 148-151.

152 ———. Fifteen ways to get more out of sex. *Sexol.,* 1971, 38(1), 4-7.

153 ———. *The folklore of sex.* New York: Charles Boni, 1951. Also published as *Sex beliefs and customs.* London: Peter Nevill, 1951; New York: Grove Press, 1961.

154 ———. Foreword to H. Beigel (Ed.), *Advances in sex research.* New York: Hoeber, 1963. Pp. xi-xii.

155 ———. Frigidity. In A. Ellis & A. Abarbanel (Eds.), *The encyclopedia of sexual behavior.* Pp. 450-456.

156 ———. From the first to the second Kinsey report. *Int. J. Sexol.,* 1953, 7, 64-72.

157 ———. Goals of psychotherapy. In A. R. Mahrer (Ed.), *The goals of psychotherapy.* Pp. 206-220.

158 ———. Group marriage: A possible alternative. In H. A. Otto (Ed.), *The family in search of a future.* New York: Appleton-Century-Crofts, 1970. Pp. 85-98.

159 **Ellis, A.** *Growth through reason: Verbatim cases in rational emotive therapy.* Palo Alto: Science & Behavior Books, 1971 (with B. N. Ard, Jr., H. J. Geis, J. M. Gullo, P. A. Hauch, & M. C. Maultsby, Jr.).

160 ———. A guide to rational homosexuality. *Drum: Sex in perspective,* 1964, 4(8), 8-12.

161 ———. *A guide to rational living in an irrational world.* Englewood Cliffs, N. J.: Prentice-Hall, 1961 (with R. A. Harper).

162 ———. Guilt, shame and frigidity. *Quart. Rev. Surg. Obstet. & Gynecol.,* 1959, 16, 259-261; *Lumière et Liberté,* Oct., 1960. P. 2.

163 ———. Havelock Ellis. In D. Sills (Ed.), *International encyclopedia of the social sciences.* New York: Macmillan, 1969.

164 ———. Healthy and disturbed reasons for having extramarital relations. In G. Neubeck (Ed.), *Extramarital relations.* Englewood Cliffs, N. J.: Prentice-Hall, 1969. Pp. 153-161; *J. hum. Relations,* 1968, 16, 490-501.

165 ———. Helping people get better rather than merely feel better. *Rat. Living,* 1972, 7(2), 2-9.

166 ———. Helping troubled people. *Past. Psychol.,* 1958, 9, No. 82. Pp. 33-41.

167 ———. A homosexual treated with rational therapy. *J. clin. Psychol.,* 1959, 15, 338-343.

168 ———. Homosexuality and creativity. *J. clin. Psychol.,* 1959, 15, 376-379.

169 ———. *Homosexuality: Its causes and cure.* New York: Lyle Stuart, 1965.

170 ———. Homosexuality: The right to be wrong. *J. Sex Res.,* 1968, 4, 96-107.

171 ———. How American women are driving American males into homosexuality. *Exposé* (Independent), 1956, No. 52. P. 4.

172 ———. How homosexuals can combat anti-homosexualism. *One,* 1957, 5(2), 7-9.

173 ———. How males contribute to female frigidity. *Independent,* 1956, No. 56. P. 4.

174 ———. How much sex freedom in marriage? *Sexol.,* 1961, 28, 292-296.

175 ———. How neurotic are you? *True Story,* 1959, 79(6), 34-35.

176 ———. How to beat antisex laws. *Innovator,* July, 1965, 2, 33.

177 ———. How to have an affair—and end it with style. *Saga,* 1964, 29(1), 44-45, 89.

178 Ellis, A. How to keep boredom out of the bedroom. *Pageant,* 1964, 20(2), 14–18.

179 ———. How to learn to relax and enjoy Women's Lib. *Chicago Sunday Tribune Mag.,* Jan. 10, 1971. Pp. 38–39, 44.

180 ———. *How to live with a neurotic.* New York: Crown, 1957; New York: Award, 1969.

181 ———. How to live with a neurotic. *Macleans Mag.,* 1957, 30, 74–78.

182 ———. How to live with a neurotic. *Fam. Living,* Aug. 17, 1958. Pp. 8–9.

183 ———. How to live with a sex deviate. *Sexol.,* 1962, 28, 580–583.

184 ———. *How to participate effectively in a marathon weekend of marital encounter.* New York: Inst. Adv. Study Rational. Psychother., 1967; 1972.

185 ———. *How to prevent your child from becoming a neurotic adult.* New York: Crown, 1966 (with Janet L. Wolfe & Sandra Mosely).

186 ———. How to vary your sex techniques. *Sex Guide,* 1965, No. 103. Pp. 26–35.

187 ———. How you can get along with a neurotic. *Today's Living, New York Herald Tribune,* Aug. 3, 1958. Pp. 4–5.

188 ———. Humanism, values, rationality [Tribute to Alfred Adler on his 100th birthday]. *JIP,* 1970, 26(2), 11–12.

189 ———. Hypnotherapy with borderline schizophrenics. *J. gen. Psychol.,* 1958, 59, 245–253.

190 ———. "I feel so guilty." *True Story,* 1957, 78(6), 18–29.

191 ———. *If this be sexual heresy. . .* New York: Lyle Stuart, 1963; New York: Tower Pub., 1966.

192 ———. Illegal communication among institutionalized female delinquents. *J. soc. Psychol.,* 1958, 48, 155–160 (with S. Kosofsky).

193 ———. An impolite interview with Dr. Albert Ellis. *Realist,* 1960, 16(1), 9–14; 1960, 17, 7–12 (with P. Krassner & R. A. Wilson). Also in P. Krassner, *Impolite interviews.* New York: Lyle Stuart, 1961. Pp. 21–71; New York: Inst. Rat. Living, 1966.

194 ———. In defense of current sex studies. *Nation,* 1952, 174, 250–252 (with D. W. Cory).

195 ———. The influence of heterosexual culture on the attitudes of homosexuals. *Int. J. Sexol.,* 1951, 5, 77–79. Also in *Mattachine Rev.,* 1955, 1(5), 11–14.

196 Ellis, A. Instinct, reason and sexual liberty. *A way out,* 1963, 19, 332–335.

197 ———. *The intelligent woman's guide to man-hunting.* New York: Lyle Stuart, 1963; New York: Dell Books, 1965.

198 ———. Interests and attitudes. *Rev. educ. Res.,* 1947, 17, 64–79.

199 ———. The International Journal of Sexology. *Int. J. Sexol.,* 1953, 6, 180–181. Also published as Introduction to A. P. Pillay & A. Ellis, *Sex, society and the individual.*

200 ———. Interrogation of sex offenders. *J. crim. Law,* 1954, 45, 41–47. Also in A. Ellis & R. Brancale, *The psychology of sex offenders.* Pp. 107–119.

201 ———. Introduction to Rey Anthony, *The housewife's handbook on selective promiscuity.* Tucson, Ariz.: Seymour Press, 1960.

202 ———. Introduction to W. Braun, *The cruel and the meek.* New York: Lyle Stuart, 1967. Pp. ix–xiv.

203 ———. Introduction to N. Chorier, *The dialogues of Louisa Sigea.* Hollywood, Cal.: Brandon House, 1965. Pp. iii–xiv.

204 ———. Introduction to D. W. Cory, *The homosexual in America.* New York: Greenberg, 1951. Pp. ix–xi.

205 ———. Introduction to D. W. Cory, *The lesbian in America.* New York: Citadel Press, 1964. Pp. 11–20.

206 ———. Introduction to M. de Martinos, *The new female sexuality.* New York: Julian Press, 1969.

207 ———. Introduction to A. Edwardes, *The jewel in the lotus.* New York: Julian Press, 1959. Pp. xv–xxi.

208 ———. Introduction to *Fanny Hill—condensed. Eros,* 1962, 1(3), 82–83.

209 ———. Introduction to *The guild dictionary of homosexual terms.* Washington, D. C.: Guild Press, 1965.

210 ———. Introduction to V. Howarth, *Secret techniques of erotic delight.* New York: Lyle Stuart, 1967. Pp. i–vii.

211 ———. Introduction to Chin Ping Mei, *The love pagoda.* Hollywood, Cal.: Brandon House, 1965. Pp. 3–8.

212 ———. Introduction to L. Maddock, *Single and pregnant.* Hollywood, Cal.: Genell, 1962. Pp. 5–7.

213 **Ellis, A.** Introduction to Victoria Morhaim, *Casebook: Nymphomania.* New York: Dell, 1964. Pp. 7–9.

214 ——. Introduction to L. R. O'Conner, *The photographic manual of sexual intercourse.* New York: Pent-R Books, 1969. Pp. 9–13.

215 ——. An introduction to the principles of scientific psychoanalysis. *Genet. Psychol. Monogr.,* 1950, 41, 147–212.

216 ——. Introduction to Pauline Reage, *The story of O.* Hollywood, Cal.: Brandon House, 1965. Pp. iii–xi.

217 ——. Introduction to K. Thornley, *Oswald.* Chicago: New Classics House, 1965. Pp. 5–12.

218 ——. Introduction to J. Wilmat, *Earl of Rochester Sodom.* Hollywood, Cal.: Brandon House, 1966. Pp. iii–ix.

219 ——. Introduction to R. W. Wood, *Christ and the homosexual.* New York: Vantage Press, 1960.

220 ——. Irrational ideas [Interview with J. Elliott]. *Explorations,* 1969–70, No. 17. Pp. 13–16.

221 ——. Is nudism anti-sexual? *Eden,* 1962, No. 11. Pp. 6–9.

222 ——. *Is objectivism a religion?* New York: Lyle Stuart, 1968.

223 ——. Is pornography harmful to children? *Realist,* 1964, No. 47. Pp. 17–18.

224 ——. Is premarital chastity desirable? *Sex. Behav.,* 1971, 1(3), 42–52 (with Rebecca Liswood).

225 ——. Is psychoanalysis harmful? *Psychiat. Opin.,* 1968, 5, 16–24; *Univ. Rev.,* Nov., 1969. Pp. 18–20; New York: Inst. Rat. Living, 1969.

226 ——. Is the vaginal orgasm a myth? In A. P. Pillay & A. Ellis (Eds.), *Sex, society and the individual.*

227 ——. Is the vaginal orgasm a myth? *Liaison,* 1963, 1(9), 2–4.

228 ——. The justification of sex without love. *Independent,* 1957, No. 64. P. 4; 1957, No. 65. P. 4; 1957, No. 66. P. 4.

229 ——. Legal status of the marriage counselor: A psychologist's view. *Marr. Fam. Living,* 1951, 13, 116–120. Also in C. E. Vincent (Ed.), *Readings in marriage counseling.* New York: Crowell, 1956.

230 ——. The legitimate pickup. *Mlle.,* 1965, No. 198. Pp. 88, 94, 126 (with Ruth Nathan).

231 **Ellis, A.** The lesbian. *Rogue,* Sept., 1962. Pp. 17–18, 28, 76.

232 ——. Letter on the suspension of Dr. Leo F. Koch. *Balanced Living,* 1960, 16, 175.

233 ——. Letter to Norman Cousins on sex censorship. *Independent,* 1960, 3, 5.

234 ——. Love and family relationships of American college girls. *Amer. J. Sociol.,* 1950, 55, 550–556.

235 ——. Marriage counseling. In E. Harms (Ed.), *Handbook of counseling techniques.* New York: Pergamon Press, 1964. Pp. 147–153.

236 ——. Marriage counseling with couples indicating sexual incompatibility. *Marr. Fam. Living,* 1953, 15, 53–59. Also in C. E. Vincent (Ed.), *Readings in marriage counseling.* New York: Crowell, 1956.

237 ——. Marriage counseling with demasculinizing wives and demasculinized husbands. *Marr. Fam. Living,* 1960, 22, 13–20.

238 ——. A marriage of two neurotics. In Amer. Assn. of Marr. Counselors, *Marriage counseling: A casebook.* New York: Association Press, 1958. Pp. 197–204.

239 ——. Masturbation. *J. soc. Ther.,* 1955, 1, 141–143.

240 ——. Masturbation by sexually isolated individuals. In R. E. L. Masters (Ed.), *Sexual self-stimulation.* Los Angeles: Sherbourne Press, 1967. Pp. 221–231.

241 ——. Morality and therapy. *Columbia Univ. Forum,* 1962, 6(2), 47–48.

242 ——. Mothers are too good for their own good. *Boston Sunday Globe Mag.,* May 11, 1969. Pp. 26–31.

243 ——. Mowrer on sin. *Amer. Psychologist,* 1960, 15, 713–714.

244 ——. Must we be guilty about premarital sex? *Mod. Sex,* 1964, 1(1), 66–75.

245 ——. The myth of nymphomania. *Gent,* 1963, 7(6), 31–33, 74–80.

246 ——. Myths about sex. *Cosmopolitan,* Feb., 1961, 82–85.

247 ——. Myths about sex compatibility. *Sexol.,* 1962, 28, 652–655.

248 ——. Neurotic interaction between marital partners. *J. couns. Psychol.,* 1958, 5, 24–28; *Lumière et Liberté,* Dec., 1959. Pp. 3–4.

249 ——. *New apporaches to psychotherapy techniques.* Brandon, Vt.: J. clin. Psychol., 1955.

250 **Ellis, A.** New dynamics in contemporary petting. *Nugget*, 1964, 9(2), 16–20.

251 ———. New hope for homosexuals. *Sexol.*, 1958, 25, 164–168; *Lumière et Liberté*, Apr., 1960. Also in I. Rubin, *The third sex*. New York: New Book Co., 1961. Pp. 53–57.

252 ———. New kooky (but workable) cures for frigidity. *Cosmopolitan*, 1966, 160(1), 30–35.

253 ———. New light on masturbation. *Exposé* (Independent), 1956, No. 51. P. 4; *Mattachine Rev.*, 1956, 3(1), 13–15.

254 ———. A new look in psychotherapy. *Independent*, 1959, No. 94. Pp. 21–22. Also published as Rationalism and its therapeutic applications. In *The place of value in the practice of psychotherapy*.

255 ———. A new sex code for modern Americans. *Pageant*, 1961, 17(6), 110–116.

256 ———. The new sexual freedoms. *Rogue*, 1967, 12(6), 12–13, 17, 83–85.

257 ———. 1953 classified bibliography on human sex relations. *Int. J. sexol.*, 1954, 7, 228–239.

258 ———. 1953 classified bibliography on marriage and family relations. *Marr. Fam. Living*, 1954, 16, 146–161, 254–263.

259 ———. Nudity and love. *Independent*, 1963, No. 135. Pp. 3, 6.

260 ———. *Nymphomania: A study of the oversexed woman*. New York: Julian Messner-Gilbert Press, 1964; New York: MacFadden-Bartell, 1965 (with E. Sagarin).

261 ———. An objective examination of prostitution. *Int. J. Sexol.*, 1954, 8, 99–105 (with H. Benjamin).

262 ———. Objectivism, the new religion. *Rat. Living*, 1967, 2(2), 1–6; Part II., 1968, 3(7), 12–19.

263 ———. On premarital sex relations. *Independent*, 1956, No. 59. P. 4; 1956, No. 60. P. 4.

264 ———. On Reiss and Durkin on Ellis on Fried on Freud. *Contemp. Psychol.*, 1961, 6, 382.

265 ———. On sex fascism. *Independent*, 1957, No. 69. P. 4; 1957, No. 70. P. 4; 1957, No. 71. P. 4.

266 ———. On the cure of homosexuality. *Int. J. Sexol.*, 1952, 5, 135–138; *Mattachine Rev.*, 1955, 1(6), 6–9.

267 ———. On the myths about love. *Independent*, 1956, No. 58. P. 6.

268 **Ellis, A.** An operational reformulation of some of the basic principles of psychoanalysis. *Psychoanal. Rev.*, 1956, 43, 163–180. Also in H. Feigl & M. Scriven (Eds.), *Minnesota studies in the philosophy of science*. Vol. 1. Minneapolis: Univ. Minnesota Press, 1956. Pp. 131–154.

269 ———. Orgasm and health. *A Way Out*, 1963, 19, 240–242.

270 ———. *The origins and the development of the incest taboo*. (Bound together with E. Durkheim, *Incest: The nature and origin of the taboo*). New York: Lyle Stuart, 1963.

271 ———. Other devices for investigating personality. *Rev. educ. Res.*, 1947, 17, 101–109 (with H. H. Abelson).

272 ———. Our soaring suicide rate. *No. Amer. Newspaper Alliance*, Jan. 18–19, 1966.

273 ———. Outcome of employing three techniques of psychotherapy. *J. clin. Psychol.*, 1957, 13, 344–350.

274 ———. Over-aggressiveness in wives. *King Features Syndicate*, July 26, 1959; *Lumière et Liberté*, Oct., 1960. P. 3.

275 ———. Penthouse casebook. *Penthouse*, 1971, 2(10), 60–63.

276 ———. Penthouse casebook: Ego! Sex and the great I am! *Penthouse*, 1971, 3(1), 66–67, 92–94.

277 ———. The personal problems of senior nursing students. *Amer. J. Psychiat.*, 1949, 106, 212–215.

278 ———. Personality questionnaires. *Rev. educ. Res.*, 1947, 17, 56–63.

279 ———. Perversions and neurosis. *Int. J. Sexol.*, 1952, 6, 232–233.

280 ———. Phone dialogue with Hugh Hefner: The American Sex revolution. *Voices*, 1967, 3, 88–97.

281 ———. The place of value in the practice of psychotherapy. *Ann. Psychother. Monogr.*, 1959, No. 2.

282 ———. A plea for polygamy. *Eros*, 1962, 1(1), 22–23; Also published as a case for polygamy. *Nugget*, 1960, 5(1), 19, 24, 26.

283 ———. Postscript to J. Z. Eglinton, *Greek love*. New York: Oliver Layton Press, 1964. Pp. 429–438.

284 ———. Premarital relations—pro. *Controversy*, 1959, 1(4), 24, 26–27.

285 ———. Premarital sex relations. In R. A. Harper (Ed.), [Symposium]. *Marr. Fam. Living*, 1952, 14, 229–236.

Also in C. E. Vincent (Ed.), *Readings in marriage counseling.* New York: Crowell, 1956.

286 **Ellis, A.** The pressures of masculinity and femininity. *Independent,* 1964, No. 143. Pp. 1, 4, 6–7.

287 ———. Private clinical practice. In E. A. Rubinstein & M. Lorr, *A survey of clinical practice in psychology.* New York: Int. Univer. Press, 1954. Pp. 186–196.

288 ———. The private practice of psychotherapy: A clinical psychologist's report. *J. gen. Psychol.,* 1958, 58, 207–216.

289 ———. Professional liability insurance. *Amer. Psychologist,* 1955, 10, 243–244 (with R. G. Anderson, I. A. Berg, J. McV. Hunt, O. H. Mowrer, H. E. O'Shea, C. H. Rush, Jr., R. B. Selover, & W. H. Wulfeck).

290 ———. Pros and cons of legislation for psychologists. *Amer. Psychologist,* 1953, 8, 551–553.

291 ———. Prostitution re-assessed. *Int. J. Sexol.,* 1951, 5, 41–42.

292 ———. Psychiatric and psychological investigations of convicted sex offenders. *Amer. J. Psychiat.,* 1952, 109, 17–21 (with R. Brancale & Ruth Doorbar.)

293 ———. Psychological aspects of discouraging contraception. *Realist,* 1959, 1(7), 11–13.

294 ———. Psychologie de la sexualité. In *Dictionnaire de sexologie.* Paris: Jean-Jacques Pauvert, 1962. Also published as The psychology of sex. *Real Life Guide,* 1960, 3(3), 6–14.

295 ———. The psychologist in private practice and the good profession. *Amer. Psychologist,* 1952, 7, 129–131.

296 ———. A psychologist looks at adultery. *Rogue,* Feb. 1963. Pp. 15–16, 32.

297 ———. A psychologist looks at the Warren Report dissenters. *Cincinnati Pictorial Enquirer,* Nov. 19, 1967. Pp. 18–26; *New York Sunday News; New Haven Register.*

298 ———. The psychology and physiology of sex. In *Sex life of the American woman and the Kinsey report.* Pp. 203–214.

299 ———. The psychology of assassination. *Independent,* 1963, No. 139. Pp. 1, 4, 5; New York: Inst. Rat. Living, 1964.

300 ———. The psychology of sex. *Real Life Guide,* 1960, 3(3), 6–14. Also published as *Psychologie de la sexualité.* In *Dictionnaire de sexologie.* Paris: Jean-Jacques Pauvert, 1962.

301 **Ellis, A.** *The psychology of sex offenders.* Springfield, Ill.: C. C. Thomas, 1956 (with R. Brancale & Ruth R. Doorbar).

302 ———. The psychology of sex offenders. In A. Ellis & A. Abarbanel (Eds.), *The encyclopedia of sexual behavior.* Pp. 949–955.

303 ———. Psychosexual and marital problems. In L. A. Pennington & I. A. Berg (Eds.), *An introduction to clinical psychology.* Pp. 264–283; New York: Ronald Press, 1966. Pp. 248–269.

304 ———. Psychotherapy and atomic warfare. *Realist,* 1962, No. 38. Pp. 1–4.

305 ———. Psychotherapy and moral laxity. *Psychiat. Opin.,* 1967, 4(5), 18–21.

306 ———. Psychotherapy techniques for use with psychotics. *Amer. J. Psychother.,* 1955, 9, 452–476.

307 ———. Psychotherapy without tears. In A. Burton (Ed.), *Twelve therapists.* San Francisco: Jossey-Bass, 1972. Pp. 103–126.

308 ———. Qualifications of the clinical psychologist for the practice of psychotherapy. *J. clin. Psychol.,* 1955, 11, 33–37 (with J. Nydes & B. F. Riess).

309 ———. Questionnaire versus interview methods in the study of human love relationships. *Amer. sociol. Rev.,* 1947, 12, 541–553; II. Uncategorized responses. *Amer. sociol. Rev.,* 1948, 13, 61–65.

310 ———. A rational approach to interpretation. In E. Hammer, *The use of interpretation in treatment.* New York: Grune & Stratton, 1968. Ch. 28, 232–239; New York: Inst. Rat. Living, 1968.

311 ———. A rational approach to premarital counseling. *Psychol. Rep.,* 1961, 8, 333–338.

312 ———. Rational emotive psychotherapy. In D. S. Arbuckle, *Counseling and psychotherapy.* New York: McGraw-Hill, 1967. Pp. 78–100.

313 ———. Rational-emotive psychotherapy: A critique of three critiques. *Bull. Essex County Soc. Clin. Psychologists in Priv. Prac.,* Spring, 1963. Pp. 6–10.

314 ———. Rational-emotive therapy. In L. Hersher, *Four psychotherapies.* New York: Appleton-Century-Crofts, 1970. Pp. 47–83.

315 ———. Rational-emotive therapy in the private practice of psychotherapy. *J. contemp. Psychother.,* 1969, 1, 82–94; *Explorations,* 1969–70, No. 17. Pp. 5–12.

316 **Ellis, A.** Rational psychotherapy. *J. gen. Psychol.*, 1958, 59, 35–49; New York: Inst. Rat. Living, 1965.

317 ———. Rational psychotherapy and Individual Psychology. *JIP*, 1957, 13, 38–44.

318 ———. A rational sexual morality. In L. A. Kirkendall & R. N. Whitehurst (Eds.), *The new sexual revolution.* New York: Donald W. Brown, 1971. Pp. 47–61; New York: Prometheus Books, 1971.

319 ———. Rational therapy applied. *Balanced Living*, 1961, 17(6), 273–278.

320 ———. Rational training: A new method of facilitating management and labor relations. *Psychol. Rep.*, 1967, 20, 1267–1284 New York: Inst. Rat. Living, 1967 (with M. L. Blum).

321 ———. Rationalism and its therapeutic applications. In *The place of value in the practice of psychotherapy.* Pp. 55–64. Also published as A new look in psychotherapy. *Independent*, 1959, No. 94. Pp. 21–22.

322 ———. Rationality in sexual morality. *Humanist*, 1969, 29(5), 17–21; New York: Inst. Rat. Living, 1970.

323 ———. Re-analysis of an alleged telepathic dream. *Psychiat. Quart.*, 1949, 23, 116–126. Also in G. Devereux, *Psychoanalysis and the occult.* New York: Int. Univer. Press, 1953. Pp. 363–370.

324 ———. Reactions of psychotherapy patients who resist hypnosis. *J. clin. exp. Hypnosis*, 1953, 1(3), 12–15.

325 ———. Reason and emotion in the Individual Psychology of Adler. *JIP*, 1971, 27(1), 50–64.

326 ———. *Reason and emotion in psychotherapy.* New York: Lyle Stuart, 1962.

327 ———. Reason and emotion in psychotherapy. *Pop. Psychol.*, 1967, 1(1), 30–32, 59–62.

328 ———. Recent research with personality inventories. *J. consult. Psychol.*, 1953, 17, 45–49.

329 ———. Recent studies on the sex and love relations of young girls: A resumé. *Int. J. Sexol.*, 1953, 6, 161–163.

330 ———. Recent trends in sex, marriage, and family research. *Marr. Fam. Living*, 1952, 14, 338–340 (with Ruth R. Doorbar).

331 ———. Recent views on sexual deviation. In A. P. Pillay & A. Ellis (Eds.), *Sex, society and the individual.* Pp. 337–349.

332 **Ellis, A.** Recommendations concerning standards for the unsupervised practice of clinical psychology. *Amer. Psychologist*, 1953, 8, 494–495.

333 ———. The relationship between personality inventory scores and other psychological test results. *J. soc. Psychol.*, 1948, 26, 287–289.

334 ———. Reply to the Humm's "Notes on the validity of personality inventories in military practice." *Psychol. Bull.*, 1949, 46, 307–308.

335 ———. Report on survey of members of the Division of Clinical and Abnormal Psychology who are presently engaged in paid private practice. *Suppl. Nwsltr., Div. Clin. Abnorm. Psychol., Amer. Psychol. Assn.*, Aug., 1951. Pp. 1–4.

336 ———. Requisite conditions for basic personality change. *J. consult. Psychol.*, 1959, 6, 538–540.

337 ———. Requisites for research in psychotherapy. *J. clin. Psychol.*, 1950, 6, 152–156.

338 ———. The requisites of the sexual revolution and their relation to nudism. *Sol*, 1966, No. 7. Pp. 30–31.

339 ———. Research in psychotherapy. *Nwsltr., Psychologists in Priv. Prac.*, Feb., 1960.

340 ———. Results of a mental hygiene approach to reading disability problems. *J. consult. Psychol.*, 1949, 13, 56–61.

341 ———. Review of W. E. O'Connell, *An odyssey of a Psychologist.* In *JIP*, 1972, 28, 92.

342 ———. The right to sex enjoyment. *Independent*, 1957, No. 72. P. 4.

343 ———. The role of coital positions in sexual relations. *Sex. Behav.*, 1971, 1(4), 11–12.

344 ———. The roots of psychology and psychiatry. In M. H. Krout, *Psychology, psychiatry and the public interest.* Minneapolis: Univ. Minnesota Press, 1956. Pp. 9–13.

345 ———. Rorschach methods and other projective techniques. *Rev. educ. Res.*, 1947, 17, 78–100 (with Marguerite R. Hertz & P. M. Symonds).

346 ———. *The search for sexual enjoyment.* New York: Lyle Stuart, 1966.

347 ———. Self acceptance and successful human relations. *Nwsltr., Inst. for*

Marr. and Friendship and Sci. Introduc. Centre, 1967, 3, 8-9.

348 Ellis, A. Self-appraisal methods. In D. Brower & L. Abt (Eds.), *Progress in clinical psychology*. Vol. II. Pp. 67-90.

349 ———. *The sensuous person: Critique and corrections.* New York: Lyle Stuart, 1972.

350 ———. The seven secrets of sexual satisfaction. *Pageant*, 1959, 14(12), 26-31.

351 ———. The seven year itch. *Dude*, 1962, 6(3), 8-10, 71-72.

352 ———. Sex and censorship in literature and the arts. *Playboy*, July, 1961. Pp. 27-28, 74-99 (with T. Arnold, R. Ginzburg, M. Girodias, N. Mailer, O. Preminger, B. Rosset, & P. Krassner).

353 ———. Sex and civilization. *Independent*, 1966, No. 167. PP. 1, 8; 1966, No. 168. Pp. 5-6, 8.

354 ———. Sex and revolution. *Mod. Utopian*, 1968, 2(5), 3.

355 ———. Sex and summer violence. *This month*, 1962, 1(6), 46-52.

356 ———. Sex and the family. In I. A. Falk (Ed.), *Prophecy for the year 2000.* New York: Julian Messner, 1970. Pp. 176-178.

357 ———. *Sex and the single man.* New York: Lyle Stuart, 1963; New York: Dell Books, 1965.

358 ———. Sex and the young adult. *Twenty-five*, 1968, 1(1), 36-39, 50-51.

359 ———. Sex and violence in society. *Independent*, 1965, No. 157. Pp. 1, 4, 6.

360 ———. *Sex beliefs and customs.* London: Peter Nevill, 1951. Also published as *The folklore of sex.* New York: Charles Boni, 1951.

361 ———. Sex freedom in marriage. *Best years*, 1954, 1(1), 3-7; *Sexol.*, 1957; *Real Life Guide*, Dec., 1959; *Lumière et Liberté*, Mar., 1962.

362 ———. Sex, frustration and aggression. *Rogue*, 1969, No. 18. Pp. 27-30.

363 ———. *Sex life of the American woman and the Kinsey report.* New York: Greenberg, 1954.

364 ———. The sex, love, and marriage questions of senior nursing students. *J. soc. Psychol.*, 1950, 31, 209-216.

365 ———. Sex: Love or hate. *Independent*, 1963, No. 132. Pp. 1, 4, 6.

366 ———. The sex offender and his treatment. In H. Toch (Ed.), *Legal*

and criminal psychology. New York: Holt, Rinehart & Winston, 1961. Pp. 400-416.

367 Ellis, A. Sex—the schizoid best seller. *Sat. Rev. Lit.*, 1951, 34(11), 42-44.

368 ———. *Sex, society and the individual.* Bombay: Int. J. Sexol., 1953 (with A. P. Pillay).

369 ———. *Sex without guilt.* New York: Lyle Stuart, 1958; New York: Hillman Books, 1959; New York: Macfadden Books, 1960; New York: Grove Press, 1965; New York: Lancer Books, 1969.

370 ———. Sex without guilt. In D. L. Grummon & A. M. Barclay (Eds.), *Sexuality: A search for perspective.* New York: Van Nostrand Reinhold, 1971. Pp. 226-244.

371 ———. Sexual adventuring and personality growth. In H. A. Otto (Ed.), *The new sexuality.* Palo Alto, Cal.: Science & Behavior Books, 1971. Pp. 94-109; New York: Inst. Rat. Living, 1972.

372 ———. The sexual criminal. *Penthouse*, 1970, 1(8), 83-86, 93.

373 ———. The sexual element in non-sex crimes. *Psychol. Nwsltr.*, 1957, 8, 122-125.

374 ———. Sexual inadequacy in the male. *Independent*, 1956, No. 57. P. 4.

375 ———. Sexual manifestations of emotionally disturbed behavior. *Ann. Amer. Acad. Pol. & Soc. Sci.*, 1968, 376, 96-105; New York: Inst. Rat. Living, 1968.

376 ———. Sexual promiscuity in America. *Ann. Amer. Acad. Pol. & Soc. Sci.*, 1968, 378, 58-67.

377 ———. The sexual psychology of human hermaphrodites. *Psychosom. Med.*, 1945, 7, 108-125.

378 ———. A sexologist looks at sexual living. *Independent*, 1968, No. 184. P. 5; 1968, No. 186. Pp. 1, 4, 6; 1969, No. 188. Pp. 7-8.

379 ———. Should men marry older women? *This Week*, July 6, 1958. Pp. 8-9. Also in Ruth Shonle Cavan, *Marriage and family in the modern world.* New York: Crowell, 1960. Pp. 157-160.

380 ———. Should non-professionals be trained to do psychotherapy? *Nwsltr., Div. Clin. Psychol., Amer. Psychol. Assn.*, 1966, 19(2), 10-11.

381 ———. Should some people be labeled mentally ill? *J. consult. Psychol.*, 1967, 31, 435-446; New York: Inst. Rat. Living, 1967.

382 **Ellis, A.** Should we ban war toys? *Realist*, 1964, No. 48. Pp. 29–31.

383 ———. Sick and healthy love. *Independent*, 1963, No. 132. Pp. 1, 8–9; No. 133. Pp. 4–6.

384 ———. Social interest. *IPNL*, 1967, 18(3–4, Whole No. 200–201). Pp. 17–18.

385 ———. Some significant correlates of love and family behavior. *J. soc. Psychol.*, 1949, 30, 3–16.

386 ———. Special review of A. C. Kinsey, W. B. Pomeroy, & C. E. Martin, *sexual behavior in the human male.* In *J. gen. Psychol.*, 1948, 39, 299–326.

387 ———. State's adopted "Kinsey" reports. *L. A. Free Press*, Jan. 20, 1967. P. 16.

388 ———. A study of human love relationships. *J. genet. Psychol.*, 1949, 75, 61–71.

389 ———. A study of the love emotions of American college girls. *Int. J. Sexol.*, 1949, 3, 15–21.

390 ———. A study of sexual preferences. *Int. J. Sexol.*, 1952, 6, 87–88; *Real Life Guide*, Aug., 1960 (with Ruth Doorbar, H. Guze, & L. Clark).

391 ———. A study of 300 sex offenders. *Int. J. Sexol.*, 1951, 4, 127–135. Also in A. P. Pillay & A. Ellis, *Sex, society and the individual.*

392 ———. A study of trends in recent psychoanalytic publications. *Amer. Imago*, 1948, 5, 306–316.

393 ———. *Suggested procedures for a weekend of rational encounter.* New York: Inst. Adv. Study Rat. Psychother., 1969, 1972.

394 ———. *Suppressed: Seven key essays publishers dared not print.* Chicago: New Classics House, 1965.

395 ——— (Ed.). *Symposium on aspects of female sexuality. Quart. Rev. Surg. Obstet. & Gynecol.*, 1959, 16, 217–263; New York: Soc. Sci. Study of Sex, 1959.

396 ———. A talk with Dr. Ellis [Interviewed by C. Averitt & L. Lipton]. *L. A. Free Press*, Sept. 10, 1964. P. 3.

397 ———. Talking to adolescents about sex. *Rat. Living*, 1967, 2(1), 7–12.

398 ———. Teaching emotional education in the classroom. *Sch. Hlth. Rev.*, Nov., 1969. Pp. 10–13.

399 ———. Teen age sex relations. *Realist*, 1962, No. 31. Pp. 30–31.

400 ———. Telepathy and psychoanalysis: A critique of recent "findings." *Psychiat.*

Quart., 1947, 21, 607–659. Also in G. Devereux (Ed.), *Psychoanalysis and the occult.* New York: Int. Univer. Press, 1953. Pp. 297–314.

401 **Ellis, A.** Ten indiscreet proposals. *Pageant*, 1958, 14(5), 6–15; *ICSE Nwsltr.*, Jan., 1960.

402 ———. Theoretical schools of psychology. In A. Weider (Ed.), *Contributions toward medical psychology.* New York: Ronald Press, 1953. Pp. 31–50.

403 ———. There is no place for the concept of sin in psychotherapy. *J. couns. Psychol.*, 1960, 7, 188–192.

404 ———. Thoughts on petting. *Independent*, 1957, No. 68. P. 4.

405 ———. Thoughts on theory vs. outcome in psychotherapy. *Psychother.*, 1964, 1, 83–87.

406 ———. To thine own psychotherapeutic self be true. *Nwsltr., Psychologists in Priv. Prac.*, 1963, 4(1), 8.

407 ———. Toward a more precise definition of "emotional" and "intellectual" insight. *Psychol. Rep.*, 1963, 13, 125–126.

408 ———. Toward an understanding of youthful rebellion. In P. R. Frank (Ed.), *A search for a meaning of a generation gap.* San Diego: San Diego Co. Dept. Educ., 1969. Pp. 85–111.

409 ———. Towards the improvement of psychoanalytic research. *Psychoanal. Rev.*, 1949, 36, 123–143.

410 ———. The treatment of a psychopath with rational psychotherapy. *Quaderni di Criminol. Clin.*, 1959, 1, 173–184; *J. Psychol.*, 1961, 51, 141–150.

411 ———. The treatment of psychotic and borderline psychotic patients with rational emotive psychotherapy. In *Symposium on therapeutic methods with schizophrenics.* Battle Creek, Mich.: VA Hosp., 1965. Pp. 5–32; New York: Inst. Rat. Living, 1965.

412 ———. The truth about nudity and sexuality. *Bachelor*, 1963, 4(5), 18–20, 67–68.

413 ———. Twelve true versus false ideas. *Balanced Living*, 1962, 18, 140–141.

414 ———. The use of printed, written and recorded words in psychotherapy. In L. Pearson (Ed.), *The use of written communications in psychotherapy.* Springfield, Ill.: C. C. Thomas, 1965. Pp. 23–36.

415 ———. Use of psychotherapy with homosexuals. *Mattachine Rev.*, 1956, 2, 14–16.

416 **Ellis, A.** The use of sex in human life: A dialogue [with D. Mace]. *J. Sex Res.*, 1969, 5, 41–49.

417 ———. The validity of personality inventories in military practice. *Psychol. Bull.*, 1948, 45, 385–420.

418 ———. The validity of personality questionnaires. *Psychol. Bull.*, 1946, 43, 385–440.

419 ———. Valuation in presenting scientific data. *Sociol. soc. Res.*, 1948, 33, 92–96.

420 ———. The value of marriage prediction tests. *Amer. sociol. Rev.*, 1948, 13, 710–718. Also in R. F. Winch & R. McGinnis (Eds.), *Selected studies in marriage and the family.* New York: Holt, 1953.

421 ———. A weekend of rational encounter. In A. Burton (Ed.), *Encounter.* San Francisco: Jossey-Bass, 1969. Pp. 112–127; *Rat. Living*, 1970, 42(2), 1–8.

422 ———. What creates sex hostility? *Sexol.*, 1964, 30, 592–594.

423 ———. What does transpersonal psychology have to offer to the art and science of psychotherapy? *Voices*, 1972, 8(3), 10–20.

424 ———. What else is new? Me! *Voices*, 1969–70, 5(3), 33–35.

425 ———. What is normal sex behavior? *Complex*, 1952, 8, 41–51. Also in A. Ellis & R. Brancale, *The psychology of sex offenders: Hlth. Dig.*, Feb., 1961; *Lumière et Liberté*, July, 1961.

426 ———. What is normal sex behavior? *Sexol.*, 1962, 28, 364–369.

427 ———. What is psychotherapy? *Ann. Psychother. Monogr.*, 1959, No. 1.

428 ———. What is psychotherapy?—varied approaches to the problem. *Ann. Psychother. Monogr.*, 1959, No. 1. Pp. 5–8.

429 ———. What kinds of research are American psychologists doing? *Amer. Psychologist*, 1949, 4, 490–494.

430 ———. What really causes therapeutic change? *Voices*, 1968, 4(2), 90–97; New York: Inst. Rat. Living, 1969.

431 ———. What should you do about an unfaithful husband? *Pageant*, 1960, 15(9), 6–11.

432 ———. What we should know about a sensuous man. *Coronet*, 1970, 8(10), 18–24.

433 ———. When are we going to quit stalling about sex education? *Independent*, 1956, No. 54. P. 4.

434 **Ellis, A.** Which intercourse position or positions are best for a woman to reach orgasm? *Sex. Behav.*, 1971, 1(8), 4.

435 ———. Why Americans are so fearful of sex. *Independent*, 1956, No. 53. P. 4; *Mattachine Rev.*, 1956, 3(1), 13–15.

436 ———. Why married men visit prostitutes. *Sexol.*, 1959, 25, 344–347; *Lumière et Liberté*, Nov., 1961.

437 ———. Why one out of every five wives is having an affair. *Pageant*, 1967, 23(3), 112–117.

438 ———. Wife swapping. *Realist*, 1964, No. 50. Pp. 19–21.

439 ———. Woman as sex aggressor. *Best Years*, 1955, 1(3), 25–29.

440 ———. A young woman convicted of manslaughter. *Case Rep. clin. Psychol.*, 1951, 2(1), 9–34.

441 **Ellis, H.** Yes to social interest. *IPNL*, 1972, 21(5), 81–82.

442 **Emerson, H.** Wer ist unheilbar? *IZIP*, 1934, 12(1), 5–10.

443 **Emerson, R. W.** Über Kompensation. *IZIP*, 1933, 11(4), 282.

444 **Emmerich, W.** Young children's discriminations of parent and child roles. *Child Developm.*, 1959, 20, 404–420.

445 **Engebretson, D.** Pastoral counseling with low-income clients. *JIP*, 1972, 28, 67–75.

446 **Engerth, G.** Review of H. Hoffman, *Das Problem des Charakteraufbaues, seine Gestaltung durch die erbbiologische Persönlichkeitsanalyse.* Berlin: J. Springer, 1926. In *IZIP*, 1928, 6(5), 423.

447 **Eppelbaum, Vera.** See Strasser, Vera.

448 **Epstein, H.** *Youth in danger becomes a danger: A symposium on juvenile delinquency.* New York: Individual Psychology Assn., 1956 (with Alexandra Adler, J. Dumpson, & E. Papanek).

449 **Erb, E. D.** *The psychology of the emerging self.* Philadelphia: Davis, 1967 (with D. Hooker).

450 **Erbstein, J.** Review of Jean S. Grossman, *Life with family.* New York: Appleton-Century-Crofts, 1948. In *IPB*, 1949, 7, 139.

451 **Eriksen, C. W.** The case for perceptual defense. *Psychol. Rev.*, 1954, 61, 175–182.

452 ———. Individual differences in defensive forgetting. *J. exp. Psychol.*, 1952, 44, 442–446.

453 **Ermalinski, R.** Action therapy intervention in human interaction training.

Nwsltr. Res. Psychol., 1972, 14(4), 23–25 (with W. E. O'Connell, R. R. Baker & P. G. Hanson).

454 **Ermalinski, R.** The generation gap on a psychiatric ward. *Nwsltr. Res. Psychol.*, 1971, 13(2), 1–5 (with P. Hanson & W. E. O'Connell).

455 ———. Toward resolution of a generation gap conflict on a psychiatric ward. *Int. J. grp. Tensions*, 1972, 2(2), 77–89 (with P. Hanson & W. E. O'Connell).

456 **Ernst, C. J.** Aus der Erziehungspraxis. *IZIP*, 1949, 18(4), 176–181.

457 ———. Individualpsychologische Gedankengänge in Vergangenheit und Gegenwart. *IZIP*, 1947, 16(4), 189–190.

458 ———. Review of H. Glaser, *Die Beziehungen der Geschlechter*. Wien: Holder-Pichler-Tempsky, 1949. In *IZIP*, 1950, 19(3), 141.

459 ———. Review of P. R. Hofstätter, *Einführung in die Tiefenpsychologie*. Wien: Bräumüller, 1948. In *IZIP*, 1949, 18(3), 137–138.

460 ———. Review of P. R. Hofstätter, *Die Psychologie der öffentlichen Meinung*. Wien: Bräumüller, 1949. In *IZIP*, 1950, 19(3), 141–142.

461 ———. Review of E. Menninger-Lerchenthal, *Das europäische Selbstmordproblem*. Wien: F. Deuticke, 1947. In *IZIP*, 1947, 17(3), 142–143.

462 ———. Review of *Nietzsche-Brevier*. Wien: G. Prachner, 1950. In *IZIP*, 1951, 20(4), 190.

463 ———. Review of H. Schwartz, *Das Buch der Lebenskunst—Schaff dir Freude*. Wien: Frau u. Mutter Verlag, 1949. In *IZIP*, 1950, 19(3), 143.

464 ———. Review of H. Schiff, *Elternfehler—Kinderschicksal*. Wien: Bräumüller, 1948. In *IZIP*, 1949, 18(3), 138–139.

465 ———. Review of W. M. Treichlinger, *Japanische Spruchweisheit*. Stuttgart: Janusbibliothek der Weltliteratur, 1950. In *IZIP*, 1950, 19(4), 191.

466 ———. Review of E. von Feuchtersleben, *Kleines Lehrbuch der Vernunft*. Wien: G. Prachner, 1949. In *IZIP*, 1950, 19(3), 40–41.

467 ———. Review of *Wiener Zeitschrift für praktische Psychologie*. Wien: Hollinek, 1949. In *IZIP*, 1950, 20(1), 45–46.

468 **Ernst, E. J.** Review of R. Dreikurs, *Manual of child guidance*. In *IZIP*, 1949, 18(1), 44–45.

469 **Ernst, K.** Review of N. Fenton, The diagnosis "Hickman". *Survey*, June, 1929. In *IZIP*, 1931, 9(4), 482–483.

470 **Escalona, Sybille K.** The effect of success and failure upon level of aspiration and behavior in manic-depressive psychoses. *Univ. Iowa Stud. Child Welf.*, 1940, 16, 199–302

471 **Espenak, Liljan.** The role of dance therapy in Adlerian psychology. *IP*, 1966, 4(1), 8–9.

472 ———. Movement diagnosis tests and the inherent laws governing their use in treatment: An aid in detecting the life style. *IP*, 1970, 7(1), 8–13.

473 **Estes, S. G.** Concerning the therapeutic relationship in the dynamics of cure. *J. consult. Psychol.*, 1948, 12, 76–81.

474 **Estes, W. K.** *Learning theory and mental development*. New York: Academic Press, 1970.

475 **Etigson, Elizabeth.** Effect of stress on earliest memory. *Arch. gen. Psychiat.*, 1968, 19, 435–444 (with S. S. Tobin).

476 **Evans, J. H.** The influence of teacher personality and pupil misbehavior upon teache impressions of pupils. Ph.D. Diss., Indiana Univ., 1971.

477 **Evans, J. W.** Alienation and learning in a hospital setting. *Amer. sociol. Rev.*, 1962, 27, 772–782 (with M. Seeman).

478 **Evans, R. I.** *Innovations in social psychiatry*. London: Avenue Publ. Co., 1969 (with J. Bierer).

479 **Exner, J. E.** Birth order and hierarchical versus innovative role requirements. *J. Pers.*, 1970, 38, 581–587 (with B. Sutton-Smith).

480 **Eysenck, H. J.** Personality in primary schoc children. III. Family background. *Brit. J. educ. Psychol.*, 1970, 40, 117–131 (with D Cookson).

F

1 **F. K.** Review of *Bericht über die dritte Tagung über Psychopathenfürsorge*. Berlin: Springer, 1925. In *IZIP*, 1926, 4(3), 168.

2 **Fagan, R. C.** The future progress of Individual Psychology. *IPB*, 1942, 2(3), 54–55.

3 Fairbairn, J. S. I. P. and psychosomatic disorders (II). *IPMP*, 1933, No. 9 (with W. M. Eccles, M. Marcus, Mary B. Ferguson, & F. G. Crookshank).

4 ———. Remarks on psychology in gynaecological practice. *IPMP*, 1933, No. 9. Pp. 7–24.

5 Falzoni, G. Translator of R. Dreikurs, *Lineamenti della psicologia di Adler.*

6 Fanning, Edna G. Translator of R. Dreikurs, *An introduction to Individual Psychology.*

7 Fanon, F. *Black skin, white masks.* Translated by C. L. Markmann. New York: Grove Press, 1967.

8 Fantl, Berta. Cultural factors in family diagnosis of a Chinese family. *Int. J. soc. Psychiat.*, 1959, 5(1), 27–32.

9 Fanucchi, K. J. Counseling lab holds spanking often harmful. *Los Angeles Times*, Feb. 27, 1972.

10 Farau, A. Alfred Adler und die Zukunft der Psychologie. *Die Heilkunst* (München), 1960, 73(2), 39–43.

11 ———. Alfred Adler zum 80. Geburtstage. *IZIP*, 1950, 19(2), 49–55.

12 ———. C. G. Jung: An Adlerian appreciation. *JIP*, 1961, 17, 135–141.

13 ———. The challenge of social feeling. In K. A. Adler & Danica Deutsch (Eds.), *Essays in Individual Psychology.* Pp. 8–16.

14 ———. (Contributions on Adlerian psychology). *Church Dictionary.* New York: Morehouse-Barlow, 1964.

15 ———. *Der Einfluss der Oesterreichischen Tiefenpsychologie auf die Psychotherapie der Gegenwart.* Vienna-Meisenheim: A. Sexl, 1953.

16 ———. Die Entwicklung der Individualpsychologie und ihre Steilung in heutigen Amerika. *Psyche* (Stuttgart), 1960, 13(12), 881–891.

17 ———. A few personal memories of Alfred Adler. *IP*, 1967, 4(2), 42–45.

18 ———. Fifty years of Individual Psychology. *Comprehen. Psychiat.*, 1962, 3, 242–254.

19 ———. The heritage of Alfred Adler. *Darshana Int.* (Moradabad, India), 1964, 4, 105–112; *Universitas* (Stuttgart), 1965, 8(1), 67–76.

20 ———. Individual Psychology and existentialism. *IP*, 1964, 2(1), 1–8.

21 ———. The influence of Alfred Adler on current psychology. *AJIP*, 1952, 10, 59–76.

22 Farau. A. The legacy of Alfred Adler. Part 1. *Pirquet Bull. clin. Med.*, 19(2, 3, 4), 10–13.

23 ———. My teacher, Alfred Adler. *Universitas* (Stuttgart), 1968, 2(1), 65–74.

24 ———. Portrait. *IPNL*, 1972, 21(6), 112.

25 ———. *A psicologia das profundidades.* Coimbra, Portugal: Atlandida, 1963 (with H. Schaffer).

26 ———. *La psicologia del profondo.* Rome: Casa Editrice Astrolabio, 1963 (with H. Schaffer).

27 ———. *La psicologia profunda.* Madrid: Espasa-Calpe, 1963 (with H. Schaffer).

28 ———. *La psychologie des profondeurs, des origins à nos jours.* Paris: Payot, 1960 (with H. Schaffer).

29 ———. Review of P. Rom, *Sigmund Freud.* In *JIP*, 1967, 23, 120.

30 ———. Sane man and sane society. *Darshana Int.* (Moradabad, India), 1963, 3(3), 17–26.

31 Farber, M. *The foundation of phenomenology.* Cambridge, Mass.: Harvard Univ. Press, 1943.

32 ———. The function of phenomenological analysis. *Phil. phenomenol. Res.*, 1941, 1, 431–441.

33 ———. *Phenomenology as a method and as a philosophical discipline.* Buffalo: Univ. Buffalo Press, 1928.

34 Farberow, N. L. (Ed.). *The cry for help.* New York: McGraw-Hill, 1961 (with E. S. Schneidman).

35 Farina, A. Birth order of recovered and nonrecovered schizophrenics. *Arch. gen. Psychiat.*, 1963, 9, 224–228 (with H. Barry, N. Garmezy, & C. Storrs).

36 Faris, M. Early memories as expressions of relationship paradigms. *Amer. J. Orthopsychiat.*, 1960, 30, 507–520 (with M. Mayman).

37 Farley, F. H. Birth order, achievement, motivation, and academic attainment. *Brit. J. educ. Psychol.*, 1967, 37, 256.

38 Farrelly, F. Weapons of insanity. *Amer. J. Psychother.*, 1967, 21, 737–749 (with A. M. Ludwig).

39 Farson, R. E. The therapeutic event in group psychotherapy: A study of subjective reports by group members. *JIP*, 1963, 19, 204–212 (with Constance Pious & Betty Berzon).

40 Feather, B. Review of D. Dinkmeyer & R. Dreikurs, *Encouraging children* *to learn.* In *Contemp. Psychol.*, 1964, 9, 187.

41 **Feather, N. T.** *A theory of achievement motivation.* New York: Wiley, 1966 (with J. W. Atkinson).

42 **Feder, D. D.** Measurement of self concept: A critique of the literature. *J. couns. Psychol.*, 1961, 8, 170-179 (with D. J. Strong).

43 **Federn, E.** (Ed.). *Minutes of the Vienna Psychoanalytic Society. Vol. 1. 1906-1908.* New York: Int. Univer. Press, 1962 (with H. Nunberg).

44 ———. Was Adler a disciple of Freud? A Freudian view. *JIP*, 1963, 19, 80-82.

45 **Feibleman, J.** Critique of the logic of psychoanalysis. *IJIP*, 1936, 2(4), 309-319.

46 **Feichtinger, F.** Early recollections in neurotic disturbances. *IPB*, 1943, 3, 44-50.

47 ———. In memoriam. *IPB*, 1947, 6, 5-7.

48 ———. The psychology of guilt feelings. *IPB*, 1950, 8, 39-43.

49 ———. Psychosomatics and psychoneuroses. *AJIP*, 1954, 10, 123-135.

50 ———. Teaching of mental hygiene. *IPB*, 1949, 7, 5-11. Also in K. A. Adler & Danica Deutsch (Eds.), *Essays in Individual Psychology.* Pp. 99-108.

51 **Feigenbaum, K.** Leisure and life style. *Amer. J. Sociol.*, 1959, 64, 396-404 (with R. J. Havighurst).

52 **Feingold, Lissy.** Suicide in twins and only children. *Amer. J. hum. Genet.*, 1949, 1, 113-126 (with F. J. Kallman, J. DePorte & E. DePorte).

53 **Feldman, Ruth C.** A study of cognitive style and some personality variables in relation to the conceptual performance of emotionally disturbed adolescents. *Diss. Abstr.*, 1965, 26, 1776-1777.

54 **Feldmann, Evelyn.** Thirty days with Alfred Adler. *JIP*, 1972, 28, 81-89.

55 **Feldstein, S.** Factors interacting with birth order in self-selection among volunteer subjects. *J. soc. Psychol.*, 1967, 72, 125-128 (with Barbara S. Dohrenwend & Gertrude Schmeidler).

56 **Fenchel, G. H.** Cognitive rigidity as a behavioral variable manifested in intellectual and perceptual tasks by an outpatient population. Unpubl. Ph.D. Diss., New York Univ., 1959.

57 ———. Review of H. Ansbacher & Rowena R. Ansbacher (Eds.), *Superiority and social interest.* In *IP*, 1964, 2(2), 23-24.

58 **Fenchel, G. H.** Review of W. Gorman, *Flavor, taste, and the psychology of smell.* Springfield, Ill.: C. C. Thomas, 1964. In *IP*, 1965, 3(1), 24.

59 ———. Review of N. Grekoski, *Psychological testing.* Springfield, Ill.: C. C. Thomas, 1964. In *IP*, 1964, 2(2), 25.

60 ———. Review of L. Kanner, *A history of the care and study of the mentally retarded.* Springfield, Ill.: C. C. Thomas, 1964. In *IP*, 1964, 2(2), 25.

61 ———. Review of M. Levine & G. Spivack, *The Rorschach index of repressive style.* Springfield, Ill.: C. C. Thomas, 1964. In *IP*, 1964, 2(2), 25.

62 ———. Review of H. Mullan & M. Rosenbaum, *Group psychotherapy.* Glencoe, Ill.: Free Press, 1962. In *IP*, 1963, 1(1), 19-20.

63 ———. Review of Hertha Orgler, *Alfred Adler—the man and his work.* In *IP*, 1964, 2(2), 25-26.

64 ———. Review of J. P. Riedy, *Zone mental health centers.* Springfield, Ill.: C. C. Thomas, 1964. In *IP*, 1965, 3(1), 24-25.

65 ———. Review of A. Wolf & E. Schwartz, *Psychoanalysis in groups.* New York: Grune & Stratton, 1962. In *IP*, 1963, 1(1), 18-19.

66 ———. Social interest—task and challenge. *IP*, 1963, 1(2), 5-12.

67 **Fenichel, O.** *Psychoanalytic theory of neurosis.* New York: Norton, 1945.

68 **Fenton, N.** The only child. *J. genet. Psychol.*, 1928, 35, 546-556.

69 **Ferguson, Eva D.** Adlerian concepts in contemporary psychology: The changing scene. *JIP*, 1960, 24, 150-156.

70 ———. Effect of ego-involvement instructions and intratest similarity on stimulus generalization errors in paired-associate learning. *Psychol. Rep.*, 1972, 31, 243-248.

71 ———. The effect of sibling competition and alliance on level of aspiration, expectation, and performance. *J. abnorm. soc. Psychol.*, 1958, 56, 213-222.

72 ———. Ego-involvement: As a stimulus, as a response, and its relationship to level of aspiration. *Amer. Psychologist*, 1959, 14, 392 (Abstract).

73 ———. Ego involvement: A critical examination of some methodological issues. *J. abnorm. soc. Psychol.*, 1962, 64, 407-417.

74 **Ferguson, Eva D.** An evaluation of two types of kindergarten attendance programs. *J. educ. Psychol.*, 1957, 48, 287–301.

75 ———. Family counseling in a nursery school. *IPB*, 1951, 9, 167–169.

76 ———. Financial assistance for master's degree students. *Amer. Psychologist*, 1968, 23(6), 456.

77 ———. Interview and test data in a diagnostic problem: A case report. *J. clin. Psychol.*, 1959, 15, 124–127 (with M. Swartz).

78 ———. Relationship between ego-involvement instructions and various motivation and performance measures. *Psychol. Rep.*, 1971, 29(5), 547–556.

79 ———. Review of Janet Chenery, *Wolfie.* In *Science Books: A quarterly Review.*

80 ———. Review of V. H. Denenberg (Ed.), *Readings in the development of behavior.* Stamford, Conn.: Sinauer, 1972. In *Science Books: A quarterly Review.*

81 ———. Review of W. K. Estes, *Learning theory and mental development.* New York: Academic Press, 1970. In *Science Books: A quarterly Review.*

82 ———. Review of H. C. Lindgren, D. Byrne, & F. Lindgren (Eds.), *Current research in psychology: A book of readings.* In *Science Books: A quarterly Review.*

83 ———. Role of individual differences in measures of ego-involvement. *Psychol. Rep.*, 1971, 29, 569–570.

84 ———. The use of early recollections in assessing life style and diagnosing psychopathology. *J. proj. Tech.*, 1964, 28, 402–412.

85 **Ferguson, J. F.** Review of Anne Anastasi, *Differential psychology.* New York: Macmillan, 1958. In *IJIP*, 1937, 3(2), 203–204.

86 ———. Review of H. S. Dimock, *Rediscovering the adolescent.* New York: Association Press, 1937. In *IJIP*, 1937, 3(3), 274–275.

87 **Ferguson, Mary B.** A case of aphonia. *IPMP*, 1933, No. 9. Pp. 41–45.

88 ———. I. P. and psychosomatic disorders (II). *IPMP*, 1933, No. 9 (with W. M. Eccles, M. Marcus, J. S. Fairbairn, & F. G. Crookshank).

89 **Ferreira, A. J.** Family myth and family life style. *JIP*, 1967, 23, 224–225.

90 ———. Family myth and homeostasis. *Arch. gen. Psychiat.*, 1963, 9, 457–463.

91 **Ferreira, A. J.** Family myths. *Amer. Psychiat. Assn., Psychiat. Res. Rep.*, 1966, 20, 85–90.

92 ———. Family myths: The covert rules of the relationship. *Confin. Psychiat.*, 1965, 8, 15–20.

93 ———. Family therapy and the concept of mental health. *Voices*, 1967, 3(2), 18–21.

94 ———. Psychosis and family myth. *Amer. J. Psychother.*, 1967, 21, 186–197.

95 **Festinger, L.** A theoretical interpretation of shifts in level of aspiration. *Psychol. Rev.*, 1942, 49, 235–250.

96 **Feuer, L. S.** Rejoinder on "The role of sexuality in the formation of ideas". *JIP*, 1961, 17, 110–111.

97 ———. The standpoints of Dewey and Freud: A contrast and analysis. *JIP*, 1960, 16, 119–136.

98 **Fey, W. F.** Acceptance by others and its relation to acceptance of self and others: A revaluation. *J. abnorm. soc. Psychol.*, 1955, 50, 274–276.

99 ———. Correlates of certain subjective attitudes towards self and others. *J. clin. Psychol.*, 1957, 13, 44–49.

100 **Fiddle, S.** *Portraits from a shooting gallery: Life styles from the drug addict world.* New York: Harper & Row, 1967.

101 **Fiedler, F.** A comparison of therapeutic relationships in psychoanalytic, nondirective, and Adlerian therapy. *J. consult. Psychol.*, 1950, 14, 436–445.

102 ———. The concept of the ideal therapeutic relationship. *J. consult. Psychol.*, 1950, 14, 239–245.

103 ———. Factor analyses of psychoanalytic, nondirective and Adlerian therapeutic relationships. *J. consult. Psychol.*, 1951, 15, 32–38.

104 ———. The psychological-distance dimension in interpersonal relations. *J. Pers.*, 1953, 22, 142–150.

105 **Fienburgh, W.** Breastplasty. *IPNL*, 1953, No. 33. Pp. 2–3.

106 **Filbert, M. S.** A study of cognitive styles in the deaf. *Diss. Abstr.*, 1965, 26, 3485. Unpubl. Ph.D. Diss., Univ. Rochester, 1965.

107 **Finch, Helen M.** Young children's concepts of parent roles. *J. Home Econ.*, 1955, 47, 99–103.

108 **Fink, H. K.** Adaptation of the family constellation in group psychotherapy. *Acta Psychother.*, 1958, 6, 189–192.

109 **Firestone, I.** Birth order and reactions to frustration. *J. abnorm. soc. Psychol.*, 1963, 66, 192–194 (with D. C. Glass & M. Horwitz).

110 **Fischel, W.** Das Zielstreben der Tiere. *Jb. Psychol. Psychother.*, 1952, 1, 37–45.

111 **Fischer, E. H.** Birth order and expressed interest in being a college professor. *J. couns. Psychol.*, 1968, 15, 111–116 (with C. F. Wells & S. L. Cohen).

112 ———. First born and last born children: Further comments. *JIP*, 1966, 22, 212–213.

113 ———. Participation in psychological research: Relation to birth order and demographic factors. *J. consult. clin. Psychol.*, 1969, 33, 610–613 (with D. Winer).

114 **Fischer, Sylvia.** Coercion in the nursery school. *Nerv. Child.*, 1946, 5, 244–246 (with Danica Deutsch).

115 **Fischer, W. F.** Review of J. Lyons, *Psychology and the measure of man.* New York: Free Press of Glencoe, 1963. In *JIP*, 1965, 21, 212–213.

116 **Fischl, J.** Hofrat Dr. Carl Furtmüller: Ein Siebziger. *Erziehung und Unterricht* (Wien), 1950,   , 383–385.

117 **Fischl, P.** Die Altersrangvertauschung. *IZIP*, 1933, 12(6), 460–464.

118 ———. Bewusstsein, bewusst, und Mitbewusst. *IZIP*, 1950, 19(3), 135–140.

119 ———. Individualpsychologie und Wissenschaft. *IZIP*, 1926, 4(4), 195–199.

120 ———. In memoriam Alfred Adler. *IZIP*, 1947, 16(2), 49–56.

121 ———. Lehrbriefe Pestalozzis über Erziehung. *IZIP*, 1947, 16(4), 182–189.

122 ———. Das Minderwertigkeitsgefühl. *IZIP*, 1951, 20(3), 129–141.

123 ———. Das Problem der Willensfreiheit. *IZIP*, 1951, 20(4), 175–182.

124 ———. Review of G. W. Allport, *Personality: A psychological interpretation.* In *IZIP*, 1949, 18(3), 14.

125 ———. Review of Gertrud Bäumer (Ed.), *Die Frau*, 1930, 7. In *IZIP*, 1931, 9(2), 160.

126 ———. Review of M. Berka *et al.*, *Kleines psychologisches Lexikon.* Wien: A. Sexl, 1949. In *IZIP*, 1950, 19(2), 93.

127 ———. Review of J. Bierer, *The day hospital.* In *IZIP*, 1951, 20(4), 185–186.

128 ———. Review of F. Birnbaum, *Versuch einer Systematisierung der Erziehungsmittel.* In *IZIP*, 1951, 20(1) 39.

129 **Fischl, P.** Review of R. Bossard, *Psychologie des Traumbewusstseins.* Zürich: Rasche 1951. In *IZIP*, 1951, 20(4), 186.

130 ———. Review of O. Brachfeld, *Inferiority feelings in the individual and the group.* In *IZIP*, 1951, 20(4), 187.

131 ———. Review of A. Dempf, *Selbstkritik der Philosophie und vergleichende Philosophiegeschichte im Umriss.* Wien: Thomas Morus, 1947. In *IZIP*, 1948, 17(2), 94–95.

132 ———. Review of W. Dieck, *Der Widerspruch im Richtigen.* Sterkrade: W. Osterkamp, 1926. In *IZIP*, 1932, 10(3), 233–234.

133 ———. Review of [   ], *Du und dein Kind.* Bielefeld: Velhagen & Klasing, 1931. In *IZIP*, 1932, 10(3), 234.

134 ———. Review of V. E. Frankl, *Homo patiens.* In *IZIP*, 1951, 20(2), 88–89.

135 ———. Review of V. E. Frankl, *Ein Psycholog erlebt das Konzentrationslager.* Wien: Verlag f. Jugend u. Volk, 1947. In *IZIP*, 1950, 19(3), 141.

136 ———. Review of V. E. Frankl, *Der unbedingte Mensch.* In *IZIP*, 1950, 19(2), 92–93.

137 ———. Review of V. E. Frankl, *Der unbewusste Gott.* In *IZIP*, 1951, 20(1), 41.

138 ———. Review of R. Goldscheid, *Grundlinien zu einer Kritik der Willenskraft.* Wien: Wilhelm Bräumüller, 1905. In *IZIP*, 1925, 3(5), 262–264.

139 ———. Review of *Individual Psychology Bulletin.* In *IZIP*, 1950, 19(4), 186–188.

140 ———. Review of B. Juhos, *Die Erkenntnis und ihre Leistung.* Wien: Springer, 1950. In *IZIP*, 1951, 20(1), 41–42.

141 ———. Review of D. Katz, *Psychologischer Atlas.* Basel: Benno Schwabe, 1945. In *IZIP*, 1948, 17(4), 191.

142 ———. Review of L. Klages, *Die Grundlagen der Charakterkunde.* Wien: Star, 1948 In *IZIP*, 1949, 18(4), 190–191.

143 ———. Review of G. Klatt, *Geschlechtsleben und Alkohol.* In *IZIP*, 1931, 9(2), 159.

144 ———. Review of V. Kraft, *Einführung in die Philosophie.* Wien: Springer, 1950. In *IZIP*, 1950, 19(4), 189–190.

145 ———. Review of V. Kraft, *Mathematik, Logik und Erfahrung.* Wien: Springer, 1947. In *IZIP*, 1949, 18(3), 137.

146 **Fischl, P.** Review of V. Kraft, *Der Wiener Kreis*. Wien: Springer, 1950. In *IZIP*, 1950, 19(4), 188.

147 ———. Review of H. Kunz, A. Mitscherlich & F. Schottländer (Eds.), *Psyche*. Heidelberg: Lambert Schneider, [   ]. In *IZIP*, 1951, 20(1), 42–43.

148 ———. Review of L. E. Lawes, *Geborene Verbrecher? Erkennbare Verbrecher?* Berlin: August Scherl, 1929. In *IZIP*, 1929, 7(5), 399–400.

149 ———. Review of R. Luchsinger & G. E. Arnold, *Lehrbuch der Stimm- und Spruchheilkunde*. Wien: Springer, 1949. In *IZIP*, 1950, 19(1), 42–44.

150 ———. Review of H. Meuter, *Zolas Rougon-Machquarts als literarische Quelle für beziehungswissenschaftliche Analysen*. In *IZIP*, 1927, 5(4), 312–314.

151 ———. Review of A. Moll, *Psychologie und Charakterologie der Okkultisten*. Stuttgart: Ferdinand Enke, 1929. In *IZIP*, 1931, 9(1), 71–72.

152 ———. Review of O. Müller, *Die Lehre vom Unbewussten in der deutschen Philosophie*. München: Otto Gmelin, 1930. In *IZIP*, 1931, 9(1), 70–71.

153 ———. Review of R. Müller-Freienfels, *Die Hauptrichtungen der gegenwärtigen Psychologie*. Leipzig: Quelle & Meyer, 1929. In *IZIP*, 1930, 8(2), 276–277.

154 ———. Review of M. Pfliegler, *Der rechte Augenblick*. Wien: Herder, 1948. In *IZIP*, 1948, 17(2), 95.

155 ———. Review of P. Polak, *Frankls Existenzanalyse in ihrer Bedeutung für Anthropologie und Psychotherapie*. Innsbruck: Tyrolia, 1949. In *IZIP*, 1949, 18(4), 188–189.

156 ———. Review of P. Popenoe, *Des Kindes Erbschaft*. Stuttgart: Deutsche Verlagsanstalt, 1930. In *IZIP*, 1931, 9(3), 255.

157 ———. Review of *Das Problem des abnormen Kindes*. Dresden: Deutscher Verlag f. Volkswohlfart, 1929. In *IZIP*, 1931, 9(2), 159.

158 ———. Review of Helen W. Puner, *Freud: His life and his mind*. London: Grey Walls Press, 1949. In *IZIP*, 1951, 20(1), 46–47.

159 ———. Review of H. Rohrarcher, *Einführung in die Psychologie*. Wien: Urban & Schwarzenberg, 1951. In *IZIP*, 1951, 20(4), 190–191.

160 **Fischl, P.** Review of B. Russel, *Ewige Ziele der Erziehung*. Heidelberg: Niels Kampmann, 1928. In *IZIP*, 1931, 9(2), 159–160.

161 ———. Review of Irma Sander, *Schwierige Kinder in der Volksschule. Das werdende Zeitalter*, 1930, 9(2-3). In *IZIP*, 1931, 9(3), 254.

162 ———. Review of O. Scheibner, *Zwanzig Jahre Arbeitsschule in Idee und Gestaltung*. Leipzig: Quelle & Meyer, 1928. In *IZIP*, 1929, 7(4), 319.

163 ———. Review of [   ], *Die schönsten Upanischaden*. Zürich: Rascher,   . In *IZIP*, 1951, 20(3), 143–144.

164 ———. Review of O. Stahlin & A. Uffenheimer, *Warum kommen die Kinder in der Schule nicht vorwärts?* München: O. Gmelin, 1927. In *IZIP*, 1929, 7(4), 319.

165 ———. Review of H. Thirring, *Homo sapiens*. Wien: Ullstein, 1948. In *IZIP*, 1948, 17(4), 190–191; 1948, 18(1), 44–45.

166 ———. Review of R. F. Tredgold, *Human relations in modern industry*. London: Duckworth, 1949. In *IZIP*, 1951, 20(1), 44–45.

167 ———. Review of A. Ulitz, *Aufruhr der Kinder*. Berlin: Propyläen, 1928. In *IZIP*, 1929, 7(4), 324.

168 ———. Review of R. von der Mühlen, *Menschenauslese für Industrie, Handwerk und Bildungwesen*. In *IZIP*, 1929, 7(1), 75.

169 ———. Review of P. von Schiller, *Aufgabe der Psychologie*. Wien: Springer, 1948. In *IZIP*, 1948, 17(4), 189–190.

170 ———. Review of A. von Winterstein, *Der gegenwärtige Stand der Parapsychologie*. In *IZIP*, 1949, 18(4), 191.

171 ———. Review of F. Werfel, *Realismus und Innerlichkeit*. Leipzig: P. Zsolnay, 1932. In *IZIP*, 1933, 12(6), 478–479.

172 ———. Review of E. Wexberg & H. Fritsch, *Our children in a changing world*. In *IZIP*, 1949, 18(3), 139–140.

173 ———. Review of F. Wilken, *Die nervöse Erkrankung als sinnvolle Erscheinung unseres gegenwärtigen Kulturzeittraumes*. In *IZIP*, 1927, 5(4), 318.

174 ———. Review of H. Winkler, *Schüler in ihrem Grundwesen*. München: Ernst Reinhardt, 1930. In *IZIP*, 1931, 9(1), 70.

175 ———. Review of Ruth Zechlin, *Beschäftigen für das kranke Kind*.

Ravensburg: Otto Maier, [   ]. In *IZIP*, 1933, 12(6), 479.

176 **Fischl, P.** Weiterentwicklung oder Revision? *IZIP*, 1948, 17(4), 172–177.

177 ———. Willensfreiheit. *IZIP*, 1950, 19(1), 26–29.

178 **Fishman, J. R.** A method for clinical and theoretical study of the earliest memory. *Arch. gen. Psychiat.*, 1960, 3, 523–534 (with R. J. Laings, M. B. Rothenberg & M. F. Reiser).

179 **Fitts, H.** The role of the self-concept in social perception. Unpubl. Ph.D. Diss., Vanderbilt Univ., 1954.

180 **Fitzgibbon, C.** Translator of M. Sperber, *The Achilles heel.*

181 **Flanagan, J.** *Men in jail.* Chicago: Loyola Univ. Press, 1965 (with C. O'Reilly, F. Cizon & S. Pflanczer).

182 **Flanagan, J. C.** Review of R. J. Corsini & D. D. Howard (Eds.), *Critical incidents in teaching.* In *Contemp. Psychol.*, 1965, 10, 152–153.

183 **Flavell, J. H.** Selective forgetting as a function of the induction and subsequent removal of ego-threat. Unpubl. M.A. thesis, Clark Univ., 1952.

184 **Fleck, S.** Family dynamics and origin of schizophrenia. *Psychosom. Med.*, 1960, 22, 333–344.

185 ———. The prediction of family interaction from a battery of projective techniques. *J. proj. Tech.*, 1957, 21, 199–208 (with Dorothy T. Sohler, J. D. Holzberg, Alice R. Cornelison, Eleanor Kay, & T. Lidz).

186 **Fleckenstein, H.** *Krankheit und Persönlichkeit.* Freiburg: 1941.

187 **Fleischl, Maria F.** The understanding and utilization of social and adjunctive therapies. *Amer. J. Psychother.*, 1962, 16, 255–265.

188 **Fletcher, F. M.** Review of A. G. Nikelly, *A guide for adjusting to college: Mental health for students.* In *Contemp. Psychol.*, 1967, 12, 370.

189 **Flournoy, H.** Poetry and the memories of childhood. *Int. J. Psychoanal.*, 1950, 31, 103–107.

190 **Foa, U. G.** Depreciation and accusation tendencies: Empirical support. *JIP*, 1972, 28, 45–50 (with M. Teichman).

191 **Forbes-Dennis, N.** Portrait. *IPNL*, 1970, 19(4), 79.

192 **Forchlander, Berta.** Rudi. *IZIP*, 1949, 18 (4), 181–188.

193 **Ford, D. H.** The Individual Psychology of Alfred Adler: A review. *JIP*, 1965, 21, 85–88 (with H. B. Urban).

194 ———. *Systems of psychotherapy: A comparative study.* New York: Wiley, 1963 (with H. B. Urban).

195 **Forer, Lucille D.** *Birth order and life roles.* Springfield, Ill.: C. C. Thomas, 1969.

196 **Forest, H. S.** Biological expansion and psychology. *JIP*, 1958, 14, 105–110.

197 **Forgione, J.** El sentimento de inferioridad en los ninos. *Boletin de Educ.* (Argentina), 1940, 22, 25–38.

198 **Forgus, R. H.** *Perception: The basic process in cognitive development.* New York: McGraw-Hill, 1966.

199 **Formica, R.** Emotional comparison and self-esteem as determinants of affiliation. *J. Pers.*, 1963, 31, 141–162 (with P. Zimbardo).

200 **Forsyth, G. A.** Selective attention and social interest. *JIP*, 1972, 28, 51–59 (with R. J. Huber).

201 **Foster, Constance.** Rules of thumb. *OSIPNL*, 1967, 8(4), 6.

202 **Foster, S.** A study of the personality make-up and social setting of fifty jealous children. *Ment. Hyg.*, 1927, 11, 53–77.

203 **Foster, W.** *Problems of the beginning elementary school teacher.* Minneapolis, Minn.: Burgess Publ. Co. (with [   ]. Jacobs).

204 **Foulds, G. A.** Attitudes toward self and others of psychopaths. *JIP*, 1960, 16, 81–83.

205 ———. Superiority-Inferiority Index in relation to frustrating situations. *J. clin. Psychol.*, 1958, 14, 163–166.

206 **Foulkes, D.** *The psychology of sleep.* New York: Scribner's, 1966.

207 ———. Theories of dream formation and recent studies of sleep consciousness. *Psychol. Bull.*, 1964, 62, 236–247.

208 **Foulkes, S. H.** *Guide du psychotherapie de group.* Translated by M. Dreyfuss. Paris: Editions Epi, 1971 (with Asya Kadis, J. D. Krasner & C. Winick).

209 ———. *A practicum of group psychotherapy.* New York: Hoeber, 1963 (with Asya Kadis, J. D. Krasner, & C. Winick).

210 **Fournier, Annie.** La contribution du Docteur Adler à la comprehension de

l'enfant. *Les Cahiers de l'Enfance inadaptée*, 1956, 6(6), 1–3.

211 **Foxe, A. N.** (Ed.). *Psychosomatic aspects of surgery.* New York: Grune & Stratton, 1956 (with A. J. Cantor).

212 **Franco, J.** *Family treatment of schizophrenia: A symposium. Fam. Proc.*, 1962, 1, 101–140 (with H. Hildreth, I. Boszormenyi-Nagy, C. Midelfort & A. Friedman).

213 **Frank, G. H.** The role of the family in the development of psychopathology. *Psychol. Bull.*, 1965, 64, 191–205. Also in M. Zax & G. Stricker (Eds.), *The study of abnormal behavior.*

214 **Frank, J. D.** The face of the enemy. *Psychol. Today*, 1968, 2(6), 24–29.

215 ———. Recent studies of the level of aspiration. *Psychol. Bull.*, 1941, 38, 218–219.

216 ———. Review of O. H. Mowrer, *The new group therapy.* In *Amer. J. Psychiat.*, 1965, 121, 829.

217 **Frank, L. K.** The cost of competition. *Plan Age*, 1940, 6, 314–324.

218 ———. Sex as an expression of personal and social values. *Pastor. Psychol.*, 1953, 4(31), 55–67.

219 ———. Teleological mechanisms. *Ann. N. Y. Acad. Sci.*, 1948, 50, 187–278.

220 **Frankel, M.** Morality in psychotherapy. *Psychol. Today,* 1967, 1(4), 24–29.

221 **Frankl, V. E.** *Ärztliche Seelsorge.* Wien: Deuticke, 1946.

222 ———. The concept of man in psychotherapy. *Past. Psychol.*, 1955, 6, 16–26.

223 ———. Dimensions of human existence. *J. Psychol. Psychother.*, 1952–53, 1, 186–194.

224 ———. *The doctor and the soul: From psychotherapy to logotherapy.* Translated by R. & Clara Winston. New York: Knopf, 1965.

225 ———. *Ein Psycholog erlebt das Konzentrationslager.* Wien: Verlag f. Jugend u. Volk, 1947.

226 ———. Existenzanalyse und Logotherapie. *4th Int. Kong. f. Psychotherapie*, Barcelona, Sept. 5, 1958.

227 ———. Forerunner of existential psychiatry. Tribute to Alfred Adler on 100th birthday. *JIP*, 1970, 26(2), 12.

228 ———. *From death camp to existentialism.* Boston: Beacon Press, 1959. Revised and reissued as *Man's search for meaning.*

229 **Frankl, V. E.** Gegenwartsprobleme der Psychotherapie. *Wien. Z. Nervenheilk. u. deren Grenzgebiete*, 1962, 22, 78–89.

230 ———. Group therapeutic experiences in a concentration camp. *Grp. Psychother.*, 1954, 7, 81–90.

231 ——— (Ed.). *Handbuch der Neurosenlehre und Psychotherapie.* München: Urban & Schwarzenberg, 1958 (with V. E. von Gebsattel & J. H. Schultz).

232 ———. *Homo patiens.* Wien: Deuticke, 1950.

233 ———. Logos and existence in psychotherapy. *Amer. J. Psychother.*, 1953, 7, 8–15.

234 ———. Logotherapie und Existenzanalyse. *Wien. Z. Nervenheilk. u. deren Grenzgebiete*, 1958, 15, 65–83.

235 ———. Logotherapy and existential analysis—a review. *Amer. J. Psychother.*, 1966, 20, 256–260.

236 ———. *Man's search for meaning.* New York: Washington Sq. Press, 1963. Paper.

237 ———. *Medische Zielsorg.* Utrecht: Bijleveld, 1959.

238 ———. *Das Menschenbild der Seelenkunde.* Stuttgart: Hippokrates Verlag, 1959.

239 ———. On logotherapy and existential analysis. *Amer. J. Psychoanal.*, 1958, 18, 28–37.

240 ———. Paradoxical intention. In H. Greenwald (Ed.), *Active psychotherapy.* Pp. 337–352.

241 ———. Paradoxical intention: A logotherapy technique. *Amer. J. Psychother.*, 1960, 14, 520–535.

242 ———. Personality and responsibility. *Schweiz. Z. Psychol. Anwend.*, 1947, 6, 83.

243 ———. *Die Psychotherapie in der Praxis.* Wien: Deuticke, 1947.

244 ———. Psychotherapie und Weltanschauung. *IZIP*, 1925, 3(5), 250–252.

245 ———. *Psychotherapy and existentialism: Selected papers on logotherapy.* New York: Washington Sq. Press, 1967.

246 ———. Review of O. Eichler, *Die Wurzeln des Frauenhasses bei Arthur Schopenhauer.* Bonn: Marcus & Weber, 1926. In *IZIP*, 1926, 4(5), 314–315.

247 ———. Review of E. Michaelis, *Die Menschheitsproblematik.* In *IZIP*, 1926, 4(6), 397.

248 ———. Rudolf Allers als Philosoph und Psychiater. *Wissensch. u. Weltbild*, 1964, 17, 150–154.

249 **Frankl, V. E.** The spiritual dimension in existential analysis and logotherapy. *JIP*, 1959, 15, 157–165.

250 ———. *Theorie und Therapie der Neurosen.* Wien: Deuticke, 1950; Wien: Urban & Schwarzenberg, 1956.

251 ———. *Der unbedingte Mensch.* Wien: Deuticke, 1949.

252 ———. *Der unbewusste Gott.* Wien: Deuticke, 1948.

253 ———. The will to meaning. *J. past. Care*, 1958, 12, 82–88.

254 ———. *The will to meaning: Foundations and applications of logotherapy.* New York: World, 1969.

255 ———. Zur geistigen Problematik der Psychotherapie. *Zbl. Psychother.*, 1937, 10, 33–45.

256 ———. Zur Grundlegung einer Existenzanalyse. *Schweiz. med. Wchnschr.*, 1939, 69, 707–709.

257 ———. Zur Psychologie des Intellektualismus. *IZIP*, 1926, 4(6), 326–333.

258 **Franks, T. W.** Foreword. *Grp. Psychother.*, 1959, 12(2), 125–126.

259 ———. A note on role playing in an industrial setting. *Grp. Psychother.*, 1952, 5, 59–64.

260 **Frederickson, E.** Competitive fighting between mice with different hereditary backgrounds. *J. genet. Psychol.*, 1954, 85, 271–280 (with E. Ann Birnbaum).

261 **Freedman, A. M.** (Ed.). *Comprehensive textbook of psychiatry.* Baltimore: Williams & Wilkins, 1967 (with H. I. Kaplan).

262 **Freedman, L. Z.** Neurosis and social class. I. Social interaction. *Amer. J. Psychiat.*, 1957, 113, 769–775 (with A. B. Hollingshead).

263 **Freedman, N.** Early childhood recollections: An integrative technique of personality test data. *AJIP*, 1953, 10, 31–42 (with Asya Kadis & Janet Greene).

264 **Freedman, R. D.** Birth order, conformity, and managerial achievement. *Personnel Psychol.*, 1969, 22, 269–279 (with P. Dubno and H. Bedrosian).

265 ———. Birth order, educational achievement, and managerial attainment. *Personnel Psychol.*, 1971, 24, 63–70 (with P. Dubno).

266 **Freeman, F. S.** Review of R. Dreikurs, *Psychology in the classroom.* In *Contemp. Psychol.*, 1957, 2(8), 209.

267 **Freeman, Lucy.** *The story of psychoanalysis.* New York: Pocket Books, 1960 (with M. Small).

268 **Freeman, N.** Concepts of Adler and Horney. *Amer. J. Psychoanal.*, 1950, 10, 18–26.

269 **Freeman, S. L.** (Ed.). *Readings in group counseling.* Scranton, Pa.: Int. Textbook Co., 1968 (with J. J. Muro).

270 **Freeman, W.** *The psychiatrist: Personalities and patterns.* New York: Grune & Stratton, 1968.

271 **Frei, B.** Sozialkritische Bemerkungen zur Individualpsychologie. *IZIP*, 1925, 3(5), 243–247.

272 **Freistadt, Else.** Ethische Bewegung in Nordamerika. *IZIP*, 1926, 4(4), 381–383.

273 ———. Review of M. T. Bohl, Die Stellung der Frauen im alten Babylonien und Israel. *Bibliothec. sacra*, 1920. In *IZIP*, 1925, 3(6), 348–350.

274 ———. Review of H. Prager, *Die Weltanschauung Dostojewskis.* In *IZIP*, 1926, 4(3), 163–165.

275 ———. Von inneren Leben der Jugend. In E. Wexberg (Ed.), *Handbuch der Individualpsychologie.* Pp. 235–275.

276 **French, J. R., Jr.** Birth order among medical students. *J. Amer. Med. Assn.*, 1966, 195, 312–313 (with S. Cobb).

277 **Freschl, R.** Eine psychologische Analyse (August Strindberg's "Corinna" aus "Heiraten"). *ZIP*, 1914, 1(1), 21–26.

278 ———. Friedrich Nietzsche and Individual Psychology. *IJIP*, 1935, 1(4), 87–98.

279 ———. Friedrich Nietzsche und die Individualpsychologie. *IZIP*, 1936, 14(1), 50–61.

280 ———. Das Streben nach Macht. *IZIP*, 1935, 13(2), 115–123.

281 ———. Vorbemerkungen zu Individualpsychologie der Persönlichkeit Friedrich Nietzsche. *ZIP*, 1914, 1(4–5), 110–115.

282 **Freud, S.** *Autobiography.* New York: Norton, 1935.

283 ———. *The basic writings of Sigmund Freud.* New York: Modern Libr., 1938.

284 ———. Childhood memories and screen memories. In *Psychopathology of everyday life.*

285 ———. A childhood recollection from Dichtung und Wahrheit. In *Collected Papers.* Vol. 4. Pp. 357–367.

286 ———. *Collected Papers.* London: Hogarth, 1925, 1953–56.

287 **Freud, S.** *A general introduction to psy-choanalysis.* New York: Garden City, 1938.

288 ———. The history of the psychoanalytic movement. In *The basic writings of Sigmund Freud.* Pp. 931-977; New York: Collier Books, 1963. Paper.

289 ———. *Leonardo da Vinci and a memory of his childhood.* Translated by A. Tyson. London: Hogarth, 1953; New York: Norton, 1964.

290 ———. On the history of the psychoanalytic movement. In *Collected papers.* Vol. 1. Pp. 287-359; New York: Norton, 1966. Paper.

291 ———. *Psychopathology of everyday life.* New York: Mentor Books, 1951. Paper; London: Hogarth, 1953.

292 ———. Repression. In *Collected papers.* Vol. 4.

293 ———. Screen memories. In *Collected papers.* Vol. 5. Pp. 47-69.

294 ———. The unconscious. In *Collected papers.* Vol. 4. Pp. 98-136.

295 **Freudenberg, Sophie.** Bericht *über* eine Tagung des Internationalen Vereines für Individualpsychologie. *IZIP,* 1925, 3(3), 132-134.

296 ———. *Erziehungs-und heilpädagogische Beratungsstellen.* Leipzig: Hirzel, 1928.

297 ———. Individualpsychologie und Jugend-fürsorge. *IZIP,* 1926, 4(5), 282-291.

298 ———. Individualpsychologie und Jugend-wohlfartspflege. In E. Wexberg (Ed.), *Handbuch der Individualpsychologie.* Pp. 367-381.

299 ———. Individualpsychologie und neue Erziehung. *IZIP,* 1927, 5(2), 148-149.

300 ———. Über die Internationale Pädagogische Konferenz in Heidelberg. *IZIP,* 1926, 4(2), 99-101.

301 **Freund, Edith.** Review of A. Kronfeld, Über einen bestimmten Typus männlichen Frauen. In *IZIP,* 1924, 2(3), 62-63.

302 **Freund, H.** Der Antagonismus in vegetativen Nervensystem. *IZIP,* 1927, 5(3), 161-168.

303 ———. *Das bettnässende Kind.* Dresden: Verlag am Andern Ufer, 1926.

304 ———. Entwicklungstendenzen in der sozialen Psychiatrie. In K. Leist, *Richter und Arzt.* München-Basel: Reinhardt Verlag. Pp. 66-73.

305 **Freund, H.** Hellmut v. Gerlach. Eine Politikeranalyse. *IZIP,* 1929, 7(5), 351-353.

306 ———. *Die Individualpsychologie.* Leipzig: Wissenschaftliche Beilage der Lehrerzeitung, No. 43.

307 ———. *Konstruktive Psychologie.* Darmstadt: Neue Darmstadter Verlagsanstalt, 1954.

308 ———. Pseudoonanie. *IZIP,* 1932, 10(4), 289-290.

309 ———. Selbsterziehung in einem Fall von genuiner Epilepsie. *IZIP,* 1930, 8(1), 119-125.

310 ———. Über Training. *IZIP,* 1928, 6(5), 370-373.

311 **Freund, J. D.** Value of the Funkenstein test in predicting psychosurgery. *Dis. nerv. Syst.,* 1957, 18(4), 134-138 (with R. Dreikurs).

312 **Frey, E. C.** The dream: A means to self-analysis. In K. A. Adler & Danica Deutsch (Eds.), *Essays in Individual Psychology.* Pp. 348-353.

313 ———. Dreams of male homosexuals and the attitude of society. *JIP,* 1962, 18, 26-34.

314 **Frick, W. B.** Healthy interpersonal relationships: An exploratory study. *JIP,* 1967, 23, 58-66.

315 **Friedland, Bernice U.** Changes in problems of ninth grade students as an outcome of Adlerian group counseling. *Diss. Abstr.,* 1972, 33(4-A), 1511-1512.

316 **Friedman, A.** Family treatment of schizophrenia: A symposium. *Fam. Proc.,* 1962, 1, 101-140 (with H. Hildreth, I. Boszormenyi-Nagy, C. Midelfort & J. Franco).

317 **Friedman, A.** Der verwöhnte Kind beim Schlafen gehen. In F. Liebling & J. Rattner (Eds.), *Psychologische Menschenkenntnis.*

318 **Friedman, Alice R.** Anfänge und Entwicklung des männlichen Protests. *IZIP,* 1925, 3(6), 290-298.

319 ———. Behavior training in a case of enuresis. *JIP,* 1968, 24, 86-87.

320 ———. Beitrag zur pädagogischen Menschenkenntnis. *IZIP,* 1929, 7(2), 129-143.

321 ———. Biologie und Psychologie der Linkshändigkeit. *IZIP,* 1926, 4(5), 257-271.

322 ———. Early childhood memories of mental patients. *J. child Psychiat.,* 1952, 2, 266-269.

323 **Friedman, Alice R.** Early childhood memories of mental patients: Preliminary report. *IPB*, 1950, 8, 111–116. Also in K. A. Adler & Danica Deutsch (Eds.), *Essays in Individual Psychology*. Pp. 200–206.

324 ——. Education as a part of group therapy program. *Ment. Hosp.*, May, 1962. P. 274.

325 ——. Eidetik und Individualpsychologie. *IZIP*, 1927, 5(3), 196–197.

326 ——. Ein Ängstlicher. *IZIP*, 1928, 6(4), 335–336.

327 ——. Ein Fall von Lernflucht. *IZIP*, 1924, 2(5), 27–28.

328 ——. Entmutigung und Heldentum. *IZIP*, 1924, 2(5), 28–33.

329 ——. Erneuerung der Erziehung. *IZIP*, 1927, 5(6), 470–471.

330 ——. Erziehung und Stottern. *IZIP*, 1928, 6(6), 496–501.

331 ——. Familie und Erziehungsberatung. *IZIP*, 1929, 7(3), 179–183.

332 ——. The family and child guidance. In A. Adler & assoc., *Guiding the child*. Pp. 53–65.

333 ——. First recollections of school. *IJIP*, 1935, 1(1), 111–116.

334 ——. Fragebogen für Untersuchung auf Linkshändigkeit. *IZIP*, 1927, 5(3), 193–195.

335 ——. Das Frauenproblem der Gegenwart. *IZIP*, 1936, 14(2), 94–104.

336 ——. Gemeinsammes Phantasieren und Dauerspiele im Geschwisterkreis. *IZIP*, 1933, 11(2), 108–119.

337 ——. Heilpädagogik. *IZIP*, 1927, 5(6), 471–475; 1928, 6(1), 68–70; 1928, 6(2), 257–259; 1928, 6(4), 333–334.

338 ——. Heilpädagogik: Neue Erziehungsmerkblätter. *IZIP*, 1931, 9(6), 478–481.

339 ——. "Ich habe es im Guten und im Bösen versucht." *IZIP*, 1928, 6(6), 496.

340 ——. If your child is a fussy eater. *IJIP*, 1937, 3(1), 46–47.

341 ——. Individualpsychologische Heilpädagogik. In E. Wexberg (Ed.), *Handbuch der Individualpsychologie*. Pp. 336–366.

342 ——. Inferiority feelings and a growing genius. *JIP*, 1958, 14, 171–172.

343 ——. In memory of Phyllis Bottome. *IPNL*, 1963-64, 14 (3–5, Whole No. 152–154). Pp. 17–18.

344 ——. Die innere Arbeit in der Charakterbildung. *IZIP*, 1930, 8(1), 78–84.

345 **Friedman, Alice R.** Kenne ich mein Kind? *IZIP*, 1930, 8(5), 532–536.

346 ——. Kind der Krise. *IZIP*, 1934, 12(1), 47–49.

347 ——. Kindertypen in individualpsychologischer Heimerziehung. *IZIP*, 1931, 9(3), 222–234.

348 ——. Die Kindheit Gandhis. *IZIP*, 1933, 11(1), 1–7.

349 ——. Die Kunst der individualpsychologischen Pädagogik. *IZIP*, 1937, 15(3–4), 150–152.

350 ——. Lieblosigkeit der Mutter. *IZIP*, 1928, 6(5), 411–412.

351 ——. Life styles observed in a foster home for Individual Psychological re-education. *IJIP*, 1936, 2(2), 62–75.

352 ——. Das Minderwertigkeitsgefühl beim kleine Kinde. *IZIP*, 1929, 7(1), 60–67.

353 ——. Das mutlose Kind vor dem Aufstehen. *Psychol, Menschenkenntnis*, 1964.

354 ——. Nietzsche, der Mensch. *IZIP*, 1924, 2(3), 16–36.

355 ——. Observations at a New York center for the care of children of working mothers in wartime. *IZIP*, 1947, 16, 28–33.

356 ——. Observations in a play group of young children. *IPB*, 1951, 9, 25–30.

357 ——. Portrait. *IPNL*, 1970, 19(4), 61.

358 ——. Psychische Stummheit. *IZIP*, 1926, 4(1), 24–30.

359 ——. Psychological diagnosis of intracranial pathology after accident. *Acta Psychother.*, 1956, 4(4), 352–357.

360 ——. Review of P. Cohn, *Um Nietzsches Untergang*, Hannover: Morris Verlag, [   ]. In *IZIP*, 1933, 11(2), 156.

361 ——. Review of Else Croner, *Die Psyche der werblichen Jugend*. Langensalza: Hermann Beyer U. Söhne, 1928. In *IZIP*, 1928, 6(6), 508.

362 ——. Review of J. Eisenstädter, *Montessorisystem und proletarische Erziehung*. Leipzig: Oldenburg, [   ]. In *IZIP*, 1924, 2(6), 42.

363 ——. Review of M. Epstein (Ed.), *Das Buch der Erziehung. IZIP*, 1924, 2(6), 43.

364 ——. Review of R. Kobler, *Der Weg des Menschen vom Links- zum Rechtshander*. Wien: Moritz Perles, 1932. In *IZIP*, 1933, 12(3), 245–255.

365 ——. Review of A. Kronfeld, *Das seelisch Abnorme und die Gemeinschaft*. In *IZIP*, 1924, 2(4), 32.

366 **Friedman, Alice R.** Review of K. Mannheim, *Mensch und Gesellschaft im Zeitalter des Umbaus.* Leiden: [   ], 1935. In *IZIP,* 1936, 14(4), 244–245.

367 ———. Review of H. Nöll, *Intentionalität, Reaktivität und Schachsinn.* Halle: Carl Marhold, 1926. In *IZIP,* 1928, 6(3), 260–261.

368 ———. Review of W. Paulsen, *Die Überwindung der Schule.* Leipzig: Quelle & Meyer, 1926. In *IZIP,* 1927, 5(3), 238.

369 ———. Review of E. F. Podach, *Nietzsches Zusammenbruch.* Freiburg: Niels Kampmann, 1930. In *IZIP,* 1931, 9(1), 73–74.

370 ———. Review of W. Rasmussen, *Psychologie des Kindes zwischen 4 und 7 Jahren.* Leipzig: Felix Meiner, 1925. In *IZIP,* 1927, 5(2), 156.

371 ———. Review of H. Sauer, *Jugendberatungsstellen, Idee und Praxis.* In *IZIP,* 1924, 2(3), 60.

372 ———. Review of M. Tramer, *Technisches Schaffen Geisteskranker.* München: Oldenbourg, 1926. In *IZIP,* 1927, 5(2), 156.

373 ———. Review of J. Wandeler, *Die Individualpsychologie Alfred Adlers in ihrer Beziehung zur Philosophie des Als Ob Hans Vaihingers.* In *IZIP,* 1936, 14(2), 122–124.

374 ———. Rorschach responses and treatment results under drug and group psychotherapy. *Acta Psychother.,* 1963, 2, 28–32.

375 ———. Das Seminar für Massenpsychologie vom Oktober 1923 bis Jänner 1924. *IZIP,* 1923–24, 2(4), 30–31.

376 ———. Some perspectives on Individual Psychology in our times. *IPB,* 1947, 6, 45–47.

377 ———. Spiegelbilder. *IZIP,* 1929, 7(5), 388.

378 ———. Warum glauben Sie, dass ihr Kind bessert, wenn Sie es schlagen? *IZIP,* 1930, 8(2), 264–265.

379 ———. Warum ist das Kind nicht? *IZIP,* 1929, 7(4), 306–307.

380 ———. Wenn ich von der Schule nach Hause komme. . . . *IZIP,* 1930, 8(3), 353–355.

381 **Friedman, F.** Portrait. *IPNL,* 1971, 20(6), 110.

382 **Friedman, J.** Early recollections of schizophrenic and depressed patients. *JIP,* 1962, 18, 57–61 (with H. Schiffman).

383 **Friedman, P.** (Ed.). *On suicide: With particular reference to suicide among young students.* (Discussions of the Vienna Psychoanalytic Society, 1910). New York: Int. Univer. Press, 1967.

384 **Friedman, P.** Reply (to H. L. Ansbacher, Adler and the 1910 Vienna Symposium on suicide). *JIP,* 1968, 24, 191–192.

385 **Friedmann, Alice R.** See Friedman, Alice R.

386 **Friedmann, F.** "Arrangement" als Flucht vor Verantwortung. *IZIP,* 1949, 18(3), 127–130.

387 ———. Beziehung zwischen Lehrform und Disziplin. *IZIP,* 19(2), 87–91.

388 ———. Escape to disease. In A. Adler & assoc., *Guiding the child.* Pp. 231–235.

389 ———. Flucht in die Krankheit. *IZIP,* 1929, 7(3), 236.

390 ———. *Lexikon der Erziehung.* Wien: Ulstein, 1956 (with K. Baumgärtel).

391 ———. Schlusswort. In Int. Verein Indivpsy., *Alfred Adler zum Gedenken.* P. 164.

392 ———. Translator of E. R. Braithwaite, *To Sir, with love.*

393 **Fries, Margaret E.** Probleme des Verhaltens bei Kindern unter drei Jahren. *IZIP,* 1929, 7(4), 296–303.

394 **Fritsch, H. E.** *Our children in a changing world: An outline of practical guidance.* New York: Macmillan, 1938 (with E. Wexberg).

395 **Fritz, Viktoria.** Das Geschwister des schwererziehbaren Kindes. *IZIP,* 1930, 8(5), 499–502.

396 **Frizelle, J.** The gap between religion and psychiatry. *Insight,* 1963, 1(3), 27–34 (with W. O'Connell, C. Harris, J. Jernigan & J. Wohl).

397 **Froeschels, E.** Anatomy and physiology (with Elly Sittig). In *Twentieth century speech and voice correction.* Pp. 1–38.

398 ———. Die Bedeutung der Vorstellungstypen für den Sprach-und Gesangsunterricht. *Wien. med. Wchnschr.,* 1928, 78, 956 (with A. Jellinek).

399 ———. Beiträge zur Symptomatologie des Stotterns. *Monatschr. Ohrenheilk.,* 1921, 55, 1109–1112.

400 ———. Cluttering. *J. Speech Disorders,* 1946, 11, 31.

401 ———. A contribution to the pathology and therapy of dysarthria due to certain cerebral lesions. *J. Speech Disorders,* 1943, 8, 301–321.

402 Froeschels, E. *The human race—a study in the nature of knowledge.* New York: Phil. Libr., 1947.

403 ———. Hygiene of the voice. *Arch. Otolaryngol.,* 1943, 38, 122–130.

404 ———. *Lehrbuch der Sprachheilkunde.* Wien: Deuticke, 1925.

405 ———. A lip reading procedure for adults. *Volta Rev.,* 1940, 42(6), 369.

406 ———. Pathologie und Therapie der Stimme und Sprache. *Fortschr. Med.,* 1926, 44.

407 ———. Pathology and therapy of stuttering. In *Twentieth century speech and voice correction.* Pp. 194–207. Also in *New Child,* 1943, 12, 148–161.

408 ———. A peculiar intermediary state between waking and sleeping. *Amer. J. Psychother.,* 1949, 3, 19–25.

409 ———. *Philosophy in wit.* New York: Phil. Libr., 1948.

410 ———. Portrait. *IPNL,* 1972, 21(6), 111.

411 ———. *Practice of voice and speech therapy.* Boston: Expression Co., 1941 (with A. Jellinek).

412 ———. The problem of auditory and visual imperceptivity in stutterers. *Folia Phoniat.,* 1936, 15, 13–20 (with R. W. Rieber).

413 ———. Psychic deafness in children. *Arch. neurol. Psychiat.,* 1944, 51, 544–549.

414 ———. Review of A. R. Luria, *The role of speech in the regulation of normal and abnormal behavior.* New York: Pergamon Press, 1961. In *Amer. J. Psychother.,* 1962, 16(1), 182–183.

415 ———. *Selected papers (1940–1964).* Amsterdam: North-Holland Publ., 1964.

416 ———. *Speech therapy.* Boston: Expression Co., 1933.

417 ———. Stuttering and psychotherapy. *Folia Phoniat.,* 1953, 3, 1–9.

418 ———. A technique for stutterers—"ventriloquism". *J. Speech Hearing Dis.,* 1950, 15, 336–337.

419 ———. Testing the hearing of new-born infants. *Arch. Otolaryngol.,* 1946, 44, 710–714 (with Helen Beebe).

420 ———. Transition phenomena. *Amer. J. Psychother.,* 1953, 7, 273–277.

421 ——— (Ed.). *Twentieth century speech and voice correction.* New York: Phil. Libr., 1948.

422 Froeschels, E. Über Auskultationsphänomin am Brustkorb. *Arch. klin. Med.,* 1923, 6, 427–436 (with F. G. Stockert).

423 ———. Über eine wenig beachtete Komponente des mangelhaften Sprachgehörs bei Schwerhörigen und ihre Bedeutung für die Hörübungen. *Monatschr. Ohrenheilkunde,* 1932, 4, 454–461.

424 ———. Über einen durch Schalreiz ausgelösten Reflex bei Hochgradig Schwerhörige *Z. Hals-Nasen-Ohren-Heilkunde,* 1930.

425 ———. Über Konstitution associativ-aphasischer Kinder. *Wien. med. Wchnschr.,* 1926, 76, No. 29 (with P. Moses).

426 ———. Vorstellungstypen von Polteren. *Wien. med. Wchnschr.,* 1930, 2, 1162 (with L. A. Kallen).

427 Fröhlich, E. M. Review of J. Lindworsky, *Die Methode die Individualpsychologie in der Erziehung.* In *IZIP,* 1927, 5(4), 314–315.

428 Fromm, E. Individual and social origins of neurosis. *Amer. sociol. Rev.,* 1944, 9, 380–384.

429 Fuller, Frances. Review of R. Dreikurs, *Psychology in the classroom.* 2nd. ed. In *Contemp. Psychol.,* 1969, 14, 72–74.

430 Furchtgott, E. Maternal parity and offspring behavior in the domestic mouse. *Developm. Psychol.,* 1969, 1, 227–230 (with J. Lazar).

431 Furtmüller, Aline. Der Kampf der Geschwisters. In A. Adler & C. Furtmüller (Eds.), *Heilen und Bilden* (1914). Pp. 262–266; (1928). Pp. 155–159.

432 ———. Zur psychologie der Frau (in Rusland). *Dokumente des Fortschritte,* 1910 (Juli-Dez.), 519.

433 Furtmüller, C. Alfred Adler: A biographical sketch. In H. L. Ansbacher & Rowena R. Ansbacher (Eds.), *Superiority and social interest.* Pp. 330–393.

434 ———. Alltägliches aus dem Kinderleben. *ZIP,* 1914, 1(2), 53–58.

435 ——— (Ed.). *Curar y educar.* [ ] (with A. Adler).

436 ———. Denkpsychologie und Individualpsychologie. *ZIP,* 1914, 1(3), 80–91.

437 ———. *Ethik und Psychoanalyse.* München: Ernst Reinhardt, 1912.

438 ———. Geleitwort. In A. Adler & C. Furtmüller (Eds.), *Heilen und Bilden* (1914). Pp. v–viii.

439 Furtmüller, C. Geleitwort. *ZIP*, 1914, 1 (1), 1–3.

440 —— (Ed.). *Heilen und Bilden: Ärztlich-pädagogische Arbeiten des Vereins für Individualpsychologie.* München: Reinhardt, 1914 (with A. Adler).

441 —— (Ed.). *Heilen und Bilden: Ein Buch der Erziehungskunst für Ärzte und Pädagogen.* München: Bergmann, 1928 (with A. Adler & E. Wexberg).

442 —— (Ed.). *Heilen und Bilden: Grundlagen der Erziehungskunst für Ärzte und Pädagogen.* München: Bergmann, 1922 (with A. Adler & E. Wexberg).

443 ——. In memory of Dr. Alexander Neuer. *IPN*, 1941, 1(8–9), 9.

444 ——. Iphigenie auf Tauris. *IZIP*, 1932, 10(5), 328–338.

445 ——. Die pädagogischen und psychologischen Auswirkungen der oesterreichischen Schulreform. In Sofie Lazarsfeld (Ed.), *Technik der Erziehung.*

446 ——. Psychoanalyse und Ethik. *Schr. Verein freie psychoanal. Forsch.*, 1912, No. 1.

447 ——. Die psychologische Bedeutung der Psychoanalyse. In A. Adler & C. Furtmüller (Eds.), *Heilen und Bilden* (1914). Pp. 168–186.

448 ——. Review of A. Messer, *Psychologie.* Stuttgart: Deutsche Verlagsanstalt, 1914. In *ZIP*, 1914, 1(3), 94–95.

449 ——. Selbsterfundene Märchen. In A. Adler & C. Furtmüller (Eds.), *Heilen und Bilden* (1914). Pp. 278–305; (1928). Pp. 305–321.

450 ——. Selbsterziehung als Berufsproblem des Lehrers. *IZIP*, 1930, 8, 70–78.

451 ——. Vorwort zur ersten Auflage. In A. Adler & C. Furtmüller (Eds.), *Heilen und Bilden* (1928). Pp. iii–v.

452 ——. Zur Entwicklung der Individualpsychologie (with E. Wexberg). In A. Adler & C. Furtmüller (Eds.), *Heilen und Bilden* (1928). Pp. 1–15.

453 Furtmüller-Klatschke, Aline. See Furtmüller, Aline.

G

1 Gabain, Marjorie. Translator of O. Brachfeld, *Inferiority feelings in the individual and the group.*

2 Gainer, Priscilla. Altruism in the albino rat. *J. comp. physiol. Psychol.*, 1962, 55(1), 123–125 (with G. E. Rice).

3 Gallen, M. The comparative effectiveness of two contrasting alcoholic treatment programs. *Nwsltr. Res. Psychol.*, 1972, 14(4), 21–23 (with Barbara Williams, W. E. O'Connell, & P. M. Sands).

4 Galton, F. *English men of science: Their nature and nurture.* London: Macmillan, 1874.

5 Gans-van Weerden, Hermine. See van Weerden, Hermine.

6 Ganz, Madeleine. *Adlers Psykologi och barnets utveckling.* Stockholm: Natur och Kultur, 1940.

7 ——. *La psychologie d'A. Adler et la developpement de l'enfant.* Neuchatel et Paris: Delachaux et Niestlé, 1935; Geneva: , 1935.

8 ——. *The psychology of Alfred Adler and the development of the child.* New York: Humanities Press, 1953; London: Routledge & Kegan Paul, 1953.

9 Gardner, Pearl L. An analysis of children's attitudes toward fathers. *J. genet. Psychol.*, 1947, 70, 3–28.

10 Gardner, Ruth. *What do you advise?* New York: Ives Washburn, 1946 (with F. Künkel).

11 Garlock, Rose. The social club as an adjunct to therapy (with Erika Mohr). In K. A. Adler & Danica Deutsch (Eds.), *Essays in Individual Psychology.* Pp. 465–467.

12 Garmezy, N. Birth order of recovered and nonrecovered schizophrenics. *Arch. gen. Psychiat.*, 1963, 9, 224–228 (with A. Farina, H. Barry, & C. Storrs).

13 Garner, H. H. The confrontation problem-solving technique: Applicability to Adlerian psychotherapy. *JIP*, 1972, 28(2), 248–259.

14 ——. Introducing Rudolf Dreikurs, M. D., Conference honoree. *JIP*, 1972, 28(2), 125–126.

15 Garner, W. R. To perceive is to know. *Amer. Psychologist*, 1966, 21, 11–19.

16 Gatch, Vera M. The belief in psychic determinism and the behavior of the psychotherapist. *Rev. existent. Psychol. Psychiat.*, 1965, 5, 16–33 (with M. K. Temerlin).

17 Gates, R. R. *Human genetics.* New York: Macmillan, 1946.

18 **Gatley, R. H.** Happiness and affiliation. *Diss. Abstr. Int.*, 1969, 30, 2890–2891.

19 **Gaudet, Hazel.** *The people's choice.* New York: Duell, Sloan & Pearce, 1944 (with P. Lazarsfeld & B. Berelson).

20 **Gayer, Isabella.** Review of A. Hoche, *Das traumende Ich.* Jena: Gustav Fischer, 1927. In *IZIP*, 1928, 6(4), 344–345.

21 ———. Review of E. Joël, *Die Behandlung der Giftsuchen.* Leipzig: Georg Thieme, [   ]. In *IZIP*, 1930, 8(2), 273.

22 ———. Review of Paula Modersohn-Becker, *Briefe und Tagebuchblätter.* München: Kurt Wolff, 1926. In *IZIP*, 1928, 6(3), 266.

23 ———. Review of H. Többen, *Neuere Beobachtungen über die Psychologie der zu lebenslänglicher Zuchthausstrafe verurteilten oder begnadigten Verbrecher.* Wien: F. Deuticke, 1927. In *IZIP*, 1928, 6(3), 261–262.

24 ———. Über einen Fall von Schizophrenie. *IZIP*, 1927, 5(1), 34–47.

25 **Gazda, G.** (Ed.). *Basic approaches to group psychotherapy and group counseling.* Springfield, Ill.: C. C. Thomas, 1968.

26 ——— (Ed.). *Innovations to group therapy.* Springfield, Ill.: C. C. Thomas, 1968.

27 **Gebhardt, J.** Childhood memories of single and recurrent incidents. *J. genet. Psychol.*, 1965, 107, 85–89 (with N. G. Hanawalt).

28 **Geiwitz, P. J.** *Non-Freudian personality theories.* Belmont, Calif.: Brooks-Cole, 1969.

29 **Gelfand, S.** The relationship of birth order to pain tolerance. *J. clin. Psychol.*, 1963, 19, 406–407.

30 **Gelsted, O.** Translator of A. Adler, *Menneskekundstab.*

31 **Gemelli, A.** Über das Wesen und die Entstehung des Charakters. *IZIP*, 1935, 13(1), 7–28.

32 **Gentile, Isolda.** Translator of R. Dreikurs, *I bambini una sfida.*

33 **George, A. L.** Power as a compensatory value for political leaders. *J. soc. Issues*, 1968, 24(3), 29–49.

34 **Georges, A.** Influence de la séquence sur les aptitudes intellectuelles. (The influence of sibling sequence on intellectual aptitudes.) *Bull. Inst. nat. Etude du Travail et d'Orientation profess.*, 1971, 27, 39–49–4024.

35 **Georgi, Gertrud.** Aus einer Beratungsstelle. *IZIP*, 1950, 19(4), 180–186.

36 **Georgi, Gertrud.** Die Bedeutung der Frage in der Beratung. *IZIP*, 1951, 20(1), 34–38

37 ———. Friederike Friedmann. *JIP*, 1969, 25, 137–138.

38 ———. Review of A. Michel, *Psychoanaly de la musique.* Paris: Hesses Universitaires de France, 1951. In *IZIP*, 1951, 20(4), 189–190.

39 **Gerard, Elisabeth.** Der Tod als Erlebnis be Kindern und Jugendlichen. *IZIP*, 1930, 8(6), 551–558.

40 **Gero-Cserna, Elisabeth.** Ein nervöse Kind. *IZIP*, 1929, 7(6), 474–475.

41 **Gerz, H. O.** Six years of clinical experienc with the logotherapeutic technique of paradoxical intention in the treatment of phobic and obsessive-compulsive patients. *Amer. J. Psychiat.*, 1966, 123, 548–553.

42 ———. The treatment of the phobic and obsessive-compulsive patient using paradox cal intention. *J. Neuropsychiat.*, 1962, 3, 375–387.

43 **Geteles, F.** Cognitive styles and stereotyping in interpersonal perception. *Diss. Abstr* 1965, 26, 2867. Unpubl. Ph.D. Diss., Columbia Univ., 1965.

44 **Getoff, L.** The earliest memories of three age groups. Unpubl. Ph.D. Diss., Columbia Univ., 1960.

45 **Ghosh, E. S.** A study of parental role-perception in siblings. *J. psychol. Researches* 1966, 10(1), 8–18 (with D. Sinha).

46 **Gibbs, J. P.** (Ed.). *Suicide.* New York: Harper & Row, 1968.

47 **Gibran, K.** Was der prophet von Kindern sagte. *IZIP*, 1929, 7(1), 1.

48 **Giddings, M. G.** Cultural deprivation: A study in mythology. *Teachers Coll. Rec.*, 1965, 66, 606–613 (with B. Mackler).

49 **Gilbert, A. R.** The concept of life style: It background and its psychological significance. *Jb. Psychol. Psychother. med. Anthropol.*, 1960, 7, 97–106.

50 **Gilbert, G. M.** The new status of experimental studies on the relationship of feeling to memory. *Psychol. Bull.*, 1938, 35, 26–35.

51 ———. Toward a comprehensive biosocial theory of human behavior. *Int. J. soc. Psychiat.*, 1963, 9, 85–93.

52 **Gilbert, Jeanne G.** Personality characteristics of young male narcotic addicts. *J. consult. Psychol.*, 1967, 31, 536–538 (with D. N. Lombardi).

53 **Gildersleeve, Alta.** Report on group counseling. *OSIPNL*, 1964, 5(1), 10-11 (with W. Peckham).

54 **Gilmore, J. B.** Birth order and social reinforcer effectiveness in children. *Child Developm.*, 1964, 35, 193-200 (with E. Zigler).

55 **Gilner, F.** Factor analysis of self-report statements of love relationships. *JIP*, 1964, 20, 186-188 (with C. H. Swenson).

56 **Gindes, B.** *Concepts of hypnosis.* New York: Julian Press, 1951.

57 ———. Delusional production under hypnosis. *Int. J. clin. exp. Hypn.*, 1963, 11, 1-10.

58 **Ginzberg, E.** Choice of the term "life style" by one research group. *JIP*, 1967, 23, 213-216.

59 ——— et al. *Life styles of educated women.* New York: Columbia Univ. Press, 1966.

60 **Ginzberg, R.** The aging and the aged: Psychological and social aspects. *IPB*, 1950, 8, 117-130.

61 ———. Geriatrics and gerontology in every-day practice. *IPB*, 1949, 7, 21-29.

62 **Ginzburg, B.** Translator of A. Adler & associates, *Guiding the child.*

63 **Glass, D. C.** Birth order and reactions to frustrations. *J. abnorm. soc. Psychol.*, 1963, 66, 192-194 (with M. Horwitz & I. Firestone).

64 **Glasser, W.** *Reality therapy: A new approach to psychiatry.* New York: Harper & Row, 1965.

65 ———. *Schools without failure.* New York: Harper & Row, 1969.

66 **Glover, E.** The screening function of traumatic memories. *Int. J. Psychoanal.*, 1929, 10, 90-93.

67 **Glueck, B.** Translator of A. Adler, *The neurotic constitution* (with J. E. Lind).

68 **Godin, A.** (Ed.). *Adult et enfant devant Dieu.* Brussels: Centre Intl. d'Etudes de la Formation Religieuse.

69 **Gold, L.** Fingerpainting as an aid in personality evaluation of 44 adult hospitalized mentally ill patients. *Psychiat. Quart. Suppl.*, 1952, 26, 59-69 (with G. M. Campbell).

70 ———. Toward an understanding of adolescent drug addiction. *Fed. Probat.*, Sept., 1958. Pp. 42-48.

71 **Goldberg, Elsa M.** *Family influences and psychosomatic illness.* London: Tavistock Publ. Ltd., 1959.

72 **Goldberg, G.** *Corrective treatment for unadjusted children.* New York: Harper, 1942 (with N. Shoobs).

73 ———. Guiding the adolescent boy. *Nerv. Child*, 1945, 4, 159-166 (with N. E. Shoobs).

74 **Goldberger, Edith.** Review of S. J. Rossolimo, *Das psychologische Profil.* In *IZIP*, 1927, 5(5), 397-398.

75 ———. Schwere Kindheit. *IZIP*, 1928, 6(6), 501.

76 **Goldberger, P.** Infektionskrankheiten und Individualpsychologie. *IZIP*, 1928, 6(1), 26-35.

77 ———. Review of R. Baerwald, *Psychologie der Selbstverteidigung.* Leipzig: J. C. Hinrichs, 1927. In *IZIP*, 1928, 6(1), 78.

78 ———. Review of V. Hähnlein, *Der Mut zur Gesundheit.* Leipzig: Hesse & Becker, [ ]. In *IZIP*, 1928, 6(1), 78.

79 ———. Review of Clara Liepmann, *Die Selbstverwaltung der Gefangenen.* Mannheim: J. Bensheimer, 1928. In *IZIP*, 1928, 6(4), 340.

80 ———. Review of [ ], *Sittlichkeit und Strafrecht.* Berlin: Verlag der Neuen Gesellschaft, [ ]. In *IZIP*, 1928, 6(1), 72-73.

81 ———. Review of A. Wenzl, *Das unbewusste Denken.* Karlsruhe: G. Braun, 1927. In *IZIP*, 1928, 6(1), 77-78.

82 ———. Review of J. Zappert, Kritisches über die Enuresis Nocturna. *Arch. Kinderheilkunde*, 1922, 1, 27-30. In *IZIP*, 1928, 6(4), 340-341.

83 **Goldfried, M. R.** Feelings of inferiority and the depreciation of others: A research review and theoretical reformulation. *JIP*, 1963, 19, 27-48.

84 **Goldin, P. C.** Experimental investigation of selective memory and the concept of repression and defense: A theoretical synthesis. *J. abnorm. soc. Psychol.*, 1964, 69, 365-380.

85 **Goldman, Margaret.** *The ABC's of guiding the child.* Chicago: North Side Unit, Comm. Child Guid. Ctrs., 1964. Paper. Also in Prine areas, B. C. Primary Teachers Assn., 1972, 15(1), (with R. Dreikurs).

86 ———. The recorder. In R. Dreikurs, R. Corsini, R. Lowe, & M. Sonstegard (Eds.), *Adlerian family counseling.* Pp. 45-52.

87 **Goldstein, A. P.** *Therapist-patient expectancies in psychotherapy.* New York: Pergamon Press, 1962.

88 **Goldstein, K.** Die ganzheitliche Betrachtung in die Medizin. In T. Brugsch (Ed.), *Einheitsbestrebungen in der Medizin.* Berlin: Steinkopff, 1930. Pp. 144–158.

89 ———. Notes on the development of my concepts. *JIP,* 1959, 15, 5–14.

90 **Gondor, E. I.** Art and play therapy. In K. A. Adler & Danica Deutsch (Eds.), *Essays in Individual Psychology.* Pp. 206–216.

91 ———. *Art and play therapy.* New York: Random House, 1954, 1958.

92 ———. Changing times. *Amer. J. Psychother.,* 1969, 23, 67–76 (with Lily Gondor). Also in Stella Chess & A. Thomas (Eds.), *Annual progress in child psychiatry and child development.* New York: Brunner-Mazel, 1970.

93 ———. Expression therapy. In W. Wolff (Ed.), *Contemporary psychotherapists examine themselves.*

94 ———. *The function of art and play therapy groups.* New York: N. Y. Med. Coll., 1969.

95 ———. Illustrations in E. A. Gutheil, *The handbook of dream analysis.* New York: Grove Press, 1960.

96 ———. Review of C. Brown, *Manchild in the promised land.* In *JIP,* 1967, 23, 248–249.

97 ———. Review of Rhoda Kelley, *The psychology of children's art.* In *Amer. J. Psychother.,* 1970, 24, 151–152.

98 ———. Review of Elizabeth Koppitz, *Psychological evaluation of children's drawings.* In *Amer. J. Psychother.,* 1969, 23, 327–328.

99 ———. Review of Edith Kramer, *Art as therapy with children.* New York: Schocken, 1971. In *JIP,* 1972, 28, 99.

100 ———. Review of Edith Kramer, *Art therapy in a children's community.* Springfield, Ill.: C. C. Thomas, 1958. In *JIP,* 1958, 14, 193–194.

101 ———. Review of J. H. Plokker, *Art from the mentally disturbed.* Boston: Little, Brown, 1965. In *Amer. J. Psychother.,* 1967, 21(3), 695–697.

102 ———. Techniques and expressive therapy integrated into the treatment of mentally retarded children. *Amer. J. ment. Defic.,* 1958, 63, 60–63.

103 ———. The use of art in therapy (with Ruth Hartley). In D. Brower & L. E. Abt (Eds.), *Progress in clinical psychology.*

104 **Gondor, Lily.** Bias and misunderstanding? *Contemp. Psychol.,* 1969, 14, 452.

105 ———. Changing times. *Amer. J. Psychother.,* 1969, 23, 67–76 (with E. I. Gondor Also in Stella Chess & A. Thomas (Eds.), *Annual progress in child psychiatry and child development.* New York: Brunner-Mazel, 1970.

106 ———. Use of fantasy communications in child psychotherapy. *Amer. J. Psychother.* 1957, 11(2), 323–335.

107 **Goodall, K.** Conscientious objection—Adlerian. *Psychol. Today,* 1971, 5(1), 18–19.

108 ———. The first-born phenomenon is a figment—"A cheap bet on a long shot." *Psychol. Today,* 1972, 6(7), 14, 16.

109 ———. Painter's views. *Psychol. Today,* 1972, 6(1), 32.

110 **Goodchilds, Jacqueline D.** Some personality and behavioral factors related to birth order. *J. appl. Psychol.,* 1963, 47, 300–303 (with E. E. Smith).

111 **Gooddy, W.** Two directions of memory. *JIP,* 1959, 15, 83–88.

112 **Goodenough, Florence.** The effect of certain family relationships upon the development of personality. *J. genet. Psychol.,* 1927, 34, 45–72 (with A. M. Leahy).

113 ———. Interrelationships in the behavior of young children. *Child Developm.,* 1930, 1, 29–47.

114 **Goodman, C. C.** Value and need as organizing factors in perception. *J. abnorm. so Psychol.,* 1947, 42, 33–44 (with J. S. Bruner).

115 **Goodstein, L.** Ego strength and types of defensive and coping behavior. *J. consult. Psychol.,* 1967, 31, 432 (with Corinda Hunter).

166 **Goodwin, Carol.** Value of the study group course to me. *OSIPNL,* 1966, 6(3), 7–8.

117 **Gordon, G.** Anorexia nervosa. *IPMP,* 1931, No. 2. Pp. 45–49.

118 ———. Anorexia nervosa. IPMP, 1931, No. 2 (with C. M. Bevan-Brown, J. C. Young, W. Langdon-Brown, & F. G. Crookshank).

119 ———. Discussion of J. C. Young & F. G. Crookshank, The treatment of sexual incompetence by the methods of Individual Psychology. *IPMP,* 1932, No. 3. Pp. 53–54

120 ———. Escape into invalidism. *IPP,* 1939, No. 21. Pp. 23–29.

121 **Gordon, K.** A study of early memories. *J. Delin.*, 1928, 12, 129–132.

122 **Gorlow, L.** (Ed.). *Readings in the psychology of adjustment.* 2nd ed. New York: McGraw-Hill, 1968 (with W. Katkovsky).

123 **Goss, A.** Abasement scores and adjustment of neuropsychiatric patients. *J. Psychol.*, 1969, 72, 17–19.

124 ———. Alcoholism and clinical symptoms. *J. abnorm. Psychol.*, 1969, 74, 482–483 (with T. Morosco).

125 ———. Predicting vocational success for neuropsychiatric patients with the Edwards Personal Preference Schedule. *J. appl. Psychol.*, 1969, 53, 250–252.

126 ———. The relationship between a dimension of internal-external control and the MMPI with an alcoholic population. *J. consult. Psychol.*, 1970, 34(2), 189–192 (with T. Morosco).

127 **Gottesfeld, H.** Changes in feelings of powerlessness in a community action program. *Psychol. Rep.*, 1966, 19, 978.

128 ———. Cooperative research in community mental health. *Prof. Psychol.*, 1971, 2, 145–147.

129 ———. Professionals and delinquents evaluate professional methods with delinquents. *Soc. Probs.*, 1965, 13, 45–59.

130 ———. A social interest scale for patients in group psychotherapy. *JIP*, 1963, 19, 77–79.

131 ———. A study of the role of paraprofessionals in community mental health. *Comm. ment. Hlth. J.*, 1970, 6(4), 285–291.

132 **Gottsegen, Gloria** (Ed.). *Professional school psychology.* New York: Grune & Stratton, 1960 (with M. G. Gottsegen).

133 **Gottsegen, M. G.** (Ed.). *Professional school psychology.* New York: Grune & Stratton, 1960 (with Gloria Gottsegen).

134 **Gould, R.** The cognitive styles of adaptation of repressors, anxiety reactors and psychopaths. *Diss. Abstr.*, 1966, 26, 6167. Unpubl. Ph.D. Diss., Univ. Florida, 1965.

135 **Gould, Shirley.** How to hold a family council. *OSIPNL*, 1964, 5(2), 9–10; 1969, 10(2), 9–11.

136 **Graber, Edith H.** Alexander Müller (1895–1968). *JIP*, 1969, 25, 139.

137 **Grace, H. A.** Children's reactions to stories depicting parent-child conflict situations. *Child Developm.*, 1952, 23, 61–74 (with Joan J. Lohman).

138 **Grace, H. A.** Conformance and performance. *J. soc. Psychol.*, 1954, 40, 333–335.

139 **Graeber, M.** In-service education in counseling. *Midland Schools*, 1960, 75, 10–12 (with M. Sonstegard).

140 **Graf, K.** Portrait. *IPNL*, 1971, 20(6), 111.

141 **Graff, R. W.** Behavioral bibliotherapy: A simple home remedy for fears. *Psychother.*, 1970, 7(2), 118–119 (with G. D. MacLean).

142 **Granville-Grossman, K. L.** Birth order and schizophrenia. *Brit. J. Psychiat.*, 1966, 112, 1119–1126.

143 **Gray, B.** Family constellations of "normal" and "disturbed" marriages: An empirical study. *JIP*, 1961, 17, 93–95 (with W. Toman).

144 **Gray, F.** Place of psychology in the medical curriculum. *IPMP*, 1936, No. 16 (with W. Langdon-Brown, R. G. M. Ladell, & F. G. Crookshank).

145 ———. The psycho-pathology of organic disease. *IPMP*, 1936, No. 16. Pp. 33–43.

146 **Great Man.** Brief, incidental hints. *IZIP*, 1923, 2(2), 15–16.

147 **Green, Betty** (Ed.). *Death education: Preparation for living.* Cambridge, Mass.: Schenkman, 1971 (with D. Irish).

148 **Green, C. E.** Birth order, family size and extra-sensory perception. *Brit. J. soc. clin. Psychol.*, 1966, 5, 150–152 (with M. E. Eastman & S. T. Adams).

149 ———. The effect of birth order and family size on extra-sensory perception. *J. soc. psychic Res.*, 1955, 43, 181–191.

150 **Green, Jane N.** The unity of the self-image. *IP*, 1970, 7(1), 3–7.

151 **Green, M.** Personality and group factors in the making of atheists. *J. abnorm. soc. Psychol.*, 1932, 27, 179–194 (with G. E. Vetter).

152 **Greenacre, Phyllis.** Contribution to study of screen memories. In *Trauma, growth and personality.* New York: Norton, 1952.

153 ———. Contribution to the study of screen memories. *Psychoanal. Stud. Child*, 1949, 3–4, 73–84.

154 **Greenberg, H.** Order of birth as a determinant of personality and attitudinal characteristics. *J. soc. Psychol.*, 1963, 60, 221–230 (with Rosemary Guerino, Marilyn Lashen, D. Mayer, & Dorothy Piskowsky).

155 **Greenburg, D.** *How to make yourself miserable.* New York: Signet Books, 1966.

156 **Greene, J. T.** Altruistic behavior in the albino rat. *Psychonom. Sci.*, 1969, 14(1), 47–48.

157 **Greene, Janet.** Early childhood recollections: An integrative technique of personality test data. *AJIP*, 1953, 10, 31–42 (with Asya Kadis & N. Freedman).

158 **Greene, M.** First born and last born children in a child development clinic. *JIP*, 1964, 20, 179–182 (with B. Cushna & B. C. F. Snider).

159 **Greenblatt, Helen J.** "I hate reading." *Understanding the Child*, 1952, 21, 78–84.

160 **Greenfield, N. S.** Some cognitive aspects of a personality dimension: Neurosis and problem solving behavior. Unpubl. Ph.D. Diss., Univ. Cal., 1953.

161 **Greenwald, H.** (Ed.). *Active psychotherapy.* New York: Atherton, 1967.

162 ———. (Ed.). *Great cases in psychoanalysis.* New York: Ballantine, 1959. Paper.

163 **Greenwood, Alice.** Das erste Halbjahr eines Säuglings. *IZIP*, 1933, 12(6), 464–467.

164 ———. John Milton. *IZIP*, 1930, 8(4), 401–416.

165 ———. Review of C. Richter, *Principles in bio-physics.* Harrisburg, Pa.: Good Books Corp., 1927. In *IZIP*, 1927, 5(5), 396–397.

166 ———. Review of E. Thorndike, *The measurement of intelligence.* New York: Columbia Univ. Press, 1925. In *IZIP*, 1927, 5(5), 396.

167 **Greever, Kathryn B.** An Adlerian approach to measuring change in entering freshmen after one semester in an open-door community college. *Diss. Abstr.*, 1972, 33(4-A), 1513.

168 **Gregerson, H.** Portrait. *Miami Herald*, Apr. 18, 1971.

169 **Gregory, W. E.** Life is therapeutic. *Ment. Hyg.* (New York), 1953, 37, 259–264.

170 **Greven, Georgia.** Counseling the reluctant child and her mother. *IP*, 1966, 4(1), 4–8. Also in R. Dreikurs (Ed.), *Education, guidance, psychodynamics.* Pp. 11–15 (with Eleanore Redwin).

171 ———. Discussion group of small children. *IP*, 1967, 5, 26–29 (with Eleanore Redwin).

172 ———. The playroom and the playroom director. In R. Dreikurs, R. Corsini, R. Lowe & M. Sonstegard (Eds.), *Adlerian family counseling.* Pp. 53–62.

173 **Grey, L.** *Como lograr la disciplina en el niño y en el adolescente.* Buenos Aires: Paidos, 1972 (with R. Dreikurs).

174 ———. A comparison of the educational philosophy of John Dewey and Alfred Adler. *AJIP*, 1954, 11, 71–80.

175 ———. *Demokrati og opdragelse. En vejledning for foraeldre.* [A parent's guide to child discipline]. Translated by Nina Lautrup-Larsen. Copenhagen: Hans Reitzels 1971 (with R. Dreikurs).

176 ———. *Discipline without tyranny: Child training in the first five years.* New York: Hawthorn Books, November, 1972.

177 ———. Humanity at the crossroads. *IPB*, 1951, 9, 170–173.

178 ———. *Logical consequences: A new approach to discipline.* New York: Meredith, 1968 (with R. Dreikurs).

179 ———. *A parent's guide to child discipline.* New York: Hawthorn Books, 1970 [A new revised edition of *Logical consequences*] (with R. Dreikurs).

180 ———. Paul Brodsky (1900–1970). *JIP*, 1971, 27(1), 124–125.

181 ———. Portrait. *Los Angeles Times*, Feb. 27, 1972.

182 ———. The social adjustment of our gifted children: An Adlerian interpretation. *AJIP*, 1954, 11, 155–162.

183 ———. The use of logical consequences in interpersonal relations. *IP*, 1968, 5(3), 12–14.

184 ———. Utilization of the earliest childhood recollection in detecting maladjustment among junior college students. Unpubl. Ph.D. Diss., Univ. So. Calif., 1959.

185 **Griffith, R. M.** Forgetting of jokes: A function of repression? *JIP*, 1963, 19, 213–215 (with Joan C. Lee).

186 **Grigg, A. E.** Superiority of childhood account over current account for judging current self impressions. *JIP*, 1960, 16, 64–66.

187 **Grigg, K.** Early memories. *Arch. gen. Psychiat.*, 1962, 7, 57–69 (with J. Levy).

188 ———. Early memories, thematic configurational analysis. *Arch. gen. Psychiat.*, 1962, 7, 83–95 (with J. Levy).

189 **Grindea, M.** [Note]. *ADAM: Int. Rev.* (London), 1970, 35(340-342), 3.

190 **Gronert, R. R.** Combining a behavioral approach with reality therapy. *Elem. Sch. Guid. Couns.*, 1970, 5, 104–112.

191 **Grosjaques, Marybelle.** Review of Judith Smith & D. E. Smith, *Child management.* Ann Arbor: Ann Arbor Publ., 1966. In *OSIPNL,* 1970, 11(1), 12 (with Nancy Pearcy).

192 **Grossack, M. M.** Some effects of co-operation and competition upon small group behavior. *J. abnorm. soc. Psychol.,* 1954, 49, 341–348.

193 **Grossen Manne.** Kurze gelegentliche Hinweise. *IZIP,* 1923, 2(2), 16–17.

194 **Grosz, H. J.** Birth order, anxiety, and affiliative tendency: Observations and comments regarding Schachter's hypothesis. *J. nerv. ment. Dis.,* 1964, 19, 588–590.

195 **Grotjahn, M.** (Ed.). *Psychoanalytic pioneers: A history of psychoanalysis as seen through the lives and works of its most eminent teachers.* New York: Basic Books, 1966 (with F. Alexander & S. Einstein).

196 **Grubbe, Marie.** Functional use of Adlerian psychology in the public school. *Amer. Soc. Adlerian Psychol. Educ. Div. Nwsltr.,* 1964, 2, 9–17 (with T. E. Grubbe).

197 **Grubbe, T. E.** Adlerian psychology as a basic framework for elementary counseling services. *Elem. Sch. Guid. Couns.,* 1968, 3, 20–26.

198 ———. Functional use of Adlerian psychology in the public schools. *Amer. Soc. Adlerian Psychol. Educ. Div. Nwsltr.,* 1964, 2, 9–17 (with Marie Grubbe).

199 ———. Possibilities of a school psychologist. *IPNL,* 1960, 10(7-8, Whole No. 108–109). Pp. 27–28.

200 **Grübl, M. A.** A case of nervous vomiting. *IJIP,* 1936, 2(2), 105–109.

201 ———. Ein Fall von nervösen Erbrechen. *IZIP,* 1932, 10(6), 433–436.

202 ———. Review of K. Springenschmid, *Das Bauernkind.* München: R. Oldenburg, 1926. In *IZIP,* 1932, 10(6), 479–480.

203 **Grün, H.** Was Wir wollen. *Ärztl. Standeszeitung* (Wien), 1902, 1(1), 1–2.

204 **Grünbaum-Sachs, Hilde.** Frauenbewegung und männlicher Protest. *IZIP,* 1926, 4(2), 88–90.

205 **Grünberger, F.** Die Grussformen des Kindes. *IZIP,* 1928, 6(1), 66–68.

206 ———. The basic discrepancy of the human mind. *IPB,* 1948, 6, 177–184.

207 ———. Beobachtungen über das Sprachen aus dem Schlaf. *IZIP,* 1927, 5(5), 384–388.

208 **Grünberger, F.** Mood fluctuations. *IJIP,* 1937, 3(1), 54–67.

209 ———. Review of O. & Alice Rühle, *Das proletarische Kind.* In *IZIP,* 1926, 4(3), 162.

210 ———. Review of T. Ziehen, *Über das Wesen der Beanlagung und ihre methodische Erforschung.* Langensalza: Hermann Beyer & Söhne, 1929. In *IZIP,* 1930, 8(4), 440.

211 ———. Über die Stimmung und deren Schwankungen. *IZIP,* 1936, 14(4), 196–209.

212 **Grunwald, Bernice.** See Grunwald, Bronia.

213 **Grunwald, Bronia.** The application of Adlerian principles in a classroom. *AJIP,* 1954, 11, 131–141.

214 ———. [Comments]. In R. J. Corsini & D. D. Howard (Eds.), *Critical incidents in teaching.* Pp. 24–25, 35–37, 75–76.

215 ———. How the group helped a discouraged boy. *IP,* 1970, 7(1), 14–26.

216 ———. Is the teacher a psychotherapist? In R. Dreikurs (Ed.), *Education, guidance, psychodynamics.* Pp. 1–6.

217 ———. *Maintaining sanity in the classroom: Illustrated teaching techniques.* New York: Harper & Row, 1971 (with R. Dreikurs & Floy Pepper).

218 ———. *Minutes of a school class council.* Corvallis, Ore.: Oregon Soc. I. P., n.d. Pp. 13. Mimeo. Also in *OSIPNL,* 1964, 5(2).

219 ———. *Motivating children to learn.* Burlington, Vt.: Univ. Vermont, 1971 (with R. Dreikurs).

220 ———. Never underestimate the power of children. *Intel. Dig.,* 1972, 11(10), 54–56 (with R. Dreikurs & Floy Pepper).

221 ———. Portrait. *IPNL,* 1972, 21(6), 110.

222 ———. Role playing as a classroom group procedure. *IP,* 1969, 6(2), 34–38.

223 ———. Strategies for behavior change in schools. *Couns. Psychologist,* 1971, 3(1), 55–57.

224 **Guerino, Rosemarie.** Order of birth as a determinant of personality and attitudinal characteristics. *J. soc. Psychol.,* 1963, 60, 221–230 (with H. Greenberg, Marilyn Lashen, D. Mayer, & Dorothy Piskowsky).

225 **Guerney, B. G., Jr.** Alfred Adler and the current mental health revolution. *JIP,* 1970, 26(2), 124–134.

226 **Guevara, C.** Attitudes of schizophrenics and normals toward success and failure. *J. abnorm. Psychol.,* 1967, 72, 303-310 (with P. McReynolds).

227 **Guilford, J. P.** Three faces of intellect. *Amer. Psychologist*, 1959, 14, 469–479.

228 **Guilford, R. B.** A comparative study of the only and non-only children. *J. genet. Psychol.*, 1930, 38, 411–426 (with D. A. Worcester).

229 **Gullion, Elizabeth.** *Living with children: New methods for parents and teachers.* Champaign, Ill.: Research Press, 1969 (with G. R. Patterson).

230 **Gunderson, E. K. E.** Body size, self-evaluation, and military effectiveness. *J. Pers. soc. Psychol.*, 1965, 2, 902–906.

231 **Gunderson, M. M.** Relationships between expressed personality needs and social background and military status variables. *J. Psychol.*, 1969, 71, 217–224.

232 **Gundlach, R.** Birth order and sex of siblings in a sample of lesbians and nonlesbians. *Psychol. Rev.*, 1967, 20, 61–62 (with B. F. Riess).

233 ———. A boon for being first born? *Contemp. Psychol.*, 1961, 6, 110–111.

234 **Gunning, Evelyn C.** Investigations into self concept: II. Stability of reported self identifications. *J. clin. Psychol.*, 1955, 11, 41–46 (with J. F. T. Bugental).

235 **Gunther, J.** Freuds Schüler und Widersacher. *Frankfurter Allg. Zeit.*, July 4, 1970.

236 ———. Review of M. Sperber, *Alfred Adler oder das Elend der Psychologie.* In *Frankfurter Allg. Zeit.*, July 4, 1970.

237 **Gurewicz, S.** *Beurteilung freier Schüleraufsätze und Schülerzeichnungen auf Grund der Adlerschen Individualpsychologie.* Zürich: Rascher, 1948.

238 **Gushurst, R. S.** The reliability and concurrent validity of an approach to the interpretation of early recollections. Unpubl. Ph.D. Diss., Univ. Chicago, 1971.

239 ———. Some therapeutic uses of psychologic testing. *Amer. J. Psychother.*, 1972, 26(4), 539–546 (with H. H. Mosak).

240 ———. The technique, utility, and validity of life style analysis. *Couns. Psychologist*, 1971, 3(1), 30–39.

241 ———. What patients say and what they mean. *Amer. J. Psychother.*, 1971, 25(3), 428–436 (with H. H. Mosak).

242 **Gutheil, E. A.** Transsexualism and transvestitism: A symposium. *Amer. J. Psychother.*, 1954, 8, 219–230 (with H. Benjamin & R. V. Sherwin).

243 **Guttman, R. R.** Sex and age differences in pattern organization in a figural-conceptual task. *Developm. Psychol.*, 1971, 5, 446–453 (with I. Kahneman).

H

1 **H. J.** Review of [   ], *Gegen Psychoanalyse.* In *IZIP*, 1932, 10(3), 237–238.

2 **Häberlin, P.** *Minderwertigkeitsgefühle.*

3 **Haberer, Maureen.** Effectiveness of Adlerian counseling with low achieving students. *JIP*, 1966, 22, 222–227 (with M. O. Nelson).

4 **Hadfield, J. A.** *Introduction to psychotherapy: Its history and modern schools.* London: Allen & Unwin, 1967.

5 ———. Reliability of infantile memories. *Brit. J. med. Psychol.*, 1928, 8, 87–111.

6 **Haeutler, A.** Idiotie. *IZIP*, 1931, 9(1), 33–39.

7 ———. Religiöse Menschlichkeit. *IZIP*, 1932, 10(2), 127–136.

8 **Hagen, Rosemarie.** Translator of D. Dinkmeyer & R. Dreikurs. *Ermutigung als Lernhilfe.*

9 **Haigh, G. B.** Changes in the relation between self-concepts and ideal concepts consequent upon client-centered counseling (with J. M. Butler). In C. R. Rogers & R. F. Dymond (Eds.), *Psychotherapy and personality change.* Chicago: Univ. Chicago Press, 1954.

10 ———. Multiple therapy as a method for training and research in psychotherapy. *J. abnorm. soc. Psychol.*, 1950, 45, 659–666 (with B. L. Kell).

11 **Haire, N.** Discussion of J. C. Young & F. G. Crookshank, The treatment of sexual incompetence by the methods of Individual Psychology. *IPMP*, 1932, No. 3. Pp. 49–50.

12 **Haldane, F. P.** A self-governed patients social club in a public mental hospital. *J. ment. Sci.*, 1941, 87, 419–426 (with J. Bierer).

13 **Hale, Phyllis.** Response to Kehas' critique. *JIP*, 1969, 25, 215–218 (with L. C. Hartlage).

14 ———. Self concept decline from psychiatric hospitalization. *JIP*, 1968, 24, 174–176 (with L. C. Hartlage).

15 Haley, J. The art of being schizophrenic. *Voices*, 1965, 1(1), 133–147.

16 ———. Family experiments: A new type of experimentation. *Fam. Proc.*, 1962, 3, 41–65.

17 ———. An interactional description of schizophrenia. *Psychiat.*, 1959, 22, 321–332.

18 ———. *Strategies of psychotherapy.* New York: Grune & Stratton, 1963.

19 ———. *Techniques of family therapy.* New York: Basic Books, 1967 (with Lynn Hoffman).

20 Hall, C. S. A cognitive theory of dreams. *J. gen. Psychol.*, 1953, 49, 273–282.

21 ———. *The meaning of dreams.* New York: McGraw-Hill, 1966.

22 ———. *Psychology: An introductory textbook.* Cleveland: Howard Allen, 1960.

23 ———. Review of R. May, *The art of counseling.* In *Contemp. Psychol.*, 1959, 4, 263.

24 ———. *Theories of personality.* New York: Wiley, 1957 (with G. Lindzey).

25 ———. *Theories of personality: Primary sources and research.* New York: Wiley, 1965 (with G. Lindzey).

26 Hall, Elizabeth. Alfred Adler, a sketch. *Psychol. Today*, 1970, 3(9), 45, 67.

27 Hall, E. Attitudinal structures of older and younger siblings. *JIP*, 1964, 20, 59–68 (with B. Barger).

28 ———. Ordinal position and success in engagement and marriage. *JIP*, 1965, 21, 154–158.

29 Hall, G. S. Note on early memories. *Pedag. Sem.*, 1899, 6, 485–512.

30 ———. Portrait. *IZIP*, 1924, 2(5), 1.

31 Hall, Mary H. A conversation with Abraham H. Maslow. *Psychol. Today*, 1968, 2(2), 34–37, 54–57.

32 ———. A conversation with Kenneth B. Clark. *Psychol. Today*, 1968, 2(1), 18–25.

33 ———. A conversation with Michael Polanyi. *Psychol. Today*, 1968, 1(12), 20–25, 66–67.

34 ———. A conversation with Viktor Frankl. *Psychol. Today*, 1968, 1(9), 57–63.

35 ———. An interview with "Mr. Humanist" —Rollo May. *Psychol. Today*, 1967, 1(5), 24–29, 72–73.

36 Hall, R. W. Alfred Adler's concept of God. *JIP*, 1971, 27(1), 10–18.

37 Hall, R. W. Review of M. Merleau-Ponty, *Signs.* Evanston, Ill.: Northwestern Univ. Press, 1964. In *JIP*, 1965, 21(2), 219–220.

38 Hamilton, Elizabeth. *Heloise.* Garden City, N. Y.: Doubleday, 1967.

39 ———. *Saint Teresa, a journey to Spain.* New York: Scribner, 1959.

40 ———. *Simon.* London: Andre Deutsch,

41 Hamilton, J. Effects of stress, communication relevance, and birth order on opinion change. *Psychonom. Sci.*, 1968, 11, 297–298 (with R. Helmreich).

42 Hammer, M. Preference for a male child: Cultural factor. *JIP*, 1970, 26, 54–56.

43 Hammond, L. K. Cognitive structure and clinical inference. *Diss. Abstr.*, 1966, 26, 6847; Unpubl. Ph.D. Diss., Univ. Colorado, 1965.

44 Hammond, Maybelle. Review of N. Copeland, *Psychology and the soldier.* Harrisburg, Pa.: Military Serv. Co., 1942. In *IPB*, 1943, 3, 97–99.

45 ———. A summer seminar in Individual Psychology. *IPB*, 1943, 3, 50–53 (with Orpha Mills).

46 Hampel, K. Pädagogische Bewegung in der Türkei. *IZIP*, 1931, 310–312.

47 Hampton, F. A. Schüchternheit. *IZIP*, 1928, 6(5), 350–358.

48 Hanawalt, N. G. Childhood memories of single and recurrent incidents. *J. genet. Psychol.*, 1965, 107, 85–89 (with J. Gebhardt).

49 Hancock, Francena T. An examination of the relationship between ordinal position, personality and conformity: An extension, replication and partial verification. *J. Pers. soc. Psychol.*, 1967, 5, 398–407 (with E. E. Sampson).

50 Handel, G. *Family worlds: A psychosocial approach to family life.* Chicago: Univ. Chicago Press, 1959 (with R. D. Hess).

51 ———. Persistence and change in working-class life style (with L. Rainwater). In A. B. Shostak & W. Gomberg (Eds.), *Blue collar world.* Englewood Cliffs, N. J.: Prentice-Hall, 1964. Pp. 36–41.

52 ———. Psychological study of whole families. *Psychol. Bull.*, 1965, 63, 19–41.

53 ———. *Workingman's wife: Her personality, world and life style.* Dobbs Ferry, N. Y.: Oceana Publ., 1959 (with L. Rainwater & R. P. Coleman).

54 Handlon, J. H. The treatment of patient and family as a group: Is it group psychotherapy? *Int. J. grp. Psychother.*, 1962, 12, 132-142 (with M. B. Perloff).

55 Hanfmann, Eugenia. Introduction [Papers in honor of Kurt Goldstein]. *JIP*, 1959, 15, 4 (with N. L. Mintz).

56 ———. Review of F. Heider, *The psychology of interpersonal relations.* In *JIP*, 1960, 16, 99-100.

57 Hanks, H. L. Review of E. Becker, *The birth and death of meaning.* In *JIP*, 1963, 19, 91-92.

58 Hanlon, T. E. Congruence of self and ideal self in relation to personality adjustment. *J. consult. Psychol.*, 1954, 18, 215-218 (with P. Hofstaetter & J. P. O'Conner).

59 Hansen, Edna. The child guidance clinic of Abraham Lincoln Center. *IPB*, 1944-45, 4, 49-58.

60 ———. Parents can be wiser. *The standard*, Feb.-Mar., 1953. Pp. 63-67.

61 Hansen, J. (Ed.). Guidance services in the elementary school. APGA Reprint Series Two, 1971.

62 Hanson, P. Action therapy intervention in human interaction training. *Newsltr. Res. Psychol.*, 1972, 14(4), 23-25 (with W. E. O'Connell, R. R. Baker, & R. Ermalinski).

63 ———. The generation gap on a psychiatric ward. *Newsltr. Res. Psychol.*, 1971, 13(2), 1-5 (with R. Ermalinski & W. E. O'Connell).

64 ———. The negative nonsense of the passive patient. *Rat. Living*, 1971, 6(1), 28-31 (with W. E. O'Connell).

65 ———. Patient's cognitive changes in human relations training. *JIP*, 1970, 26, 57-63 (with W. E. O'Connell).

66 ———. Some basic concepts in human relations training for psychiatric patients. *Hosp. Comm. Psychiat.*, 1970, 21, 137-143 (with W. E. O'Connell, P. Rothaus, & G. Wiggins).

67 ———. Toward resolution of a generation gap conflict on a psychiatric ward. *Int. J. grp. Tensions*, 1972, 2(2), 77-89 (with R. Ermalinski & W. E. O'Connell).

68 ———. Training patients for effective participation in back-home groups. *Amer. J. Psychiat.*, 1969, 126, 857-862 (with P. Rothaus, W. O'Connell, & G. Wiggins).

69 ———. Verbal participation and group behavior. *Newsltr. Res. Psychol.*, 1970, 12(2), 36-39 (with W. E. O'Connell & K. Pate).

70 Harden, L. A quantitative investigation of early memories. *J. soc. Psychol.*, 1931, 2, 252-255 (with M. N. Crook).

71 Hardy, K. R. An appetitional theory of sexual motivation. *Psychol. Rev.*, 1964, 71, 1-18.

72 Hare, E. [Birth order and the month of birth in schizophrenia]. *Vestnik Akad. med. Nauk SSSR*, 1971, 26(5), 39-42.

73 Hare, E. H. Associations: Important or trivial. *Int. J. Psychiat.*, 1967, 3(6), 537-538.

74 Hargreaves, R. The flight into normality. *IPP*, 1940, No. 22. Pp. 18-30.

75 Harlow, H. F. Motivational forces underlying learning. In *Learning theory, personality theory, and clinical research: The Kentucky symposium.* New York: Wiley, 1954. Pp. 36-53.

76 Harlow, R. G. Masculine inadequacy and compensatory development of physique. *J. Pers.*, 1951, 19, 312-324.

77 Harms, E. Alfred Adler in American psychotherapy. *IPB*, 1947, 6, 41-44.

78 ——— (Ed.). *Handbook of child guidance.* New York: Child Care Publ., 1946, 1948, 1951.

79 ———. Inferiority and superiority as primarily psychological concepts. *Stud. Gen.*, 1965, 18, 361-364.

80 ——— (Ed.). *Pathogenesis of nervous and mental diseases.* New York: Libra, 1968.

81 Harper, R. A. *A guide to rational living.* Englewood Cliffs, N. J.: Prentice-Hall, 1961; Hollywood, Cal.: Wilshire Books, 1971 (with A. Ellis).

82 ———. Marriage counseling as rational process-oriented psychotherapy. *JIP*, 1960, 16, 197-207.

83 ———. *Psychoanalysis and psychotherapy: 36 systems.* Englewood Cliffs, N. J.: Prentice-Hall, 1959. Paper.

84 ———. Review of Frieda Fromm-Reichmann, *Psychoanalysis and psychotherapy.* Chicago: Univ. Chicago Press, 1959. In *JIP*, 1960, 16, 105-106.

85 Harrell, S. N. Patterns of parental child-rearing and subsequent vulnerability to cognitive disturbance. *J. consult. Psychol.*, 1966, 30, 51-59 (with A. B. Heilbrun, Jr. & Helen K. Orr).

86 **Harriman, P. L.** (Ed.). *Encyclopedia of psychology.* New York: Phil. Libr., 1947.

87 **Harris, A.** (Ed.). *Readings on reading instruction.* New York: David McKay, 1972 (with E. Sipay).

88 **Harris, C.** The gap between religion and psychiatry. *Insight,* 1963, 19, 69–76 (with W. O'Connell, J. Frizelle, J. Jernigan & J. Wohl).

89 **Harris, I.** Birth order and creative styles. In J. H. Masserman (Ed.), *Science and psychoanalysis.* Vol. 8. Pp. 74–90.

90 ———. *The promised seed: A comparative study of eminent first and later sons.* New York: Free Press of Glencoe, 1964.

91 **Harris, N. G.** *Modern trends in psychological medicine.* London: Butterworth, 1948; New York: Hoeber, 1948.

92 **Harris, T. G.** The Devil & Rollo May. *Psychol. Today,* 1969, 3(3), 13–16.

93 **Hart, D. L.** *Der tiefenpsychologische Begriff der Kompensation.* Zürich: Origo Verlag, 1956.

94 **Hart, J. L.** Pastoral counseling and Individual Psychology. *JIP,* 1971, 27(1), 36–43.

95 ———. Steve: A case study using Adlerian concepts in college counseling. *IP,* 1969, 6(2), 39–41.

96 **Harten, R.** Heimerziehung. In Sofie Lazarsfeld (Ed.), *Technik der Erziehung.*

97 **Hartford, Claire** (Ed.). *The firstborn.* Cambridge, Mass.: Harvard Univ. Press, 1968 (with M. J. E. Senn).

98 **Hartlage, L. C.** Response to Kehas' critique. *JIP,* 1969, 25, 215–218 (with Phyllis Hale).

99 ———. Self-concept decline from psychiatric hospitalization. *JIP,* 1968, 24, 174–176 (with Phyllis Hale).

100 **Hartley, E. L.** (Ed.). *Outside readings in psychology.* New York: Crowell, 1950 (with Ruth E. Hartley & H. G. Burch).

101 ———. Review of M. Rokeach, *The open and closed mind.* New York: Basic Books, 1960. In *JIP,* 1960, 16, 212–214.

102 **Hartley, Margaret.** Changes in the self-concept during psychotherapy. Unpubl. Ph.D. Diss., Univ. Chicago, 1951.

103 **Hartley, Ruth E.** (Ed.). *Outside readings in psychology.* New York: Crowell, 1950 (with E. L. Hartley & H. G. Burch).

104 ———. Personal characteristics and the acceptance of secondary groups as reference groups. *JIP,* 1957, 13, 45–55.

105 **Hartley, Ruth E.** The use of art in therapy (with E. I. Gondor). In D. Brower & L. E. Abt (Eds.), *Progress in clinical psychology.*

106 **Hartmann, G. W.** The rigidity of a basic attitudinal frame. *J. abnorm. soc. Psychol.,* 1939, 34, 314–335 (with W. S. Watson).

107 **Hartmann, H.** (Ed.). *Essays on ego psychology.* New York: Int. Univer. Press, 1964.

108 **Hartogs, R.** *Das Minderwertigkeitsgefühl.* Bad Homburg: J. Siemens, 1933.

109 **Hartwich, A.** Translator of Alexandra Adler. *Individualpsychologie.*

110 **Harvey, O. J.** Level of aspiration as a case of judgmental activity in which ego-involvements operate as factors. *Sociom.,* 1951, 14, 141–147 (with M. Sherif).

111 **Hathaway, S. R.** Review of S. Standal & R. J. Corsini (Eds.), *Critical incidents in psychotherapy.* In *Contemp. Psychol.,* 1960, 5, 164–166.

112 **Haupt. H. J.** On reading George Brandes' autobiography. *IPNL,* 1954, No. 38. P. 7.

113 **Hauser, Andrée.** L'acquisition du courage. *L'Ecole des Parents,* 1952, No. 7.

114 ———. Alfred Adler. *Méthodes Actives,* 1947, No. 9.

115 ———. L'association départmentale favorise la réussité de nos enfants. *L'Ecole de Region Parisienne,* 1953, No. 31 (with M. Dreyfus).

116 ———. Le cas d'un jeune delinquant. *Méthodes Actives,* 1947, No. 9.

117 ———. Changement dans le milieu familial. *La Famille et l'Ecole de la Region Parisienne,* 1955, No. 48.

118 ———. La colêre. *Le Travail Vivant,* 1939, No. 19.

119 ———. Compte-rendu d'une consultation psycho-pédagogique donnée selon la technique d'Alfred Adler. *L'Ecole des Parents,* 1953, No. 2. Pp. 39–41 (with M. Dreyfus).

120 ———. Consultations pour parents et instituteurs. *Actes des Journées Internationales des Centres Psychopédagogiques de Langue Française,* 1954, No. 5.

121 ———. Difficulté scolaire après un sejour en privetorium. *L'Ecole des Parents,* 1955, No. 4.

122 ———. The drawing as a help in child-psychotherapy. *AJIP,* 1956, 12, 53–58.

123 ———. Etude d'un cas. *Bull. du Centre de Psychol. Adlérienne,* 1950, No. 1, Pp. 7–10.

124 Hauser, Andrée. La femme et le couple. *Le Groupe familial,* 1965.

125 ———. Journées d'études internationales sur l'éducation des parents. *L'Ecole des Parents,* 1956, No. 3.

126 ———. Les parents nerveux. *Bull. de liaison des Cercles de Parents,* 1956, No. 2.

127 ———. Les parents ont voulu très bien faire. *La Famille et l'Ecole de la Region Parisienne,* 1955, No. 48.

128 ———. Le sentiment d'infériorité. *L'Ecole des Parents,* 1961, No. 4.

129 ———. Utilisation de la psychologie adlérienne pour les enfants difficiles. *L'Homoed. Française,* 1947, Nos. 6-7.

130 ———. La vie familiale de l'educateur intervient-elle dans les attitudes auprès des parents? *Le Groupe familial,* 1961, No. 13.

131 Hauser, E. Individualpsychologie und Kriminalpolitik. *ZIP,* 1914, 1(6-9), 174-185.

132 Hauser, Mme. Portrait. *IPNL,* 1971, 20(6), 111.

133 Hauser, R. *Lehrbuch der Psychologie.* Wien: Herder, 1933.

134 Havighurst, R. J. *et al.* Development of the ideal self in childhood and adolescence. *J. educ. Res.,* 1946, 40, 41-57.

135 ———. Leisure and life style. *Amer. J. Sociol.,* 1959, 64, 396-404 (with K. Feigenbaum).

136 ———. *Problems and methods of cross-national research.* New York: Houghton-Mifflin, 1970 (with G. Manaster).

137 Healy, Kathleen. *The demon and the dove: Personality growth through literature.* Pittsburgh: Duquesne Univ. Press, 1967 (with A. van Kaam).

138 Heaney, S. Personal helicon. *IPNL,* 1969, 19(2), 40.

139 Hedvig, Eleanor B. Children's early recollections as diagnostic technique. *JIP,* 1965, 21, 187-188.

140 ———. Stability of early recollections and Thematic Apperception stories. *JIP,* 1963, 19, 49-54.

141 ———. A study of the effects of immediately preceding experiences upon early childhood recollections. Unpubl. Ph.D. Diss., Northwestern Univ., 1960.

142 Heffron, A. R. Differences in performance on the chromatic vs. achromatic H-T-P drawings.

J. clin. Psychol., 1960, 16, 334-335 (with V. J. Bieliauskas).

143 Hegel, G. W. F. *Phenomenology of mind.* London: Unwin, 1931.

144 Hegeler, S. *Peter and Caroline: A child asks about childbirth and sex.* Introduction by Alexandra Adler. New York: Abelard-Schuman, 1961.

145 Heger, H. Individualität und Religion. *Mitteilungsbl. Int. Verein Indivpsy.,* [ ], 1(1), [ ].

146 Hegligers-Gunning, C. I. "Alles kan ook anders zijn." *MNWIP,* 1970, 19(2), 4-8.

147 Heider, F. *The psychology of interpersonal relations.* New York: Wiley, 1958.

148 Heilbrun, A. B., Jr. Patterns of parental childrearing and subsequent vulnerability to cognitive disturbance. *J. consult. Psychol.,* 1966, 30, 51-59 (with Helen K. Orr & S. N. Harrell).

149 Heimrich, R. Stress: Under the sea. *Psychol. Today,* 1969, 3(4), 28-29, 59-60 (with R. Radloff).

150 Hein, G. W. A. Neue Wege in der Behandlung der Verbrecher. In Int. Verein Indivpsy. *Alfred Adler zum Gedenken.* Pp. 32-63.

151 Heine, R. W. A comparison of patients' reports on psychotherapeutic experience with psychoanalytic, nondirective, and Adlerian therapists. *Amer. J. Psychother.,* 1953, 7, 16-23.

152 ———. *Concepts of personality.* Chicago: Aldine, 1963 (with J. M. Wepman).

153 ———. *Psychotherapy.* Englewood Cliffs, N. J.: Prentice-Hall, 1970.

154 ———. Review of B. H. Shulman, *Essays in schizophrenia.* In *Contemp. Psychol.,* 1968, 13(10), 536.

155 Heinrichs, Annie. Child-home-school: A successful child. *IPN,* 1941, 1(10), 3-4.

156 ———. Child-home-school: An everyday problem. *IPN,* 1941, 1(8-9), 13-14 (with Assja Kadis).

157 Heisler, V. T. Goal setting behavior of crippled and noncrippled children in situations of success and failure. Unpubl. Ph.D. Diss., Stanford Univ., 1951.

158 Hellkamp, D. T. Race, sex, ordinal position of birth, and self-disclosure in high school students. *Psychol. Rep.,* 1969, 25, 235-238 (with R. E. Dimond).

159 Helmreich, R. Effects of stress, communication relevance, and birth order on opinion change. *Psychonom. Sci.,* 1968, 11, 297-298 (with J. Hamilton).

160 **Helmreich, R.** Effects of stress and birth order on attitude change. *J. Pers.*, 1968, 36, 466-473 (with D. Kwiken & B. Collins).

161 **Helper, M. M.** Learning theory and the self-concept. *J. abnorm. soc. Psychol.*, 1955, 51, 184-194.

162 **Helson, H.** *Contemporary approaches to psychology.* Princeton, N. J.: Van Nostrand, 1967 (with W. Bevan).

163 **Helson, R.** Effects of sibling characteristics and parental values on creative interest and achievement. *J. Pers.*, 1968, 36, 589-607.

164 **Hemming, J. A.** Alfred Adler: The neglected innovator. *New Soc.* (London), Feb. 5, 1970.

165 ———. *The alternative society.* London: South Place Ethical Soc., 1969.

166 ———. A propos: Teilhard de Chardin. *IPNL*, 1969, 19(2), 27-28.

167 ———. *The child is right: A challenge to parents and other adults.* London: Longmans, 1947, 1950 (with Josephine Balls).

168 ———. Citizenship through social experience. In D. C. Thomson (Ed.), *Training worker citizens.* London: Macdonald & Evans, 1949.

169 ———. Comment. *IPNL*, 1964, 14(8-9, Whole No. 157-158). P. 31.

170 ———. *Democracy in school life.* London: Oxford Univ. Press, 1947.

171 ———. From minus to plus. *IPNL*, 1959, 9(11, Whole No. 100). Pp. 39-41.

172 ———. Humanism and Christianity (with H. Marrath). In C. Macey (Ed.), *Let's teach them right.* London: Pemberton, 1969.

173 ———. The humanist signpost. *New Statesman*, Oct. 27, 1967.

174 ———. *Individual morality.* London: Thomas Nelson, 1969; London: Panther, 1970.

175 ———. Letter on moral education. *Freethinker* (London), June 20, 1970. P. 200.

176 ———. *Mankind against the killers.* London-New York: Longmans, Green, 1956.

177 ———. Moral education. In A. J. Ayer (Ed.), *The humanist outlook.* London: Pemberton, 1968.

178 ———. Moral education in chaos. In T. Raison (Ed.), *Youth in new society.* London: Rupert Hart-Davis, 1966.

179 ———. Morals without religion. In *An enquiry into humanism.* London: BBC Publications, 1966.

180 **Hemming, J. A.** The motivation crisis. *IPNL*, 1972, 21(5), 86-88.

181 ———. A perspective on man and education—Adlerian viewpoint. *New Era in Home and School*, 1956, 37(1), 7-17.

182 ———. Points on writing letters for the press. *IPNL*, 1968, 18(7-8, Whole No. 204-205). Pp. 55-56.

183 ———. Portrait. *IPNL*, 1970, 19(4), 80; 1971, 20(6), 109.

184 ———. *The problem of child crime.* London: Common Wealth, 1949.

185 ———. *Problems of adolescent girls.* London: Heinemann, 1960.

186 ———. *Pupil guidance in secondary schools.* Berkshire Educ. Comm., 1964.

187 ———. *Ready reading for backward readers.* London: Longmans, Green, 1950.

188 ———. Reply to L. Way. *IPNL*, 1972, 21(2), 29.

189 ———. The road to sexual maturity. *Freethinker* (London), Apr. 3, 1971.

190 ———. *Sex and love.* London: Heinemann, 1972 (with Z. Maxwell).

191 ———. Sex-phobic pseudo-moralists. *IPNL*, 1972, 21(2), 27-28.

192 ———. *Sixth-form citizens.* London: Oxford Univ. Press, 1950.

193 ———. The struggle for self-fulfilment. In M. Chazan (Ed.), *The psychology of adolescence.* Swansea: Swansea Univ. Press, 1966.

194 ———. *Teach them to live.* London: Heinemann, 1948; London: Longmans, 1957.

195 ———. *The teaching of social studies in secondary schools.* London: Longmans, 1949, 1951.

196 ———. Values of humanity. *IPNL*, 1968, 18(9-10, Whole No. 206-207). Pp. 65-66.

197 **Hendershot, G. E.** Familial satisfaction, birth order, and fertility values. *J. Marr. Fam.*, 1969, 31, 27-33.

198 **Hendrick, D.** Effects of extraneous fear arousal and birth order on attitude change. *Psychonom. Sci.*, 1970, 18, 225-226 (with R. Borden).

199 **Henningsen, N.** In welche Schule schicke ich meine Kinder? In Sofie Lazarsfeld (Ed.), *Technik der Erziehung.*

200 **Henri, B.** Earliest recollections. *Pop. Sci. Month.*, 1898, 53, 108-115 (with C. Henri).

201 ———. Enquête sur les premiers souvenirs de l'enfance. *L'année Psychol.*, 1897, 3, 184 (with C. Henri).

202 **Henri, C.** Earliest recollections. *Pop. Sci. Month.*, 1898, 53, 108-115 (with B. Henri).

203 ———. Enquête sur les premiers souvenirs de l'enfance. *L'année Psychol.*, 1897, 3, 184 (with B. Henri).

204 **Henry, G. W.** *A history of medical psychology.* New York: Norton, 1941 (with G. Zilboorg).

205 **Hepner, H. W.** *Finding yourself in your work.* New York: Appleton-Century, 1937.

206 **Herbst, P. G.** The measurement of family relationships. *Hum. Relat.*, 1952, 5, 3-36.

207 **Herrell, J. M.** Birth order and the military: A review from an Adlerian perspective. *JIP*, 1972, 28, 38-44.

208 **Herrmann, I.** Grundlagen und Ziel der vergleichenden Individualpsychologie. *Die Frau im Staate*, July, 1923.

209 **Herrman, R. S.** Dogmatism, time perspective and anomie. *JIP*, 1960, 16, 67-72 (with A. H. Roberts).

210 **Herst, Louise.** Around the International Congress on Mental Health. *IPB*, 1949, 7, 38-40.

211 ———. Review of J. Bierer (Ed.), *Therapeutic social clubs.* In *IPB*, 1949, 7, 186-187.

212 **Hervat, Adele.** See Horvat, Adele.

213 **Herzog, E.** Erziehungsmöglichkeiten in den öffentlichen Internaten. *IZIP*, 1932, 10(4), 290-303.

214 **Herzog-Dürck, Johanna.** *Menschsein als Wagnis.* Stuttgart: Ernst Klett,

215 **Hess, K. E.** Ordinal position and acceptance of conventional morality. *Diss. Abstr. Int.*, 1971, 32(2A), 1073.

216 **Hess, L.** Non-public vocational education: A trend of the future? *Guidelines for Pupil Services*, 1972, 11(1), 18-21 (with L. Sperry & C. Piskula).

217 **Hess, R. D.** *Family worlds: A psychosocial approach to family life.* Chicago: Univ. Chicago Press, 1959 (with G. Handel).

218 **Heydweiller, Erna.** Beitrag zur Psychologie des Hundes. *IZIP*, 1929, 7(6), 450-458.

219 **Heynemann, Marie.** Pampering is not love. *New Health* (London), 1953, 25-28.

220 ———. Review of M. A. Payne, *Oliver untwisted.* London: Edward Arnold, [   ]. In *IZIP*, 1934, 12(3), 194-195.

221 **Hickman, Lorraine.** A goal, that's what the uptight generation needs [about Hertha Orgler]. *Austral. Women's J.*, Feb. 25, 1970.

222 **Hildreth, H.** Family treatment of schizophrenia: A symposium. *Fam. Proc.*, 1962, 1, 101-140 (with I. Boszormenyi-Nagy, C. Midelfort, J. Franco, & A. Friedman).

223 **Hilferding, Margret.** Durchschnittliche Entwicklung und Ernährung während der Schulzeit. In Sofie Lazarsfeld (Ed.), *Technik der Erziehung.*

224 ———. Geburtenregelung. In S. Lazarsfeld (Ed.), *Richtige Lebensführung.*

225 ———. Individualpsychologische Gedankengänge eines Kinderarztes. *IZIP*, 1935, 13(4), 206-213.

226 **Hilferding-Hönigsberg, Margret.** See Hilferding, Margret.

227 **Hilgard, E. R.** Human motives and the concept of self. *Amer. Psychologist*, 1949, 4, 374-382. Also in H. Brand (Ed.), *The study of personality.* New York: Wiley, 1954. Pp. 347-361.

228 **Hill, A. S.** A study of juvenile theft. *J. educ Res.*, 1929, 20, 81-87 (with H. J. Baker & F. J. Decker).

229 **Hillman, B. W.** Composition of the family constellation and its effect on school achievement: A test of an Adlerian hypothesis. *Diss. Abstr. Int.*, 1970, 30, 4829-4830.

230 **Hillson, J. S.** Self concept and defensive behavior in the maladjusted. *J. consult. Psychol.*, 1957, 21, 83-88 (with P. Worchel).

231 ———. The self-concept in the criminal: An exploration of Adlerian theory. *JIP*, 1958, 14, 173-181 (with P. Worchel).

232 **Hilton, I.** Differences in the behavior of mothers towards first and later born children. *J. Pers. soc. Psychol.*, 1967, 7, 282-290.

233 **Himelstein, Jacqueline.** Leading authority on wit and humor [about W. E. O'Connell] *Nat. Enquirer*, Dec. 5, 1971.

234 **Himmelsberger, T.** Review of K. Albrecht, *Struktur und Entwicklung des sachrechnerischen Bewusstseins.* Langensalza: H. Beyer & Söhne, 1926. In *IZIP*, 1927, 5(4), 316.

235 **Hinrichsen, O.** Unser Verstehen der seelischen Zusammenhänge in der Neurose und Freuds und Adlers Theorien. *Zbl. Psychoanal.*, 1913, 3, 369-393.

236 ———. Zur Psychologie der Dementia praecox. *ZIP*, 1914, 1(6-9), 207-227.

237 **Hinsie, L. E.** Introduction to A. Adler, *Understanding human nature.*

238 Hion, V. Zur Aetiologie, Symptomatologie und Pathogenese des Stotterns. *Folia Neuro-Esthon.*, 1932, 12, 190–195.

239 Hirsch, B. We must help win the war. *IPB*, 1942, 2(4), 67.

240 Hirsch, T. Over troubled waters. *Psychol. Today*, 1970, 3(12), 36–39 (with M. Reznikoff).

241 Hobbs, N. Sources of gain in psychotherapy. *Amer. Psychologist*, 1962, 17, 741–747.

242 Hoch, P. H. Influence of Alfred Adler on psychoanalysis. *AJIP*, 1952, 10, 54–58.

243 ———— (Ed.). *Psychopathology of schizophrenia.* New York: Grune & Stratton, 1966 (with J. Zubin).

244 Hoefbauer, Margarethe. Portrait. *IPNL*, 1970, 19(4), 80.

245 Hoek, A. Conjoint psychotherapy of married couples: A clinical report. *Int. J. soc. Psychiat.*, 1966, 12(3), 209–216 (with S. Wolstein).

246 Hoff, H. *Aktuelle Probleme der psychosomatischen Medizin.* Munich: Jolis Verlag, (with E. Ringel).

247 ————. Beitrag zur Lehre vom Phantomgliede. *Monatschr. Psychiat. Neurol.*, 1930, 76, 80–86 (with Alexandra Adler).

248 ————. Gehauftes Auftreten von Polyneuritiden unter dem Bild der Landry'schen Paralyse. *Deutsche med. Wchnschr.*, 1929, 55, 1880–1882 (with Alexandra Adler).

249 ————. A modern psychosomatic view of the theory of organ inferiority by Alfred Adler (with E. Ringel). In A. Jores & B. Stokvis (Eds.), *Advances in psychosomatic medicine.* Vol. 1. Pp. 120–127.

250 ————. Psychotherapie in Amerika. *IZIP*, 1950, 19(4), 145–161.

251 ————. *Die Zeit und ihre Neurose.* Wien: UNESCO-Schriftenreche, 1957 (with P. Berner & E. Ringel).

252 Hoffman, Joyce. Review of A. Adler, *The problem child.* In *Contemp. Psychol.*, 1964, 9, 452.

253 ————. Review of A. Adler, *Problems of neurosis.* In *Contemp. Psychol.*, 1965, 10, 216.

254 Hoffman, Lynn. *Techniques of family therapy.* New York: Basic Books, 1967 (with J. Haley).

255 Hoffman, M. A note on the origins of ego psychology. *Amer. J. Psychother.*, 1962, 16, 230–234.

256 Hoffstätter, R. Psyche und Schwangerschaft. *IZIP*, 1926, 4(4), 199–216.

257 Hofstaetter, P. Congruence of self and ideal self in relation to personality adjustment. *J. consult. Psychol.*, 1954, 18, 215–218 (with T. E. Hanlon & J. P. O'Conner).

258 Hogan, R. The three self images of the patient in psychotherapy. *JIP*, 1966, 22, 94–99.

259 ————. Review of J. F. Rychlak, A *philosophy of science for personality theory.* In *JIP*, 1971, 27(1), 103–104.

260 Holland, G. A. Clinical usefulness. [Tribute to Alfred Adler on his 100th birthday]. *JIP*, 1970, 26(2), 12–13.

261 Hollerman, J. L. Explorations in human development with an early memories inventory. *Diss. Abstr.*, 1965, 26, 493; Unpubl. Ph.D. diss., Univ. Oklahoma, 1965.

262 Hollingshead, A. B. Neurosis and social class. I. Social interaction. *Amer. J. Psychiat.*, 1957, 113, 769–775 (with L. Z. Freedman).

263 Hollingsworth, S. Work with large groups in mental hospitals. *JIP*, 1963, 19, 61–68 (with M. Jones).

264 Holloway, H. Relationships between memories of their parents' behavior and psychodiagnosis in psychiatrically disturbed soldiers. *J. consult. Psychol.*, 1964, 28, 126–132 (with C. G. Lauterbach & M. Livingston).

265 Holmberg, Joyce. *"We love to learn."* Rockford, Ill.: Rockford Pub. Schools, 1972.

266 Holmes, D. S. Early recollections and vocational choice. *J. consult. Psychol.*, 1965, 29, 486–488 (with R. I. Watson).

267 ————. Security feelings and tone of early recollections: A re-evaluation. *J. proj. Tech.*, 1965, 29, 314–318.

268 Holmes, J. H. Manche übel, die die moderne Psychologie angerichtet hat. *IZIP*, 1931, 9(4), 274–282.

269 ————. Three evils of present-day psychology. *JIP*, 1971, 27(1), 19–24.

270 Holt, H. Existential analysis, Freud and Adler. *J. Exis.*, 1967, 8, 203–222.

271 Holt, R. R. Level of aspiration: Ambition or defense? *J. exp. Psychol.*, 1946, 36, 398–416.

272 Holtgrew, Annemarie. Die Bedeutung "wahrer" und "nicht-wahrer" Kunst für unser Leben. *IZIP*, 1932, 10(6), 439–446.

273 **Holtzman, W. H.** Adjustment and the discrepancy between self concept and inferred self. *J. consult. Psychol.*, 1953, 17, 39–44 (with A. D. Calvin).

274 **Holub, A.** Alfred Adler in seiner Bedeutung für die somatische Medizin. *IZIP*, 1937, 15(3–4), 134–141.

275 ———. Alfred Adler 60 Jahre. *IZIP*, 1930, 8(2), 219–220.

276 ———. Aus der neuesten Literatur über Organminderwertigkeit. *IZIP*, 1929, 7(5), 325–328.

277 ———. Ausbreitung der Individualpsychologie. *IZIP*, 1935, 13(1), 30–35.

278 ———. Beziehungen zwischen Auge und Dichtung. *IZIP*, 1931, 9(6), 448–455.

279 ———. Das Bronchialasthma als neurotisches Symptom. *IZIP*, 1933, 11(3), 216–223.

280 ———. Bronchial asthma as neurotic symptom. *IJIP*, 1935, 1(1), 18–29.

281 ———. A case of deaf-mutism (with Elly Rothwein). In A. Adler & assoc., *Guiding the child.* Pp. 193–194.

282 ———. Character development of twins (with Martha Holub). In H. Hartmann (Ed.), *Essays on ego psychology.*

283 ———. Ein Fall von Hörrstummheit. *IZIP*, 1929, 7(3), 227 (with Elly Rothwein).

284 ———. Das einzige Kind. *IZIP*, 1929, 7(3), 230 (with Elly Rothwein).

285 ———. Individualpsychologische Gedankengänge in der somatischen Medizin. *IZIP*, 1932, 10(2), 89–94.

286 ———. Das kindliche Minderwertigkeitsgefühl und seine Kompensation. *IZIP*, 1934, 12(2), 112–123.

287 ———. Körperdefekt und Organminderwertigkeit als Faktoren der Selbsterziehung. *IZIP*, 1930, 8(1), 115–119.

288 ———. Krankheit und Psyche. *IZIP*, 1934, 12(2), 72–84.

289 ———. *Die Lehre von der Organminderwertigkeit.* Leipzig: Hirzel, 1931.

290 ———. Missbrauch des Anlagebegriffs. *IZIP*, 1930, 8(3), 295–297.

291 ———. Psychologie des Tuberkulosen und Asthmatikers. *IZIP*, 1928, 6(5), 363–369.

292 ———. Review of L. Alkan, *Anatomische Organkrankheiten aus seelische Ursache.* Stuttgart: Hippokrates-Verlag, 1930. In *IZIP*, 1930, 8(6), 598.

293 ———. Review of F. Alverdes, *Die Tierpsychologie in ihren Beziehungen zur Psychologie des Menschen.* Leipzig: C. L. Hirschfeld, [   ]. In *IZIP*, 1932, 10(4), 315–316.

294 **Holub, A.** Review of F. Alverdes, *Tiersoziologie.* Leipzig: C. L. Hirschfeld, 1925. In *IZIP*, 1928, 6(3), 261.

295 ———. Review of K. H. Baumgärtner, *Krankenphysiognomik.* Berlin: Madaus, 1928. In *IZIP*, 1929, 7(2), 159.

296 ———. Review of C. E. Benda, Probleme der modernen Psychotherapie. *Mediz. Welt*, 1932, No. 11. In *IZIP*, 1932, 10(4), 316.

297 ———. Review of E. Braun, Hysterischer Charakter, hysterische Einzelsymptome und die hysterische Reaktion. *Klin. Wchnschr.*, 1928, 21, [   ]. In *IZIP*, 1929, 7(1), 80.

298 ———. Review of E. Braun, *Krankheit und Tod in Schicksal bedeutender Menschen.* Stuttgart: Ferdinand Enke, 1934. In *IZIP*, 1936, 14(4), 239.

299 ———. Review of Dorothea Chaplin, *Das ärztliche Denken der Hindu.* Leipzig: Astra, 1930. In *IZIP*, 1931, 9(5), 409.

300 ———. Review of F. Curtius, Organminderwertigkeit und Erbenlage. *Klin. Wchnschr*, 1932, 5, [   ]. In *IZIP*, 1932, 10(3), 235.

301 ———. Review of H. Dogen & O. Lipmann, *Gang und Charakter.* Leipzig: J. A. Barth, 1931. In *IZIP*, 1931, 9(5), 409.

302 ———. Review of E. Ebstein, *Tuberkulose als Schicksal.* Stuttgart: Ferdinand Enke, 1931. In *IZIP*, 1933, 12(3), 255.

303 ———. Review of W. Eliasberg (Ed.), *Psychotherapie.* Leipzig: S. Hirzel, 1927. In *IZIP*, 1928, 6(5), 418.

304 ———. Review of W. Fischer-Defoy, *Der Schularzt.* Karlsruhe: G. Braun, 1928. In *IZIP*, 1928, 6(5), 417–418.

305 ———. Review of G. Flatau, *Unfälle-Neurosen.* Stuttgart: Ferdinand Enke, 1931 In *IZIP*, 1933, 12(3), 255.

306 ———. Review of E. Flusser, Für und wider die Individualpsychologie. *Med. Klin.*, 1930, No. 11. In *IZIP*, 1930, 8(6), 597–598.

307 ———. Review of H. Freund, *Sozialismus und Volksgesundheit.* Dresden: Bezirkausschuss f. sozialist. Bildungsarbeit Ostachsen, [   ]. In *IZIP*, 1932, 10(1), 79.

308 ———. Review of J. K. Friedjung, Schlimm oder Krank? *Münch. med. Wchnschr.*, 1929, 9, 376–377 & Erziehung und Kinderheilkunde. *Wiener med. Wchnschr.*,

1929, 79, 366–378. In *IZIP*, 1929, 7(5), 400.

309 Holub, A. Review of *Führende Psychiater in Selbstdarstellungen.* Leipzig: Felix Meiner, 1930. In *IZIP*, 1935, 13(2), 128.

310 ———. Review of F. V. Gagern, *Geister, Gänger, Gesichte, Gewalten.* Leipzig: L. Staackman, 1932. In *IZIP*, 1932, 10(4), 315.

311 ———. Review of Erna Gläsner, *Körperbau und Sexualfunktion.* Stuttgart: Ferdinand Enke, 1930. In *IZIP*, 1931, 9(5), 409.

312 ———. Review of G. Grossman, *Sich selbst rationalisieren.* Verlag Wissensch. u. Verkehr, [   ]. In *IZIP*, 1929, 7(6), 480.

313 ———. Review of A. Heidenhain, *Über den Menschenhass: Eine pathographische Untersuchung über Jonathan Swift.* Stuttgart: Ferdinand Enke, 1935. In *IZIP*, 1936, 14(4), 239.

314 ———. Review of H. F. Hoffmann, *Über Ärzte und Patienten.* Stuttgart: Ferdinand Enke, 1934. In *IZIP*, 1936, 13(3), 190–191.

315 ———. Review of G. Kaufmann, Praktischer Arzt und Psychotherapeut. *Mediz. Welt*, 1932, No. 11. In *IZIP*, 1932, 10(4), 317.

316 ———. Review of Elga Kern, *Wie sie dazu kamen.* München: E. Reinhardt, 1928. In *IZIP*, 1929, 7(2), 159–160.

317 ———. Review of E. Klein, *Naturheilverfahren.* Leipzig: Felix Meiner, 1938. In *IZIP*, 1929, 7(2), 161.

318 ———. Review of F. Kobler (Ed.), *Gewalt und Gewaltlosigkeit.* Zurich: Rotapfel, 1929. In *IZIP*, 1929, 7(6), 481.

319 ———. Review of K. Krayl, *Hippokrates-Brevier.* Stuttgart: Ferdinand Enke, 1929. In *IZIP*, 1931, 9(5), 409.

320 ———. Review of E. Metzer, *Der Einfluss der Tuberkulose auf das Seelenleben.* In *IZIP*, 1934, 12(3), 195–196.

321 ———. Review of F. Mohr, *Psychotherapie bei organischen Erkrankungen.* Leipzig: Georg Thieme, 1930. In *IZIP*, 1931, 9(5), 408–409.

322 ———. Review of G. Pick, *Sinn und Wert der Sozialversicherung.* Brünn: R. M. Rohrer, 1933. In *IZIP*, 1934, 12(3), 196.

323 ———. Review of F. Reuter, Zwei interessante Fälle von Tötung aus sexuellem Motiv. *Deutsche Z. gesam. gericht. Med.*, 1927, 9. In *IZIP*, 1928, 6(3), 261.

324 Holub, A. Review of E. Ruedin, *Die Bedeutung der Eugenik und Genetik für die psychische Hygiene.* In *IZIP*, 1930, 8(6), 598.

325 ———. Review of [   ], *Der schreiende Säugling.* Berlin: Urban & Schwarzenberg, 1928. In *IZIP*, 1929, 7(2), 157.

326 ———. Review of Hedwig Schulhof, *Das Glück als Aufgabe.* In *IZIP*, 1928, 6(1), 79.

327 ———. Review of E. Schweninger, *Der Arzt.* Radeburg: Madaus, 1926. In *IZIP*, 1927, 5(4), 311.

328 ———. Review of E. Stein, *Die Psyche des Lungenkranken.* Halle: Carl Marhold, 1925. In *IZIP*, 1926, 4(5), 311–312.

329 ———. Review of E. Stern, *Émigration als psychologisches Problem.* Paris: Author, 1937. In *IZIP*, 1937, 15(2), 91.

330 ———. Review of E. Stern, *Gesundheitliche Erziehung.* Karlsruhe: G. Braun, 1928. In *IZIP*, 1928, 6(5), 417.

331 ———. Review of E. Stransky, Beiträge zur Zwillingspathologie. *Monatschr. Kinderheilkunde.* In *IZIP*, 1932, 10(1), 79.

332 ———. Review of L. v. Krehl, *Krankheitsform und Persönlichkeit.* Leipzig: Georg Thieme, 1929. In *IZIP*, 1929, 7(1), 157.

333 ———. Review of A. v. Muralt, *August Forel.* Zurich: Orell Füssli, [   ]. In *IZIP*, 1929, 7(6), 481.

334 ———. Review of W. H. v. Wyss, *Körperlich-seelische Zusammenhänge in Gesundheit und Krankheit.* Leipzig: Georg Thieme, 1931. In *IZIP*, 1932, 10(3), 235.

335 ———. Review of J. Weiss, *Der Kranke und die Krankheit.* Stuttgart: Ferdinand Enke, 1930. In *IZIP*, 1931, 9(5), 409.

336 ———. Review of P. Wenger, Über Erfolge der Psychotherapie im Rahmen einer Poliklinik für intern Kranke. *Klin. Wchnschr.*, 1930, No. 49. In *IZIP*, 1931, 9(5), 410.

337 ———. Review of H. Winkler, *Psychische Entwicklung und Krüppeltum.* Leipzig: Leopold Vosz, 1931. In *IZIP*, 1932, 10(4), 316–317.

338 ———. Review of J. F. Wolf, *Lingner und sein Vermächtnis.* Hellerau: Jakob Hegner, [   ]. In *IZIP*, 1932, 10(1), 79.

339 ———. Review of H. Würtz, *Goethes Wesen und Umwelt im Spiegel der Krüppelpsychologie.* Leipzig: Leopold Vosz, 1932. In *IZIP*, 1933, 12(3), 255.

340 **Holub, A.** Review of H. Würtz, *Zerbrecht die Krücken.* Leipzig: Leopold Vosz, 1932. In *IZIP*, 1932, 10(4), 316.

341 ———. Review of *Z. psychoanal. Pädagogik*, 1927, Vol. 1. In *IZIP*, 1927, 5(6), 478–479; 1927, Vol. 2. In *IZIP*, 1928, 6(1), 76.

342 ———. Review of *Z. Sexual wissenschaft*, Vol. 14. In *IZIP*, 1928, 6(4), 343–344.

343 ———. Die Rezeption der Individualpsychologie durch die medizinische Wissenschaft. *IZIP*, 1928, 6(4), 320–324.

344 ———. Sickness and psyche. *IZIP*, 1936, 2(1), 91–103.

345 ———. Wege zu besonderen Fähigkeiten ("Begabung"). *IZIP*, 1933, 12(5), 350–353.

346 ———. Zur Frage der Charakterentwicklung bei Zwillingen. *IZIP*, 1933, 11(4), 264–281 (with Martha Holub).

347 **Holub, Martha.** Auch eine einzige Besprechung kann genügen–Das "Trauma". *IZIP*, 1929, 7(3), 237 (with Lydia Sicher).

348 ———. Die Bedeutung der Geschwisterreihe. In Sofie Lazarsfeld (Ed.), *Technik der Erziehung.*

349 ———. Character development of twins (with A. Holub). In H. Hartmann (Ed.), *Essays on ego psychology.*

350 ———. Conversations with parents and children. *IJIP*, 1935, 1(2), 96–112.

351 ———. Drei Fälle aus der Praxis. *IZIP*, 1929, 7(6), 407–412.

352 ———. Ein Betnässer. *IZIP*, 1937, 15(1), 29–34 (with A. Zanker).

353 ———. Ein mittleres Kind, das sich wie ein erstgeborenes benimmt. *IZIP*, 1928, 6(5), 414.

354 ———. Die Entwicklung der individualpsychologischen Bewegung in Amerika. *IZIP*, 1931, 9(2), 140–144.

355 ———. Das gehasste Kind. *IZIP*, 1929, 7(3), 230–235.

356 ———. Gespräche mit Eltern und Kindern. *IZIP*, 1930, 8(5), 441–458.

359 ———. *Geschwisterkampf.* Wien: Moritz Perles, 1928.

358 ———. Geschwisterkampf. In Sofie Lazarsfeld (Ed.), *Richtige Lebensführung.*

359 ———. The hated child. *IJIP*, 1936, 2(2), 97–104 (with A. Zanker).

360 ———. The hated child. In A. Adler & assoc., *Guiding the child.* Pp. 210–231.

361 ———. Individualpsychologische Tests. *IZIP*, 1932, 10(1), 59–71.

362 **Holub, Martha.** Infantile inferiority-feelings. *IJIP*, 1935, 1(1), 76–87.

363 ———. On education methods which are based upon Individual Psychology (with A. Neuer). In A. Adler & assoc., *Guiding the child.* Pp. 148–156.

364 ———. Review of A. Adler, *The case of Mrs. A.* In *IZIP*, 1931, 9(5), 407.

365 ———. Review of E. Bagby, *The psychology of personality.* New York: Holt, 1928. In *IZIP*, 1929, 7(2), 161.

366 ———. Review of F. G. Crookshank, Individual Psychology and general medicine. In *IZIP*, 1931, 9(2), 154.

367 ———. Review of Elinor Deutsch, *The dream imagery of the blind.* In *IZIP*, 1929, 7(4), 324.

368 ———. Review of J. Dewey, *Die menschliche Natur, ihr Wesen und ihr Verhalten.* Stuttgart: Deutsche Verlagsanstalt, 1931. In *IZIP*, 1932, 10(1), 80.

369 ———. Review of F. N. Freeman, Die Vererbung geistiger charaktereigenschaften bein Menschen. *Ment. Hyg. Bull.*, 1930 (Feb.). In *IZIP*, 1931, 9(3), 254–255.

370 ———. Review of A. Gesell, *Körperseelische Entwicklung in der frühen Kindheit.* Halle: Carl Marhold, [   ]. In *IZIP*, 1931, 9(5), 407–408.

371 ———. Review of E. Haller, Die Entweichungen von Kindern und Jugendlichen. *Z. Kinderschutz*, Vol. 3. In *IZIP*, 1927, 5(2), 159.

372 ———. Review of H. Hanselmann, *Einführung in die Heilpädagogik.* Erlenbach: Rotapfel, 1930. In *IZIP*, 1931, 9(3), 253–254.

373 ———. Review of I. C. Heinrich, *Conflict attitude.* In *IZIP*, 1934, 12(1), 54.

374 ———. Review of Doris Jaehner, *Zwei Tage aus dem Leben dreier Geschwister.* Leipzig: J. A. Barth., 1930. In *IZIP*, 1932, 10(1), 80.

375 ———. Review of F. Kramer, *Die Willenskrankheiten und ihre pädagogische Therapie.* Langensalza: H. Beyer & Söhne, 1924. In *IZIP*, 1928, 6(4), 342–343.

376 ———. Review of Sofie Lazarsfeld (Ed.), *Richtige Lebensführung.* In *IZIP*, 1926, 4(3), 245–246.

377 ———. Review of A. J. Murphy, Child guidance only sure cure for crime. *N. Y. World Telegram*, Oct., 1934. In *IZIP*, 1935, 13(1), 59.

378 **Holub, Martha.** Review of C. S. Myers, *The association of psycho-neurosis with mental deficiency.* In *IZIP*, 1926, 4(3), 167–168.

379 ———. Review of F. Schlotte (Ed.), *Pädagogisch-psychologische Arbeiten aus dem Institut des Leipziger Lehrervereins.* Leipzig: Verlag der Dürrschen Buchhandlung, 1931. In *IZIP*, 1933, 11(1), 78.

380 ———. Review of Helene Stöcker, *Die neue Generation.* Vol. 24. In *IZIP*, 1928, 6(6), 507.

381 ———. Review of F. Strus, *Sprüche der Liebe.* Charlottenberg: Author, [ ]. In *IZIP*, 1933, 11(2), 158.

382 ———. Review of E. Wexberg, *Das nervöse Kind.* In *IZIP*, 1926, 4(3), 167.

383 ———. Review of *Das Wiener Jugendhilfswerk.* Wien: Verlag des Jugendamtes der Stadt Wien, 1930. In *IZIP*, 1932, 10(1), 80.

384 ———. Review of W. B. Wolfe, *How to be happy though human.* In *IZIP*, 1932, 10(6), 477.

385 ———. Review of S. Wronsky, *Methoden der Fürsorge.* Berlin: Carl Heymanns, 1930. In *IZIP*, 1931, 9(5), 410.

386 ———. Review of Z. *Kinderschutz, Familien- und Berufsorge.* In *IZIP*, 1926, 4(5), 314; In *IZIP*, 1928, 6(4), 345.

387 ———. Richtlinien und Indikationen für die Zuweisung an eine individualpsychologische Erziehungsberatungsstelle. *IZIP*, 1929, 7(3), 177–178.

388 ———. Translator of P. Mairet, *Hamlet der neurotiker.*

389 ———. Translator of Marie J. Rasey, Über Kinder, die keine Freunde haben.

390 ———. Translator of C. Washburne, *Die Volksschulen von Winnetka.*

391 ———. Two cases (with Lydia Sicher). In A. Adler & assoc., *Guiding the child.* Pp. 236–240.

392 ———. Über nicht-individualpsychologische Erziehungsberatungsmethoden. *IZIP*, 1929, 7(3), 215–217 (with A. Neuer).

393 ———. When to refer children to guidance clinics (with A. Zanker). In A. Adler & assoc., *Guiding the child.* Pp. 47–52.

394 ———. Zur Frage der Charakterentwicklung bei Zwillingen. *IZIP*, 1933, 11(4), 264–281 (with A. Holub).

395 **Holzberg, J. D.** The prediction of familial interaction from a battery of projective techniques. *J. proj. Tech.,* 1957, 21, 199–208 (with Dorothy T. Sohler, S. Fleck, Alice R. Cornelison, Eleanor Kay & T. Lidz).

396 **Hölzl, A.** Der Alkohol, ein Feind richtiger Lebensführung. In Sofie Lazarsfeld (Ed.), *Richtige Lebensführung.*

397 **Homra, D.** Task group report (with T. W. Allen, J. Krumboltz, F. Robinson, J. Cody, W. Cottle, & J. Ray). In J. Whiteley (Ed.), *Research problems in counseling.* Pp. 219–237.

398 **Hooker, D.** *The psychology of the emerging self.* Philadelphia: Davis, 1967 (with E. D. Erb).

399 **Hooker, Evelyn.** Male homosexual life styles and venereal disease. *Pub. Hlth. Serv. Publ. 997,* 1962. Pp. 431–437.

400 **Hooker, H. F.** The study of the only child at school. *J. genet. Psychol.,* 1931, 39, 122–126.

401 **Hoover, K.** Therapeutic democracy. *Proc. Int. Soc. Soc. Psychiat.,* 1965 (with B. H. Shulman).

402 ———. Therapeutic democracy: Some changes in staff-patient relationships. *Int. J. soc. Psychiat.,* 1964, Spec. ed. 3, 16–23 (with B. H. Shulman).

403 **Hoppe, Johanna.** Ein verkrüppeltes Kind. *IZIP*, 1933, 12(5), 399–400.

404 ———. Erziehung zur Gemeinschaft durch die Schule. *IZIP*, 1930, 8(5), 519–522.

405 ———. Review of E. Fischer, Graphologie als pädagogische Hilfswissenschaft. *Sächsischen Schulzeit.* In *IZIP*, 1934, 12(1), 54–55.

406 ———. Review of O. Ludwig, *Zwischen Himmel und Erde.* Verlag Deutsche Bibliothek, 1926. In *IZIP*, 1933, 12(4), 336.

407 **Hora, T.** Epistemological aspects of existence and psychotherapy. *JIP*, 1959, 15, 166–173.

408 **Hörl, R.** (Ed.). *Kinder in ihrer Welt—Kinder in unserer Welt: Kleines Praktikum für Eltern und Erzieher.* Hamburg: Furche, 1968.

409 **Horn, R.** Review of A. Messer, *Mein Weg.* Hamburg: [ ], 1933. In *IZIP*, 1933, 12(4), 330–331.

410 **Horney, Karen.** *Neurosis and human growth.* New York: Norton, 1950.

411 **Horton, D. L.** Father identification as a function of mother-father relationship. *JIP*, 1964 20, 167–171 (with J. C. Baxter & R. E. Wiley).

412 Horvat, Adele. Ambivalenz der Gefühle. *IZIP*, 1933, 11(3), 230–237.

413 ———. Concerning stagefright. *IJIP*, 1937, 3(4), 350–355.

414 ———. Individual Psychology and sexual difficulties (I). *IPP*, 1932, No. 3 (with A. Adler, R. Dreikurs, E. Wexberg, J. C. Young, F. G. Crookshank, Mary C. Luff & others).

415 ———. Lord Byrons Charakter. *IZIP*, 1936, 14(1), 37–49.

416 ———. Naturwissenschaft und Individual-psychologie. *IZIP*, 1932, 10(2), 94–101.

417 ———. Review of F. Birnbaum, *Die seelischen Gefahren des Kindes*. In *IZIP*, 1932, 10(1), 72.

418 ———. Review of K. Fahrenkamp, *Der Herzkranke*. Stuttgart: Hippokrates-Verlag, [   ]. In *IZIP*, 1932, 10(5), 394–395.

419 ———. Review of G. C. Ferrari, Psichologia de lavoro. *Rass. di Studi Psychiat.* Vol. 19. In *IZIP*, 1933, 12(5), 401–403.

420 ———. Review of F. Künkel, *Eine Angstneurose und ihre Behandlung*. In *IZIP*, 1932, 10(2), 152–153.

421 ———. Review of A. Maurois, *Ariel ou La vie de Shelley*. In *IZIP*, 1933, 12(6), 479.

422 ———. Review of F. Werfel, *Die Geschwister von Neapel*. In *IZIP*, 1932, 10(5), 399–400.

423 ———. Review of R. Wilhelm, *Der Mensch und das Sein*. Jena: Eugen Diederichs, 1931. In *IZIP*, 1933, 12(4), 335–336.

424 ———. Schwierigkeiten bei der individual-psychologischen Behandlung. *IZIP*, 1934, 12(4), 84–92.

425 ———. The technique of treatment. *IPP*, 1932, No. 3. Pp. 21–28.

426 ———. Über das Lampenfieber. *IZIP*, 1932, 10(1), 29–34.

427 Horwitz, H. Sinn und Problematik der Ichfunktion. *IZIP*, 1927, 5(4), 252–262.

428 Horwitz, M. Birth order and reaction to frustration. *J. abnorm. soc. Psychol.*, 1963, 66, 192–194 (with D. C. Glass & I. Firestone).

429 Hott, L. Relating self-conception to curriculum development. *J. educ. Res.*, 1965, 58, 348–351 (with M. Sonstegard).

430 House, S. D. Mental hygiene: The quintessence of dynamic psychology. *IZIP*, 1927, 5(6), 418–438.

431 ———. Review of A. S. Neill, *The problem child*. New York: MacBride, 1927. In *IZIP*, 1928, 6(6), 508.

432 House, S. D. Review of E. Wexberg, *Your nervous child*. In *IZIP*, 1927, 5(4), 311–312.

433 ———. Sex and wisdom. *IZIP*, 1926, 4(2), 77–80.

434 Houston, T. J. Measurement of neurotic tendency in women with uncommon names. *J. gen. Psychol.*, 1948, 39, 289–296 (with F. C. Sumner).

435 Howard, D. D. (Ed.). *Critical incidents in teaching*. Englewood Cliffs, N. J.: Prentice-Hall, 1964 (with R. J. Corsini).

436 ———. Training through roleplaying. *Concept*, 1960 (with R. J. Corsini).

437 Howard, K. I. Birth order and responsibility. *J. Marr. Fam.*, 1968, 30, 427–432 (with I. D. Harris).

438 Howes, Elizabeth B. The ethics of self-fulfillment. *J. Psychother. rel. Proc.*, 1954, 1, 22–30.

439 Hsia, J. A study of the sociability of elementary school children. *Teachers Coll. Contrib. Educ.*, 1928, No. 322.

440 Hsiao, H. H. The status of the first-born with special reference to intelligence. *Genet. Psychol. Monogr.*, 1931, No. 9(1–2).

441 Huber, R. J. Double-aspect perception and social interest. *Percep. mot. Skills*, 1970, 30, 387–392 (with R. J. Skiggins).

442 ———. Selective attention and social interest. *JIP*, 1972, 28, 51–59 (with G. A. Forsyth).

443 Huckabee, M. W. Cognitive attitudes as residual factors in adaptation level. *Diss. Abstr.*, 1966, 26, 4075.

444 Hückel-Rohm, Hella. Jugendgericht. *IZIP*, 1929, 7(6), 432–435.

445 Hudnut, Jean. The contributions of a psychiatric nurse on a medical service. *Perspec. psychiat. Care*, 1966, 4(2), 22–37 (with B. H. Shulman, D. Corrigan, & Zoe Pfouts).

446 Hughes, T. Keith. *IPNL*, 1965, 15(9–10, Whole No. 170–172). Pp. 34–35.

447 Hulse, W. C. *Sources of conflict in contemporary group therapy*. Basel: S. Karger, 1960 (with Asya L. Kadis, H. S. Leopold, & A. Wolf).

448 Humphries, R. The dreams of Aeneas. *IZIP*, 1927, 5(5), 344–348.

449 Hunt, J. McV. Further studies utilizing the discomfort-relief quotient (with O. H. Mowrer & L. Kogan). In O. H. Mowrer (Ed.), *Psychotherapy: Theory and research*. Pp. 257–295.

450 **Hunt, J. McV.** Tension changes during psychotherapy (with O. H. Mowrer & L. S. Kogan). In O. H. Mowrer (Ed.), *Psychotherapy: Theory and research.* Pp. 596-640.

451 **Hunt, W.** Review of K. R. Eissler, *Medical orthodoxy and the future of psychoanalysis.* New York: Int. Univer. Press, 1965. In *IP*, 1966, 3(2), 23-25.

452 **Hunter, Corinda.** Ego strength and types of defensive and coping behavior. *J. consult. Psychol.*, 1967, 31, 432 (with L. Goodstein).

453 **Hunter, Katharine J.** Sibling position in the family and personality of offspring. *J. Marr. Fam.*, 1965, 27, 65-68 (with A. L. Stroup).

454 **Huschka, Mabel.** Psychopathological disorders in the mother. *J. nerv. ment. Dis.*, 1941, 94, 76-83.

455 **Husserl, E.** *Ideas: General introduction to pure phenomenology.* London: Allen & Unwin, 1931.

456 **Hutter, L.** Ein "normales" Mädchen. *IZIP*, 1926, 4(2), 80-86.

457 ———. Review of F. Cleff, *Die Weltwirklichkeit.* In *IZIP*, 1927, 5(2), 158.

458 ———. Review of M. de Unamuno, *Abel Sanchez.* München: Meyer & Jensen, [   ]. In *IZIP*, 1926, 4(4), 243-245.

459 ———. Review of H. Driesch, *Grundprobleme der Psychologie.* Leipzig: E. Reinicke, [   ]. In *IZIP*, 1926, 4(5), 310-311.

460 ———. Review of *Jahrbuch der Charakterologie.* Vols. 2-3. In *IZIP*, 1926, 4(6), 396-397.

461 ———. Review of J. Marcinowski, *Der Mut zu sich selbst.* Berlin: Otto Salle, 1912. In *IZIP*, 1927, 5(2), 157-158.

462 ———. Review of O. Ritschl, *Die doppelte Wahrheit in der Philosophie des "als ob".* Göttingen: Vandenoeck & Ruprecht, [   ]. In *IZIP*, 1927, 5(1), 80.

463 **Hutton, Laura.** Individual Psychology and the child (II). *IPP*, 1933, No. 8 (with Hilda Weber & W. B. Wolfe).

464 ———. Parental influences in the formation of the neurotic character. (1) Lack of parental love. *IPP*, 1933, No. 8. Pp. 7-19.

465 ———. Translator of A. Adler, The fear of woman.

466 **Huysamen, G. K.** Correlates of the communication organ score on the Harris-Goodenough drawing test. *JIP*, 1968, 24, 60-62 (with D. J. W. Strumpfer).

I

1 **Iaquinta, R.** Review of Lisa Appignanesi, D. Holmes, & Monica Holmes, *The language of trust.* New York: Science House, 1971. In *IP*, 1972, 9(1), 32.

2 ———. Review of D. D. Runes, *Handbook of reason.* New York: Phil. Libr., 1972. In *IP*, 1972, 9(1), 31.

3 **Ichheiser, G.** The image of the other man. *Sociom.*, 1940, 3, 277-291.

4 ———. Misunderstandings in human relations: A study in false perception. *Amer. J. Sociol.*, 1949, 55 (Part 2), 110-112.

5 ———. On Freud's blind spots concerning some obvious facts. *JIP*, 1960, 16, 45-55. Reprinted in part in H. D. Werner (Ed.), *New understandings of human behavior.* Pp. 41-43.

6 ———. Structure and dynamics of interpersonal relations. *Amer. sociol. Rev.*, 1943, 8, 302-305.

7 **Immergluck, L.** Determinism-freedom in contemporary psychology: An ancient problem revisited. In M. Zax & G. Stricker (Eds.), *The study of abnormal behavior.*

8 **Institute for Individual Psychology, Los Angeles.** Report from the Institute for Individual Psychology, Inc. *IPB*, 1950, 8, 167-168.

9 **International Vereinigung für Individualpsychologie.** *Alfred Adler zum Gedenken.* Wien: Verein für Individualpsychologie, 1957.

10 ———. *Fragebogen zum Verständnis und zur Behandlung schwererziehbar Kinder.* Wien: Verein für Individualpsychologie, 1924.

11 **Irish, D.** (Ed.). *Death education: Preparation for living.* Cambridge, Mass.: Schenkman, 1971 (with Betty Green).

12 **Irvine, P.** Pioneers in special education—Alfred Adler. *J. spec. Educ.*, 1968, 2, 234-235.

13 **Isaacs, D. A.** Helping the adolescent delinquent. *N. Y. St. Educ.*, Nov., 1961.

14 ———. Rehabilitation through a residential treatment center. *Educ.*, 1961, 81, 413-414.

15 Isaacson, G. S. Meaningfulness of personal versus common constructs. *JIP*, 1965, 21, 160-166 (with A. W. Landfield).

16 Isele, F. W. Differential responses of addicts and non-addicts on the MMPI. *J. proj. Tech.*, 1968, 32(5), 479-482 (with D. N. Lombardi & B. J. O'Brien).

17 ———. The young drug addict. *N. J. educ. Rev.*, Feb., 1967 (with D. N. Lombardi).

18 Izard, C. E. Personal similarity and friendship. *J. abnorm. soc. Psychol.*, 1960, 61, 47-51.

19 ———. Personal similarity and friendship: A follow up study. *J. abnorm. soc. Psychol.*, 1963, 66, 598-600.

20 ———. Personal similarity, positive affect, and interpersonal attraction. *J. abnorm. soc. Psychol.*, 1960, 61, 484-485.

J

1 J. H. W. Alfred Adler—February 7, 1870—May 28, 1937. *N. Y. St. med. J.*, 1970, 70(4), 507.

2 J. L. M. Review of Blanche C. Weill, *Through children's eyes*. In *Bull. Menninger Clin.*, 1942, 6, 167.

3 Jackson, D. D. The question of family homeostasis. *Psychiat. Quart. Suppl.*, 1957, 31, 79-90.

4 Jackson, L. *A test of family attitudes.* London: Methuen, 1952.

5 Jackson, Marilyn. Early recollections in four neurotic diagnostic categories. *JIP*, 1962, 18, 52-56 (with L. Sechrest).

6 Jacobs, [   ]. *Problems of the beginning elementary school teacher.* Minneapolis: Burgess Publ. Co., [   ] (with W. Foster).

7 Jacobs, G. L. Review of J. Haley, *Strategies of psychotherapy*. In *JIP*, 1967, 23, 125-126.

8 Jacobs, May. The comparative Individual Psychology of Alfred Adler. [Review of A. Adler, *The neurotic constitution*]. *Ped. Sem.*, 1923, 30, 16-23.

9 ———. The family Aksakoff. *IZIP*, 1926, 4(6), 363-368.

10 ———. Individual Psychology and common sense. *IZIP*, 1925, 3(2), 22-29.

11 Jacobson, J. Z. Paul: A boy who escaped. *IJIP*, 1936, 2(2), 22-29.

12 Jacobson, J. Z. Review of J. Jastrow (Ed.), *The story of human error.* In *IJIP*, 1937, 3(2), 202-203.

13 ———. Review of T. Mann, Freud, Goethe, Wagner. In *IJIP*, 1937, 3(3), 272-273.

14 ———. Review of S. F. Mendelsohn, *Mental healing in Judaism*. Chicago: Jewish Gift Shop, 1936. In *IJIP*, 1937, 3(2), 204.

15 Jacobson, Leonore. *Pygmalion in the classroom: Teacher expectation and pupils' intellectual development.* New York: Holt, Rinehart & Winston, 1968 (with R. Rosenthal).

16 ———. Teacher expectations for the disadvantaged. *Sci. Amer.*, 1968, 218, 19-23 (with R. Rosenthal).

17 Jacoby, H. Bemerkungen über biologistische Tendenzen. *IZIP*, 1933, 12(5), 345-350.

18 ———. *Die Bürokratisierung der Welt.* Neuwied: Luchterhand, 1969.

19 ———. Ein jugendlicher Verbrecher. *IZIP*, 1928, 6(2), 117-121.

20 ———. Der Machtkampf der Generationen. *IZIP*, 1934, 12(3), 156-165.

21 ———. Mythology. *IPNL*, 1972, 21(3), 47-48.

22 ———. Die Nervosität des Alltags. *IZIP*, 1929, 7(4), 269-275.

23 ———. Once more: A strange footnote. *IPNL*, 1972, 21(5), 82-83.

24 ———. Der Seelenbegriff im Wandel der Zeiten: Eine geschichtsmaterialistische Betrachtung. *Der Kampf*, 1927.

25 ———. A strange footnote. *IPNL*, 1972, 21(2), 25-27.

26 ———. Wie Ich zum Verbrecher wurde. *IZIP*, 1931, 9(5), 389-395.

27 Jahn, E. *Machtwille und Mindwertigkeitsgefühl: Eine kritische Analyse der Individualpsychologie.* Berlin: Warneck, 1931.

28 ———. Religion und Individualpsychologie. In E. Jahn & A. Adler, *Religion und Individualpsychologie: Eine prinzipelle Auseinandersetzung über Menschenführung.* Vienna: Rolf Passer, 1933.

29 ———. *Wege und Grenzen der Psychoanalyse.* Schwerin: Bahn, 1927.

30 Jakobson, R. Linguistic glosses to Goldstein's Wortbegriff. *JIP*, 1959, 15, 62-65.

31 Jakoby, H. *Das jähzornige Kind.* Dresden: Verlag am andern Ufer, 1926.

32 James, B. E. Attitudes toward premarital behavior as a function of behavioral commitment. *Coll. Stud. J.*, Sept.-Oct., 1972, 6(3) (with J. W. Croake).

33 **James, B. E.** Group marriage counseling: A review and proposal. *Marr. Couns. Quart.*, Winter, 1971 (with J. W. Croake).

34 ———. How far are students ready to go? *Sexol.*, May, 1970 (with J. W. Croake).

35 **James, W. T.** Karen Horney and Erich Fromm in relation to Alfred Adler. *IPB*, 1947, 6, 105–116.

36 **Jarrett, R. F.** Sex differences in attitudes about sex differences. *J. Psychol.*, 1953, 35, 161–168 (with A. C. Sherriffs).

37 **Jelliffe, S. E.** Translator of A. Adler, *Study of organ inferiority and its psychical compensation.*

38 **Jellinek, A.** Die Bedeutung der Vorstellungstypen für den Sprach-und Gesangsunterricht. *Wien. Med. Wchnschr.*, 1928, 78, 956 (with E. Froeschels).

39 ———. *Practice of voice and speech therapy.* Boston: Expression Co., 1941 (with E. Froeschels).

40 **Jenkin, N.** Birth order and academic achievement. *JIP*, 1967, 23, 103–110 (with M. Oberlander). Also in H. J. Vetter & B. D. Smith (Eds.), *Personality theory: A source book.*

41 **Jenkins, R. L.** Birth order and intelligence. *J. educ. Psychol.*, 1929, 20, 641–651 (with L. L. Thurstone).

42 **Jensen, Eleanore.** Translator, with F. Jensen, of A. Adler, *The case of Miss R.*

43 ———. Translator, with F. Jensen, of A. Adler, *The education of children.*

44 ———. Translator of F. Künkel, *Let's be normal!*

45 **Jensen, F.** Translator, with Eleanore Jensen, of A. Adler, *The case of Miss R.*

46 ———. Translator, with Eleanore Jensen, of A. Adler, *The education of children.*

47 **Jernigan, J.** The gap between religion and psychiatry. *Insight*, 1963, 19, 69–76 (with W. O'Connell, J. Frizelle, C. Harris, & J. Wohl).

48 **Jessor, R.** Issues in the phenomenological approach to personality. *JIP*, 1961, 17, 27–38.

49 ———. Phenomenological personality theories and the data language of psychology. *Psychol. Rev.*, 1956, 63, 173–180.

50 ———. The problem of reductionism in psychology. *Psychol. Rev.*, 1958, 65, 170–178.

51 **Jessor, R.** Social values in psychotherapy. *J. consult. Psychol.*, 1956, 20, 264–266.

52 **Jimenez de Asua, L.** Psicoanalysis delito y pena. *Arqui. Med. legal e Identificacao*, 1939, 9, 407–433.

53 **Johanson, E.** Inmates of youth prisons compared with controls for family structure. *Acta psychiat. Scand.*, 1968, 44, 289–297.

54 **Johnson, Elizabeth Z.** In defense of Standal and Corsini. *Contemp. Psychol.*, 1960, 5, 350–351.

55 **Johnson, E. L.** Existential trends toward Individual Psychology. *IP*, 1966, 3(2), 11–13.

56 ———. Existential trends toward Individual Psychology, *JIP*, 1966, 22, 33–42.

57 **Johnson, F. L.** Responsibility. *Bull. Inst. Child Study* (Toronto), 1955, 17, 1–4.

58 **Johnson, P. E.** *Psychology of religion.* Rev. ed. New York & Nashville: Abingdon Press, 1959.

59 **Jones, Diane.** Generality of continuity on two tasks. *JIP*, 1969, 25, 48–51 (with R. Eisenman).

60 **Jones, E.** *The life and work of Sigmund Freud.* New York: Basic Books. Vol. 1, 1953; Vol. 2, 1955; Vol. 3, 1957.

61 **Jones, E. M.** An application of the Q-technique to the study of religious concepts. *Psychol. Rep.*, 1957, 3, 293–297 (with M. O. Nelson).

62 ———. Les concepts religieux dans leur relation aux images parentals. In A. Godin (Ed.), *Adult et enfant devant Dieu* (with M. O. Nelson).

63 **Jones, H.** Habit strength as a function of the pattern of reinforcement. *J. exp. Psychol.*, 1945, 35, 293–311 (with O. H. Mowrer).

64 **Jones, H. E.** Order of birth in relation to the development of the child. In C. Murchison (Ed.), *A handbook of child psychology.* Pp. 204–241.

65 **Jones, M.** Work with large groups in mental hospitals. *JIP*, 1963, 19, 61–68 (with S. Hollingsworth).

66 **Jones, M. R.** Ordinal position, age, anxiety, and defensiveness in unwed mothers. *Proceed. 75th Ann. Conv. Amer. Psychol. Assn.*, 1967, 2, 177–178 (with P. E. Wohlford).

67 **Joseph, E. D.** Memory and conflict. *Psychoanal. Quart.*, 1966, 35(1), 1–17.

68 Jourard, S. M. I-thou relationship versus manipulation in counseling and psychotherapy. *JIP*, 1959, 15, 174–179.

69 ———. Perceived parental attitudes, the self, and security. *J. consult. Psychol.*, 1955, 19, 364–366 (with R. M. Remy).

70 Joy, K. The anxious child. *SDEA J.* Sept., 1966 (with J. W. Croake).

71 Julian, J. W. Sex and birth-order differences in conformity as a function of need affiliation arousal. *J. Pers. soc. Psychol.*, 1966, 3, 479–483 (with W. C. Carrigan).

K

1 Kadis, Asya L. L'age critique est-il critique? *Psyché* (Paris), 1954, 9, 152, 163 (with Sofie Lazarsfeld).

2 ———. Alfred Adler's theory of compensation applied to current studies of sidedness. *IPB*, 1947, 6, 27–31 (with Danica Deutsch).

3 ———. The alternate meeting in group psychotherapy. *Amer. J. Psychother.*, 1956, 10, 275–291.

4 ———. "Change of life"—End of life? *JIP*, 1958, 14, 167–170 (with Sofie Lazarsfeld).

5 ———. Child-home-school: An every day problem. *IPN*, 1941, 1(8–9), 13–14 (with Anna Heinrichs).

6 ———. Coordinated meetings in group psychotherapy. In M. Rosenbaum & M. Berger (Eds.), *Group psychotherapy and group function.* Pp. 437–448.

7 ———. Early childhood recollections: An integrative technique of personality test data. *AJIP*, 1953, 10, 31–42 (with Janet Greene & N. Freedman).

8 ———. Early childhood recollections as aids in group psychotherapy. *JIP*, 1957, 13, 182–187.

9 ———. Fees in group therapy. *Amer. J. Psychother.*, 1968, 22, 66–67 (with C. Winick).

10 ———. Finger painting in the psychotherapy of children. *Amer. J. Orthopsychiat.*, 1946, 16, 134–146 (with J. A. Arlow).

11 ———. The group as a psychotherapeutic factor. *Nerv. Child*, 1945, 4, 226–235 (with Sofie Lazarsfeld).

12 ———. Group psychotherapy (with M. Markowitz). In D. Brower &

L. E. Abt (Eds.), *Progress in clinical psychology.* Pp. 154–183.

13 Kadis, Asya L. *Group psychotherapy today: Selected papers presented at the scienfific meetings of the Eastern Group Psychotherapy Society, 1960–1963.* Basel, Switzerland: Karger, 1965. Paper (with C. Winick).

14 ———. *Guide du psychothérapie de groupe.* Translated by M. Dreyfus. Paris: Editions Epi, 1971 (with J. D. Krasner, C. Winick & S. H. Foulkes).

15 ———. A new approach to marital therapy. *Int J. soc. Psychiat.*, 1964, 10(4), 261–264.

16 ———. A new group supervisory technique for group therapists. *Voices*, 1971, 7(1), 31–32.

17 ———. Parental interaction as a determining factor in social growth of the individual. *Int. J. soc. Psychiat.*, Spec. Ed. 2, 81–89 (with M. Markowitz).

18 ———. Portrait. *Frontiers Hosp. Psychiat.*, 1968, 5(11), 6; *Voices*, 1971, 7(1), 31.

19 ———. *A practicum of group psychotherapy.* New York: Hoeber, 1963 (with J. D. Krasner, C. Winick & S. H. Foulkes).

20 ———. Re-experiencing the family constellation in group psychotherapy. *AJIP*, 1956, 12, 63–68. Also in K. A. Adler & Danica Deutsch (Eds.), *Essays in Individual Psychology.* Pp. 256–263.

21 ———. The respective roles of earliest recollections and images. *Amer. J. Psychother.*, 1948, 2, 250–255 (with Sofie Lazarsfeld).

22 ———. The role of the deviant in the therapy group. *Int. J. soc. Psychiat.*, 1960, 6, 277–287 (with C. Winick).

23 ——— (Ed.). *Sources of conflict in contemporary group therapy.* Basel, Switzerland: Karger, 1960 (with W. C. Hulse, H. S. Leopold & A. Wolf).

24 ———. *Topical problems in group psychotherapy.* Basel, Switzerland: S. Karger, 1964.

25 Kagan, Esther. Couple multi-therapy for marriages in crisis. *Psychother.*, 1972, 9(4), 332–336 (with M. Zaks).

26 Kagan, J. The concept of identification. *Psychol. Rev.*, 1958, 65, 296–305.

27 ———. On the need for relativism. *Amer. Psychologist*, 1967, 22, 131–142.

28 **Kagan, J.** The child's differential perception of parental attributes. *J. abnorm. soc. Psychol.*, 1960, 61, 440–447 (with Judith Lemkin).

29 **Kagan, S.** Competition: The star-spangled scramble. *Psychol. Today*, 1972, 6(4), 53–56, 90–91 (with L. L. Nelson).

30 ———. Cooperation and competition of Mexican, Mexican-American, and Anglo-American children of two ages under four instructional sets. *Developm. Psychol.*, 1971, 5, 32–39.

31 **Kahana, E.** *A freudizmus után. Bevezetes Alfred Adler Individualpszichologiajaba.* Brasov, Romania: Wilhelm Grünfeld, 1924.

32 **Kahana, R.** The value of early memories in psychotherapy. *Psychiat. Quart.*, 1953, 27, 73–82 (with I. Weiland, B. Snyder & M. Rosenbaum).

33 **Kahane, M.** (Ed.). *Medizinische Handlexikon praktiz. Aerzte.* Wien: Urban & Schwarzenberg, 1908.

34 **Kahn, E.** *The craving for superiority.* New Haven: Yale Univ. Press, 1931 (with R. Dodge).

35 **Kahn, P. J.** *Author-title index for Individual Psychology Bulletin, 1940–1951, Vols. 1–9.* Palo Alto, Cal.: Author, 1972.

36 ———. *Author-title index for International Journal of Individual Psychology, 1935–1937, Vols. 1–3.* Palo Alto, Cal.: Author, 1972.

37 ———. *Author-title index of Journal of Individual Psychology, 1952–1972.* Palo Alto, Cal.: San Francisco Bay Area Society for Adlerian Psychology, 1972.

38 ———. Progress of Individual Psychology work at University of Oregon. *OSIPNL*, 1966, 7(3), 4–5.

39 **Kahneman, I.** Sex and age differences in pattern organization in a figural-conceptual task. *Develpm. Psychol.*, 1971, 5, 446–453 (with R. Guttman).

40 **Kaiser, J. W.** Einführung in die Interpretation des Dramas. *IZIP*, 1929, 7(2), 112–124.

41 **Kal, E.** Portrait. *Frontiers Hosp. Psychiat.*, 1967, 4(12), 6.

42 ———. Survey of contemporary Adlerian clinical practice. *JIP*, 1972, 28(2), 261–266.

43 **Kalhorn, Joan.** Patterns of parent behavior. *Psychol. Monogr.*, 1945, 58, No. 3 (Whole No. 268) (with A. L. Baldwin & Fay Breese).

44 **Kallen, L. A.** Vorstellungstypen von Polteren. *Wien med. Wchnschr.*, 1930, 2, 1162 (with E. Froeschels).

45 **Kallman, F. J.** Suicide in twins and only children. *Amer. J. hum. Genet.*, 1949, 1, 113–126 (with J. De Porte & E. De Porte).

46 **Kalmann, H.** Angebliche Spukphänomene und ihre individualpsychologische Deutung. *IZIP*, 1930, 8(2), 249–251.

47 **Kamano, D. K.** Selectivity in memory of personally significant material. *J. gen. Psychol.*, 1961, 65, 25–32 (with Janet E. Drew).

48 **Kameny, A.** Normal children as aids in child psychotherapy. *JIP*, 1964, 20, 90–95.

49 **Kammeyer, K.** Birth order and the feminine sex role among college women. *Amer. sociol. Rev.*, 1966, 34, 508–515.

50 ———. Birth order as a research variable. *Soc. Forces*, 1967, 46, 71–80.

51 **Kanitz, O. F.** *Das proletarische Kind in der bürgerlichen Gesellschaft.* Jena: Urania Verlag, 1925.

52 **Kanter, H. L.** Birth order, background factors, and teacher referral for emotional disturbance. *Diss. Abstr. Int.*, 1971, 31(7A), 3341–3342.

53 **Kanter, M.** Toward a halacha of personality. Unpubl. Ph.D. Diss., Univ. Chicago, 1969.

54 **Kantor, V. F.** A study of the relationship between birth order and achievement by overachieving early school starters and underachieving late school starters at the sixth grade level. *Diss. Abstr. Int.*, 1970, 31(1A), 70–71.

55 **Kanungo, R. N.** Retention of affective material: Frame of reference or intensity. *J. Pers. soc. Psychol.*, 1966, 4, 27–35.

56 **Kapit, Hanna.** Relationships between attitudes toward therapists and attitudes toward parents. Unpubl. Ph.D. Diss., Columbia Univ., 1956.

57 **Kaplan, H. B.** Self-derogation and childhood family structure: Family size, birth order, and sex distribution. *J. nerv. ment. Dis.*, 1970, 151, 13–23.

58 **Kaplan, H. I.** (Ed.). *Comprehensive textbook of psychiatry.* Baltimore: Williams & Wilkins, 1967 (with A. M. Freedman).

59 **Kaplan, M. L.** Maintaining continuity of experience in organic deficit. *JIP*, 1964, 20, 48–54.

60 **Kapuste, E.** Individualpsychologie im Unterricht. *IZIP*, 1932, 10(4), 312–313.

61 **Karabenick, S. A.** On the relationship between personality and birth order. *Psychol. Rep.*, 1971, 28, 258.

62 **Karl, E. A.** An innovation in conduct of parent study groups. *IP*, 1972, 9(1), 25-28.

63 **Karpf, Fay B.** The Adlerian background—Individual Psychology. In *The psychology and psychotherapy of Otto Rank*. New York: Phil. Libr., 1953. Ch. IV.

64 **Karon, B. P.** The resolution of acute schizophrenic reactions: A contribution to the development of non-classical psychotherapeutic techniques. *Psychother.*, 1963, 1, 27-43.

65 ———. Suicidal tendency as the wish to hurt someone else, and resulting treatment technique. *JIP*, 1964, 20, 206-212.

66 ———. Suicide (with A Nikelly). In A. Nikelly (Ed.), *Techniques for behavior change*. Pp. 185-188.

67 **Karydi, G.** Translator of F. Künkel, *Eisagogi eis tin Charaktirologian*.

68 **Kass, Miriam.** What's so funny and why [about W. E. O'Connell]. *Houston Post*, Aug. 13, 1967.

69 **Kastenbaum, R.** Cognitive and personal futurity in later life. *JIP*, 1963, 19, 216-222.

70 **Kates, S. L.** Authoritarian ideology and attitudes on parent-child relationships. *J. abnorm. soc. Psychol.*, 1955, 51, 13-16 (with L. N. Diab).

71 **Katkovsky, W.** The efficacy of brief clinical procedures in alleviating children's behavior problems. *JIP*, 1961, 17, 205-211 (with B. A. Maher).

72 ———. *Readings in the psychology of adjustment*. 2nd ed. New York: McGraw-Hill, 1968. Paper (with L. Gorlow).

73 **Katz, D.** Gespräche mit Kindern. *IZIP*, 1930, 8(5), 459-470.

74 **Katz, J.** President Kennedy's assassination. *Psychoanal. Rev.*, 1964, 51(4), 121-124; *JIP*, 1967, 23, 20-23.

75 **Katz, Paula.** Körperliche Erziehung. In Sofie Lazarsfeld (Ed.), *Technik der Erziehung*.

76 ———. Turnen. In Sofie Lazarsfeld (Ed.), *Technik der Erziehung*.

77 **Katz, Rosa.** *Gespräche mit Kindern*. Berlin: J. Springer, 1928 (with D. Katz).

78 **Katzoff, E. T.** Personality as related to birth order and family size. *J. appl. Psychol.*, 1936, 20, 340-346 (with R. Stagner).

79 **Kaufmann, Elvira F.** The fear of defeat. In K. A. Adler & Danica Deutsch (Eds.), *Essays in Individual Psychology*. Pp. 353-360.

80 ———. The "progress chart". *IPN*, 1941, 1(10), 2-3.

81 **Kaufman, I.** The family constellation and overt incestuous relations between father and daughter. *Amer. J. Orthopsychiat.*, 1954, 24, 266-279 (with Alice L. Peck & C. K. Tagiuri).

82 **Kaufmann, W.** Nietzsche's concept of the will to power. *JIP*, 1972, 28(1), 3-11.

83 **Kaus, Gina.** Die seelische Entwicklung des Kindes. In E. Wexberg (Ed.), *Handbuch der Individualpsychologie*. Pp. 137-168.

84 ———. *Die Verliebten*. Berlin: Ullstein,

85 **Kaus, O.** *Die Angst vor der Frau*. Leipzig: S. Hirzel, 1927.

86 ———. Der Begriff der Norm in der Individualpsychologie. *IZIP*, 1930, 8(4), 426-435.

87 ———. Bemerkungen zum Leib-Seelenproblem. *IZIP*, 1926, 4(3), 124-140.

88 ———. *Das einzige Kind*. Dresden: Verlag am andern Ufer, 1926.

89 ———. *Der Fall Gogol*. München: Ernst Reinhardt, 1912.

90 ———. Der Fall Gogol. *Schr. Verein freie psychoanal. Forsch.*, 1912, No. 2.

91 ——— (Ed.). *Individuum und Gemeinschaft*. München: Bergmann, 1926-27 (with A. Adler & L. Seif).

92 ———. Pestalozzi und Wir. *IZIP*, 1927, 5(2), 129-148.

93 ———. Review of J. H. Schultz, *Die Schicksalsstunde der Psychotherapie*. In *IZIP*, 1926, 4(5), 312-313.

94 ———. Die Traume in Dostojewskis "Raskolnikoff". In A. Adler, L. Seif & O. Kaus (Eds.), *Individuum und Gemeinschaft*.

95 ———. Über Lügenhaftigkeit beim Kinde. In A. Adler & C. Furtmüller (Eds.), *Heilen und Bilden* (1914). Pp. 207-226.

96 ———. Über sexuelle Verirrungen (with F Künkel). In E. Wexberg (Ed.), *Handbuch der Individualpsychologie*. Pp. 555-582.

97 **Kausen, R.** Laius Complex and mother-child symbiosis. *JIP*, 1972, 28, 33-37.

98 **Kay, Eleanor.** The prediction of family interaction from a battery of projective techniques. *J. proj. Tech.*, 1957, 21, 199–208 (with Dorothy T. Sohler, J. D. Holzberg, S. Fleck, Alice R. Cornelison & T. Lidz).

99 **Kayton, L.** Birth order and the obsessive-compulsive character. *Arch. gen. Psychiat.*, 1967, 17, 751–754 (with F. F. Borge).

100 **Keedy, T. C.** Anomie and religious orthodoxy. *Sociol. soc. Res.*, 1958, 43, 34–47.

101 **Keenleyside, Marjorie C.** Masculine protest by feminine methods. *IJIP*, 1937, 3(2), 171–178.

102 ———. Review of E. Wexberg & H. E. Fritsch, *Our children in a changing world: An outline of practical guidance.* In *IJIP*, 1937, 3(3), 275–276.

103 **Kehas, C. D.** Self-concept decline from psychiatric hospitalization. *JIP*, 1969, 25, 213–214.

104 **Keimowitz, R. I.** Personality and achievement in mathematics. *JIP*, 1960, 16, 84–87 (with H. L. Ansbacher).

105 **Keleher, R. V.** Individual Psychology used in police training. *IPB*, 1947, 6, 61–64.

106 **Kell, B.** Multiple psychotherapy as a method for training and research in psychotherapy. *J. abnorm. soc. Psychol.*, 1950, 45, 659–666 (with G. Haigh).

107 **Keller, W.** *Das Selbstwertstreben: Wesen, Formen und Schicksale.* München: Reinhardt, 1963.

108 **Kelley, E. C.** *Education for what is real.* New York: Harper, 1947.

109 **Kelley, E. L.** Consistency of the adult personality. *Amer. Psychologist*, 1955, 10, 659–681.

110 **Kelly, G. A.** The language of hypothesis: Man's psychological instrument. *JIP*, 1964, 20, 137–152.

111 ———. Nonparametric factor analysis of personality theories. *JIP*, 1963, 19, 115–147.

112 ———. *Psychology of personal constructs.* New York: Norton, 1955.

113 **Kelman, H. C.** Group therapy, group work, and adult education. *J. soc. Issues*, 1952, 8(2), 3–10 (with H. H. Lerner).

114 **Kemper, T. D.** Mate selection and marital satisfaction according to sibling type of husband and wife. *J. Marr. Fam.*, 1966, 28, 346–349.

115 **Kemper, W.** "Organwahl" und psychosomatische Medizin. *Z. Psychother. u. med. Psychol.*, 1954, 4(3), 101–113.

116 **Kent, D. P.** Subjective factors in mate selection; an exploratory study. *Sociol. soc. Res.*, 1951, 35, 391–398.

117 **Kerckhoff, A.** Value consensus and need complementarity in mate selection. *Amer. sociol. Rev.*, 1962, 27, 295–303 (with K. A. Davis).

118 **Kerr, Rose Netzorg.** *Costume personality charts.* Waldwick, N. J.: Fairbairn Publishers,

119 **Kessen, W.** Stimulus variability and cognitive change. *Psychol. Rev.*, 1966, 73, 164–178 (with H. Munsinger).

120 **Keyserling, H.** (Ed.). *Buch der Ehe.* Celle: Chapman, 1925.

121 **Kiernan, T.** *A pictorial history of psychology and psychiatry.* New York: Phil. Libr., 1969 (with A. A. Roback).

122 **Kiersch, T. A.** The schizophrenic in college. *Arch. gen. Psychiat.*, 1966, 15, 54–58 (with A. G. Nikelly).

123 **Kilpatrick, D. G.** The relationship of ordinal position, dogmatism, and personal sexual attitudes. *J. Psychol.*, 1969, 73, 115–120 (with N. R. Cauthen).

124 **Kilpatrick, F. P.** Hadley Cantril (1906–1969): The transactional point of view. *JIP*, 1969, 25, 219–225.

125 ———. Personality in transactional psychology. *JIP*, 1961, 17, 12–19.

126 ———. Review of C. M. Solley & G. Murphy, *Development of the perceptual world.* New York: Basic Books, 1960. In *JIP*, 1961, 17, 118–119.

127 ———. Self-anchoring scaling: A measure of individual's unique reality worlds. *JIP*, 1960, 16, 158–173 (with H. Cantril).

128 **King, G. (Ed.).** *The Mexican American Directory.* Washington, D. C.: Executive Systems Corp., 1969 (with A. Palacios & P. Scarth).

129 **King, Marian.** Die andere Seit des Tores. *IZIP*, 1933, 11(2), 137–151.

130 **Kinsolving, D. L.** First borns, only children, sex and field independence. *Psychol. Rep.*, 1971, 29, 126 (with R. N. Bone).

131 **Kirby, J.** Mobile facilities—an innovation in counselor training. *IP*, 1970, 8(2), 49–54 (with Jonell Kirby).

132 **Kirby, Jonell.** Adlerian group counseling in the elementary schools: Report

of a program. *JIP*, 1969, 25, 155–163 (with G. E. Stormer).

133 **Kirby, Jonell.** Mobile facilities—an innovation in counselor training. *IP*, 1970, 8(2), 49–54 (with J. Kirby).

134 **Kirkham, Sandra L.** An evaluation of the organic signs in the H-T-P drawings. *J. clin. Psychol.*, 1958, 14, 50–54 (with V. Bieliauskas).

135 **Klages, L.** Das persönliche Leitbild. In *Graphol. Monatshefte*. München: Ackermann, 1906.

136 **Klaiber, E. L.** Ability to automatize and automatization cognitive style: A validation study. *Percep. mot. Skills*, 1966, 23, 419–437 (with D. M. Broverman & Inge Broverman).

137 **Klapman, H.** Organ inferiority and psychiatric disorders in childhood (with B. H. Shulman). In E. Harms (Ed.), *Pathogenesis of nervous and mental diseases*. Pp. 49–62.

138 ———. Rehabilitation of children discharged from a psychiatric hospital. *Amer. J. Orthopsychiat.*, 1964, 34(5), 942–947 (with Sarah Slagle & I. Morino).

139 **Klapman, J. W.** The case for didactic group psychotherapy. *Dis. nerv. Sys.*, 1950, 11(2), 35–41. Also in M. Rosenbaum & M. Berger (Eds.), *Group psychotherapy and group functions*. Pp. 328–339.

140 ———. A didactic approach to group psychotherapy. *Ill. Psychiat. J.*, 1941, 1, 6–10.

141 ———. Group psychotherapy (with R. J. Corsini). In E. A. Spiegel (Ed.), *Progress in neurology and psychiatry*. 1955, Vol. 10; 1956, Vol. 11; 1957, Vol. 12; 1958, Vol. 13; 1959, Vol. 14.

142 ———. Group psychotherapy: Social activities as an adjunct to treatment. *Grp. Psychother.*, 1951, 3, 327–338.

143 ———. *Group therapy: Theory and practice.* New York: Grune & Stratton, 1946.

144 ———. *Is insanity shameful?* Chicago: Resurgo Associates, 1950.

145 ———. Objective appraisal of textbook mediated group psychotherapy with psychotics. *Int. J. grp. Psychother.*, 1952, 3, 116–126 (with W. H. Lundin).

146 ———. An observation on the interrelationship of group and individual psychotherapy. *J. nerv. ment. Dis.*, 1945, 101, 242–246.

147 **Klapman, J. W.** Observations on the "shuttle" process in individual-group psychotherapy. *Psychiat. Quart.*, 1950, 24, 124–130.

148 ———. Preface to R. J. Corsini, *Methods of group psychotherapy.*

149 ———. Psychiatric social club therapy. *Grp. Psychother.*, 1953, 6, 43–49.

150 ———. Psychoanalytic or didactic group psychotherapy? *Psychiat. Quart.*, 1954, 28, 279–286.

151 ———. Public relations of the mental hospital. *Ment. Hyg.*, 1944, 28, 381–396.

152 ———. Reactions of patients to textbook-mediated group psychotherapy. *Dis. nerv. Sys.*, 1953, 14, 144–148.

153 ———. *Social adjustment: A textbook for group psychotherapy.* Chicago: Resurgo Associates, 1950.

154 ———. Some impressions of group psychotherapy. *Psychoanal. Rev.*, 1944, 31(3), 322–328.

155 ———. Supportive psychotherapy. *Psychiat. Quart.*, 1945, 19, 605–617.

156 ———. The team approach in group psychotherapy. *Dis. nerv. Sys.*, 1957, 18, 95–99 (with Ruth E. Meyer).

157 ———. Therapeutic value of institutional journalism. *J. occup. Ther. Rehab.*, 1943, 22, 126–131.

158 ———. Use of autobiography in pedagogical group psychotherapy. *Dis. nerv. Sys.*, 1947, 8, 175–180.

159 **Klatt, G.** *Die Alkoholfrage.* Berlin: Newland-Verlag, 1931.

160 ———. Geschlechtsleben und Alkohol. *Int. Z. gesam. Alkohol*, 1928, 4,

161 ———. *Psychologie des Alkoholismus: Ein Versuch.* Halle: Carl Marhold, 1932.

162 ———. Rausch. *IZIP*, 1932, 10(2), 110–124.

163 ———. Traume eines Abstinenten. *IZIP*, 1929, 7(1), 50–57.

164 **Kleber, D. A.** [Letter on college activists and internal-external control]. *Psychol. Today*, 1971, 5(4), 4 (with G. Manaster).

165 **Klein-Greenwood, Alice.** See Greenwood, Alice.

166 **Kleist, F.** Erfahrungen eines Individualpsychologen im Strafvollzug. *IZIP*, 1931, 9(5), 381–388.

167 ———. Der Ermutigungsgedanke in preussischen Strafvollzug. *IZIP*, 1931, 9(1), 40–50.

168 Kleist, F. *Jugend am Gesetz*. Berlin: Gottfried Martin, 1928.

169 ———. Die Jugend, die man prügelt. *IZIP*, 1929, 7(2), 144–148.

170 ———. *Jugend hinter Gittern*. Jena: Karl Zwing, 1931.

171 ———. Review of Im Jugendgefangnis. In P. Ostreich (Ed.), *Die neue Erziehung*. Berlin: Hensel, [   ]. In *IZIP*, 1928, 6(3), 265–266.

172 ———. Review of E. Schmidt, *Das Verbrechen als Ausdrucksform sozialer Entmutigung*. München: J. Schweitzer, [   ]. In *IZIP*, 1933, 11(2), 154–155.

173 ———. "Th. K." Zur Psychologie eines jugendlichen Kriminellen. *IZIP*, 1928, 6(2), 108–116.

174 Kleist, K. The brain and mental life. *An. Port. Psiquiat.*, 1951, 3, 112–119.

175 ——— (Ed.). *Richter und Arzt*. München-Basel: Reinhardt,

176 ———. Adler et la Psychologie Individuelle. *Strasbourg Médical*, 1957 (juillet), 578–586.

177 ———. L'evolution de la psychothérapie depuis ses origines en Allemagne. M. D. Diss.

178 Klinghammer, Irma. "I'm not as much of a brat as I used to be." *OSIPNL*, 1966, 7(4), 16.

179 Klingholtz, Emmy. Psychologische Betrachtungen zur Methode Coué. *IZIP*, 1929, 7(1), 44–47.

180 Klockars, A. J. Relationship between personality dimensions and the familial variables of birth order, sex of siblings and family size. *Diss. Abstr.*, 1968, 29, 327.

181 Kluckhohn, C. A dynamic theory of personality (with O. H. Mowrer). In J. McV. Hunt (Ed.), *Personality and the behavior disorders*. Pp. 69–135.

182 Kluckhohn, Lucy. Birth order and achievement in eighteenth century Scotland. *JIP*, 1971, 27(1), 80 (with Bonnie Bullough, V. L. Bullough, & Martha Voight).

183 Knopf, Olga. Der "Angstbeisser". *IZIP*, 1928, 6(4), 336–337.

184 ———. *The art of being a woman*. London: Rider, 1932; Boston: Little, Brown, 1932.

185 ———. Arzt und Erziehungsberatung. *IZIP*, 1929, 7(3), 170–176 (with E. Wexberg).

186 ———. Drei Traume. *IZIP*, 1928, 6(3), 192–195.

187 Knopf, Olga. Individualpsychologie und Gynäkologie. *IZIP*, 1929, 7(4), 276–286.

188 ———. Individual Psychology and gynecology. *IPMP*, 1932, No. 6, Pp. 22–33.

189 ———. Individual Psychology and practice (I). *IPMP*, No. 6 (with E. Wexberg & H. C. Squires).

190 ———. The physician and educational guidance (with E. Wexberg). In A. Adler & assoc., *Guiding the child*. Pp. 28–46.

191 ———. Prophylactic educational guidance in parents' associations. In A. Adler & assoc., *Guiding the child*. Pp. 89–101.

192 ———. Prophylaktische Erziehungsberatung. *IZIP*, 1929, 7(3), 192–195.

193 ———. Review of H. A. Adam, *Geisteskrankheiten in alter und neuer Zeit*. Regensburg: Ludwig Rath, 1928. In *IZIP*, 1929, 7(1), 78–80.

194 ———. Review of H. Blüher, *Traktat über die Heilkunde, insbesondere die Neurosenlehre*. Jena: E. Diederichs, 1926. In *IZIP*, 1929, 7(1), 70–71.

195 ———. Review of O. Flake, *Die erotische Freiheit*. Berlin: S. Fischer, 1928. In *IZIP*, 1930, 8(2), 275.

196 ———. Review of F. Giese, *Erlebensformen des Alterns*. Halle: Carl Marhold, 1928. In *IZIP*, 1929, 7(1), 80.

197 ———. Review of P. Haberlin, *Über die Ehe*. Zurich: Schweizer Spiegel, 1928. In *IZIP*, 1929, 7(1), 152–153.

198 ———. Review of C. G. Jung, *Die Frau in Europa*. Zurich: Verlag der neuen Schweizer Rundschau, 1929. In *IZIP*, 1930, 8(2), 276.

199 ———. Review of Elga Kern (Ed.), *Führende Frauen Europas*. München: Ernst Reinhardt, 1928. In *IZIP*, 1930, 8(2), 275–276.

200 ———. Review of F. Künkel, *Die Arbeit am Charakter*. In *IZIP*, 1929, 7(5), 396.

201 ———. Review of Sofie Lazarsfeld, *Die Ehe von Heute und Morgen*. In *IZIP*, 1928, 6(3), 262.

202 ———. Review of T. Mann, *Spannungen*. Woltersdorf Jugenbund, 1928. In *IZIP*, 1928, 6(6), 507.

203 ———. Review of G. Maranon, *Über das Geschlechtsleben*. Heidelberg: Niels Kampmann,   . In *IZIP*, 1929, 7(1), 77–78.

204 ———. Review of M. Marcuse (Ed.), *Die Ehe*. Berlin: A. Markus & E. Webers, 1927. In *IZIP*, 1928, 6(1), 76–77.

205 **Knopf, Olga.** Review of P. Schmidt, *Das überwundene Alter.* Leipzig: P. List, [   ]. In *IZIP*, 1929, 7(4), 319–320.

206 ———. Review of E. E. Schwabach, *Revolutionierung der Frau.* Leipzig: Der Neue Geist Verlag, 1928. In *IZIP*, 1929, 7(5), 400.

207 ———. Review of H. Sellheim, *Hygiene und Diätetic der Frau.* München: J. F. Bergmann, 1926. In *IZIP*, 1929, 7(5), 479–480.

208 ———. Review of H. Sperber, *Die Lüge im Strafrecht.* In *IZIP*, 1927, 5(2), 159.

209 ———. Review of H. Vignes, *Physiologie gynécologique et médicine des femmes.* Paris: S. Masson, [   ]. In *IZIP*,

210 ———. Review of Else Volk-Friedland, *Die Frau von 50 Jahren und ihre richtige Lebensführung.* Wien: Schwartz, [   ]. In *IZIP*, 1928, 6(6), 507.

211 ———. Review of P. Wenger, *Sexualpädagogik. Med. Klin.*, No. 25. In *IZIP*, 1930, 8(2), 275.

212 ———. Review of R. S. Woodworth, *Psychologies of 1930.* In *IZIP*, 1931, 9(5), 408.

213 ———. Das "sexuelle Traume". *IZIP*, 1931, 9(6), 457–461.

214 ———. Die Stellung des Kindes in der Familie. *IZIP*, 1930, 8(2), 237–249.

215 ———. Translator of J. Dewey, *Individualität in der Gegenwart.*

216 ———. Über Frigidität. *IZIP*, 1930, 8(1), 151–159.

217 ———. *Die Ursache des Vaginismus und seine Behandlung. Monatschr. ungarisch. Med.*, , 3, .

218 **Knox, F.** Attitudes toward authority figures. *Coll. Stud. Survey,* Fall, 1970 (with J. W. Croake).

219 ———. Common fears. *Florida Pupil Personnel Quart.*, 1971, 3(3) (with J. W. Croake).

220 ———. A reinvestigation of fear retention and dissonance. *Psychol.*, 1971, 6(23) (with J. W. Croake).

221 ———. A second look at adolescent fears. *J. Adolesc.*, 1971, 6(23), (with J. W. Croake).

222 **Knutson, A. L.** The concept of personal security. *J. soc. Psychol.*, 1954, 40, 219–236.

223 **Ko, Y-H.** Ordinal position and the behavior of visiting the child guidance clinic. *Acta psychol. Taiwanica*, 1965, 7, 10-16 (with L-C Sun).

224 **Ko, Y-H.** Ordinal position and the behavior of visiting the child guidance clinic. II. *Acta psychol. Taiwanica*, 1966, 8, 92–95 (with L-C Sun).

225 ———. The relationships between personality development and ordinal positions. *Acta psychol. Taiwanica*, 1966, 8, 29–37 (with L. Lin).

226 **Kobler, F.** (Ed.). *Gewalt und Gewaltlosigkeit: Handbuch des aktiven Pazifismus.* Zurich: Rotapfel-Verlag, 1928.

227 **Koch, Helen L.** Attitudes of young children toward their peers as related to certain characteristics of their siblings. *Psychol. Monogr.*, 1956, 70(19), No. 426.

228 ———. The influence of some affective factors upon recall. *J. gen. Psychol.*, 1930, 4, 171–190.

229 ———. The relation in young children between characteristics of their playmates and certain attributes of their siblings. *Child Devlpm.*, 1957, 28, 175–202.

230 ———. Sibling influence on children's speech. *J. Speech Hearing Dis.*, 1956, 21, 322–328.

231 ———. Some emotional attitudes of the young child in relation to characteristics of his sibling. *Child Develpm.*, 1957, 27, 393–426.

232 ———. Some personality correlates of sex, sibling position, and sex of sibling among five- and six year-old children. *Genet. Psychol. Monogr.*, 1955, 52, 3–50.

233 ———. *Twin and twin relations.* Chicago: Univ. Chicago Press, 1966.

234 **Koch, Joanne.** Help at hand for the mentally ill. Part II. *Chicago Today Mag.*, Oct. 4, 1970.

235 **Koenig, F.** Definitions of self and ordinal position of birth. *J. soc. Psychol.*, 1969, 78, 287–288.

236 **Kogan, L.** Further studies utilizing the discomfort-relief quotient (with O. H. Mowrer & J. McV. Hunt). In O. H. Mowrer (Ed.), *Psychotherapy: Theory and research.* Pp. 257–295.

237 ———. Tension changes during psychotherapy (with O. H. Mowrer & J. McV. Hunt). In O. H. Mowrer (Ed.), *Psychotherapy: Theory and research.* Pp. 596–640.

238 **Kohlmann, [   ].** Review of W. Daim, *Umwertung der Psychoanalyse.* Wien: Herold, 1951. In *IZIP*, 1951, 20(4), 187–188.

MOSAK, HAROLD H AND BIRDIE MOSAK

VN0001 AUTHOR AREA

BIBLIOGRAPHY FOR ADLERIAN PSYCHOLOGY
HEMISPHERE PUB CORP (DIST BY HALSTED DIV OF WILE

TITLE AREA

DATE PUB 75 IDENTIFICATION CHARACTERISTICS AREA

JOSEPH ACCT 94100

TR CODE	CALL NUMBER	LIBRARY OF CONGRESS NUMBER	SELECTION LIST NUMBER	SYMBOLS	QUANTITY ORDERED	ORDER LIST PRICE
33		7426938			1	1750

ORDER CARD MESSAGE AREA

AGENCY	P	R/C	QTY	AGENCY	P	R/C	QTY	AGENCY	P	R/C	QTY	AGENCY	P	R/C	QTY	AGENCY	P	R/C	QTY

TR CODE	LIBRARY NUMBER	BOOK NUMBER	INVOICE NUMBER	PURCHASE	QTY	INVOICE LIST PRICE	INVOICE	DISCOUNT	INVOICE NET PRICE
HPY	C001								

239 **Kohn, M.** Social class and the exercise of parental authority. *Amer. sociol. Rev.*, 1954, 24, 352–366.

240 **Kohut, N. C.** (Ed.). *Therapeutic family law.* Chicago: Family Law Publications, 1968.

241 **Koltuv, M.** Toleration for psychiatric rehabilitation as a function of coping style. *J. consult. Psychol.*, 1967, 31, 364–370 (with W. S. Neff).

242 **Konstantinidi, G. D.** Translator of A. Adler, *Synkretiki Atomiki Psychologia kai Psychotherapeia.*

243 **Kopkind, A.** An alien in his world. *IPNL*, 1966, 17(1–2, Whole No. 186–187). P. 4.

244 **Kopp, R. R.** The use of early recollections in the study of adolescents. M.A. thesis, Univ. Chicago, 1971.

245 **Korchin, S.** Memory for socially-relevant material. *J. abnorm. soc. Psychol.*, 1952, 47, 25–37 (with Thelma S. Alper).

246 **Korn, E. M. F.** The relationship existing between order of birth intelligence and temperament. Master's essay, Columbia Univ., 1923.

247 **Kosofsky, S.** An attempt at weight control through group psychotherapy. *JIP*, 1957, 13, 68–71.

248 **Kosse, W.** Education as encouragement. Historic-systematic analysis of the educational phenomenon. *Pädagog. Heute*, 1969, 3–4.

249 **Kotchen, T. A.** Existential mental health: An empirical approach. *JIP*, 1960, 16, 174–181.

250 **Kovács, Ilonka.** Das Opfer. *IZIP*, 1933, 12(6), 471–477.

251 **Kramer, Hilde C.** A comparative study of non-blooded related and a blood related case of *folie à deux. IPB*, 1950, 8, 131–149.

252 ———. Elternliebe. In Sofie Lazarsfeld, *Richtige Lebensführung.*

253 ———. Family interrelationships and their bearing upon the development of psychotic conditions. *IPB*, 1946, 5, 35–52.

254 ———. Fantasías profesionales. In A. Adler & C. Furtmüller (Eds.), *Curar y educar.*

255 ———. The first guidance clinic and its first patient. *IPB*, 1942, 2(2), 32–37.

256 ———. The function of dreams. *IPB*, 1943, 3, 37–43.

257 **Kramer, Hilde C.** Häufigkeit und Bedeutung von Mindwertigkeitsgefühlen in Psychosen. *IZIP*, 1947, 16(2), 65–74.

258 ———. An Individual Psychological approach to a case of *folie imposée. IPB*, 1947, 6, 117–129.

259 ———. Individualpsychologische Analyse eines Falles von Folie Imposée. *IZIP*, 1947, 16(3), 122–136.

260 ———. Inferiority feelings in psychotic conditions. *IPB*, 1944–45, 4, 67–74.

261 ———. Is punishment a method of education? *Educ. Method*, 1942, 21(4), 188–191.

262 ———. Laughing spells in patients after lobotomy. *J. nerv. ment. Dis.*, 1954, 119, 517–522.

263 ———. Obstacles and their solutions. *IPN*, 1940, 1(1), 3.

264 ———. *Das phantastische Kind.* Dresden: Verlag am andern Ufer, 1927.

265 ———. Preventive psychiatry. *IPB*, 1947, 7, 12–18.

266 ———. Selbsterziehung des Körperbehinderten. *IZIP*, 1930, 8(3), 332–334.

267 ———. Situational neuroses in childhood. *Nerv. Child*, 1944, 3, 127–144.

268 **Kramer, J.** Kindliche Phantasien über Berufswahl. In A. Adler & C. Furtmüller (Eds.), *Heilen und Bilden* (1914). Pp. 321–355; (1928). Pp. 328–341.

269 **Kras, Shari.** Anti-social behavior. *Int. J. soc. Psychiat.*, 1955, 1(2), 41–46.

270 ———. A discussion group for seriously disturbed mental patients. *Int. J. soc. Psychiat.*, 1957, 2(4), 299–303.

271 ———. Maladjustment, a result of social stress. *Int. J. soc. Psychiat.*, 1955.

272 ———. Report on the annual conference of the British Psychological Society. *Int. J. soc. Psychiat.*, 1955, 1(1), 72–77.

273 ———. Review of Marion Langer, *Learning to live as a widow.* New York: Gilbert Press, 1957. In *Int. J. soc. Psychiat.*, 1959, 5(1), 79.

274 ———. Review of C. MacLean, *Child guidance and the school.* London: Methuen, 1946. In *Int. J. soc. Psychiat.*, 1967–68, 14(1), 78.

275 ———. Review of *The psychoanalytic study of the child.* Vol. XI. New York: Int. Univer. Press, 1956. In *Int. J. soc. Psychiat.*, 1959, 5(1), 80.

276 **Kras, Shari.** Review of H. Zulliger, *Helfen Anstalt strafen jugendlichen Dieben.* Stuttgart: E. Klett, 1956. In *Int. J. soc. Psychiat.*, 1957, 3(3), 23.

277 ———. Review of S. Zurukzoglu & P. Nussbaum, *Die Bedeutung des Minderwertigkeitsgefühle für den Alkoholismus.* In *Int. J. soc. Psychiat.*, 1955, 1(2), 76–77.

278 **Krasner, J. D.** *Guide du psychothérapie de groupe.* Translated by M. Dreyfus. Paris: Ed. Epi, 1971 (with S. H. Foulkes, Asya Kadis, & C. Winick).

279 ———. *A practicum of group psychotherapy.* New York: Hoeber, 1963 (with S. H. Foulkes, Asya Kadis, & C. Winick).

280 **Krasnow, Anita.** An Adlerian approach to the problem of school maladjustment. *Sch. Psychol. Dig.*, 1972, 1(2), 10–13. Condensed from *Acad. Ther.*, 1972, 7(2), 171–183.

281 **Kraus, O.** Franz Brentano's Psychologie und die Individualpsychologie. *IZIP*, 1925, 3(5), 257–259.

282 **Krausz, E. O.** Biozentrische oder individualpsychologische Charakterkunde. *IZIP*, 1932, 10(1), 19–29.

283 ———. The commonest neurosis. In K. A. Adler & Danica Deutsch (Eds.), *Essays in Individual Psychology.* Pp. 108–118.

284 ———. Die Fehlerquellen der Psychoanalyse. *IZIP*, 1933, 12(6), 416–450.

285 ———. The homeostatic function of dreams (abstract). *IPNL*, 1959, No. 9. P. 48.

286 ———. Homosexualität und Neurose. *IZIP*, 1933, 11(3), 224–230.

287 ———. Homosexuality as neurosis. *IJIP*, 1935, 1(1), 30–39.

288 ———. Is stuttering primarily a speech disorder? *J. Speech Dis.*, 1940, 5(3), 227–231.

289 ———. Pessimismus. *IZIP*, 1933, 11(2), 90–103.

290 ———. The pessimistic attitude. *IJIP*, 1935, 1(3), 86–99.

291 ———. Portrait. *IPNL*, 1970, 19(4), 61.

292 ———. Psychologie und Moral. *IZIP*, 1931, 9(4), 257–269.

293 ———. Psychology and morals. *IJIP*, 1935, 1(2), 51–69.

294 ———. Review of R. N. Coudenhove-Kalergi, *Held oder Heiliger.* Wien: Paneuropa, 1931. In *IZIP*, 1933, 11(1), 77–78.

295 ———. Review of F. G. Crookshank, *Individual Psychology and sex difficulties.* In *IZIP*, 1932, 10(4), 314.

296 **Krausz, E. O.** Review of F. G. Crookshank, *Individual sexual problems.* In *IZIP*, 1932, 10(4), 314.

297 ———. Review of M. Dessoir, *Vom Jenseits der Seele.* Stuttgart: Ferdinand Enke, 1931. In *IZIP*, 1932, 10(4), 315.

298 ———. Review of L. Deutsch, *Individualpsychologie im Musikunterricht und in der Musikerziehung.* In *IZIP*, 1932, 10(1), 73.

299 ———. Review of F. Künkel, Grundzüge der politischen Charakterkunde. In *IZIP*, 1932, 10(4), 317–318.

300 ———. Review of W. Schmied-Kowarzik, *Ethik.* Osterwieck am Harz: A. W. Zickfeldt, 1932. In *IZIP*, 1932, 10(4), 320.

301 ———. Review of F. Seifert, *Die Wissenschaft von Menschen in der Gegenwart.* Leipzig: Pan-Bucherei, [   ]. In *IZIP*, 1931, 9(5), 414.

302 ———. Review of J. Vach *et al.*, *Das Problem der Kultur und die ärztliche Psychologie.* In *IZIP*, 1932, 10(4), 319–320.

303 ———. Translator of J. C. Smuts, *Das wissenschaftliche Weltbild der Gegenwart.*

304 ———. Das Triebleben in der Psychoanalyse. *IZIP*, 1934, 12(4), 203–221.

305 ———. Die Weiblichkeit in der Psychoanalyse. *IZIP*, 1934, 12(1), 16–31.

306 **Krausz, Tilde.** Portrait. *IPNL*, 1972, 21(6), 110.

307 **Krawiec, T. S.** *Systems and theories of psychology.* 2nd ed. New York: Holt, Rinehart & Winston, 1968 (with J. F. Chaplin).

308 **Krech, D.** Notes toward a psychological theory. *J. Pers.*, 1949, 18, 66–87.

309 **Krieger, Margery H.** A test of the psychoanalytical theory of identification. *JIP*, 1960, 16, 56–63 (with P. Worchel).

310 **Kris, E.** The recovery of childhood memories in psychoanalysis. *Psychoanal. Stud. Child.*, 1956, 11, 54–88.

311 **Krische, P.** Die psychologie Erweiterung des Marxismus. *IZIP*, 1926, 4(4), 189–194.

312 **Krishnan, B.** Order of birth and temperament. *Indian J. Psychol.*, 1951, 26, 85–87.

313 **Kroger, W. S.** (Ed.). *Psychosomatic obstetrics, gynecology and endocrinology.* Springfield, Ill.: C. C. Thomas, 1962.

314 **Kroll, Leona.** Correlated with language and art. *OSIPNL*, 1966, 7(2), 6.

315 **Kronenberger, E. J.** Review of A. G. Nikelly, *Mental health for students*. In *JIP*, 1966, 22, 250–251.

316 **Kronfeld, A.** Der V. Internationale Kongress für Individualpsychologie. *IZIP*, 1930, 8(5), 537–550 (with G. Voigt).

317 ———. Die Individualpsychologie als Wissenschaft. In E. Wexberg (Ed.), *Handbuch der Individualpsychologie*. Pp. 1–29.

318 ———. Neurosenwahl. *IZIP*, 1931, 9(2), 81–87.

319 ———. *Perspektiven der Seelenheilkunde.* Leipzig: Georg Thieme, 1930.

320 ———. Psychagogik oder psychotherapeutische Erziehungslehre. In K. Birnbaum (Ed.), *Die psychischen Heilmethoden.*

321 ———. *Das seelisch Abnorme und die Gemeinschaft.* Berlin: J. Püttman, 1923.

322 ———. *Sexualpathologie.* Wien: Deuticke, 1923.

323 ———. Über einen bestimmten Typus männlicher Frauen. *Jb. sex. Zwischenstufen*, 1923, 23, 38–45.

324 ———. Über seelische Selbstumstellung eines jugendlichen Gewohnheitsverbrecher. *IZIP*, 1930, 8(1), 177–181.

325 ———. Die weltanschauliche Bedeutung der Individualpsychologie. *IZIP*, 1926, 4(1), 1–17.

326 ———. Zur Theorie der Individualpsychologie. *IZIP*, 1929, 7(4), 252–263.

327 **Kronstein, I.** Die tödlichen Wünsche. *IZIP*, 1924, 2(6), 34–36.

328 **Kropotkin, P.** On sociability. *IPNL*, 1967, 17(7–8, Whole No. 192–193). P. 53.

329 **Krueger, F.** *Die Lehre von dem Ganzen.* Bern: H. Huber, 1948.

330 **Krumboltz, J.** Task group report (with T. W. Allen, F. Robinson, W. Cottle, J. Cody, D. Homra & J. Ray). In J. Whiteley (Ed.), *Research problems in counseling.* Pp. 219–237.

331 **Ktsanes, T.** Empirical elaboration of the theory of complementary needs in mate selection. *J. abnorm. soc. Psychol.*, 1955, 51, 508–514 (with R. F. Winch & Virginia Ktsanes).

332 ———. The theory of complementary needs in mate selection. *Amer. sociol. Rev.*, 1954, 19, 241–249 (with R. F. Winch & Virginia Ktsanes).

333 **Ktsanes, Virginia.** Empirical elaboration of the theory of complementary needs in mate selection. *J. abnorm. soc. Psychol.*, 1955, 51, 508–514 (with R. F. Winch & T. Ktsanes).

334 ———. The theory of complementary needs in mate selection. *Amer. sociol. Rev.*, 1954, 19, 241–249 (with R. F. Winch & T. Ktsanes).

335 **Kuenzli, A. E.** (Ed.). *The phenomenological problem.* New York: Harper, 1959.

336 ———. *Reconstruction in religion.* Boston: Beacon Press, 1961.

337 ———. Review of M. Farber, *Naturalism and subjectivism.* Springfield, Ill.: C. C. Thomas, 1959. In *JIP*, 1960, 16, 100–101.

338 ———. Review of G. A. Miller, E. Galanter & K. H. Pribram, *Plans and the structure of behavior.* New York: Holt, 1960. In *JIP*, 1961, 17, 117–118.

339 ———. Review of Ruth C. Wylie, *The self concept.* In *JIP*, 1962, 18, 190–191.

340 ———. Symposium on phenomenological conceptions of personality: Introduction by the chairman. *JIP*, 1961, 17, 4.

341 **Kühnel, G.** Review of P. Bjerre, *Von der Psychoanalyse zur Psychosynthese.* Halle: Carl Marhold, 1925. In *IZIP*, 1927, 5(1), 79–80.

342 ———. Tiefenperson. *IZIP*, 1927, 5(5), 336–343.

343 ———. Über die organischen Grundlagen der Individualpsychologie. *IZIP*, 1926, 4(2), 90–94.

344 **Kuiken, D.** Effects of stress and birth order on attitude change. *J. Pers.*, 1968, 36, 466–473 (with R. Helmreich and B. Collins).

345 **Kulcsar, I.** *Bevezetis az individuálpszichológiábe* [Introduction to Individual Psychology]. Budapest: Ungarischen Ver. f. Indivpsy., 1931.

346 **Künkel, F.** *Die Arbeit am Charakter.* Meckl.-Schwer.: Bahn, 1931, 1939, 1969.

347 ———. Beitrag zur Kritik der Ambivalenz. *IZIP*, 1925, 3(2), 62–79.

348 ———. *Character, growth, education.* New York: Lippincott, 1938.

349 ———. *Charakter, Einzelmensch und Gruppe.* Leipzig: S. Hirzel, 1933.

350 ———. *Charakter, Krisis und Weltanschauung.* Leipzig: S. Hirzel, 1935.

351 ———. *Charakterkunde.* Leipzig: S. Hirzel, 1950.

352 **Künkel, F.** *Charakter, Leiden und Heilung.* Leipzig: S. Hirzel, 1934.

353 ——. *Charakter, Liebe, und Ehe.* Leipzig: S. Hirzel, 1932, 1936.

354 ——. *Charakter, Wachstum und Erziehung.* Leipzig: S. Hirzel, 1931, 1934, 1965.

355 ——. *Conquer yourself: The way to self-confidence.* New York: Ives Washburn, 1936.

356 ——. *Creation continues: A psychological interpretation of the first Gospel.* New York: Scribner, 1947.

357 ——. *Del yo al nosotros.* Barcelona: L. Miracle, 1940, 1943. Buenos Aires: , 1940.

358 ——. *Das dumme Kind.* Dresden: Verlag am andern Ufer, 1926.

359 ——. *Eine Angstneurose und ihre Behandlung.* Leipzig: S. Hirzel, 1931.

360 ——. *Einführung in die Charakterkunde.* Leipzig: S. Hirzel, 1928, 1931, 1936, 1971.

361 ——. *Der Einzelunterricht für nervöse Kinder.* Z. Kinderforsch., 1926, 31, 480–491.

362 ——. *Eisagogi eis tin charaktirologian* [The work on character]. Translated by G. Karydi. Athens: Ekdotikon Ergastirion Graphikon Technon tis Christianikis Enoseos Ergazomenis Neolaios, 1960.

363 ——. *Entwurf eines Lehrplanes für die individualpsychologische Ausbildung der Lehrer und Soziolbeamten.* IZIP, 1926, 4(2), 57–68.

364 ——. Die geheime Distanz zwischen Mann und Frau. *IZIP*, 1925, 3(6), 269–286.

365 ——. *God helps those.* New York: Ives Washburn, 1931.

366 ——. *Die Grundbegriffe der Individualpsychologie und ihre Anwendung in der Erziehung.* Berlin: A. Hoffmans, 1927 (with Ruth Künkel).

367 ——. *Grundzüge der politischen Charakterkunde.* Berlin: Junker & Dünnhaupt, 1931.

368 ——. *Grundzüge der praktischen Seelenheilkunde.* Berlin: Junker & Dünnhaupt, 1934.

369 ——. *How character develops.* New York: Scribner's, 1940 (with R. E. Dickerson).

370 ——. *In search of maturity.* New York: Scribner, 1943.

371 ——. The integration of religion and psychology. *J. Psychother. rel. Proc.*, 1954, 1, 3–11.

372 **Künkel, F.** *Introducción a la caracterologia.* Edited by O. Brachfeld. Barcelona: Ed. Victoria, 1945; Barcelona: Condal,

373 ——. *Jugendcharakterkunde.* Meckl.-Schwer.: Bahn, 1932, 1967.

374 ——. Der Kampf um die Vererbung. *IZIP*, 1930, 8(3), 282–294.

375 ——. *Krisenbriefe (Die Beziehung zwischen Wirtschaftskrise und Charakterkrise).* Meckl.-Schwer.: Bahn, 1932, 1933.

376 ——. Die Kritik der Triebe. *IZIP*, 1927, 5(1), 19–34; 1927, 5(2), 97–112; 1927, 5(3), 207–224; 1927, 5(4), 292–304; 1927, 5(6) 458–467.

377 ——. *Let's be normal! The psychologist comes to his senses.* Translated by Eleanore Jensen. New York: Ives Washburn, 1929.

378 ——. *Mensch und Gemeinschaft.* Berlin: M. A. Hoffmans, 1927 (with Ruth Künkel).

379 ——. *My dear ego.* Boston: Pilgrim Press 1947, 1962.

380 ——. Neurasthenie und Hysterie. In E. Wexberg (Ed.), *Handbuch der Individualpsychologie.* Pp. 460–506.

381 ——. Die Rolle der seelischen Krise. *IZIP*, 1930, 8(1), 36–43.

382 ——. Self-review of *Charakter, Wachstum und Erziehung.* In *IZIP*, 1931, 9(4), 318–319.

383 ——. Sex and society. *J. abnorm. soc. Psychol.*, 1932–33, 27, 1–28.

384 ——. Über sexuelle Verirrungen (with O. Kaus). In E. Wexberg (Ed.), *Handbuch der Individualpsychologie.* Pp. 555–582.

385 ——. *Vitale Dialektik, theoretische Grundlagen der individualpsychologischen Charakterkunde.* Leipzig: S. Hirzel, 1929.

386 ——. Vorwort to N. Sylvus, *Herkologische Graphologie.*

387 ——. *What do you advise?* New York: Ives Washburn, 1946 (with Ruth Gardner).

388 ——. *What it means to grow up.* New York: Scribner, 1936.

389 ——. *Das Wir: Die Grundbegriffe der Wir-Psychologie.* Schwer.-Meckl.: Bahn, 1939, 1972.

390 **Künkel, Ruth.** Die Entwicklung des Säuglings und des Kleinkindes bis zur Aufnahme der Gemeinschaft. In Sofie Lazarsfeld (Ed.), *Technik der Erziehung.*

391 ——. *Die Grundbegriffe der Individualpsychologie und ihre Anwendung in der Erziehung.* Berlin: A. Hoffmans, 1927 (with F. Künkel).

392 **Künkel, Ruth** (Ed.). *Mensch und Gemeinschaft.* Berlin: M. A. Hoffmans, 1927 (with F. Künkel).

393 ———. Psychologie des Geschlechtsbeziehungen. In E. Wexberg (Ed.), *Handbuch der Individualpsychologie.* Pp. 114-133.

394 ———. Die Rolle der Sexualität in der Neurose. *IZIP,* 1926, 4(5), 277-282.

395 ———. Die Rolle des Trainings in der Entwicklungsgeschichte einer Konversionsneurose. *IZIP,* 1925, 3(3), 120-124.

396 ———. *Das sexuell Frühreife Kind.* Dresden: Verlag am andern Ufer, 1926.

397 ———. Die Strafe in der Erziehung. *IZIP,* 1924, 3(1), 33-38.

398 **Kunwald, Ella.** Review of Maria von Brissen, *Entwicklung der Musikalität in der Reifejahren.* Langensalza: Hermann Beyer u. Söhne, 1929. In *IZIP,* 1931, 9(3), 253.

399 **Kunz, B.** Professor Dr. Rudolf Dreikurs, 1897-1972. *OSIPNL,* 1972, 13(1), 12-13.

400 **Kunz, H.** Erwiderung auf A. Kronfelds "Zur Theorie der Individualpsychologie". *IZIP,* 1929, 7(5), 353-358.

401 ———. Rudolf Dreikurs, 1897-1972. *Schweiz. Lehrerzeit,* 1972, 25, 969.

402 **Kunzel, Helga.** Translator of W. Beecher & Marguerite Beecher, *Besser leben ohne Neid und Eifersucht.*

403 **Kuo, Y-Y.** Family constellation in the Chinese language. *JIP,* 1971, 27(2), 181-184.

404 ———. The renaissance of Adler's Individual Psychology. *Inst. Educ. Res. Letters* (Natl. Chengchi Univ.), Sept., 1970. Pp. 19-22.

405 **Kusano, S.** A sketch of the nervous temperament. *Jap. J. Psychol.,* 1940, 15, 331-341.

L

1 **L. R.** Review of A. Maeder, *Selbsterhaltung und Selbstheilung.* Zürich: Rascher, 1949. In *IZIP,* 1949, 18(3), 141-142.

2 ———. Review of E. Neumann, *Tiefenpsychologie und neue Ethik.* Zürich: Rascher, 1949. In *IZIP,* 1949, 18(3), 142-143.

3 **La Barba, R. C.** The psychopath and anxiety: A reformulation. *JIP,* 1965, 21, 167-170. Also in H. D. Werner (Ed.), *New understandings of human behavior.* Pp. 75-79.

4 **Ladell, R. G. M.** Medical psychology: Prewar, war time and post-war. *IPMP,* 1936, No. 16. Pp. 19-32.

5 ———. Place of psychology in the medical curriculum. *IPMP,* 1936, No. 16 (with W. Langdon-Brown, F. Gray, & F. G. Crookshank).

6 **Lakin, M.** Bias in psychotherapists of different orientation. *Amer. J. Psychother.,* 1958, 12, 79-86 (with B. Lebovits).

7 ———. Guilt and groups [Review of O. H. Mowrer, The new group therapy]. In *Contemp. Psychol.,* 1965, 10, 50-51.

8 **Lallus, J. F.** *Guidance: Theory and practice.* New York: American Book Co., 1964 (with F. N. Zeran & K. W. Wegner).

9 **Lambert, L. J.** Change: A result, not a target. *Texas Outlook,* July, 1970 (with E. J. Chambliss & J. W. Tidrow).

10 **Lambert, W.** (Ed.). *Handbook of personality theory.* Chicago: Rand McNally, 1968 (with E. Borgatta).

11 **Lamoreaux, R. R.** Avoidance conditioning and signal duration—a study of secondary motivation and reward. *Psychol. Monogr.,* 1942, 54, Whole No. 247 (with O. H. Mowrer).

12 ———. Fear as an intervening variable in avoidance conditioning. *J. comp. Psychol.,* 1946, 39, 29-50 (with O. H. Mowrer).

13 **Lamper, N.** Biography and photograph. *Voices,* 1966, 2(4), 60; 1967, 3(2), 114.

14 ———. Great God Pavlov. *Voices,* 1966, 2(4), 60-65.

15 ———. Growing pains. *Voices,* 1967, 3(2), 114-130.

16 ———. "The village idiot". *Voices,* 1971, 7, 66-77.

17 **Landfield, A. W.** Meaningfulness of personal versus common constructs. *JIP,* 1965, 21, 160-166 (with G. S. Isaacson).

18 ———. Reflexivity: An unfaced issue of psychology. *JIP,* 1962, 18, 114-124.

19 **Landsman, T.** Discussion of the papers by Patterson, Kilpatrick, Luchins and Jessor. *JIP,* 1961, 17, 39-42.

20 ———. Four phenomenologies. *JIP,* 1958, 14, 29-37.

21 ———. Review of A. W. Combs & D. Snygg, *Individual behavior.* In *JIP,* 1959, 15, 246-247.

22 Landsman, T. Review of A. E. Kuenzli, *The phenomenological problem.* In *JIP*, 1960, 16, 101.

23 Langdon-Brown, W. Adler's contribution to general medicine. *IPMP*, 1938, No. 19.

24 ———. Anorexia nervosa. *IPP*, 1931, No. 2 (with F. G. Crookshank, J. C. Young, G. Gordon, & C. M. Bevan-Brown).

25 ———. The birth of modern endocrinology: Inaugural address. *Proc. Royal Soc. Med.*, 1946, 39, 507-510.

26 ———. Early phases of medical psychology. *IPP*, 1943, No. 23. Pp. 9-11.

27 ———. Individual Psychology and psychosomatic disorders (I). *IPMP*, 1932, No. 4 (with O. H. Woodcock, J. C. Young, S. V. Pearson, M. B. Ray, M. Robb, & F. G. Crookshank).

28 ———. Place of psychology in the medical curriculum. *IPP*, 1936, No. 16 (with R. G. M. Ladell, F. Gray, & F. G. Crookshank).

29 ———. The place of psychology in the medical curriculum. *IPP*, 1936, No. 16. Pp. 7-19.

30 ———. The return to Aesculapius. *IPMP*, 1932, No. 4. Pp. 11-27.

31 Lange, B. The teaching of drawing as preparation of attitudes toward life. *IJIP*, 1935, 1(4), 67-72.

32 ———. Zur Psychologie des Zeichenunterrichts. *IZIP*, 1933, 11(4), 295-300.

33 Langer, Marianne. Das Kind im Spital. *IZIP*, 1931, 9(3), 243-251.

34 ———. Review of C. Bonheim, *Kinderpsychotherapie in der Praxis.* Berlin: Springer, [ ]. In *IZIP*, 1933, 11(1), 75-76.

35 ———. Review of R. Menzel & Rudolfine Menzel, *Wesenserprobung.* Selbstverlag, [ ]. In *IZIP*, 1930, 8(6), 598-599.

36 Langman, L. Adlerian thought in Asch's social psychology. *JIP*, 1960, 16, 137-145.

37 Langner, L. *The importance of wearing clothes.* New York: Hastings House, 1959.

38 Langs, R. Earliest memories and personality. *Arch. gen. Psychiat.*, 1965, 12, 379-390.

39 ———. First memories and characterologic diagnosis. *J. nerv. ment. Dis.*, 1965, 141, 318-320.

40 ———. *A manual for the scoring of earliest memories, revised.* New York: Albert Einstein Coll. Med., 1960 (with M. Reiser).

41 ———. A method for clinical and theoretical study of the earliest memory. *Arch. gen. Psychiat.*, 1960, 3, 523-534 (with M. B. Rothenberg, J. R. Fishman, & M. F. Reiser).

42 Langs, R. Stability of earliest memories under LSD-25 and placebo. *J. nerv. ment. Dis.*, 1967, 144, 171-184.

43 Lansky, L. M. The obviousness of two masculinity-femininity tests. *J. consult. clin. Psychol.*, 1968, 32(3), 314-318 (with V. J. Bieliauskas & S. B. Miranda).

44 Lapinsohn, L. The application of Individual Psychology to Psychosomatic medicine. *AJIP*, 1956, 12, 143-156.

45 ———. Review of H. P. Laughlin, *The neuroses in clinical practice.* Philadelphia: W. B. Saunders, 1956. In *JIP*, 1957, 13, 203.

46 La Porte, G. H. Editor of A. Adler, *Sex, personality and the Establishment.*

47 ———. Preface to A. Adler, *Sex, personality and the Establishment.* Pp. i-ii.

48 ———. Social interest in action: A report on one attempt to implement Adler's concept. *IP*, 1966, 4(1), 22-26.

49 Lapsley, J. N. Adler centennial. *Past. Psychol.*, 1970, 21(207), 5-6.

50 Larsen, R. P. *Studying effectively.* Stanford Cal.: Stanford Univ. Press, 1941, 1955, 1956 (with C. G. Wrenn).

51 Lashen, Marilyn. Order of birth as a determinant of personality and attitudinal characteristics. *J. soc. Psychol.*, 1963, 60, 221-230 (with H. Greenberg, Rosemarie Guerino, D. Mayer, & Dorothy Piskowsky).

52 Lasko, Joan. Parental behavior toward first and second children. *Genet. Psychol. Monogr.*, 1954, 48, 97-137.

53 Laskowitz, D. The adolescent drug addict: An Adlerian view. *JIP*, 1961, 17, 68-79.

54 ———. Drug addiction. In A. Nikelly (Ed.), *Techniques for behavior change.* Pp. 165-175.

55 Lasswell, H. D. Power and personality. *Psychol. Today*, 1968, 2(5), 64-67. Abridged from *Power and personality.*

56 ———. *Power and personality.* New York: Norton, 1948.

57 Laufketter, Sally. Is it more important to be wrong than right? *Couns. Interviewer*, 1969, 2(1), 48-49 (with G. McKay).

58 Lauterbach, C. G. Sibling patterns and social adjustment among normal and psychiatrically disturbed soldiers. *J. consult. Psychol.*, 1963, 27, 236-242 (with W. Vogel).

59 **Lautrup-Larsen, Nina.** Translator of R.
Dreikurs & L. Grey, *Demokrati og opdragelse.*

60 **Lavastine, L.** Introduction to A. Adler,
Sens de la vie.

61 **Lavender, A.** Editorial postscript on testing.
IP, 1967, 5, 14–16.

62 **la Viete, Ruth.** Day treatment center and
school: Seven years experience. *Amer. J.
Orthopsychiat.*, 1965, 15(1), 160–169
(with Ruth E. Ronall, Rosalyn Cohn, &
Renee Reens).

63 **Lawson, T. E.** *The Robinsons: Character
studies of a family in a nutshell.* London:
C. W. Daniel, 1932.

64 **Layton, F. G.** Individual Psychology and
practice (II). *IPMP*, No. 12 (with C. M.
Bevan-Brown, O. H. Woodcock, & F.
Marjory Edwards).

65 ———. Purpose and some neuroses. *IPMP*,
, No. 12.

66 **Lazarsfeld, P.** Hinter der Kulissen der
Schule. In Sofie Lazarsfeld (Ed.), *Technik
der Erziehung.*

67 ———. *The people's choice.* New York:
Duell, Sloan & Pearce, 1944 (with B.
Berelson & Hazel Gaudet).

68 ———. Das Weltbild des Jugendlichen
(with [   ] Reininger & M. Jahoda). In
Sofie Lazarsfeld (Ed.), *Technik der Erziehung.*

69 **Lazarsfeld, R.** Johannes Chrysostomus und
Olympias. *IZIP*, 1926, 4(1), 33–40.

70 ———. Mythos und Komplex. *IZIP*, 1930,
8(2), 261–263.

71 ———. Das Problem der Ambivalenz in
der Antiken Psychologie. *IZIP*, 1932, 10(2),
125–126.

72 ———. Review of R. Bechterew, *Allgemeine Grundlagen der Reflexologie des
Menschen.* Wien: Deuticke, 1926. In *IZIP*,
1927, 5(1), 77–78.

73 ———. Review of A. Lenz, *Grundriss der
Kriminalbiologie.* Berlin: Springer, [   ].
In *IZIP*, 1930, 8(2), 274–275.

74 ———. Zum Entwurf des österreichischen
Gesetzes über die Behandlung jugendlicher
Rechtsbrecher. *IZIP*, 1926, 4(4), 235–
237.

75 ———. Zur individualpsychologischen
Traumlehre. *IZIP*, 1930, 8(6), 587.

76 **Lazarsfeld, Sofie.** "L'age critique" est-il
un age critique? *Psyché* (Paris), 1954,
9, 152–163 (with Asya Kadis).

77 **Lazarsfeld, Sofie.** "Change of life"—end of
life? *JIP*, 1958, 14, 167–170 (with Asya
Kadis).

78 ———. Le coin du rire. *IPNL*, 1966, 17
(1–2, Whole No. 186–187). P. 6.

79 ———. The courage for imperfection. *New
Age* (London), 1927,   ; *JIP*, 1966, 22,
163–165.

80 ———. Dare to be less than perfect. *IJIP*,
1936, 2(2), 76–82.

81 ———. Did Oedipus have an Oedipus
complex? *Amer. J. Orthopsychiat.*, 1944,
14, 226–229. Also in K. A. Adler & Danica
Deutsch (Eds.), *Essays in Individual Psychology.* Pp. 118–125.

82 ———. Dreamlife and dream of life. *IPB*,
1949, 7, 87–93.

83 ———. Die Ehe von Heute und Morgen.
In A. Adler, L. Seif, & O. Kaus (Eds.),
Individuum und Gemeinschaft. Pp.
323–335.

84 ———. Erotischer Gedächtnis und erotische
Treue. *IZIP*, 1924, 3(1), 31–33.

85 ———. *Erziehung zur Ehe.* Vienna: M.
Perles, 1928.

86 ———. Familien oder Gemeinschaftserzie-
hung. In E. Wexberg (Ed.), *Handbuch der
Individualpsychologie.*

87 ———. The group as a therapeutic factor.
Nerv. Child, 1945, 4, 228–235 (with Asya
L. Kadis).

88 ———. Grundbegriffe der modernen Erziehung. In *Technik der Erziehung.*

89 ———. *Hur Kvinnan Upplever Mannen.*
Stockholm: Natur och Kultur, 1945.

90 ———. *Hvordan Kvinnen Opplever Mannen.* Oslo: Dreyer, 1947.

91 ———. Jarl Skules Weg zu Gott. *IZIP*,
1936, 14(3), 176–191.

92 ———. Kleist im Lichte der Individualpsychologie. In *Jahrbuch der Kleistgesell-
schaft.* Berlin: Weidemann, 1927.

93 ———. Kleists Pentisilea. *IZIP*, 1927,
5(6), 450–457.

94 ———. *Das lügenhafte Kind.* Dresden:
Am andern Ufer, 1927.

95 ———. *Maenniskan I Diktens Spegel.*
Stockholm: Natur och Kultur, 1950.

96 ———. Der Mut zur Unvollkommenheit.
IZIP, 1926, 4, 375–381.

97 ———. On social interest in psychotherapy.
JIP, 1961, 17, 181–183.

98 ———. Organ inferiority and crimin-
ality. *IPB*, 1944–45, 4, 88–90.

99 **Lazarsfeld, Sofie.** Pitfalls in psychotherapy. *AJIP*, 1952, 10, 20–26.

100 ———. The respective roles of earliest recollections and images. *Amer. J. Psychother.*, 1948, 2, 250–255 (with Asya L. Kadis).

101 ———. Review of Ada Beil, *Die unbekannte Männerseele.* Leipzig: S. Hirzel, 1927. In *IZIP*, 1927, 5(3), 238.

102 ———. Review of H. de Man, *Der Kampf um die Arbeitsfreude.* Jena: E. Diederichs, 1927. In *IZIP*, 1928, 6(5), 415.

103 ———. Review of A. Farau & H. Schaffer, *La psychologie des profondeurs, des origines à nos jours.* In *JIP*, 1960, 16, 218–219.

104 ———. Review of L. Rattner. *Individualpsychologische Berufsberatung.* In *AJIP*, 1954, 11, 90–91.

105 ———. Review of Sidonie Reiss, *Mental readjustment.* In *IPB*, 1950, 8, 73.

106 ———. Review of G. Robin, *Noel Mathias.* Paris: Ed. Kra, [   ]. In *IZIP*, 1931, 9(1), 77–78.

107 ———. Review of B. Springer, *Der Schlüssel zu Goethes Liebesleben.* Berlin: Nikolassee, [   ]. In *IZIP*, 1926, 4(6), 392–393.

108 ———. Review of Viktoria T. Wolf, *Eine Frau wie Du und Ich.* Dresden: Carl Keissner, [   ]. In *IZIP*, 1932, 10(6), 480–481.

109 ———. *Rhythm of life.* New York: Greenberg, 1934; London: Routledge & Kegan Paul, 1934.

110 ———. *Le rhythme de l'amour.* Paris: Editions de Paris, 1950.

111 ——— (Ed.). *Richtige Lebensführung.* Wien-Leipzig: M. Perles, 1926. Includes Sofie Lazarsfeld, Vom hauslichen Frieden; E. Wexberg, Seelische Entwicklungshemmungen; Margret Hilferding, Geburtenregelung; L. Stein, Die Sprache des Kindes und ihre Fehler; A. Adler, Liebesbeziehungen und deren Störungen; Martha Holub, Geschwisterkampf; Hilde Krampflitschek, Elternliebe; Anon., Aus der Schule geplaudert (von einem Lehrer); and Sofie Lazarsfeld, Sexuelle Erziehung.

112 ———. Sexual cases in child guidance clinics. *IJIP*, 1935, 1(4), 40–46.

113 ———. Sexual cases in child guidance clinics. In A. Adler & assoc., *Guiding the child.* Pp. 166–182.

114 **Lazarsfeld, Sofie.** Sexuelle Erziehung. In *Richtige Lebensführung.*

115 ———. Sexuelle Fälle in der Erziehungsberatung. *IZIP*, 1929, 7(3), 220–224.

116 ———. *Some Kvinden uplever Manden.* Copenhague: Reitzel, 1947.

117 ———. Sources of obstacles in the course of therapy. *AJIP*, 1956, 12, 136–156.

118 ——— (Ed.). *Technik der Erziehung.* Leipzig: S. Hirzel, 1928.

119 ———. Über Eheberatung. *IZIP*, 1930, 8(1), 160–164.

120 ———. The use of fiction in psychotherapy. *Amer. J. Psychother.*, 1949, 3, 26–33

121 ———. Vom hauslichen Frieden. In *Richtige Lebensführung.*

122 ———. *De vrouw en haar levengezel.* Amsterdam: G. W. Breughel, 1952, 1955; Antwerpen; Merten & Stappaets, 1952.

123 ———. War and peace between the sexes. *IPB*, 1947, 6, 74–79.

124 ———. *Wie die Frau den Mann erlebt.* Leipzig-Wien: Verlag f. Sexualwissenschaft, 1931.

125 ———. *Woman's experience of the male.* New York: Wehmann, 1938; London: Encyclopaedic Press, 1967.

126 ———. *Zehn Jahre Wiener Beratungsarbeit* Berlin: J. Springer, 1931.

127 ———. Zehn Jahre Wiener Beratungsstellen arbeit. *Z. Kinderforsch.*, 1931, 39, 68–80.

128 **Lazowick, L. M.** On the nature of identification. *J. abnorm. soc. Psychol.*, 1955, 51, 175–183.

129 **Leahy, A. M.** The effect of certain family relationships upon the development of personality. *J. genet. Psychol.*, 1927, 34, 45–72 (with F. L. Goodenough).

130 **Leahy, M. P.** Discussion of J. C. Young & F. G. Crookshank, The treatment of sexual incompetence by the methods of Individua Psychology. *IPMP*, 1932, No. 3. Pp. 50–52.

131 **Leary, T.** Interpersonal diagnosis: Some problems of methodology and validation. *J. abnorm. soc. Psychol.*, 1955, 50, 110–124 (with H. S. Coffey).

132 **Lebenstein, H.** Über die neuere Konstitutions-und Vererbungslehre. *IZIP*, 1926, 4(1), 17–22.

133 **Lebovic, S.** *Child guidance centers.* Geneva: World Health Org., 1960 (with D. Buckle).

134 **Lebovits, B.** Bias in psychotherapists of different orientation. *Amer. J. Psychother.*, 1958, 12, 79–86 (with M. Lakin).

135 **Lecky, P.** Review of J. B. Watson, *Die psychische Beeinflussung des Säuglings und des Kleinkindes.* New York: Norton, 1928. In *IZIP*, 1928, 6(6), 506–507.

136 ———. *Self-consistency.* New York: Island Press, 1945, 1951; New York: Doubleday Anchor Books, 1969. Paper.

137 **Lecomte Du Noüy, P.** *Human destiny.* New York: Longmans, Green, 1947.

138 **Ledermann, E. K.** Existentialism and psychiatry: Comment on the article by Frank Fish. *J. ment. Sci.*, 1962, 108, 525–527.

139 ———. *Philosophy and medicine.* London: Tavistock Publ., 1970.

140 ———. A review of the principles of Adlerian psychology. *Int. J. soc. Psychiat.*, 1956, 2(3), 172–184.

141 ———. Review of V. E. Frankl, *Das Menschenbild der Seelenheilkunde.* In *Int. J. soc. Psychiat.*, 1959, 5(2), 158–159.

142 ———. Review of H Häfner, *Schulderleben und Gewissen.* Stuttgart: Ernst Klett, 1956. In *Int. J. soc. Psychiat.*, 1957, 2(4), 314–315.

143 ———. Review of H. Meng (Ed.), *Psychohygienische Vorlesungen.* Basel: Benno Schwab, [   ]. In *Int. J. soc. Psychiat.*, 1960, 5(4), 315.

144 ———. Review of R. Meyer *et al., Essentials of pediatric psychiatry.* New York: Appleton-Century-Crofts, 1962. In *Int. J. soc. Psychiat.*, 1964, 10(4), 320.

145 **Lee, Joan C.** Forgetting of jokes: A function of repression? *JIP*, 1963, 19, 213–215 (with R. M. Griffith).

146 **Lee, Victoria.** Delinquent has no mind of his own. *New York World Telegram*, Feb. 21, 1958.

147 **Leeper, R. W.** Learning and the fields of perception, motivation, and personality. In S. Koch (Ed.), *Psychology: A study of a science.* Vol. 5. Pp. 365–487.

148 ———. What contributions might cognitive learning theory make to our understanding of personality? *J. Pers.*, 1953, 22, 32–40.

149 **Lees, J. P.** Family or sibship position and some aspects of juvenile delinquency. *Brit. J. Delinqu.*, 1954, 5, 46–65 (with L. J. Newson).

150 **Lefcourt, H. M.** Belief in personal control: Research and implications. *JIP*, 1966, 22, 185–195.

151 ———. Internal versus external control: A review. *Psychol. Bull.*, 1966, 65, 206–220.

152 **Lefton, M.** Decision-making in a mental hospital: Real, perceived, ideal. *Amer. sociol. Rev.*, 1959, 24, 822–829 (with S. Dinitz & B. Pasaminick).

153 **Lehrman, S. R.** Goals, procedures and achievements in clinic psychotherapy. *J. Mt. Sinai Hosp.*, 1951, 18, 221–227 (with Alexandra Adler, M. Schatner & F. Spiegel).

154 **Lehrmann, N. S.** After the fall the fall continues. *Reconstructionist*, 1964, 30(6), 20–26.

155 ———. Anti-therapeutic and anti-democratic aspects of Freudian dynamic psychiatry. *JIP*, 1963, 19, 167–181.

156 **Leifer, R.** Avoidance and mastery: An interactional view of phobias. *JIP*, 1966, 22, 80–93. Also in H. D. Werner (Ed.), *New understandings of human behavior.* Pp. 108–117.

157 ———. Review of E. Becker, *The revolution in psychiatry.* In *JIP*, 1966, 22, 132–133.

158 ———. Review of N. S. Greenfield & W. C. Lewis (Eds.), *Psychoanalysis and current biological thought.* Madison, Wis.: Univ. Wisconsin Press, 1965. In *JIP*, 1966, 22, 245–247.

159 **Leimert, Virginia.** [Community Child Guidance Centers]. *Chicago Daily News*, May 25–27, 1949.

160 **Leistner, Renée.** Die Grenzen der Methodik. *IZIP*, 1950, 19(4), 174–177 (with H. Branton).

161 **Leitner, H.** Über Musikbegabung. *IZIP*, 1927, 5(5), 379–383.

162 ———. Zur Theorie der kindlichen Haltung. *ZIP*, 1914, 1(2), 58–60.

163 **Le May, M. L.** Birth order and college misconduct. *JIP*, 1968, 24, 167–169.

164 ———. The uncontrollable nature of control groups. *J. couns. Psychol.*, 1968, 15, 63–67 (with O. C. Christensen, Jr.).

165 **Lemkin, Judith.** The child's differential perception of parental attributes. *J. abnorm. soc. Psychol.*, 1960, 61, 440–447 (with J. Kagan).

166 **Lenarduzzi, P.** Hallowed myths of juvenile delinquency. *OSIPNL*, 1971, 12(1), 6–7.

167 **Lennhoff, F. G.** Einige persönliche Erinnerungen an Alfred Adler. *Heilpädag. Werkbl.*, 1962, 31, 98–99.

168 **Lenzberg, K.** Concerning wit and humor. *IJIP*, 1937, 3(1), 81–87.

169 Lenzberg, K. Kunstler und Neurose. *IZIP*, 1927, 5(4), 263–272.

170 ———. Review of L. Frank, *Die psychokathartische Behandlung nervöser Störungen*. Leipzig: Georg Thieme, 1927. In *IZIP*, 1927, 5(6), 478.

171 ———. Review of H. Henning, *Psychologie der Gegenwart*. Berlin: Mauritius, 1925. In *IZIP*, 1927, 5(1), 76.

172 ———. Review of J. Neumann, *Das Gefühle und das Ich*. In *IZIP*, 1929, 7(1), 73.

173 ———. Review of E. Rignano, *Die Gestalttheorie*. Berlin: J. Springer, 1928. In *IZIP*, 1929, 7(5), 398.

174 ———. Review of G. A. Roemer, Atmung und musikalisches Erleben. *Psychol. u. Med.*, 1925, 1(1). In *IZIP*, 1927, 5(2), 156–157.

175 ———. Review of G. A. Roemer, Über die Auffindung des aktuellen Kernproblems einer Persönlichkeit durch die Tiefentestmethode. *Z. Menschenkunde*, 1925, 1(6). In *IZIP*, 1927, 5(1), 77.

176 ———. Review of E. Utitz (Ed.), *Jahrbuch der Charakterologie*. Berlin: Rolf Heise, 1927. In *IZIP*, 1928, 6(1), 75–76.

177 ———. Review of F. G. von Stockert, Kliniks und Ätiologie der Kontaktneurosen. *Klin. Wchnschr.*, 1929, 8. In *IZIP*, 1929, 7(5), 399.

178 ———. Review of A. A. Weinberg, Psyche und unwillkürliches Nervensystem. *Z. Neurol. Psychiat.* Vols. 85, 86, 93. In *IZIP*, 1927, 5(2), 156.

179 ———. Review of H. Werner, *Tagebuch eines alten Irrenarztes*. Lindenthal: Wellersberg-Verlag, 1928. In *IZIP*, 1931, 9(2), 159.

180 ———. Review of G. Zenker, *Traumdeutung und Traumforschung*. Leipzig: Astra-Verlag, 1928. In *IZIP*, 1931, 9(2), 159.

181 ———. Review of S. Zurukzoglu, *Biologische Probleme der Rassehygiene und die Kulturvölker*. München: J. F. Bergmann, 1925. In *IZIP*, 1928, 6(1), 78.

182 ———. Traumform und Traumsinn. *IZIP*, 1928, 6(3), 201–221.

183 ———. Über Konfliktneurosen. In *IZIP*, 1931, 9(2), 112–116.

184 ———. Über Witz und Humor. *IZIP*, 1930, 8(1), 188–194.

185 ———. Der vierte internationale Kongress für Individualpsychologie. *IZIP*, 1927, 5(5), 467–469.

186 Lenzberg, K. Der zweite allg. ärztliche Kongress für Psychotherapie. *IZIP*, 1927, 5(4), 308–309.

187 Leonard, Lynn. Review of J. A. Peterson, *Counseling and values: A philosophical examination*. In *JIP*, 1971, 27(1), 104–106

188 Leopold, H. S. (Ed.). *Sources of conflict in contemporary group therapy*. Basel: S. Karger, 1960 (with W. C. Hulse, Asya L. Kadis & A. Wolf).

189 Lepicard, Marie-Hélène. Ecole maternelle et prophylaxie mentale. *BISFPA*, 1970, No. 7. Pp. 19–21.

190 ———. Education du sens social à l'école maternelle. *BSFPA*, 1971, No. 10. Pp. 16–23.

191 ———. La structure du caracteré chez le jeune enfant. *BSFPA*, 1972, No. 13. Pp. 20–27.

192 Lerner, H. H. Group therapy, group work, and adult education. *J. soc. Issues*, 1952, 8(2), 3–10 (with H. C. Kelman).

193 ———. Methodological convergence and social action. *J. soc. Issues*, 1952, 8, 75–80.

194 ———. The next decade: The role of the students and alumni society of Alfred Adler Institute for Individual Psychology. In K. A. Adler & Danica Deutsch (Eds.), *Essays in Individual Psychology*. Pp. 460–464.

195 Lerner, M. J. Conformity as a function of birth order, payoff, and type of group pressure. *J. abnorm. soc. Psychol.*, 1964, 69, 318–323 (with S. W. Becker & J. Carroll).

196 Leschallier de l'Isle, Y. Translator of R. Dreikurs, *Le defi de l'enfant*.

197 Lessing, Elise F. Ordinal position and childhood psychopathology as evaluated from four perspectives. *Proc. 75th Ann. Conv. Amer. Psychol. Assn.*, 1967, 2, 179–180 (with M. Oberlander).

198 ———. Developmental study of ordinal position and personality adjustment of the child as evaluated by the California Test of Personality. *J. Pers.*, 1967, 35, 487–497 (with M. Oberlander).

199 Lester, D. Sibling position and suicidal behavior. *JIP*, 1966, 22, 204–207.

200 ———. Studies on death-attitude scales. *Psychol. Rep.*, 1969, 24, 182.

201 ———. Suicide and sibling position. *JIP*, 1970, 26(2), 203–204.

202 **Lester, J. T.** Stress: On Mount Everest. *Psychol. Today*, 1969, 3(4), 30–32, 62.

203 **Levine, D.** Rorschach genetic level and psychotic symptomatology. *J. clin. Psychol.*, 1960, 16, 164–167.

204 **Levinger, G.** Birth order and need for achievement. *Psychol. Rep.*, 1965, 16, 73–74 (with G. H. Walker).

205 ———. Complementarity in marital adjustment: Reconsidering Toman's family constellation hypothesis. *JIP*, 1965, 21, 137–144 (with M. Sonnheim).

206 ———. Note on need complementarity in marriage. *Psychol. Bull.*, 1964, 61, 153–157.

207 ———. Rejoinder. *JIP*, 1965, 21, 147–148.

208 ———. Task and social behavior in marriage. *Sociom.*, 1964, 27, 433–448.

209 **Levitt, L. P.** Introduction. *JIP*, 1972, 28 (2), 123–124.

210 **Levy, D. M.** "Individual Psychology" in a Vienna public school. *Soc. Serv. Rev.*, 1929, 3, 207–216.

211 ———. *Maternal overprotection.* New York: Norton, 1966.

212 **Levy, J.** Early memories. *Arch. gen. Psychiat.*, 1962, 7, 57–69 (with K. Grigg).

213 ———. A quantitative study of behavior problems in relation to family constellation. *Amer. J. Psychiat.*, 1930–31, 10, 637–654.

214 **Levy-Suhl, M.** Ein literarische Beitrag zur Kriegsneurosenfrage. *IZIP*, 1927, 5(4), 273.

215 **Lewin, K.** Behavior and development as a function of the total situation. In L. Carmichael, *Manual of child psychology.* Pp. 791–844.

216 ———. Patterns of aggressive behavior in experimentally created "social climates". *J. soc. Psychol.*, 1939, 10, 271–299 (with Rosemary Lippitt & R. K. White).

217 ———. Psychology of success and failure. *Occupations*, 1936, 14, 926–930.

218 **Lewis, Annabelle.** Developing social feeling in the young child through his play life. *IPB*, 1947, 6, 58–60.

219 **Lhermitte, J.** Introduction to Hertha Orgler, *Alfred Adler et son oeuvre.*

220 **Liberty, P. G., Jr.** Perceptual defense, dissimulation, and response styles. *J. consult. Psychol.*, 1964, 28, 529–535 (with C. E. Lunneborg & G. C. Atkinson).

221 **Lichtenberg, P.** Mutual achievement striving and social interest. *JIP*, 1963, 19, 148–160.

222 **Lichtenberger, A.** *La petite soeur de Trott.* Paris: Libraire Plan, 1898. Translated by Blanche & Irma Weill as *Trott and his little sister.* New York: Viking Press, 1931.

223 ———. *Mon petit Trott,* Translated by Blanche and Irma Weill. Paris: Libraire Plan, 1896.

224 **Lichtenwalner, J. S.** The relationship of birth order and socioeconomic status to the creativity of preschool children. *Child Developm.*, 1969, 40, 1241–1247.

225 **Lichtstein, R.** Translator, with B. Bodluck, of A. Adler, *Der zin fun leben.*

226 **Lickorish, J. R.** The casket scenes from The Merchant of Venice: Symbolism or life style. *JIP*, 1969, 25, 202–212.

227 **Liddell, Margaret.** Freddy Frog: A story for grades 1–4. *OSIPNL*, 1964, 5(1), 9–10.

228 **Lidrich, Pat.** Class council for first grade. *IPNL*, 1968, 18(9–10, Whole No. 206–207). P. 77.

229 ———. Class council for first grade. *OSIPNL*, 1968, 8(5), 8.

230 **Lidz, T.** The prediction of family interaction from a battery of projective techniques. *J. proj. Tech.*, 1957, 21, 199–208 (with Dorothy T. Sohler, J. D. Holzberg, S. Flack, Alice R. Cornelison & Eleanor Kay).

231 **Lieben, Beatrice.** Analysis of results of the Harris Tests of Hand Dominance used as group tests. Unpubl. M.S. Diss., City Coll. N. Y., 1951.

232 ———. Attitudes, platitudes and conferences in teacher-parent relations involving the child with a reading problem. *Elem. Sch. J.*, 1958, 58(5), 279–286.

233 ———. Does advice suffice? *Educ.*, 1959, 79(6), 1–8. Also in *Child Fam. Dig.*, Mar.-Apr., 1959 (with E. Shefrin).

234 ———. Individual differences in learning and retention. Unpubl. Ph.D. Diss., The New School, 1961.

235 ———. Reading disability and life style: A case. *JIP*, 1967, 23, 226–231.

236 ———. Ricky. *Psychol. Today*, 1969, 3(4), 16. Also in *JIP*, 1967, 23, 226–231.

237 **Lieber, L.** Farewell to Freud. *This Week Mag.*, Sept. 18, 1966. Pp. 4–5.

238 **Lieberman, Martha G.** Childhood memories as a projective technique. *J. proj. Tech.*, 1957, 21, 32–36.

239 **Lieberman, Nina J.** A developmental analysis of playfulness as a clue to

cognitive style. *J. creat. Behav.*, 1967, 1.

240 **Liebmann, A.** *Untersuchung und Behandlung geistig zurückgebliebener Kinder.* 3rd. ed. München: Reinhardt, 1970.

241 **Leibmann, Suzanne.** Alfred Adler Lebensdaten. *Schule u. Psychol.* (München), Dec., 1970.

242 ———. Auswahl individualpsychologischer Schriften. *Schule u. Psychol.* (München), Dec., 1970.

243 ———. Co-editor, with W. Metzger, of A. Liebmann, *Untersuchung und Behandlung geistig zurückgebliebener Kinder.*

244 ———. The founder of Individual Psychology. *A. J. R. Info.*, March, 1970.

245 ———. Individualpsychologische Arbeit mit gestörten Kindern. *Schule u. Psychol.* (München), 1970.

246 ———. Individualpsychologische Neurosenlehre in Stichworten. *Schule u. Psychol.* (München), Dec., 1970.

247 ———. Leben und Werke von Dr. med. Albert Liebmann. *Heilpädagog. Forsch.*, 1971, 3(1).

248 ———. On the 100th birthday of Alfred Adler. *Schule u. Psychol.*, (München), Dec., 1970.

249 ———. Review of W. Köhler, *Gestalt psychology.* In *IZIP*, 1933, 11(2), 157–158.

250 ———. Die Schriften von Alfred Adler. *Schule u. Psychol.* (München), Dec., 1970.

251 ———. Zur Theorie der Begabungs-und Eignungsprüfungen. *IZIP*, 1930, 8(2), 257–260.

252 **Limbrecht, R. E.** A new compensation system for counselors. *Concept*, 1959 (with R. J. Corsini).

253 **Lin, L-H.** Relationship between ordinal position and personality development: Part II. *Acta Psychol. Taiwanica*, 1966, 8, 29–37 (with J-H Ko).

254 **Lind, J. E.** Translator, with B. Glueck, of A. Adler, *The neurotic constitution.*

255 **Lindenfeld, Elda.** Adler's contribution to social adjustment. *IPB*, 1947, 6, 22–26 (with B. A. MacDonald).

256 ———. Kosmetik und Psychologie. *IZIP*, 1933, 11(1), 44–54.

257 ———. The lesson I learned in Nazi Austria. *Univ. Manitoba med. J.*, 1941, 13(2), 42–47.

258 **Lindgren, F.** (Ed.). *Current research in psychology: A book of readings.* New York Wiley, 1971 (with H. C. Lindgren & D. Byrne).

259 **Lindgren, H. C.** *Current research in psychology: A book of readings.* New York: Wiley, 1971 (with F. Lindgren & D. Byrne).

260 **Lindzey, G.** (Ed.). *The history of psychology in autobiography.* New York: Appleton Century-Crofts, 1972.

261 ———. *Theories of personality.* New York: Wiley, 1957 (with C. S. Hall).

262 ———. *Theories of personality: Primary sources and research.* New York: Wiley, 1965 (with C. S. Hall).

263 **Linn, E.** The boy who survived Auschwitz. *Saturday Evening Post*, April 11, 1964 (with E. Papanek).

264 ———. The wild ones. *Readers Digest*, Feb., 1958.

265 **Lint, F.** Der Kampf des Kindes gegen Autorität. In A. Adler & C. Furtmüller (Eds.), *Heilen und Bilden* (1914). Pp. 374–379; (1928). Pp. 175–179.

266 **Linton, J.** Translator, with R. Vaughan, of A. Adler, *Social interest.*

267 **Lippitt, Rosemary.** An experimental study of the effect of democratic and authoritarian group atmospheres. *Univ. Iowa Stud., Stud. Child Welfare*, 1940, 16, No. 3. Pp. 43–195.

268 ———. Patterns of aggressive behavior in experimentally created "social climates". *J. soc. Psychol.*, 1939, 10, 271–299 (with K. Lewin & R. K. White).

269 **Litwin, G. H.** Achievement motive and test anxiety conceived as motive to success and motive to avoid failure. *J. abnorm. soc. Psychol.*, 1960, 60, 52–63 (with J. Atkinson).

270 **Litzky, L.** Case study of Edna. *IP*, 1964, 2(2), 11–22.

271 **Liverant, S.** Review of D. H. Lawrence & L. Festinger, *Deterrents and reinforcements.* Stanford, Calif.: Stanford Univ. Press, 1962. In *JIP*, 1962, 18, 191–192.

272 **Livingston, W. K.** The concept of transaction in psychology and neurology. *JIP*, 1963, 19, 3–16 (with H. Cantril).

273 **Löbl, Henriette.** Die Entmutigung durch das Märchen. *IZIP*, 1930, 8(5), 531–532.

274 **Loeffler, F. J.** The co-therapist method: Special problems and

advantages. *Grp. Psychother.*, 1954, 6, 189–192 (with H. M. Weinstein).

75 **Loehlin, J. C.** Word meanings and self-descriptions. *J. abnorm. soc. Psychol.*, 1961, 62, 28–34.

76 **Loewenstein, J.** Asthma und Psychotherapie. *Med. Klin.*, 1926, 22, 994–997.

77 **Lohman, Joan J.** Children's reactions to stories depicting parent-child conflict situations. *Child Developm.*, 1952, 23, 61–74 (with H. A. Grace).

278 **Lohmeyer, G.** The upbringing of twins. *IJIP*, 1935, 1(2), 113–117.

279 ———. Zwillingserziehung. *IZIP*, 1931, 9(6), 461–465.

280 **Lombardi, D. N.** Differential responses of addicts and non-addicts on the MMPI. *J. proj. Tech.*, 1968, 32(5), 479–482 (with B. J. O'Brien & F. W. Isele).

281 ———. Factors affecting changes in attitudes toward Negroes among high school students. *J. Negro Educ.*, 1963 (Spring). *Diss. Abstr.*, 1962, 23, 4.

282 ———. First memories of drug addicts. *IP*, 1967, 5(1), 7–13 (with W. P. Angers).

283 ———. Heroin and God. *Cath. psychol. Rec.*, 1965, 3(1), 35–38 (with J. B. Di Peri).

284 ———. Peer group influence on attitude. *J. educ. Sociol.*, 1963, 36(7), 307–309.

285 ———. Personality characteristics of young male narcotic addicts. *J. consult. Psychol.*, 1967, 31, 536–538 (with Jeanne G. Gilbert).

286 ———. Self reliance and social cooperation. *J. drug Educ.*, 1971, 1(3), 279–284.

287 ———. The special language of the addict. *Past. Psychol.*, 1969, 20 (June), 51–52.

288 ———. What do you want to be when you grow up? *Child & Fam.*, 1966, 5, 29–31 (with V. J. Adesso).

289 ———. *You the counselor.* Newark, N. J.: Essex County Youth House, 1972.

290 ———. The young drug addict. *New Jersey educ. Rev.*, Feb., 1967 (with F. W. Isele).

291 **London, P.** Review of H. S. Sullivan, *The fusion of psychiatry and social sciences.* New York: Norton, 1964. In *JIP*, 1965, 21(2), 217–218.

292 **London Student.** On being taught Individual Psychology. *IPNL*, 1952, Whole No. 15–16. Pp. 5–6.

293 **Long, L. M. K.** Alfred Adler and Gordon W. Allport: A comparison of certain topics in personality theory. *AJIP*, 1952, 10, 43–53.

294 ———. Alfred Adler and the problem of the unconscious. *AJIP*, 1954, 11, 163–166.

295 **Longstreth, L. E.** Birth order and avoidance of dangerous activities. *Developm. Psychol.*, 1970, 2, 154.

296 **Looft, W. R.** Birth order, sex, and complexity-simplicity: An attempt at replication. *Percep. mot. Skills*, 1971, 32, 303–306 (with M. D. Baranowski).

297 **Lord, Mae M.** Activity and effect in early memories of adolescent boys. *J. Pers. Assess.*, 1971, 35, 448–456.

298 **Lossart, E.** Los sentimentos de inferioridad. *Boletin de Educ.* (Argentina), 1939, No. 20. Pp. 19–21.

299 **Louis, B.** Portrait. *IPNL*, 1971, 20(6), 111; 1972, 21(6), 112.

300 **Louis, V.** Adlerian point of view on health insurance. *AJIP*, 1956, 12, 59–62.

301 ———. *Charakter und seelische Leiden.* Solothurn, Switzerland: Konkordat Schweiz. Krankenkassen, 1961. Paper.

302 ———. *Einführung in die Individualpsychologie.* Bern-Stuttgart: Paul Haupt, 1969.

303 ———. Gruppendynamik als Faktor der Rehabilitationsbehandlung. *Praxis*, 1965, 55(1), 13–18.

304 ———. Das individualpsychologisch-therapeutische Gespräch. *Prax. Psychother.*, 1966, 11(5), 217–227.

305 ———. Obituary [Suzanne Rolo]. *JIP*, 1961, 17, 250.

306 ———. Portrait. *IPNL*, 1971, 20(6), 111; 1972, 21(6), 112.

307 ———. Preliminary report on the formation of an International Association of Adlerian (Individual) Psychology. *IPNL*, 1954, No. 38. Pp. 2–6 (with A. Müller & J. Bierer).

308 ———. Probleme der Prophylaxe sozialer und chronischer Krankheiten bei Jugendlichen. *Praxis*, 1958, 47(28), 899–901.

309 ———. Der Revierbegriff beim Menschen. *Praxis*, 1970, 59(3), 87–89.

310 ———. Review of M. Sperber, *Alfred Adler: Oder das Elend der Psychologie.* In *JIP*, 1970, 26, 228–230.

311 ———. Vergleich der Belastung in der sozialen Krankenversicherung durch schweizerische und ausländische Arbeiter. *Praxis*, 1966, 55(1), 13–18.

312 Lovell, L. L. *Parent Practices Research Scale.* Iowa City: St. Univ. Iowa, 1956 (with J. G. Chantiny & B. R. McCandless).

313 Lowe, C. M. The self-concept: Fact or artifact? *Psychol. Bull.*, 1961, 58, 325–336.

314 ———. Values versus sickness in the mental health field. *JIP*, 1964, 20, 196–201.

315 Lowe, R. N. (Ed.). *Adlerian family counseling.* Eugene, Ore.: Univ. Oregon Press, 1959 (with R. Dreikurs, R. J. Corsini & M. Sonstegard).

316 ———. Family counseling and socio-emotional problems. In J. S. Roucek, *The difficult child.* New York: Phil. Libr., 1964.

317 ———. Goal recognition. In A. Nikelly (Ed.), *Techniques for behavior change.* Pp. 65–75.

318 ———. Parent education. In F. N. Zeran, J. F. Lallus & K. Wegner (Eds.), *Guidance: Theory and practice.* Ch. 12.

319 ———. Parent-teacher education and child development. *Educ.*, 1960, 81, 28–31.

320 ———. Parent-teacher education through family counseling. *Fam. Life Coordinator*, 1962, 2, 87–90.

321 ———. Portrait. In K. Stokes, *Mommy's Mad.*

322 ———. Pupil personnel services. In F. N. Zeran, J. F. Lallus & K. Wegner (Eds.), *Guidance: Theory and practice.* Ch. 5.

323 ———. *A rationale and model for organizing and administering programs of pupil personnel services.* Eugene, Ore.: Ore. Univ. Press, 1962.

324 ———. Review of D. Dinkmeyer & R. Dreikurs, *Encouraging children to learn.* In *JIP*, 1963, 19, 241–242.

325 ———. Review of O. Spiel, *Discipline without punishment.* In *JIP*, 1962, 18, 192–193. Also in *OSIPNL*, 1962, 3(2), 3.

326 ———. Sense and nonsense about raising children. *Ore. Parent Teacher Bull.*, Dec. 1956–Jan. 1957, 37(4–9).

327 ———. Teacher education through child guidance centers. In R. Dreikurs, R. Corsini, R. Lowe & M. Sonstegard (Eds.), *Adlerian family counseling.* Pp. 87–100.

328 ———. What are the factors in effective pedagogy? *Trans. Amer. Acad. Ophthalmol. Otolaryngol.*, Nov.-Dec., 1959.

329 Lowe, W. L. Group beliefs and socio-economic factors in religious delusions. *J. soc. Psychol.*, 1954, 40, 267–274.

330 Lowe, W. L. Psychodynamics in religious delusions and hallucinations. *Amer. J. Psychother.*, 1953, 7, 454–462.

331 ———. Value systems in the psychotherape process. *Int. Rec. Med. & Gen. Prac. Clin.* 1955, 168, . Also in K. A. Adler & Danica Deutsch (Eds.), *Essays in Individu Psychology.* Pp. 125–132.

332 Löwenstein, E. Self-review of *Nervöse Leute.* Leipzig: Kurt Wolff, 1914. In *ZIP*, 1914, 1(3), 91–92.

333 Löwy, Ida. Aus der Praxis der Beratungsstellen. In Sofie Lazarsfeld (Ed.), *Technik der Erziehung.*

334 ———. Bekenntnis. *IZIP*, 1930, 8(2), 21(218.

335 ———. Du und dein Kind. In J. Neumann (Ed.), *Du und der Alltag.*

336 ———. Dummheit als Enthebungsmittel. *IZIP*, 1930, 8(5), 478–486.

337 ———. Eindrücke beim Jugendricht. *IZIP*, 1931, 9(5), 369–370.

338 ———. Individualpsychologische Erziehun, *IZIP*, 1925, 3(3), 129–132.

339 ———. Irrtumer der Erziehung. In E. Wex berg (Ed.), *Handbuch der Individualpsychologie.* Pp. 276–288.

340 ———. Das Kleinkind in der Erziehungsbe ratung. *IZIP*, 1929, 7(3), 218–220.

341 ———. Kränkung und Verwahrlosung. In A. Adler & C. Furtmüller (Eds.), *Heilen und Bilden* (1928). Pp. 145–149.

342 ———. Portrait. *IPNL*, 1971, 20(6), 109.

343 ———. Review of P. Oestreich, *Strafanstalt oder Lebensschule.* Karlsruhe: G. Braun, [ ]. In *IZIP*, 1925, 3(3), 139.

344 ———. Small children in guidance clinics. In A. Adler & assoc., *Guiding the child.* Pp. 157–165.

345 ———. Stupidity as exemption. *IJIP*, 1935 1(1), 102–110.

346 ———. "Und was haben Sie dazu, damit es besser wird?" *IZIP*, 1937, 15(3–4), 167–168.

347 Lu, Y. Mother-child role relationships in schizophrenia: A comparison of schizophrenic patients with non-schizophrenic siblings. *Psychiat.*, 1961, 24, 133–142.

348 ———. Parent-child relationship and marital role. *Amer. sociol. Rev.*, 1952, 17, 357–361.

349 ———. Parental role and parent-child relationship. *Marr. Fam. Living*, 1952, 14, 294–297.

50 Lubner, S. H. The parent-child relation. *IPMP*, 1937, No. 17 (with H. G. Baynes, S. Crown, A. AC. Court, M. Marcus & F. G. Crookshank).

51 ———. Psychotherapy in general practice. *IPMP*, 1937, No. 17. Pp. 34-39.

52 Luchins, A. S. *Group therapy: A guide.* New York: Random House, 1964. Paper.

53 ———. Some aspects of Wertheimer's approach to personality. *JIP*, 1961, 17, 20-26.

54 Ludwig, A. M. Weapons of insanity. *Amer. J. Psychother.*, 1967, 21, 737-749 (with F. Farrelly).

55 Luff, Mary C. Individual Psychology and sexual difficulties (I). *IPP*, 1932, No. 3 (with A. Adler, R. Dreikurs, E. Wexberg, Adele Hervat, J. C. Young, F. G. Crookshank & others).

356 ———. Report of a case of obsessional neurosis closely allied to schizophreniá. *IPP*, 1932, No. 3. Pp. 54-66.

357 Lundin, W. H. Objective appraisal of textbook mediated group psychotherapy with psychotics. *Int. J. grp. Psychother.*, 1952, 3, 116-126 (with J. W. Klapman).

358 ———. Use of co-therapists in group psychotherapy. *J. consult. Psychol.*, 1952, 16, 76-80 (with B. M. Aronov).

359 Lunneborg, C. E. Perceptual defense, dissimulation, and response styles. *J. consult. Psychol.*, 1964, 28, 529-535 (with P. G. Liberty, Jr. & G. C. Atkinson).

360 Lunneborg, Patricia. Birth order, aptitude and achievement. *J. consult. clin. Psychol.*, 1968, 32, 101.

361 ———. Birth order and sex of sibling effects on intellectual abilities. *J. consult. Psychol.*, 1971, 37, 445.

362 Lüps, A. Co-editor of L. Seif, *Wege der Erziehungshilfe.* 2nd. ed.

363 Lüps, Frau. Portrait. *IPNL*, 1972, 21(6), 109.

364 Luquet, J. Les caractères dans le théâtre de Molière. *BSFPA*, 1972, No. 14. Pp. 30-34.

365 Lüttich, R. Review of H. R. G. Günther, *Jung-Stilling.* München: E. Reinhardt, 1928. In *IZIP*, 1929, 7(2), 158-159.

366 Lynn, D. B. A note on sex differences in the development of masculine and feminine identification. *Psychol. Rev.*, 1959, 66, 126-135.

367 Lynn, D. B. Personal philosophies in psychotherapy. *JIP*, 1961, 17, 49-55.

368 Lyons, J. Heidegger, Adler, and the paradox of fame. *JIP*, 1961, 17, 149-161.

369 ———. Review of M. Heidegger, *Essays in metaphysics.* New York: Phil. Libr., 1960. In *JIP*, 1961, 17, 120.

370 ———. Review of S. Kierkegaard, *The diary of Soren Kierkegaard.* New York: Phil. Libr., 1960. In *JIP*, 1961, 17, 119.

371 Lyssons, A. M. Sex, birth order and volunteering behavior. *Austral. J. Psychol.*, 1966, 18, 158-159 (with P. R. Wilson & J. R. Patterson).

M

1 M. B. Review of Alexandra David-Neel, *Mönche und Strauchritter.* Leipzig: F. A. Brockhaus, [   ]. In *IZIP*, 1935, 13(1), 59-60.

2 M. E. Dr. Alfred Adler (1870-1970). *Morley Mag.*, 1970, 75 (with T. T.).

3 Mabry, J. Review of H. W. Dunham, *Community and schizophrenia.* Detroit: Wayne St. Univ. Press, 1965. In *JIP*, 1966, 22, 249-250.

4 MacArthur, C. Personalities of first and second children. *Psychiat.*, 1956, 19, 47-54.

5 Macchitelli, F. J. Alcoholism and ethical risk taking. *Quart. J. Studies in Alcohol*, 1971, 32(3), 775-781 (with F. Krauss & G. J. Mozdzierz).

6 ———. Botulinum toxin, type A: Effects on central nervous system. *Science*, 1965, 147, 1036-1037 (with E. Polley, J. A. Vick, H. P. Cinchta, D. Fischetti & N. Montanarelli).

7 ———. Changes in behavior and electrocortical activity in the monkey following administration of 5-hydroxytryptophan (5-HTP). *Psychopharmacol.*, 1966, 9, 444-456.

8 ———. Negative ion preference in "old" rats. *Psychol. Rep.*, 1963, 12, 439-440 (with R. Maier & J. Oriessen).

9 ———. A simple chronic cortical electrode for the monkey. *J. exp. Anal. Behav.*, 1965, 8, 436 (with N. Montanarelli).

10 ———. Temperament characteristics of chronic alcoholics as measured by the

Guilford-Zimmerman Temperament Survey. *J. gen. Psychol.*, 1971, 79, 97–102 (with G. J. Mozdzierz, L. Flaherty, & R. deVito).

11 MacDonald, B. A. Adler's contribution to social adjustment. *IPB*, 1947, 6, 22–26 (with Elda Lindenfeld).

12 Mackler, B. An assessment of sensory style. *Percep. mot. Skills*, 1964, 18, 841–848 (with F. C. Shontz).

13 ———. Black on white or white on black: Harlem and white professionals. *Prof. Psychol.*, 1971, 2(3), 247–250.

14 ———. Children should be seen and not heard. In A. Rubenstein (Ed.), Crisis in the New York schools. *New York Monthly Rev.*, 1970.

15 ———. Cultural deprivation: A study in mythology. *Teachers Coll. Rec.*, 1965, 66, 606–613 (with M. G. Giddings).

16 ———. Life style and creativity: An empirical investigation. *Percep. mot. Skills*, 1965, 20, 873–896 (with F. C. Shontz).

17 ———. *The little black school house.* New York: Atheneum, 1970.

18 ———. On being human. *J. Existent.*, 1964, 17, 67–76 (with E. A. Dreyfus).

19 ———. Review of U. Bronfenbrenner, *The worlds of childhood: U.S. and U.S.S.R.* New York: Russell Sage Foundation, 1970. In *JIP*, 1971, 27(1), 106–107.

20 ———. Review of E. H. Erickson, *Childhood and society.* New York: Norton, 1963. In *JIP*, 1964, 20(1), 110.

21 MacLean, G. D. Behavioral bibliotherapy: A simple home remedy for fears. *Psychother.*, 1970, 7(2), 118–119 (with R. W. Graff).

22 MacLeod, R. B. The phenomenological approach to social psychology. *Psychol. Rev.*, 1947, 54, 193–210.

23 ———. The place of phenomenological analysis in social psychological theory. In J. H. Rohrer & M. Sherif (Eds.), *Social psychology at the crossroads.* Pp. 215–241.

24 ———. Teleology and theory of human behavior. *Science*, 1957, 125, 477–480.

25 Macmurray, J. A philosopher looks at psychotherapy. *IPP*, 1938, No. 20. Pp. 9–22.

26 Maddi, S. R. Alfred Adler and the fulfillment model of personality theorizing. *JIP*, 1970, 26(2), 153–160.

27 Maddi, S. R. *Personality theories: A comparative analysis.* Homewood, Ill.: Dorsey, 1968.

28 ——— (Ed.). *Perspectives on personality: A comparative approach.* Boston: Little, Brown, 1970.

29 Madsen, M. C. Cooperation and competition of Mexican, Mexican-American, and Anglo-American children of two ages under four instructional sets. *Developm. Psychol.*, 1971, 5, 32–39 (with S. Kagan).

30 ———. Cooperative and competitive behavior of Kibbutz and urban children in Israel. *Child Developm.*, 1969, 40, 609–617 (with Ariella Shapira).

31 ———. Cooperative and competitive behavior of urban Afro-American, Anglo-American and Mexican village children. *Developm. Psychol.*, 1970, 3, 16–20 (with Ariella Shapira).

32 ———. Cooperative and competitive motivation of children in three Mexican subcultures. *Psychol. Rep.*, 1967, 20(3), 1307–1320.

33 Magary, J. (Ed.). *School psychological services in theory and practice.* Englewood Cliffs, N. J.: Prentice-Hall, 1967.

34 Magruder, W. W. *Folie à deux* in identical twins treated with electroshock therapy. *J. nerv. ment. Dis.*, 1946, 103, 181–186.

35 Maher, B. A. Effect of construct type on recall. *JIP*, 1962, 18, 177–179 (with E. K. Renner).

36 ———. The efficacy of brief clinical precedures in alleviating children's behavior problems. *JIP*, 1961, 17, 205–211 (with W. Katkovsky).

37 ———. (Ed.). *Progress in experimental personality research.* New York: Academic Press, 1964 (Vol. 1); 1965 (Vol. II); 1967 (Vol. IV).

38 Mahler, Wera. *Psikhologia.* 2 vols. Tel Aviv: Mifaley Tarbut Vechinuch, 1967.

39 Maholick, L. T. The case for Frankl's "will to meaning". *J. existent. Psychiat.*, 1963, 4, 43–48 (with J. C. Crumbaugh).

40 ———. An experimental study in existentialism: The psychometric approach to Frankl's concept of *noogenic* neurosis. *J. clin. Psychol.*, 1964, 20, 200–207.

41 Mahrer, A. R. (Ed.). *Goals in psychotherapy.* New York: Appleton-Century-Crofts, 1967.

42 ———. Interpretation of patient behavior through goals, feelings, and context. *JIP*, 1970, 26(2), 186–195.

43 Mairet, P. *ABC of Adler's psychology.* London: Kegan Paul, Trench, Trubner, 1928; New York: Greenberg, 1929.

44 ——— (Ed.). *Christian essays in psychiatry.* New York: Phil. Libr., 1956.

45 ———. The contributions of Alfred Adler to psychological medicine. *IPMP*, 1938, No. 19.

46 ———. Editor of A. Adler, *Problems of neurosis.*

47 ———. Hamlet der Neurotiker. *IZIP*, 1931, 9(6), 424–437.

48 ———. Hamlet as study in Individual Psychology. *JIP*, 1969, 25, 71–88.

49 ———. A note on the author and his work. In A. Adler, *The science of living* (1929). Pp. 9–30.

50 ———. Preface to A. Adler, *The science of living.*

51 ———. Presuppositions of psychological analysis. In *Christian essays in psychiatry.* Pp. 40–73.

52 ———. Review of F. Alexander. *The medical value of psychoanalysis.* New York: Norton, 1932. In *IPMP*, 1933, No. 8. Pp. 57–58.

53 ———. Translator of Madelaine Ganz, *The psychology of Alfred Adler and the development of the child.*

54 Majumdar, K. An experimental study of the relative influence of reward and punishment on learning. *Indian J. Psychol.*, 1951, 26, 67–72.

55 Malamud, D. I. Difference in the early childhood memories of authoritarian and non-authoritarian personalities. Unpubl. Ph.D. Diss., New York Univ., 1956.

56 ———. Toward self-understanding: A new approach in mental health education. In K. Adler and Danica Deutsch (Eds.), *Essays in Individual Psychology.* Pp. 264–268.

57 ———. The use of early recollections as a teaching device. *Teaching Psychol. Nwsltr.*, Skidmore, Coll., June 1969. Pp. 8–10.

58 Maller, J. B. Size of family and personality of offspring. *J. soc. Psychol.*, 1931, 2, 3–27.

59 Malleson, N. Panic and phobia: A possible method of treatment. *Lancet*, 1959, No. 7066. Pp. 225–227.

60 Maltz, M. *New faces—new futures: Rebuilding character with plastic surgery.* Introduction by A. Adler. New York: R. R. Smith, 1936.

61 ———. *Psycho-cybernetics.* New York: Prentice-Hall, 1960. New York: Pocket Books, 1969. Paper.

62 Manaster, G. [Letter on college activists and internal-external control]. *Psychol. Today*, 1971, 5(4), 4 (with D. A. Kleber).

63 ———. *Problems and methods of cross-national research.* New York: Houghton-Mifflin, 1970 (with R. Havighurst).

64 ———. Traditionalism and risk-taking in Puerto Rican adolescents. *Proc. Inter-American Psychol. Congr.*, April, 1969.

65 Mandell, Sibyl. Adleriana. *IPN*, 1941, 1(5), 5.

66 ———. Adler's contribution to the varying functions of a psychologist. *IPB*, 1947, 6, 65–68.

67 ———. Drei Fälle aus der Praxis. *IZIP*, 1928, 5.

68 ———. The future progress of Individual Psychology. *IPB*, 1942, 2(3), 55–56.

69 ———. Individualpsychologische Behandlung von Sprachfehlern. *IZIP*, 1933, 12(6), 409–416.

70 ———. Individual Psychology in the high school. *IJIP*, 1937, 3(3), 263–271.

71 ———. An only girl among brothers. *IPB*, 1942, 2(2), 25–31.

72 ———. The orientation of Individual Psychology as applied to the reading of a case study in criminal psycho-pathology. *IPB*, 1944–45, 4, 104–109.

73 ———. The persistence of the individual life pattern in war psychoses. *IPB*, 1944–45, 4, 9–19.

74 ———. The process of identification in the Adlerian sense, as used in interviewing in a public health setting. *AJIP*, 1954, 11, 47–59. Also in K. A. Adler and Danica Deutsch (Eds.), *Essays in Individual Psychology.* Pp. 216–231.

75 ———. Die Psychologie des Stotterns. *IZIP*, 1930, 8(4), 369–375.

76 ———. Review of J. M. Fletcher, *The problem of stuttering.* New York: Longmans, Green, 1928. In *IZIP*, 1930, 8(3), 359.

77 ———. Review of S. Huddleston, *Louis XIV in love and in war.* New York: Harper, 1929. In *IZIP*, 1929, 7(5), 478.

78 Mandell, Sibyl. Review of D. M. Levy, *Finger sucking and accessory movements in early infancy. Amer. J. Psychiat.,* May, 1928. In *IZIP,* 1928, 6(5), 418-419.

79 ———. Review of P. Mairet, *ABC of Adler's Psychology.* In *IZIP,* 1928, 6(5), 418.

80 ———. Review of I. S. Wile, *Schwierigkeiten im Verhalten der Kinder.* New York: Nat. Comm. Ment. Hyg., 1927. In *IZIP,* 1928, 6(6), 507.

81 ———. School problems and the family constellation. *IJIP,* 1936, 2(3), 83-94.

82 ———. Wo Tugend Laster ist. *IZIP,* 1929, 7(6), 472-473.

83 Marais, D. C. A tribute. *IZIP,* 1923, 2(2), 28-30.

84 Marcinowski, J. Die erotischen Quellen der Minderwertigkeitsgefühle. *Z. Sex. Wissensch.,* 1918, 4, Nos. 11 & 12.

85 Marcus, M. Individual Psychology and psychosomatic disorders (II). *IPP,* 1933, No. 9 (with J. S. Fairbairn, W. M. Eccles, Mary B. Ferguson & F. G. Crookshank).

86 ———. The parent-child relation. *IPMP,* 1937, No. 17 (with H. G. Baynes, S. Crown, S. H. Lubner, A. C. Court & F. G. Crookshank).

87 ———. Psychological investigation in general medicine. *IPMP,* 1933, No. 9. Pp. 37-41.

88 ———. Psychotherapy in general practice. *IPP,* 1937, No. 17. Pp. 42-46.

89 ———. Review of W. B. Wolfe, *How to be happy though human.* In *IPMP,* 1932, No. 5. Pp. 59-60.

90 ———. Translator of A. Adler, Sexual perversions.

91 Marcuse, F. L. (Ed.). *Areas of psychology.* New York: Harper, 1954.

92 Marcuse, M. (Ed.). *Verhandlung I. Int. Kongr. Sex. Forschung, Berlin, 1926.* Berlin-Köln: Marcus & Webers, 1928.

93 Margetts, E. L. The concept of the unconscious in the history of medical psychology. *Psychiat. Quart.,* 1953, 27, 115-138.

94 Margolis, M. The mother-child relationship in bronchial asthma. *J. abnorm. soc. Psychol.,* 1961, 63, 360-367.

95 Marketou, S. G. Translator of E. Wexberg, *Ergasia kai Koinonia.*

96 ———. Translator of E. Wexberg, *Nevrika Paidia.*

97 Markin, R. J. Consumer motivation and behavior: Essence vs. Existence. *Business & Society,* 1970, 2, 30-36.

98 Marko, J. [Family and adjustment of children to school]. *Psychol. Patapsychol. Dietata,* 1967-1968, 3, 519-533.

99 Markowitz, M. Group psychotherapy (with Asya Kadis). In D. Brower & L. E. Abt (Eds.), *Progress in clinical psychology.* Vol. 3. New York: Grune & Stratton, 1958. Pp. 154-183.

100 ———. Parental interaction as a determining factor in social growth of the individual. *Int. J. soc. Psychiat.,* Spec. Ed. 2, 81-89 (with Asya Kadis).

101 Marks, P. A. *Actuarial description of abnormal personality.* Baltimore: Williams and Wilkins, 1963 (with W. Seeman).

102 Marley, H. Beginnings in America. In R. Dreikurs, R. Corsini, R. Lowe & M. Sonstegard (Eds.), *Adlerian family counseling.* Pp. 7-16.

103 ———. Three psychological imperatives. *IP,* 1969, 6(1), 18-22.

104 ———. When humanism becomes a religion. *Humanist,* 1944 (Spring), 24-26.

105 Marmor, J. The feeling of superiority: An occupational hazard in the practice of psychotherapy. *Amer. J. Psychiat.,* 1953, 110, 370-376.

106 ———. Holistic conception and points of mild issue. *JIP,* 1972, 28(2), 153-154.

107 ——— (Ed.). *Modern psychoanalysis: New directions and perspectives.* New York: Basic Books, 1968.

108 ———. Psychoanalytic therapy as an education process: Common denominators in the therapeutic approaches of different psychoanalytic "schools". *Sci. & Psychoanal.,* 1962, 5, 286-299.

109 Marratt, H. Humanism and Christianity (with J. Hemming). In *Let's teach them right.* London: Pemberton, 1969.

110 Marriott, Anne. Search. *IPNL,* 1972, 21(6), 103.

111 Marsten, B. H. Specificity of attitudes toward paternal and non-parental authority figures. *JIP,* 1961, 17, 96-101 (with J. C. Coleman).

112 Marti-Ibanez, F. Individual Psychologist. *MD,* 1970, 14(2), 185-190 (with K. A. Adler).

113 Martin, R. M. Review of H. J. Eysenck (Ed.), *Handbook of abnormal* *psychology.* New York: Basic Books, 1961. In *JIP*, 1961, 17, 120.

114 **Marty, J.** Translator of A. Adler, *Connaissance de l'homme.*

115 **Marx, A. M.** Vertaald. In Sidonie Reiss, *Levenskoers en Levensverniewing.*

116 **Marx, Beatrice.** Conflicting schools of analysis. *IZIP*, 1927, 5(3), 180-186.

117 ———. Individual Psychology in America. *IZIP*, 1927, 5, xx-xxi.

118 **Masling, J.** Birth order and the need for affiliation. *Psychol. Rep.*, 1965, 16, 631-632.

119 ———. Relationships of oral imagery to yielding behavior and birth order. *J. consult. clin. Psychol.*, 1968, 32, 89-91 (with Lillie Weiss & B. Rothschild).

120 **Maslow, A. H.** Critique of self-actualization. I. Some dangers of being-cognition. *JIP*, 1959, 15, 24-32.

121 ———. Deficiency motivation and growth motivation. In M. R. Jones (Ed.), *Nebraska symposium on motivation: 1955.* Lincoln, Nebr.: Univ. Nebraska Press, 1955. Pp. 1-30.

122 ———. Emotional blocks to creativity. *JIP*, 1958, 14, 51-56.

123 ———. Higher needs and personality. *Dialectica*, 1951, 5, 257-265.

124 ———. Holistic emphasis. [Tribute to Alfred Adler on his 100th birthday]. *JIP*, 1970, 26(2), 13.

125 ———. Individual Psychology and the social behavior of monkeys and apes. *IJIP*, 1935, 1(4), 47-59.

126 ———. *Eupsychian management: A journal.* Homewood, Ill.: R. D. Irwin and Dorsey Press, 1965.

127 ———. *Motivation and personality.* New York: Harper, 1954.

128 ———. Neurosis as a failure of personal growth. *Humanitas*, 1967, 3, 153-169.

129 ———. Das soziale Verhalten der niedern und höheren Affen. *IZIP*, 1936, 14(1), 14-25.

130 ———. Synergy in the society and in the individual. *JIP*, 1964, 20, 153-164. Also in *Humanitas*, 1965, 1, 161-173.

131 ———. A theory of metamotivation: The biological rooting of the value-life. *J. humanist. Psychol.*, 1967, 7, 93-127.

132 ———. *Toward a psychology of being.* Princeton, N. J.: Van Nostrand, 1962.

133 **Maslow, A. H.** Was Adler a disciple of Freud? A note. *JIP*, 1962, 18, 125.

134 **Massarik, F.** Review of R. J. Corsini, M. E. Shaw, & R. R. Blake, *Roleplaying in business and industry.* In *Contemp. Psychol.*, 1964, 9, 54-55.

135 **Masserman, J. H.** "Altruistic" behavior in rhesus monkeys. *Amer. J. Psychiat.*, 1964, 21, 584-585 (with S. Wechkin & W. Terris).

136 ———. (Ed.). *Current psychiatric therapies.* New York: Grune & Stratton. Vol. 2, 1962; Vol. 5, 1965.

137 ———. (Ed.). *Science and psychoanalysis.* Vol. 8. New York: Grune & Stratton, 1965.

138 ——— (Ed.). *Science and psychoanalysis.* Vol. 20. *The dynamics of power.* New York: Grune & Stratton, 1972. Pp. 53-63.

139 **Masters, Yvonne J.** Selection and engagement of patients in family therapy. *Amer. J. Orthopsychiat.*, 1968, 38(4), 715-723 (with Ruth Ronall, C. J. Sager & W. G. Norman).

140 **Masterson, M. L.** Family structure variables and need approval. *J. consult. clin. Psychol.*, 1971, 36, 12-13.

141 **Mather, K.** Group differences in size estimation. *Psychometrika*, 1945, 10, 37-56 (with H. L. Ansbacher).

142 **Matfus, Olga.** [Ida Loewy—biographical data]. *IPN*, 1941, 1(8-9), 13.

143 **Matson, F. W.** *The broken image: Man, science and society.* Garden City, N. Y.: Anchor Books, 1966. Paper.

144 **Mattauschek, E.** Über Coffetylin. *Wien. klin. Wchnschr.*, 1927, 40(2), (with R. Dreikurs).

145 ———. Über die Verschlimmerung von alten Neurosen bei Kriegsbeschädigten aus sozialen Gründen (soziale Verschlimmerung). *Z. ges. Neurol. Psychiat.*, 1929, 119, 679-700 (with R. Dreikurs).

146 **Matthew, A. V.** *Depth psychology and education.* Bombay: Sch. Coll. Bookstall, 1944.

147 **Maultsby, M. C.** Yes, you can live rationally without loving your neighbor. *IPNL*, 1972, 21(5), 84-86.

148 **Maxwell, Z.** *Sex and love.* London: Heinemann, 1972 (with J. Hemming).

149 **May, R.** *The art of counseling: A practical guide with case studies and demonstrations.* New York: Abingdon Press, n.d. Paper.

150 **May, R.** *Existence.* New York: Basic Books, 1958 (with C. Angel & H. F. Ellenberger).

151 ———. *Existential psychology.* New York: Random House, 1964.

152 ———. *Love and will.* New York: Norton, 1969.

153 ———. *The meaning of anxiety.* New York: Ronald Press, 1950.

154 ———. Myth and guiding fiction. [Tribute to Alfred Adler on his 100th birthday]. *JIP*, 1970, 26(2), 13.

155 ———. *Psychology and the human dilemma.* Princeton, N. J.: Van Nostrand, 1967.

156 **Mayer, D.** Order of birth as a determinant of personality and attitudinal characteristics, *J. soc. Psychol.*, 1963, 60, 221–230 (with H. Greenberg, Rosemarie Guerino, Marilyn Lashen & Dorothy Piskowski).

157 **Mayeroff, M.** *On caring.* New York: Harper & Row, 1971.

158 **Mayman, M.** Early memories and abandoned ego states. In *Proceedings of the Academic Assembly on Clinical Psychology.* Montreal: McGill Univ. Press, 1963. Pp. 97–117.

159 ———. Early memories and character structure. *J. proj. Tech.*, *1968*, **32**, 303–316.

160 ———. Early memories as expressions of relationship paradigms. *Amer. J. Orthopsychiat.*, 1960, 30, 507–520 (with M. Faris).

161 **McArthur, C.** Personalities of first and second children. *Psychiat.*, 1956, 19, 47–54.

162 **McArthur, H.** The necessity of choice. *JIP*, 1958, 14, 153–157.

163 **McCall, R. J.** Review of A. H. Maslow, *The psychology of science.* New York: Grune & Stratton, 1972. In *JIP*, 1967, 23, 240–242.

164 **McCandless, B. R.** Anxiety in children, school achievement, and intelligence. *Child Developm.*, 1956, 27, 379–382 (with A. Castaneda).

165 ———. *Parent Practices Research Scale.* Iowa City: St. Univ. Iowa, 1956 (with J. G. Chantiny & L. L. Lovell).

166 **McCarter, D. E.** Early recollections as predictors of the Tompkins-Horn Picture Arrangement Test performance. *JIP*, 1961, 17, 177–180 (with H. M. Schiffman & S. S. Tompkins).

167 **McCarter, R. E.** Affective components of early recollections. *Diss. Abstr.*, 1961, 20, 2090.

168 **McCarthy, C.** Thinkers and their thoughts (I): Alfred Adler and Individual Psychology *Washington Post*, Oct. 29, 1970.

169 **McClelland, R. A.** *The errant dawn* [Adlerian poems]. Homestead, Fla.: Olivant Press, 1969.

170 **McClure, R. F.** Birth order and school related attitudes. *Psychol. Rep.*, 1969, 25, 657–658.

171 ———. Birth order, income, sex, and schoo related attitudes. *J. exp. Educ.*, 1971, 39, 73–74.

172 **McCord, Joan.** The familial genesis of psychoses. *Psychiat.*, 1962, 25, 60–71 (with W. McCord & Judith Porta).

173 ———. *The psychopath.* New York: Van Nostrand, 1964 (with W. McCord). Paper.

174 ———. *Psychopathy and delinquency.* New York: Grune & Stratton, 1956 (with W. McCord).

175 **McCord, W.** The familial genesis of psychoses. *Psychiat.*, 1962, 25, 60–71 (with Joan McCord & Judith Porta).

176 ———. *The psychopath.* New York: Van Nostrand, 1964 (with Joan McCord). Paper

177 ———. *Psychopathy and delinquency.* New York: Grune & Stratton, 1956 (with Joan McCord).

178 **McEachern, Lilly Downing.** *Adlerian psychology and present trends in personality theory.* Urbana, Ill.: Univ. Illinois, 1967. Mimeo.

179 **McEachern, W. A.** Review of R. Dreikurs & L. Grey, *A parents' guide to discipline.* In *Relig. Humanism*, 1971, 5(2), 94–95.

180 **McFarland, R.** Group psychotherapy. Annual review of the year's literature. In E. A Spiegel (Ed.), *Progress in neurology and psychiatry*, 1960, Vol. XV. Pp. 526–534 (with R. J. Corsini & R. Daniels).

181 **McGee, T. P.** Conjunctive use of psychodrama and group psychotherapy in a group living program with schizophrenic patients. *Grp. Psychother.*, 1965, 18(3), 127–135 (with Adaline Starr, Joanne Powers, Frances A. Racusen, & A. Thornton).

182 **McGinnies, E.** Personal values as selective factors in perception. *J. abnorm. soc. Psychol.*, 1948, 42, 142–154 (with L. Postman & J. S. Bruner).

183 **McGlynn, F. D.** Academic performance among first-born students. *JIP*, 1969, 25, 181–182.

184 **McGuckin, H. E. Jr.** An experimental study in the persuasive force of similarity in cognitive style between advocate and audience. *Diss. Abstr.*, 1966, 27, 551. Unpubl. Ph.D. Diss., Stanford Univ., 1966.

185 **McGraw, Myrtle B.** The pediatric anamnesis: Inaccuracies in eliciting developmental data. *Child Developm.*, 1941, 12, 255–265 (with Louise B. Molloy).

186 **McIntyre, C. J.** Acceptance by others and its relation to acceptance of self and others. *J. abnorm. soc. Psychol.*, 1952, 47, 624–625.

187 **McKay, G.** Is it more important to be wrong than right? *Couns. Interviewer*, 1969, 2(1), 48–49 (with Sally Laufketter).

188 **McKeithen, E. Jean.** Patterns of motivation as related to ordinal position. *Diss. Abstr.*, 1965, 25, 4845–4846. Unpubl. Ph.D. Diss., Syracuse Univ., 1962.

189 **McKelvie, W. H.** Involvement in corrections. *IP*, 1972, 9(1), 13–15.

190 ———. Review of W. Petersen, *Population.* Toronto: Macmillan, 1969. In *IP*, 1969, 6(1), 23.

191 ———. Review of C. Rogers, *On encounter groups.* New York: Harper & Row, 1970. In *IP*, 1970, 8(2), 55–56.

192 **McKinney, M. R.** An assessment of the effectiveness of small group counseling on selected eighth grade junior high school students having moderate emotional problems. Unpubl. Ph.D. Diss., Oregon St. Univ., 1963.

193 **McLaughlin, J.** Sane Ben Franklin: An Adlerian view of his autobiography. *JIP*, 1971, 27(2), 189–207 (with R. R. Ansbacher).

194 **McReynolds, P.** Attitudes of schizophrenics and normals toward success and failure. *J. abnorm. Psychol.*, 1967, 72, 303–310 (with C. Guevara).

195 ———. The motives to attain success and to avoid failure: Historical note. *JIP*, 1968, 24, 157–161.

196 ———. The Obscure Figures Test: An instrument for measuring "cognitive innovation." *Percep. mot. Skills*, 1965, 21, 815–821 (with Mary Acker).

197 **McReynolds, P.** Review of S. Coopersmith, *The antecedents of self-esteem.* In *JIP*, 1969, 25, 234–237.

198 **Medical Society of Individual Psychology.** A discussion on anorexia nervosa. *Med. Press and Circ.*, Apr. 5, 1931. Pp. 308–309, 315; *Lancet*, Apr. 18, 1931. P. 865.

199 **Mednick, S. A.** The associative basis of the creative process. *Psychol. Rev.*, 1962, 69, 220–232.

200 **Meer, S. J.** Authoritarian attitudes and dreams. *J. abnorm. soc. Psychol.*, 1955, 51, 74–78.

201 **Meerloo, J. A. M.** Pervasiveness of terms and concepts. [Tribute to Alfred Adler on his 100th birthday]. *JIP*, 1970, 26(2), 14.

202 ———. Why do we sympathize with each other? *Arch. gen. Psychiat.*, 1966, 15, 390–397.

203 **Mehling, Elisabeth.** Zur Psychologie der Frau. *IZIP*, 1926, 4(6), 333–348.

204 **Mehrabian, A.** *An analysis of personality theories.* Englewood Cliffs, N. J.: Prentice-Hall, 1968.

205 **Mehta, P. H.** Birth order, vocational preference and vocational expectation. *Indian J. Psychol.*, 1969, 44, 57–70 (with S. Juneja).

206 **Meiers, J.** Adlerian concepts in relation to the mental hygiene system in the U.S.A. *Nwsltr., IPA, New York City*, 1962, 1(2), 4.

207 ———. An Adlerian "turn" inside the International Psychoanalytic Association. *IPNL*, 1971, 20(4), 61–62.

208 ———. Bibliography of published writings of Kurt Goldstein. In M. L. Simmel (Ed.), *The reach of the mind.* New York: Springer, 1968. Pp. 271–295.

209 ———. Compte-rendu médical p. la première année de la consultation de l'OSE. *Rev. OSE* (Paris), 1935.

210 ———. Dr. Rudolf Dreikurs, 70 Jahre. *Aufbau* (New York), Feb. 10, 1967. P. 4.

211 ———. Epilogue. *IP*, 1967, 4(2), 41.

212 ———. Die Individualpsychologische Newsletter is Twintig Jaar. *MNWIP*, 1972, 21(2),

213 ———. IP methods observable. *IPNL*, 1965, 16(1–3, Whole No. 174–176). P. 3.

214 ———. IPNL: Coming of age. *IPNL*, 1971, 20(4), 68–69.

215 ———. In memoriam: John F. Kennedy, 1917–1963. *The Bagpipe*, (New York, Oct., 1964. P. 4 (with H. Weiner & A. Bassin)).

216 **Meiers, J.** In memorium [Sidonie Reiss]. *IP*, 1970, 7(2), 61.

217 ———. Intermediary distantal therapy: A subspecies of group psychotherapy for those who do not want to be treated. In K. A. Adler & Danica Deutsch (Eds.), *Essays in Individual Psychology*. Pp. 268-274.

218 ———. Is environment protection an Adlerian concern? *IPNL*, 1972, 21(6), 103-104.

219 ———. Kurt Goldstein bibliography: 1936-1959. *JIP*, 1959, 15, 15-19 (with N. L. Mintz).

220 ———. Kurt Goldstein bibliography: Supplement, 1945-1965. *JIP*, 1966, 22, 126-127.

221 ———. Leonard I. Lapinsohn (1919-1970). *JIP*, 1970, 26, 250.

222 ———. A less known facet of Rudolf Dreikurs' work: Multiple psychotherapy. *IP*, 1967, 5, 1-2.

223 ———. Mental hygiene clinic. *The Morningsider*, July 20, 1961. P. 6.

224 ———. Obituary [Leonard I. Lapinsohn]. *IPNL*, 1970, 19(6), 108.

225 ———. Obituary [Irvin Neufeld (1903-1969)]. *IPNL*, 1970, 19(3), 45-46.

226 ———. Obituary [Sidonie Reiss]. *IPNL*, 1971, 20(2), 22-23.

227 ———. On deterioration and inveteration in mental disease. *Psychiat. Quart.*, 1947, 21(1), 33-37.

228 ———. Origins and development of group therapy. *Psychodrama & Grp. Psychother. Monogr.*, No. 17.

229 ———. Origins and developments of group psychotherapy. *Sociom.*, 1945, 8, 499-534.

230 ———. Personal notes on Paul Federn [Obituary]. *Amer. J. Psychother.*, 1950, 4, 509-510.

231 ———. Portrait. *IPNL*, 1970, 19(4), 79.

232 ———. Protection environmentale. *BSFPA*, 1972, 14, 47-49.

233 ———. The relevance of Alfred Adler's ideas and methods in today's need in the U.S.A. and in the world. *IPNL*, 1970, 19, 130-131.

234 ———. Remarks on psychotherapy with aged persons. *IP*, 1968, 5(2), 59-60.

235 ———. Remarques sur la psychotherapie des personnes agées. Translated by Emilia Munoz-Cuesta. *BISFPA*, 1970, No. 8. Pp. 24-27.

236 **Meiers, J.** Review of O. E. Byrd, *Health instruction yearbook*. Stanford, Cal.: Stanford Univ. Press, 1950. In *Amer. J. Psychother.*, 1950, 4, 670-671.

237 ———. Review of A. Deutsch, *The shame of the states*. New York: Harcourt, Brace, 1948. In *Amer. J. Psychother.*, 1950, 4, 360-362.

238 ———. Review of K. Goldstein, On emotions—considerations from the organism's point of view. *J. Psychol.*, 1951, 31, 37-49. In *JIP*, 1954, 11, 93.

239 ———. Review of J. L. Moreno & Zerka T. Moreno (Eds.), *Psychodrama*. Vol. 3. In *Amer. J. Psychiat.*, 1971, 127(7), 160.

240 ———. Review of Marianne L. Simmel (Ed.), *The reach of the mind: Essays in memory of Kurt Goldstein*. New York: Springer, 1968. In *JIP*, 1968, 24, 198.

241 ———. Review of B. Stokvis (Ed.), *Second International Congress of Psychotherapy*. Basel: Karger, 1959. In *Grp. Psychother.*, 1959, 12, 347-349.

242 ———. Sidonie Reiss (1882-1970). *JIP*, 1970, 26, 250.

243 ———. Sur la théorie de la consultation médico-psychologique des enfants arriérés. *Rev. OSE* (Paris), 1935 (with Minna Elias).

244 ———. Techniques and statistics in the evaluation of results of the psychotherapie *Amer. J. Psychother.*, 1964, 18 (Suppl.I), 59-60.

245 ———. Therapy at a distance. *Int. J. Sociom. Sociat.*, 1957, 1, 2-3; 1957, 1, 109-111.

246 ———. Thoughts on recent advances in group psychotherapy (1945-1950). *Grp. Psychother.*, 1952, 3, 244-273.

247 ———. Tragedy and triumph of psycho-socio-drama. *Grp. Psychother.*, 1967, 20, 187-188.

248 ———. Translator of C. A. Brouilhet, Individual Psychology: An interview with Alfred Adler.

249 ———. Translator of J. De Busscher, Alfred Adler and psychotherapy.

250 ———. Translator of B. Kunz, Rudolf Dreikurs, 1897-1972. *ASAP Nwsltr.*, 1972, 9, 4-5.

251 ———. What is "intermediary-distantal" therapy? What is the "invisible group" technique? *Brooklyn Psychologist*, Feb., 1963. P. 8.

252 ———. Women-Power: Letter to the editor. *IPNL*, 1970, 19, 119.

253 **Meignant, P.** Le point de vue de l'"Individualpsychologie" sur le crime et la délinquence, spécialement sur la délinquence juvénile. *L'Hygiene ment.*, 1932,

254 **Meister, O.** Geschichtsforschung und Individualpsychologie. *IZIP*, 1934, 12(1), 37–44.

255 **Meltzer, H.** The present status of experimental studies on the relationship of feeling to memory. *Psychol. Rev.*, 1930, 37, 124–139.

256 **Menge, J. W.** *What we learn from children.* New York: Harper, 1956 (with Marie I. Rasey).

257 **M[enninger]. K. A.** Reading notes. *Bull. Menninger Clin.*, 1971, 35, 54–55.

258 **Menninger, W.** Seven characteristics of the mature person. *OSIPNL*, 1967, 8(2), 8.

259 **Mensen, H.** Die "geheimen" Verführer und Wir. *Allg. Therapeutik*, 1969, 9, 99–110.

260 **Menser, Edyth B.** The individual faces his problem—how? *IJIP*, 1937, 3(2), 128–136.

261 **Menzel, R.** Nationalismus und Menschentum. *IZIP*, 1927, 5(4), 274–282.

262 ———. Review of E. Baur, E. Fischer & F. Lenz, *Menschliche Erbliehkeitslehre.* München: Lehmann, 1927. In *IZIP*, 1933, 12(5), 403–404.

263 ———. Review of [   ] Behr-Pinnow, *Die Zukunft der menschlichen Rasse.* Berlin: F. Fontaine, 1927. In *IZIP*, 1931, 9(2), 155.

264 ———. Review of W. Gemünd, *Liebe und Ahnerbe.* München: Otto Gmelin, 1928. In *IZIP*, 1931, 9(2), 154–155.

265 ———. Review of E. Hauck, *Das seelische Verhalten des Pferdes und des Hundes.* Wien: Urban & Schwarzenberg, 1928. In *IZIP*, 1930, 8(3), 359–360.

266 ———. Review of W. Scheidt, *Rassenkunde.* München: J. F. Lehmann, 1925. In *IZIP*, 1933, 12(6), 178.

267 ———. Review of E. Zacharias, *Die Gesundheit der Familie und des Volkes das Ziel der "ärztlichen Eheberatung".* Berlin: A. Metzner, [   ]. In *IZIP*, 1929, 7(2), 159.

268 ———. Über die Geltung individualpsychologischer Gesetzmässigkeit in der Tierwelt. *IZIP*, 1929, 7(1), 22–26 (with Rudolfine Menzel).

269 ———. Der Unverbesserliche. *IZIP*, 1928, 6(5), 398–408.

270 **Menzel, R.** *Wesenserprobung.* Selbstverlag, (with Rudolfine Menzel).

271 **Menzel, Rudolfine.** Über die Geltung individualpsychologischer Gesetzmässigkeiten in der Tierwelt. *IZIP*, 1929, 7(1), 22–26 (with R. Menzel).

272 ———. *Wesenserprobung.* Selbstverlag, (with R. Menzel).

273 **Meredith, C. W.** The AANA and public relations—A study of morale and work. *AANA Bull.*, 1955, 9(5), 10–14.

274 ———. Evaluation and the teaching of educational psychology. *APA Nwsltr.*, 1957, 3, 1–7.

275 ———. Humanizing relationships in the family. *Insights*, 1971, 8(1), 6.

276 ———. Improvement of instruction. *Current Issues in Higher Education.* 1956, 168–169.

277 ———. The magic of involvement. *IP*, 1972, 9(1), 1–3.

278 ———. My philosophy of discipline in a democratic atmosphere. *School News and Views from Oswego*, 1957, 2(1), 1–4.

279 ———. Personality and social development during childhood and adolescence. *Rev. educ. Res.*, 1955, 25(5), 469–476.

280 ———. Philosophy of evaluation. *APA Nwsltr.*, 1957, 2, 7–8.

281 ———. Problem solving and creativity. *J. Amer. Assn. Nurse Anesthetists*, 1962, 30(2), 83–89.

282 ———. Psychology and the nurse anesthetist. *J. AANA*, 1958, 26(1), 18–25.

283 ———. Psychology and the nurse anesthetist—A follow-up of actual experiences. *J. AANA*, 1959, 27(1), 36–47.

284 ———. The reading of projected books with special reference to rate and visual fatigue. *J. educ. Res.*, 1948, 41(6), 453–460 (with I. Anderson).

285 ———. Super humanity problems of teachers. *Insights*, 1967, 4(3), 6–7.

286 ———. Year round school—A challenge to change. *Insights*, 1968, 5(1), 3–4.

287 ———. You as an individual learner. *Teachers Coll. J.*, 1955, 26(6), 110–113.

288 **Merrill, B. A.** A measurement of mother-child interaction. *J. abnorm. soc. Psychol.*, 1946, 41, 37–49.

289 **Merton, R. K.** The self-fulfilling prophecy. *Antioch Rev.*, 1948, 8, 193–210.

290 **Merzbach, Therese.** Eine Zwangsbewegung. *IZIP*, 1930, 8(6), 588–589.

291 **Messer, A.** *Einführung in die Psychologie und die psychologischen Richtungen der Gegenwart.* Leipzig: Felix Meiner, 1931.

292 ———. Individualpsychologie und Wertphilosophie. *IZIP*, 1927, 5(5), 321–323.

293 **Messer, M.** *Sex and the single mother: A do-it-yourself guide to illegitimacy prevention.* Chicago: Illegit. Prevention Inc., 1969.

294 **Messick, S.** Content and style in personality assessment. *Psychol. Bull.*, 1958, 55, 243–252.

295 **Metzer, E.** *Der Einfluss der Tuberkulose auf das Seelenleben.* Stuttgart: Ferdinand Enke, 1933.

296 **Metzger, Juliana.** "Schon von Adler entdeckt". *Frankfurter Allgem. Zeit.*, Nov. 29, 1963. P. 10.

297 **Metzger, W.** Alfred Adler—Forgotten or repressed. *Pädagog. Heute*, 1969, 3–4.

298 ———. Co-editor, with Suzanne Liebmann, of A. Liebmann, *Untersuchung und Behandlung geistig zurückgebliebener Kinder.*

299 ———. Geleitwort to P. Rom, *Alfred Adler und die wissenschaftliche Menschenkenntnis.*

300 ———. The historical background for actional trends in psychology: German psychology. *J. Hist. Behav. Sci.*, 1965-66, 1-2, 109–115.

301 ———. Introduction to A. Liebmann, *Untersuchung und Behandlung geistig zurückgebliebener Kinder.*

302 ———. Obituary [O. Brachfeld, 1908–1967]. *Psychol. Rundsch.* (Göttingen), 1968, 19, 56; *JIP*, 1968, 24, 124–125.

303 ———. Obituary [W. Köhler, 1897-1960]. *Psychol. Rundsch.* (Göttingen), 1968, 19.

304 ———. *Schöpferische Freiheit.* Frankfurt-am-Main: Waldemar Kramer, 1962.

305 ———. Über die Verifikation tiefenpsychologischer Thesen. *Schule u. Psychol.* (München), Dec., 1970.

306 **Metzger, Zerline.** *Individual voice patterns.* New York: Carlton Press, 1966.

307 **Meyer, A.** Alfred Adler. In *Encyclopaedia Universalis*, 1969, Vol. 1. P. 239.

308 ———. Aperçu sur les principes particuliers de la psychologie adlérienne. *Premier Cong. mond. de Psychiat., 1950.* Paris: Hermann, 1952. P. 199.

309 ———. Aspects de la névrose dans le cas affections causales et des traumatismes accidentels. *BSFPA*, 1971, No. 11. Pp. 23–26.

310 **Meyer, A.** Généralités sur la psychologie d'Alfred Adler. *Bull. du Centre de Psychol Adlérienne*, 1950, No. 1. Pp. 3–5.

311 ———. La notion du temps dans la psychologie de la profondeur. *BSFPA*, 1972, No. 13. Pp. 16–19.

312 ———. Le peur névrotique. *BSFPA*, 1972, No. 14. Pp. 11–18.

313 ———. Principes de la psychologie adlérie [Congres mondial, 1950]. *Psychothérapie.* Tome 5. Paris: Hermann, 1952.

314 ———. Problème du travail et psychothérapie adlérienne. *BISFPA*, 1970, No. 7. Pp. 6–11.

315 ———. Psychothérapie adlérienne. In H. Ey (Ed.), *Psychiatrie, l'encyclopédie médico-chirurgicale.* Paris: , 1955, 1960.

316 ———. Reflexions sur la Psychologie Individuelle d'Adler. *BSFPA*, 1971, No. 9. Pp. 11–13.

317 ———. Le rôle de l'imaginations dans le style de vie, fiction et realité. *BSFPA*, 1971, No. 10. Pp. 8–15.

318 **Meyer, E.** (Ed.). *Didaktische Studien.* Stutgart: Ernst Klett, 1969.

319 ——— (Ed.). *Sozialerziehung und Grupper unterricht.* Stuttgart: Ernst Klett, 1963.

320 **Meyer, Ruth E.** The team approach in group psychotherapy. *Dis. nerv. Sys.*, 1957 18, 95–99 (with J. W. Klapman).

321 **Meyer, W. F.** Review of Phyllis Bottome, *Alfred Adler.* In *OSIPNL*, 1962, 3(2), 3–4.

322 **Meyers, C. E.** The effect of conflicting authority on the child. *Univ. Iowa Stud. Child Welf.*, 1944, 20, No. 409. Pp. 31–98.

323 ———. *What I like to do: An inventory o children's interests.* Chicago: Science Research Assoc., 1954 (with M. R. Bonsall & L. P. Thorpe).

324 **Mezer, R. R.** Review of A. Adler, *The Individual Psychology of Alfred Adler.* In *Amer. J. Sociol.*, 1957, 62, 532–533.

325 **Michotte, A.** *The perception of causality.* New York: Basic Books, 1963.

326 **Midelfort, C. F.** *The family in psychotherapy.* New York: McGraw-Hill, 1957.

327 ———. Family treatment of schizophrenia A symposium. *Fam. Proc.*, 1962, 1, 101–140 (with H. Hildreth, I Boszormenyi-Nagy, J. Franco, & A. Friedman).

328 **Mieth-Arnold, Nita.** See Arnold, Nita.

329 **Mignard, M.** *L'unité psychique et les troubles mentaux.* Paris: Alcan, 1928.

330 **Mikesell, R. H.** Masculinity-femininity and self-concept. *Percep. mot. Skills,* 1972, 34, 163-167.

331 **Miles, C.** Study of individual psychology. *Amer. J. Psychol.,* 1893, 6, 534-558.

332 **Miley, C. H.** Birth-order research 1963-1967; Bibliography and index. *JIP,* 1969, 25, 64-70.

333 **Mill, J. S.** Utilitarianism. In *Utilitarianism, liberty, and representative government.* New York: Dutton, 1951. Pp. 1-80.

334 **Millard, R. M.** *Personality and the good: Psychological and ethical perspectives.* New York: David McKay, 1963 (with P. A. Bertocci).

335 **Miller, G.** Psychology in prison. *Amer. Psychologist,* 1954, 19, 184-185 (with R. J. Corsini).

336 **Miller, J. G.** *Unconsciousness.* New York: Wiley, 1942.

337 **Miller, K. S.** The effects of need-achievement and self-ideal discrepancy on performance under stress. *J. Pers.,* 1956, 25, 176-189 (with P. Worchel).

338 **Miller, M. H.** Obsessive and hysterical syndromes in the light of existential considerations. *J. exis. Psychiat.,* 1960, 1, 315-329 (with J. W. Chotlos).

339 **Mills, G.** *Elementary guidance and counseling: An introduction through essays and commentaries.* New York: Random House, 1971.

340 **Mills, Orpha.** A summer seminar in Individual Psychology. *IPB,* 1943, 3, 50-53 (with Mabelle Hammond).

341 **Minder, R.** Review of M. Sperber, *Alfred Adler oder das Elend der Psychologie.* In *Süddeutsche Zeitung,* May, 1970.

342 **Mink. O. G.** *Foundations of guidance counseling.* New York: Lippincott, 1969 (with C. E. Smith).

343 **Minor, Margareta.** Elternsünden. *IZIP,* 1928, 6(5), 387-396.

344 ———. Review of Hedwig Schulhof, *Henrik Ibsen, der Mensch und sein Werk im Lichte der Individualpsychologie.* In *IZIP,* 1924, 3(1), 43-44.

345 ———. Ursachen und triebende Kräfte der Frauenbewegung im Lichte der Individualpsychologie. *IZIP,* 1925, 3(6), 310-314.

346 **Minton, H. L.** Contemporary concepts of power and Adler's views. *JIP,* 1968, 24, 46-55.

347 **Minton, H. L.** Power as a personality construct. In B. A. Maher (Ed.), *Progress in experimental personality research* Vol. 4 Pp. 229-267.

348 **Mintz, Elizabeth.** Transference in co-therapy groups. *J. consult. Psychol.,* 1963, 27(1), 34-39.

349 **Mintz, L.** Concerning Goethe's approach to the theory of color. *JIP,* 1959, 15, 33-49.

350 **Mintz, N. L.** Kurt Goldstein bibliography: 1936-1959. *JIP,* 1959, 15, 15-19 (with J. Meiers).

351 ———. Introduction [Papers in honor of Kurt Goldstein]. *JIP,* 1959, 15, 4 (with Eugenia Hanfmann).

352 **Miranda, S. B.** The obviousness of two masculinity-femininity tests. *J. consult. clin. Psychol.,* 1968, 32(3), 314-318 (with V. J. Bieliauskas & L. M. Lansky).

353 **Misra, D.** The concept of "set" in modern psychology. *Indian J. Psychol.,* 1949, 24, 26-46.

354 **Misra, S. L.** Effect of birth order, education and rank status on insecurity. *Psychol. Annu.,* 1969, 3, 17-19.

355 **Mitscherlich, A.** *Freiheit und Unfreiheit in der Krankheit.* Hamburg: , 1945.

356 **Mittag, W.** Die Grundlagen der individualpsychologischen Didaktik. *IZIP,* 1931, 9(3), 214-221.

357 **Mittelman, B.** The concurrent analysis of married couples. *Psychoanal. Quart.,* 1948, 17, 182-197.

358 **Miyamoto, M.** Review of J. Needham, *Science and civilisation in China.* Vol. 2. Cambridge, England: Univ. Press, 1956. In *JIP,* 1960, 16, 215-216.

359 **Miyamoto, S. F.** A test of interactionalist hypotheses of self-conception. *Amer. J. Sociol.,* 1956, 61, 399-403 (with S. M. Dornbush).

360 **Moawad, B.** Democracy, does it work? *OSIPNL,* 1970, 11(3), 11.

361 **Moens, J. F.** An investigation of the validity of the H-T-P as an intelligence test for children. *J. clin. Psychol.,* 1961, 17, 178-180 (with V. J. Bieliauskas).

362 **Mohr, Erika.** The role of emotions in pregnancy and delivery. *AJIP,* 1954, 10, 169-174.

363 ———. The social club as an adjunct to therapy (with Rose Garlock). In

K. A. Adler & Danica Deutsch (Eds.), *Essays in Individual Psychology*. Pp. 465-467.

364 **Molish, H. B.** (Ed.). *Reflexes to intelligence: A reader in clinical psychology*. Glencoe, Ill.: Free Press, 1959 (with S. J. Beck).

365 **Molitor, K.** Drei Beiträge zur Problem des Schülerselbstmord (with A. Adler & D. E. Oppenheim). In A. Adler & C. Furtmüller (Eds.), *Heilen und Bilden* (1914). Pp. 341-373; (1928) Same with F. Künkel instead of K. Molitor. Pp. 206-227.

366 **Molloy, Louise B.** The pediatric anamnesis: Inaccuracies in eliciting developmental data. *Child Developm.*, 1941, 12, 255-265 (with Myrtle B. McGraw).

367 **Monashkin, I.** Acceptance of self, parents, and people in patients and normals. *J. clin. Psychol.*, 1956, 12, 327-332 (with M. Zuckerman & M. Baer).

368 **Monne, R. H.** A piano lover. *IPNL*, 1961, 11(9-10, Whole No. 125-126). P. 50.

369 **Monro, A. B.** The self-referent attitudes of neurotic and inadequate personalities. *J. ment. Sci.*, 1962, 108, 37-46.

370 ———. The social attitudes of neurotic and inadequate personalities. *Brit. J. Psychiat.*, 1963, 109, 775-778.

371 **Montagu, A.** *The biosocial nature of man.* New York: Grove Press, 1956.

372 ———. Chromosomes and crime. *Psychol. Today*, 1968, 2(5), 42-49.

373 ———. *The direction of human development.* New York: Harper, 1955.

374 ———. *The natural superiority of women.* New York: Macmillan, 1954.

375 ———. Review of H. Cleckley, *The mask of sanity.* St. Louis: C. V. Mosby, 1964. In *JIP*, 1965, 21(1), 97-98.

376 ———. Review of J. D. Frank, *Sanity and survival.* New York: Random House, 1969. In *JIP*, 1969, 25, 118.

377 ———. Social interest and aggression as potentialities. *JIP*, 1970, 26, 17-31.

378 **Moor, J.** Portrait. *IPNL*, 1970, 19(4), 79.

379 **Moore, M.** Adleriana. *IPN*, 1941, 1(6), 5; 1941, 1(7), 4-5.

380 ———. Alfred Adler—creative personality. *AJIP*, 1954, 11, 1-8.

381 **Moore, T. V.** Language and intelligence: A longitudinal study of the first eight years. II. Environmental correlates of mental growth. *Hum. Developm.*, 1968, 11, 88-106.

382 **Moorhouse, G.** The man who stood out against Freud. *Guardian*, Feb. 7, 1970.

383 **Mora, G.** 1970 anniversaries. *Amer. J. Psychiat.*, 1971, 127(7), 901-907.

384 **Moraitis, D.** *Atomiki Psychologia* [Individual Psychology]. Athens: J. Sideris, 1930.

385 ———. *I Atomiki Psychologia kai ai Epharmogai avtis* [Individual Psychology]. Athens: Ekdosis Paidiatrikos Kosmos, 1947.

386 ———. *I Atomiki Psychologia kai ai epharmogai avtis eis tin Psychotherapeian kai tin agogin* [The theory of Individual Psychology]. Athens: Typois "Ekdotikis", n.d.

387 ———. A case of recurring fainting spells. *IJIP*, 1936, 2(1), 71-76.

388 ———. Ein Fall von Epilepsie. *IZIP*, 1934, 12(3), 179-184.

389 ———. Free composition of an adolescent girl. *IPB*, 1946, 5, 112-118.

390 ———. Der lebende Tote. *IZIP*, 1937, 15(2), 80-82.

391 ———. *I Praktiki tis Atomokis Psychologia* [The practice of Individual Psychology]. Athens: 1940.

392 ———. Self-review of *Atomiki Psychologia.* In *IZIP*, 1931, 9(3), 252-253.

393 **Moran, G.** Ordinal position and approval motivation. *J. consult. Psychol.*, 1967, 31, 319-320.

394 **Morano, N. T.** Complexity-simplicity: An investigation of cognitive, motivational personality correlates. *Diss. Abstr.*, 1966, 26, 4079. Unpubl. Ph.D. Diss., Fordham Univ., 1965.

395 **Moreno, J. L.** (Ed.). *Handbook of group therapy.* New York: Phil. Libr., 1966.

396 **Morgan, J. J. B.** *Child psychology.* New York: Richard Smith, 1931.

397 **Morino, I.** Rehabilitation of children discharged from a psychiatric hospital. *Amer. J. Orthopsychiat.*, 1964, 34(5), 942-947 (with H. Klapman & Sarah S. Slagle).

398 **Morosco, T.** Alcoholism and clinical symptoms. *J. abnorm. Psychol.*, 1969, 74, 482-483 (with A. Goss).

399 ———. The relationship between a dimension of internal-external control and the MMPI with an alcoholic population. *J. consult. clin. Psychol.*, 1970, 34(2), 189-192 (with A. Goss).

400 **Moroose, D. A.** Pre-service training in Adleria psychology. *IP*, 1972, 9(1), 16-21.

401 Morris, C. Alfred Adler and George H. Mead. *JIP*, 1965, 21, 199–200.

402 Morrison, Lillian. To a friend. *IPNL*, 1953, Whole No. 26–27. Pp. 6–7.

403 ———. Too much devotion. *IPNL*, 1953, Whole No. 25. P. 4.

404 Morse, J. Review of G. S. Hall, *Life and confessions of a psychologist*. New York: Appleton, 1923. In *IZIP*, 1924, 2(6), 31–34.

405 Mosak, Birdie. Portrait. *IPNL*, 1972, 21(6), 110.

406 Mosak, H. H. Aggression as a secondary phenomenon. *JIP*, 1967, 23, 232–235 (with Lydia Sicher). Also in H. D. Werner (Ed.), *New understandings of human behavior*. Pp. 168–172.

407 ———. A comparison of client-centered and adlerian psychotherapy. *Couns. Ctr. Discussion Papers* (Univ. Chicago), 1960, 6, No. 8 (with J. M. Shlien & R. Dreikurs).

408 ———. Early recollections as a projective technique. *J. proj. Tech.*, 1958, 22, 302–311. Also in G. Lindzey & C. S. Hall (Eds.), *Theories of personality: Primary sources and research*. Pp. 105–113. Also *Alfred Adler Inst. Monogr., No. 2.* Chicago: Alfred Adler Inst., 1972.

409 ———. Early recollections: Evaluation of some recent research. *JIP*, 1969, 25, 56–63.

410 ———. Effect of time limits: A comparison of client-centered and Adlerian psychotherapy (Abstract). *Amer. Psychologist*, 1960, 15, 415 (with J. M. Shlien & R. Dreikurs).

411 ———. Effect of time limits: A comparison of two psychotherapies. *J. couns. Psychol.*, 1962, 9, 31–34 (with J. M. Shlien & R. Dreikurs).

412 ———. Evaluation in psychotherapy: A study of some current measures. Unpubl. Ph.D. Diss., Univ. Chicago, 1950.

413 ———. A full time internship in private practice. *Clin. Psychologist*, 1970, 14(1), 5–6.

414 ———. The getting type, a parsimonious social interpretation of the oral character. *JIP*, 1959, 15, 193–198.

415 ———. *Individual psychotherapy: A syllabus*. Chicago: Alfred Adler Inst., 1963 (with B. H. Shulman).

416 ———. The interrelatedness of the neuroses through central themes. *JIP*, 1968, 24, 67–70.

417 Mosak, H. H. The inter-relationship of the neuroses. In R. Dreikurs (Ed.), *Education, guidance, psychodynamics*. Pp. 24–28.

418 ———. *Introductory Individual Psychology: A syllabus*. Chicago: Alfred Adler Inst., 1961 (with B. H. Shulman).

419 ———. Language and the interpretation of "sexual" symbolism. *J. consult. Psychol.*, 1955, 19, 108.

420 ———. Life style assessment: A demonstration focused on family constellation. *JIP*, 1972, 28(2), 232–247.

421 ———. *The life style inventory*. Chicago: Alfred Adler Inst., 1971 (with B. H. Shulman).

422 ———. Lifestyle. In A. Nikelly (Ed.), *Techniques for behavior change*. Pp. 77–81.

423 ———. The life tasks III. The fifth life task. *IP*, 1967, 5, 16–22 (with R. Dreikurs).

424 ———. *The neuroses: A syllabus*. Chicago: Alfred Adler Inst., 1966 (with B. H. Shulman).

425 ———. Patient-therapist relationship in multiple psychotherapy. I. Its advantages to the therapist. *Psychiat. Quart.*, 1952, 26, 219–227 (with R. Dreikurs & B. H. Shulman). Also in R. Dreikurs (Ed.), *Group psychotherapy and group approaches*. Pp. 114–120.

426 ———. Patient-therapist relationship in multiple psychotherapy. II. Its advantages for the patient. *Psychiat. Quart.*, 1952, 26, 590–596 (with R. Dreikurs & B. H. Shulman). Also in R. Dreikurs (Ed.), *Group psychotherapy and group approaches*. Pp. 121–126.

427 ———. Portrait. In G. Alcock, Guiding children back to happiness. *Chicago Tribune* (Grafic Section), June 17, 1951: In F. Ruch, *Psychology and life; IPNL*, 1972, 21(6), 110.

428 ———. Predicting the relationship to the psychotherapist from early recollections. *JIP*, 1965, 21, 77–81.

429 ———. Performance on the Harrower-Erickson Multiple Choice Test of patients with spinal cord injuries. *J. consult. Psychol.*, 1951, 15, 346–349.

430 ———. Problems in the definition and measurement of success in psychotherapy. In W. Wolff & J. A. Precker (Eds.), *Success in psychotherapy*. Pp. 1–25.

431 ———. The psychological attitude in rehabilitation. *Amer. Arch. Rehab. Ther.*, 1954, 2, 9–10.

432 Mosak, H. H. Review of Camilla Anderson, *Beyond Freud.* In *JIP*, 1958, 14, 89–90.

433 ———. Review of L. Langner, *The importance of wearing clothes.* In *JIP*, 1960, 16, 107–108.

434 ———. Selective perception in the interpretation of symbols. *J. abnorm. soc. Psychol.*, 1952, 47, 255–256 (with F. J. Todd).

435 ———. Some therapeutic uses of psychologic testing. *Amer. J. Psychother.*, 1972, 26(4), 539–546 (with R. S. Gushurst).

436 ———. Strategies for behavior change in schools: Consultation strategies: A personal account. *Couns. Psychologist*, 1971, 3(1), 58–62.

437 ———. Subjective criteria of normality. *Psychother.*, 1967, 4, 159–161.

438 ———. A suggestion—and invitation. *IPNL*, 1971, 20(1), 11.

439 ———. The tasks of life. I. Adler's three tasks. *IP*, 1966, 4(1), 18–22 (with R. Dreikurs).

440 ———. The tasks of life. II. The fourth life task. *IP*, 1967, 4(2), 51–56 (with R. Dreikurs).

441 ———. Various purposes of symptoms. *JIP*, 1967, 23, 79–87 (with B. H. Shulman).

442 ———. What patients say and what they mean. *Amer. J. Psychother.*, 1971, 25(3), 428–436 (with R. S. Gushurst).

443 Moses, P. Über Konstitution associativ-aphasischer Kinder. *Wien. med. Wchnschr.*, 1926, 76, No. 29 (with E. Froeschels).

444 Mosher, D. L. The influence of Adler on Rotter's social learning theory of personality. *JIP*, 1968, 24, 33–45.

445 Moskalski, D. D. Sex and birth order and future expectations of occupational status and salary. *JIP*, 1968, 24, 170–173 (with J. J. Platt & R. Eisenman).

446 Moskowitz, I. P. [Letter on birth order and internal-external control]. *Psychol. Today*, 1971, 5(4), 4.

447 Motlagh, H. Selected non-academic factors related to creativity. *Diss. Abstr.*, 1968, 29, 1453.

448 Moulyn, A. C. Purposeful and non-purposeful behavior. *Phil. Sci.*, 1951, 18, 154.

449 Moustakas, C. E. *Psychotherapy with children; The living relationship.* New York: Harper, 1959.

450 Moustakas, C. E. Self explorations of teachers in a seminar in interpersonal relations. *JIP*, 1957, 13, 72–93.

451 ———. The significance of individual creativity for psychotherapy. *JIP*, 1957, 13, 159–164 (with D. Smillie).

452 ———. *The teacher and the child.* New York: McGraw-Hill, 1956.

453 Mowrer, O. H. Abnormal reactions or actions?—An autobiographical answer. In J. Vernon (Ed.), *Introduction to general psychology.* Dubuque, Ia.: Brown, 1966. Pp. 1–42.

454 ———. Adler's basic concepts: Neurotic ambition and social interest. In A. Nikelly (Ed.), *Techniques for behavior change.* Pp. 5–12.

455 ———. Anxiety-reduction and learning. *J. exp. Psychol.*, 1940, 27, 497–516.

456 ———. Anxiety theory as a basis for distinguishing between counseling and psychotherapy. In R. F. Berdie (Ed.), *Concepts and programs of counseling.* Minneapolis: Univ. Minnesota Press, 1951. Pp. 7–26.

457 ———. Autobiography. In G. Lindzey (Ed. *The history of psychology in autobiography.*

458 ———. Avoidance conditioning and signal duration—A study of secondary motivation and reward. *Psychol. Monogr.*, 1942, 54, Whole No. 247 (with R. R. Lamoreaux).

459 ———. The basis of psychopathology: Malconditioning or misbehavior. In C. D. Speelberger (Ed.), *Anxiety and behavior.* New York: Academic Press, 1966.

460 ———. The behavior therapies with special reference to "modeling" and imitation. *Amer. J. Psychother.*, 1966, 20, 439–461.

461 ———. Biography and photograph. *Voices*, 1965, 1(1), 14; 1966, 2(2), 7.

462 ———. Changes in verbal behavior during therapy. In O. H. Mowrer (Ed.), *Psychotherapy: Theory and research.* Pp. 463–545.

463 ———. Changing conceptions of the unconscious. *J. nerv. ment. Dis.*, 1959, 129, 222–234.

464 ———. Civilization and its malcontents. *Psychol. Today*, 1967, 1(5), 48–52.

465 ———. Comments on Trude Weiss—Rosmarin's "Adler's psychology and the Jewish tradition." *JIP*, 1959, 15, 128–129.

466 ———. Conflict, contract, conscience, confession. *Transactions*, 1969, 1, 7–19.

467 **Mowrer, O. H.** *The crisis in psychiatry and religion.* Princeton, N. J.: D. Van Nostrand, 1961.

468 ——. Critique of Patterson's article. *Couns. Psychologist,* 1964, 1(2), 48–57.

469 ——. A dynamic theory of personality (with C. Kluckhohn). In J. McV. Hunt (Ed.), *Personality and the behavior disorders.* New York: Ronald Press, 1943, Pp. 69–135.

470 ——. Enuresis—a method for its study and treatment. *Amer. J. Orthopsychiat.,* 1938, 8, 436–459 (with W. M. Mowrer).

471 ——. Even there, thy hand. *Chicago Theol. Semin. Register,* 1962, 52, 1–17.

472 ——. Existentialism and integrity therapy. *Int. J. Psychol. in the Orient,* 1967, 10(3–4).

473 ——. An experimental analogue of fear from a sense of helplessness. *J. abnorm. soc. Psychol.,* 1948, 43, 193–200 (with P. Viek).

474 ——. Fear as an intervening variable in avoidance conditioning. *J. comp. Psychol.,* 1946, 39, 29–50 (with R. R. Lamoreaux).

475 ——. Foreword to W. Glasser, *Reality therapy.*

476 ——. Further studies utilizing the discomfort—relief quotient (with J. McV. Hunt & L. Kogan). In O. H. Mowrer (Ed.), *Psychotherapy: Theory and research.* Pp. 257–295,

477 ——. A great opportunity not exploited. Review of [   ]. Belgium, *Religion and medicine.* In *Contemp. Psychol.,* 1969, 15, 531–532.

478 ——. Identification: A link between learning theory and psychotherapy. In *Learning theory and personality dynamics.* Pp. 573–616.

479 ——. Implications of a two-factor learning theory. *Psychol. Serv. Ctr. J.,* 1950, 2, 116–122.

480 —— et al. Individual differences and "racial experience" in the rat, with special reference to vocalization. *J. genet. Psychol.,* 1948, 73, 3–28.

481 ——. *Integrity groups: Basic principles and objectives.* Urbana, Ill.: Univ. Illinois, 1971. Mimeo.

482 ——. Integrity therapy: A self-help approach. *Psychother.,* 1966, 3, 114–119.

483 ——. Inter-trial responses as "rehearsal". *Amer. J. Psychol.,* 1947, 60, 608–616 (with H. Coppock).

484 **Mowrer, O. H.** Introduction to K. Dabrowski, *Personality-shaping through positive disintegration.* Boston: Little, Brown, 1967.

485 ——. The law of effect and ego psychology. *Psychol. Rev.,* 1946, 53, 321–334.

486 ——. *Learning theory and behavior.* New York: Wiley, 1960.

487 ——. Learning theory and behavior therapy. In B. B. Wolman (Ed.), *Handbook of clinical psychology.* Pp. 242–276.

488 ——. Learning theory and the neurotic fallacy. *Amer. J. Orthopsychiat.,* 1952, 22, 679–689.

489 ——. Learning theory and the neurotic paradox. *Amer. J. Orthopsychiat.,* 1948, 18, 571–610.

490 ——. *Learning theory and personality dynamics.* New York: Ronald Press, 1950.

491 ——. Loss and recovery of community: A guide to theory and practice of integrity therapy. In G. M. Gazda (Ed.), *Innovations to group therapy.* Pp. 130–189.

492 ——. Mental health study requires historical dimension. *Champaign* (Ill.). *News-Gazette,* June 19, 1966.

493 ——. A method of measuring tension in written documents. *J. abnorm. soc. Psychol.,* 1947, 42, 3–32 (with J. Dollard).

494 ——. *Morality and mental health.* Chicago: Rand-McNally, 1967.

495 ——. Neurosis and its treatment as learning phenomena. In D. Brower & L. E. Abt (Eds.), *Progress in clinical psychology.* Pp. 312–323.

496 ——. New directions in the understanding and management of depression. In C. J. Frederick (Ed.), *The future of psychotherapy.* Boston: Little, Brown, 1969.

497 ——. *The new group therapy.* Princeton, N. J.: Van Nostrand, 1964. Paper.

498 ——. Notes. In Anon., A new theory of schizophrenia. *J. abnorm. soc. Psychol.,* 1958, 57, 226–236.

499 ——. On the dual nature of learning—A reinterpretation of "conditioning" and "Problem-solving." *Harvard educ. Rev.,* 1947, 17, 102–148.

500 ——. Pain, punishment, guilt, and anxiety. In P. H. Hoch & J. Zubin (Eds.), *Anxiety.* New York: Grune & Stratton, 1950. Pp. 27–40.

501 ——. Peer groups and medication, the best "therapy" for professionals and laymen alike. *Psychother.,* 1971, 8(1), 44–53.

502 Mowrer, O. H. *Personality.* New York: Ronald Press, 1953.

503 ———— (Ed.). *Psychotherapy: Theory and research.* New York: Ronald Press, 1953.

504 ————. Q-technique—Description, history, and critique. In *Psychotherapy: Theory and research.* Pp. 316-375.

505 ————. Review of Margaretta K. Bowers, E. N. Jackson, J. A. Knight & L. Le Shan, *Counseling the dying.* New York: Thomas Nelson, 1964. In *Contemp. Psychol.,* 1965, 10, 426-427.

506 ————. Review of K. Dabrowski, *Positive disintegration.* Boston: Little, Brown, 1964. In *Contemp. Psychol.,* 1965, 10, 538-540.

507 ————. Review of W. W. Wood, *Culture and personality aspects of the Pentecostal Holiness religion.* The Hague: Mouton, 1965. In *Contemp. Psychol.,* 1967, 12, 212, 214.

508 ————. Review of R. S. Woodworth, *Dynamics of behavior.* New York: Holt, 1958. In *Contemp. Psychol.,* 1954, 4, 129-133.

509 ————. Revolution in integrity? *Voices,* 1967, 3(1), 26-33.

510 ————. The role of the concept of sin in psychotherapy. *J. couns. Psychol.,* 1960, 7, 185-188.

511 ————. Sigmund Freud: Psychotherapist or "theologian?" *Psychiat. Dig.,* June, 1965. Pp. 39-47.

512 ————. "Sin": The lesser of two evils. *Amer. Psychologist,* 1960, 15, 301-304. Also in M. Zax & G. Stricker (Eds.), *The study of abnormal behavior.*

513 ————. A stimulus-response analysis of anxiety and its role as a reinforcing agent. *Psychol. Rev.,* 1939, 46, 553-565.

514 ————. Tension changes during psychotherapy (with J. McV. Hunt & L. S. Kogan). In *Psychotherapy: Theory and research.* Pp. 596-640.

515 ————. Time as a determinant in integrative learning. *Psychol. Rev.,* 1945, 52, 61-90 (with A. D. Ullman).

516 ————. Too little and too late. *Int. J. Psychiat.,* 1969, 7, 536-556.

517 ————. Training in therapy. *J. consult. Psychol.,* 1951, 15, 274-277.

518 ————. What is normal behavior? In L. A. Pennington & I. A. Berg (Eds.), *An introduction to clinical psychology.* Pp. 58-88.

519 Mowrer, W. M. Enuresis—A method for its study and treatment. *Amer. J. Orthopsychiat.,* 1938, 8, 436-459 (with O. H. Mowrer).

520 Mozdzierz, G. J. Alcoholism and ethical risk taking. *Quart. J. Studies in Alcohol,* 1971, 32(3), 775-781 (with H. Krauss & F. Macchitelli).

521 ————. Anxiety and temporal perspective among normals in a stressful life situation. *Psychol. Rep.,* 1967, 21, 721-724 (with H. Krauss, R. Ruiz & J. Button).

522 ————. Classroom status and perceived performance in sixth graders. *J. soc. Psychol.,* 1968, 75, 185-190 (with M. McConville & H. Krauss).

523 ————. Comments on the automated interview. *Nwsltr. Res. Psychol.,* 1971, 13, 39-40.

524 ————. How you can improve your married life. *New World,* 1971, 79(41), 11.

525 ————. Husband-wife games: What they really mean. *New World,* 1972, 80(8), 9. Also in *Fam. Dig.,* 1972, 27, 49-54.

526 ————. New dimension in the treatment of alcoholism. *Ill. med. J.,* 1969, 135, 24-27 (with R. de Vito & L. Flaherty).

527 ————. Summation of thirst and maternal drives in the white rat. *Loyola Behav. Lab. Series,* 1962-63, 3 (11) (with R. Meier & M. McConnville).

528 ————. Temperament characteristics of chronic alcoholics as measured by the Guilford-Zimmerman Temperament Survey. *J. gen. Psychol.,* 1971, 79, 97-102 (with F. Macchitelli, L. Flaherty & R. de Vito).

529 ————. Toward a psychodynamic theory in alcoholism. *Dis. nerv. Sys.,* 1970, 31, 43-49 (with R. de Vito & L. Flaherty).

530 ————. Vietnam era veterans and AMA discharges: A further look. *Nwsltr. Res. Psychol.,* 1972, 14(2), 17.

531 Mukherjee, B. N. Birth order and verbalized need for achievement. *J. soc. Psychol.,* 1968, 75, 223-229.

532 Mulgrave, N. An investigation of the cognitive factor structure of two types of concept attainment tasks and two tests of cognitive style. *Diss. Abstr.,* 1966, 27, 1283. Unpubl. Ph.D. Diss., Univ. Pittsburgh, 1965.

533 Mullahy, P. *Oedipus: Myth and complex.* New York: Hermitage Press, 1948.

534 Mullahy, P. *Psychoanalysis: Evolution and development.* New York: Hermitage House, 1950; New York: Grove, 1950 (with Clara Thompson).

535 Müller, A. Anthropology and Individual Psychology. *AJIP*, 1956, 12, 106–111.

536 ———. A case of speech disturbance (with T. Vértes). In A. Adler & assoc., *Guiding the child.* Pp. 241–246.

357 ———. Contribution to understanding of the nature and management of the so-called organ neuroses. *AJIP*, 1954, 10, 136–139.

538 ———. *Du sollst ein Segen sein: Grundzüge eines religiösen Humanismus.* Schwarzenburg, Switzerland: Gerber, 1954.

539 ———. Ein Fall von Organmindwertigkeit. *IZIP*, 1929, 7(3), 238–239 (with T. Vértes).

540 ———. Erlebnis. *IZIP*, 1926, 4(1), 40–42.

541 ———. Errors in the technique of guidance work. In A. Adler & assoc., *Guiding the child.* Pp. 119–126.

542 ———. *Gij zult een zegen zijn.* Den Haag: N. V. Servier, 1963.

543 ———. Kunstfehler in der Beratungstechnik. *IZIP*, 1929, 7(3), 204–206.

544 ———. Portrait. *IPNL*, 1971, 20(6), 110.

545 ———. The positive emotional attitude. *IJIP*, 1937, 3(1), 30–37.

546 ———. Positive Gefühleinstellung. *IZIP*, 1930, 8(1), 98–102.

547 ———. Preliminary report on the foundation of an International Association of Adlerian (Individual) Psychology. *IPNL*, 1954, No. 38. Pp. 2–6 (with J. Bierer & V. Louis).

548 ———. Über sensitiven Beziehungswahn. *IZIP*, 1927, 5(6), 412–418.

549 ———. Zur Theorie und Therapie der Organneurosen. In Int. Verein Indivpsy., *Alfred Adler zum Gedenken.* Pp. 64–77.

550 Müller, Mrs. A. Portrait. *IPNL*, 1971, 20(6), 110.

551 Müller, O. Anna Freuds Technik der Kinderanalyse. *IZIP*, 1927, 5(5), 356–361.

552 ———. Review of Alice Rühle-Gerstel, *Der Weg zum Wir.* In *IZIP*, 1927, 5(6), 482.

553 ———. *Sexuelle Verirrung.* Berlin: A. Hoffmans, 1929.

554 Multatuli, [   ]. Geschichte von der Autorität. *IZIP*, 1929, 7(3), 243–244.

555 Mundy, Sister Jean. [Funeral services for R. Dreikurs]. *Nwsltr.,* (Family Educ. Ctrs. of Hawaii), 1972 3(1).

556 Munkh, Mira. Fortschritte und Ausblicke der Individualpsychologie. *IZIP*, 1951, 20(1), 1–15.

557 Munoz-Cuesta, Emilia. Translator of J. Meiers, Remarques sur la psychothérapie des personnes agées.

558 Munroe, R. H. Overrepresentation of first borns in East African secondary schools. *J. soc. Psychol.,* 1971, 84, 151–152 (with R. L. Munroe).

559 Munroe, R. L. Overrepresentation of first borns in East African secondary schools. *J. soc. Psychol.,* 1971, 84, 151–152 (with R. H. Munroe).

560 Munroe, Ruth L. *Schools of psychoanalytic thought.* New York: Dryden Press, 1955.

561 Munsinger, H. Stimulus variability and cognitive change. *Psychol. Rev.,* 1966, 73, 164–178 (with W. Kessen).

562 Munz, D. C. Achievement motivation and ordinal position of birth. *Psychol. Rep.,* 1968, 23, 175–180 (with A. D. Smouse & G. Letchworth).

563 ———. Ordinal position of birth and self-disclosure in high school students. *Psychol. Rep.,* 1968, 21, 829–833 (with R. E. Dimond).

564 Murchison, C. (Ed.). *A handbook of child psychology.* Worcester, Mass.: Clark Univ. Press, 1931.

565 ——— (Ed.). *Psychologies of 1930.* Worcester, Mass.: Clark Univ. Press, 1930.

566 Murdock, P. H. Birth order and affiliation. *Brit. J. soc. clin. Psychol.,* 1969, 8, 235–245 (with G. F. Smith).

567 ———. Birth order and age at marriage. *Brit. J. soc. clin. Psychol.,* 1966, 5, 24–29.

568 Murdock, B. B. Jr. Perceptual defense and threshold measurements. *J. Pers.,* 1954, 22, 565–571.

569 Muro, J. J. *Group counseling theory and practice.* Itasca, Ill.: Peacock Press, 1971 (with D. C. Dinkmeyer).

570 ——— (Ed.). *Readings in group counseling.* Scranton, Pa.: Int. Textbook Co., 1968 (with S. L. Freeman).

571 Murphy, G. *Experimental social psychology.* New York: Harper, 1937. Pp. 345–373 (with Lois B. Murphy & T. M. Newcomb).

N

572 Murphy, G. The factor of attitude in associative memory. *J. exp. Psychol.*, 1943, 33, 228–238 (with L. Postman).

573 ———. *Fulfillment of one's individuality and milieu.* (Tribute to Alfred Adler on his 100th birthday). *JIP*, 1970, 26(2), 14–15.

574 ———. *Historical introduction to modern psychology.* Rev. ed. New York: Harper, 1949.

575 ———. *Personality: A biosocial approach to origins and structure.* New York: Harper, 1947, 1966.

576 ———. The third human nature. *JIP*, 1957, 13, 125–133.

577 Murphy, Lois B. *Experimental social psychology.* New York: Harper, 1937. Pp. 345–373 (with G. Murphy & T. M. Newcomb).

578 Murray, E. J. Review of K. A. Adler & Danica Deutsch (Eds.), *Essays in Individual Psychology.* In *Contemp. Psychol.*, 1960, 5, 332–333.

579 Murray, N. Prolonged sneezing. *Psychosom. Med.*, 1951, 13, 56–58 (with J. Bierer).

580 Murstein, B. L. The complementary need hypothesis in newlyweds and middle-aged married couples. *J. abnorm. soc. Psychol.*, 1961, 63, 194–197.

581 Mussen, P. H. The effects of feeding, weaning, and scheduling procedures on childhood adjustment and the formation of oral symptoms. *Child Developm.*, 1952, 23, 185–191 (with W. H. Sewell).

582 ———. Infant feeding gratification and adult personality. *J. Pers.*, 1951, 19, 449–458 (with J. R. Thurston).

583 Mutschmann, H. *Der andere Milton.* Bonn: Kurt Schroeder, 1920.

584 ———. *Milton und das Licht.* Halle a.d. Saale: Max Niemeyer, 1920.

585 Myasishchev, V. N. Treatment of neuroses: Soviet and American, pros and cons. *Soviet Life*, 1966, No. 6(117). Pp. 16–17.

586 Myers, J. S. Schizophrenia in the youngest male child of the lower middle class. *Amer. J. Psychiat.*, 1955, 112, 129–134 (with B. H. Roberts).

587 Myrdal, G. Foreward to K. B. Clark, *Dark ghetto.*

1 N. Review of R. Sandek, *Experimentelle Graphologie.* Berlin: Pan-Verlag, 1929. In *IZIP*, 1929, 7(4), 316.

2 Nadaud, L. Aspects adlériennes de la "Bhagavad Ghita". *BSFPA*, 1972, No. 12. Pp. 24–29.

3 ———. Le névrose obsessionelle de SALAVIN (Duhamel) dans l'optique adlérienne. *BSFPA*, 1972, No. 13. Pp. 28–36.

4 ———. Quelques points communs à la psychologie adlérienne et à la sagesse orientale. *BISFPA*, 1970, No. 7. Pp. 29–34.

5 Naegele, O. Der Erziehungsgedanke im Jugendrecht. In D. Oestreich (Ed.), *Entschiedene Schulreform.* Vol. 48. Leipzig: Oldenberg, 1925.

6 ———. Jugendlicher und Justiz. In E. Wexberg (Ed.), *Handbuch der Individualpsychologie.* Pp. 382–415.

7 ———. Kriminalität und Justiz. *IZIP*, 1931, 9(5), 350–357.

8 ———. *Das kriminelle Kind.* Dresden: Verlag am andern Ufer, 1926.

9 ———. Menschenkenntnis und Selbsterkenntnis des Richters. *IZIP*, 1930, 8(1), 181–188.

10 ———. Review of *Beiträge zur Kriminalpsychologie und Strafrechtsreform.* Heidelberg: C. Winter's, 1926. In *IZIP*, 1927, 5(4), 316–317.

11 ———. Review of Fürst, Herschfeld, Riese & Steinschneider, *Der Fall Weichmann.* Stuttgart: Julius Püttman, 1928. In *IZIP*, 1930, 8(4), 439.

12 ———. Review of *Mitteilungen der Kriminalbiologischen Gesellschaft.* Graz: Ulrich Mosers, 1929. In *IZIP*, 1930, 8(4), 438–439.

13 ———. Review of O. Monkmöller, *Psychologie und Psychopathologie der Aussage.* In *IZIP*, 1930, 8(4), 595–596.

14 ———. Review of [   ], *Die Münchner Fürsorgergemeinschaft.* In *IZIP*, 1924, 2(5), 35.

15 ———. Review of R. Sieverts, *Die Wirkungen der Freiheitsstrafe und Untersuchungschaft auf die Psyche der Gefangenen.* Mannheim: J. Bensheimer, 1929. In *IZIP*, 1931, 9(1), 75.

16 **Naegele, O.** Review of E. Wulffen, *Kriminalpsychologie.* Berlin: Langenscheidt, 1926. In *IZIP*, 1930, 8(4), 235-238.

17 ———. *Richter und Jugendlicher.* Selbstverlag, 1923.

18 ———. Schule und Justiz. *IZIP*, 1926, 4(3), 115-124.

19 **Nagel, E.** (Ed.). *Scientific psychology: Principles and approaches.* New York: Basic Books, 1965 (with B. B. Wolman).

20 **Nagelschmidt, Stephanie.** Review of M. Burns, *Mr. Lyward's answer.* In *IPNL*, 1956, 6(3-4, Whole No. 67-69). Pp. 12-14.

21 **Nagge, J. W.** *Psychology of the child.* New York: Ronald Press, 1942.

22 **Nathorff, Hertha.** A case of rare deviation. In K. A. Adler & Danica Deutsch (Eds.), *Essays in Individual Psychology.* Pp. 360-365.

23 **National Committee for Children and Youth.** The American Society of Adlerian Psychology. *NCCY Follow Up Reporter,* 1969, 9(1), 18-19.

24 **Nawas, M. M.** A future-oriented theory of nostalgia. *JIP*, 1965, 21, 51-57 (with J. J. Platt).

25 ———. Review of E. H. Erikson, *Insight and responsibility.* New York: Norton, 1964. In *JIP*, 1965, 21(2), 213-214.

26 **Necheles, Stefanie.** The social worker. In R. Dreikurs, R. Corsini, R. Lowe & M. Sonstegard (Eds.), *Adlerian family counseling.* Pp. 41-44.

27 **Nedzielski, H.** La democratie au foyer. *La Tribune de l'Enfance,* 1970, 8, 41-45.

28 **Neff, W. S.** Toleration for psychiatric rehabilitation as a function of coping style. *J. consult. Psychol.,* 1967, 31, 364-370 (with M. Koltuv).

29 **Neilson, Ethel.** Portrait. *IPNL*, 1970, 19(4), 79.

30 **Neisser, Edith F.** *The eldest child.* New York: Harper, 1957.

31 **Nelson, L. L.** Competition: The star-spangled scramble. *Psychol. Today,* 1972, 6(4), 53-56, 90-91 (with S. Kagan).

32 **Nelson, M. O.** An application of the Q-technique to the study of religious concepts. *Psychol. Rep.,* 1957, 3, 293-297 (with E. M. Jones).

33 ———. The concept of God and feeling toward parents. *JIP*, 1971, 27(1), 46-49.

34 **Nelson, M. O.** Les concepts religieux dans leur relation aux images parentals (with E. M. Jones). In A. Godin (Ed.), *Adult et enfant devant Dieu.*

35 ———. Effectiveness of Adlerian counseling with low achieving students. *JIP*, 1966, 22, 222-227 (with Maureen Haberer).

36 ———. Individual Psychology as a basis for the counseling of low achieving students. *Pers. Guid. J.,* 1967, 46(3), 283-287.

37 ———. Scene in a consulting room. *IPNL*, 1968, 18(3-4, Whole No. 212-213). Pp. 19-21.

38 **Netherlands Institute for Individual Psychology.** Report for the year 1949. *IPB*, 1950, 8, 158-161.

39 **Neto, T. N.** Translator of A. Adler, *A ciencia de viver.*

40 **Nettler, G.** A measure of alienation. *Amer. sociol. Rev.,* 1957, 22, 670-677.

41 **Neuda, P.** Individualpsychologische Gedankengänge in Vergangenheit und Gegenwart. *IZIP*, 1926, 4(4), 237-239.

42 **Neuer, A.** Adlers "absolute Wahrheit" und Künkel's "Infinale". *IZIP*, 1928, 6(3), 222-228.

43 ———. Courage and discouragement. *IJIP*, 1936, 2(2), 30-50.

44 ———. Ist Individualpsychologie als Wissenschaft möglich? *IZIP*, 1913, 1(1), 3-8.

45 ———. Die moderne Ehe als neurotisches Symptom. *IZIP*, 1929, 7(1), 36-44.

46 ———. Mut und Entmutigung: Die Prinzipien der Psychologie Alfred Adlers. In A. Adler, L. Seif, & O. Kaus (Eds.), *Individuum und Gemeinschaft.*

47 ———. A note on modern marriage and neurosis. *IJIP*, 1936, 2(4), 49-54.

48 ———. On education methods which are based upon Individual Psychology (with Martha Holub). In A. Adler & assoc., *Guiding the child.* Pp. 148-156.

49 ———. Die Psychoanalyse gesehen mit den Augen eines Individual-Psychologen. *IZIP*, 1927, 5(6), 409-411.

50 ———. Review of K. Bonhoeffer & W. His, *Beurteilung, Begutachtung und Rechtsprechung bei den sogenannten Unfallsneurosen.* Leipzig: Georg Thieme, 1926. In *IZIP*, 1928, 6(6), 505.

51 ———. Review of F. Brentano, *Psychologie vom empirischen Standpunkt.* Leipzig: Felix Meiner, [   ]. In *IZIP*, 1932, 10(1), 76-77.

52 **Neuer, A.** Review of K. Bühler, *Die Krise der Psychologie.* Jena: Gustav Fischer, 1927. In *IZIP*, 1928, 6(4), 342.

53 ———. Review of *Festschrift zu Karl Bühlers 50 Geburtstag.* Jena: Gustav Fischer, 1929. In *IZIP*, 1932, 10(1), 75–76.

54 ———. Review of S. Freud, *Die Zukunft einer Illusion.* Wien: Int. Psychoanal. Verlag, 1927. In *IZIP*, 1928, 6(6), 503.

55 ———. Review of R. Hamburger, *Neue Theorie der Wahrnehmung und des Denkens.* Berlin: Geo. Stilke, n.d. In *IZIP*, 1932, 10(1), 76.

56 ———. Review of C. G. Jung, *Die Bedeutung des Vaters für das Schicksal des Einzelnen.* Wien: Deuticke, 1927. In *IZIP*, 1929, 7(1), 76–77.

57 ———. Review of C. G. Jung, *Die Beziehungen zwischen dem Ich und dem Unbewussten.* Darmstadt: Reichl, 1928. In *IZIP*, 1928, 6(6), 504–505.

58 ———. Review of F. Linke, *Grundfragen der Wahrnehmungslehre.* München: Ernst Reinhardt, [   ]. In *IZIP*, 1932, 10(1), 77.

59 ———. Review of H. Lungwitz, *Die Entdeckung der Seele.* Leipzig: Ernst Oldenberg, [   ]. In *IZIP*, 1932, 10(1), 77–78.

60 ———. Review of A. Maeder, *Die Richtung im Seelenleben.* Zürich: Rascher, 1928. In *IZIP*, 1929, 7(1), 77.

61 ———. Review of M. Nachmannsohn, *Die wissenschaftlichen Grundlagen der Psychoanalyse Freuds.* Berlin: S. Karger, 1928. In *IZIP*, 1929, 7(1), 77.

62 ———. Review of M. Rosenfeld, *Die Störungen des Bewusstseins.* Leipzig: Georg Thieme, n.d. In *IZIP*, 1932, 10(1), 76.

63 ———. Review of E. Stier, *Über die sogenannten Unfallsneurosen.* Leipzig: Georg Thieme, 1926. In *IZIP*, 1928, 6(3), 260.

64 ———. Review of H. Vaihinger, *Philosophie des Als Ob.* Leipzig: Felix Meiner, 1928. In *IZIP*, 1930, 8(2), 273–274.

65 ———. Das Training im Traume. *IZIP*, 1928, 6(3), 187–191.

66 ———. Über den III. allgemeinen ärztlichen Kongress für Psychotherapie. *IZIP*, 1928, 6(4), 325–333.

67 ———. Über nicht-individualpsychologische Erziehungsberatungs-methoden.

IZIP, 1929, 7(3), 215–217 (with Martha Holub).

68 **Neufeld, I.** Adler and creative power. *IP*, 1967, 4(2), 41–42.

69 ———. Application of Individual-Psychological concepts in psychosomatic medicine. *AJIP*, 1955, 11, 104–117.

70 ———. Application of the stress concept in the management of psychosomatic cases in nonpsychiatric medical practice. *Int. Rec. Med.*, 1958, 171, 134–145.

71 ———. The authentic life style. *IP*, 1964, 2(1), 9–21.

72 ———. An editorial. *AJIP*, 1954, 10, 97–98.

73 ———. Evaluation of "psychic" superstructure of "somatic" symptoms. *Amer. J. Psychother.*, 1955, 9, 27–42.

74 ———. Fibropathic syndromes in geriatric patients. *Geriatrics*, 1955, 10, 318–323.

75 ———. Holistic medicine versus psychosomatic medicine. *AJIP*, 1954, 10, 140–168.

76 ———. Mechanical factors in the pathogenesis, prophylaxis, and management of "fibrositis". *Arch. phys. Med. Rehab.*, 1955, 36, 759–765.

77 ———. Outline of teleo-psychological principles in rehabilitation of physically handicapped persons. *IPB*, 1951, 9, 47–69.

78 ———. Pathogenetic concepts of "fibrositis". *Arch. phys. Med.*, 1952, 33, 363–369.

79 ———. Psychological implication of the causality-finality schism. *IPB*, 1951, 9, 127–132.

80 ———. Psychosomatic medicine in geriatric practice. *IP*, 1968, 5, 40–48.

81 ———. Recognition and management of post-traumatic psychosomatic manifestations. In A. J. Cantor & A. N. Foxe (Eds.), *Psychosomatic aspects of surgery.* New York: Grune and Stratton, 1956. Pp. 159–175.

82 ———. Referred pain. In *Proceed. Rudolf Virchow Med. Soc.*, 1959, 16.

83 ———. Review of L. E. Cole, *Human behavior: Psychology as bio-social science.* Yonkers-on-Hudson, N. Y.: World Book Co., 1953. In *AJIP*, 1956, 12, 93–94.

84 ———. Review of A. Farau, *Der Einfluss der Oesterreichischen Tiefenpsychologie auf die Amerikanische Psychotherapie der Gegenwart.* In *AJIP*, 1956, 12, 92–93.

85 **Neufeld, I.** Review of E. Podolsky, *Music therapy.* New York: Phil. Libr., 1954. In *AJIP*, 1956, 12, 186-187.

86 ———. Review of D. D. Runes, *Pictorial history of philosophy.* New York: Phil. Libr., 1959. In *IP*, 1962, 2(1), 28.

87 ———. Review of C. Taylor, *The explanation of behaviour.* New York: Humanities Press, 1964. In *IP*, 1965, 3(1), 25.

88 ———. Review of W. Toman, *Family constellation.* In *IP*, 1963, 1(1), 17-18.

89 ———. Talking about Alfred Adler, *IPNL*, 1967, 17 (11-12, Whole No. 196-197). P. 81.

90 ———. A teleo-analytic approach to the application of the stress concept in dynamic psychology. In K. A. Adler & Danica Deutsch (Eds.), *Essays in Individual Psychology.* Pp. 132-139.

91 **Neumann, A.** Die individualpsychologische Deutung und Behandlung der Neurose. *IZIP*, 1936, 14(2), 80-94.

92 **Neumann, E.** *The origin and history of consciousness.* New York: Pantheon, 1954; New York: Harper Torchbooks, 1962. Paper.

93 **Neumann, Frau.** Portrait. *IPNL*, 1972, 21 (6), 109.

94 **Neumann, J.** Diebstahl als Enmutigungserscheinung. *IZIP*, 1928, 6(5), 412-414.

95 ——— (Ed.). *Du und der Alltag: Eine Psychologie des täglichen Lebens.* Berlin: Warneck, 1926.

96 ——— (Ed.). *Einführung in die Psychotherapie für Pfarrer auf individualpsychologischer Grundlage.* Gütersloh: Bertelsmann, 1930.

97 ——— (Ed.). *Die Entwicklung der sittlichen Persönlichkeit.* Gütersloh: C. Bertelsmann, 1930.

98 ———. Expressionismus als Lebensstil. *Z. angew. Psychol.*, 1932, 43, 414-460.

99 ———. Die Gefühle und das Ich. In A. Adler, L. Seif & O. Kaus (Eds.), *Individuum und Gemeinschaft.*

100 ——— (Ed.). *Gemeinschaft mit Freunden der Individualpsychologie.* Berlin: Martin Warneck, 1926.

101 ———. Grundlegung einer individualpsychologischen Soziologie. *IZIP*, 1925, 3(5), 228-242.

102 ———. Grundlinien des Menschenbildes der Individualpsychologie. In Int. Verein Indivpsy., *Alfred Adler zum Gedenken.* Pp. 78-91.

103 **Neumann, J.** Hauterkrankungen aus Eitelkeit. *IZIP*, 1951, 20(4), 159-165.

104 ———. Kierkegaards "Pfahl im Fleisch". *IZIP*, 1949, 18(1), 7-13.

105 ———. *Leben ohne Angst: Psychologische Seelenheilkunde.* Stuttgart: Hippokrates Verlag, 1938, 1948.

106 ———. *Leven zon der angst: Psychologie en psychotherapie van den modernen mensch.* Amsterdam: Kosmos, 1938.

107 ———. Macht und Liebe: Ein Grundproblem einer Psychopolitik. *IZIP*, 1949, 18(3), 97-121; 18(4), 155-166.

108 ———. Möglichkeiten, Erfolge, Grenzen der Selbsterziehung. *IZIP*, 1930, 8(1), 43-51.

109 ———. *Der nervöse Charakter und seine Heilung.* Stuttgart: Hippokrates-Verlag, 1954; Buenos Aires: , 1955.

110 ———. Portrait. *IPNL*, 1972, 21(6), 109.

111 ———. Die Problematik der Angst im Lichte der Individualpsychologie. *Z. Psychosomat. Med.* (Göttingen), 1963, 9, 108-115.

112 ———. *Psychiatrische Seelsorge im Lichte der Individualpsychologie.* Schwerin i. Meckl.: F. Balm, 1927.

113 ——— (Ed.). *Religionpsychologische Reihe.* Gütersloh: C. Bertelsmann, 1930.

114 ———. Religiöse Erlösung und individualpsychologische Heilung. *IZIP*, 1928, 6(6), 482-492.

115 ———. Review of R. Allers, *Das Werden der sittlichen Person.* In *IZIP*, 1929, 7(6), 477-478.

116 ———. Review of D. P. Blau, *Seelsorge an den Jugendlichen.* Gütersloh: Author, 1931. In *IZIP*, 1933, 12(4), 332-333.

117 ———. Review of W. Burkamp, *Die Struktur der Ganzheiten.* Berlin: Junker & Dünnhaupt, 1929. In *IZIP*, 1931, 9(5), 408.

118 ———. Review of M. Flesch, *Gehirn und Veranlagung des Verbrechers.* Berlin: Walter de Gruyter, 1929. In *IZIP*, 1930, 8(2), 271.

119 ———. Review of J. Fröbes, *Lehrbuch der experimentellen Psychologie.* Freiburg: Herder, 1929. In *IZIP*, 1933, 12(4), 333.

120 ———. Review of G. Füllkrug, *Seelenkunde der weiblichen Jugend.* Schwerin i. Meckl.: Bahn, 1927. In *IZIP*, 1928, 6(4), 346.

121 **Neumann, J.** Review of K. J. Grau, *Eitelkeit und Schamgefühl.* Leipzig: Felix Meiner, 1928. In *IZIP*, 1929, 7(2), 314.

122 ———. Review of W. Gruehn, *Religionspsychologie.* Breslau: Jedermanns Bucherei, 1926. In *IZIP*, 1927, 5(3), 238-239.

123 ———. Review of L. Klages, Persönlichkeit, Einführung in die Charakterkunde & H. Prinzhorn, Leib—Seele—Einheit & G. R. Heyer, Seelenführung. All in *Das Weltbild.* Potsdam: Müller & Kiepenhauer, . In *IZIP*, 1929, 7(2), 313-314.

124 ———. Review of R. Koch, *Ärztliche Studie über zwölf theologische Schriften Hohenheims aus der Philosophia magna.* Leipzig: J. A. Barth, 1927. In *IZIP*, 1928, 6(5), 416–417.

125 ———. Review of H. Leitner, *Psychologie jugendlicher Religiosität innerhalb des deutschen Methodismus.* München: Becksche, 1930. In *IZIP*, 1933, 12(4), 334.

126 ———. Review of R. Liertz, *Erziehung und Seelsorge.* München: J. Kösel & F. Pustet, 1927. In *IZIP*, 1927, 5(5), 392-393.

127 ———. Review of O. Rank, *Grundzüge einer genetischen Psychologie.* Wien: F. Deuticke, 1927 & *Gestaltung und Ausdruck der Persönlichkeit.* [   ]: Ebenda, 1928. In *IZIP*, 1930, 8(3), 358.

128 ———. Review of F. Seifert, *Charakterologie.* München: Oldenbourg, 1929. In *IZIP*, 1934, 12(1), 54.

129 ———. Review of M. Wertheimer, *Über Gestalttheorie.* Erlangen: Verlag der philosoph. Akademie, 1925. In *IZIP*, 1927, 5(2), 157.

130 ———. Review of L. V. Wiese, *Allgemeine Soziologie als Lehre von den Beziehungen und den Beziehungsbilden der Menschen.* In *IZIP*, 1933, 12(3), 256.

131 ———. *Schleiermacher—Existenz, Ganzheit, Gefühl als Grundlagen seiner Anthropologie.* Berlin: Neue deutsche Forschungen, 1936.

132 ———. Soeren Kirkegaards Individuationsprozess nach seinen Tagebüchern. *Z. Psychother. med. Psychol.*, 1952, 2, 152–168.

133 ———. Über den Münchener Kurs über Psychotherapie an Kindern und Jugendlichen. *IZIP*, 1928, 6(6), 492–495.

134 ———. Über den IV allg. ärztlichen Kongress für Psychotherapie. *IZIP*, 1929, 7(4), 303-305.

135 **Neumann, J.** Wetzlar, die Entstehung des Selbst aus der Angst. In W. Bitter (Ed.), *Angst und Schuld in theologischer und psychotherapeutischer Sicht, ein Tagungbericht.* 2nd ed. Stuttgart: Ernst Klett, 1959.

136 ———. Zur Psychologie des anachronistischen Mönchtums. *IZIP*, 1927, 5(1), 50-62.

137 **Newbert, N.** A study of certain personality correlates of the middle child in a three-child family. *Diss. Abstr.*, 1969, 29, 4333-4334.

138 **Newcomb, T. M.** *Experimental social psychology.* New York: Harper, 1937. Pp. 345-373 (with G. Murphy & Lois B. Murphy).

139 **Newcombe, H. B.** Screening for effects of maternal age and birth order in a register of handicapped children. *Ann. hum. Genet.*, 1964, 27, 367-382.

140 **Newell, A. W.** The psychodynamics of maternal rejection. *Amer. J. Orthopsychiat.*, 1934, 4, 387–401.

141 **Newell, J. F.** The relationship of social concept development and children's social perception. *Diss. Abstr. Int.*, 1969, 30, 812.

142 **Newman, Daisy.** Review of C. Wilson, *Religion and the rebel.* Boston: Houghton Mifflin, 1957. In *JIP*, 1959, 15, 134-135.

143 **Newson, L. J.** Family or sibship and some aspects of juvenile delinquency. *Brit. J. Delin.*, 1954, 5, 46-65 (with J. P. Lees).

144 **Nichols, K.** Selecting the Nazi officer. *Infantry J.*, 1941, 49(Nov.), 44–48 (with H. L. Ansbacher).

145 **Nicole, J. E.** *Psychopathology: A survey of modern approaches.* London: Tindall & Cox, 1930.

146 ———. Review of L. Way, *Adler's place in psychology.* In *J. ment. Sci.*, 1951, 97, 597.

147 **Niederland, W. G.** The ego in the recovery of early memories. *Psychoanal. Quart.*, 1965, 34, 564-571.

148 **Nielsen, J.** Translator of R. Dreikurs, *Psykologi i klassaevaerelset.*

149 **Nielsen, J. M.** Birth primacy and idiopathic epilepsy. *Bull. Los Angeles Neurol. Soc.*, 1948, 13, 176–   (with F. O. Butler).

150 **Nikelly, A. G.** Action-oriented methods (with W. E. O'Connell). In *Techniques for behavior change.* Pp. 85-90.

151 Nikelly, A. G. The Adlerian concept of the unconscious in psychotherapy. *JIP*, 1966, 22, 214–221.

152 ———. Alfred Adler's contribution to modern education and its goals. *IP*, 1971, 8(1), 1–6.

153 ———. Basic processes in psychotherapy. In *Techniques for behavior change*. Pp. 27–32.

154 ———. The centennial of Alfred Adler. *Acta Neurol. Psychiat. Hellenica*, 1970, 9(3), 165–178.

155 ———. Democratic assumptions in Adler's psychology. *JIP*, 1963, 19, 161–166.

156 ———. The dependent adolescent. *Adolescence*, 1971, 6(22), 139–144.

157 ———. Developing social feeling in psychotherapy. In *Techniques for behavior change*. Pp. 91–95.

158 ———. Early recollections (with D. Verger). In *Techniques for behavior change*. Pp. 55–60.

159 ———. Ethical issues in research on student protest. *Amer. Psychologist*, 1971, 26(5), 475–478.

160 ———. Existential-humanism in Adlerian psychotherapy (with E. A. Dreyfus). In *Techniques for behavior change*. Pp. 13–20.

161 ———. Extentialism and education for mental health. *J. Existent.*, 1964, 5, 205–212.

162 ———. Family constellation (with B. H. Shulman). In *Techniques for behavior change*. Pp. 35–40.

163 ———. Fundamental concepts of maladjustment. In *Techniques for behavior change*. Pp. 21–25.

164 ———. Goal-directedness: A practical goal for psychotherapy. *Ment. Hyg.*, 1962, 46, 523–526.

165 ———. A guide for adjusting to college: *Mental health for students*. Springfield, Ill.: C. C. Thomas, 1966.

166 ———. Individual and social ethics of clinical psychology. *Clin. Psychologist*, 1972, 26(1), 8–9.

167 ———. Maternal indulgence and neglect and maladjustment in adolescents. *J. clin. Psychol.*, 1967, 23, 148–150.

168 ———. *Mental health for students*. Springfield, Ill.: C. C. Thomas, 1966.

169 ———. Multiple therapy. In *Techniques for behavior change*. Pp. 129–133.

170 Nikelly, A. G. Parsimony in Freud and Adler. *Psychiat. Quart. Suppl.* 1962, 36(1), 100–106.

171 ———. Private logic. In *Techniques for behavior change*. Pp. 61–64.

172 ———. The process of encouragement (with D. Dinkmeyer). In *Techniques for behavior change*. Pp. 97–101.

173 ———. The protesting student. In *Techniques for behavior change*. Pp. 159–164.

174 ———. Psychodrama (with Adaline Starr). In *Techniques for behavior change*. Pp. 135–139.

175 ———. The psychologic problems of democratization. *Amer. J. Psychother.*, 1964, 18, 52–58.

176 ———. Psychotherapy as reorientation and readjustment (with J. A. Bostrom). In *Techniques for behavior change*. Pp. 103–107.

177 ———. Review of H. L. Ansbacher, Utilization of creativity in Adlerian psychotherapy. In *Amer. J. Psychother.*, 1972, 26(3), 455–456.

178 ———. The schizophrenic in college. *Arch. gen. Psychiat.*, 1966, 15, 54–58 (with T. A. Kiersch).

179 ———. Social interest: A paradigm for mental health education. *JIP*, 1962, 18, 147–150.

180 ——— (Ed.). *Techniques for behavior change*. Springfield, Ill.: C. C. Thomas, 1971.

181 ———. Toward effective mental health education. *Coll. Hlth.*, 1962, 11, 148–152.

182 Nisbett, R. E. Birth order and participation in dangerous sports. *J. Pers. soc. Psychol.*, 1968, 8, 351–353.

183 Nissen, I. *Absolute monogamy, the attitude of woman, and war*. Oslo: Aschehoug, 1961.

184 ———. *The dictatorship of psychopaths*. Oslo: 1945.

185 ———. *Menneskelige oppgaver og utveier: Ledende ideer i mitt forfatterskap*. Oslo: Aschehoug (Nygaard), 1966. Paper.

186 ———. *Moral philosophy and the techniques of ruling, a study of George Edward Moore's theory of value*. Oslo: 1948.

187 ———. Psychological motifs in the works of the Norwegian sculptor, Gustav Vigeland. *Int. Rec. Med.*, 1952, 165, 177–183.

188 ———. Das psychologische Problem in Ibsens "Rosmersholm". *IZIP*, 1931, 9(2), 132–136.

189 **Nissen, I.** Self-review of *Sjelelig forsvar.*
In *IZIP,* 1931, 9(1), 74–75.
190 ———. Self-review of *Sjelelige Kuser i
menueskets liv. Henrik Ibsen og den
moderne psykologie.* In *IZIP,* 1932, 10(3),
233.
191 ———. *Sjelelig forsvar.* Oslo: Aschehoug,
1930.
192 ———. *Sjelelig kuser i menueskets liv.
Henrik Ibsen og den moderne psykologie.*
Oslo: Aschehoug, 1931.
193 ———. *The structure of the methodology
of the cultural sciences.* Oslo: Acad. of
Sci., 1942.
194 **Noble, R.** Psychiatry and the community.
IPP, 1938, No. 20. Pp. 42–53.
195 **Noetzel, Elinor.** A study of birth order
and behavior. *J. soc. Psychol.,* 1931, 2,
52–71 (with I. S. Wile).
196 **Norman, W. G.** Selection and engagement
of patients in family therapy. *Amer. J.
Orthopsychiat.,* 1968, 38(4), 715–723
(with Ruth Ronall, C. J. Sager & Yvonne
J. Masters).
197 **Novotny, S.** *Betrachtungen zur Individualpsychologie.* Wien: Wilhelm Mandrich,
1947.
198 **Nowotny, K.** Alfred Adler. In Int. Verein
Indivpsy., *Alfred Adler zum gedenken.* Pp.
3–10.
199 ———. Bericht über das individualpsychologische Ambulatorium der psychiatrisch-
neurologischen Abteilung des Wiener allgemeinen Krankenhaus. *IZIP,* 1931, 9(6),
474–477.
200 ———. Individualpsychologie als Wirklich-
keitswissenschaft. *IZIP,* 1949, 18(1), 1–7.
201 ———. Nervosität. *IZIP,* 1933, 11(1), 20–
28.
202 ———. Nervousness. *IJIP,* 1936, 2(1), 62–
70.
203 ———. Portrait. *IPNL,* 1972, 21(6), 111.
204 ———. Review of K. Birnbaum, *Die psychischen Heilmethoden.* In *IZIP,* 1927,
5(4), 309–311.
205 ———. Review of A. Flinker, *Studien
über Kretinismus.* Leipzig: Franz Deuticke,
1930. In *IZIP,* 1932, 10(6), 478.
206 ———. Review of M. Hirschfeld, *Sexualpathologie.* Bonn: A. Marcus & E. Webers,
1921, 1922, 1928. In *IZIP,* 1931, 9(2),
151–152.
207 ———. Review of M. Löwy, *Über Wahn-
bildung.* In *IZIP,* 1924, 2(6), 39–40.

208 **Nowotny, K.** Review of F. Mauz, *Die
Prognostik der endogenen Psychosen.*
Leipzig: Georg Thieme, 1930. In *IZIP,*
1932, 10(6), 477–478.
209 ———. Review of H. Prinzhorn, *Psychotherapie.* Leipzig: Georg Thieme. [   ].
In *IZIP,* 1931, 9(1), 63–64.
210 ———. Review of W. N. Speranski, *Innere
Sekretion und psychische Prozesse.* Berlin:
S. Karger, 1929. In *IZIP,* 1933, 11(1), 77.
211 ———. Review of O. Tuszkai, *Ärztliche
Pädagogie.* In *IZIP,* 1927, 5(2), 159–160.
212 ———. Die Technik der Individualpsychologie. In E. Wexberg (Ed.), *Handbuch
der Individualpsychologie.* Pp. 646–661.
213 **Nunberg, H.** (Ed.). *Minutes of the Vienna
Psychoanalytic Society.* Vol. 1. 1906–1908.
New York: Int. Univer. Press, 1962 (with
E. Federn).
214 **Nussbaum, P.** *Die Bedeutung des Minderwertigkeitsgefühle für den Alkoholismus.*
Schwarzenburg, Switz.: Verlag Gerber-
Buchdruck, 1954 (with S. Zurukzoglu).
215 **Nuttall, R.** Sibling order, premorbid adjustment, and remission in schizophrenia. *J.
nerv. ment. Dis.,* 1967, 144, 37–46 (with
L. Solomon).
216 **Nuttal, W.** Observations on occupational
psychology and fatigue. *IZIP,* 1924, 2(3),
12–16.
217 **Nuttin, J.** *Psychoanalysis and personality:
A dynamic theory of normal personality.*
Translated by George Lamb. New York:
New Amer. Libr., 1962.

O

1 **O. K.** Review of W. Jurinatz, *Psychoanalyse und Marxismus.* Wien: Verlag f.
Literatur u. Politik, 1925. In *IZIP,* 1925,
3(5), 264–265.
2 **Oakes, R. H.** Social perception of one
other self. *J. soc. Psychol.,* 1961, 53, 235–
242 (with R. J. Corsini).
3 **Oberholzer, E.** An infantile cover memory,
a fragment of an analysis. *J. nerv. ment.
Dis.,* 1931, 74, 212–213.
4 **Oberlander, M.** Birth order and academic
achievement. *JIP,* 1967, 23, 103–110 (with
N. Jenkin). Also in H. J. Vetter & B. D.
Smith (Eds.), *Personality theory: A
source book.*

5 Oberlander, M. Ordinal position and childhood psychopathology as evaluated from four perspectives. *Proc. 75th Ann. Conv. Amer. Psychol. Assn.*, 1967, 2, 179–180 (with Elise F. Lessing).

6 O'Brien, B. J. Differential responses of addicts on the MMPI. *J. proj. Tech.*, 1968, 32(5), 479–482 (with D. N. Lombardi & F. W. Isele).

7 O'Connell, W. E. Action-oriented methods (with A. G. Nikelly). In A. G. Nikelly (Ed.), *Techniques for behavior change.* Pp. 85–90.

8 ———. Action therapy intervention in human interaction training. *Nwsltr. Res. Psychol.*, 1972, 14(4), 23–25 (with R. R. Baker, P. G. Hanson & R. Ermalinski).

9 ———. Action therapy is fun. *Voices,* 1969, 5(3), 43.

10 ———. The adaptive functions of wit and humor. *J. abnorm. soc. Psychol.,* 1960, 61, 263–270. Cited in *Annual Review of Psychology,* 1962, 13, 506. Abridged in D. Byrne, *An introduction to personality: A research approach.* Pp. 180–182.

11 ———. Adlerian action therapy. *Voices,* 1971, 7(2), 22–27.

12 ———. Adlerian action therapy technique. *JIP,* 1972, 28(2), 184–191.

13 ———. Adlerian psychodrama with chronic schizophrenics. *JIP,* 1963, 19, 69–76.

14 ———. Alfred Adler: A psychological heretic. *Explorations,* 1966, 7, 19–25.

15 ———. Being alive. *IPNL,* 1970, 19(4), 67–68.

16 ———. Beyond Gemeinschaftsgefühl. *JIP,* 1964, 20, 233–234.

17 ———. Biography and photograph. *Voices,* 1965, 1(1), 14.

18 ———. Community confrontations: A challenge to the practice of psychotherapy. *JIP,* 1969, 25, 38–47.

19 ———. The comparative effectiveness of two contrasting alcoholic treatment programs. *Nwsltr. Res. Psychol.,* 1972, 14(4), 21–23 (with Barbara Williams, M. Gallen & P. M. Sands).

20 ———. Creativity in humor. *J. soc. Psychol.,* 1969, 78, 237–241. Also in *Psychiat. Dig.,* 1970, 31(9), 49.

21 ———. Death attitudes and humor appreciation among medical students. *Existent. Psychiat.,* 1967, 6(24), 433–442 (with C. Covert).

22 O'Connell, W. E. A defense of Mowrer's eros. *Insight,* 1967, 6(2), 66–67.

23 ———. Demands on self and others (Therapist on vacation). *Voices,* 1966, 2(2), 86.

24 ———. Democracy in human relations. *Desert Call,* 1970, 5(2), 8–9.

25 ———. Developing psychological treatment with "ancillary" personnel. *J. Assn. Med. Phys. Rehab.,* 1964, 18(1), 10–16.

26 ———. Diagnosis as a predictor of social behavior in human relations training. *Nwsltr. Res. Psychol.,* 1970, 12(3), 29–33 (with P. Hanson, P. Rothaus & G. Wiggins).

27 ———. A "do-it-with-others" method of psychotherapy. Review of R. J. Corsini, *Role playing in psychotherapy: A manual.* In *JIP,* 1967, 23, 123–124.

28 ———. The enigma of brotherly love. *IP,* 1968, 5(3), 6–9.

29 ———. The equal collaborator. *IPNL,* 1969, 19(2), 25–26.

30 ———. Equality in encounter groups. *IP,* 1971, 8(1), 1–6.

31 ———. The eternal incident. *Voices,* 1969, 5(3), 112–113.

32 ———. The failure of psychotherapy in mental hospitals. *IP,* 1964, 2(1), 24–27.

33 ———. Failures of mental hospitals—or of society? *Psychiat. Opin.,* 1970, 7(5), 8–12.

34 ———. Foreword to V. Salz, *Communication: Parent and child.*

35 ———. Frankl, Adler, and spirituality. *J. Relig. & Hlth.,* 1972, 11(2), 134–138.

36 ———. The gap between religion and psychiatry. *Insight,* 1963, 1(3), 27–34 (with J. Frizelle, C. Harris, J. Jernigan & J. Wohl).

37 ———. Gemeinschaftsgefühl: Discussion continues. *IPNL,* 1966, 16(11–12, Whole No. 184–185). P. 43.

38 ———. The generation gap on a psychiatric ward. *Newsltr. Res. Psychol.,* 1971, 13(2), 1–5 (with R. Ermalinski & P. Hanson).

39 ———. How do we study a killer? *IPNL,* 1967, 17(5–6, Whole No. 190–191). Pp. 35–37.

40 ———. Humanistic identification, a new translation for Gemeinschaftsgefühl. *JIP,* 1965, 21, 44–47.

41 ———. Humanizing religion, race and sex. In W. Pew (Ed.), *The war between the generations.* Pp. 17–32.

42 ———. Humanizing versus dehumanizing in somatotherapy and psychotherapy. *JIP,* 1966, 22, 49–55.

43 O'Connell, W. E. Humor and death. *Psychol. Rep.*, 1968, 22, 391–402.

44 ———. Humor and repression. *J. exis. Psychiat.*, 1964, 4, 309–316 (with Penny Peterson). Abridged in B. Maher (Ed.), *Progress in experimental personality research.* Vol. 1. Pp. 184–185.

45 ———. The humor of the gallows. *Omega,* 1966, 1, 32–33; *Moreana,* 1967, 4(13), 108–110; *IPNL,* 1967, 17, 54–56.

46 ———. Humor: The therapeutic impasse. *Voices,* 1969, 5(2), 25–27.

47 ———. Identification and curability of the mental hospital patient. *JIP,* 1962, 18, 68–76. Also in O. H. Mowrer (Ed.), *Morality and mental health.* Pp. 430–436.

48 ———. In defense of Civil War romanticism. *Psychiat. Quart. Suppl.,* 1961, 35 (Part 1), 28–35; *Bay State Bugle,* 1964, 4(4).

49 ———. Individual Psychology. In *The New Catholic Encyclopedia.* Vol. 7. New York: McGraw-Hill, 1967. Pp. 472–474.

50 ———. An item analysis of the Wit and Humor Appreciation Test. *J. soc. Psychol.,* 1962, 56, 271–276.

51 ———. Is the "third Viennese school of psychotherapy" real? *JIP,* 1970, 26, 85–86.

52 ———. Jest appreciation and interaction in leaderless groups. *Int. J. grp. Psychother.,* 1969, 19, 454–462 (with P. Rothaus, P. Hanson, & R. Moyer).

53 ———. Lest we forget. *JIP,* 1967, 23, 124.

54 ———. Maturity, sex and wit-humor appreciation. *Nwsltr. Res. Psychol.,* 1969, 11, 14–15.

55 ———. Mental health proposals by a clinical psychologist. *JIP,* 1964, 20, 202–206.

56 ———. Metaphysician of madness. *JIP,* 1970, 26, 98–99.

57 ———. Motives of joke-tellers. *Sexual Behav.,* 1971, 1(2), 57.

58 ———. Movies for therapists: The Prisoner and Bridge on the River Kwai (Guinness and Hawkins Transactions). *Voices,* 1966, 2(1), 54–55.

59 ———. Multidimensional scaling of humor. *Psychiat. Quart.,* 1964, 38, 1–12.

60 ———. The negative nonsense of the passive patient. *Rat. Living,* 1971, 6(1), 28–31 (with P. G. Hanson).

61 ———. New concepts in psychotherapy: Morality and ethics. *Amer. Acad. Psychotherapists. Nwsltr.,* 1964, 9(3), 29–30.

62 O'Connell, W. E. A note on Thomas More. *IPNL,* 1967, 17(7–8, Whole No. 192–193). Pp. 54–56.

63 ———. *An odyssey of a psychologist.* New York: MSS Educational Publ. Co., 1971.

64 ———. On our love for magnicide. *Amer. Psychol.-Law Nwsltr.,* 1969, 2(1), 6–7. Also in *IPNL,* 1969, 18(7–8, Whole No. 216–217). Pp. 51–54.

65 ———. Organic and schizophrenic differences in wit and humor appreciation. *Dis. nerv. Syst.,* 1968, 29, 276–281. Abridged in *Proceedings (APA),* 1966, 171–172.

66 ———. Ossified institutional concerns. *Teilhard Today,* 1972, March-April. P. 1.

67 ———. Pastoral dimensions in counseling and psychotherapy (an exploration): Purposes for "pastoral". *J. past. Couns.,* 1970, 5, 4–5.

68 ———. Patients' cognitive changes in human relations training. *JIP,* 1970, 26, 57–63 (with P. Hanson).

69 ———. Peer rankings of friendliness and staff rankings of mental health with chronic schizophrenic patients. *J. soc. Psychol.,* 1964, 63, 339–351.

70 ———. Portrait. *Houston Post,* Aug. 13, 1967; *IPNL,* 1971, 20(6), 109; *Nat. Enquirer,* Dec. 5, 1971. P. 11.

71 ———. Postscript: Hatred and alienation. *Voices,* 1966, 2(2), 119–122.

72 ———. Practicing Christianity and humanistic identification. *J. humanis. Psychol.,* 1964, 4, 118–129.

73 ———. The protagonist in human relations training. *Grp. Psychother. Psychodrama,* 1970, 23, 45–55.

74 ———. Psychodrama and science. *Voices,* 1971, 7, 24.

75 ———. Psychodrama: Involving the audience. *Rational Living,* 1967, 2(1), 22–25. Abridged in *IPNL,* 1967, 18, 4.

76 ———. Psychotherapy for everyman: A look at action therapy. *J. Existent.,* 1966, 7(25), 85–91.

77 ———. Rap on race. *JIP,* 1971, 27, 235.

78 ———. Rehabilitation and behavior. *J. Assn. Med. Phys. Rehab.,* 1964, 18(4), 107.

79 ———. Repression, observation, and inference. Review of P. Madison, *Freud's concept of repression and defense.* Minneapolis:

Univ. Minnesota Press, 1961. In *JIP*, 1965, 21, 95–96.

80 **O'Connell, W. E.** Resignation, humor, and wit. *Psychoanal. Rev.*, 1964, 51, 49–56.

81 ———. Review of R. J. Corsini, *Roleplaying in psychotherapy.* In *JIP*, 1967, 23, 123–124.

82 ———. Review of V. E. Frankl, *The will to meaning.* In *JIP*, 1970, 26, 85–86.

83 ———. Review of E. Fromm, *The heart of man;* and F. T. T. Severin, *Humanistic viewpoints in psychology.* In *Cath. psychol. Rec.*, 1965, 3(2), 141–145.

84 ———. Review of I. A. Greenberg, *Psychodrama and audience attitude change.* Beverly Hills: Thyrsus Publ. Co., 1968. In *Prof. Psychol.*, 1972, 3(1), 89–92.

85 ———. Review of B. Justice, *Violence in the city.* Ft. Worth: Texas Christian Univ. Press, 1969. In *JIP*, 1969, 25, 238–239.

86 ———. Review of J. L. Moreno (Ed.), *The international handbook of group psychotherapy.* New York: Phil. Libr., 1966. In *JIP*, 1967, 23, 124.

87 ———. Review of R. Piddington, *The psychology of laughter.* New York: Gamut Press, 1963. In *JIP*, 1964, 20, 118.

88 ———. Review of Hertha Orgler, *Alfred Adler, the man and his work.* In *JIP*, 1964, 20, 108–109.

89 ———. Review of A. van Kaam, *Religion and personality.* In *JIP*, 1964, 20(2), 233–234.

90 ———. Sensitivity training and Adlerian theory. *JIP*, 1970, 26, 165–166; 1971, 27(1), 65–72.

91 ———. Small group dialogue: An approach to police–community relations. *J. crim. Law, Criminol., Police Sci.*, 1969, 60, 242–246 (with R. Bell, S. Cleveland, & P. Hanson). Also in H. C. Lindgren, D. Byrne & F. Lindgren (Eds.), *Current research in psychology: A book of readings.* Pp. 487–493.

92 ———. The social aspects of wit and humor. *J. soc. Psychol.*, 1969, 79, 183–187.

93 ———. Social interest and humor. *Int. J. soc. Psychiat.*, 1969, 15, 179–188 (with R. Worthen).

94 ———. Some basic concepts in human relations training for psychiatric patients. *Hosp. Commun. Psychiat.*, 1970, 21, 137–143 (with P. Hanson, P. Rothaus, & G. Wiggins).

95 **O'Connell, W. E.** Spitting and stroking. *IP*, 1967, 5(1), 29–31.

96 ———. Team therapy: An antidote to the double bind. *JIP*, 1967, 24, 239.

97 ———. Teleodrama. *IP*, 1969, 6(2), 42–45.

98 ———. The third force: Psychotherapy's *aggiornamento. Cath. psychol. Rec.*, 1965, 3, 141–145.

99 ———. Toward resolution of a generation gap conflict on a psychiatric ward. *Intl. J. Grp. Tensions*, 1972, 2(2), 77–89 (with R. Ermalinski & P. Hanson).

100 ———. Training patients for effective participation in backhome groups. *Amer. J. Psychiat.*, 1969, 126, 857–862 (with P. Hanson, P. Rothaus, & G. Wiggins).

101 ———. The value of role reversal in psychodrama and action therapy. *Handb. Int. Sociom.*, 1971, 6, 98–104 (with Deanna Brewer).

102 ———. Verbal participation and group behavior. *Nwsltr. Res. Psychol.*, 1970, 12 (2), 36–39 (with K. Pate & P. Hanson).

103 ———. Viktor Frankl, the Adlerian? *Psychiat. Spectator*, 1970, 6(11), 13–14.

104 ———. Wandering with an open heart. *Voices*, 1966, 2(2), 52–54.

105 ———. Ward psychotherapy with schizophrenics through concerted encouragement. *JIP*, 1961, 17, 193–204.

106 ———. Watch our language. *Amer. J. Nursing*, 1967, 67, 1406–1407.

107 ———. What is action therapy? *IPNL*, 1971, 20(6), 102–103.

108 ———. Wit, humor, and defensiveness. *Nwsltr. Res. Psychol.*, 1970, 12, 32–33 (with Sallie Cowgill).

109 **O'Conner, J. P.** Congruence of self and ideal self in relation to personality adjustment. *J. consult. Psychol.*, 1954, 18, 215–218 (with T. E. Hanlon & P. Hofstaetter).

110 **Oden, T. C.** A theologian's view of the process of psychotherapy. *JIP*, 1964, 20, 69–78.

111 **Oeser, R.** Individuum und Gemeinschaft im Tierreich. *IZIP*, 1929, 7(1), 15–22.

112 **Offner, M.** Die seelischen Nöte des ostjüdischen Kindes. *IZIP*, 1932, 10(2), 136–146.

113 **Ohlsen, M. M.** Counseling within a group setting. *J. Natl. Assn. Women Deans & Counselors*, 1960, 23, 104–109.

114 **Olsen, R. S.** The recordings of psychotherapeutic sessions. *Lancet*, 1948, 254, 957–958 (with J. Bierer).

115 **Oman, J. B.** The doctrines of predestination and freedom of will in the light of Individual Psychology. *Past. Psychol.*, 1972, 23(220), 63–66.

116 ———. One parish's educational counseling plan and how it grew. *Past. Psychol.*, 1968, 19, 37–44.

117 **Omwake, Katharine T.** The relationship between acceptance of self and acceptance of others shown by three personality inventories. *J. consult. Psychol.*, 1954, 18, 443–446.

118 **Opedal, L. E.** Analysis of the earliest memory of a delinquent. *IJIP*, 1935, 1(3), 52–58.

119 ———. Die erste Kindheitserinnerung eines Delinquenten. *IZIP*, 1936, 14(1), 7–13.

120 ———. Jim's Frankenstein. *IJIP*, 1936, 2(3), 35–45; *IZIP*, 1936, 14(4), 227–238.

121 **Ophey, R.** Review of W. Gruehn (Ed.), *Arch. für Religionspsychologie und Seelenführung*. Leipzig: Eduard Pfeiffer, 1929. In *IZIP*, 1930, 8(6), 600.

122 **Oppenheim, D.** *Dreams in folklore.* New York: Int. Univer. Press, 1958 (with S. Freud).

123 **Oppenheim, D. E.** *Dichtung und Menschenkenntnis: Psychologische Streifzüge durch alte und neue Literatur.* München: Bergmann, 1926.

124 ———. Drei Beiträge zum Problem des Schülerselbstmord (with A. Adler & K. Molitor). In A. Adler & C. Furtmüller (Eds.), *Heilen und Bilden* (1914). Pp. 341–373; Same with F. Künkel instead of K. Molitor (1928). Pp. 206–207.

125 ———. Der Kampf der Frau um ihre gesellschaftliche Stellung im Spiegel der antiken Literatur. *IZIP*, 1925, 3(6), 287–290.

126 ———. Der Mann in Schönherrs "Weibsteufel". *IZIP*, 1923, 2(1), 26–31.

127 ———. Selbsterziehung und Fremderziehung nach Seneca. *IZIP*, 1930, 8(1), 62–70.

128 ———. Vergils Dido. *IZIP*, 1925, 3(2), 79–91.

129 ———. Ziel und Weg der Menschenkenntnis. *IZIP*, 1930, 8(2), 221–233.

130 ———. Zu Schillers Novelle: Der Verbrecher aus verlorener Ehre. *IZIP*, 1928, 6(5), 358–362.

131 **Oppenheim, G.** What's group psychiatry really like? *N. Y. Herald Tribune*, March 10, 1957.

132 **Oppenheimer, Jo.** Drawing of Alfred Adler *IPNL*, 1970, 19(6), 104.

133 **Oppenheimer, O.** "I" and time—a study in memory. *Psychol. Rev.*, 1947, 54, 222–228.

134 **O'Reilly, C.** *Men in jail.* Chicago: Loyola Univ., 1965 (with F. Cizon, J. Flanagan & S. Pflanczer).

135 **Orgler, Hertha.** Adlerian psychology: A help in solving the current crime problem. *IP*, 1969, 6(2), 25–28.

136 ———. *Alfred Adler, der Mann und sein Werk: Triumph über den Minderwertigkeitskomplex.* Wien Urban & Schwarzenberg, 1956, 1972.

137 ———. *Alfred Adler en zÿn Werk.* Utrech Bijleveld, 1939, 1951.

138 ———. *Alfred Adler e la sua opera il trionfo sul complesso di inferiorita.* Roma: Astrolabio, 1970.

139 ———. *Alfred Adler, l'homme et son oeuvre.* Paris: Stock, 1955, 1968.

140 ———. *Alfred Adler: The man and his work: Triumph over the inferiority complex.* London: Daniel, 1939; London: Vision Press, 1947; London: Sidgwick & Jackson, 1963; New York: Liveright, 1963; New York: Capricorn Books, 1965; New York: New American Libr., 1972.

141 ———. Comparative study of two first recollections. *AJIP*, 1952, 10, 27–30.

142 ———. Identical twins separately reared. *IJIP*, 1935, 1(3), 120–131.

143 ———. Identische, getrennt aufgezogene Zwillinge. *IZIP*, 1935, 13(1), 35–46.

144 ———. Mistrust in love. *The Psychologist* (London), 1952,

145 ———. Overcoming the effects of an unhappy and unhelpful upbringing. *The Psychologist* (London), July, 1962. Pp. 22–24.

146 ———. Über Zwillingsbeobachtungen. *IZIP*, 1932, 10(5), 353–357.

147 **Orlansky, H.** Infant care and personality. *Psychol. Bull.*, 1949, 46, 1–48.

148 **Orr, Helen K.** Patterns of parental childrearing and subsequent vulnerability to cognitive disturbance. *J. consult. Psychol.*, 1966, 30, 51–59 (with A. B. Heilbrun, Jr., & S. N. Harrell).

149 **Ortega y Gasset, J.** Adler's psychology: Science of living. *JIP*, 1971, 27(2), 134.

150 **Osgood, C. E.** *Contemporary approach to cognition.* Cambridge, Mass.: Harvard Univ. Press, 1957.

151 **Osherson, S.** An Adlerian approach to Goethe's Faust. *JIP*, 1965, 21, 194–198.

152 **Osler, [   ].** Review of K. S. Lashley (Ed.), *Studies in the dynamics of behavior.* Chicago: Univ. Chicago Press, 1932. In *IZIP*, 1933, 11(2), 157.

153 **Osofsky, J. D.** Children's effects upon parental behavior: Mother's and father's responses to dependent and independent child behaviors. *Proc. Annu. Convent. Amer. Psychol. Assn.*, 1971, 6, 143–144 (with S. Oldfield).

154 **Ottenheimer, L.** Nature and development of the ego ideal. *Amer. J. Psychother.*, 1955, 9, 612–623.

155 **Otto, H. A.** (Ed.). *Explorations in human potentialities.* Springfield, Ill.: C. C. Thomas, 1966.

156 ——— (Ed.). *Human potentialities.* St. Louis: Warren H. Green, 1968.

157 **An outsider.** Adlerians, Rankians, and Jungians in U.S.A. *IPNL*, 1968, 18(5–6, Whole No. 202–203). Pp. 35–37.

158 **Overton, R. K.** Experimental studies of organ inferiority. *JIP*, 1958, 14, 62–63.

159 ———. Unrecognized weakness and compensatory learning. *Amer. J. Psychol.*, 1957, 70, 126–127 (with W. L. Brown).

160 **Owen, I.** Adlerian counseling in racially mixed groups of elementary school children. *IP*, 1970, 7(2), 53–58.

161 **Owens, Karen.** Guidance and instruction: Complementary for the educative process. *Elem. Sch. Guid. Counsel.*, 1969, 3(4), 260–268 (with D. Dinkmeyer).

P

1 **P. L.** [Alfred Adler]. *Arbejderbladet* (Oslo), Aug. 12, 1970.

2 **Pabbruwe, A. C.** Translator, with P. Ronge, of R. Dreikurs, *Alfred Adler's Individual-psychologie.*

3 **Painter, Genevieve.** Academic failure prevention starting in infancy. In J. Arena (Ed.), *Successful programming.* Assn. for Children with Learning Disabilities, 1969.

4 **Painter, Genevieve.** Application of Adlerian psychology to recreational therapy. *OSIPNL*, 1965, 5(4), 14.

5 ———. *Baby-Schule.* Translated by W–E August. Berlin: Bertelsmann Ratgebe Verlag, 1972.

6 ———. The effect of rhythmic and sensory-motor activity program on perceptual motor spatial abilities of kindergarten children. *Excep. Children*, 1966, 33, 113–118.

7 ———. The effect of a structured tutorial program on the cognitive and language development of culturally disadvantaged infants. *Merrill-Palmer Quart. Behav. & Developm.*, 1969, 15(3), 279–294.

8 ———. *Infant education.* San Rafael, Cal.: Dimensions Publ. Co., 1968.

9 ———. Joint counseling with parents and teens. In A. Nikelly (Ed.), *Techniques for behavior change.* Pp. 205–209.

10 ———. Portrait. *IPNL*, 1972, 21(6), 112.

11 ———. Remediation of maladaptive behavior and psycholinguistic deficits in a group sensory-motor activity program. *Acad. Ther. Quart.*, 1968, 3, 233–243.

12 ———. A sensory-motor approach to readiness. In J. Arena (Ed.), *Management of the child with learning disabilities: An interdisciplinary challenge.* Assn. for Children with Learning Disabilities, 1969.

13 ———. *Teach your baby.* New York: Simon & Schuster, 1971.

14 ———. A tutorial language program for disadvantaged infants. In Celia Stendler Lavatelli (Ed.), *Language training in early childhood education.* ERIC Clearinghouse on Early Childhood Education. Urbana, Ill.: Univ. of Illinois Press, 1971.

15 ———. Why are Adlerian techniques still being ignored in formulating curricula for training counselors and teachers? *OSIPNL*, 1967, 7(4), 12.

16 **Palacios, A.** (Ed.). *The Mexican American Directory.* Washington: Executive Systems Corp., 1969 (with G. King & P. Scarth).

17 **Paleologos, G.** Translator of A. Adler, *Anthropognosia.*

18 **Pally, S.** Cognitive rigidity as a function of threat. Unpubl. Ph.D. Diss., Univ. Penn., 1953.

19 **Palmer, R. D.** Birth order and identification. *J. consult. Psychol.*, 1966, 30, 129–130.

20 **Pantle, A. J.** Neostriatal and hippocampal functions in the behavior

variability of the chick. *J. genet. Psychol.*, 1967, 110, 59–60 (with V. J. Bieliauskas).

21 **Papageorgis, D.** Repression and the unconscious: A social-psychological reformulation. *JIP*, 1965, 21, 18–31. Also reprinted in H. D. Werner (Ed.), *New understandings of human behavior.* Pp. 43–54.

22 **Papanek, E.** Air raid alarms and the schools: Experiences in France. *Sch. & Soc.*, 1942, 55, 156–157.

23 ———. American youth for world youth: Social interest in Kilpatrick's concept of education. *Educ. Theory*, 1966, 16, 59–70.

24 ———. *The Austrian school reform: Its bases, principles and development—The twenty years between the two World Wars.* New York: Fell, 1962.

25 ———. The boy who survived Auschwitz. *Sat. Eve. Post*, Apr. 11, 1964 (with E. Linn).

26 ———. Children during air raids. *Prog. Educ.*, 1942, 19, 151–159.

27 ———. Consider the children. *Christian Regis.*, 1946.

28 ———. Contributions of Individual Psychology to social work. *AJIP*, 1954, 11, 142–150.

29 ———. Creative restitution. *IPNL*, 1972, 21(3), 41–42.

30 ———. Creative restitution, a correctional technique and a theory. *JIP*, 1959, 15, 226–232 (with A. Eglash).

31 ———. Delinquency. In A. Nikelly (Ed.), *Techniques for behavior change.* Pp. 177–183.

32 ———. The delinquent child. In M. G. Gottsegen & G. B. Gottsegen (Eds.), *Professional school psychology.* Pp. 237–248.

33 ———. Education in Austria after the fall of Hitler. In *Austria's problems after Hitler's Fall.* New York: Austrian Labor News, 1943. Pp. 31–40.

34 ———. Erste Fürsorgemassnahmen nach dem Krieg. *Austr. Labor Inform.*, 1943, No. 10.

35 ———. Erziehungsberatung and child guidance (with Alexandra Adler). In V. Frankl (Ed.), *Handbuch der Neurosenlehre und Psychotherapie.* Wien: Urban & Schwarzenberg, 1958. Pp. 569–583.

36 ———. États mental des enfants déportées. *Vers l'Educ. Nouvelle*, 1946, 8.

37 ———. Individual Psychology today (with Helene Papanek). *Amer. J. Psychother.*, 1961, 15, 4–26.

38 **Papanek, E.** Initial problems of the refugee children's homes in Montmorency, France. *Sch. & Soc.*, 1943, 57, 141–145.

39 ———. In-service training of educators for maladjusted youth. *Proc. Fourth Cong. Int. Assn. Workers Maladj. Childr.*, Lausanne-Paris, 1958.

40 ———. International post-war problems: Austria. *Rev. Amer. Labor Conf. Int. Affairs*, 1944.

41 ———. International trends in treatment in training schools and institutions. *Amer. J. Orthopsychiat.*, 1952, 22, 119–126.

42 ———. *Joseph Gerl und seine Freunde: Die Idee steht mir hoeher als das Leben.* Prague: 1934.

43 ———. Juvenile delinquency: The community's contribution to its solution. *Pathways in Child Guidance*, 1959, 1(1), 3–4.

44 ———. Das Kinderheim, sein Theorie und Praxis im Lichte der Individualpsychologie. *Acta Psychotherapeutica*, 1956, 4, 53–72.

45 ———. Lend-lease help to re-educate Axis countries after the war. *Educ. Forum*, 1944, 2 (Part 1), 197–201.

46 ———. Lessons from a film: "The Quiet One". *The Way Forum* (Paris), Dec., 1956. Pp. 14–16.

47 ———. Management of the acting-out adolescent. *Amer. J. Psychother.*, 1964, 18, 418–434.

48 ———. Management of acting out adolescents. In L. E. Abt & S. L. Weissman (Eds.), *Acting out: Theoretical and clinical aspects.* Pp. 208–232.

49 ———. Modern techniques of Adlerian therapy (with Helene Papanek). In J. H. Masserman (Ed.), *Current psychiatric therapies.* Vol. 2. Pp. 86–93.

50 ———. *The Montmorency period of the child-care program of the OSE.* World Union OSE and the American Committee of OSE, 1968. Pp. 116–134. Also in L. Wulman (Ed.), *In fight for the health of the Jewish people: 50 years of OSE.* New York: World Union OSE & Amer. Comm. OSE, 1968.

51 ———. My experiences with refugee children in Europe. *Nerv. Child*, 1943, 2, 301–307.

52 ———. A new approach to institutional care for children. In K. A. Adler & Danica Deutsch (Eds.), *Essays in Individual Psychology.* Pp. 139–151.

53 **Papanek, E.** Re-education and treatment of juvenile delinquents. *Amer. J. Psychother.*, 1958, 12, 269-296.

54 ———. Residential treatment of children: Adlerian approach. *Forum resident. Ther.*, 1963, 1(1), 5-8.

55 ———. Response to T. E. Linton's "The European educateur program for disturbed children". *Forum resident. Ther.*, 1969, 7.

56 ———. Review of R. Lindner, *Must you conform?* In *The Socialist Call*, 1956, 24(2), 22-23.

57 ———. Review of A. H. Moehlman, *Comparative educational systems*. In *Harvard educ. Rev.*, 1965, 35, 412-414.

58 ———. The role of reward and punishment in education and correction. *Fed. Probat.*, 1958, 22(2), 41-46.

59 ———. Social interest, a purposeful motive for constructive or destructive behavior. *IP*, 1964, 2(2), 1-5.

60 ———. Social interest in Kilpatrick's concept of education: American youth for world youth. *Educ. Theory*, 1966, 16, 59-70.

61 ———. Social orientation aids the young delinquent. *J. Assn. Psychiat. Treat. Offenders*, 1957, 1(2), 1, 4.

62 ———. Social services for European Jewish children. *Jewish Soc. Serv. Quart.*, 1948, 24, 412-417.

63 ———. Society and its schools—Bridging the educational gap. *The Socialist Call*, 1958, 26(7-8), 12-13.

64 ———. Society and juvenile delinquency: What makes the youthful criminal? *The Socialist Call*, 1955, 23(2), 13-16.

65 ———. Society and the delinquent: Tracing the pattern of rebellion. *The Socialist Call*, 1956, 24(2), 21-24.

66 ———. Some factors in the treatment of juvenile delinquency. *Int. J. soc. Psychiat.*, 1961, 7, 212-221.

67 ———. Some psycho-social aspects of crime and delinquency. *Dimensions*, 1971, 5(4), 13-19.

68 ———. Specific psycho-pedagogical topics. *Symposium Int. Orthopädäg.*, (Louvain, Belgium), 1962. Pp. 43-53.

69 ———. Statement of Dr. Ernst Papanek at Hearings before Subcommittee to Investigate Juvenile Delinquency of the Committee on the Judiciary, U.S. Senate, 85th Congress, Second Session, Mar. 4, 1958.

70 **Papanek, E.** Symposium on feelings of abandonment. Univ. Louvain (Belgium), 1962.

71 ———. They are not expendable [The homeless children]. *Soc. Serv. Rev.*, 1946, 20, 312-319.

72 ———. The training school: Its program and leadership. *Fed. Probat.*, 1953, 17(2), 16-22.

73 ———. The underground in Austria. *Quart. Rev. Amer. Labor Conf. Int. Affairs*, 1944, 1(3), 308-317.

74 ———. [Untitled chapter]. In *Summerhill: For and against*. New York: Hart Publ. Co., 1970. Pp. 156-173.

75 ———. Treatment by group work: A case in a group of problem children. *Amer. J. Orthopsychiat.*, 1945, 15, 223-229.

76 ———. Why is American youth "shook up"? *The Socialist Call*, 1958, 26(5), 8-9.

77 ———. William Heard Kilpatrick, Lehrer der Lehrerschaft in aller Welt. *Erzieh. und Unterricht* (Wien), 1957. Pp. 5-9.

78 ———. William Heard Kilpatrick's international influence: Teacher of world teachers. *Prog. Educ.*, 1957, 34(2), 54-57.

79 ———. Wiltwyck School for Boys. *United Teacher*, May 15, 1968.

80 ———. The working mother. *The Journal* (Parents without Partners), 1961, 5(2).

81 ———. *Youth after the catastrophe*. New York: Yiddish Scientific Inst., 1948.

82 ——— (Ed.). *Youth in danger becomes a danger*. New York: Individual Psychology Assn. of N. Y., 1956. Pp. 24-26 (with Alexandra Adler, J. Dumpson, & H. Epstein).

83 **Papanek, Helene.** About Adlerian group psychotherapy. *IPNL*, 1970, 19(1), 1-3. Extracted from "Therapeutic and antitherapeutic factors in group relations".

84 ———. The Adlerian viewpoint in group psychoanalysis. *J. Psychoanal. Grps.*, 1963, 1(1), 36-42.

85 ———. Adler's concepts in community psychiatry. *JIP*, 1965, 21, 117-126.

86 ———. Adler's psychology and group psychotherapy. *Amer. J. Psychiat.*, 1970, 127, 783-786.

87 ———. Alfred Adler. In A. M. Freedman & H. I. Kaplan (Eds.), *Comprehensive textbook of psychiatry*. Pp. 320-327.

88 ———. The borderline schizophrenic in group psychotherapy (Summary). *JIP*, 1958, 14, 74-75.

89 **Papanek, Helene.** Bridging dichotomies through group psychotherapy. *JIP*, 1964, 20, 38–47.

90 ———. Change in ethical values in group psychotherapy. *Int. J. grp. Psychother.*, 1958, 8, 435–444.

91 ———. Change of therapist during treatment: Case report with emphasis on psychodynamics. *Amer. J. Psychother.*, 1952, 6, 725–729.

92 ———. Combined group and individual therapy in the light of Adlerian psychology. *Int. J. grp. Psychother.*, 1956, 6, 136–146.

93 ———. Combined group and individual therapy in private practice. *Amer. J. Psychother.*, 1954, 8, 679–686.

94 ———. Comparative goals of psychoanalytic training. *IP*, 1965, 3(1), 10–13.

95 ———. Contributor to S. W. Standal & R. Corsini (Eds.), *Critical incidents in psychotherapy.*

96 ———. Developments and implications of the Adlerian theory for clinical psychology. In L. E. Abt & B. F. Riess (Eds.), *Progress in clinical psychology.* Pp. 137–148.

97 ———. Diagnosis and treatment of borderline psychosis. *Med. Circle Bull.*, 1959, 6(6), 6–11.

98 ———. Dreams in group psychoanalysis. *J. Psychoanal. Grps.*, 1964, 1, 36–37.

99 ———. Dynamics and treatment of borderline schizophrenia from the Adlerian viewpoint. *AJIP*, 1954, 11, 60–70.

100 ———. Editorial responsibilities for crossfertilization in the fields of psychotherapy. *IPNL*, 1961, 11(9–10, Whole No. 125–126). Pp. 43–44.

101 ———. Emotions and intellect in psychotherapy. *Amer. J. Psychother.*, 1959, 13, 150–173.

102 ———. Ethical values in psychotherapy. *JIP*, 1958, 14, 160–166.

103 ———. Experiences in group psychotherapy. *Grp. Psychother.*, 1967, 20, 162–165.

104 ———. Expression of hostility: Its value in the psychotherapy group. *JIP*, 1962, 18, 62–67.

105 ———. Group process and individual psychodynamics as factors in group therapy. *J. Psychoanal.*, 1965, 1(3), 12–17.

106 ———. Group psychotherapy at the Alfred Adler Consultation Center. In K. A. Adler & Danica Deutsch (Eds.), *Essays in Individual Psychology.* Pp. 274–280.

107 **Papanek, Helene.** Group psychotherapy interminable. *Frontiers clin. Psychiat.*, 1969, 6(14), 3.

108 ———. Group psychotherapy interminable. *Int. J. grp. Psychother.*, 1970, 20, 219–223.

109 ———. Group psychotherapy with married couples. In J. H. Masserman (Ed.), *Current psychiatric therapies.* Vol. 5. Pp. 157–163.

110 ———. Group therapy for schizophrenics. *Frontiers clin. Psychiat.*, 1967, 4(16), 8.

111 ———. Group therapy helps spouses maintain constructive equilibrium. *Frontiers hosp. Psychiat.*, 1965, 2(11), 2.

112 ———. Group therapy with married couples. In *Sandoz Psychiat. Spectator*, 1970, 6(11), 8–9.

113 ———. Group therapy with married couples. In H. I. Kaplan & B. J. Sadock (Eds.), *Comprehensive group psychotherapy.* Pp. 691–723.

114 ———. The hysterical personality in combined individual and group psychotherapy: A case report. *Int. J. grp. Psychother.*, 1962, 12, 89–98.

115 ———. Inconstant coupling. *Psychiat. Spectator*, 1965, 2(4).

116 ———. Individual Psychology today. *Amer. J. Psychother.*, 1961, 15, 4–26 (with E. Papanek).

117 ———. Individual Psychology today. *Nwsltr., Council Psychoanal. Psychotherapists*, Feb., 1965. Pp. 3–4.

118 ———. The management of anxiety in group psychoanalysis: A round table discussion. *Amer. J. Psychoanal.*, 1961, 21, 82–84.

119 ———. Mental health and psychotherapy. *IP*, 1963, 1(1), 11–16.

120 ———. Modern techniques of Adlerian therapy (with E. Papanek). In J. Masserman (Ed.), *Current psychiatric therapies.* Vol. 2. Pp. 86–93.

121 ———. Pathology of power striving and its treatment. *JIP*, 1972, 28, 25–32.

122 ———. Portrait. *Frontiers clin. Psychiat.*, 1967, 4(16), 1; *IPNL*, 1970, 20(6), 111.

123 ———. Projective test evaluation of changes effected by group psychotherapy. *Int. J. grp. Psychother.*, 1960, 10, 446–455.

124 **Papanek, Helene.** Psychothérapie collective des schizophrenes. *Méd. et Hyg.* (Génève), 1968, 26, 844.

125 ———. Psychotherapy without insight: Group therapy as milieu therapy. *JIP*, 1961, 17, 184–192.

126 ———, Recent developments and implications of the Adlerian theory for clinical psychology. In L. Abt & B. Riess (Eds.), *Progress in clinical psychology.* Vol. 5. Pp. 157–163.

127 ———. Review of R. J. Corsini, *Methods of group psychotherapy.* In *JIP*, 1958, 14, 91–92.

128 ———. Review of O. H. Mowrer (Ed.), *Morality and mental health.* In *JIP*, 1968, 24, 100–102.

129 ———. Review of M. Rosenbaum & M. Berger (Eds.), *Group psychotherapy and group function.* In *JIP*, 1964, 20(1), 110–111.

130.———. Review of B. H. Shulman, *Essays in schizophrenia.* In *JIP*, 1968, 24, 199–200.

131 ———. Satisfactions and frustrations of a supervisor of group psychotherapists. *Amer. J. Psychother.*, 1958, 12, 500–503.

132 ———. The school in a sane society, mental health and the teacher. *The Socialist Call,* 1958, 26(7–8), 18–20.

133 ———. Shared group resistance may reflect various problems. *Frontiers clin. Psychiat.*, 1966, 3(8), 6.

134 ———. Therapeutic and anti-therapeutic factors in group relations. *Amer. J. Psychother.*, 1969, 23, 396–404. Also summarized in *Frontiers clin. Psychiat.*, 1969, 6(13).

135 ———. Therapeutic factors in the group setting. *Int. ment. Hlth. Nwsltr.*, 1961, 3, 11–13.

136 ———. The use of early recollections in psychotherapy. *JIP*, 1972, 28(2), 169–176.

137 **Pappas, Mary Ann.** Review of D. Brown, *Changing student behavior: A new approach to discipline.* Dubuque, Ia.: W. C. Brown, 1971. In *IP*, 1970, 8(2), 57–58.

138 ———. Review of the *Counseling Psychologist*, 1971, 3(1). In *IP*, 1972, 9(1), 30.

139 ———. Review of R. Dreikurs, Bernice Grunwald, & Floy C. Pepper, *Maintaining sanity in the classroom.* In *IP*, 1972, 9(1), 29–30.

140 **Pappas, Mary Ann.** Review of J. Holt, *How children learn.* New York: Pitman, 1967. In *IP*, 1970, 8(1), 28–29.

141 ———. Review of W. E. O'Connell, *An odyssey of a psychologist.* In *IP*, 1970, 8(2), 58.

142 ———. Review of N. Postman & C. Weingartner, *Teaching as a subversive activity.* New York: Delacorte Press, 1969. In *IP*, 1970, 8(1), 29–30.

143 **Parenti, F.** Anticipacioni psicosomatiche nel pensiero di Alfred Adler. *Pagine di Storia della Med.*, 1967, 11(1).

144 ———. Introduction to A. Adler, *Il temperamento nervosa.*

145 ———. *Manuele di psicotherapia su base Adlerians.* Milano: Hoepli, 1970.

146 **Parks, C.** Birth order, aggression training and authoritarianism. *Psychol. Rec.*, 1970, 20, 69–71 (with G. Schwendiman & K. S. Larsen).

147 **Parks, J.** Review of McKelvie review of C. Rogers, *On encounter groups.* In *IP*, 1972, 9(1), 32–33.

148 **Parloff, M. B.** The treatment of patient and family as a group: Is it group psychotherapy? *Int. J. grp. Psychother.*, 1962, 12, 132–142 (with J. H. Handlon).

149 **Parsley, M.** The delinquent girl in Chicago: The influence of ordinal position and size of family. *Smith Coll. Stud. Soc. Work,* 1932, 3, 274–283.

150 **Parson, B. S.** *Lefthandedness.* New York: Macmillan, 1924.

151 **Parsons, T.** (Ed.). *The negro American.* Foreword by L. B. Johnson. Boston: Houghton Mifflin, 1966; Boston: Beacon, 1966. Paper (with K. B. Clark).

152 **Partridge, E. J.** *Baby's point of view.* New York: Oxford Univ. Press, 1937.

153 ———. Early infancy, puberty and adolescence. *IPMP*, 1937, No. 18 (with H. Crichton-Miller, T. A. Ross & F. G. Crookshank).

154 ———. The management of early infancy. *IPMP*, 1937, No. 18. Pp. 9–27.

155 **Pasaminick, B.** Decision-making in a mental hospital: Real, perceived, ideal. *Amer. sociol. Rev.*, 1959, 24, 822–829 (with M. Lefton & S. Dinitz).

156 **Paschal, B. J.** The role of self-concept in achievement. *J. Negro Educ.*, 1968, 37, 392–396.

157 **Paschalis, A. P.** Points of friction between parents and children and how to avoid them. *Fam. & Sch.*, 1972, 2(3), 22-25.

158 ———. Some fallacies in child rearing. *Fam. & Sch.*, 1972, 3(2), 30-33.

159 **Pate, K.** Verbal participation and group behavior. *Nwsltr. Res. Psychol.*, 1970, 12(2), 36-39 (with W. E. O'Connell & P. Hanson).

160 **Patterson, C. H.** The self in recent Rogerian theory. *JIP*, 1961, 17, 5-11.

161 ———. A unitary theory of motivation and its counseling implications. *JIP*, 1964, 20, 17-31.

162 **Patterson, F.** *Victory over myself.* New York: Bernard Geis Assoc., 1962.

163 **Patterson, G. R.** *Living with children: New methods for parents and teachers.* Champaign, Ill.: Research Press, 1969 (with Elizabeth Gullion).

164 **Patterson, J. R.** Sex, birth order and volunteering behavior. *Austral. J. Psychol.*, 1966, 18, 158-159 (with P. R. Wilson & A. M. Lyssons).

165 **Pattie, F. A.** Unpleasantness of early memories and maladjustment of children. *J. Personnel*, 1952, 20, 315-321 (with D. Cornett).

166 **Patton, W. F.** Birth-order and ruralism as potential determinants of attendant nature. *Amer. J. ment. Defic.*, 1967, 72, 428-434 (with C. C. Cleland & N. Seitz).

167 ———. Birth order, sex, and achievement gain of institutionalized retardates. *Psychol. Rep.*, 1966, 19, 327-330 (with C. C. Cleland).

168 **Paulmier, B.** Alfred Adler et la pédagogie contemporaine. *BSFPA*, 1972, No. 12. Pp. 30-32; 1972, No. 13. Pp. 37-42.

169 ———. L'apport de la doctrine d'Alfred Adler à la vie d'un école. *BISFPA*, 1970, No. 8. Pp. 18-23.

170 ———. L'ascendant du maître sur ses élèves. *BSFPA*, 1971, No. 9. Pp. 14-19.

171 ———. Compte-rendu de l'assemblée du janvier 1971. *BSFPA*, 1971, No. 10. Pp. 28-29.

172 ———. La discussion scolaire, modalité d'entrainement à la co-opération vitale. *BISFPA*, 1970, No. 6.

173 ———. L'éducation du sens social. Beaumont sur Oise: , 1971.

174 ———. Pourquoi Alfred Adler? *BISFPA*, 1970, No. 7. Pp. 26-28.

175 **Paulmier, B.** The work of Alfred Adler. *Éducation à la fraternité*, Jan.-Fev., 1965. P. 7.

176 **Payne, D. L.** Birth order, personality and performance at the Air Force Academy. *JIP*, 1971, 27(2), 185-187.

177 **Pear, T. H.** Personal recollections. *IPNL*, 1968, 18(9-10, Whole No. 206-207). Pp. 66-67.

178 **Pearcy, F.** Technique of retraining in psychotherapy. *Dis. nerv. Sys.*, 1948, 9, 80-83.

179 **Pearcy, Nancy.** Additions to parent study group leaders guide. *OSIPNL*, 1969, 10(1), insert.

180 ———. Child's mistaken goals. *OSIPNL*, 1968, 8(5).

181 ———. How to present and follow through with an incident in a parent discussion group. *OSIPNL*, 1969, 10(3), 8.

182 ———. Outline using *Children: The challenge. OSIPNL*, 1969, 10(1), insert (with M. Bullard).

183 ———. The parent study group program. *OSIPNL*, 1966, 7(4), 13-14.

184 ———. Parent study group sitter guidelines. *OSIPNL*, 1969, 10(1), insert.

185 ———. Review of A. Adler, *The science of living.* In *OSIPNL*, 1969, 10(3), 9-10.

186 ———. Review of Alexandra Adler, *Guiding human misfits.* In *OSIPNL*, 1969, 10(2) 8.

187 ———. Review of W. Glasser, *Reality therapy.* In *OSIPNL*, 1969, 9(3), 6.

188 ———. Review of W. Glasser, *Schools without failure.* In *OSIPNL*, 1969, 9(5), 8-9.

189 ———. Review of J. Holt, *How children fail.* New York: Pitman, 1964, & *How children learn.* New York: Pitman, 1967. In *OSIPNL*, 1969, 9(4), 12-13.

190 ———. Review of Judith Smith & D. E. Smith, *Child management.* Ann Arbor: Ann Arbor Publ., 1966. In *OSIPNL*, 1970, 11(1), 12 (with Marybelle Grosjaques).

191 ———. Suggestions to participants, parent study groups. *OSIPNL*, 1969, 10(1), insert.

192 ———. Working toward increased social responsibility. *OSIPNL*, 1969, 10(1), insert.

193 **Pearson, S. V.** Individual Psychology and psychosomatic disorders (I). *IPMP*, 1932, No. 4 (with F. G. Crookshank, W. Langdon-

Brown, M. B. Ray, M. Robb, O. H. Woodcock & J. C. Young).

194 Peck, Alice L. The family constellation and overt incestuous relations between father and daughter. *Amer. J. Orthopsychiat.*, 1954, 24, 266-279 (with I. Kaufman & C. K. Tagiuri).

195 Peck, C. P. Hi-lights in VA psychology [about Ralph Nelson]. *Clin. Psychologist*, 1968, 22(1), 35.

196 Peckham, W. Report on group counseling. *OSIPNL*, 1964, 5(1), 10-11 (with Alta Gildersleeve).

197 Pelzman, O. Ambulatory insulin treatment for chronic schizophrenics. *Psychiat. Quart.*, 1950, 24, 153-159 (with C. L. Wittson).

198 ———. The contribution of Individual Psychology to the understanding of psychoses. *AJIP*, 1954, 11, 118-122. Also in K. A. Adler & Danica Deutsch (Eds.), *Essays in Individual Psychology*. Pp. 152-157.

199 ———. A group therapy service in a psychiatric hospital: The place of social service in the program. *Psychiat. Quart. Suppl.*, Part 2, 1949, 23, 332-344 (with Ethel B. Bellsmith).

200 ———. Review of J. J. Berruezo, *Complejo de inferioridad*. In *AJIP*, 1956, 12, 94-95.

201 ———. Some problems in the use of psychotherapy. *Psychiat. Quart. Suppl.*, Part 1, 1952, 26, 53-58.

202 ———. Tranylcypromine in the office treatment of depression. *Psychiat. Quart.*, 1961, 35, 261-267.

203 Penaloza, Maria Martinez. Translator of H. L. Ansbacher & Rowena R. Ansbacher (Eds.), *Superioridad y interes social: Una colección de sus ultimos escritos*.

204 Pendennis, [   ]. Anniversary of a complex. *Observer* (London), Feb. 8, 1970.

205 Pennington, L. A. *An introduction to clinical psychology*. 2nd ed. New York: Ronald, 1954 (with I. A. Berg).

206 Pennington, L. W., Jr. Developmental trends in children's H-T-P drawings of a person. *Virginia J. Sci.*, 1954, 4, 323 (with V. J. Bieliauskas).

207 Pepper, Floy C. Birth order. In A. Nikelly (Ed.), *Techniques for behavior change*. Pp. 49-54.

208 Pepper, Floy C. The characteristics of the family constellation. *OSIPNL*, 1964, 4(3), 15-19.

209 ———. *Maintaining sanity in the classroom: Illustrated teaching techniques*. New York: Harper & Row, 1971 (with R. Dreikurs & Bernice Grunwald).

210 ———. Never underestimate the power of children. *Intel. Dig.*, 1972, 11(10), 54-56 (with R. Dreikurs & Bernice Grunwald).

211 Peregrin, [   ]. Review of H. Ellis, Marcel Jouhandeau. In *Life & Letters*. London: Chalboad Wind, 1933. In *IZIP*, 1933, 11 (4), 330.

212 Perestello, Maria. Translator, with O. Rocha, of R. Dreikurs, *Psicologia do casamento*.

213 Perestrello, D. Biotipologia e Psicologia Individual de Adler. In W. Berardinelli, *Tratado de Biotipologia*. Part 5.

214 Perlberger, Klara. Avodah Individual-Psikhologit bakitah layelodim mefagrim [Individual Psychological work in classes for retarded children]. In Anon., *Kovets Individual-Psikhologie*. Pp. 65-87.

215 Perry, R. B. *Realms of value: A critique of human civilization*. Cambridge, Mass.: Harvard Univ. Press, 1954.

216 Perth, R. E. The psychiatric patient. *Anglo-German med. Rev.*, 1965, 3.

217 ———. Psychosomatic problems. *Mod. Med.*, 1958, 3.

218 ———. Psychosomatic problems in general practice. *J. R. Coll. gen. Pract.*, 1957, 4.

219 ———. Psychotherapeutic afterthoughts. *Proc. Int. Cong. Psychother.*, Vienna, 1961.

220 ———. Psychotherapy on Adlerian lines. *Proc. Int. Cong. Indiv. Psychol.*, 1960.

221 Pesman, Sandra. First, get rid of report cards. *San Francisco Sunday Examiner and Chronicle*, Feb. 13, 1972.

222 ———. Home start. The case for teaching infants [about Genevieve Painter]. *Chicago Daily News*, Sept. 14, 1971.

223 ———. How to head off a teen suicide [about Bernice Grunwald]. *Chicago Daily News*, Nov. 9, 1971.

224 ———. Unique aid for routine family woes. *Chicago Daily News*, Sept. 29, 1970.

225 Peters, H. (Ed.). *Guidance: An introduction— selected readings*. Charles E. Merrill Publ. Co., 1972 (with J. R. Cochran).

226 ——— (Ed.). *Guidance in the elementary school: A book of readings*. New York: Macmillan, 1963 (with A. Riccio & J. Quaranta).

227 **Peters, H.** (Ed.). *School counseling: Perspectives and procedures.* Itasca, Ill.: F. E. Peacock, 1968 (with M. Bathory).

228 **Peters, J. S.** Attitudes of delinquents as measured by the semantic differential scales. *JIP*, 1958, 14, 182–184.

229 **Peters, R. S.** *The concept of motivation.* London: Routledge & Kegan Paul, 1958.

230 **Peterson, J. A.** Co-editor of R. Dreikurs, *Student guidebook for "Understanding your children": 26 television sessions* (with Neysa M. Peterson).

231 ———. Review of D. C. Dinkmeyer & J. J. Muro, *Group counseling: Theory and practice.* In *JIP*, 1972, 28, 100–101.

232 ——— (Ed.). *Study guide: A guide to accompany an in-service television series of ten 30-minute lessons.* Burlington, Vt.: Vermont Educ. Network & Univ. Vt., 1971 (with Neysa M. Peterson).

233 ———. Review of R. Dreikurs & L. Grey, *Logical consequences.* In *JIP*, 1969, 25, 112–113.

234 **Peterson, M.** Birth order effects in juvenile patients with diabetes mellitus. *Diss. Abstr. Int.*, 1971, 31, 5004.

235 **Peterson, Neysa M.** Co-editor of R. Dreikurs, *Student guidebook for "Understanding your children": 26 television sessions* (with J. A. Peterson).

236 ——— (Ed.). *Study guide: A guide to accompany an in-service television series of ten 30-minute lessons.* Burlington, Vt.: Vermont Educ. Network & Univ. Vt., 1971 (with J. A. Peterson).

237 **Peterson, Penny.** Humor and repression. *J. exis. Psychiat.*, 1964, 4, 309–316 (with W. O'Connell). Abridged in B. Maher (Ed.), *Progress in experimental personality research.* Vol. 1. Pp. 184–185.

238 **Petrilowitsch, N.** (Ed.). *Die Sinnfrage in der Psychotherapie.* Darmstadt: Wissenschaftl. Buchgesellsch., 1972.

239 **Peven, Dorothy.** Sex for domination. *Med. Asp. hum. Sexual.*, 1971, 5(10), 34–45 (with B. Shulman).

240 ———. Graffiti therapy. *Perspec. psychiat. Care*, 1972, 10(1), 34–36 (with B. Shulman & Anne Byrne).

241 ———. The use of religious revival techniques to indoctrinate personnel: The home party sales organizations. *Sociol. Quart.*, 1968, 9(1), 97–106. Also in R. Olsen & T. T. Wotruba

(Eds), *Sales management.* New York: Holt, Rinehart & Winston, 1971.

242 **Pew, Miriam L.** Adlerian marriage counseling. *JIP*, 1972, 28(2), 192–202 (with W. L. Pew).

243 ———. *Manual for life style assessment. Part I.* Minneapolis: Hennepin County Court Services, 1971 (with W. L. Pew, R. Dreikurs, & Vicki Soltz Statton).

244 ———. Marital therapy (with W. L. Pew). In A. Nikelly (Ed.), *Techniques for behavior change.* Pp. 125–128.

245 ———. Parent study group evaluation for the Eugene, Oregon area, Sept. 1961–Sept. 1962. *OSIPNL*, 1963, 3(3), 6–8.

246 ———. Why study groups succeed or fail. *OSIPNL*, 1964, 5(3), 8–9.

247 **Pew, W. L.** Adlerian marriage counseling. *JIP*, 1972, 28(2), 192–202 (with Miriam L. Pew).

248 ———. An alternative to autocracy. *IP*, 1970, 8(2), 35–40.

249 ———. [Contribution]. In Betty Green & D. Irish (Eds.), *Death education: Preparation for living.* Cambridge, Mass.: Schenkman, 1971.

250 ———. How it can be done. *IPNL*, 1967, 17(9–10, Whole No. 194–195). P. 75.

251 ———. Instant rapport with children. *Elem. Sch. Guid. & Couns.*, 1969, 4(1), 67–68.

252 ———. International summer school. *IPNL*, 1969, 18 (11–12, Whole No. 220–221). Pp. 85–87. Also in *OSIPNL*, 1969, 10(1), 13–14.

253 ———. *Manual for life style assessment. Part I.* Minneapolis: Hennepin County Court Services, 1971 (with R. Dreikurs, Miriam L. Pew & Vicki Soltz Statton).

254 ———. Marital therapy (with Miriam L. Pew). In A. Nikelly (Ed.), *Techniques for behavior change.* Pp. 125–128.

255 ———. Portrait. *IPNL*, 1972, 21(6), 112.

256 ———. Quantified LSD effects on ego strength (with A. S. Marazzi, R. A. Meish, & T. G. Bieter). In J. Wortis (Ed.), *Recent advances in biological psychiatry.* New York: Plenum Press, 1967.

257 ———. Review of W. & Marguerite Beecher, *Parents on the run.* In *OSIPNL*, 1964, 4(4), 12.

258 ———. Review of J. E. Bell, *Family group therapy.* In *OSIPNL*, 1964, 4(3), 10–11.

259 **Pew, W. L.** Review of W. E. Oates, *What psychology says about religion.* New York: Association Press, 1958. In *OSIPNL*, 1963, 4(2), 9.

260 ———. *A team approach: Pre-disposition report: An innovative delivery perspective.* Minneapolis: Hennepin County Court Services, 1972 (with J. Stoeckel & I. Schwartz).

261 ——— (Ed.). *The war between the generations.* St. Paul: Amer. Soc. Adlerian Psychol., 1969. Mimeo.

262 **Pfeifer, Rosa.** Review of P. Vachet, *Der Gedanke, der heilt.* Paris: Grassets, 1926. In *IZIP*, 1928, 6(6), 509.

263 **Pflanczer, S.** *Men in jail.* Chicago: Loyola Univ., 1965 (with C. O'Reilly, F. Cizon, & J. Flanagan).

264 **Pfouts, Zoe.** The contributions of a psychiatric nurse on a medical service. *Perspec. psychiat. Care,* 1966, 4(2), 22-37 (with B. H. Shulman, D. Corrigan, & Jean Hudnut).

265 **Phillips, E. L.** Attitudes toward self and others: A brief questionnaire report. *J. consult. Psychol.,* 1951, 15, 79-81.

266 ———. *Psychotherapy: A modern theory and practice.* Englewood Cliffs, N. J.: Prentice-Hall, 1956.

267 **Pick, R.** Erleben der Gemeinschaft durch die Kunst. *IZIP*, 1924, 2(3), 46.

268 ———. Der Gemeinschaftsgedanke als Zielpunkt der neueren Philosophie. *IZIP*, 1929, 7(5), 359-366.

269 ———. Die Geschichte des Gemeinschaftsgefühls und der Unsterblichkeitsgedanke. *IZIP*, 1926, 4(5), 300-303.

270 ———. Die Jugend des Themistokles. *IZIP*, 1929, 7(6), 462-469.

271 ———. Review of A. Bjerre, *Zur Psychologie des Mordes.* Heidelberg: Karl Winters, 1925. In *IZIP*, 1926, 4(6), 396.

272 ———. Review of A. Grimme, *Vom Sinn und Widersinn der Reifeprufung.* Leipzig: Oldenburg, [   ]. In *IZIP*, 1924, 2(6), 40-41.

273 ———. Review of G. S. Hall, *The psychology of the Nativity.* In *IZIP*, 1924, 2(3), 54-56.

274 ———. Review of O. Juliusberger, *Schopenhauer und die Psychotherapie der Gegenwart.* In *IZIP*, 1929, 7(2), 154-155.

275 ———. Review of O. Kaus, Die Träume in Dostojewskys "Raskalnikoff." In *IZIP*, 1927, 5(6) 482-483.

276 **Pick, R.** Review of D. E. Oppenheim, *Dichtung und Menschenkenntnis.* In *IZIP*, 1927, 5(2), 155-156.

277 ———. Review of T. Schramek, *Freiherr von Egloffstein.* Berlin: Verlag die Schmiede, [   ]. In *IZIP*, 1926, 4(6), 394.

278 ———. Review of A. Seidel, *Bewusstsein als Verhängnis.* Bonn: F. Cohn, 1927. In *IZIP*, 1927, 5(5), 398-399.

279 ———. Review of A. Tridon, *Psychoanalysis* and *Psychoanalysis and behaviour.* In *IZIP*, 1923, 2(1), 41-42.

280 ———. Review of P. G. Vorbrodt, *Arbeitsprogram für zukünftige Religionspsychologie.* Wien: W. Bräumüller, 1926.

281 ———. Zum Führerproblem. In A. Adler & C. Furtmüller (Eds.), *Heilen und Bilden* (1928). Pp. 299-304.

282 ———. Zur Führerproblem. *IZIP*, 1926, 4(6), 368-371.

283 **Pick-Seewart, R.** See Pick, R.

284 **Pickens, Marleen.** Review of Betty Friedan, *The feminine mystique.* New York: Norton, 1963. In *OSIPNL*, 1964, 4(3), 8.

285 ———. Review of K. Kesey, *One flew over the cuckoo's nest.* New York: Viking Press, 1962. In *OSIPNL*, 1963, 4(1), 9.

286 ———. Review of H. Nunberg & P. Federn, *Minutes of the Vienna Psychoanalytic Society.* In *OSIPNL*, 1964, 4(3), 9.

287 ———. Review of H. F. Peters, *My sister, my spouse.* New York: Norton, 1962. In *OSIPNL*, 1963, 4(1), 9.

288 ———. Review of Ayn Rand, *Atlas shrugged.* New York: Random House, 1957. In *OSIPNL*, 1963, 4(2), 8-9.

289 ———. Review of Ruth Sprang & G. Morris, *Third force psychology.* New York: Macmillan, 1964. In *OSIPNL*, 1965, 5(3), 14-15.

290 **Pienaar, W. D.** Dominance in families. *Diss. Abstr. Int.,* 1969, 30, 2914-2915.

291 **Pierce, J. V.** Personality and achievement among able high school boys. *JIP*, 1961, 17, 102-107.

292 **Pierce, K. K.** The personality inventory correlates of the level of aspiration. Ph.D. Diss., Univ. Arizona, 1954.

293 **Pijnaker, J. N.** *Reclassering in deze Tijd.* *MNWIP*, 1971, 20(3).

294 **Piskowski, Dorothy.** Order of birth as a determinant of personality and attitudinal characteristics. *J. soc. Psychol.,*

1963, 60, 221-230 (with H. Greenberg, Rosemarie Guerino, Marilyn Lashen & D. Mayer).

295 **Pious, Constance.** The therapeutic event in group psychotherapy: A study of subjective reports by group members. *JIP*, 1963, 19, 204-212 (with Betty Berzon & R. E. Farson).

296 **Piskula, C.** Non-public vocational education: A trend of the future? *Guidelines for Pupil Services*, 1972, 11(1), 18-21 (with L. Sperry & L. Hess).

297 **Plank, R.** The family constellation of a group of schizophrenic patients. *Amer. J. Orthopsychiat.*, 1953, 23, 817-825.

298 **Platt, J.** The efficiency of the Adlerian model in elementary school counseling. Ed.D. Diss., Univ. Arizona, 1970.

299 **Platt, J. J.** Birth order and sex differences in future time perspective. *Developm. Psychol.*, 1969, 1, 70 (with R. Eisenman).

300 ———. A future-oriented theory of nostalgia. *JIP*, 1965, 21, 51-57.

301 ———. Group discussion at high school level. *OSIPNL*, 1965, 6(3), 6.

302 ———. Homesickness, future time perspective, and the self concept. *JIP*, 1967, 23, 94-97 (with R. E. Taylor).

303 ———. Sex and birth order, and future expectations of occupational status and salary. *JIP*, 1968, 24, 170-173 (with D. D. Moskalski & R. Eisenman).

304 **Plaut, P.** Bericht über den Kongress für Sexualforschung. *IZIP*, 1927, 5(3), 228-232.

305 **Pleune, F. G.** All dis-ease is not disease: A consideration of psycho-analysis, psychotherapy, and psycho-social engineering. *Int. J. Psychoanal.*, 1965, 46, 358-366.

306 **Plewa, F.** Adler und der Evolutionsgedanke. *IZIP*, 1937, 15(3-4), 142-149.

307 ———. The meaning in childhood recollections. *IJIP*, 1935, 1(1), 88-101.

308 ———. Psychic difficulties. *IJIP*, 1936, 2(1), 114-126.

309 ———. Review of R. Dreikurs, *Einführung in die Individualpsychologie*. In *IZIP*, 1934, 12(1), 53-54.

310 ———. Review of F. Hoppe, *Erfolg und Miserfolg*. Berlin: Julius Springer, 1930. In *IZIP*, 1934, 12(2), 126-127.

311 ———. Review of M. Serog, *Nervenärztliche Gutachtertätigkeit*. Leipzig: Geo. Thieme, 1931. In *IZIP*, 1933, 12(3), 255-256.

312 **Plewa, F.** Review of D. A. Thom, *Ausrotung der Eifersucht*. *N. Y. Herald Tribune*, March 12, 1933. In *IZIP*, 1934, 12(3), 196-197.

313 ———. Seelische Schwierigkeiten. *IZIP*, 1935, 13(3), 146-158.

314 ———. Shakespeare und die Macht. *IZIP*, 1936, 14(1), 26-36.

315 ———. Der Sinn in den Kindheitserinnerungen. *IZIP*, 1934, 12(3), 142-155.

316 ———. Die Stellung der Frau zur Gesellschaft. *IZIP*, 1936, 14(2), 104-118.

317 ———. Über seelische Behandlung. *IZIP*, 1935, 13(2), 65-76.

318 ———. Zur Frage der psychischen Kompensation der Augenminderwertigkeit. *IZIP*, 1931, 9(6), 455-456.

319 ———. Zur Psychologie der Jugendbewegung, namentlich in ihrer Ausdrucksform als Wandervogebewegung. *IZIP*, 1933, 12(5), 353-368.

320 **Plewa, H.** See Plewa, F.

321 **Plosky, Joyce.** Factors interacting with birth order in self-selection among volunteer subjects. *J. soc. Psychol.*, 1967, 72, 125-128 (with Barbara S. Dohrenwend, S. Feldstein & Gertrude Schmeidler).

322 **Plottke, P.** See Rom, P.

323 **Polak, Elise.** Individualpsychologische Betrachtungen über Tolstoi. *IZIP*, 1928, 6(6), 456-481.

324 **Pollak, O.** (Ed.). *Family dynamics and female sexual delinquency*. Palo Alto: Science & Behavior Books, 1969 (with A. S. Friedman).

325 **Pollak, S. W.** Theory and techniques for a therapeutic milieu. *JIP*, 1969, 25, 164-173.

326 **Polony, Marie.** Über das Erwecken der Kontakt Fähigkeit. *IZIP*, 1929, 7(1), 59-60.

327 **Ponce, A.** *Diario intimo de una adolescente*. Buenos Aires: Ateneo, 1943.

328 **Popper, V.** Review of L. Deutsch, *Guided sight reading*. In *IPB*, 1951, 9, 36-37; 1951, 9, 92.

329 **Porta, Judith.** The familial genesis of psychoses. *Psychiat.*, 1962, 25, 60-71 (with W. McCord & Joan McCord).

330 **Porter, A.** Editor of A. Adler, *What life should mean to you*.

331 **Porter, B. M.** The relationship between marital adjustment and parental acceptance of children. *J. Home Econ.*, 1955, 47, 157-164.

332 **Postel, R.** New approaches in Adlerian group psychotherapy. In R. Dreikurs (Ed.), *Education, guidance, psychodynamics.* Pp. 28–32.

333 **Postman, L.** The factor of attitude in associative memory. *J. exp., Psychol.*, 1943, 33, 228–238 (with G. Murphy).

334 ———. Personal values as selective factors in perception. *J. abnorm. soc. Psychol.*, 1948, 42, 142–154 (with J. S. Bruner & E. McGinnies).

335 ———. Personal values, visual recognition and recall. *Psychol. Rev.*, 1951, 58, 271–284 (with B. H. Schneider).

336 **Potwin, E. B.** Study of early memories. *Psychol. Rev.*, 1901, 8, 596–601.

337 **Powers, Joanne.** Conjunctive use of psychodrama and group psychotherapy in a group living program with schizophrenic patients. *Grp. Psychother.*, 1965, 18(3), 127–135 (with T. P. McGee, Adaline Starr, Frances A. Racusen, & A. Thornton).

338 **Powers, R. L.** The minister as psychotherapist: Role-conflict and convergence. In R. Dreikurs (Ed.), *Education, guidance, psychodynamics.* Pp. 15–19.

339 ———. Portrait. *IPNL*, 1972, 21(6), 110.

340 **Prakash, J.** The effect of family size, economic condition, and order of birth on adolescent adjustment. *Manas*, 1963, 10, 83–88 (with P. K. Srwastava).

341 **Precker, J. A.** (Ed.). *Success in psychotherapy.* New York: Grune & Stratton, 1952 (with W. Wolff).

342 **Preparatory Commission to the Congress of Mental Hygiene.** The basic needs of children. *IPB*, 1950, 8, 49–71.

343 **Price, J.** Personality differences within families: Comparison of adult brothers and sisters. *J. biosoc. Sci.*, 1969, 1, 177–205.

344 **Price, J. S.** Birth order and family size: Bias caused by changes in birth rate. *Brit. J. Psychiat.*, 1969, 115, 647–657 (with E. H. Hare).

345 ———. Birth order studies: Some sources of bias. *Brit. J. Psychiat.*, 1969, 115, 633–646 (with E. H. Hare).

346 ———. Birth rank in schizophrenia: With a consideration of the bias due to changes in birth rate. *Brit. J. Psychiat.*, 1970, 116, 409–420 (with E. H. Hare).

347 **Prince, Gloria.** The ballade of Careful Joan (or neurotic distance-creating). *New Statesman & Nation*, Dec. 29, 1956. Also in *IPNL*, 1957, 6(6–7, Whole No. 70–71). P. 24

348 **Prince, M.** Über die Notwendigkeit, das systematische Studium der funktionellen Krankheiten in die medizinische Studienordnung aufzunehmen. *IZIP*, 1928, 6(1), 2–4.

349 **Progoff, I.** *The death and rebirth of psychology.* New York: Julian Press, 1956; New York: Delta, 1964. Paper.

350 ———. Personal concern and integrity (Tribute to Alfred Adler on his 100th birthday). *JIP*, 1970, 26(2), 15.

351 ———. Psychology as a road to personal philosophy. *JIP*, 1961, 17, 43–48.

352 ———. The psychology of Lee Harvey Oswald: A Jungian approach. *JIP*, 1967, 23, 37–47.

353 ———. Review of W. & Marguerite Beecher, *Beyond success and failure.* In *JIP*, 1967, 23, 120–121.

354 **Pronko, N. H.** On learning to play the violin at the age of four without tears. *Psychol. Today*, 1969, 2(12), 52–53, 66.

355 **Prothro, E. T.** Birth order and age at marriage in the Arab Levant. *Psychol. Rep.*, 1968, 23, 1236–1238 (with L. N. Diab).

356 ———. Cross-cultural study of some correlates of birth order. *Psychol. Rep.*, 1968, 22, 1137–1142 (with L. Diab).

357 **Prull, R. W.** Birth order, personality development, and the choice of law as a profession. *J. genet. Psychol.*, 1970, 116, 219–221 (with P. S. Very).

358 **Prunkl, P. R.** Factors in predicting Army aviator performance: Birth order and participation in dangerous sports and activities. *Human RRO prof. Papers*, 1969.

359 **Przywara, E.** Zur Metaphysik der Person. *IZIP*, 1926, 4.

360 **Puig, F.** La genèse de la volonté chez l'enfant et la doctrine du Professeur Adler. *IZIP*, 1931, 9(2), 138.

361 **Puner, Helen W.** *Freud: His life and his mind.* London: Grey Walls Press, 1949.

362 **Purcell, K.** Memory and psychological security. *J. abnorm. soc. Psychol.*, 1952, 47, 433–440.

363 **Purpura, P. A.** A study of the relations between birth order, self-esteem and conformity. *Diss. Abstr. Int.*, 1971, 31, 6266.

Q

1 Quaatz, P. G. *Verlorene Gemeinschaft.* Berlin: Verlag Haus u. Schule, 1950.

2 Quaranta, J. (Ed.). *Guidance in the elementary school: A book of readings.* New York: Macmillan, 1963 (with H. Peters & A. Riccio).

3 Quarrick, E. A. Personality and attitude toward a political event. *JIP,* 1964, 20, 189–193 (with R. E. Rankin).

4 Quay, H. C. The effect of verbal reinforcement on the recall of early memories. Ph.D. Diss., Univ. Illinois, 1958; *J. abnorm. soc. Psychol.,* 1959, 59, 254–257.

R

1 R. L. Psychische Charakteristiks der Schizophrene bei Dämmerzuständen und manisch-depressiven Irresein. *IZIP,* 1929, 7(6), 403–406.

2 Rabkin, L. Y. The disturbed child's perception of his parents. *JIP,* 1964, 20, 172–178.

3 Racamato, C. P. The relationship of birth order to seeking counseling. *Diss. Abstr.,* 1969, 29, 4294.

4 Racusen, Frances A. Conjunctive use of psychodrama and group psychotherapy in a group living program with schizophrenic patients. *Grp. Psychother.,* 1965, 18(3), 127–135 (with T. P. McGee, Adaline Starr, Joanne Powers & A. Thornton).

5 Racz, E. Die Behandlung der depressiven Neurosen nach Adler. *IZIP,* 1926, 4(5), 303–307.

6 Radin, P. Translator of A. Adler, *The practice and theory of Individual Psychology.*

7 Radke, Marian J. Relationship of parental authority to children's behavior and attitude. *Univ. Minn. Inst. Child Welf. Monogr.,* 1946, No. 22.

8 Radl, Lucia. An adult school phobia. *Voices,* 1967, 3(3), 20–22. Also in *Treatm. Monogr. on Analyt. Psychother.,* 1967, 1(1).

9 ———. Biography and photograph. *Voices,* 1967, 3(3), 20.

10 ———. Existentialism and Adlerian psychology. In K. A. Adler & Danica Deutsch (Eds.), *Essays in Individual Psychology.* Pp. 157–167.

11 Radl, Lucia. Review of A. Stern, *Sartre: His philosophy and psychoanalysis.* New York: Liberal Arts Press, 1953. In *JIP,* 1958, 14, 94–95.

12 Radloff, R. Stress: Under the sea. *Psychol. Today,* 1969, 3(4), 28–29, 59–60 (with R. Heimrich).

13 Raimy, V. C. The self concept as a factor in counseling and personality organization. Unpubl. Ph.D. Diss., Ohio St. Univ., 1943.

14 Rainer, O. Der moderne Zeichen-und Kunstunterricht. In Sofie Lazarsfeld (Ed.), *Technik der Erziehung.*

15 Rainwater, L. Persistence and change in working-class life style (with G. Handel). In A. B. Shostak & W. Gomberg (Eds.), *Blue-collar world.* Englewood Cliffs, N. J.: Prentice-Hall, 1964. Pp. 36–41.

16 ———. *Workingman's wife: Her personality, world and life style.* Dobbs Ferry, N. Y.: Oceana Publications, 1959 (with R. P. Coleman & G. Handel).

17 Ralph, Elisabeth R. Miss Edna—a perfectionist. *IJIP,* 1937, 3(3), 254–262.

18 Ranchetti, C. Translator of R. Dreikurs, *Psicologia in classe.*

19 Rancurello, A. C. *A study of Franz Brentano.* New York: Academic Press, 1968.

20 Rankin, R. Personality and attitude toward a political event. *JIP,* 1964, 20, 189–193 (with E. A. Quarrick).

21 Rao, M. S. S. Sibling position and mental disorders. *Psychiat. Quart.,* 1965, 39, 27–47.

22 Rapaport, D. *Emotions and memory.* Baltimore: Williams & Wilkins, 1942.

23 Rapoport, R. Early and later experiences as determinants of adult behavior: Married women's family and career patterns. *Brit. J. Sociol.,* 1971, 22, 16–30 (with R. N. Rapoport).

24 Rapoport, R. N. Early and later experiences as determinants of adult behavior: Married women's family and career patterns. *Brit. J. Sociol.,* 1971, 22, 16–30 (with R. Rapoport).

25 Rasey, Marie. Peter Brown's Geheimnis. *IZIP,* 1929, 7(5), 382–383.

26 ———. Test für moralische Meinung. *IZIP,* 1928, 6(5), 347–349 (with June Dennerline).

27 ———. *This is teaching.* New York: Harper, 1950.

28 **Rasey, Marie.** *Toward maturity, the psychology of child development.* New York: Hinds, Hayden & Eldridge, 1947.

29 ———. Toward the end. In C. E. Moustakas (Ed.), *The self: Explorations in personal growth.* New York: Harper, 1956. Pp. 247–260.

30 ———. Über Kinder, die keine Freunde haben. *IZIP*, 1931, 9(3), 235–238.

31 ———. *What we learn from children.* New York: Harper, 1956 (with J. W. Menge).

32 **Rattner, J.** *Alfred Adler in Selbstzeugnissen und Bilddokumenten.* Hamburg: Rowohlt, 1972.

33 ———. *Individualpsychologie: Eine Einführung in die tiefenpsychologische Lehre Alfred Adlers.* Munich-Basel: Reinhardt, 1962.

34 ———. Die Neurose Peer Gynts. *Der Psychologe*, 1963, 14.

35 ———. *Psychologie und psychopathologie des Liebeslebens.* Berne: Hans Huber, 1965.

36 ———. *Psychosomatische Medizin Heute.* Zürich: Werner Classen, 1964.

37 ———. Self review of *Individualpsychologie.* In *JIP*, 1963, 19, 98.

38 ———. *Verwöhnung und Neurose.* Zürich: Werner Classen, 1968.

39 ———. *Das Wesen der Schizophrenen Reaktion.* München: E. Reinhardt, 1963.

40 **Rattner, L.** Hemmungen und Minderwertigkeitsgefühle. *Tages-Anzeiger* (Zürich), May 14, 1949.

41 ———. *Individualpsychologische Berufsberatung.* Schwarzenburg, Switzerland: Gerber-Buchdruck, 1952.

42 ———. Das individualpsychologische Berufswahlgespräch. *IZIP*, 1948, 17(2), 77–84. Also in *Caritas* (Luzern), Oct., 1954.

43 ———. Individual Psychology and democracy. *AJIP*, 1954, 11, 167–171.

44 ———. The Individual Psychology of proper training for the job. *AJIP*, 1954, 11, 23–33. Also in *Connaissance de l'homme*, No. 15, Jan., 1956.

45 ———. Kritik der Psychoanalyse. *Tages-Anzeiger* (Zürich), Apr. 30, 1949.

46 ———. The pampered child. *Today's Educ.*, 1972, 61(1), 22–24. Reprinted in condensed form in *Educ. Digest*, 1972, 37(7), 14–16.

47 ———. The pampered lifestyle. In A. Nikelly (Ed.), *Techniques for behavior change.* Pp. 143–150.

48 **Rattner, L.** Praktische Menschenkenntnis. *Tages-Anzeiger* (Zürich), Oct. 9, 1948.

49 ———. *Psychologie und Sozialismus.* Wien: Die Zukunft, 1947.

50 ———. Review of L. E. Abt & B. F. Riess (Eds.), Dreams and dreaming. *Progress in clinical psychology.* Vol. 8. New York: Grune & Stratton, 1969, In *IP*, 1968, 5(3), 24.

51 ———. Review of G. W. Burns, *The science of genetics.* New York: Macmillan, 1969. In *IP*, 1968, 5(3), 24.

52 ———. Review of S. Endleman (Ed.), *Violence in the streets.* Chicago: Quadrangle Books, 1969. In *IP*, 1969, 6(2), 47.

53 ———. Review of J. Ehrenwald. *Psychotherapy: Myth and method.* New York: Grune & Stratton, 1966. In *IP*, 1966, 4(1), 33–34.

54 ———. Review of A. P. Goldstein & A. J. Dean (Eds.), *The investigation of psychotherapy: Commentaries and reading.* New York: Wiley, 1966. In *IP*, 1967, 4(2), 71–72.

55 ———. Review of E. Jones, *The life and work of Sigmund Freud.* In *AJIP*, 1956, 12, 184–185.

56 ———. Review of H. Kahn & A. J. Weiner, *The year 2000: A framework for speculation on the next thirty-three years.* New York: Macmillan, 1967. In *IP*, 1968, 5, 70.

57 ———. Review of R. May, *Love and will.* In *IP*, 1970, 7(2), 59–60.

58 ———. Review of J. L. Moreno et al., *The international handbook of group psychotherapy.* New York: Phil. Libr., 1956. In *IP*, 1966, 4(1), 34.

59 ———. Review of D. Offer & M. Sabshin, *Normality.* New York: Basic Books, 1966. In *IP*, 1969, 6(2), 46.

60 ———. Review of H. A. Otto, *Guide to developing your potential.* New York: Scribner's, 1967. In *IP*, 1968, 5, 69.

61 ———. Review of B. S. Phillips, *Social research: Strategy and tactics.* New York: Macmillan, 1966. In *IP*, 1967, 5(1), 37.

62 ———. Review of J. P. Sartre, *Ist der Existentialismus ein Humanismus?* Zurich: Europa, 1947. In *IZIP*, 1948, 17(4), 187–189.

63 ———. Review of W. K. Schaie & R. Heiss, *Color and personality.* New York: Grune & Stratton, 1964. In *IP*, 1966, 3(2), 22–23.

64 **Rattner, L.** Review of E. Singer, *Key concepts in psychotherapy.* New York: Random House, 1966. In *IP,* 1967, 4(2), 71–72.

65 ———. Review of I. B. Weiner, *Psychodiagnosis in schizophrenia.* New York: Wiley, 1967. In *IP,* 1968, 5, 70.

66 ———. Review of B. Wolstein, *Theory of psychoanalytic therapy.* New York: Grune & Stratton, 1967. In *IP,* 1967, 5, 37.

67 ———. The social theory of personality in Alfred Adler's Individual Psychology and contemporary American sociology. Unpubl. master's thesis, New Sch. for Soc. Res., 1955.

68 ———. A study of excessive dependency in mother-son relationships. *AJIP,* 1956, 12, 171–176. Also in K. A. Adler & D. Deutsch (Eds.), *Essays in Individual Psychology.* Pp. 365–371.

69 **Rau, Charlotte.** Eine persönliche Begegnung mit der Jugendrichter Lindsey. *IZIP,* 1928, 6(2), 146–154.

70 **Raush, H. L.** Identification and the adolescent boy's perception of his father. *J. abnorm. soc. Psychol.,* 1952, 47, 855–856 (with Esther L. Cava).

71 **Rawlings, Margaret.** Disillusion and Thomas Mann's approach to the individual in society. *IJIP,* 1936, 2(2), 87–96.

72 ———. "Enttäuschung" und Thomas Manns Annäherung an das Individuum in der Gesellschaft. *IZIP,* 1937, 15(1), 34–45.

73 **Ray, J.** Task group report (with T. W. Allen, J. Krumboltz, F. Robinson, W. Cottle, J. Cody, & D. Homra). In J. Whiteley (Ed.), *Research problems in counseling.* Pp. 219–237.

74 **Ray, M. B.** Individual Psychology and psychosomatic disorders (I). *IPMP,* 1932, No. 4 (with F. G. Crookshank, W. Langdon-Brown, S. V. Pearson, M. Robb, O. H. Woodcock, & J. C. Young).

75 ———. The psychological factor in the rheumatic syndrome. *IPMP,* 1932, No. 4. Pp. 58–60.

76 ———. *Rheumatic diseases.* London: Routledge & Kegan Paul,

77 **Ray, Marie B.** *The importance of feeling inferior.* New York: Harper, 1957. Condensed in *Readers Digest,* Sept., 1958.

78 ———. *Doctors of the mind.* Boston: Little, Brown, 1942.

79 **Rayner, Doris.** Individual Psychology and the child (I). *IPMP,* 1933, No. 7 (with L. Seif & Agnes Zilahi).

80 ———. Individual Psychology and the children's clinic. *IPMP,* 1933, No. 7.

81 **Record, R. G.** The relation of measured intelligence to birth order and maternal age. *Ann. hum. Genet.,* 1969, 33, 61–69 (with T. McKeown and J. H. Edwards).

82 **Reddy, N. Y.** A study of the relationship between ordinal position of adolescents and their adjustment. *Psychol. Studies,* 1967, 12, 91–100.

83 **Redl, F.** Die Idee der Erziehungsgemeinschaft und ein Versuch ihrer Verwirklichung. *IZIP,* 1929, 7(6), 419–432.

84 **Redwin, Eleanore.** Adlerian psychotherapy with disturbed children. *IP,* 1965, 3(1), 2–9.

85 ———. Aus einer individualpsychologischer Kindergemeinschaft. *IZIP,* 1931, 9(6), 466–468.

86 ———. A case of deaf-mutism (with A. Holub). In A. Adler & assoc., *Guiding the child.* Pp. 193–194.

87 ———. Child guidance with Adlerian techniques in Chicago. *AJIP,* 1956, 12, 70–77.

88 ———. Counseling the reluctant child and her mother. *IP,* 1966, 4(1), 4–8 (with Georgia Greven). Also in R. Dreikurs (Ed.), *Education, guidance, psychodynamics.* Pp. 11–15.

89 ———. The development of a power contest. *AJIP,* 1954, 11, 172–177 (with Letitia Wainwright).

90 ———. Discussion group of small schildren *IP,* 1967, 5, 26–29 (with Georgia Greven).

91 ———. Ein Fall von Hörstummheit. *IZIP,* 1929, 7(3), 227 (with A. Holub).

92 ———. Das einzige Kind. *IZIP,* 1929, 7(3), 230 (with A. Holub).

93 ———. Mothers' therapy groups. In R. Dreikurs, R. Corsini, R. Lowe, & M. Sonstegard (Eds.), *Adlerian family counseling.* Pp. 63–68.

94 ———. Portrait. *IPNL,* 1971, 20(6), 112; 1972, 21(6), 110.

95 ———. Re-education through counseling. *IPB,* 1949, 7, 162–170.

96 ———. Über Einfügung in die Geschlechts-rolle bei Schulekindern. *IZIP,* 1925, 3(4), 195–199 (with Melka Schlamm).

97 Redwin, Eleanore. Work. in a settlement house. *IPB*, 1944–45, 4, 91–92.

98 Reed, Muriel. Mother study groups. In R. Dreikurs, R. Corsini, R. Lowe, & M. Sonstegard (Eds.), *Adlerian family counseling.* Pp. 83–86.

99 Reed, R. Y. A qualitative study of the self concept as revealed in the counseling situation. Unpubl. Ph.D. Diss., Univ. Chicago, 1952.

100 Reed, T. R. The effect of imagined context, sex, and birth order on the connotative meaning of selected social interaction concepts. *Diss. Abstr. Int.*, 1970, 30, 5069.

101 Reens, Renee. Day treatment center and school: Seven years experience. *Amer. J. Orthopsychiat.*, 1965, 15(1), 160–169 (with Ruth Ronall, Ruth la Viete, & Rosalyn Cohn).

102 Rees, A. H. Factors related to change in mental test performance. *Developm. Psychol.*, 1970, 3, (2, Pt. 2), 57 (with F. H. Palmer).

103 Reeve, G. H. A method of coordinated treatment. *Amer. J. Orthopsychiat.*, 1939, 9, 743.

104 Reeves, J. Strange overcompensations: Academic. *New Statesman & Nation*, Dec. 29, 1956. Also in *IPNL*, 1958, 8 (10–12, Whole No. 86–88). P. 48.

105 Reeves, Margaret P. The psychologies of McDougall and Adler—A comparison. *IPB*, 1949, 7, 147–161.

106 Regan, R. A. Ordinal position and behavior problems in children. *J. Hlth. & soc. Behav.*, 1967, 8(1), 32–39 (with J. Tuckman).

107 Regan, T. F. ESOL and the Mexican-American. *Linguist Reporter*, 1968, 10 (25), 1–2 (with P. Scarth).

108 Reich, Luna. An adolescent's behavior problem. In K. A. Adler & Danica Deutsch (Eds.), *Essays in Individual Psychology.* Pp. 371–382.

109 Reider, N. Reconstruction and screen function. *J. Amer. Psychoanal. Assn.*, 1953, 1, 389–405.

110 Reiff, R. *Memory and hypnotic age regression: Developmental aspects of cognitive function explored through hypnosis.* New York: Int. Univer. Press, 1959 (with M. Scheerer).

111 Reik, T. Emotional differences of the sexes. *Psychoanal.*, 1953, 2(1), 3–13.

112 Reilly, Mary St. Anne. The complementarity of personality needs in friendship choice. *J. abnorm. soc. Psych.*, 1960, 61, 292–294 (with W. D. Commins & E. C. Steffic).

113 Reimanis, G. Childhood experience memories and anomie in adults and college students. *JIP*, 1966, 22, 56–64.

114 ———. Relationship of childhood experience memories to anomie in later life. *J. genet. Psychol.*, 1965, 106, 245–252.

115 ———. The role of anomie as a psychological concept. *JIP*, 1959, 15, 215–225 (with H. Davol).

116 Reimer, C. Some words of encouragement. *OSIPNL*, 1967, 7(4), 7; 1972, 3(5), 8.

117 Reinhardt, J. M. Cultural factors in personality problems. *IJIP*, 1937, 3(1), 72–80.

118 Reis, M. *Das kränkelnde Kind.* Dresden: Verlag am andern Ufer, 1927.

119 ———. Minderwertigkeit von Organen. In E. Wexberg (Ed.), *Handbuch der Individualpsychologie.* Pp. 30–46.

120 ———. Review of E. Utiz, *Jahrbuch der Charakterologie, 1924.* Vol. 1. In *IZIP*, 1926, 4(1), 45–46.

121 Reiser, M. F. *A manual for the scoring of earliest memories, revised.* New York: Albert Einstein Coll. Med., 1960 (with R. Langs).

122 ———. A method for clinical and theoretical study of the earliest memory. *Arch. gen. Psychiat.*, 1960, 3, 523–524 (with R. J. Langs, M. B. Rothenberg & J. R. Fishman).

123 Reisman, J. M. *The development of clinical psychology.* New York: Appleton-Century-Crofts, 1966. Paper.

124 Reiss, Sidonie. Die Anwendung der individualpsychologischen Therapie als Problem. *IZIP*, 1937, 15(1), 4–17.

125 ———. Betrachtungen einer "Untertaucherin". *IZIP*, 1947, 16(2), 74–83.

126 ———. Eine "Spiel" Behandlung. *IZIP*, 1934, 12(3), 169–178.

127 ———. *Levenskoers en Levensverniewing.* Vertaald door P. Th. Van Enckevort en A. M. Marx. Utrecht: Bijleveld, 1951.

128 ———. *Mental readjustment.* London: Allen & Unwin, 1949.

129 ———. Psychotherapy in a case of chronic illness. In K. A. Adler &

Danica Deutsch (Eds.), *Essays in Individual Psychology.* Pp. 382–400.

130 **Reissner, A.** The medicine of the person. *The Witness, for Christ and His Church,* 1964, 49(39).

131 ———. Prologue. In A. Adler, *Sex, personality and the Establishment.* Pp. iii–xi.

132 ———. Religion and classical psychotherapy: How Freud, Jung and Adler evaluated the role of religious faith in relation to mental well-being. *Christian Century,* 1961, 78, 453–455.

133 ———. Religion and psychotherapy. *JIP,* 1957, 13, 165–170. Also in K. A. Adler & Danica Deutsch (Eds.), *Essays in Individual Psychology.* Pp. 167–174.

134 ———. Three great schools of psychology and their attitude towards religion. *Ministerium Medici,* 1961, 2, 55–63.

135 **Reitman, W. R.** Performance as a function of motive strength and expectance of goal attainment. *J. abnorm. soc. Psychol.,* 1956, 53, 361–367 (with J. W. Atkinson).

136 **Remits, E. L.** The feeling of superiority and anxiety-superior. Unpubl. M. A. thesis, Univ. Ottawa, 1952.

137 **Remy, R. M.** Perceived parental attitudes, the self, and security. *J. consult. Psychol.,* 1955, 19, 364–366 (with S. Jourard).

138 **Renck, R.** *Verbal reasoning.* Education-Industry Service, University of Chicago, 1961 (with R. J. Corsini).

139 **Renner, E. K.** Effect of construct type on recall. *JIP,* 1962, 18, 177–179 (with B. A. Maher).

140 **Renner, Maria.** Ein Fall von Sprachstörung. *IZIP,* 1951, 20(2), 49–66.

141 **Revers, W. J.** Über das Problem des Stils im persönlichen Lebenslauf. *Studium Generale,* 1955, 8, 15ff.

142 **Reymert, M. L.** (Ed.). *Feelings and emotions: The Wittenberg symposium.* Worcester, Mass.: Clark Univ. Press, 1928.

143 **Reynell, W. R.** Escape into invalidism. *IPP,* 1939, No. 21. Pp. 30–33.

144 **Reznikoff, M.** Over troubled waters. *Psychol. Today,* 1970, 3(12), 36–39.

145 **Rheinstein, M.** Individualpsychologie und Staatsauffassung. *IZIP,* 1928, 6(2), 172–182.

146 **Rhine, W. R.** Birth order differences in resistance to conformity pressure related to social class and level of achievement arousal. *Proc. Ann. Conv. Amer. Psychol. Assn.,* 1969, 4, 265–267.

147 **Rhine, W. R.** Conformity behavior in children as related to socio-economic status, birth order, and level of arousal. *Diss. Abstr.,* 1966, 27, 295. Unpubl. Ph.D. Diss., Univ. Texas, 1965.

148 ———. Motivational and situational determinants of birth order differences in conformity among preadolescent girls. *Proc. Ann. Conv. Amer. Psychol. Assn.,* 1968, 3, 351–352.

149 **Riard, E. H.** [The nature and development of sparetime activities of school-age boys as a function of age and family environment]. *Bull. Psychol.,* 1969–1970, 23, 221 229 (with F. Winnykamen).

150 **Riccio, A.** (Ed.). *Guidance in the elementary school: A book of readings.* New York: Macmillan, 1963 (with H. Peters & J. Quaranta).

151 **Rice, G. E.** Altruism in the albino rat. *J. comp. physiol. Psychol.,* 1962, 55(1), 123–125 (with Priscilla Gainer).

152 **Rice, Katherine K.** The importance of including fathers. *Int. J. grp. Psychother.,* 1952, 2, 232–238.

153 **Rice, R. P.** Idea exchange column. *IP,* 1966, 4(1), 27–29; 1967, 4(2), 66–67; 1967, 5(1), 31–32; 1968, 5(2), 63–65.

154 **Richards, J. M.** Accuracy of interpersonal perception—a general trait? *J. abnorm. soc. Psychol.,* 1960, 60, 1–7 (with V. B. Cline).

155 **Richards, L. G.** Cognitive grouping and material culture. *Diss. Abstr.,* 1965, 26, 520. Unpubl. Ph.D. Diss., Cornell Univ., 1965.

156 **Richardson, Helen M.** Studies of mental resemblance between husbands and wives and between friends. *Psychol. Bull.,* 1939, 36, 104–120.

157 **Richter, G.** Das Ich und die Umwelt. *IZIP,* 1925, 3(3), 125–128.

158 ———. Individualpsychologie und Staatsauffassung. *IZIP,* 1928, 6(5), 396–398.

159 ———. Die Jagd nach Zeit, Macht und Genialität. *IZIP,* 1927, 5(2), 125–129.

160 **Richter, H. E.** *Eltern, Kind und Neurose: Psychoanalyse der kindlichen Rolle.* Stuttgart: Ernst Klett Verlag, 1963.

161 **Rie-Andro, T.** Der Richter Ben Lindsey. *IZIP,* 1928, 6(2), 141–145.

162 **Riese, W.** On causal thought in psychological medicine. *Episteme* (Milan), 1967, 1(1), 3–16.

163 **Riess, B. F.** Birth order and sex of siblings in a sample of lesbians and nonlesbians. *Psychol. Rev.*, 1967, 20, 61-62 (with R. Gundlach).

164 ———. *Progress in clinical psychology.* New York: Grune & Stratton, 1963 (with L. E. Abt).

165 **Riggs, M. D.** An exploratory study of the concepts of God reported by selected samples of physical scientists, biologists, psychologists and sociologists. Unpubl. Ph.D. Diss., Univ. So. Calif., 1959.

166 ———. Review of J. Wortis, *Fragments of an analysis with Freud.* In *AJIP*, 1956, 12, 185-186.

167 **Rigney, Kleona.** *The family council.* Chicago: Family Educ. Assn., 1970 (with R. Corsini).

168 **Ringel, E.** Psychotherapie and Seelsorge. In Int. Verein Indivpsy., *Alfred Adler zum Gedenken.* Pp. 92-109.

169 ———. Religion und Individualpsychologie. *IZIP*, 1949, 18(4), 145-155.

170 ———. Seelsorge und Neurose. *IZIP*, 1951, 20(3), 97-110 (with W. van Lun).

171 ———. *Die Selbstmord—Abschluss einer krankhaften psychischen Entwicklung.* Wien: Maudrich, 1953.

172 ———. *Die Tiefenpsychologie hilft dem Seelsorger.* Wien: Herder-Verlag, 1953 (with W. van Lun).

173 ———. Der Wertbegriff in der Individualpsychologie. *IZIP*, 1950, 19(3), 122-129.

174 ———. *Zum Problem des Unbewussten vom Standpunkt der Individualpsychologie.* Stuttgart: Ernst Klett, 1954 (with W. Spiel).

175 ———. Zur Problematik des Undbewussten vom Standpunkt der Individualpsychologie. *Psyche* (Stuttgart), 1952, 6, 378-388 (with W. Spiel).

176 **Ringold, Evelyn S.** Dr. Rudolf Dreikurs—An Adlerian force. *SK&F Psychiat. Reporter,* Jan.-Feb., 1969, No. 42. Also in *OSIPNL*, 1969, 10(5), 11-15.

177 **Ripin, Rowena.** See Ansbacher, Rowena R.

178 **Roback, A. A.** *A pictorial history of psychology and psychiatry.* New York: Phil. Libr., 1969 (with T. Kiernan).

179 ——— (Ed.). *Present-day psychology.* New York: Phil. Libr., 1955.

180 **Robb, M.** Individual Psychology and psychosomatic disorders (I). *IPMP*, 1932, No. 4 (with F. G. Crookshank, W. Langdon-Brown, S. V. Pearson, M. B. Ray, O. H. Woodcock & J. C. Young).

181 **Robb, M.** Organ jargon. *IPMP*, 1932, No. 4. Pp. 61-68.

182 **Robbins, Lillian C.** The accuracy of parental recall of aspects of child development and of child rearing practices. *J. abnorm. soc. Psychol.*, 1963, 66, 261-270.

183 **Roberts, A. H.** Dogmatism, time perspective and anomie. *JIP*, 1960, 16, 67-72 (with R. S. Herrmann).

184 **Roberts, B. H.** Schizophrenia in the youngest male child of the lower middle class. *Amer. J. Psychiat.*, 1955, 112, 129-134 (with J. S. Myers).

185 **Roberts, C. S.** Ordinal position and its relation to some aspects of personality. *J. genet. Psychol.*, 1938, 53, 173-213.

186 **Roberts, Loma.** Individual Psychology and Dalcroze Eurythmics. *IJIP*, 1937, 3(4), 303-308.

187 **Robinson, E. S.** A concept of compensation and its psychological setting. *J. abnorm. soc. Psychol.*, 1923, 17, 383-394.

188 **Robinson, F.** Task group report (with T. W. Allen, J. Krumboltz, W. Cottle, J. Cody, D. Homra & J. Ray). In J. Whiteley (Ed.), *Research problems in counseling.* Pp. 219-237.

189 **Robinson, Marcelle.** Review of D. C. Dinkmeyer (Ed.), *Guidance and counseling in the elementary school.* In *JIP*, 1968, 24, 201-202.

190 ———. A study of recall set utilizing early childhood recollections and recent recollections. Unpubl. Ph.D. Diss., Univ. So. Calif., 1961.

191 **Rocha, O.** Translator (with Maria Perestello) of R. Dreikurs, *Psicologia do casamento.*

192 **Rochester, D. E.** The use of Porter's Test of Counselor Attitudes to discriminate between Adlerian- and phenomenologically-oriented students. *J. couns. Psychol.*, 1968, 15, 427-429.

193 **Rodenberg, Katharina.** Soziale Arbeit und individualpsychologische Therapie im Dienste des Christentums. *IZIP*, 1930, 8(4), 422-425.

194 **Roff, M.** Peer acceptance-rejection and birth order. *Psychol. Schools*, 1964, 1, 156-162 (with S. B. Sells).

195 **Rogers, C. R.** Freedom and commitment. *ETC*, 1965, 22, 133-152.

196 **Rogg, S. G.** Time of decision. *Psychiat. Quart.*, 1950, 24, 437-447.

197 **Roe, Anne.** Man's forgotten weapon. *Amer. Psychologist*, 1959, 6, 261-266.

198 **Roeder, Marianne.** Gregorovius über Lucrezia Borgia. *IZIP*, 1937, 15(3), 82-89.

199 **Roland, A.** Three therapeutic approaches . . . one patient. *IP*, 1966, 3(2), 1-10 (with N. E. Shoobs & J. Sacks).

200 **Rolo, Susanne.** Portrait. *IPNL*, 1970, 19(4), 80; 1971, 20(6), 110.

201 **Rom, Elfreda.** Portrait. *IPNL*, 1971, 20(6), 111, 112.

202 **Rom, P.** À la découverte du style de vie. *Rééducation* (Paris), Feb., 1950.

203 ———. About beards. *IPNL*, 1963, 14(1-2, Whole No. 150-151). P. 8.

204 ———. About maturity. *IPNL*, 1963-64, 14(3-5, Whole No. 152-154). P. 13.

205 ———. Abstract of Alexandra Adler, *Individualpsychologie*. In *IPNL*, 1958, 9(3-5, Whole No. 91-93). Pp. 18-19.

206 ———. Abstract of H. L. Ansbacher, Fetishism: An Adlerian interpretation. In *IPNL*, 1958, 9(3-5, Whole No. 91-93). P. 18.

207 ———. Abstract of O. Brachfeld, Change and resistance to change in the field of human relations. In *IPNL*, 1960, 11 (3-4, Whole No. 117-118). Pp. 15-16.

208 ———. Abstract of L. Deutsch, *Piano: Guided sight reading*. In *IPNL*, 1959, 9(6-7, Whole No. 94-95). P. 24.

209 ———. Abstract of R. Dreikurs *et al.*, *Adlerian family counseling*. In *IPNL*, 10(1, Whole No. 102-103). P. 3.

210 ———. Abstract of R. Dreikurs, Music therapy with psychotic children. In *IPNL*, 1961, 11(7-8, Whole No. 121-122). P. 29.

211 ———. Abstract of Frieda Fromm-Reichman, *Intensive Psychotherapie*. Stuttgart: Hippokrates-Verlag, 1959. In *IPNL*, 1959, 10(1, Whole No. 102-103). P. 5.

212 ———. Abstract of L. Kling, *Adler et la psychologie individuelle*. In *IPNL*, 1957, 8(1-3, Whole No. 77-79). P. 3.

213 ———. Abstract of H. March (Ed.), *Verfolgung und Angst in ihren leibseelischen Auswirkung*. In *IPNL*, 1961, 11(9-10, Whole No. 123-124). P. 38.

214 ———. Abstract of J. I. Meiers, Therapy at a distance. In *IPNL*, 1957, 8(1-3, Whole No. 77-79). Pp. 3-4.

215 **Rom, P.** Abstract of H. H. Mosak & B. H. Shulman, *Introductory Individual Psychology: A syllabus*. In *IPNL*, 1961, 11(9-10, Whole No. 123-124). Pp. 33-34.

216 ———. Abstract of J. Neumann, *Wetzlar, die Entstehung des Selbst aus der Angst*. In *IPNL*, 1959, 9(12, Whole No. 101). P. 46.

217 ———. Abstract of Helene Papanek, Change of ethical values in group psychotherapy. In *IPNL*, 1959, 9(8, Whole No. 96-97). Pp. 31-32.

218 ———. Abstract of Helene Papanek, Emotion and intellect in psychotherapy. In *IPNL*, 1959, 9(8, Whole No. 96-97). P. 32.

219 ———. Abstract of Helene Papanek, The hysterical personality in combined individual and group psychotherapy. In *IPNL*, 1962, Whole No. 130-131. P. 22.

220 ———. Abstract of Helene Papanek & E. Papanek, Individual Psychology today. In *IPNL*, 1961, 11(9-10, Whole No. 123-124). P. 33.

221 ———. Abstract of Helene Papanek, Projective test evaluation of changes effected by group psychotherapy. In *IPNL*, 1961, 11(7-8, Whole No. 121-122). P. 28.

222 ———. Abstract of Helene Papanek, Satisfactions and frustrations of a supervisor of group psychotherapists. In *IPNL*, 1959, 9(8, Whole No. 96-97). P. 31.

223 ———. Abstract of Elisabeth Plattner, *Gehorsam, eine Hilfe für Eltern, Lehrer und vem sonst Gehorsam gebührt*. In *IPNL*, 1961, 11(-10, Whole No. 123-124). P. 38.

224 ———. Abstract of R. M. Singer, Adlerian psychology in dentistry. In *IPNL*, 1961, 11(11-12, Whole No. 125-126). Pp. 48-49.

225 ———. Abstract of A. Stern, *La psychologie individuelle d'Alfred Adler et la philosophie*. In *IPNL*, 1961, 11(7-8, Whole No. 121-122). P. 31.

226 ———. Un acte manqué. *IPNL*, 1972, 21 (5), 91.

227 ———. Acting out. *IPNL*, 1969, 18(5-6, Whole No. 214-215). Pp. 37-38.

228 ———. Adaptation v. contribution. *IPNL*, 1968, 18(9-10, Whole No. 206-207). P. 68.

229 ———. Adler amongst a thousand. *IPNL*, 1969, 18(11-12, Whole No. 220-221). P. 89.

230 **Rom, P.** Adler and aggression. *IPNL*, 1970, 19(5), 85.

231 ———. "Adler and the Freudians". *IPNL*, 1969, 18(9–10, Whole No. 218–219). Pp. 68–69.

232 ———. Adler and Goethe. *IP*, 1963, 1(2), 2–4.

233 ———. Adler and the inferiority complex. *IPNL*, 1965, 15(12, Whole No. 173). Pp. 45–46.

234 ———. Adler and the others. *IPB*, 1947, 6, 130–136.

235 ———. Adler and Prohibition. *IPNL*, 1961, 11(9–10, Whole No. 125–126). P. 49.

236 ———. Adler and religion. *IPNL*, 1958, 9(3–5, Whole No. 91–93). Pp. 10–11.

237 ———. Adler and Socrates. *IPNL*, 1961, 12(1–2, Whole No. 127–128). Pp. 2–4.

238 ———. Adler misquotes Kleist. *IPNL*, 1962, 13(1–2, Whole No. 138–139). Pp. 1–2.

239 ———. Adler on twist. *IPNL*, 1964, 14(8–9, Whole No. 157–158). P. 34.

240 ———. Adler remembered at Aberdeen. *IPNL*, 1971, 20(1), 19–20.

241 ———. Adler seen afresh. *IPNL*, 1970, 19(6), 105–106.

242 ———. Adler u'trumato la'Higiene Hanafshit [Adler's teaching and social hygiene]. *Eitanim*, July, 1966. Pp. 240–241.

243 ———. Adler versus Plato. *IPNL*, 1959, 10(2, Whole No. 104–105). Pp. 9–10.

244 ———. An Adlerian case or a character by Sartre. *JIP*, 1965, 21, 32–40 (with H. L. Ansbacher).

245 ———. Adlerian concepts in creative writing. *IPNL*, 1972, 21(1), 4–5.

246 ———. Adlerian concepts in other writers. *IPNL*, 1964, 14(6–7, Whole No. 155–156). P. 28; 1965, 15(5–6, Whole No. 166–167). Pp. 19–22; 1965, 15(7–8, Whole No. 168–169). P. 26.

247 ———. Adlerian concepts in other writings. *IPNL*, 1963, 14(1–2, Whole No. 150–151). P. 4.

248 ———. Adlerian concepts in various writings. *IPNL*, 1963, 13(7–8, Whole No. 144–145). Pp. 26–28; 1963–64, 14(3–5, Whole No. 152–154). Pp. 15–16.

249 ———. Adlerian concepts occurring in works of fiction. *IPNL*, 1961, 11(9–10, Whole No. 125–126). P. 46.

250 ———. Adlerian concepts occurring in works of fiction and poetry. *IPNL*, 1962, 12(11–12, Whole No. 136–137). P. 52.

251 **Rom, P.** Adlerian concepts used by other writers. *IPNL*, 1964, 14(10–12, Whole No. 159–161). P. 40; 1964, 15(1–2, Whole No. 162–163). P. 3.

252 ———. Adlerian notions in other writing. *IPNL*, 1964, 14(10–12, Whole No. 159–161). Pp. 44–45.

253 ———. Un Adlerien sans le savoir (Gleanings from Antoine de Saint-Exupery, *Vol de nuit*). *IPNL*, 1953, Whole No. 25. P. 5.

254 ———. "Adlerisms". *IPNL*, 1963, 13(11–12, Whole No. 148–149). P. 48.

255 ———. Adler's individuum v. Jung's "Undiscovered self". *IPNL*, 1958, 8(10–12, Whole No. 86–88). Pp. 37–38.

256 ———. Adler's later writings. [Review of H. L. Ansbacher & Rowena Ansbacher (Eds.), *Superioritiy and social interest*]. In *IPNL*, 1965, 15(7–8, Whole No. 168–169). Pp. 25–26.

257 ———. Adler's letters. *IPNL*, 1968, 18(9–10, Whole No. 206–207). P. 76; 1968, 18 (3–4, Whole No. 212–213). P. 21.

258 ———. Adler's main concepts. *IPNL*, 1968, 18(1–2), 3–8.

259 ———. Adlers Verhältnis zu Freud. *Psyche* (Stuttgart), 1955, 9, 117–123.

260 ———. Adler's work in France. *IPNL*, 1955, 4(9–10, Whole No. 49–50). Pp. 4–5.

261 ———. Again beards. *IPNL*, 1964, 14(8–9, Whole No. 157–158).

262 ———. Again: The International Congress of the Psychoanalytic Association. *IPNL*, 1971, 20(5), 81.

263 ———. The ages of turmoil. *IPNL*, 1972, 21(1), 11–12.

264 ———. Albert Camus (1913–1960). *IPNL*, 1960, 10(7-8, Whole No. 108-109). Pp. 28-29.

265 ———. Alfred Adler. *Geist und Tat* (Frankfurt), 1970, 1, 37–38.

266 ———. Alfred Adler and Alfred Doeblin. *IPNL*, 1971, 20(4), 70–71.

267 ———. Alfred Adler and music. *IPNL*, 1969, 19(3), 41–42.

268 ———. Alfred Adler centenary. *Humanist*, 1970, 85(2), 51–53.

269 ———. Alfred Adler en France. *Les Cahiers de l'Enfance Inadaptée* (Paris), 1957, 7(4).

270 ———. Alfred Adler, notice biographique. In A. Adler, *Le tempérament nerveux*. 2nd ed. Pp. 7–10.

271 **Rom, P.** *Alfred Adler und die wissenschaftliche Menschenkenntnis.* Frankfurt am Main: Waldemar Kramer, 1966.

272 ———. American English v. English English. *IPNL*, 1958, 9(1–2, Whole No. 89–90). Pp. 2–3.

273 ———. Americans criticizing their English. *IPNL*, 1969, 19(2), 36.

274 ———. Analysis of the fanatic. *IPNL*, 1962, 12(11–12, Whole No. 136–137). Pp. 47–48.

275 ———. Anarchism. *IPNL*, 1967, 17(7–8, Whole No. 192–193). P. 53.

276 ———. Another big step forward. *IPNL*, 1960, 10(3–4, Whole No. 106). Pp. 13–14.

277 ———. Another encourager [R. G. Collingwood]. *IPNL*, 1970, 19(4), 75.

278 ———. Another Herostratus. *IPNL*, 1962, 11(7–8, Whole No. 132–133). P. 129.

279 ———. Another Maigret. *IPNL*, 1972, 21 (3), 54.

280 ———. Are you a C.O.? *IPNL*, 1971, 20 (5), 88.

281 ———. Are you able to become aware of falling asleep? *IPNL*, 1969, 18(9–10, Whole No. 218–219). P. 67.

282 ———. Association experiments. *IPNL*, 1960, 10(11–12, Whole No. 112–114). P. 44.

283 ———. Authority. . . *IPNL*, 1971, 20(5), 85.

284 ———. Autobiographie. In *Autobiographies of the members of the Centre of German-speaking Writers Abroad.* London: P.E.N., 1968.

285 ———. Avant-propos de la seconde edition français of Alfred Adler, *Le tempérament nerveux.* Pp. 7–10.

286 ———. Avertissement pour l'edition française. In A. Adler *Connaissance de l'homme.* P. 7.

287 ———. The avoidance of discouragement. *IPNL*, 1968, 18(7–8, Whole No. 204–205). Pp. 49–51.

288 ———. Balzac's understanding of human behaviour. *IPNL*, 1964, 14(6–7, Whole No. 155–156). P. 21.

289 ———. The bathroom technique. *IPNL*, 1970, 19(2), 39–40.

290 ———. Un bébé de 13 ans. *IZIP*, 1948, 17(2), 91–93.

291 ———. The beginning sfor the end. *Voices*, 1969, 5(1), 40–41. Discussion by H. L. Ansbacher. Pp. 41–42.

292 **Rom, P.** Being and becoming. *IPNL*, 1959, 9(9–10, Whole No. 98–99). P. 34.

293 ———. Bertrand Russell, 1872–1970. *IPNL*, 1970, 19(4), 68–69.

294 ———. Beyond. . . *IPNL*, 1967, 17(5–6, Whole No. 190–191). Pp. 37–38.

295 ———. Biased apperception and attitudes towards scientific discoveries. *IPNL*, 1966, 16(4–6, Whole No. 177–179). Pp. 13–14.

296 ———. Bibliographie de l'"Individualpsychologie". *Courage, Feuilles de Psychologie Adlérienne*, 1939, 2(1), 15–16.

297 ———. Bist du ein Menschenkenner? *Geist und Tat* (Frankfurt), 1963, 18, 309–311.

298 ———. Bist du hilfreich? *Prakt. Psychol.*, 1972, 26(6), 142–143.

299 ———. Brief an eine depriemerte Frau. *Prakt. Psychol.*, 1968, 22, 125–127.

300 ———. Bruder-Rivalität. *IZIP*, 1950, 19(1) 29–35.

301 ———. Büchner–Adler–Freud. *IPNL*, 1953, Whole No. 25. P. 5.

302 ———. C. G. Jung a Nazi? *IPNL*, 1966, 16(11–12, Whole No. 184–185). P. 45.

303 ———. C. P. Snow reveals three technique to justify . . . DOING NOTHING. *IPNL*, 1963, 13(9–10, Whole No. 146–147). P. 34.

304 ———. Can you be rational without loving your neighbour? *IPNL*, 1972, 21(1), 1–3.

305 ———. Can you reap a page of Adler's? *IPNL*, 1955, 4(6–7, Whole No. 46–47). P. 1.

306 ———. A case of neurotic abstention from alcohol. *IJIP*, 1936, 2(2), 83–86.

307 ———. Cases of over-compensation. *IPNL*, 1972, 21(5), 88–89.

308 ———. Centenary celebrations. *IPNL*, 1970, 19(4), 63–64.

309 ———. The challenge of. . . *IPNL*, 1963, 13(5–6, Whole No. 142–143). P. 19.

310 ———. Charles Baudouin. *IPNL*, 1963–64, 14(3–5, Whole No. 152–154). P. 11.

311 ———. Chief Inspector Maigret: A spiritual brother of Adler. *IPNL*, 1970, 19(5), 95–98.

312 ———. The child and his name. *IPB*, 1950 8, 150–157.

313 ———. Cinquante écolières racontent leur premier souvenir d'enfance. *Méthodes actives* (Pairs), 1948, 3(7), 194–198.

314 ———. Le coin du rire. *IPNL*, 1962, 12 (11–12, Whole No. 136–137). Pp. 45–46;

1968, 18(5-6, Whole No. 202-203). Pp. 39-40; 1969, 18(5-6, Whole No. 214-215). P. 40; 1969, 19(2), 40; 1969, 19(3), 54-55; 1970, 19(6), 118-119; 1972, 21(4), 61-65.

315 **Rom, P.** Le coin due Rire (Amer.). *IPNL*, 1963-64, 14(3-5, Whole No. 152-154). P. 17.

316 ————. Comparative? *IPNL*, 1969, 18(9-10, Whole No. 218-219). Pp. 65-66.

317 ————. Compensation means mental health. *IPNL*, 1961, 11(9-10, Whole No. 123-124). Pp. 35-36.

318 ————. Concerning dreams. *IPNL*, 1959, 9(9-10, Whole No. 98-99). Pp. 33-34.

319 ————. Concerning earliest recollections. *IPNL*, 1965, 15(7-8, Whole No. 168-169). P. 27.

320 ————. Concerning noses. *IPNL*, 1957, 8(4-5, Whole No. 80-81). Pp. 14-15.

321 ————. The constancy of a life style [St. Augustine]. *IPNL*, 1962, 12(11-12, Whole No. 136-137). P. 45.

322 ————. Contemporary application of Alfred Adler's theories [A review of K. A. Adler & Danica Deutsch (Eds.), *Essays in Individual Psychology*]. *IPNL*, 1967, 17(7-8, Whole No. 192-193). Pp. 49-50.

323 ————. Courage et la guerre des nerfs. *Rev. d'Alger*, 1945, 11(7), 209-216.

324 ————. A courageous encourager [Churchill]. has left us. *IPNL*, 1965, 15(5-6, Whole No. 166-167). Pp. 17-18.

325 ————. D. H. Lawrence's understanding of human behavior. *IPNL*, 1952, Whole No. 21-22. Pp. 3-4.

326 ————. Death of Albert Einstein. *IPNL*, 1955, 4(9-10, Whole No. 49-50). P. 4.

327 ————. Death of C. G. Jung. *IPNL*, 1962, 12(5-6, Whole No. 130-131). P. 17.

328 ————. Death of Dr. Neufeld. *IPNL*, 1969, 18(11-12, Whole No. 220-221). P. 92).

329 ————. Deep, deeper, deepest, *IPNL*, 1963-64, 14(3-5, Whole No. 152-154). P. 9.

330 ————. Depth or context? *IPNL*, 1965, 15(7-8, Whole No. 168-169). Pp. 27-28.

331 ————. "Depth" psychology. *IPNL*, 1969, 19(2), 37.

332 ————. Did you enjoy reading this American writer [Saul Bellow]? *IPNL*, 1967, 17(5-6, Whole No. 190-191). Pp. 40-42.

333 ————. Dieptepsychologie? *MNWIP*, 1972, 21(2).

334 **Rom, P.** Discouragement, new insight, training. *IPNL*, 1963, 14(1-2, Whole No. 150-151). P. 2.

335 ————. The displeasure of reading. *IPNL*, 1972, 21(6), 105-106.

336 ————. Do computers think about themselves, live in a society? *Freethinker* (London), April 18 & 25, 1970. Pp. 123, 131.

337 ————. Do you know a better name for Adler's teaching than Individual Psychology? *IPNL*, 1971, 20(4), 73-74.

338 ————. Do you understand your dreams? *IPNL*, 1966, 16(7-8, Whole No. 180-181). P. 25.

339 ————. Dr. Edmund Schletter [An obituary]. *IPNL*, 1964, 15(1-2, Whole No. 162-163). P. 4.

340 ————. Dr. Otto Peter Radl [An obituary]. *IPNL*, 1965, 15(9-10, Whole No. 170-172). P. 39.

341 ————. Doctor Zhivago. *IPNL*, 1958, 9(3-5, Whole No. 91-93). Pp. 12-15.

342 ————. Does professional crime run in families? *IPNL*, 1963-64, 14(3-5, Whole No. 152-154). P. 11.

343 ————. Dozent Dr. Karl Nowotny [An obituary]. *IPNL*, 1965, 15(9-10, Whole No. 170-172). Pp. 38-39.

344 ————. A dream. *IPNL*, 1969, 18(9-10, Whole No. 218-219). P. 67.

345 ————. A dream about Adler. *IPNL*, 1969, 19(2), 29.

346 ————. Dreams. *IPNL*, 1964, 14(10-12, Whole No. 159-161). P. 38.

347 ————. Du und dein Lebenstil. *Prakt. Psychol.*, 1968, 22, 158-162.

348 ————. Le dynamisme de la personnalité. *Psyché*, 1947, 2(9-10), 869-873.

349 ————. Il dynamismo della personalita nella dottrina di Adler. *Revista di Psicol.*, 1944-45,   , 40-41.

350 ————. E. A. Poe versus James Russell Lowell. *IPNL*, 1959, 9(12, Whole No. 101). P. 45.

351 ————. Eagles. *IPNL*, 1958, 8(10-12, Whole No. 86-88). P. 47.

352 ————. Ecce Homo. *IPNL*, 1969, 18(5-6, Whole No. 214-215). Pp. 33-35.

353 ————. Eclecticism or convergence of doctrines. *IPNL*, 1968, 18(5-6, Whole No. 202-203). Pp. 37-39.

354 ————. Economic circumstances affect character. *IPNL*, 1968, 18(11-12, Whole No. 208-209). P. 95.

355 **Rom, P.** Ein Fall von neurotischer Alko-
holabstinenz. *IZIP*, 1932, 10(6), 436–439.
356 ———. Eine Fehlleistung Alfred Adlers.
Der Psychologe (Berne), 1963, 15, 280–
283.
357 ———. Eine gute Nachricht. *IPNL*, 1969,
18(5–6, Whole No. 214–215). Pp. 38–39.
358 ———. Das Elend der Vollkommenheits-
sucht. *Prakt. Psychol.*, 1971, 25(4) 73–76.
359 ———. Encouragement between great men
[A. Einstein & B. Russell]. *IPNL*, 1970,
19(4), 74.
360 ———. Encouragements. *IPNL*, 1965, 16(1-
3, Whole No. 174–176). P. 1.
361 ———. Encouragements [A review of N.
Kazantzakis, *Zorba the Greek*]. *IPNL*,
1967, 17(9–10, Whole No. 194–195). P.
72.
362 ———. Epilepsy, masculine protest and
gynecophobia. *IPNL*, 1962, 12(11–12,
Whole No. 136–137). Pp. 46–47.
363 ———. Epistolary guidance: An Adlerian
contribution. *IPB*, 1949, 7, 171–185.
364 ———. Epistolary guidance to "mental
health." *Brit. J. soc. Psychol. & Comm.
Hlth.*, 1971, 5(2), 129–132.
365 ———. Epistolary guidance to mental
health (Abstract). *IPNL*, 1968, 18(5–6,
Whole No. 202–203). Pp. 41–42.
366 ———. Ernest Jones, "Freud's Huxley".
IPNL, 1961, 12(5–6, Whole No. 130–131).
P. 18.
367 ———. Errare humanum est. *IPNL*, 1955-
56, 5(5–7, Whole No. 57–59). Pp. 4–5.
368 ———. Existentialist outraged about lack
of recognition of Adler. *IPNL*, 1962, 11(7-
8, Whole No. 132–133). Pp. 29–30.
369 ———. Faith in man [Review of R.
Dreikurs, *Equality, the challenge of our
times*]. *IPNL*, 1969, 18(11–12, Whole No.
220–221). P. 93.
370 ———. Der Fall Hans N. Randbemerkungen
zum Bericht einer Stiefmutter. *Schola*
(Mainz), 1950–52.
371 ———. The fallacy of the "trauma".
IPNL, 1961, 12(5–6, Whole No. 130–131).
P. 19.
372 ———. Family council. *IPNL*, 1968, 18(5-
6, Whole No. 202–203). Pp. 33–34; 1971,
20(2), 32.
373 ———. Fear in the schoolroom. *IPB*, 1944-
45, 4, 85–87.
374 ———. First memories of "normal" and of
"delinquent" girls. *IPB*, 1949, 7, 15–20.

375 **Rom, P.** Fremde Sprachen in Traumleben.
Ling. Rev., 1956, No. 135. Pp. 17–18.
376 ———. Fremde Sprachen in Traumleben.
Der Psychologe (Berne), 1963, 15, 23–26.
377 ———. Freud as "depreciator". *IPNL*,
1955, 5(5–7, Whole No. 57–59). Pp. 4–5;
1957, 8(4–5, Whole No. 80–81). P. 15;
1958, 8(6–7, Whole No. 82–83). P. 26.
378 ———. Freud? No, Adler. *IPNL*, 1964,
14(10–12, Whole No. 159–161). P. 41.
379 ———. Freud's shadow over Adler. *IPNL*,1961
11(9–10, Whole No. 125–126). Pp. 45–46.
380 ———. From A. A. to N. N. *IPNL*, 1958,
8(10–12, Whole No. 86–88). P. 45.
381 ———. From the life of a courageous
man. *IPNL*, 1964, 15(3–4, Whole No. 164–
165). Pp. 11–12.
382 ———. Fromm, Freud, Marx, Adler. *IPNL*,
1968, 18(3–4, Whole No. 212–213). Pp.
22–24.
383 ———. Gemeinschaftsgefühl. *IPNL*, 1957,
8(4–5, Whole No. 80–81). Pp. 17–18.
384 ———. Gemeinschaftsgefühl, solidarité,
love of neighbour. *IPNL*, 1961, 11(5–6,
Whole No. 119–120). P. 18.
385 ———. Georges Simenon et les psychiatres.
BSFPA, 1971, No. 11. Pp. 29–37.
386 ———. Giftedness. *IPNL*, 1963, 13(5–6,
Whole No. 142–143). P. 17.
387 ———. Gleanings. *IPNL*, 1972, 21(1), 12–
13; 1972, 21(5), 91.
388 ———. "The goal" [Review of Phyllis
Bottome, *The goal*]. *IPNL*, 1962, 11(7–8,
Whole No. 121–122). Pp. 28–29.
389 ———. Goethe, a pre-Adlerian Individual
Psychologist. *IPNL*, 1960, 10(7–8, Whole
No. 108–109). P. 32.
390 ———. Goethe as an interpreter of dreams.
Lit. Psychol., 1962, 12(2), 37–38.
391 ———. Goethe on psychotherapy. *JIP*,
1963, 19, 182–184.
392 ———. Goethe's earliest recollection. *JIP*,
1965, 21, 189–193.
393 ———. Gottes Lachen [E. Froeschels
(1887-1972)]. *IPNL*, 1972, 21(4), 65–66.
394 ———. Grandeur and misery of the university. *IPNL*, 1968, 18(7–8, Whole No.
204–205). Pp. 63–64.
395 ———. Great Britain "goes metric". *IPNL*,
1970, 19(3), 43–44.
396 ———. The growing recognition of Adler [A
review of L. J. Bischof, *Interpreting personality theories*]. *IPNL*, 1964, 14(8-9, Whole No.
157–158). Pp. 30–31.

397 **Rom, P.** Growth of Individual Psychology. *World Psychol.*, 1957, 10(11), 19-21.

398 ——. Guessing. *IPNL*, 1971, 20(5), 81.

399 ——. Gynecophobia. *IPNL*, 1960, 11(1-2, Whole No. 115-116). P. 7.

400 ——. Half a century of Individual Psychology. *IPNL*, 1961, 11(9-10, Whole No. 123-124). Pp. 33-34.

401 ——. Hamlet. *IPNL*, 1964, 15(3-4, Whole No. 164-165). Pp. 12-13.

402 ——. Hang your neighbour and feel fine. *IPNL*, 1965, 15(9-10, Whole No. 170-172). Pp. 33-34.

403 ——. Happy readings. *IPNL*, 1963, 13 (7-8, Whole No. 144-145). Pp. 25-26.

404 ——. Die Hauptgestalten des Niebelungenliedes im Lichte der vergleichenden Individualpsychologie Alfred Adlers. Unpubl. Diss., Sorbonne, 1939.

405 ——. Hear! Hear! *IPNL*, 1968, 18(11-12, Whole No. 208-209). Pp. 89-90.

406 ——. Helping each other. *IPNL*, 1962, 12(5-6, Whole No. 130-131). P. 19.

407 ——. High, higher, highest. *IPNL*, 1964, 14(8-9, Whole No. 157-158). P. 32.

408 ——. History of the International Association of Individual Psychology. In *Directory of International Association of Individual Psychology*, 1962, 1965. Pp. 4-8.

409 ——. How one can do it. *IPNL*, 1963, 13(9-10, Whole No. 146-147). P. 35.

410 ——. How permissive. *IPNL*, 1972, 21 (1), 7.

411 ——. How to deal with compulsive teachers. *IPNL*, 1971, 20(5), 96.

412 ——. How to discourage a piano pupil [A review of L. Deutsch, *Guided sight-reading*]. *IPNL*, 1964, 15(3-4, Whole No. 164-165). Pp. 10-11.

413 ——. How to encourage. *IPNL*, 1960, 10(3-4, Whole No. 106). Pp. 14-15.

414 ——. A humanist's attitude to dying. *Freethinker* (London), 1970, 90, No. 20.

415 ——. Humour: Sick and healthy. *IPNL*, 1962, 13(1-2, Whole No. 138-139). Pp. 3-4.

416 ——. Hydrophobia. *IPNL*, 1970, 19(4), 74.

417 ——. I—afraid? *IPNL*, 1967, 17(5-6, Whole No. 190-191). P. 35.

418 ——. The IPNL loses two more eminent and faithful friends [Raissa Adler & Lydia Sicher]. *IPNL*, 1962, 11(7-8, Whole No. 132-133). P. 25.

419 **Rom, P.** In memoriam Elisabeth Sorge-Boehmke. *IPNL*, 1960, 10(7-8, Whole No. 108-109). Pp. 29-30.

420 ——. In memoriam Ian Fleming. *IPNL*, 1964, 15(3-4, Whole No. 164-165). P. 15.

421 ——. In memoriam Fritz Künkel. *IPNL*, 1970, 19(5), 85-87.

422 ——. In memoriam of a great president [J. F. Kennedy]. *IPNL*, 1964, 15(3-4, Whole No. 164-165). P. 16:

423 ——. In memoriam Oskar Spiel (1892-1961). *IPNL*, 1961, 12(1-2, Whole No. 127-128). Pp. 1-2.

424 ——. In memoriam Raissa Adler. *IPNL*, 1962, 12(9-10, Whole No. 134-135). Pp. 33-34.

425 ——. Increase in impotency. *IPNL*, 1972, 21(3), 48.

426 ——. Individualpsychologie ist keine Religion. *Hamburger Echo*, May 27, 1952.

427 ——. Individualpsychologische Bemerkungen zu Fichtes deutscher Nationalerziehung. *IZIP*, 1933, 11, 468-470.

428 ——. Individualpsychologisches Betrachtung von Schillers Don Carlos. *Revue de la Société des Etudes Germaniques* (Paris), 1947 (avril-juin *et pass.*).

429 ——. Individual Psychologists and novelists. *IPNL*, 1970, 19(4), 75.

430 ——. Individual Psychology and literary cristicism. *IPNL*, 1972, 21(3), 45-46.

431 ——. Individual Psychology and politics. *IPNL*, 1959, 10(2) Whole No. 104-105). Pp. 8-9.

432 ——. Individual Psychology for teachers. *IPNL*, 1962, 12(9-10, Whole No. 134-135). Pp. 36-37.

433 ——. Individual Psychology in the analysis of literature. Dr. Jekyll and Mr. Hyde. *IPB*, 1951, 9, 9-17.

434 ——. Individual Psychology manifesting itself as a school. *IPNL*, 1972, 21(4), 71-76.

435 ——. Individualpsycholophobie. *IZIP*, 1934, 12, 221-223.

436 ——. Inferiority complex as an alibi. *IPNL*, 1961, 11(7-8, Whole No. 121-122). Pp. 25-26.

437 ——. "Interdisciplinary." *IPNL*, 1969, 18(7-8, Whole No. 216-217). Pp. 49-50.

438 ——. An interesting criticism of Freud's death instinct. *IPNL*, 1962, 12(9-10, Whole No. 134-135). P. 42.

439 ——. International Adlerian summer school. *IPNL*, 18(5-6, Whole No. 214-215). Pp. 41-42.

440 **Rom, P.** International congresses in Europe. *IPNL*, 1968, 18(11–12, Whole No. 208–209). Pp. 81–83.

441 ———. Introduzione to H. Ellis, *I carrateri sessuali psichici*. Roma: Newton Compton Italiana, 1972.

442 ———. Invitation à la valse. *IPNL*, 1965, 15(7–8, Whole No. 168–169). P. 28.

443 ———. Invitation to a perfectionist. *IPNL*, 1969, 18(9–10, Whole No. 218–219). P. 68.

444 ———. J. M. Barrie's *Peter Pan*. *IPNL*, 1955, 4(6–7, Whole No. 46–47). Pp. 5–6.

445 ———. Jolly slips. *IPNL*, 1968, 18(11–12, Whole No. 208–209). P. 90.

446 ———. Julian's withdrawal. *IP*, 1963, 1(1), 2–4.

447 ———. Juvenile delinquency. *IPNL*, 1961, 11(5–6, Whole No. 119–120). P. 20.

448 ———. A king in the realm of vision. *IPNL*, 1960, 11(3–4, Whole No. 117–118). Pp. 9–11.

449 ———. Kunst und Psychologie. *MNWIP*, 1967, 17, 3–6.

450 ———. Learning the humorous way. *IPNL*, 1963–64, 14(3–5, Whole No. 152–154). Pp. 10–11.

451 ———. Legalised violence. *IPNL*, 1971, 20 (2), 23–24.

452 ———. Legio Patria Nostra. *The Sinjum, Sir Walter St. John's Sch. Mag.* (London), Mar., 1954.

453 ———. Lena Frender [Obituary]. *IPNL*, 1966, 16(4–6, Whole No. 177–179). P. 20.

454 ———. Libido-ego-unit of personality. *IPNL*, 1963, 13(5–6, Whole No. 142–143). P. 23.

455 ———. Life and literature. *IPNL*, 1971, 20 (6), 101–102.

456 ———. Life style of an immature 13 yr. old. *Freethinker* (London), June 20, 1970. Pp. 197–198.

457 ———. Like father, like daughter. *IPNL*, 1971, 20(4), 69.

458 ———. A little algebra. *IPNL*, 1965, 15(5–6, Whole No. 166–167). P. 17.

459 ———. A little excursion into American literature. *IPNL*, 1959, 9(8, Whole No. 96–97). P. 32.

460 ———. Looking back. *IPNL*, 1968, 18(3–4, Whole No. 212–213). Pp. 17–18.

461 ———. Looking backwards & forwards! *IPNL*, 1954, Whole No. 38. Pp. 1–2.

462 **Rom, P.** L'zichro shel Alfred Adler [In memory of Alfred Adler]. *Urim*, 1952–53, 10, 23–24.

463 ———. Magister Adler. *IPNL*, 1968, 18(5–6, Whole No. 202–203). P. 45.

464 ———. Ma Hu Signon Ha-chaim shelcha? [What is your life style?]. *Urim la-horim*, 1966 (Feb.). Pp. 26–28.

465 ———. Maigret—der Mann ohne Komplexe. *Prakt. Psychol.*, 1972, 26(10), 240–241; 1972, 26(11), 262–265.

466 ———. Maigret dreams. . . *IPNL*, 1971, 20(4), 63–65.

467 ———. Many happy returns, Phyllis Bottome. *IPNL*, 1962, 12(9–10, Whole No. 134–135). P. 38.

468 ———. Man's nothingness and greatness. *IPNL*, 1970, 20(3), 46–47.

469 ———. Marijuana and painting. *IPNL*, 1967, 18(3–4, Whole No. 200–201). P. 30.

470 ———. Masculine protest with feminine means. *IPNL*, 1964, 14(10–12, Whole No. 159–161). Pp. 40–41.

471 ———. Memorial meeting for Alfred Adler. *IPB*, 1944–45, 4, 102–103.

472 ———. Memories of an Individual Psychologist. *Freethinker* (London), Mar. 7, 1970.

473 ———. The misery of perfectionism. *IP*, 1970, 8(1), 18–20.

474 ———. Misquotations: An Adlerian contribution to the psychology of errors. *JIP*, 1961, 17, 172–176.

475 ———. More news about centenary events. *IPNL*, 1970, 19(5), 84.

476 ———. Mrs. Alfred Adler's 85th birthday. *IPNL*, 1958, 9(3–5, Whole No. 91–93). Pp. 12–15.

477 ———. Music and poetry. *IPNL*, 1969, 18(11–12, Whole No. 220–221). P. 95.

478 ———. Mutual aid. *IPNL*, 1960, 10(11–12, Whole No. 112–114). P. 45.

479 ———. My uncle Toby, the fly, and universal good will. *IPNL*, 1964, 14(10–12, Whole No. 159–161). P. 37.

480 ———. A new start. *IPNL*, 1950, No. 0. Pp. 1–2.

481 ———. XIX International Congress of Psychology. *IPNL*, 1969, 18(11–12, Whole No. 220–221). Pp. 90–92.

482 ———. Le nom et le style de vie. *Culture Humaine* (Paris), Nov., 1947.

483 ———. Note on Alfred Adler. *Urim*, 1957, 99(1), 23–24.

484 Rom, P. Note on Friedrich Schiller. *IPNL*, 1955, 4(9-10, Whole No. 49-50). Pp. 7-8.

485 ———. The notion of solidarity in the work of Albert Camus. *JIP*, 1960, 16, 146-150.

486 ———. Notre Mâitre Adler. *IPNL*, 1954, 4(4-5, Whole No. 44-45). P. 9.

487 ———. Obituaries [A. Müller & E. O. Krausz (1887-1968)]. *IPNL*, 1969, 18(3-4, Whole No. 212-213). Pp. 26-28.

488 ———. Obituaries [J. Ronge-Haslinghuis, G. J. Winter-de Graff & J. Vinkenborg]. *IPNL*, 1970, 19(3), 44-45.

489 ———. Obituaries [Edmond R. Schlesinger (1893-1968) & F. Friedmann]. *IPNL*, 1969, 18(5-6, Whole No. 214-215). Pp. 35-37.

490 ———. Obituary [O. Brachfeld]. *IPNL*, 1967, 18(1-2, Whole No. 198-199). Pp. 4-5.

491 ———. Obituary [P. Brodsky]. *IPNL*, 1971, 20(1), 4-7.

492 ———. Obituary [J. B. Delhez]. *IPNL*, 1971, 20(6), 116.

493 ———. Obituary [E. Froeschels]. *IPNL*, 1972, 21(3), 45-46.

494 ———. Obituary [Margot Levy]. *IPNL*, 1963, 13(11-12, Whole No. 148-149). Pp. 44-45.

495 ———. Obituary [B. A. Longfield]. *IPNL*, 1966, 17(1-2, Whole No. 186-187). P. 11.

496 ———. Obituary [J. Neumann]. *IPNL*, 1964, 14(8-9, Whole No. 157-158). P. 33.

497 ———. Obituary [F. Ray]. *IPNL*, 1972, 21(1), 4-5.

498 ———. Obituary [P. H. Ronge]. *IPNL*, 1969, 18(9-10, Whole No. 218-219). P. 81.

499 ———. Obituary [Regine Seidler 1895-1967]. *IPNL*, 1967, 17(9-10, Whole No. 194-195). Pp. 68-69.

500 ———. Obituary [Lydia Sicher]. *Int. J. soc. Psychiat.*, 1963, 9(2), 103.

501 ———. Obituary [K. Sulzer]. *IPNL*, 1971, 20(4), 74.

502 ———. Obituary [Henri Wallon]. *IPNL*, 1963, 13(5-6, Whole No. 142-143). P. 23.

503 ———. Observations—correct or false. *IPNL*, 1968, 18(5-6, Whole No. 202-203). P. 35.

504 ———. Old brother and young sister [The JIP and the IP]. *IPNL*, 1964, 14(6-7, Whole No. 155-156). Pp. 21-23.

505 Rom, P. On becoming an Adlerian. *OSIPNL*, 1963, 4(2), 10; 1964, 4(3), 12.

506 ———. On being an Adlerian. *IPB*, 1951, 9, 152-155.

507 ———. On being a "fellow". *IPNL*, 1956, 5(8, Whole No. 60). Pp. 7-8.

508 ———. On corporal punishment. *IPNL*, 1957, 6(6-7, Whole No. 70-71). Pp. 20-21.

509 ———. On depth psychology. *IPNL*, 1960, 10(9-10, Whole No. 110-111). P. 37.

510 ———. On having learned to drive a car. *IPNL*, 1970, 19(3), 56-59.

511 ———. On the epic [about F. Brachfeld]. *IPNL*, 1970, 19(4), 76-77.

512 ———. On the psychology of proper names. *IPB*, 1946, 5, 106-111.

513 ———. On the way [about Lydia Sicher]. IPNL, 1969, 18(11-12, Whole No. 220-221). P. 104.

514 ———. Once more garlic. . . *IPNL*, 1963, 13(5-6, Whole No. 142-143). P. 24.

515 ———. Once more homosexuality. *IPNL*, 1969, 19(1), 6-7.

516 ———. Open letter [to Bertrand Russell]. *IPNL*, 1963, 13(9-10, Whole No. 146-147). Pp. 33-34.

517 ———. "Orgtalk". *IPNL*, 1963, 13(1-2, Whole No. 138-139). Pp. 1-2.

518 ———. Our XIth International Congress. *IPNL*, 1970, 19(6), 101-102.

519 ———. Our International Congresses. *AJIP*, 1956, 12, 97-98.

520 ———. Overcompensation. *IPNL*, 1967, 17(9-10, Whole No. 194-195). P. 70; 1968, 17(5-6, Whole No. 202-203). P. 48.

521 ———. *La paix des nerfs: Exposé d'une psychologie pratique.* Geneva: Editions du Mont Blanc, 1942, 1945.

522 ———. A pampering father's sad end. . . *IPNL*, 1964, 14(6-7, Whole No. 155-156). P. 21.

523 ———. Perhaps. . . *IPNL*, 1969, 18(7-8, Whole No. 216-217). Pp. 50-51.

524 ———. Peter Pelikan helps. *IPNL*, 1967, 17(11-12, Whole No. 196-197). P. 86.

525 ———. Philo the psychotherapist. *IPNL*, 1969, 19(2), 59-60.

526 ———. Philosophers and poets teach us the science of living. *IPNL*, 1972, 21(6), 113-114.

527 ———. Phyllis Bottome died a week before our Congress. *IPNL*, 1963, 13(11-12, Whole No. 148-149). P. 44.

528 Rom, P. Physician, help yourself. *IPNL,* 1970, 19(6), 106-107.

529 ———. Pollution: A "position of cosmic inferiority". *IPNL,* 1971, 20(4), 66.

530 ———. Ponderings. *IPNL,* 1971, 20(6), 107.

531 ———. Poor Adolf. . . *IPNL,* 1971, 20(6), 103-104.

532 ———. Portrait. *IPNL,* 1970, 19(4), 62, 79, 70; 1971, 20(6), 110, 111, 112; 1972, 20(6), 112.

533 ———. The problem of distance in sex behaviour. *IPNL,* 1955, 4(6-7, Whole No. 46-47). P. 7.

534 ———. The problem of "distance" in sex behaviour. *Int. J. soc. Psychiat.,* 1957, 3(2), 145-151.

535 ———. Le problème de l'alcoholisme considéré du point de vue de l'Individual-psychologie d'Alfred Adler. *L'Hyg. ment.* (Paris), Dec., 1934. Pp. 250-256. Also in *Méthodes actives,* Oct., 1947.

536 ———. The programme of our International Congress for Vienna. [Aug. 28-Sept. 1, 1960]. *IPNL,* 1960, 10(5-6, Whole No. 107). Pp. 19-20.

357 ———. Psychiatry in modern novels. *Int. J. soc. Psychiat.,* 1965, 11(1), 70-77.

538 ———. Psychology in Italy. *IPB,* 1946, 5, 89-90.

539 ———. Psychology of proper names. *IPNL,* 1957, 6(8-9, Whole No. 72-73). Pp. 34-35.

540 ———. Purpose of this News Letter. *IPNL,* 1951, No. 1. P. 1.

541 ———. Quelques souvenirs à l'occasion du 10e anniversaire de la mort d'Alfred Adler. *Action et Pensée* (Génève), 1947, 23, 169-173.

542 ———. Question of names and languages. *IPNL,* 1951, No. 1. Pp. 1-2.

543 ———. *Qui était Sigmund Freud?* Toulouse: Privat, 1971.

544 ———. "Race, intelligence, and education". *IPNL,* 1971, 20(6), 105-106.

545 ———. Reactivity and productivity. *IPNL,* 1966, 16(7-8, Whole No. 180-181). P. 28.

546 ———. A recollection of the editor's. *IPNL,* 1970, 20(3), 47.

547 ———. Reflections on the "sense of humour". *Int. J. soc. Psychiat.,* 1971, 17, 225-229.

548 ———. Remarks on the interpretation of one's own dreams. *AJIP,* 1956, 12, 84-87.

549 Rom, P. Reply to a note on the psychology of proper names. *IPB,* 1947, 6, 144-145.

550 ———. Review of A. Adler, *The case of Mrs. A.* In *IPNL,* 1970, 20(3), 52.

551 ———. Review of A. Adler, *Connaissance de l'homme.* In *IZIP,* 1949, 18(4), 189-190.

552 ———. Review of A. Adler, *Les névroses: Commentaires, observations et présentations de cas.* In *IPNL,* 1972, 21(3), 53-54.

553 ———. Review of A. Adler, *Pratique et théorie de la psychologie individuelle comparée.* In *IPNL,* 1961, 11(9-10, Whole No. 123-124). P. 37.

554 ———. Review of A. Adler, *Problems of neurosis.* In *IPNL,* 1964, 15(3-4, Whole No. 164-165). P. 10.

555 ———. Review of A. Adler, *Le tempérament nerveux.* In *IZIP,* 1949, 18(4), 189-190.

556 ———. Review of R. Affeman, *Psychologie und Bibel.* Stuttgart: Ernst Klett, 1957. In *IPNL,* 1957, 8(1-3, Whole No. 77-79). P. 10.

557 ———. Review of H. L. Ansbacher, Love and violence in the view of Adler. In *IPNL,* 1967, 17(11-12, Whole No. 196-197). Pp. 89-90.

558 ———. Review of H. L. & Rowena Ansbacher & D. & Kathleen Shiverick, Lee Harvey Oswald: An Adlerian interpretation In *IPNL,* 1967, 17(5-6, Whole No. 190-191). Pp. 43-44.

559 ———. Review of Phyllis Bottome, *Against whom?* In *IPNL,* 1954, Whole No. 36-37. P. 4.

560 ———. Review of Phyllis Bottome, *Alfred Adler, apostle of freedom.* In *IPNL,* 1957, 7(10-12, Whole No. 74-76). P. 44.

561 ———. Review of Phyllis Bottome, *Search for a soul.* In *IZIP,* 1948, 17(3), 141.

562 ———. Review of A. Boutinaud, A propos de l'enurésie. *Rééducation* (Paris), July-Aug., 1949. In *IZIP,* 1950, 19(1), 42.

563 ———. Review of Brigid Brophy, *Black ship to Hell.* In *IPNL,* 1967, 17(7-8, Whole No. 192-193). Pp. 52-53.

564 ———. Review of *Bulletin d'Information, Société Française de Psychologie Adlérienne,* Nos. 8 & 9. In *IPNL,* 1971, 20(3), 53-54.

565 ———. Review of L. Deutsch, *Guided sight reading.* In *IZIP,* 1951, 20(1), 40.

566 Rom, P. Review of D. Dinkmeyer & R. Dreikurs, *Encouraging children to learn.* In *IPNL*, 1963-64, 14(3-5, Whole No. 152-154). Pp. 11-12.

567 ———. Review of *Doctor Erich Kästners Lyrische Hausapotheke.* Zürich: Atrium, 1946. In *IZIP*, 1950, 19(1), 42.

568 ———. Review of R. Dreikurs, *Psychologie im Klassenzimmer.* In *IPNL*, 1967, 18(3-4, Whole No. 200-201). P. 28.

569 ———. Review of R. Dreikurs, *Social equality.* In *IPNL*, 1971, 20(5), 97.

570 ———. Review of A. Farau & H. Schaffer, *La psychologie des profondeurs des origines à nos jours.* In *IPNL*, 1960, 10(9-10, Whole No. 110-111). P. 41.

571 ———. Review of H. Freund, *Konstruktive Psychologie.* In *IPNL*, 1954, Whole No. 36-37. P. 5.

572 ———. Review of N. Friedman, *The social nature of psychological research.* New York: Basic Books, 1967. In *IPNL*, 1967, 17(11-12, Whole No. 196-197). Pp. 87-88.

573 ———. Review of E. Fromm, *You shall be as Gods.* London: Jonathan Cape, 1967. In *IPNL*, 1969, 18(9-10, Whole No. 218-219). Pp. 70-71.

574 ———. Review of M. M. Glatt, D. J. Pittman, D. G. Gillespie, & D. R. Hills, *The drug scene in Great Britian.* In *IPNL*, 1967, 18(3-4, Whole No. 200-201). Pp. 28-29.

575 ———. Review of N. G. Harris, *Modern trends in psychological medicine.* In *IPB*, 1949, 7, 138-139. Also in *IZIP*, 1949, 18(1), 44.

576 ———. Review of Johanna Herzog-Duerck, *Menschsein als Wagnis.* In *IPNL*, 1961, 11 (9-10, Whole No. 123-124). Pp. 38-39.

577 ———. Review of M. Hill & M. Lloyd Jones, *Sex education (The erroneous zone).* London: Nat. Secular Soc., 1970.

578 ———. Review of *Individual Psychology Bulletin.* In *IZIP*, 1950, 19(2), 94.

579 ———. Review of E. Jahn & A. Adler, *Religion et psychologie individuelle comparée,* and G. Wittgenstein (Ed.), *Psychotherapie und Theologie.* Stuttgart: Hippokrates, 1959. In *Int. J. soc. Psychiat.*, 1959, 4(4), 313-314.

580 ———. Review of E. Koestner, *When I was a little boy.* In *IPNL*, 1967, 17(9-10, Whole No. 194-195). P. 79.

581 ———. Review of W. Kosse, *Erziehung und Lebenssinn.* Oberursel:

Finken, 1967. In *IPNL*, 1967, 18(3-4, Whole No. 200-201). Pp. 27-28.

582 Rom, P. Review of Sari Kras, A discussion group for seriously disturbed mental patients. In *IPNL*, 1957, 7(10-12, Whole No. 74-76). P. 44.

583 ———. Review of G. di Lampedusa, *The leopard.* In *IPNL*, 1966, 16(11-12, Whole No. 184-185). P. 47.

584 ———. Review of T. Lidz, *Zur Familienumwelt des Schizophrenen.* Stuttgart: Ernst Klett, 1959, In *IPNL*, 1960, 10(7-8, Whole No. 108-109). P. 31.

585 ———. Review of A. Liebmann, *Untersuchung und Behandlung geistig zurückgebliebener Kinder.* 3rd ed. München: Reinhardt, 1970. In *IPNL*, 1971, 20(2), 28-29.

586 ———. Review of H. Mensen, *Psychologische und sozialische Aspekte der Nachbehandlung des Herzinfarktes.* Bad Woerishofen: Sanitas-Verlag, 1968. In *IPNL*, 1968, 17 (11-12, Whole No. 208-209). P. 85.

587 ———. Review of H. H. Mosak & B. H. Shulman, *Introductory psychotherapy,* Part I. In *IPNL*, 1963-64, 14(3-5, Whole No. 152-154). P. 16.

588 ———. Review of H. H. Mosak & B. H. Shulman, *The neuroses: A syllabus.* In *IPNL*, 1967, 17(7-8, Whole No. 192-193). P. 58.

589 ———. Review of I. Neufeld, Recognition and management of post-traumatic manifestations. In *IPNL*, 1956, 5(8, Whole No. 60). P. 5.

590 ———. Review of Hertha Orgler, *Alfred Adler et son oeuvre.* In *Int. J. soc. Psychiat.*, 1956, 1(4), 72.

591 ———. Review of Hertha Orgler, *Alfred Adler, the man and his work.* In *IPNL*, 1963, 14(1-2, Whole No. 150-151). Pp. 4-5; *IPB*, 1949, 7, 187.

592 ———. Review of Hertha Orgler, *Alfred Adler, Triumph über den Minderwertigkeitskomplex.* In *IPNL*, 1956, 6(3-4, Whole No. 67-69). P. 16.

593 ———. Review of Genevieve Painter, *Infant education.* In *IPNL*, 1971, 20(2), 34.

594 ———. Review of Genevieve Painter, *Teach your baby.* In *IPNL*, 1972, 21(3), 54.

595 ———. Review of J. B. Priestley, *Delight.* London: Heinemann, 1949. In *IZIP*, 1950, 19(2), 94-95.

596 Rom, P. Review of J. Rattner, *Alfred Adler in Selbstzeugnissen und Bilddokumenten.* In *IPNL*, 1972, 21(6), 119.

597 ———. Review of J. Rattner, *Individualpsychologie, eine Einführung in die tiefenpsychologische Lehre von Alfred Adler.* In *IPNL*, 1963, 14(1–2, Whole No. 150–151). P. 4.

598 ———. Review of A. A. Roback & T. Kiernan, *Pictorial history of psychology and psychiatry.* In *IPNL*, 1971, 20(2), 28.

599 ———. Review of C. Rolo (Ed.), *Psychiatry in American life.* New York: Delta, 1966. In *IPNL*, 1967, 18(3–4, Whole No. 200–201). P. 27.

600 ———. Review of A. O. Schorb, *Erzogenes Ich—erziehendes Du.* Stuttgart: Ernst Klett, 1928. In *IPNL*, 1959, 10(1, Whole No. 102–103). P. 4.

601 ———. Review of B. H. Shulman, Schizophrenia and sexual behavior. In *IPNL*, 1971, 20(3), 53.

602 ———. Review of M. M. Simons, *Making citizens.* London: His Majesty's Stationery Office, 1946. In *IZIP*, 1949, 18(1), 42–44.

603 ———. Review of S. R. Slavson, *Child-centered group guidance of parents.* New York: Int. Univer. Press, 1958. In *Int. J. soc. Psychiat.*, 1959, 4(4), 313.

604 ———. Review of M. Sperber, *The Achilles heel.* In *IPNL*, 1959, 10(2, Whole No. 104–105). P. 10.

605 ———. Review of M. Sperber (Ed.), *Wir und Dostojevskij.* In *IPNL*, 1972, 21(6), 119–120.

606 ———. Review of O. Spiel, *Einmal anders gesehen.* In *IPNL*, 1956, 5(8, Whole No. 60). P. 6.

607 ———. Review of O. Spiel & F. Birnbaum, *Die Reise ins Leben.* In *IPNL*, 1954, No. 36–37. Pp. 4–5.

608 ———. Review of A. Storr, *Human aggression.* London: Allen Lane, 1968. In *IPNL*, 1968, 18(3–4, Whole No. 212–213). Pp. 31–32.

609 ———. Review of K. L. Tank, *Gunter Grass.* Berlin: Colloquium Verlag, 1965. In *IPNL*, 1966, 16(11–12, Whole No. 184–185). P. 46.

610 ———. Review of Margarethe von Andics, *Suicide and the meaning of life.* London: Wm. Hodge, 1947. In *IPNL*, 1954, No. 36–37. P. 4.

611 Rom, P. Review of M. von Register, *Indie ist anders.* In *IPNL*, 1964, 15(1–2, Whole No. 162–163). P. 5.

612 ———. Review of L. Way, *Adler's place in psychology.* In *IZIP*, 1951, 20(2), 89–90.

613 ———. Review of L. Way, *Alfred Adler, an introduction to his psychology.* In *IPNL*, 1956, 6, 2.

614 ———. Review of L. Way, *Man's quest for significance.* In *IZIP*, 1951, 20(2), 90–91.

615 ———. Review of H. Weicker, *Der Helfer des Alkoholkranken.* Berlin: Verlag Deutscher Arbeiter-Abstinenbund. In *IZIP*, 1932, 10(2), 154.

616 ———. Review of E. Weisenhütter, *Werde und Handeln.* Stuttgart: Hippokrates Verlag 1963. In *IPNL*, 1963, 13(7–8, Whole No. 144–145). P. 32.

617 ———. Review of H. Zulliger. *Die Angst unsere Kinder.* Stuttgart: Ernst Klett, 1966. In *IPNL*, 1966, 16(11–12, Whole No. 184–185). P. 46.

618 ———. Right or wrong: My friend. . . . *IPNL*, 1972, 21(5), 89–90.

619 ———. Rudolf Dreikurs—a young 70-year old. *IPNL*, 1967, 17(5–6, Whole No. 190–191). Pp. 33–34.

620 ———. Rudolf Dreikurs, an encourager. *IPNL*, 1972, 21(4), 61–65.

621 ———. St. Augustine versus Pelagius. *IPNL*, 1963–64, 14(3–5, Whole No. 152–154). Pp. 14–15.

622 ———. St. Augustine's biased apperception. *IPNL*, 1962, 13(1–2, Whole No. 138–139). P. 5.

623 ———. Schiller bicentenary. *IPNL*, 1959, 10(2, Whole No. 104–105). Pp. 7–8.

624 ———. Schillers Don Carlos. *Etudes Germaniques*, 1947 (avril-juin), 600–604.

625 ———. Scientology alias dianetics: A fountain of . . . what? *IPNL*, 1967, 17(9–10, Whole No. 194–195). Pp. 73–74.

626 ———. Seelische Gesundheitspflege. *Geist und Tat* (Frankfurt), 1967, No. 1. Pp. 53–54.

627 ———. "Seelische" Krankheit und Gesundheit. *Prakt. Psychol.*, 1971, 25(5), 111–114.

628 ———. A self confessed case. *IPNL*, 1965, 16(1–3, Whole No. 174–176). P. 9.

629 ———. Sexualité et Individualpsychologie. *Laennec* (Paris), 1947, 7(3), 3–10.

630 Rom, P. Should I bequeath my corpse to a teaching hospital? *Omega*, 1970, 1(2), 141–142.

631 ———. *Sigmund Freud.* Berlin: Colloquium Verlag, 1966.

632 ———. Simenon et les psychiatres. *Med. et Hyg.* (Génève), 1971, 17, 1797–1803.

633 ———. Sin or error? *IPNL*, 1962, 12(11–12, Whole No. 136–137). Pp. 44–45.

634 ———. Sixteen years of I.P.N.L. *IPNL*, 1966, 16(11–12, Whole No. 184–185). P. 41.

635 ———. Skating. *IPNL*, 1965, 16(1–3, Whole No. 174–176). P. 4.

636 ———. Slips. *IPNL*, 1963, 13(5–6, Whole No. 142–143). P. 20; 1964, 15(3–4, Whole No. 164–165). P. 16; 1965, 15 (7–8, Whole No. 160–161). P. 32; 1967, 18(1–2, Whole No. 198–199). P. 11; 1968, 18(5–6, Whole No. 202–203). P. 41; 1969, 18(5–6, Whole No. 214–215). Pp. 40–41.

637 ———. Slips interpreted. *IPNL*, 1965, 15 (5–6, Whole No. 166–167). Pp. 17–18.

638 ———. Slips self interpreted. *IPNL*, 1964, 14(10–12, Whole No. 159–161). P. 40.

639 ———. Slips, strange and funny. *IPNL*, 1966, 16(7–8, Whole No. 180–181). P. 26.

640 ———. Solidarity. *IPNL*, 1965, 15(12, Whole No. 173). P. 46.

641 ———. Sourire amer. *IPNL*, 1962, 12(11–12, Whole No. 136–137). P. 46.

642 ———. Souvenirs de quelques delinquantes. *IZIP*, 1951, 20(4), 182–185.

643 ———. Stars and ensemble players. *IPNL*, 1969, 18(11–12, Whole No. 220–221). Pp. 87–88.

644 ———. Stekel died 20 years ago. *IPNL*, 1960, 10(9–10, Whole No. 110–111). P. 42.

645 ———. "STOPP". *IPNL*, 1969, 18(7–8, Whole No. 216–217). Pp. 61–62.

646 ———. Suicide. *IPNL*, 1957, 8(4–5, Whole No. 80–81). Pp. 15–16.

647 ———. Tailpiece. *IPNL*, 1963, 13(5–6, Whole No. 142–143). P. 24.

648 ———. Talk and music. *IPNL*, 1963, 14 (1–2, Whole No. 150–151). P. 3.

649 ———. Teleoanalysis. *IP*, 1968, 5(3), 10–11.

650 ———. A test: Old age. *IPNL*, 1971, 20(5), 81.

651 ———. Testing socialmindedness. *OSIPNL*, 1966, 6(5), 16–17.

652 Rom, P. Therapies galore. *IPNL*, 1971, 20 (5), 83–85.

653 ———. These feelings of guilt. *IPB*, 1950, 8, 32–38.

654 ———. These foreign languages. *IPNL*, 1965, 16(1–3, Whole No. 174–176). P. 5.

655 ———. They have stopped it. *IPNL*, 1972, 21(2), 32–33.

656 ———. This is not Adler! *IPNL*, 1957, 6(8–9, Whole No. 72–73). P. 36.

657 ———. This question of fellowship. *IPNL*, 1956, 5(11–12, Whole No. 63–64). Pp. 5–6.

658 ———. Thoughts on an old Book. *Freethinker* (London), 1969, 89, 331.

659 ———. Thoughts on perfectionism. *Freethinker* (London), 1971, 91(18), 139, 141.

660 ———. To appreciate or depreciate—that is the question. *IPNL*, 1971, 20(4), 66–67.

661 ———. Toda'a Hevratit (Social mindedness). *Eitanim*, May, 1966. P. 167.

662 ———. Tolerance—not easy. *IPNL*, 1968, 18(11–12, Whole No. 208–209). Pp. 88–89.

663 ———. A touching slip. *IPNL*, 1965, 16 (1–3, Whole No. 174–176). Pp. 11–12.

664 ———. Towards wholeness in teaching. *IPNL*, 1956, 5(8, Whole No. 60). Pp. 2–3.

665 ———. Tribune. *IPNL*, 1971, 20(1), 8.

666 ———. Two earliest memories [of Robert Graves]. *IPNL*, 1962, 13(1–2, Whole No. 138–139). Pp. 2–3.

667 ———. Two systems of reference. *IPNL*, 1963, 13(5–6, Whole No. 142–143). P. 18.

668 ———. Two unpublished letters by Alfred Adler. *IPNL*, 1961, 11(9–10, Whole No. 123–124). Pp. 34–35.

669 ———. Two variations on a famous theme. *IPNL*, 1962, 12(9–10, Whole No. 134–135). P. 42.

670 ———. Über ein entmutigendes Buch. *Psychol. Menschenkenntnis* (Zurich), 1964, 1, 191–194.

671 ———. Über einige Grundbegriffe der Individualpsychologie. *Prakt. Psychol.*, 1969, 23, 65–69.

672 ———. Über Hoffmans Struwwelpeter-Buch. *IZIP*, 1948, 17(3), 126–130.

673 ———. Über Linkshändigkeit. *IZIP*, 1948, 17(4), 177–178.

674 ———. Über Linkshändigkeit. *Gleichheit* (Bonn), 1960, No. 7.

675 **Rom, P.** Über das Verhalten der schönen Kriemhild. *IZIP*, 1947, 16(3), 112-122.

676 ———. Über zwei Lehrer rechten Lebens. *Psychol. Menschenkenntnis* (Zurich), 1965, 1, 318-322.

677 ———. Understanding human behaviour: Alfred Adler's key to the problem. *Mon. Rec.*, 1963, 68(12), 16-18.

678 ———. Understanding man. *IPNL*, 1971, 20(5), 91.

679 ———. The understanding of human behaviour. *Railway Rev.*, Mar. 15-22, 1946.

680 ———. Understanding the life-style of Moses. *IPNL*, 1952, Whole No. 20. P. 4.

681 ———. An "unpleasant and humiliating" method. *IPNL*, 1970, 19(3), 43.

682 ———. The useful side of life. *IPNL*, 1960, 10(9-10, Whole No. 110-111). Pp. 37-38.

683 ———. Vanity. *IPNL*, 1962, 13(1-2, Whole No. 138-139). P. 2.

684 ———. Vienna, 1960. *IPNL*, 1960, 11(1-2, Whole No. 115-116). Pp. 1-2.

685 ———. The villain. *IPNL*, 1972, 21(5), 91-92.

686 ———. Vive Georges Simenon! *IPNL*, 1965, 16(1-3, Whole No. 174-176). Pp. 10-11.

687 ———. Vorbereitung aufs Sterben. Zu Alfred Adlers 100. Geburtstag am 7. Februar, 1970. *Prakt. Psychol.*, 1970, 24(3), 80-81.

688 ———. Vyvyan Holland: Son of Oscar Wilde. *IPNL*, 1958, 8(10-12, Whole No. 86-88). P. 47.

689 ———. Was Darwin a neurotic? *IPNL*, 1971, 20(1), 1-3.

690 ———. Was Goethe a Nazi? *IPNL*, 1954, 4(4-5, Whole No. 44-45). P. 9.

691 ———. Waterpower: Misinterpreted. *IPNL*, 1969, 18(5-6, Whole No. 214-215). P. 38.

692 ———. "We are all on the way. . ." *IPNL*, 1960, 11(1-2, Whole No. 115-116). Pp. 4-5.

693 ———. We need more research. *IPNL*, 1963, 13(5-6, Whole No. 142-143). P. 23.

694 ———. What a dwarf. *IPNL*, 1972, 21(6), 105-106.

695 ———. What about hypnotism? *IPNL*, 1963, 13(11-12, Whole No. 148-149). Pp. 46-47; 1964, 15(3-4, Whole No. 164-165). P. 13.

696 ———. What did you do with your inferior organs? *IPNL*, 1967, 18(3-4, Whole No. 200-201). P. 32.

697 **Rom, P.** What do computers think about themselves? *Freethinker* (London), April 16, 1970.

698 ———. What do you do with your sexuality? [A review of B. H. Shulman, Uses and abuses of sex]. *IPNL*, 1968, 18(5-6, Whole No. 202-203). P. 47.

699 ———. What is "comparative, individualistic psychology?" *IPNL*, 1964, 14(10-12, Whole No. 159-161). P. 45.

700 ———. What is in a nickname? *IPNL*, 1963-64, 14(3-5, Whole No. 152-154). P. 9.

701 ———. What is "personology"? *IPNL*, 1972, 21(2), 23-24.

702 ———. What is the meaning of "depth" in psychology? *IPNL*, 1962, 12(5-6, Whole No. 130-131). Pp. 19-20.

703 ———. What is your style of life? *Humanist* (London), 1965, 80, 205-207.

704 ———. What some poets and philosophers thought about dreams. *IPNL*, 1972, 21(5), 94-96.

705 ———. What stuttering may mean. *IPNL*, 1964, 14(8-9, Whole No. 157-158). P. 30.

706 ———. What's in a name? *IPNL*, 1971, 20(1), 4-7.

707 ———. Where we stand. *IPNL*, 1956, 5 (11-12, Whole No. 63-64). Pp. 1-2.

708 ———. Who are they? [Work of Alexis Carrel]. *IPNL*, 1967, 17(9-10, Whole No. 194-195). Pp. 72-73.

709 ———. Why become a physician? *IPNL*, 1962, 13(3-4, Whole No. 140-141). Pp. 3-4.

710 ———. (Wo)mens Lib. . . *IPNL*, 1971, 20 (5), 92-93.

711 ———. Writers and speakers. *IPNL*, 1965, 15(9-10, Whole No. 170-172). P. 34.

712 ———. Yale's new dean. *IPNL*, 1967, 17 (7-8, Whole No. 192-193). P. 54.

713 ———. A year of grace. *IPNL*, 1955-56, 5(5-7, Whole No. 57-59). P. 1.

714 ———. You & I = We?! *IPNL*, 1963, 14 (1-2, Whole No. 150-151). Pp. 7-8.

715 ———. You and your name. *IPNL*, 1971, 20(5), 90-91.

716 ———. Zusammengehörigkeit (Alfred Adler's "Gemeinschaftsgefühl" und Camus' "Solidarität"). *Geist und Tat* (Frankfurt), March 16, 1961.

717 **Römer, R.** Störungen der Liebesfähigkeit. *IZIP*, 1951, 20(3), 110-129.

718 Ronall, Ruth E. Day treatment center and school: Seven years experience. *Amer. J. Orthopsychiat.*, 1965, 35(1), 160–169 (with Ruth la Viete, Rosalyn Cohen & Renee Reens).

719 ———. Selection and engagement of patients in family therapy. *Amer. J. Orthopsychiat.*, 1968, 38(4), 715–723 (with C. J. Sager, Yvonne J. Masters, & W. G. Norman).

720 Ronge, P. Die Entwicklung einiger Grundgedanken der Individualpsychologie. *IZIP*, 1951, 20(1), 17–27.

721 ———. The "feminine protest". *AJIP*, 1956, 12, 112–115.

722 ———. In memoriam Alfred Adler. *Psychiat. en neurolog. Bladen*, 1937, No. 3.

723 ———. *Individualpsychologie, een systematische Uitenzetting.* Utrecht: Bijleveld, 1934, 1948.

724 ———. Over de "Individualpsychologie" van Alfred Adler. *Nederl. Tijdschr. voor Geneeskunde*, 1930, No. 20.

725 ———. *Over de Psychologie der Levenstijdperken.* Utrecht: Bijleveld, 1951.

726 ———. Portrait. *IPNL*, 1970, 19(4), 80; 1971, 20(6), 110, 112.

727 ———. *Psychische Obbouw der Personlijkheid.* Utrecht: Bijleveld, 1945.

728 ———. Psychoanalysis and Individual Psychology. *Nederl. Tijdschr. Psychol.*, 1939, 7, 199–209.

729 ———. Translator of A. Adler, *Levensproblemen.*

730 ———. Translator, with A. C. Pabbruwe, of R. Dreikurs, *Alfred Adler's Individualpsychologie.*

731 ———. Translator of R. Dreikurs, *Hoe voed ik mijn kind op?*

732 ———. Über Kausalität und Finalität in der Psychologie. *Psychiat. en neurol. Bladen*, 1932, No. 3.

733 ———. Uit Kliniek en Praktijk. *Geneeskundige Gids*, 1932, 10, 529–532.

734 ———. Vergleich einiger psychoanalytischer und individualpsychologischer Begriffe. In Int. Verein Indivpsy., *Alfred Adler zum gedenken.* Pp. 110–124.

735 ———. Vertaald. In R. Dreikurs, *Hoe voed ik mijn kind op?*

736 ———. Vertaald. In L. Way, *Adler's Psychologie en Philosophie.*

737 Ronge, Mrs. P. Portrait. *IPNL*, 1971, 20(6), 112.

738 Roodin, P. A. Birth order and cooperativeness: Peer ratings. *Psychol. Rep.*, 1971, 29, 590.

739 Rosen, B. Family structure and value transmission. *Merrill-Palmer Quart.*, 1964, 10(1), 59–75.

740 Rosenbaum, M. *Group psychotherapy and group function.* New York: Basic Books, 1963 (with M. Berger).

741 ———. The value of early memories in psychotherapy. *Psychiat. Quart.*, 1953, 27, 73–82.

742 Rosenberg, B. G. The dramatic sibling. *Percep. mot. Skills*, 1966, 22, 993–994 (with B. Sutton-Smith).

743 ———. Modeling and reactive components of sibling interaction (with B. Sutton-Smith). In J. P. Hill (Ed.), *Minnesota symposia on child psychology*, 1969, 3, 131-152.

744 ———. Ordinal position and sex-role identification. *Genet. Psychol. Monogr.*, 1964, 70, 297–328 (with B. Sutton-Smith).

745 ———. The relationship of ordinal position and sibling sex status to cognitive abilities. *Psychonom. Sci.*, 1964, 1, 81–82 (with B. Sutton-Smith).

746 ———. *The sibling.* New York: Holt, Rinehart & Winston, 1970 (with B. Sutton-Smith).

747 ———. Sibling age spacing effects upon cognition. *Developm. Psychol.*, 1969, 1, 661–668 (with B. Sutton-Smith).

748 ———. Sibling association, family size and cognitive abilities. *J. genet. Psychol.*, 1966, 109, 271–279 (with B. Sutton-Smith).

749 ———. Sibling consensus on power tactics. *J. genet. Psychol.*, 1968, 112, 63–72 (with B. Sutton-Smith).

750 Rosenberg, Bina. The counselor. In R. Dreikurs, R. Corsini, R. Lowe, & M. Sonstegard (Eds.), *Adlerian family counseling.* Pp. 33–40.

751 ———. Family counseling. In A. Nikelly (Ed.), *Techniques for behavior change.* Pp. 117–123.

752 ———. Mechanisms of group psychotherapy. *J. abnorm. soc. Psychol.*, 1955, 51, 406–411 (with R. J. Corsini). Also in M. Rosenbaum & M. Berger (Eds.), *Group psychotherapy and group function.* Pp. 340–351.

753 Rosenberg, M. J. Cognitive structure and attitudinal affect. *J. abnorm. soc. Psychol.*, 1956, 53, 367–373.

754 Rosenberg, R. D. Adleriana. *IPB*, 1941, 2 (1), 19.

755 Rosenberg, S. Cognitive styles and overt symptomatology in schizophrenia. *Diss. Abstr.*, 1966, 27, 614. Unpubl. Ph.D. Diss., Columbia Univ., 1966.

756 Rosenblith, Judy F. Review of D. C. Dinkmeyer, *Child development: The emerging self.* In *Contemp. Psychol.*, 1967, 12, 293-294.

757 Rosenbluh, E. S. Birth order, need for achievement, college attendance, & sociocultural learning. *Psychol.*, 1970, 7(2), 8-12 (with G. B. Haarman).

758 Rosenfeld, H. Relationships of ordinal position to affiliation and achievement motives: Direction and generality. *J. Pers.*, 1966, 34, 467-479.

759 Rosenow, C. The incidence of first born among problem children. *J. genet. Psychol.*, 1930, 37, 145-151.

760 ———. The ordinal position of problem children. *Amer. J. Orthopsychiat.*, 1931, 1, 430-434 (with A. H. Whyte).

761 Rosenthal, H. Die Idee des Wortes in der altisraelitischen Kulturentwicklung. *IZIP*, 1932, 10(6), 414-418.

762 ———. Die Musikalität der Juden. *IZIP*, 1931, 9(2), 122-131.

763 ———. Die schauspielerische Begabung bei den Juden. *IZIP*, 1930, 8(3), 325-332.

764 Rosenthal, Hattie R. The fear of death as an indispensable factor in psychotherapy. *Amer. J. Psychother.*, 1963, 17, 619-631.

765 ———. The final dream: A criterion for the termination of therapy. In K. A. Adler and Danica Deutsch (Eds.), *Essays in Individual Psychology.* Pp. 400-409.

766 ———. Psychotherapy for the aging. *Amer. J. Psychother.*, 1959, 13, 55-65.

767 ———. Psychotherapy for the dying. *Amer. J. Psychother.*, 1959, 13, 626-633.

768 ———. Review of Margaretta K. Bowers *et al., Counseling the dying.* New York: Thomas Nelson & Sons, 1964. In *Amer. J. Psychother.*, 1965, 19(3), 509-510.

769 ———. Thinking, feeling, and perceiving in psychotherapy: An application of the principle of self-consistency. *IP*, 1963, 1(1), 5-10.

770 Rosenthal, I. Perceived parent attitudes as determinants of ego structure. *Child Developm.*, 1955, 25, 173-183 (with D. P. Ausubel, E. E. Balthazar, L. S. Blackman, S. N. Schpoont & J. Welkowitz).

771 Rosenthal, R. *Experimenter effects in behavioral research.* New York: Appleton-Century-Crofts, 1966.

772 ———. *Pygmalion in the classroom: Teacher expectation and pupils' intellectual development.* New York: Holt, Rinehart, & Winston, 1968 (with Lenore Jacobson).

773 ———. Self-fulfilling prophecy. *Psychol. Today*, 1968, 2(4), 44-51.

774 ———. Teacher expectations for the disadvantaged. *Sci. Amer.*, 1968, 218, 19-23 (with Lenore F. Jacobson).

775 Rosenzweig, S. The place of the individual and of idiodynamics in psychology: A dialogue. *JIP*, 1958, 14, 3-21.

776 Rosler, Gisa. Fighting attitude of a second born child. *IJIP*, 1937, 3(1), 68-71.

777 ———. Kampfstellung einer Zweitgeborenen. *IZIP*, 1929, 7(4), 307-309.

778 Rosler, Marie. Das einzige Kind. *IZIP*, 1929, 7(3), 227-230 (with R. Schaller).

779 ———. Review of V. K. Mikulski, *Psychologische Untersuchungen in Mittelschulen.* Warschav: [   ], 1930. In *IZIP*, 1932, 10(5), 395.

780 Rosman, Bernice L. Analytic cognitive style in children. *Diss. Abstr.*, 1966, 27, 21-26. Unpubl. Ph.D. Diss., Yale Univ., 1962.

781 Rosow, I. Issues in the concept of need complementarity. *Sociom.*, 1957, 20, 216-233.

782 Ross, B. M. Some traits associated with sibling jealousy in problem children. *Smith Coll. Stud. Soc. Work*, 1931, 1, 364-378.

783 Ross, J. Three cognitive dimensions. *Psychol. Rep.*, 1965, 16, 291-300.

784 Ross, T. A. Early infancy, puberty, and adolescence. *IPMP*, 1937, No. 18 (with Joyce Partridge, H. Crichton-Miller & F. G. Crookshank).

785 ———. The psychological approach. *IPMP*, 1937, No. 18. Pp. 33-48.

786 Rossi, A. S. Naming children in middle class families. *Amer. sociol. Rev.*, 1965, 30, 499-513.

787 Roth, S. M. Alfred Adler, the man. *OSIPNL*, 1963, 4(2), 10-11.

788 ———. The future progress of Individual Psychology. *IPB*, 1942, 2(3), 56-57.

789 Rothaus, P. Some basic concepts in human relations training for psychiatric patients. *Hosp. Commun. Psychiat.*, 1970, 21, 137-143 (with W. E. O'Connell, P. Hanson & G. Wiggins).

790 **Rothaus, P.** Training patients for effective participation in back-home groups. *Amer. J. Psychiat.*, 1969, 126, 857–862 (with P. Hanson, W. O'Connell, & G. Wiggins).

791 **Rothbart, M. K.** Birth order and mother-child interaction in an achievement situation. *J. Pers. soc. Psychol.*, 1971, 17, 113–120.

792 ——. Sibling configuration and interpersonal dominance. *Proc. Ann. Conv. Amer. Psychol. Assn.*, 1970, 5, 367–368.

793 **Rothenberg, M. B.** A method for clinical and theoretical study of the earliest memory. *J. consult. clin. Psychol.*, 1960, 3, 523–534 (with R. J. Langs, J. R. Fishman & M. F. Reiser).

794 **Rothschild, B.** Relationships of oral imagery to yielding behavior and birth order. *J. consult. clin. Psychol.*, 1968, 32, 89–91 (with J. Masling & Lillie Weiss).

795 **Rothwein, Elly.** See Redwin, Eleanore.

796 **Rotter, J. B.** An analysis of Adlerian psychology from a research orientation. *JIP*, 1962, 18, 3–11.

797 ——. Children's feelings of personal control as related to social class and ethnic group. *J. Pers.*, 1963, 31, 482–490 (with Esther S. Battle).

798 ——. *Clinical psychology*. Englewood Cliffs, N. J.: Prentice-Hall, 1964.

799 ——. External control and internal control. *Psychol. Today*, 1971, 5(1), 37–42, 58–59.

800 ——. Psychotherapy. *Annu. Rev. Psychol.*, 1960, 11, 381–414.

801 ——. Review of K. A. Adler & Danica Deutsch (Eds.), *Essays in Individual Psychology*. In *Contemp. Psychol.*, 1960, 5, 334–335.

802 **Rouquette, Madeleine.** Conferences sur la psychologie adlérienne. *L'Ecole due Grand Paris*, 1952, No. 62.

803 ——. Nouvelles conferences sur la psychologie adlérienne. *L'Ecole du Grand Paris*, 1953, No. 76. P. 10.

804 **Roussel, [   ].** Translator of A. Adler, *Le tempérament nerveux*.

805 **Rubin, Z.** The birth order of birth-order researchers. *Developm. Psychol.*, 1970, 3, 269–270.

806 **Rubiner, L.** Zur Krise des geistigen Lebens. *ZIP*, 1914, 1(6–9), 231–240.

807 **Rubinstein, A.** (Ed.). *Crisis in the New York Schools.* New York: Monthly Rev. Press, 1970.

808 **Ruch, F. L.** *Psychology and life.* Chicago: Scott, Foresman, 1963.

809 **Rudikoff, Esselyn C.** A comparative study of the changes in the concept of self, the ordinary person, and the ideal in eight cases. In C. R. Rogers and Rosalind F. Dymond (Eds.), *Psychotherapy and personality change.* Chicago: Univ. Chicago Press, 1954. Pp. 85–98.

810 **Rühle, Alice.** Am andern Ufer. 5 vols. Dresden: Verlag am andern Ufer, 1926 (with O. Rühle).

811 ——. Analyse der Psychoanalyse. *IZIP*, 1929, 7(4), 264–268.

812 ——. Autoritätsproblem. In Sofie Lazarsfeld (Ed.), *Technik der Erziehung.*

813 ——. Die drei Salvinbücher. *IZIP*, 1927, 5(4), 284–292.

814 ——. Die entthronte Libido. *IZIP*, 1930, 8(5), 558–566.

815 ——. *Das Frauenproblem der Gegenwart.* Leipzig: S. Hirzel, 1932.

816 ——. *Freud and Adler.* Dresden: Verlag am andern Ufer, 1924, 1927.

817 ——. *Freud y Adler.* Mexico, D. F.: Ed. Atlarte, 1941.

818 ——. Individualpsychologie und Klassenkampf. *IZIP*, 1924, 2(5), 18–22.

819 ——. Individualpsychologische Autodidaktic. *IZIP*, 1930, 8(1), 56–61.

820 —— (Ed.). *Moeilijke Kinderen*. 3rd ed. Translated by F. Dijkema. Amsterdam: Wereldbibliotheek, 1935 (with O. Rühle).

821 ——. *La nueva actitud ante la vida.* Mexico, D. F.: El National, 1941 (with O. Rühle).

822 ——. Portrait. *IPNL*, 1972, 21(6), 109.

823 ——. Review of H. de Man, *Zur Psychologie des Sozialismus.* Jena: Diederichs, 1926. In *IZIP*, 1926, 4(4), 240–243.

824 ——. Review of Gina Kaus, *Die Verlieb-ten.* & Toni, *Eine Schulmädchenkömodie.* Berlin: Propyläenverlag, [   ]. In *IZIP*, 1929, 7(1), 69–70.

825 ——. Review of W. M. Kranefeldt, *Die Psychoanalyse.* In *IZIP*, 1931, 9(4), 320.

826 ——. Review of H. Schulte-Vaerting, *Neubegründung der Psychoanalyse.* Berlin: M. Pfeiffer, [   ]. In *IZIP*, 1931, 9(1), 64–65.

827 ——. *Schwererziebare Kinder: Eine Schriftenfolge.* Dresden: Verlag am andern Ufer, 1926 (with O. Rühle).

828 **Rühle, Alice.** *Sexual-analyse: Psychologie des Liebes- und Ehelebens.* Rudolstadt: Graifenverlag, 1929.

829 ———. *Das Stiefkind.* Dresden: Verlag am andern Ufer, 1927.

830 ———. Über die Eifersucht als weibliche Sicherung. *IZIP*, 1925, 3(6), 314–320.

831 ———. *Der Weg zum Wir.* Dresden: Verlag am andern Ufer, 1927.

832 **Rühle, O.** *Am andern Ufer.* 5 vols. Dresden: Verlag am andern Ufer, 1926 (with Alice Rühle).

833 ———. *Atemgymnastik.* Arbeiter-Gesundheits-Bibliothek, 1909.

834 ———. *Grundfragen der Erziehung.* Dresden: Verlag am andern Ufer,

835 ———. *Karl Marx, his life and work.* London: Allen & Unwin, 1929.

836 ———. *Karl Marx, Leben und Werk.* Dresden: Avalun, 1928.

837 ———. *Karl Marx, sa vie et son oeuvre.* Paris: Grasset, 1933.

838 ———. Kindliche Kriminalität. In Sofie Lazarsfeld (Ed.), *Technik der Erziehung.*

839 ———. *Moeilijke Kinderen.* 3rd ed. Translated by P. Dijkema. Amsterdam: Wereldbibliotheek, 1935 (with Alice Rühle).

840 ———. *La nueva actitud ante la vide.* Mexico, D. F.: El National, 1941 (with Alice Rühle).

841 ———. *Das proletarische Kind.* München: A. Langen, 1911, 1922.

842 ———. Das proletarische Mädchen. *IZIP*, 1925, 3(6), 328–332.

843 ———. Review of F. Bryk, *Neger-Eros.* Berlin: A. Markus & E. Webers, 1928. In *IZIP*, 1928, 6(6), 506.

844 ———. *Schwererziehbare Kinder: Eine Schriftenfolge.* Dresden: Verlag am andern Ufer, 1926 (with Alice Rühle).

845 ———. *Die Seele des proletarischen Kindes.* Dresden: Verlag am andern Ufer, 1925.

846 ———. *Die Sozialisierung der Frau.* Dresden: Verlag am andern Ufer,

847 ———. *Umgang mit Kindern.* Dresden: Verlag am andern Ufer, 1926.

848 ———. *Das verwahrloste Kind.* Dresden: Verlag am andern Ufer, 1926.

849 **Rühle-Gerstel, Alice.** See Rühle, Alice.

850 **Ruitenbeek, H. M.** (Ed.). *Group therapy today: Styles, methods and techniques.* New York: Atherton Press, 1969.

851 ——— (Ed.). *Varieties of personality theory.* New York: Dutton, 1964.

852 **Ruman, E.** Helping student teachers utilize consultant services. Cedar Falls, Ia.: *Assn. for Student Teaching, Bull.* #10, 1959 (with M. Sonstegard).

853 **Runes, D. D.** *Pictorial history of philosophy.* New York: Phil. Libr., 1959.

854 **Russell, B.** *Power, a new social analysis.* New York: Norton, 1938.

855 **Russell, E. S.** *The directiveness of organic activities.* Cambridge, England: Univ. Press, 1945.

856 **Russell, R. W.** et al. *Frontiers of psychology.* Chicago: Scott, Foresman, 1965.

857 **Russo, C.** Bemerkungen über die pädagogischen Anschauungen Kants. *IZIP*, 1924, 2(5), 13–18.

858 **Rychlak, J. F.** *A philosophy of science for personality theory.* Boston: Houghton Mifflin, 1968.

859 ———. The similarity, compatibility or incompatibility of need in interpersonal selection. *J. Pers. soc. Psychol.*, 1965, 2, 334–340.

860 ———. The two teleologies of Adler's Individual Psychology. *JIP*, 1970, 26(2), 144–152.

861 **Ryerson, R.** Psychodynamic significance of the first conscious memory. *Bull. Menninger Clin.*, 1951, 15, 213–220 (with V. Eisenstein).

S

1 **S. K.** Review of F. Dell, Warst du je ein Kind? Leipzig: [   ], 1924. In *IZIP*, 1926, 4(1), 47–48.

2 **Sachs, E.** Abnormal delay of visual perception. *Arch. Neurol. Psychiat.*, 1946, 56, 198–206.

3 ———. The action currents of the retina in man. *Klin. Wchnschr.*, 1929, 8(3), 136.

4 ———. Antagonism between adrenergic drugs and atropine in the isolated iris dilator. *Arch. Ophthalm.*, 1940, 24, 142–148 (with P. Heath).

5 ———. Application of filters in color blindness: Contribution to palliative therapy. *Arch. Augenheilk.*, 1929, 102, 271–307 (with H. Ahlenstiel & H. Streckfuss).

6 ———. Calibration of the color sense of normal and abnormal trichromates under photopic and scotopic conditions.

In A. Bethe *et al.*, *Handb. norm. path. Physiol.* Berlin: Springer, 1931. Vol. 12. Pp. 1544-1570.

7 **Sachs, E.** A contribution to heredity in the disturbances of color vision. *Klin. Mbl. Augenheilk.*, 1928, 81, 231-233.

8 ———. A contribution to the Kataforesis of bacteria. *Z. Immunitätsforsch. u. exp. Ther.*, 1924, 40, 57-68.

9 ———. "The Fall" by Albert Camus: A study in Adlerian psychology. *JIP*, 1972, 28, 76-80.

10 ———. Human genetics. *Ärztl. Monatschr.*, Mar., 1925. Pp. 78-86.

11 ———. Mass testing of color vision. *J. Amer. Med. Assn.*, 1941, 116, 1769-1770.

12 ———. The pharmacological behavior of the intraocular muscles. I. The problem of sensitization and methods for its study. *Amer. J. Ophthalm.*, 1940, 23, 1199-1209 (with P. Heath).

13 ———. The pharmacological behavior of the intraocular muscles. II. Sensitization phenomena in the dilator and sphincter iridis. *Amer. J. Ophthalm.*, 1940, 23, 1376-1387 (with P. Heath).

14 ———. The pharmacological behavior of the intraocular muscles. III. "Cholinergic" behavior of the dilator iridis. *Amer. J. Ophthalm.*, 1941, 24, 34-39(with P. Heath).

15 ———. The pharmacological behavior of the intraocular muscles. IV. The action of strychnine on the dilator and sphincter iridis. *J. Pharmacol. & exp. Ther.*, 1942, 74, 262-265.

16 ———. The pharmacological behavior of the intraocular muscles. V. The action of yohimbine and ergotamine on the dilator iridis. *J. Pharmacol. & exp. Ther.*, 1942, 75, 105-110 (with F. F. Yonkman).

17 ———. Principles of tonometer standardization. *Arch. Ophthalm.*, 1943, 29, 782-792 (with F. L. MacCracken).

18 ———. The problem of "differential" factors in the action current of the ventricle of the heart. *Z. Biol.*, 1928, 88(2), 125-131 (with E. Holzloehner).

19 ———. The retinal currents in man (with A. Kohlrausch). In A. Bethe *et al.*, *Handb. norm. path. Physiol.* Berlin: Springer, 1931. Vol. 12. Pp. 1459-1464.

20 ———. The sensitivity to differences in hue in different color systems. *Z. Sinnesphys.*, 1928, 59, 243-256.

21 **Sachs, E.** Some observations and experimental studies on the physiology of the ciliary muscle. *Amer. J. Ophthalm.*, 1942, 25, 1277-1291.

22 ———. Surrealism—A passing phase of antirational painting. In *Neue Perspektiven aus Wirtschaft und Recht: Festschrift für Hans Schaeffer.* Berlin: Ducker & Humblot, 1966.

23 ———. The visual sensations (with A. Kohlrausch). In C. Oppenheimer & L. Pincussen (Eds.), *Tabulae Biologicae.* Berlin: W. Junk, 1927. Vol. 4. Pp. 520-538.

24 **Sachs, F. H.** Einige kritisch kanttekenende Beschouwingen over diverse Visies open Behandelingswijzen van Stotteraars. *MNWIP*, 1970, 19(2), 13-16.

25 **Sackett, Barbara.** "Baby Sitter", part of the team. *OSIPNL*, 1966, 6(3), 8-9.

26 **Sacks, J.** Three therapeutic approaches . . . one patient. *IP*, 1966, 3(2), 1-10 (with N. E. Shoobs & A. Roland).

27 **Sadler, A. W.** Dream and folk-tale: A cognitive venture. *JIP*, 1969, 25, 89-100.

28 **Sager, C. J.** The concept of aggression in modern psychiatry. *Ment. Hyg., N. Y.*, 1952, 36, 210-219.

29 ———. Selection and engagement of patients in family therapy. *Amer. J. Orthopsychiat.*, 1968, 38(4), 715-723 (with Ruth Ronall, Yvonne J. Masters, & W. G. Norman).

30 **Sahakian, W. S.** Ahead of his time [Tribute to Alfred Adler on his 100th birthday]. *JIP*, 1970, 26(2), 15.

31 ——— (Ed.). *History of psychology: A source book in systematic psychology.* Itasca, Ill.: F. E. Peacock, 1968.

32 ——— (Ed.). *Psychology of personality: Readings in theory.* Chicago: Rand McNally, 1965.

33 ——— (Ed.). *Psychotherapy and counseling: Studies in technique.* Chicago: Rand McNally, 1969.

34 ———. Stoic philosophical psychotherapy. *JIP*, 1969, 25, 32-35.

35 **Saint-Jean de la Croix, Marie.** La Psychologie Individuelle Comparée d'Alfred Adler. *Rééducation*, 1948, 12(5), 28-32.

36 **Sakel, M. J.** The importance of the Adlerian orientation in psychotherapy. *JIP*, 1958, 14, 158-159.

37 **Salas, J.** Translator of A. Adler, *La Psicologia Individual en la escuela.*

38 **Salles, Yedda.** Translator, with Terezinha Eboli, of D. Dinkmeyer & R. Dreikurs, *Encorojando crianças a aprender.*

39 **Salz, V.** Basic Christian attitudes and styles of authority. *Crossroads,* Mar., 1971.

40 ———. *Communication: Parent and child.* Louisville, Ky.: Passionist Press, 1970.

41 ———. Family council. *Crossroads,* Mar., 1971.

42 ———. Goals of behavior. *Crossroads,* Mar., 1971.

43 ———. Logical consequences vs. punishment. *Crossroads,* Mar., 1971.

44 ———. Process of encouragement. *Crossroads,* Mar., 1971.

45 **Salzman, L.** Masochism and psychopathy as adaptive behavior. *JIP,* 1960, 16, 182–188. Also in H. D. Werner (Ed.), *New understandings of human behavior.* Pp. 135–139.

46 ———. The role of sexuality in the formation of ideas: A critique. *JIP,* 1961, 17, 108–109.

47 **Sambrooks, J. E.** Paired-associate learning as influenced by birth order and the presence of others. *Psychonom. Sci.,* 1969, 16, 109–110 (with J. M. Innes).

48 **Sammani, D.** Le problème de fumer. *IPNL,* 1972, 21(1), 10.

49 **Samples, Fleury P.** A teleoanalytic approach to coordinate counseling: Teacher and counseling. *IP,* 1969, 6(1), 8–17 (with M. A. Sonstegard).

50 **Sampson, E. E.** Birth order, need achievement, and conformity. *J. abnorm. soc. Psychol.,* 1962, 64, 155–159.

51 ———. An examination of the relationship between ordinal position, personality and conformity: An extension, replication and partial verification. *J. Pers. soc. Psychol.,* 1967, 5, 398–407 (with Francena T. Hancock).

52 ———. The study of ordinal position: Antecedents and outcomes. In B. Maher (Ed.), *Progress in experimental personality research.* Vol. 2. Pp. 175–228.

53 **Sanborn, M. P.** Ordinal position of high school students identified by teachers as superior. *J. educ. Psychol.,* 1969, 60, 41–45 (with R. W. Bradley).

54 **Sandison, A.** Escape into activities. *IPP,* 1940, No. 22. Pp. 7–17.

55 **Sands, P. M.** The comparative effectiveness of two contrasting alcoholic treatment programs. *Nwsltr. Res. Psychol.,* 1972, 14(4), 21–23 (with Barbara Williams, M. M. Gallen & W. E. O'Connell).

56 **Sanford, E. G.** The bright child who fails. *Understanding the Child,* 1952, 21, 85–88.

57 **Sanford, R. N.** The dynamics of identification. *Psychol. Rev.,* 1955, 62, 106–118.

58 **Sangsted, R. C.** Level of aspiration and sociometric distance. *Sociom.,* 1952, 15, 318–325 (with R. N. Cassel).

59 **Sarason, D.** (Ed.) *Jahreskurse für ärztliche Fortbildung.* München: Lehrmann, 1913.

60 **Sarason, I. G.** Birth order, test anxiety, and learning. *J. Pers.,* 1969, 37, 171–177.

61 **Sauer, H.** *Jugendberatungsstellen, Idee und Praxis 1914–1923.* Leipzig: Oldenburg, 1923.

62 **Saul, L.** On earliest memories. *Psychoanal. Quart.,* 1956, 25, 228–237 (with E. Sheppard & T. Snyder).

63 **Saupe, E.** (Ed.) *Einführung in die neuere Psychologie.* Osterwick-Harz: Zickfeldt, 1931.

64 **Savage, B. M.** A note on singularity in given names. *J. soc. Psychol.,* 1948, 27, 271–272 (with F. L. Wells).

65 **Savitz, H. A.** The cultural background of the patient as part of the physicians' armamentarium. In D. A. McClelland (Ed.), *Studies in motivation.* New York: Appleton-Century-Crofts, 1955.

66 **Scarth, P.** *Adult migrant education bibliography.* Washington: Educational Projects Inc., 1967.

67 ———. ESOL and the Mexican-American. *Linguist. Reporter,* 1968, 10(25), 1–2 (with T. F. Regan).

68 ———. *The high school equivalency program.* Washington: Educational Projects Inc., 1967.

69 ———. Implications of Individual Psychology for the school psychologist. *JIP,* 1969, 25, 146–154.

70 ———. Individual Psychology: Its implications for school psychology. Unpubl. doctoral diss., Boston Univ., 1966.

71 ———. (Ed.) *The Mexican American Directory.* Washington: Executive Systems Corp., 1969 (with A. Palacios & G. King).

72 ———. *Principles to be used by parents for developing improved relationships.* Washington: Educational Systems Corp., 1968.

73 **Scarth, P.** *Recommendations for parents.* Washington: Educational Systems Corp., 1968.

74 ———. *Study manual.* Washington: Educational Systems Corp., 1968.

75 **Schachtel, E.** On memory and childhood amnesia. *Psychiat.*, 1947, 10, 1–26. Also in P. Mullahy (Ed.), *A study of interpersonal relations.* New York: Hermitage Press, 1949. Pp. 3–49.

76 **Schachter, S.** Birth order, eminence, and higher education. *Amer. sociol. Rev.*, 1963, 28, 757–768.

77 ———. Birth order and sociometric choice. *J. abnorm. soc. Psychol.*, 1964, 68, 453–456.

78 ———. Ordinal position and fighter pilot effectiveness (from *The psychology of affiliation*). In G. Lindzey & C. S. Hall, *Theories of personality: Primary sources and research.* Pp. 114–116.

79 ———. *The psychology of affiliation.* Stanford, Cal.: Stanford Univ. Press, 1959.

80 **Schaffer, H.** L'agressivité. *BSFPA*, 1971, No. 11. Pp. 11–22.

81 ———. [Alfred Adler]. *Rev. Psychol.* (Paris), 1970, 6, 7–13.

82 ———. Alfred Adler et la psychologie contemporaine. *BISFPA*, 1970, No. 7. Pp. 1–5.

83 ———. Un chercheur et ses idées: Alfred Adler enquète de l'animal social. *Psychol.*, 1970 (Juillet). Pp. 7–13.

84 ———. Emancipation féminine et équilibre du couple. *BSFPA*, 1972, No. 12. Pp. 1–4. Also in *Ann. Psychothér.*, 1972, No. 5. Pp. 54–57.

85 ———. *La fonction créatrice dans la vie et dans la névrose: Creativité et guérison.* Paris: Expansion scientifique, 1969. Pp. 101–105.

86 ———. La fonction d'imagination dans la vie et dans certains états psychopathologiques. *BSFPA*, 1972, No. 14. Pp. 1–10.

87 ———. Imperfect, immature or sick society: Its therapy by education. *IPNL*, 1969, 19 (1), 15–16.

88 ———. Individual Psychology theory displayed in recent French psychiatric literature. *AJIP*, 1956, 12, 88–90.

89 ———. Introduction to C. Allen, *Les découvertes modernes de la psychiatrie.*

90 ———. Necrologie [Mme. René Cialix]. *BISFPA*, 1970, No. 8. P. 30.

91 **Schaffer, H.** Obituary [P. Meignant]. *IPNL*, 1961, 11 (5–6, Whole No. 119–120). Pp. 21–22.

92 ———. [Obituary for Lydia Sicher]. *IPNL*, 1962, 11(7–8, Whole No. 132–133). Pp. 27–28.

93 ———. Parallelerscheinungen in pädagogischen und therapeutischen Methoden. In Int. Verein Indivpsy., *Alfred Adler zum Gedenken.* Pp. 125–133.

94 ———. Parallélisme entre certaines methodes pédagogiques et psychothérapiques, Adler in memoriam. Vienna: , 1957. Pp. 125–133.

95 ———. Portrait. *IPNL*, 1970, 19(4), 79, 80; 1971, 20(6), 112.

96 ———. Preface to and translator of A. Adler, *Pratique et théorie de la psychologie individuelle comparée.*

97 ———. Preface to and translator of A. Adler, *La psychologie de l'enfant difficile.*

98 ———. Preface to and translator of A. Adler & E. Jahn, *Religion et psychologie individuelle comparée* suivi de: *La névrose obsessionnelle* et *Les enfants difficile.*

99 ———. Preface to and translator of O. Spiel, *La doctrine d'Alfred Adler dans ses applications à l'éducation écolaire.*

100 ———. Psychologie adlérienne et société. *BSFPA*, 1971, No. 9. Pp. 1–10. Also in *Ann. Psychother.*, 1971, No. 3. Pp. 28–35.

101 ———. *La psychologia dal profondo, dalli origini ai nostri giorni.* Roma: Astrolabio, 1962 (with A. Farau).

102 ———. *La psychologie des profondeurs des origins à nos jours.* Paris: Payot, 1960 (with A. Farau).

103 ———. Psychosomatic medicine and Adler's concept of psychophysical unity. *AJIP*, 1954, 10, 182–185.

104 ———. Psychothérapie adlérienne. In H. Ey (Ed.), *Encyclopedie médico-chirurgicale.* Paris: , 1955, 1970.

105 ———. Religion y Psychologia Individual comparada (Adleriana). In *Psiquiatria y psicologia.* Barcelona: 1962. Pp. 552–556.

106 ———. La résistance au cours du traitement psychothérapique. *BSFPA*, 1972, No. 13. Pp. 1–15. Also in *Ann. Psychothér.*, 1972, Suppl. No. 5. Pp. 107–118.

107 ———. Review of H. F. Ellenberger, *The discovery of the unconscious.* In *BSFPA*, 1972, No. 12. Pp. 35–39.

108 **Schaffer, H.** Sur l'étiologie des troubles caractériels. *Bull. du Centre de Psychol. Adlérienne*, 1950, No. 1. Pp. 5-7.

109 ———. Survey on psychopedagogy. *AJIP*, 1956, 12, 116-122.

110 ———. *Symposium sur la schizophrénie dans la perspective adlérienne*. Zurich: Fussli, 1959.

111 ———. Tour d'horizon psychopédagogique. Introduction to O. Spiel, *La doctrine d'Alfred Adler dans les applications à l'école*. Pp. 7-13.

112 ———. La toxicomanie contemporaine accidentale. *BISFPA*, 1970, No. 8. Pp. 1-10.

113 ———. Translator of A. Adler, *Le compensation psychique de l'état d'inferiorité des organes* suivi de: *Le problème de homosexualité*.

114 ———. Translator of A. Adler, *Sens de la vie*.

115 ———. Le triple rôle de l'enseignement, agent d'instruction, agent d'education, et de fait, agent de prophylaxie mentale. *BSFPA*, 1971, No. 10. Pp. 1-7.

116 ———. The triple role of the teacher. *OSIPNL*, 1971, 12(1), 11.

117 **Schaffzin, B.** A technique for the analysis of affect in early memories. *Psychol. Rep.*, 1965, 17, 933-934 (with R. D. Wynne).

118 **Schairer, J. B.** Ein Traum von 1828 und seine Erfüllung. *IZIP*, 1929, 7(2), 125-129.

119 ———. Das frühreife Kind. *IZIP*, 1932, 10(5), 357-362.

120 ———. Die Individualpsychologie als Wissenschaft von den aktiven Seelenkräften. *IZIP*, 1932, 10(2), 102-110.

121 **Schalit, Alice.** Ein stotterndes Kind. *IZIP*, 1929, 7(2), 95-108.

122 **Schalit, Susanne.** Über Schlafstellungen. *IZIP*, 1925, 3(3), 97-103.

123 **Schaller, R.** Das einzige Kind. *IZIP*, 1929, 7(3), 227-230 (with Maria Rosler).

124 **Scharmer, F.** Review of H. Hanselmann, *Einführung in die Heilpädagogik*. Erlenbach: Rotapfel, 1946. In *IZIP*, 1948, 17(3), 139-140.

125 ———. Review of H. Hanselmann, *Grundlinien zu einer Theorie der Sondererziehung*. Zürich: Rotapfel, n.d. In *IZIP*, 1949, 18(1), 41-42.

126 ———. Die Schulklasse: Eine Arbeits- und Lebensgemeinschaft. *IZIP*, 1928, 6(3), 236-251 (with O. Spiel).

127 **Schatner, M.** Goals, procedures and achievements in clinic psychotherapy. *J. Mt. Sinai Hosp.*, 1951, 18, 221-227 (with Alexandra Adler, S. R. Lehrmann & F. Spiegel).

128 **Schatzman, M.** Paranoia or persecution: The case of Schreber. *Fam. Proc.*, 1971, 10, 177-207.

129 **Schauer, F.** Review of A. Appelt, *Die Entwicklung und praktische Durchführung der heilpädagogischen Beeinflussung sprach gestörter Kinder in den Sonderschulen Deutschlands*. In *IZIP*, 1931, 9(2), 151.

130 ———. Über den Begriff der Verantwortu *IZIP*, 1929, 7(2), 125-129.

131 **Schauer-von Unruh, Lonny.** Review of E. Lesch (Ed.), *Bericht über den fünften Kongress für Heilpädagogik*. München: Rudolf Müller & Steinicke, 1931. In *IZIP*, 1933, 12(5), 404-408.

132 ———. Review of Mathilde Vaertung, *Wahrheit und Irrtum in der Geschlechterpsychologie*. Weimar: Erich Lichtenstein, [   ]. In *IZIP*, 1932, 10(5), 395.

133 **Scheerer, M.** Cognitive theory. In G. Lindzey (Ed.), *Handbook of social psychology*. Cambridge, Mass.: Addison-Wesley, 1954. Pp. 91-142.

134 ———. *Memory and hypnotic age regression: Developmental aspects of cognitive function explored through hypnosis*. New York: Int. Univer. Press, 1959 (with R. Reiff).

135 ———. Spheres of meaning: An analysis of stages of perception to abstract thinking. *JIP*, 1959, 15, 50-61.

136 **Scherke, F.** Die Bedeutung der Gruppe für das Leben im Betrieb. In [   ], *Die Grup im Betrieb*. Dortmund: [   ], 1953.

137 ———. *Die Betriebsatmosphäre. Mensch und Arbeit*, 1950,

138 ———. *Betriebspsychologie, ihre Methode und ihre Technik*. Berlin: , 1948.

139 ———. Konsum-Leitbilder und Leitlinien. *Psychologe*, 1963, 15, 269-280.

140 ———. Leitungssteigerung durch Betriebspsychologie. *Mensch und Arbeit*, 1949,

141 ———. Die Mitarbeiterbeurteilung im Indu triebetrieb. In [   ], *Handbuch der Rationalisierung*. [   ], 1954.

142 ———. Mut und Entmutigung. *Prakt. Psychol.*, 1968, 22, 115-121.

143 ———. Portrait. *IPNL*, 1970, 19(4), 79; 1971 20(6), 110.

44 **Scherke, F.** The problem of pupil charac-
terization. *IJIP*, 1935, 1(4), 113–129.

45 ———. Soziale Betriebsgestaltung. *Nürnberger Abh.*, 1951,

46 ———. Sozialpsychohygiene im Betrieb.
In *Soziale Betriebsgestaltung* (Heidelberg),
1948,

47 ———. Über den Charakter. *Prakt. Psychol.*,
1969, 23(10),

48 ———. Über den Umgang mit Menschen
im Betrieb, ein Betriebsknigge für Be-
triebsführer, Personalchefs und Meister. In
[   ], *Handbuch der Rationalisierung*.
[   ], 1954.

49 ———. Vom Wesen und Umwesen der
Bürokratie in Verwaltung und Betrieb. In
[   ], *Wirtschaft und Gesellung*. Erlangen:
[   ], 1954.

50 ———. Zeitnot im Leben und im Betrib.
Der Psychologe, 1949,

51 ———. Zur Frage der Schülercharakter-
istik. *IZIP*, 1933, 11(4), 301–316.

52 ———. Zur Psychologie der Jugendlichen
von Heute. *Nürnberger Abh.*, 1952–53,

53 **Schick, A.** Betrachtungen über Psychotherapie. *Ars Medici*, 1963,

54 ———. The cultural background of Adler's
and Freud's work. *Amer. J. Psychother.*,
1964, 18, 7–24.

55 ———. Etiologic aspects of psychiatric
disorders and their implications for therapy.
Amer. J. Psychother., 1962, 16, 235–250.

56 ———. The Vienna Medical School:
Glimpses of the past. *Pirquet Bull. clin.
Med.*, 1967, No. 2–3.

57 **Schiffman, H. M.** Early recollections as
predictors of the Tompkins-Horn Picture
Arrangement Test performance. *JIP*, 1961,
17, 177–180 (with R. E. McCarter & S. S.
Tompkins).

58 ———. Early recollections of schizophrenic
and depressed patients. *JIP*, 1962, 18, 57–
61 (with J. Friedman).

59 **Schilder, P.** *Goals and desires of man*. New
York: Columbia Univ. Press, 1942.

160 **Schirrmeister, M.** *Das verwöhnte Kind*.
Dresden: Verlag am andern Ufer, 1926.

161 **Schlamm, Melka.** Über Einführung in die
Geschlechtsrolle bei Schulekinderen. *IZIP*,
1925, 3(4), 195–199 (with Elli Rotwein).

162 **Schlesinger, E.** Ermutigung und Ermuting-
ungsanstalten. *IZIP*, 1927, 6(2), 81–85.

163 ———. A fighter for youth [Ida Loewy].
IPN, 1941, 1(8–9), 10–11.

164 **Schlesinger, E.** Der Gaunervater: In memory of my friend Hugo Sperber. *IPN*,
1941, 1(8–9), 14–16.

165 ———. Hat der Verbrecher Gemeinschaftsgefühl? *IZIP*, 1931, 9(5), 345–350.

166 **Schletter, E.** Concerning a case of suicide.
IJIP, 1936, 2(2), 54–61.

167 ———. A contribution to the psychology
of suicide. *IPB*, 1946, 5, 119–123.

168 ———. Psychotherapy with mental patients and counseling with their relatives.
JIP, 1957, 13, 56–67.

169 ———. Review of C. Midelfort, *The
family in psychotherapy*. In *JIP*, 1958,
14, 93–94.

170 ———. Some techniques used in psychotherapy with mental patients. *AJIP*, 1956,
12, 25–45.

171 ———. The treatment of a juvenile de-
linquent. In K. A. Adler & Danica Deutsch
(Eds.), *Essays in Individual Psychology*.
Pp. 412–423.

172 ———. Zur Psychologie des Selbstmordes.
IZIP, 1929, 7(1), 7–14.

173 **Schmeidler, Gertrude R.** Factors interacting
with birth order in self-selection among
volunteer subjects. *J. soc. Psychol.*, 1967,
72, 125–128 (with Barbara S. Dohrenwend,
S. Feldstein, & Joyce Plosky).

174 **Schmid, A.** Zum Verständnis von Schillers
Frauengestalten. *ZIP*, 1914, 1(3), 72–80.

175 **Schmideberg, Melita.** Infant memories and
constructions. *Psychoanal. Quart.*, 1950,
19, 468–481.

176 **Schmidt, E.** Formen der Solidarität. *IZIP*,
1930, 8(1), 194–200.

177 ———. Individualpsychologie und Strafvollzug. *IZIP*, 1926, 4(3), 109–115.

178 ———. Individualpsychologische Bemerkungen zur Politik. *IZIP*, 1925, 3(5), 252–
256.

179 ———. Neurose, Verbrechtum und Hoch-
staplertum. *IZIP*, 1933, 11(4), 283–295.

180 ———. Review of R. Heindl, *Der Berufs-
verbrecher*. Charlottenberg: Rolf Heise,
1926. In *IZIP*, 1927, 5(5), 394–395.

181 ———. Review of [   ] Helbing-Bauer,
Die Tortur. Berlin: P. Langenscheit, [   ].
In *IZIP*, 1930, 8(6), 596.

182 ———. *Das Verbrechen als Ausdrucksform
sozialer Entmutigung*. München: J. Schweitzer, 1931.

183 ———. Verbrecher und Strafe. In E. Wexberg
(Ed.), *Handbuch der Individualpsychologie*.

184 **Schmidt, E.** Vorgeschichte eines Attentes. *IZIP*, 1939, 9(5), 358-367.

185 ———. Zur deutschen Strafrechts- und Strafvollzugsreform. *IZIP*, 1928, 6(2), 86-95.

186 **Schmidt, Linda L. M.** Idiodynamic associated set and cognitive styles. *Diss. Abstr.*, 1965, 26, 1163-1164. Unpubl. Ph.D. Diss., Univ. Texas, 1965.

187 **Schmidt, Margarete.** Kinderträume. *IZIP*, 1929, 7(6), 471-472.

188 **Schmidt, R.** Alfred Adler, an invitation to socialism? *Schule und Psychol.* (Munich), Dec., 1970.

189 ———. Alfred Adler, eine Herausforderung zum Sozialismus? *Schule und Psychol.* (München), Dec., 1970.

190 **Schmidt-Beil, Ada.** See Beil, Ada.

191 **Schmuck, R.** Sex of sibling, birth order position, and female dispositions to conform in two-child families. *Child Developm.*, 1963, 34, 913-918.

192 **Schneider, B. H.** Personal values, visual recognition, and recall. *Psychol. Rev.*, 1951, 58, 271-284 (with L. Postman).

193 **Schneider, J.** Aufsatz eines kriminellen Jugendlichen. *IZIP*, 1932, 10(6), 431-433.

194 **Schneider, J. M.** College students belief in personal control, 1966-1970. *JIP*, 1971, 27(2), 188.

195 **Schneiderman, L.** Individualism and the problem of guilt. *Psychoanal. Rev.*, 1969, 56, 313-326.

196 **Schneidman, E.** (Ed.). *The cry for help.* New York: McGraw-Hill, 1961 (with N. L. Farberow).

197 **Schonbar, Rosalea A.** Differential dream recall frequency as a component of "life style". *J. consult. Psychol.*, 1965, 29, 468-474.

198 **Schoo, J.** Der Degenschlucker. *IZIP*, 1926, 4(2), 76-77.

199 ———. Ein Mädchen das mit den Augen zwinkerte. *IZIP*, 1925, 3(6), 320-322.

200 **Schooler, C.** Birth order and hospitalization for schizophrenia. *J. abnorm. soc. Psychol.*, 1964, 69, 574-579.

201 ———. Birth order and schizophrenia. *Arch. gen. Psychiat.*, 1961, 4, 91-97.

202 ———. Birth order effects: Not here, not now! *Psychol. Bull.*, 1972, 78(3), 161-175.

203 **Schooler, E.** Birth order and preference between visual and tactual

204 **Schpoont, S. N.** Perceived parent attitude as determinants of ego structure. *Child Developm.*, 1955, 25, 173-183 (with D. F Ausubel, E. E. Balthazar, I. Rosenthal, L. S. Blackman, & J. Welkowitz).

205 **Schrecker, P.** Henri Bergsons Philosophie der Persönlichkeit. *Schr. Verein freie psychoanal. Forsch.*, 1912, No. 3. Münch E. Reinhardt, 1912.

206 ———. Die individualpsychologische Bedeutung der ersten Kindheitserinnerungen. *Zbl. psychoanal. Psychother.*, 1913-14, 4, 121-130.

207 **Schröder, K.** Evangelischer Christ und Individualpsychologie. *IZIP*, 1934, 12(1), 3: 33.

208 **Schubert, F.** Tiefenpsychologie in Dienst am Kinde. *Geesthachter Zeitung*, 1952, (with Elizabeth Sorge-Boehmke).

209 **Schulhof, Hedwig.** *Ein Buch vom Leben und Gelebtwerden.* Reichenberg: Erich Spiethoff, 1932.

210 ———. Erinnerungen an Alfred Adler. *IZIP*, 1937, 15(3-4), 168-171.

211 ———. *Das Glück als Aufgabe.* Reichenberg: E. Spiethoff,

212 ———. Goethes Weg vom Ich zum Wir. *IZIP*, 1937, 12(3), 184-193.

213 ———. *Henrik Ibsen: Der Mensch und sein Werk im Lichte der Individualpsychologie.* Reichenberg: Erich Spiethoff, 1923.

214 ———. Individualpsychologie und Frauenfrage. München: E. Reinhardt, 1914.

215 ———. Die Lebenfragen der Frau. *IZIP*, 1930, 8(1), 165-170.

216 ———. Der liebe Niemand. In A. Adler & C. Furtmüller (Eds.), *Heilen und Bilden* (1928). Pp. 345-354.

217 ———. Life problems of "woman". *IJIP*, 1937, 3(1), 48-53.

218 ———. Review of E. Schönebeck, *Strindberg als Erzieher.* Leipzig: Oldenburg, [In *IZIP*, 1924, 2(4), 32-33.

219 ———. Ricarda Huch. *ZIP*, 1914, 1(4-5), 130-136.

220 ———. Romantik und Individualpsychologie. *IZIP*, 1929, 7(6), 443-446.

221 ———. "Schwachsinn" als Waffe. *IZIP*, 1929, 7(5), 394-395.

222 ———. Self-review of *Individualpsychologi und Frauenfrage.* In *ZIP*, 1913, 1(1), 60.

receptors. *Percep. mot. Skills*, 1966, 22, 74.

223 **Schulhof, Hedwig.** Zur Psychologie Strindbergs. *IZIP*, 1923, 2(2), 20-25.

224 **Schulman, J. L.** Effect of mother-child separation and birth order on young children's responses to two potentially stressful experiences. *J. Pers. soc. Psychol.*, 1967, 5, 162-174 (with D. T. Vernon & Jeanne M. Foley).

225 **Schultz, D. P.** Birth order of volunteers for sensory restriction research. *J. soc. Psychol.*, 1967, 73, 71-73.

226 **Schultz, J. H.** (Ed.). *Handbuch der Neurosenlehre und Psychotherapie.* München: Urban & Schwarzenberg, 1958 (with V. E. Frankl & V. E. Gebsattel).

227 **Schultz, U.** Alfred Adler und die verdrängte Individualpsychologie [Review of M. Sperber, Alfred Adler oder das Elend der Psychologie]. *Christ und Welt* (Hamburg), July 10, 1970.

228 ———. Oedipus without complexes: Alfred Adler and the repressed Individual Psychology. *Christ und Welt* (Hamburg), July 10, 1970.

229 **Schussell, N. R.** Creativity, birth order and preference for symmetry. *J. consult. clin. Psychol.*, 1970, 34, 275-280 (with R. Eisenman).

230 **Schuster, W.** Die naturliche Entfaltung der Intelligenz. *IZIP*, 1937, 15(2), 52-65.

231 ———. Pädagogische Kontakttypen. *IZIP*, 1935, 13(4), 221-245.

232 ———. Schüleraufsätze als Material für die Schülercharakterkunde. *IZIP*, 1934, 12(4), 233-257.

233 **Schutz, A.** *The phenomenology of the social world.* Evanston, Ill.: Northwestern Univ. Press, 1967.

234 **Schutz, H. J.** (Ed.). *Kontexte.* Stuttgart: Krauz Verlag, 1969.

235 **Schuurman, J. C.** De huidige krisis in het waardebesef. *MNWIP*, 1971, 20(3).

236 **Schwabach, E.** Psychoanalyse und Individualpsychologie. *IZIP*, 1927, 5(5), 349-351.

237 ———. Simulation oder Neurose? *IZIP*, 1929, 7(6), 401-403.

238 **Schwartz, I.** A team approach: Pre-disposition report: An innovative delivery perspective. Minneapolis, Minn., Hennepin County Court Services, June 1972 (with W. L. Pew & J. Stoeckel).

239 **Schwarz, O.** Liebe, Sexualität und Gesellschaft. *IZIP*, 1924, 2(6), 27-31.

240 **Schwarz, O.** (Ed.). *Psychogenese und Psychotherapie körperliche Symptome.* Wien: Springer, 1925.

241 ———. Review of S. Alrutz, Gist Es eine rein nervöse Fernwerkung. *Psychiat. Neurol. Wchnschr.* 1923, Nos. 11-12. In *IZIP*, 1923, 2(1), 44.

242 ———. Self review of Die Sinnfindung als Kategorie des Ärztlichen Denkers. In *IZIP*, 1923, 2(1), 44-45.

243 ———. *Sexualität und Persönlichkeit.* : Weidmann, 1934.

244 ———. Sexualpathologie. *IZIP*, 1924, 2(3), 50-53.

245 ———. Die Sinnfindung als Kategorie des Ärztlichen Denkers. *Klin. Wchnschr.*, 1923, No. 24.

246 **Schwendiman, G.** Birth order, aggression training and authoritarianism. *Psychol. Rec.*, 1970, 20, 69-71 (with K. S. Larsen and C. Parks).

247 **Seagull, A. A.** Le nom c'est tout: The psychopathology of everyday life—a bird's eye view of the influence of names on choice of research topic or vocation. *Voices*, 1967, 3(3), 100-102.

248 ———. Two cases illustrating different approaches to the treatment of a suicide threat. *Psychother.*, 1967, 4, 41-43.

249 **Sears, R. R.** Experimental studies of projection. I. Attribution of traits. *J. soc. Psychol.*, 1936, 7, 151-163.

250 ———. et al. *Patterns of child rearing.* Evanston, Ill.: Row, Peterson, 1957.

251 **Sechrest, L.** Early recollections in four neurotic diagnostic categories. *JIP*, 1962, 18, 52-56 (with Marilyn Howard).

252 ———. Personal constructs and personal characteristics. *JIP*, 1968, 24, 162-166.

253 ———. Stimulus equivalents of the psychotherapist. *JIP*, 1962, 18, 172-176.

254 **Secter, I.** Personality factors of the MMPI and hypnotizability. *Amer. J. clin. Hypnosis*, 1961, 3, 185-188.

255 **Seegen, Marie.** Schülerselbstmord. *IZIP*, 1933, 11(2), 152-153.

256 **Seeger, S.** Review of P. Rom, *Alfred Adler und die wissenschaftliche Menschenkenntnis.* In *JIP*, 1967, 23, 119-120.

257 **Seelbach, H.** Verstehende Psycholgie und Individualpsychologie: Ein Vergleich der psychologischen Richtungen von Dilthey, Jaspers und Spranger mit der

Individualpsychologie Alfred Adlers. *IZIP*, 1932, 10(4), 262–288; 1932, 10(5), 368–391; 1932, 10(6), 452–472.

258 **Seelhammer, N.** *Die Individualpsychologie Alfred Adlers, dargestellt und kritisch untersucht vom Standpunkte der katholischen Moraltheologie.* Düsseldorf: L. Schwann, 1934.

259 **Seelman, K.** A case of seeming feeble-mindedness and its treatment in the elementary school. *IJIP*, 1935, 1(3), 100–108.

260 ———. Co-editor of L. Seif, *Wege der Erziehungshilfe.* 2nd ed.

261 ———. *Kind, Sexualität und Erziehung.* München-Basel: Reinhardt, 1955, 1968.

262 ———. *Das jüngste und älteste Kind.* Dresden: Verlag am andern Ufer, 1926.

263 ———. Ein Beitrag zur Erziehung nervöser Kinder in der Schule. *IZIP*, 1924, 2(5), 8–13.

264 ———. Ein Fall von Schwachsinn und seine Behandlung in der Normalschule. *IZIP*, 1931, 9(3), 192–199.

265 ———. Limniat hithavut kshay-chinuch bakitot-hayesod. [The prevention of educational problems in the primary grades.] In Anon., *Kovets Individual-Psykhologie.* Pp. 50–64.

266 ———. Das nervöse und schwererziehbare Kind. In E. Wexberg (Ed.), *Handbuch der Individualpsychologie.* Pp. 169–208.

267 ———. Portrait. *IPNL*, 1972, 21(6), 109.

268 ———. School education for becoming a fellowman: Teachers and pupils in the contact circle of school reality. *Pädagog. Heute*, 1969, 3–4.

269 ———. Schulkinderpsychologie. *IZIP*, 1925, 3(4), 146–194 (with A. Simon).

270 ———. Die Seele des Kindes und des Jünglings in der Weltliteratur. *IZIP*, 1926, 4(2), 86–88.

271 ———. Verhütung von Schwererziehbarkeit in der Volkschule. *IZIP*, 1927, 5(3), 169–190.

272 ———. *Wie soll ich mein Kind aufklären?* München: Ernst Reinhardt, 1965.

273 ———. *Woher kommen die kleiner Buben und Mädchen?* München: Ernst Reinhardt, 1970.

274 ———. *Zwischen 15 und 19: Information über sexuelle und andere Fragen des Erwachsenwerdens.* München: Reinhardt, 1971.

275 **Seeman, M.** Alienation and learning in a hospital setting. *Amer. sociol. Rev.*, 1962, 27, 772–782 (with J. W. Evans).

276 **Seeman, M.** Alienation and social learning in a reformatory. *Amer. J. Sociol.*, 1963, 69, 270–28

277 ———. On the meaning of alienation. *Amer. sociol. Rev.*, 1959, 24, 783–791.

278 **Seeman, W.** *Actuarial description of abnormal personality.* Baltimore: Williams & Wilkins, 1963 (with P. A. Marks).

279 **Segal, Alzire.** The prediction of expressed attitudes toward the mother. Ph.D. Diss., Univ. Michigan, 1954.

280 **Seidler, Regine.** Alfred Adler als Erziehungsberater. *IZIP*, 1937, 15(3–4), 159–162.

281 ———. Children's dreams. *IJIP*, 1936, 2(2), 11–21.

282 ———. Die Entwicklung der individualpsychologischen Erziehungsberatungsstellen in Wien. *IZIP*, 1946, 5, 79–83.

283 ———. Die Erfassung der Schülerpersönlichkeit. *IZIP*, 1930, 8(5), 522–529.

284 ———. Escape into delinquency: The case of Robert E. *IPB*, 1946, 5, 79–83.

285 ———. Ferdinand Birnbaum's contribution to Individual Psychology. *IPB*, 1948, 6, 162–163.

286 ———. Hattie the marionette. *IPB*, 1946, 5, 99–105.

287 ———. Die individualpsychologischen Erziehungsberatungsstellen im Wien. *IZIP*, 1929, 7(3), 161–170 (with L. Zilahi).

288 ———. The Individual Psychologist looks at testing. *IP*, 1967, 5(1), 3–6.

289 ———. Individual Psychology in activity group therapy. *IP*, 1966, 4(1), 1–4.

290 ———. Kinderträume. *IZIP*, 1933, 12(6), 450–459.

291 ———. The phenomenon of overcompensation. *IPB*, 1948, 6, 185–194.

292 ———. Portrait. *IPNL*, 1967, 17(9–10, Whole No. 194–195). P. 69.

293 ———. Review of Sophie Freudenberg, *Erziehungs—und heilpädagogische Beratungsstellen.* In *IZIP*, 1929, 7(1), 151.

294 ———. Review of H. Horrix, *Begriffsbildung und Gedankenausdruck in der Hilfsschule.* Halle: Carl Marhold, 1925. In *IZIP*, 1928, 6(4), 346.

295 ———. Review of Margaret E. Mathias, *The beginnings of art in the public schools.* In *IZIP*, 1931, 9(3), 255–256.

296 ———. Rivalität der Geschwister. *IZIP*, 1929, 7(3), 225–226.

297 ———. Rivalry among children of the same family. In A. Adler & assoc., *Guiding the child.* Pp. 183–192.

298 **Seidler, Regine.** School compositions help disclose life-style. *IJIP*, 1937, 3(3), 233–242.

299 ———. School guidance clinics in Vienna. *IJIP*, 1936, 2(4), 75–78.

300 ———. Die Schule als Erlebnis. *IZIP*, 1935, 3(3), 167–176.

301 ———. Die Schüleraufsatz als Ausdruck der kindlichen Persönlichkeit. *IZIP*, 1932, 10(4), 304–311.

302 ———. Understanding the pupil's personality. *IJIP*, 1935, 1(3), 71–78.

303 ———. The Vienna child guidance clinics (with L. Zilahi). In A. Adler & assoc., *Guiding the child*. Pp. 9–27.

304 **Seidman, P.** *Der Weg der Tiefenpsychologie.* Zürich: Rascher, 1959.

305 **Seif, L.** (Ed.). *Alfred Adler zum 60 Geburtstage gewidmet von seinen Schülern und Mitarbeitern der Individualpsychologie.* Leipzig: S. Hirzel, 1930 (with L. Zilahi).

306 ———. Autorität und Erziehung. In A. Adler, C. Furtmüller & E. Wexberg (Eds.), *Heilen und Bilden* (1928). Pp. 168–174.

307 ———. *Courage in life.*

308 ———. Ein Fall von Essphobie. *IZIP*, 1925, 3(2), 50–56.

309 ———. Erziehung der Erzieher. In Sofie Lazarsfeld (Ed.), *Technik der Erziehung.*

310 ———. Erziehungsberatung und Schule. *IZIP*, 1925, 3(4), 199–201.

311 ———. Individualpsychologie und Weltanschauung. *IZIP*, 1925, 3(3), 132.

312 ———. Individual Psychology and the child (I). *IPMP*, 1933, No. 7 (with Doris Rayner & A. Zilahi).

313 ———. Individual Psychology and life-philosophy. *IPMP*, 1934, No. IIa.

314 ———. (Ed.). *Individuum und Gemeinschaft.* Munich: Bergmann, 1926–27 (with A. Adler & O. Kaus). Includes J. Neumann, *Die Gefühle und das Ich*, 1926; A. Neuer, *Mut und Entmutigung: Die Prinzipien der Psychologie Alfred Adlers*, 1926; O. Kaus, *Die Traume in Dostojewskis "Raskolnikoff"*, 1926; Elisabeth Bellott, *Individualpsychologie und Schule*, 1926; Sofie Lazarsfeld, *Die Ehe von Heute und Morgen*, 1927; F. Wilken, *Die nervöse Erkrankung als sinnvolle Erscheinung unseres gegenwärtigen Kulturzeit-traumes: Eine Untersuchung über Sozialelebens*, 1927.

315 ———. *Das Musterkind.* Dresden: Verlag am andern Ufer, 1926.

316 **Seif, L.** Neurose und Willenschwäche. *IZIP*, 1933, 11(3), 201–207.

317 ———. Neurosis and weakness of will. *IJIP*, 1935, 1(3), 79–85.

318 ———. Portrait. *IPNL*, 1972, 21(6), 109.

319 ———. Psychology and education. *IPMP*, 1933, No. 7. Pp. 7–

320 ———. Review of A. Adler, *Studie über Minderwertigkeit von Organen.* In *IZIP*, 1927, 5(2), 154.

321 ———. Review of A. Appelt, *Die wirkliche Ursache des Stotterns und seine dauernde Heilung.* In *IZIP*, 1926, 4(6), 397.

322 ———. Review of R. M. Holzapfel, *Panideal.* Jena: Diederichs, 1923. In *IZIP*, 1926, 4(2), 104–105.

323 ———. Review of F. Künkel, *Psychotherapie und Seelsorge* & J. Neumann, *Psychiatrische Seelsorge im Lichte der Individualpsychologie.* In *IZIP*, 1926, 4(6), 396.

324 ———. Review of K. E. Rankes, *Die Kategorien des Liebendigen.* München: C. H. Beck, 1928. In *IZIP*, 1929, 7(1), 71–72.

325 ———. Review of O. Rühle, *Die Seele des proletarischen Kindes.* In *IZIP*, 1925, 3(5), 265.

326 ———. Review of I. L. Schmidt, *Das hohe Lied vom Atem.* Augsburg: Dom-Verlag, [   ]. In *IZIP*, 1929, 7(1), 72–73.

327 ———. Review of E. Wexberg, *Individualpsychologie.* In *IZIP*, 1928, 6(6), 503–504.

328 ———. *Selbsterziehung des Charakters: Alfred Adler zum 60 Geburtstag.* Leipzig: S. Hirzel, 1930 (with L. Zilahi).

329 ———. Selbstständigkeit und Gemeinschaft. *IZIP*, 1926, 4(6), 321–326.

330 ———. Self-knowledge and self-education. *IJIP*, 1936, 2(4), 23–31.

331 ———. Tendenz zur Konfliktlosigkeit. *IZIP*, 1923, 2(1),

332 ———. Über den Zwang im Leben und in der Neurose. *IZIP*, 1923, 2(2), 9–15.

333 ———. Über Eigenliebe und Eitelkeit. In A. Adler & C. Furtmüller (Eds.), *Heilen und Bilden* (1928). Pp. 249–254.

334 ———. Über Individualpsychologie und Erziehung. *Hamburger Lehrerzeitung*, August, 1922.

335 ———. Über Massenerziehung. *IZIP*, 1925, 3(5), 247–250.

336 ———. *Wege die Erziehungshilfe.* Munich: Lehmann, 1940, 1952.

337 ———. Wesen und Ursachen der Narkotomanie. *IZIP*, 1927, 5(1), 1–11.

338 Seif, L. Die Zwangsneurose. In E. Wexberg (Ed.), *Handbuch der Individualpsychologie.* Pp. 507–531.

339 ———. Zum Problem der Psychosen. *IZIP,* 1928, 6(4), 273–279.

340 ———. Zum Problem der Selbsterkenntnis und Selbsterziehung. *IZIP,* 1930, 8(1), 1–8.

341 ———. Zur Problematik der Psycho- und Somatotherapie der Neurosen. *IZIP,* 1931, 9(2), 106–107.

342 ———. Zur Synergie der Gegensätze. *IZIP,* 1931, 9(4), 269–274.

343 Seif, Trudi. Translator of F. G. Crookshank, *Individualpsychologie und allgemeine Medizin.*

344 Seiler, Elisabeth. Review of F. Dell, *Love in the machine age.* New York: Farrar & Rinehart, 1930. In *IZIP,* 1932, 10(3), 238–240.

345 ———. Review of E. K. Wickmann, *Verhalten der Kinder und Haltung der Lehrer.* New York: Commonwealth Fund, 1928. In *IZIP,* 1933, 9(3), 256.

346 Seitz, S. Birth-order and ruralism as potential determinants of attendant tenure. *Amer. J. ment. Defic.,* 1967, 72, 428–434 (with C. C. Cleland & W. E. Patton).

347 Selesnick, S. Alfred Adler: The psychology of the inferiority complex. In F. Alexander, S. Einstein and M. Grotjahn (Eds.), *Psychoanalytic pioneers: A history of psychoanalysis as seen through the lives and works of its most eminent teachers.* Pp. 78–86.

348 ———. *The history of psychiatry: An evaluation of psychiatric thought and practice from prehistoric times to the present.* New York: Harper & Row, 1965. New York: Mentor, 1966. Paper (with F. G. Alexander).

349 Sells, S. B. Peer acceptance-rejection and birth order. *Psychol. Schools,* 1964, 1, 156–162 (with M. Roff).

350 Sen, I. The urge for wholeness. *Indian J. Psychol.,* 1946, 21, 1–32.

351 Senior, C. Adler's reach beyond psychology. *IP,* 1967, 4(2), 47–48.

352 Senn, M. J. E. *The firstborn.* Cambridge, Mass.: Harvard Univ. Press, 1968 (with Claire Hartford).

353 Servin, C. Juvenile delinquency—A psychological challenge. *IPB,* 1943, 3(1), 6–13.

354 Severson, W. The separation capacity of the Rorschach. *J. consult. Psychol.,* 1955, 19, 194–196 (with T. Tunney, H. Vehling & R. J. Corsini).

355 Sewall, M. Some causes of jealousy in young children. *Smith Coll. Stud. soc. Work,* 1930, 1, 6–22.

356 Sewell, W. H. The effects of feeding, weaning and scheduling procedures on childhood adjustment and the formation of oral symptoms. *Child Developm.,* 1952, 23, 185–191 (with P. H. Mussen).

357 ———. Infant training and the personality of the child. *Amer. J. Sociol.,* 1952, 63, 150–159.

358 Shafer, V. W. A construct validation of Adler's social interest. *Diss. Abstr.,* 1959, 19, 3374–3375. Unpubl. Ph.D. Diss., Ohio St. Univ., 1958.

359 Shapiro, Ariella. Cooperative and competitive behavior of Kibbutz and urban children in Israel. *Child Developm.,* 1969, 40, 609–617 (with M. C. Madsen).

360 ———. Cooperative and competitive behavior of urban Afro-American, Anglo-American and Mexican village children. *Developm. Psychol.,* 1970, 3, 16–20 (with M. C. Madsen).

361 Shapiro, D. *Neurotic styles.* New York: Basic Books, 1965.

362 Sharadamba-Rao, M. Sibling position and mental disorders. *Psychiat. Quart. Suppl.,* 1965, 39(1), 27–47.

363 Sharan, S. Birth order and level of task performance: A cross-cultural comparison. *J. soc. Psychol.,* 1969, 78, 157–163 (with Y. Amir & Y. Kovarsky).

364 Sharp, Florence A. The child impostor: Pseudomental retardation. *Brit. J. Disord. Commun.,* 1966, 1, 91–98.

365 ———. Review of Marguerite & W. Beecher, *Parents on the run.* In *JIP,* 1967, 23, 121–122.

366 Shaver, P. Birth order of medical students and the occupational ambitions of their parents. *Int. J. Psychol.,* 1970, 5, 197–207 (with J. R. French & S. Cobb).

367 Shaw, F. J. Laughter, paradigm of growth. *JIP,* 1960, 16, 151–157.

368 ———. The problem of acting and the problem of becoming. *J. humanis. Psychol.,* 1961, 1, 64–69.

369 Shaw, M. E. *Role-playing in business and industry.* New York: Free Press of Glencoe, 1961 (with R. J. Corsini & R. R. Blake).

370 Shedd, C. L. The effects of ego-involvement on learning. *Proc. Okla. Acad. Sci.,* 1952, 33, 285–288 (with H. R. Angelino).

371 Sheehan, Mary R. *Contemporary schools of psychology.* New York: Ronald Press, 1969 (with R. S. Woodworth).

372 Sheerer, Elizabeth T. An analysis of the relationship between acceptance of and respect for self and acceptance of and respect for others. *J. consult. Psychol.,* 1949, 13, 169–175.

373 Shefrin, E. Does advice suffice? *Educ.,* 1959, 79(6). Also in *Child Fam. Dig.,* Mar.–Apr., 1959 (with Beatrice Lieben).

374 Sheppard, Edith. On earliest memories. *Psychoanal. Quart.,* 1956, 25, 228–237 (with L. J. Saul & T. Snyder).

375 Sherif, M. Level of aspiration as a case of judgmental activity in which ego-involvements operate as factors. *Sociom.,* 1951, 14, 141–147 (with O. J. Harvey).

376 Sherman, S. E. Empathy, attraction and birth order. *Diss. Abstr. Int.,* 1971, 32 (5B), 2989–2990.

377 Sherrick, C. E. Review of R. H. Forgus, *Perception: The basic process in cognitive development.* In *Contemp. Psychol.,* 1967, 12, 116–117.

378 Sherriffs, A. C. Sex differences in attitudes about sex differences. *J. Psychol.,* 1953, 35, 161–168 (with R. F. Jarrett).

379 Sherwin, R. V. Transsexualism and transvestitism: A symposium. *Amer. J. Psychother.,* 1954, 8, 219–230 (with H. Benjamin & E. A. Gutheil).

380 Shipley, T. (Ed.). *Classics in psychology.* New York: Phil. Libr., 1961.

381 Shiverick, D. Lee Harvey Oswald: An Adlerian interpretation. *JIP,* 1967, 23, 24–36 (with H. L. Ansbacher, Rowena R. Ansbacher, & Kathleen Shiverick). Also in *Psychoanal. Rev.,* 1966, 53(3), 55–66. Condensed in *OSIPNL,* 1967, 8(3), 9–11.

382 Shiverick, Kathleen. Lee Harvey Oswald: An Adlerian interpretation. *JIP,* 1967, 23, 24–36 (with H. L. Ansbacher, Rowena R. Ansbacher, & D. Shiverick). Also in *Psychoanal. Rev.,* 1966, 53(3), 55–66. Condensed in *OSIPNL,* 1967, 8(3), 9–11.

383 Shlien, J. M. A comparison of client-centered and Adlerian therapy. *Couns. Ctr. Discussion Papers,* 1960, 6, No. 8 (with H. H. Mosak & R. Dreikurs).

384 ———. Comparison of results with different forms of psychotherapy. *Amer. J. Psychother.,* 1964, 18 (Suppl. I), 15–22, 63–66.

385 Shlien, J. M. Effect of time limits: A comparison of client-centered and Adlerian psychotherapy (abstract). *Amer. Psychologist,* 1960, 15, 415 (with H. H. Mosak & R. Dreikurs).

386 ———. Effect of time limits: A comparison of two psychotherapies. *J. couns. Psychol.,* 1962, 9, 31–34 (with H. H. Mosak & R. Dreikurs).

387 Shoben, E. J. Jr. Love, loneliness and logic. *JIP,* 1960, 16, 11–24.

388 ———. Review of I. D. Suttie, *The origins of love and hate.* Hammondsworth, Middlesex: Penguin Books, 1960. In *JIP,* 1960, 16, 210–211.

389 ———. Toward a concept of normal personality. *Amer. Psychologist,* 1957, 12, 183–189.

390 Shontz, F. C. An assessment of sensory style. *Percep. mot. Skills,* 1964, 18, 841–848 (with B. Mackler).

391 ———. Life style and creativity: An empirical investigation. *Percep. mot. Skills,* 1965, 20, 873–896 (with B. Mackler).

392 Shoobs, N. E. Adler's sense of personal commitment. *IP,* 1967, 4(2), 48.

393 ———. Alfred Adler's sense of humor. *IP,* 1968, 5(2), 60–61.

394 ———. The application of Individual Psychology through psychodramatics. *IPB,* 1946, 5(1), 3–21.

395 ———. A case of pretended stupidity. *Nerv. Child,* 1948, 7(4), 421–424.

396 ———. *Corrective treatment for unadjusted children.* New York: Harper, 1942 (with G. Goldberg).

397 ———. The curriculum as a means of personality adjustment. *IPB,* 1951, 9, 70–85.

398 ———. The formative years of Adlerian psychology in the United States—1937–1943. *IP,* 1967, 4(2), 49–51; New York: Author, n.d. Mimeo; *OSIPNL,* 1964, 4(5), 11–13.

399 ———. Frederic Feichtinger (1900–1970). *JIP,* 1971, 27(1), 125.

400 ———. The future progress of Individual Psychology. *IPB,* 1942, 2(3), 57.

401 ———. Group methods of non-interpretive guidance of school children. *IP,* 1966, 4(1), 9–14.

402 ———. Guiding the adolescent boy. *Nerv. Child,* 1945, 4, 159–166 (with G. Goldberg). Also in *Child Fam. Dig.,* Jan. 1951,

14-24. Also in *Urim* (Israel), 1955.

403 Shoobs, N. E. Idea exchange column. *IP*, 1965, 3(1), 22-23; 1966, 3(2), 16-17.

404 ———. In memorium [F. Feichtinger]. *IPNL*, 1970, 20(2), 23.

405 ———. Individual Psychology and psychodrama. *AJIP*, 1956, 12, 46-52. Also in K. A. Adler & Danica Deutsch (Eds.), *Essays in Individual Psychology*. Pp. 280-289.

406 ——— (Ed.). *International book list for Individual Psychology. Section 1. English language titles*. New York: Amer. Soc. Adlerian Psychol., 1961. Mimeo.

407 ———. New York City institutions. *IP*, 1968, 5, 62-63.

408 ———. Our duty. *IPB*, 1947, 6, 88.

409 ———. Our impressions of Adlerians we met in Europe. *IPNL*, 1954, No. 36-37. Pp. 1-2.

410 ———. Psychodrama in the classroom. *Sociom.*, 1944, 7(2), 152-169.

411 ———. The psychodramatic approach to classroom problems. *Sociom.*, 1943, 6(3), 264-265.

412 ———. Review of Marguerite & W. Beecher, *The mark of Cain*. In *IP*, 1970, 8(1), 26.

413 ———. Review of W. Beecher & Marguerite Beecher, *Beyond success and failure: Ways to self reliance and maturity*. In *IP*, 1967, 4(2), 71.

414 ———. Review of C. Brown, *Manchild in the promised land: An autobiography*. In *IP*, 1965, 3(1), 25-26.

415 ———. Role-playing in the individual psychotherapy interview. *JIP*, 1964, 20(1), 84-89.

416 ———. 70 years young [about R. Dreikurs]. *IP*, 1967, 5(1), 1.

417 ———. Sociometry in the classroom. *Sociom.*, 1945, 8(1), 87-88; 1946, (2-3), 145-146; 1947, 10(2), 155-164; *Urim* (Israel), 1956.

418 ———. Three therapeutic approaches—One patient. *IP*, 1966, 3(2), 1-10 (with J. Sacks & A. Roland).

419 ———. We all need security. *Self*, 1946, 1(9), 19-23.

420 Shorkey, C. Power motivation in male paranoid children. *Psychiat.*, 1969, 32, 459-466 (with H. M. Wolowitz).

421 Shortell, J. R. Physical aggression in children as a function of sex of

subject and sex of opponent. *Diss. Abstr. Int.*, 1970, 30, (11-B), 5229.

422 Shrader, W. K. Birth order of children and parental report of problems. *Child Developm.*, 1968, 39, 1164-1175 (with T. Leventhal).

423 Shulman, B. H. An Adlerian approach to counseling. *Proc. Christian Psychol. Assn. 17th Ann. Meeting.* Pp. 27-36.

424 ———. The Adlerian theory of dreams. Discussion by K. Adler. In M. Kramer *et al.* (Eds.), *Dream psychology and the new biology of dreaming*. Pp. 117-137.

425 ———. An Adlerian view of the Schreber case. *JIP*, 1959, 15, 180-192.

426 ———. Adler's place in psychology [A review]. In *IPB*, 1951, 9, 31-35.

427 ———. Army medicine in Chicago. *Chi. Med. Sch. Quart.*, 1943, 4(3), 20-22.

428 ———. Art therapy with psychiatric patients. *Perspec. psychiat. Care*, 1969, 7(3), 142-143 (with Sadie G. Dreikurs).

429 ———. A comparison of Allport's and the Adlerian concepts. *IP*, 1965, 3(1), 14-21.

430 ———. Confrontation techniques. *JIP*, 1972, 28(2), 177-183.

431 ———. Confrontation techniques in Adlerian psychotherapy. *JIP*, 1971, 27(2), 167-175.

432 ———. The contributions of a psychiatric nurse on a medical service. *Perspec. psychiat. Care*, 1966, 4(2), 22-37 (with D. Corrigan, Jean Hudnut & Zoe Pfouts).

433 ———. Dermatomyositis. *Ill. med. J.*, Feb., 1950 (with D. Cohen).

434 ———. *The Downey lectures: A syllabus for first year psychiatric residents.* Downey, Ill.: V. A. Hosp., 1963. Paper.

435 ———. Editor of E. Wexberg, *Individual psychological treatment*. 2nd ed.

436 ———. *Essays in schizophrenia*. Baltimore: Williams & Wilkins, 1968.

437 ———. Family constellation (with A. G. Nikelly). In A. G. Nikelly (Ed.), *Technique for behavior change*. Pp. 35-40.

438 ———. The family constellation in personality diagnosis. *JIP*, 1962, 18, 35-47.

439 ———. Flocculation tests in the diagnosis of hepato-biliary disease. *Gastroenterol.*, 1949, 13, 9-19 (with F. Steigmann & H. Pepper).

440 ———. Graffiti therapy. *Perspec. psychiat. Care*, 1972, 10(1), 34-36 (with Ann Byrne & Dorothy Peven).

441 Shulman, B. H. Group counseling for adolescents. In R. Dreikurs, R. Corsini, R. Lowe & M. Sonstegard (Eds.), *Adlerian family counseling*. Pp. 69–74.

442 ———. Group psychotherapy in a post stockade. *J. soc. Ther.*, 1957, 3, 14–18. Also in *Fed. Probat.*, 1957, 21,

443 ———. Group therapy with adolescents: An experiment. *IPB*, 1951, 9, 86–91.

444 ———. *Individual psychotherapy: A syllabus*. Chicago: Alfred Adler Inst., 1963 (with H. H. Mosak).

445 ———. *Introductory Individual Psychology: A syllabus*. Chicago: Alfred Adler Inst., 1961 (with H. H. Mosak).

446 ———. *The life style inventory*. Chicago: Alfred Adler Inst., 1971 (with H. H. Mosak).

447 ———. The meaning of people to the schizophrenic and the manic-depressive. *JIP*, 1962, 18, 151–156.

448 ———. The mute patient. *IP*, 1966, 3(2), 14–16;

449 ———. *The neuroses: A syllabus*. Chicago: Alfred Adler Inst., 1966 (with H. H. Mosak).

450 ———. On the theory of schizophrenic ontology: A phenomenologic-holistic synthesis. *J. Exis.*, 1965, 5, 353–358.

451 ———. Organ inferiority and psychiatric disorders in childhood (with H. Klapman). In E. Harms (Ed.), *Pathogenesis of nervous and mental diseases in children*. Pp. 49–62.

452 ———. Patient-therapist relationship in multiple psychotherapy: I. Its advantages to the therapist. *Psychiat. Quart.*, 1952, 26, 219–227 (with R. Dreikurs & H. H. Mosak). Also in R. Dreikurs, *Group psychotherapy and group approaches*. Pp. 114–120.

453 ———. Patient-therapist relationship in multiple psychotherapy: II. Its advantages for the patient. *Psychiat. Quart.*, 1952, 26, 590–596 (with R. Dreikurs & H. H. Mosak). Also in R. Dreikurs, *Group psychotherapy and group approaches*. Pp. 121–126.

454 ———. Portrait. *IPNL*, 1972, 21(6), 110.

455 ———. Psychiatric aspects of headache: A symposium. *Headache*, 1967, 7, 1–12.

456 ———. A psychodramatically oriented action technique in group psychotherapy. *Grp. Psychother.*, 1960, 22, 34–39.

457 Shulman, B. H. Psychological disturbances which interfere with the patient's cooperation. *Psychosomatics*, 1964, 5, 213–220.

458 ———. Purpose of the American Society of Adlerian Psychology. *IP*, 1963, 1(2), 1.

459 ———. Reaction of troop commanders to a mental hygiene consultation service. *U. S. Armed Forces med. J.*, 1954, 11, 1657–1662.

460 ———. Review of Magda B. Arnold, *Emotion and personality*. In *JIP*, 1961, 17, 231–232.

461 ———. Review of A. Burton, *Modern humanistic psychotherapy*. San Francisco: Jossey-Bass, 1967. In *JIP*, 1971, 27(1), 107–108.

462 ———. Review of H. C. B. Denber, *Research conference on therapeutic community, held at Manhattan State Hospital, Ward's Island, New York*. Springfield, Ill.: C. C. Thomas, 1960. In *JIP*, 1961, 17, 122–123.

463 ———. Review of H. Spotnitz, *Modern psychoanalysis of the schizophrenic patient*. New York: Grune & Stratton, 1969. In *JIP*, 1970, 26, 92.

464 ———. Schizophrenia and sexual behavior. *Med. Asp. hum. Sexual.*, 1971, 5(1), 144–156.

465 ———. Sex for domination. *Med. Asp. hum. Sexual.*, 1971, 5(10), 34–45 (with Dorothy Peven).

466 ———. Some necessary conditions for schizophrenia. *IP*, 1967, 4(2), 64–66.

467 ———. Takata-Ara test in differential diagnosis of jaundice. *Amer. J. diges. Dis.*, 1950, 17, 305–311 (with F. Steigmann).

468 ———. Therapeutic democracy. *Proc. Int. Soc. soc. Psychiat.*, 1965 (with K. Hoover).

469 ———. Therapeutic democracy: Some changes in staff-patient relationships. *Int. J. soc. Psychiat.*, 1964, Spec. ed. 3, 16–23 (with K. K. Hoover).

470 ———. The time of healing of gastric ulcers. *Gastroenterol.*, 1952, 20, 20–26 (with F. Steigmann).

471 ———. The use of dramatic confrontation in group psychotherapy. *Psychiat. Quart. Suppl.*, 1962 (part I), 36, 93–99.

472 ———. The uses and abuses of sex. *J. Relig. Hlth.*, 1967, 6, 317–325.

473 ———. Various purposes of symptoms. *JIP*, 1967, 23, 79–87 (with H. H. Mosak).

474 **Shulman, Phyllis.** Portrait. *IPNL*, 1972, 21(6), 110.

475 **Shyne, A. W.** The contribution of Alfred Adler to the development of dynamic psychology. *Amer. J. Orthopsychiat.*, 1942, 12, 352-364.

476 **Sicher, H.** Adleriana. *IPN*, 1940, 1(1), 3; 1940, 1(2), 4.

477 ———. A biologic basis for an holistic philosophy in medicine. *AJIP*, 1954, 11, 151-154.

478 ———. Review of J. S. Haldane, *Die philosophischen Grundlagen der Biologie.* Berlin: Prismen-Verlag, 1932. In *IZIP*, 1934, 12(1), 51.

479 ———. Review of V. Hammerschlag, Über kombinierte Heredopathien und ihren mutnasslichen Erbgang. *Wien. klin. Wchnschr.*, 1932, Nos. 25-26. In *IZIP*, 1933, 11(1), 76-77.

480 **Sicher, Lydia.** A propos "Heurigen". *IPNL*, 1961, 11(5-6, Whole No. 119-120). P. 23.

481 ———. Adlers Bedeutung für die medizinische Psychologie. *IZIP*, 1937, 15(3-4), 128-133.

482 ———. Aggression as a secondary phenomenon. *JIP*, 1967, 23, 232-235 (with H. H. Mosak). Also in H. D. Werner (Ed.), *New understandings of human behavior.* Pp. 168-172.

483 ———. Auch eine einzige Besprechung kann genügen—Das "Trauma". *IZIP*, 1929, 7(3), 237 (with Martha Holub).

484 ———. Case history of a stutterer. *IPN*, 1941, 1(7), 2.

485 ———. A case of manic-depressive insanity. *IJIP*, 1935, 1(1), 40-56.

486 ———. "Change of life". *Amer. J. Psychother.*, 1949, 3, 399-409.

487 ———. A declaration of interdependence. *IPB*, 1944-45, 4, 20-25.

488 ———. Dedication address at the cornerstone laying ceremony of Childhouse. *IZIP*, 1947, 16(3), 111.

489 ———. Dr. Ferdinand Birnbaum. *IPB*, 1948, 6, 155-156.

490 ———. Education for freedom. *AJIP*, 1954, 11, 97-103. Also in K. A. Adler & Danica Deutsch (Eds.), *Essays in Individual Psychology.* Pp. 16-24.

491 ———. Einige theoretische und praktische Ergebnisse der Persönlichkeitsbetrachtung. *IZIP*, 1933, 11(3), 237-247.

492 **Sicher, Lydia.** Das erste individualpsychologische Ambulatorium in Wien. *IZIP*, 1931, 9(4), 312-317.

493 ———. The family constellation (in the Old Testament). *Life & Letters*, 1950, 64, 12-24, 88-104.

494 ———. Freedom or liberty? *IZIP*, 1949, 18(4), 166-173.

495 ———. Guilt and guilt feelings. *IPB*, 1950, 8, 4-11.

496 ———. The individual in society. *IJIP*, 1935, 1(2), 40-50.

497 ———. Das Individuum in der Gemeinschaft. *IZIP*, 1935, 13(2), 76-88.

498 ———. In memory of Ida Loewy. *IPN*, 1941, 1(8-9), 12.

499 ———. Is the human race a mistake of nature? *Humanist*, 1953, 13(5), 208-212.

500 ———. A modern Diogenes. *AJIP*, 1952, 10, 89-91.

501 ———. The murdered one, too, is "guilty". *IJIP*, 1936, 2(4), 37-48.

502 ———. My son, you suffer from a hunchbacked soul. *Occup. Ther. Rehab.*, 1943, 22(5), 207-221.

503 ———. Neurotic sovereignty. *JIP*, 1958, 14, 139-141.

504 ———. Obituary [O. Spiel]. *JIP*, 1961, 17, 249-250.

505 ———. Portrait. *IPNL*, 1970, 19(4), 80.

506 ———. Review of Abély & Carrette, Hepatische Autointoxikation. *L'Encéphale*, 1925. In *IZIP*, 1926, 4(6), 314.

507 ———. Review of *Actas de la primera conferencia latino-americano de neurologia, psiquiatria y medicina legal.* Buenos Aires: Imprenta de la Universidad, 1929. In *IZIP*, 1932, 10(2), 160.

508 ———. Review of R. Allendy, *Le problème de la destinée.* Paris: Librarie Gallimard, 1927, & *Wille oder Bestimmung.* Stuttgart: Hippokrates-Verlag, 1930. In *IZIP*, 1932, 10(5), 392-393.

509 ———. Review of R. & Y. Allendy, *Capitalisme et sexualité.* Paris: Ed. Denoël, 1932. In *IZIP*, 1936, 14(4), 246-247.

510 ———. Review of A. Antheaume, *Die Legende von der Kleptomanie.* In *IZIP*, 1926, 4(6), 394-395.

511 ———. Review of E. Arlt, *Pflege und Behandlung entlassener Geisteskranker.* Wien: Wilhelm Mandrich, 1933. In *IZIP*, 1936, 14(4), 246.

512 **Sicher, Lydia.** Review of F. Asnaourow, *Fortschritte der Psychologie.* In *IZIP,* 1923, 2(2), 46–47.

513 ———. Review of F. Asnaourow, Die Manischen Ideen und ihre Rolle in menschlichen Leben. In *IZIP,* 1923, 2(2), 47.

514 ———. Review of M. J. Barilari, Reflexiones sobre psicoterapia. *El Dia Medico,* 1932, 6. In *IZIP,* 1937, 15(1), 46.

515 ———. Review of M. J. Barilari & F. Asnaourow, Sintonopsiquia y neurosis. *Revista med. Latino-Amer.,* 1932. In *IZIP,* 1934, 12(1), 52.

516 ———. Review of C. Baudouin, *L'âme enfantine et la psychanalyse.* Neuchatel: Delachaux & Niestlé, 1931. In *IZIP,* 1932, 10(4), 318–319.

517 ———. Review of C. Baudouin, L'inconscient dans la contemplation esthétique. *Arch. Psychol.,* 1928, 81. In *IZIP,* 1929, 7(2), 314.

518 ———. Review of H. Baudouin & R. Briau, Sur les méconnaissances systématiques. *L'Encéphale,* 1934, 5. In *IZIP,* 1935, 13(2), 128–129.

519 ———. Review of G. Bermann, Die sokratische Methode in der klinischen Psychologie. *El Pais,* July, 1927. In *IZIP,* 1928, 6(1), 77.

520 ———. Review of Marie Bonaparte, La structure psychique d'Edgar Poe. *L'Hyg. ment.,* 1933, 8–9. In *IZIP,* 1935, 13(1), 60.

521 ———. Review of L. Bopp, *Allgemeine Heilpädagogik in systematischer Grundlegung und mit erziehungspraktischer Einstellung.* In *IZIP,* 1932, 10(5), 393–394.

522 ———. Review of K. M. Bowman, Endocrine and biochemical studies in schizophrenia. *J. nerv. ment. Dis.,* 1927, 65, 465–483. In *IZIP,* 1930, 8(2), 273.

523 ———. Review of K. M. Bowman & J. Kasanin, The sugar content of blood in emotional states. *Arch. Neurol. Psychiat.,* 1929, 21, 342–362. In *IZIP,* 1930, 8(2), 273.

524 ———. Review of O. Brachfeld, *Inferiority feelings in the individual and the group.* In *AJIP,* 1954, 11, 182–184.

525 ———. Review of Elisabeth Busse-Wilson, *Das lebender Heiligen Elisabeth von Thüringen.* München: C. H. Becksche, 1931. In *IZIP,* 1932, 10(3), 236.

526 **Sicher, Lydia.** Review of G. Calligaris, La Fabbrica dei Pensieri sulla pelle dell' uoma. *Arch. gen. Neurol. Psiciat. Psicoanal.,* 1929, 10. In *IZIP,* 1930, 8(3), 356–357.

527 ———. Review of H. Claude, L'hystérie dans ses rapports avec divers états psychopathiques. *L'Encéphale,* 1932, No. 6. In *IZIP,* 1933, 11(2), 160.

528 ———. Review of H. Claude, E. Minkowski & [   ] Tison, Contribution à l'étude des mecanismes schizophréniques. *L'Encéphale,* 1925. In *IZIP,* 1926, 4(6), 398–399.

529 ———. Review of K. Clauss, *Mutter und Sohn.* Langensalza: Hermann Beyer & Söhne, 1931. In *IZIP,* 1933, 11(2), 160.

530 ———. Review of F. G. Crookshank, *The Mongol in our midst.* In *IZIP,* 1932, 10(3), 231.

531 ———. Review of M. Culpin, *Recent advances in the study of psychoneuroses.* London: J. Churchill, 1931. In *IZIP,* 1933, 11(2), 158–159.

532 ———. Review of F. Del Greco, I "subiettivismi psicopatici" nelle commune mentalità. *Quad. Psiciat.,* 1928, 7–8. In *IZIP,* 1929, 7(5), 396–397.

533 ———. Review of F. Del Greco, Sulla anormalita dei carattere di alcuni grandi intellettuali. *Arch. gen. Neurol. Psiciat. Psicoanal.,* 1929, 10. In *IZIP,* 1930, 8(3), 357.

534 ———. Review of H. F. Delgado, *Notwendigkeit der Aufnahme der Psychologie in den medizinischen Lehrplan.* In *IZIP,* 1924, 2(3), 60.

535 ———. Review of F. Decurtius, Hinrichsens Beziehungen zur Individualpsychologie. In *IZIP,* 1932, 10(5), 396–397.

536 ———. Review of G. Destounis, Délire d'interprétation chez un daltonien. *L'Encéphale,* 1934. In *IZIP,* 1934, 12(4), 260.

537 ———. Review of C. S. Dopff, La importancia de l'autoestimacio. *Rev. Psicol. Pedagog.* (Barcelona), 1933, 1. In *IZIP,* 1935, 13(3), 191.

538 ———. Review of R. Dreikurs, *Das nervöse Symptom.* In *IZIP,* 1934, 10(1), 52.

539 ———. Review of R. Dreikurs, *Seelische Impotenz.* In *IZIP,* 1932, 10(2), 152.

540 ———. Review of J. Dretter, Des relations entre la croyance hallucine

et sa conviction de l'universalité des hallucinations. *L'Encéphale*, 1934, 6. In *IZIP*, 1935, 13(2), 129.

541 Sicher, Lydia. Review of R. Dupouy & M. Delaville, Du traitement des toxicomanes par les lipoides végétaux. *L'Encéphale*, 1934, 3. In *IZIP*, 1935, 13(1), 128.

542 ———. Review of J. Endara (Ed.), *Los temperamentos.* Quito: Verlag der Universidad Central, 1930. In *IZIP*, 1932, 10(5), 397.

543 ———. Review of G. Ewald, *Biologische und "reine" Psychologie im Persönlichkeits-aufbau.* Berlin: S. Karger, 1932. In *IZIP*, 1934, 12(1), 55–56.

544 ———. Review of L. Faivre, Les jeunes vagabondes prostituées en prison. *L'Hyg. ment.*, 1932, No. 4. In *IZIP*, 1933, 12(4), 336.

545 ———. Review of A. Fittipaldi, Contributo allo conoscenza delle sindromi psicopatiche da scompenso. *Arch. gen. Neurol. Psiciat. Psicoanal.*, 1928, 9. In *IZIP*, 1929, 7(5), 397–398.

546 ———. Review of *Forschungen zur Völkerpsychologie und Soziologie*, 1931, 10. In *IZIP*, 1936, 14(4), 245–246.

547 ———. Review of A. Gemelli, *Sulla natura e sull genesi del carattere.* Florence: Atti della Società Italiana per il Progreso della Scienze, 1929. In *IZIP*, 1932, 10(5), 397–399.

548 ———. Review of G. Genil-Perrin & Madeleine Lebreuil, Le paranoiaque et le législation des loyers. *L'Hyg. ment.*, 1934, 7. In *IZIP*, 1936, 14(1), 62.

549 ———. Review of F. Giese, *Psychologisches Wörterbuch.* Halle: Carl Marhold, 1935. In *IZIP*, 1935, 13(4), 256.

550 ———. Review of [   ] Godard, Chronische Manie und unvollständige Demenz. *L'Encéphale*, 1925. In *IZIP*, 1926, 4(6), 398.

551 ———. Review of M. Gomes, Le rêve. *Arch. Brasil de Med.*, 1928 (March). In *IZIP*, 1930, 8(3), 356.

552 ———. Review of J. M. Grimes, *When minds go wrong.* Chicago: Author, 1949. In *AJIP*, 1954, 11, 92.

553 ———. Review of C. Hartwestbrook & D. G. Lai, The height and weight measurements and their correlation with the mental traits of Chinese students in Shanghai. *China med. J.*, 1930, 44. In *IZIP*, 1932, 10(5), 392.

554 Sicher, Lydia. Review of A. Holub, *Die Lehre von der Organminderwertigkeit.* In *IZIP*, 1932, 10(2), 152.

555 ———. Review of Individual Psychology and psychosomatic disorders (I). *IPMP*, 1932, No. 4. In *IZIP*, 1933, 11(1), 75.

556 ———. Review of H. Jacoby, *Handschrift und Sexualität.* Berlin: A Marcus & E. Webers Verlag, 1932. In *IZIP*, 1934, 12(1), 59–60.

557 ———. Review of E. Jaensch & L. Grunhüt, *Über Gestaltpsychologie und Gestalttheorie.* Langensalza: Hermann Beyer & Söhne, 1929. In *IZIP*, 1930, 8(4), 437.

558 ———. Review of L. Kaplan, *Versuch einer Psychologie der Kunst.* Baden-Baden: Merlin-Verlag, 1930. In *IZIP*, 1932, 10(4), 319.

559 ———. Review of Mathilde Kelchner, *Die Frau und der weibliche Arzt.* Leipzig: Adolf Klein, 1934. In *IZIP*, 1937, 15(1), 45.

560 ———. Review of Olga Knopf, *The art of being a woman.* In *IZIP*, 1933, 11(1), 78.

561 ———. Review of K. Kolle, *Die primäre Verrücktheit.* Leipzig: Georg Thieme, 1931 In *IZIP*, 1931, 9(5), 408.

562 ———. Review of Amalie Körpeth-Tippel, *Kind und Bild.* Wien: Deutscher Verlag f. Jugend u. Volk, [   ]. In *IZIP*, 1936, 14(4), 243–244.

563 ———. Review of D. Kouretas : P. Scouras, La cauchemar. *Progrès médical*, 1931, 21. In *IZIP*, 1937, 15(1), 46–47.

564 ———. Review of J. M. Lahy & G. Heuyer Dépistage des psychopaties chez les écoliers par la méthode psychologique et l'examen clinique. *L'Hyg. ment.*, 1931, 8. In *IZIP*, 1937, 15(1), 47.

565 ———. Review of W. Langdon-Brown *et al.*, Anorexia nervosa. In *IZIP*, 1932, 10(3), 231.

566 ———. Review of Sofie Lazarsfeld, *Wie die Frau den Mann erlebt.* In *IZIP*, 1931, 9(2), 152–153.

567 ———. Review of R. Lenoble, *Psychologie et traitement des scrupuleux.* Paris: Oritoriana, [   ]. In *IZIP*, 1935, 13(4), 257.

568 ———. Review of Luisa Levi, Sulla decadenza etica dei fanciulli da encephalite epidemica. *Quad. Psiciat.*, 1928, 5–6. In *IZIP*, 1929, 7(1), 75–76.

569 Sicher, Lydia. Review of M. Levi Bianchini, La maternita cosidetta illegitima e l'aborto criminoso. *Arch. gen. Neurol. Psichiat.*, 1928, 9. In *IZIP*, 1929, 7(5), 397.

570 ———. Review of J. Levy-Valensi, L'inspiration poétique et la psychopathologie. *Hyg. ment.* [   ]. In *IZIP*, 1935, 13(4), 257.

571 ———. Review of S. Lifschitz, *Hypnoanalyse*. Stuttgart: Ferdinand Enke, 1930. In *IZIP*, 1931, 9(1), 67–69.

572 ———. Review of G. De Loverdo, Directives d'hygiene mentale. *Action et Pensée*, 1933. In *IZIP*, 1934, 12(1), 51–52.

573 ———. Review of P. Meignant, Le point de vue de l'Individual Psychologie Adlérienne sur le crime et la délinquance specialement sur la délinquance juvenile. *L'Hyg. ment.*, 1932, No. 6.

574 ———. Review of E. Minkowski, *La schizophrénie*. Paris: Payot, 1927. In *IZIP*, 1929, 7(5), 476–477.

575 ———. Review of E. Mira, Assaig psicològic sobre el dolor. *Rev. Psicol. Pedagog.* (Barcelona), 1933, 1. In *IZIP*, 1935, 13 (3), 191.

576 ———. Review of E. Mira, La nova concepció experimental de la conducta moral. *Rev. Psicol. Pedagog.* (Barcelona), 1933, 3. In *IZIP*, 1935, 13(3), 192.

577 ———. Review of W. Morgenthaler, *Die Pflege der Gemüts- und Geisteskranken*. Bern: Hans Huber, 1930. In *IZIP*, 1931, 9(3), 252.

578 ———. Review of E. Morselli, La psicopatologia de climaterio maschile. *Quad. Psiciat.*, 1928, 11–12. In *IZIP*, 1929, 7(4), 396.

579 ———. Review of J. Nagler, *Anlage, Umwelt und Persönlichkeit des Verbrechers*. Stuttgart: Ferdinand Enke, 1933. In *IZIP*, 1937, 15(1), 45–46.

580 ———. Review of I. Nissen, *Die methodische Einstellung*. In *IZIP*, 1930, 8(4), 437–438.

581 ———. Review of G. Paul-Boncour, *Quelques considerations* sur la prostitution des mineures. *L'Hyg. ment.*, 1932, No. 4. In *IZIP*, 1933, 12(4), 333.

582 ———. Review of M. Pinner & B. F. Miller (Eds.), *When doctors are patients*. New York: Norton, 1952. In *AJIP*, 1954, 11, 181–182.

583 Sicher, Lydia. Review of P. Plottke, Le problème de l'alcoolisme considéré du point de vue de "l'Individualpsychologie" de l'Alfred Adler. *L'Hyg. ment.*, Dec., 1934. In *IZIP*, 1936, 14(2), 125.

584 ———. Review of V. Prihoda, *Rationalisierung des Schulwesens*. Wien: Deutscher Verlag f. Jugend u. Volk, 1935. In *IZIP*, 1936, 14(4), 242–243.

585 ———. Review of Lorine Prouette, *G. Stanley Hall: A biography of a mind*. New York: D. Appleton, 1926. In *IZIP*, 1933, 11(2), 159–160.

586 ———. Review of W. Riese, Le determinisme de Claude Bernard et ses rapports avec la neurologie contemporaine. *L'Encéphale*, 1934, 10. In *IZIP*, 1936, 14(1), 61–62.

587 ———. Review of E. Rignano, Premiers linéaments d'une morale fondée sur l'harmonie de la vie. *Scientia*, 1928, 7–8. In *IZIP*, 1929, 7(2), 315.

588 ———. Review of E. Rignano, *Problemi della psiche*. Bologna: Nicola Zanichelli, 1928. In *IZIP*, 1929, 7(5), 398.

589 ———. Review of H. Rohleder, *Monographien über die Zeugung beim Menschen*. Leipzig: Georg Thieme, 1924. In *IZIP*, 1927, 5(3), 395–396.

590 ———. Review of P. H. Ronge, Over de "Individualpsychologie" van Alfred Adler. In *IZIP*, 1934, 12(1), 52.

591 ———. Review of A. Rouquir & J. Michel, Anorexie pithiatique elective. *L'Encéphale*, 1934. In *IZIP*, 1934, 12(4), 260–261.

592 ———. Review of J. Sanz, La seleccio dels bendotats. *Rev. Psicol. Pedagog.* (Barcelona), 1933, 2. In *IZIP*, 1935, 13(3), 191–192.

593 ———. Review of M. Schaechter, Les sévices moraux. *L'Hyg. ment.*, 1932, 8. In *IZIP*, 1936, 14(4), 246.

594 ———. Review of S. D. Schmalhausen, *Why we misbehave*. New York: Macauley, 1928. In *IZIP*, 1932, 10(3), 234–235.

595 ———. Review of O. A. H. Schmitz, *Wege zur Reife*. Freiburg: Niels Kampmann, 1931. In *IZIP*, 1932, 10(5), 399.

596 ———. Review of H. Sellheim, *Gemütsverstimmungen der Frau*. Stuttgart: Ferdinand Enke, 1930. In *IZIP*, 1931, 9(2), 152.

597 ———. Review of O. Spiel, *Einmal anders gesehen*. . . In *AJIP*, 1956, 12, 91–92.

598 **Sicher, Lydia.** Review of E. Stransky (Ed.), *Leitfaden der psychischen Hygiene.* Wien: Urban & Schwarzenberg, 1931. In *IZIP,* 1931, 9(5), 410.

599 ———. Review of S. Tissi, *La psicoanalisi.* Marland: Ulrico Hoepli, 1929. In *IZIP,* 1930, 8(2), 272-273.

600 ———. Review of Ukrainisches psychoneurologisches Staatsinstitut. In *IZIP,* 1930, 8(4), 438.

601 ———. Review of T. H. Van Der Velde, *Die Fruchtbarkeit in der Ehe und ihre wunschgemasse Beeinflussung.* Horw-Luzern: Benno Konegen, 1929. In *IZIP,* 1931, 9(1), 77.

602 ———. Review of H. Van Etten, La musique dans les prisons. *L'Hyg. ment.,* 1933, 10. In *IZIP,* 1935, 13(1), 61.

603 ———. Review of C. von Monakow & R. Mourgue, *Biologische Einführung in das Studium der Neurologie und Psychopathologie.* Stuttgart: Hippokrates-Verlag, 1930. In *IZIP,* 1931, 9(1), 69.

604 ———. Review of J. Xirau, El concepte de libertat i el problema de l'educació. *Rev. Psicol. Pedagog.* (Barcelona), 1933, 2. In *IZIP,* 1935, 13(2), 129.

605 ———. Review of J. C. Young, Individual Psychology, psychiatry and holistic medicine. In *IZIP,* 1934, 12(1), 50-51.

606 ———. Review of [   ], Zivilisation und Neurose. *La Prensa,* 1927 (June). In *IZIP,* 1928, 6(4), 341-342.

607 ———. The scope of Individual Psychology. *IPN,* 1941, 1(5), 2-3.

608 ———. Thanks to Alfred Adler. *IPB,* 1942, 2(4), 61-62.

609 ———. Two cases (with Martha Holub). In A. Adler & assoc., *Guiding the child.* Pp. 236-240.

610 ———. Über einen Fall von manisch-depressiven Irresein. *IZIP,* 1928, 6(4), 299-312.

611 ———. Versuch einer graphischen Darstellung psychischer Bewegungsarten. *IZIP,* 1934, 12(2), 96-104.

612 ———. War neuroses. *Med. women's J.,* 1944, 51, 1-8.

613 ———. Wer ist "man"? *I P Medelingenblad van de Nederlandse.* 1963, 12, Also in *IZIP,* 1950, 19(1), 1-8.

614 **Sieburg, Lilli.** Review of Trude Salinger-Perls, *Gymnastische Spiele für die Kleinen.* Dresden: Wilhelm Limpert, [   ]. In *IZIP,* 1931, 9(1), 80.

615 **Siegel, S.** Level of aspiration and decision making. *Psychol. Rev.,* 1957, 64, 253-263.

616 **Siemsen, Anna.** Berufsausbildung. In *Sofie Lazarsfeld* (Ed.), *Technik der Erziehung.*

617 **Silverman, H.** Determinism, choice, responsibility and the psychologist's role as an expert witness. *Amer. Psychologist,* 1969, 24, 5-9.

618 **Simon, A.** A case of sibling rivalry. *IJIP,* 1935, 1(3), 14-23.

619 ———. Ein Anwand gegen die Individualpsychologische Erziehungsberatungsarbeit. *IZIP,* 1933, 11(1), 54-63.

620 ———. Das Kind in der Schule. In E. Wexberg (Ed.), *Handbuch der Individualpsychologie.* Pp. 289-322.

621 ———. Pädagogische Bemerkungen zur Frage der Unbegabung. *IZIP,* 1929, 7(5), 370-382.

622 ———. Schulkinderpsychologie. *IZIP,* 1925, 3(4), 146-194 (with K. Seelman).

623 ———. So-called "inaptitude" in school children. *IJIP,* 1937, 3(4), 356-373.

624 ———. Review of M. Keilhacker, *Der ideale Lehrer nach der Auffassung der Schüler.* Freiburg: Herder, 1932. In *IZIP,* 1933, 12(4), 335.

625 ———. Volksschule oder Hilfsschule. *IZIP,* 1931, 9(3), 199-206.

626 **Simon, R.** Alfred Adlers Bedeutung für die Strafrechtswissenschaften. *IZIP,* 1937, 15 (3-4), 162-166.

627 **Simon, W. E.** Ordinal position of birth, field dependency and Forer's measure of gullibility. *Percep. mot. Skills,* 1971, 33, 677-678 (with V. Wilde).

628 **Simonov, P.** Dostoevsky as a social scientist. *Psychol. Today,* 1971, 7(7), 59-61, 102-106.

629 **Simpson, H. N.** *Stoic apologetics.* Oak Park, Ill.: Author, 1966. Paper.

630 **Simpson, Lola J.** Wide, wide world (Interview with A. Adler). *Good Housekeeping,* Oct., 1931. Pp. 40-41.

631 **Singer, Eleanor.** Birth order, educational aspiration, and educational attainment. *Diss. Abstr.,* 1967, 27, 2638. Unpubl. Ph.D. Diss., Columbia Univ., 1966.

632 **Singer, J. E.** Social concern, body size and birth order. *J. soc. Psychol.,* 1966, 68, 143-151 (with Patricia F. Lamb).

633 ———. The use of manipulative strategies: Machiavellianism and attractiveness. *Sociom.,* 1964, 27, 128-150.

634 **Singer, R. M.** Adlerian psychology in dentistry. *Canad. Dent. Assn. J.*, 1961, 27, 419–425.

635 ———. Dental psychotherapy. *Canad. Dent. Assn. J.*, 1960, 26, 203–209.

636 ———. The dentist-patient relationship— A psychological approach. *J. Ontario Dent. Assn.*, 1965, 42, 8–12.

637 ———. Should dentists shun hypnosis? *Canad. Dent. Assn. J.*, 1960, 26, 705–710.

638 **Singer, S. N.** Family interaction with schizophrenic and non-schizophrenic siblings. *Diss. Abstr.*, 1966, 26, 6859–6860. Unpubl. Ph.D. Diss., Yeshiva Univ., 1965.

639 **Sinha, D.** The effect of one experience upon the recall of another. *Quart. J. exp. Psychol.*, 1950, 2, 43–52 (with D. R. Davis).

640 ———. A study of parental role-perception in siblings. *J. psychol. Res.*, 1966, 10(1), 8–18 (with E. S. Ghosh).

641 **Sinha, J. B.** Birth order and sex differences in n-achievement and n-affiliation. *J. psychol. Res.*, 1967, 11, 22–27.

642 **Sinha, S.** Level of aspiration and culture. *Indian J. Psychol.*, 1953, 28, 55–58.

643 **Sinnott, E. W.** A biological basis for teleology. *JIP*, 1957, 13, 14–23.

644 ———. *The biology of the spirit.* New York: Viking Press, 1955.

645 ———. *Cell and psyche: The biology of purpose.* Chapel Hill, N. C.: Univ. North Carolina Press, 1950.

646 **Sipay, E.** (Ed.). *Readings on reading instruction.* New York: David McKay, 1972.

647 **Sister Mary Estelle.** An observer's viewpoint—A feature story. *OSIPNL*, 1963, 3 (6), 4–5.

648 **Sister Rachel, OSH.** Individual Psychology in a church school. *IPB*, 1951, 9, 156–166.

649 **Sittig, Elly.** Anatomy and physiology (with E. Froeschels). In E. Froeschels (Ed.), *Twentieth century speech and voice correction.* Pp. 1–38.

650 **Sivadon, P.** Adlerian psychology and mental hygiene. *JIP*, 1964, 20, 194–195.

651 ———. Introduction to A. Adler, *Les nevrosés: Commentaires, observations, presentation de cas.*

652 **Skinner, C. E.** *Elementary educational psychology.* New York: Prentice-Hall, 1945.

653 **Skinner, Olivia.** Solving family fusses democratically. *St. Louis Post-Dispatch*, July 26, 1971.

654 **Skotton, Elisabeth.** Aus meiner Praxis. *IZIP*, 1948, 17(3), 120–126.

655 **Slagle, Sarah.** Rehabilitation of children discharged from a psychiatric hospital. *Amer. J. Orthopsychiat.*, 1964, 34(5), 942–947 (with H. Klapman & I. Morino).

656 **Slagter, S.** Het belied van de Kinderrechter bij vithuisplaatsing van Kinderen. *MNWIP*, 1971, 20(3),

657 **Slamecka, N. J.** Review of H. J. Eysenck (Ed.), *Behaviour therapy and the neuroses.* New York: Pergamon Press, 1960. In *JIP*, 1961, 17, 121.

658 ———. Review of E. L. Phillips, *Psychotherapy: A modern theory and practice.* In *JIP*, 1958, 14, 90–91.

659 **Sletto, R. F.** Sibling position and juvenile delinquency. *Amer. J. Sociol.*, 1934, 39, 657–669.

660 **Small, M.** *The story of psychoanalysis.* New York: Pocket Books, 1960 (with Lucy Freeman).

661 **Smalley, R. E.** The influence of differences in age, sex and intelligence in determining the attitudes of siblings toward each other. *Smith Coll. Stud. soc. Work*, 1930, 1, 23–29.

662 **Smart, Mollie.** *An introduction to family relationships.* Philadelphia: Saunders, 1953 (with R. Smart).

663 **Smart, R.** *An introduction to family relationships.* Philadelphia: Saunders, 1953 (with Mollie Smart).

664 **Smart, R. G.** Alcoholism, birth order, and family size. *J. abnorm. soc. Psychol.*, 1963, 66, 103–105.

665 ———. Social group membership, leadership, and birth order. *J. soc. Psychol.*, 1965, 67, 221–225.

666 **Smelser, W. T.** Where are the siblings? A re-evaluation of the relationship between birth order and college attendance. *Sociom.*, 1968, 31, 294–303 (with L. H. Stewart).

667 **Smillie, D.** The significance of individual creativity for psychotherapy. *JIP*, 1957, 13, 159–164 (with C. E. Moustakas).

668 **Smith, B. D.** (Ed.). *Personality theory: A source book.* New York: Appleton-Century-Crofts, 1971.

669 **Smith, C. E.** *Foundations for guidance and counseling.* New York: Lippincott, 1969 (with O. G. Mink).

670 **Smith, C. M.** Family size in alcoholism. *J. abnorm. Psychol.*, 1965, 70, 230.

671 **Smith, C. P.** Childrearing practices, birth order, and the development of achievement-related motives. *Psychol. Rep.*, 1966, 19, 1201-1216 (with E. W. Bartlett).

672 **Smith, E. E.** Some personality and behavioral factors related to birth order. *J. appl. Psychol.*, 1963, 47, 300-303 (with Jacqueline D. Goodchilds).

673 **Smith, G. F.** Birth order and affiliation. *Brit. J. soc. clin. Psychol.*, 1969, 8, 235-245 (with P. H. Murdoch).

674 **Smith, I. C.** Retired schoolmistress. *IPNL*, 1972, 21(3), 49.

675 **Smith, M. B.** The phenomenological approach in personality theory: Some critical remarks. *J. abnorm. soc. Psychol.*, 1950, 45, 516-522.

676 ———. Rationality and social process. *JIP*, 1960, 16, 25-35.

677 **Smith, M. E.** Childhood memories compared with those of adult life. *J. genet. Psychol.*, 1952, 80, 151-182.

678 **Smith, Mary Ann.** Fresh topics for a series, from D. Cruickshank. *OSIPNL*, 1972, 13(3), 7.

679 **Smith, Sheila.** Review of Helen Riley, If your child is handicapped. *St. Joseph's Mag.* (Oregon), March, 1965. In *OSIPNL*, 1965, 5(5), 15.

680 **Smith, W. H.** Measurement of existential mental health: Further exploration. *JIP*, 1968, 24, 71-73 (with E. Brown).

681 **Smouse, A. D.** Achievement motivation and ordinal position of birth. *Psychol. Rep.* 1968, 23, 175-180 (with D. C. Munz & G. Letchworth).

682 **Smuts, J. C.** *Holism and evolution.* New York: Macmillan, 1926; London: Macmillan, 1927; New York: Viking Press, 1961. Paper.

683 ———. The scientific world picture of today. *Rep. Brit. Assn. Adv. Sci.*, 1931, , 1-18.

684 ———. Das wissenschaftliche Weltbild der Gegenwart. Translated by E. O. Krausz, *IZIP*, 1932, 10, 244-261.

685 **Snider, B. C. F.** First born and last born children in a child development clinic. *JIP*, 1964, 20, 179-182 (with B. Cushna & M. Greene).

686 **Snoad, Shari.** See Kras, Shari.

687 **Snyder, B.** The value of early memories in psychotherapy. *Psychiat. Quart.*, 1953, 27, 73-82 (with R. Kahana, I. Weiland & M. Rosenbaum).

688 **Snyder, T. R.** On earliest memories. *Psychoanal. Quart.*, 1956, 25, 228-237 (with L. J. Saul & Edith Sheppard).

689 **Snygg, D.** Individual behavior. New York: Harper, 1949, 1959 (with A. W. Combs).

690 ———. The need for a phenomenological system of psychology. *Psychol. Rev.*, 1941, 48, 404-424.

691 ———. Review of F. P. Kilpatrick (Ed.), *Explorations in transactional psychology.* New York: New York Univ. Press, 1961. In *JIP*, 1961, 17, 230-231.

692 **Sohler, Dorothy T.** The prediction of family interaction from a battery of projective techniques. *J. proj. Tech.*, 1957, 21, 199-208 (with J. D. Holzberg, S. Fleck, Alice R. Cornelison, Eleanor Kay, & T. Lidz).

693 **Söhngen, F. A.** Doel van de Gezins verzorging en de Opleiding tot Gezinsverzorgster. *MNWIP*, 1971, 21(1),

694 **Solomon, G. F.** Earliest memories and ego functions. *Arch. gen. Psychiat.*, 1964, 11, 556-567 (with G. M. Burnell).

695 **Solomon, L.** Sibling order, premorbid adjustment. and remission in schizophrenia. *J. nerv. ment. Dis.*, 1967, 144, 37-46 (with R. Nuttall).

696 **Solomon, R. L.** Punishment. *Amer. Psychologist*, 1964, 19, 239-253.

697 **Soltz, Vicki.** The application of democratic principles in the classroom. In A. Nikelly (Ed.), *Techniques for behavior change.* Pp. 197-204.

698 ———. *Children: The challenge.* New York: Duell, Sloan & Pearce, 1964 (with R. Dreikurs).

699 ———. *Le défi de l'enfant.* Translated by J. Leschallier del'Isle. Paris: Editions Robert Laffont, 1972 (with R. Dreikurs).

700 ———. The frightened parent syndrome. *IP*, 1969, 6(1), 1-7.

701 ———. *Happy children: The challenge for parents.* London: Souvenir Press, 1970 (with R. Dreikurs).

702 ———. *Kinder fordern uns heraus: Wie erziehen wir sie zeitgemass?* Translated by E. Blumenthal. Stuttgart: Ernst Klett Verlag, 1966 (with R. Dreikurs).

703 ———. *Manual for life style assessment: Part I.* Minneapolis, Minn.: Hennepin County Court Services, May, 1971 (with R. Dreikurs, Miriam L. Pew & W. L. Pew).

704 ———. *Study group leader's manual: To be used with Children: The*

challenge. Wilmington, Del: Author, 1967. Mimeo.; Chicago: Alfred Adler Inst., 1967.

705 Soltz, Vicki. *Your child and discipline: A briefing for parents.* Washington, D. C.: Natl. Educ. Assn., 1964; *NEA J.,* 1965, 54, 32–47 (with R. Dreikurs).

706 Sonn, A. Review of H. N. Casson, *Erfolge und Lebensfreude.* Berlin: J. Singer, 1927. In *IZIP,* 1928, 6(5), 415–416.

707 Sonneman, U. *Existence and therapy: An introduction to phenomenological psychology and existential analysis.* New York: Grune & Stratton, 1954.

708 Sonnheim, M. Complementarity in marital adjustment: Reconsidering Toman's family constellation hypothesis. *JIP,* 1965, 21, 137–144 (with G. Levinger).

709 Sonstegard, M. A. Academic adjustment: Ready or not and a comedy of errors. In R. J. Corsini & D. Howard (Eds.), *Critical incidents in teaching.* Pp. 153–154.

710 ———. The Adlerian or teleoanalytic group counseling approach (with R. Dreikurs). In G. M. Gazda (Ed.), *Basic approaches to group psychotherapy and group counseling.* Pp. 197–232.

711 ———. Allowance—A three "W" approach. *IP,* 1972, 9(1), 22–24.

712 ———. Applying Adlerian principles to counselor education. *IP,* 1967, 5, 22–25.

713 ———. *The basic principles and rationale of group counseling.* Moravia, N. Y.: Chronicle Guid. Publ., 1968.

714 ———. A center for the guidance of parents and children in a small community. *AJIP,* 1954, 11, 81–89.

715 ———. The fiasco of 1970. *ASAP Calendar Nwsltr.,* Jan., 1971. Pp. 8–11.

716 ———. Group dynamics. *IPNL,* 1965, 15(9–10, Whole No. 170–172). P. 33.

717 ———. *Helping student teachers utilize consultant services.* Cedar Falls, Ia.: The Assn. for Student Teaching, 1959 (with E. Ruman).

718 ———. How a center is organized. In R. Dreikurs, R. Corsini, R. Lowe & M. Sonstegard (Eds.), *Adlerian family counseling.* Pp. 101–108.

719 ———. In-service education in counseling. *Midland Schools,* 1960, 75, 10–12 (with M. Graeber).

720 ———. Interaction processes and the personality growth of children. *Grp. Psychother.,* 1958, 2(1), 40–45.

721 Sonstegard, M. A. Mechanisms and practical techniques in group counseling in the elementary school. In J. J. Muro & S. L. Freeman (Eds.), *Readings in group counseling.* Pp. 127–136.

722 ———. Points for principals to ponder. *Ill. elem. Principal,* Sept. 14–16, 1966.

723 ———. Rationale of group counseling (with R. Dreikurs). In D. Dinkmeyer (Ed.), *Guidance and counseling inthe elementary school.* Pp. 278–287.

724 ———. A rationale for interviewing parents. *Sch. Counselor,* 1964, 12, 72–76.

725 ———. A rationale for interviewing parents. *Personnel Guid. J.,* 1957, 175–183.

726 ———. Relating self-conception to curriculum development. *J. educ. Res.,* 1965, 58, 348–351 (with L. Hott).

727 ———. Review of D. C. Dinkmeyer & C. E. Caldwell, *Developmental counseling and guidance.* In *IP,* 1970, 8(1), 28.

728 ———. Review of R. Dreikurs, *Social equality.* In *IP,* 1970, 8(1), 26–27.

729 ———. Review of R. Dreikurs & L. Grey, *A parents' guide to discipline.* In *IP,* 1969, 6(2), 46–47.

730 ———. Review of H. Helson & W. Bevan, *Contemporary approaches to psychology.* In *IP,* 1970, 7(1), 28.

731 ———. Review of H. James, *Children in trouble: A national scandal.* Boston: Christian Science Publ. Soc., 1969. In *IP,* 1970, 7(1), 27.

732 ———. Review of A. G. Nikelly (Ed.), *Techniques for behavior change.* In *IP,* 1970, 8(1), 27.

733 ———. Review of A. A. Roback & T. Kiernan, *Pictorial history of psychology and psychiatry.* In *IP,* 1968, 5(3), 25.

734 ———. A specific approach to practicum supervision. *Counselor educ. Supervis.,* 1966, 6, 18–25 (with R. Dreikurs).

735 ———. The steps taken by the people of Jamaica, West Indies, to develop a child guidance programme. *IPNL,* 1959, 10(1, Whole No. 102–103). P. 2.

736 ———. Symbolic cover designs. *IP,* 1970, 8(2), 31–34.

737 ———. A teleoanalytic approach to coordinate counseling: Teacher and counselor. *IP,* 1969, 6(1), 8–17 (with Fleury P. Samples).

738 Sonstegard, M. A. *The teleoanalytic approach to group counseling.* Chicago: Alfred Adler Inst., 1967 (with R. Dreikurs).

739 ———. Toward a therapeutic community. *IP,* 1966, 4(1), 14–17.

740 Soper, D. The self, its derivative terms, and research. *JIP,* 1957, 13, 134–145 (with A. W. Combs). Also in A. E. Kuenzli (Ed.), *The phenomenological problem.* Pp. 31–48.

741 Sorge, Elisabeth. See Sorge-Boehmke, Elisabeth.

742 Sorge-Boehmke, Elisabeth. Änderung der Perspektive—Änderung des Lebensstils. *IZIP,* 1950, 19(1), 35–41.

743 ———. Aus einem Flüchtlingsleben. *IZIP,* 1948, 17(4), 179–184.

744 ———. Drei Jahre Erziehungsberatungsstelle in Geesthacht. *Schles.-Holst. Schule,* 1952, 6,

745 ———. Eine dreizehnjährige Brandshiftern. *IZIP,* 1931, 9(5), 371–375.

746 ———. Erziehungsberatung unter den Gesichtpunkten der Individualpsychologie A. Adlers. *Prax. Kinderpsychol. Kinderpsychiat.* (Göttingen), 1958, 7(2–3),

747 ———. Frauen in Belzenprozess. *IZIP,* 1947, 16, 44–46.

748 ———. Kindheitseindrücke und ihre Folgen. In Int. Verein Indivpsy., *Alfred Adler zum Gedenken.* Pp. 134–136.

749 ———. Portrait. *IPNL,* 1971, 20(6), 110.

750 ———. A thirteen-year old incendiary. *IJIP,* 1935, 1(3), 44–51.

751 ———. Tiefenpsychologie in dienst am Kinde. *Geesthachter Zeitung,* 1952, (with F. Schubert).

752 ———. Vom Ankläger zum Helfer. *IZIP,* 1948, 17(3), 130–135.

753 ———. Was geht unssonst noch an. *Gesundheitsfürsorge* (Stuttgart), 1952.

754 Spencer, H. *Education—Intellectual, moral, and physical.* New York: P. D. Alden, 1885.

755 Spencer, T. E. Cremation, an expression of life style. *JIP,* 1972, 28, 60–66.

756 Sperber, H. *Die Lüge im Strafrecht.* Wien: Zahn & Diamant, 1926.

757 ———. *Todesgedanke und Lebensgestaltung.* Wien-Leipzig: M. Perles, 1930.

758 Sperber, M. *The Achilles heel.* Translated by C. FitzGibbon. London: Andre Deutsch, 1959; New York: Doubleday, 1960.

759 ———. *Alfred Adler: Der Mensch und seine Lehre.* München: Bergmann, 1926.

760 Sperber, M. *Alfred Adler oder das Elend der Psychologie.* Wien: Fritz Molden, 1970.

761 ———. Alfred Adler revisited. *JIP,* 1970, 26, 32–35.

762 ———. *The burned bramble.* New York: Doubleday, 1951.

763 ———. *Journey without end.* Translated by C. FitzGibbon. New York: Doubleday, 1954.

764 ———. Knut Hamsen. Zu seinem 70 Geburtstag. *IZIP,* 1929, 7(6), 447–449.

765 ———. *The lost bay.* Translated by C. FitzGibbon. London: Andre Deutsch, 1956.

766 ———. A miracle [Excerpt from *The lost bay*]. *IPNL,* 1956, 6(3–4, Whole No. 67–69). Pp. 11–12.

767 ———. Meeting Adler [Excerpt from *Alfred Adler oder das Elend der Psychologie*]. *IPNL,* 1971, 20(5), 86–87.

768 ———. Review of E. Ludwig, *Wilhelm der Zweite.* Berlin: Rowohlt, 1925. In *IZIP,* 1926, 4(3), 165–166.

769 ———. Review of H. F. Wolf, *Strategie der männliche Annäherung.* In *IZIP,* 1927, 5(1), 778–779.

770 ———. Die Selbstkontrolle in Therapie und Erziehung. *IZIP,* 1930, 8(1), 102–107.

771 ———. *Le talon d'Achille.* Paris: Calmann-Lévy, 1957.

772 ———. Typische seelische Störungen des Schulkindes. In Sofie Lazarsfeld (Ed.), *Technik der Erziehung.*

773 ———. *Das Unglück begabt zu sein.* Paris: Science et Littérature, 1938.

774 ——— (Ed.). *Wir und Dostojevskij: Eine Debatte mit Heinrich Boll, Siegfried Lenz, André Malraux, Hans Erich Nossack geführt von Manes Sperber.* Hamburg: Hoffman & Campe, 1972.

775 ———. *Zur Analyse der Tyrannis* und *Das Unglück begabt zu sein.* Paris: Science et Littérature, 1938.

776 ———. *Zur täglichen Weltgeschichte.* Köln: Kiepenhauer & Witsch, 1949.

777 ———. Zur Technik der Traumdeutung. *IZIP,* 1928, 6(3), 195–201.

778 Sperry, L. Changing teacher attitudes toward human relations problems. *Res. Educ.,* July, 1972. Pp. 1–40.

779 ———. The curriculum system operating in urban education: A psychological consultant's view. *Res. Educ.,* Mar., 1971. Pp. 1–14.

780 Sperry, L. The effects of expectation, experience and social class on group productivity. *Res. Educ.*, July, 1971. Pp. 1–9 (with G. Beauchamp).

781 ———. Expectations and the future of education. *Phi Delta Kappa Nwsltr.*, 1969, 6(1), 3–4.

782 ———. *Learning performance and individual differences.* Glenview, Ill.: Scott, Foresman, 1972.

783 ———. Non-public vocational education: A trend of the future? *Guidelines for Pupil Services*, 1972, 11(1), 18–21 (with L. Hess & C. Piskula).

784 ———. A study of planned attitude change in an integrated school. *Elem. Sch. Guid. Couns.*, 1972, 7(2), 162–165.

785 ———. Understanding urban school problems: A systems approach. *Contemp. Educ.*, 1972, 44(1), 29–33.

786 Spiegel, E. A. (Ed.). *Progress in neurology and psychiatry.* New York: Grune & Stratton, 1946–

787 Spiegel, F. Goals, procedures and achievements in clinic psychotherapy. *J. Mt. Sinai Hosp.*, 1951, 18, 221–227 (with Alexandra Adler, S. R. Lehrman, & M. Schatner).

788 Spiegelberg, H. *The phenomenological movement: A historical introduction.* 2 vols. The Hague: Martinus Nijhoff, 1960.

789 Spiel, Lona. Aha-Erlebnis und Therapie. *IZIP*, 1948, 17(4), 184–185.

790 ———. Review of F. Pokorny (Ed.), *Konsilium.* Wien: Urban & Schwarzenberg, 1949. In *IZIP*, 1950, 19(4), 190.

791 Spiel, O. Adlers Verdienst: "Der Weg vom Ich zum Wir." *Neues Oesterreich*, May 29, 1957.

792 ———. Alfred Adler: Zu seinem zwansigsten Todestag. *Arbeiter-Zeitung* (Wien), May 26, 1957. P. 9.

793 ———. Am Schallbrett der Erziehung. *IZIP*, 1937, 15(1), 17–28; Wien: Jugend und Volk, 1947.

794 ———. Änderung des Lebensstils—Begabungswandel. *IZIP*, 1932, 10(3), 183–200.

795 ———. *Briefe am eine junge Mutter.* Wien: Jungbrunnen, 1957.

796 ———. Change of life style—Change of talent. *IJIP*, 1936, 2(1), 17–38.

797 ———. Consultation hour in school. *IJIP*, 1935, 1(3), 24–32.

798 Spiel, O. *Discipline without punishment.* Edited by L. Way. Translated by E. Fitzgerald. London: Faber & Faber, 1962.

799 ———. Dr. Ferdinand Birnbaum. *IZIP*, 1948, 17(1), 1–13.

800 ———. *La doctrine de A. Adler et ses applications à l'éducation écolaire.* Translated and preface by H. Schaffer. Paris: Payot, 1954.

801 ———. *Einmal anders gesehen . . . Reflections on problems of education in school.* Wein: Jungbrunnen, 1954.

802 ———. Emil, ein Fall charakterlicher Fehlentwicklung zum Einsidler. *IZIP*, 1947, 16(3), 136–139.

803 ———. Die Entwurzelungssituation (Kohärenz als Grundlage zwischen-menschlicher Beziehungen). In *Beiträge zur Sexualforschung.* Stuttgart: F. Enke, 1956.

804 ———. Ferdinand. *IJIP*, 1935, 1(4), 13–33.

805 ———. Foreword to Hertha Orgler, *Alfred Adler: The man and his work.*

806 ———. Franz. *IZIP*, 1947, 16, 33–44.

807 ———. Gemeinschaft als Idee und Realität. *IZIP*, 1948, 17(4), 145–156.

808 ———. The Individual Psychological Experimental School in Vienna. *AJIP*, 1956, 12, 1–11.

809 ———. Individualpsychologie als Beziehungslehre. In Int. Verein Indivpsy., *Alfred Adler zum gedenken.* Pp. 137–150.

810 ———. Individualpsychologie und Schule. *IZIP*, 1937, 15(3–4), 152–159.

811 ———. Mein Ältester. Bericht eines Mutter. *IZIP*, 1929, 7(6), 413–419.

812 ———. "My eldest": A mother's story. *IJIP*, 1937, 3(2), 137–150.

813 ———. Optimistische Lebensführung. *IZIP*, 1948, 17(3), 108–120.

814 ———. Die pädagogische Beratungsstunde in der Schule. *IZIP*, 1931, 9(3), 183–191.

815 ———. Portrait. *IPNL*, 1970, 19(4), 80; 1971, 20(6), 110, 112; 1972, 21(6), 112.

816 ———. Program for a school education. Individual Psychology as reconciliation between striving for personal significance and social obligation. *Pädagog. Heute*, 1969, 3–4.

817 ———. Punishment in school. *IJIP*, 1935, 1(1), 117–125.

818 ———. *Die Reise ins Leben.* Wien: Verlag für Jugend u. Volk, 1954 (with F. Birnbaum).

819 **Spiel, O.** Review of A. Dempf, *Theoretische Anthropologie.* Bern: A. Francke, 1951. In *IZIP*, 1951, 20(4), 188.

820 ———. Review of S. Guerewicz, *Beurteilung freier Schüleraufsätze und Schülerzeichnungen auf Grund der Adlerschen Individualpsychologie.* In *IZIP*, 1948, 17(4), 185–187.

821 ———. Review of R. Heiss, *Die Lehre vom Charakter.* Berlin: W. de Gruyter, 1949. In *IZIP*, 1951, 20(2), 91.

822 ———. Review of F. Horburger & A. Simonie, *Handbuch der Pädagogik.* Wien: Oesterreichischer Verlag, 1948. In *IZIP*, 1951, 20(2), 91–92.

823 ———. Review of C. G. Jung, *Seelenprobleme der Gegenwart.* Zürich: Rascher, 1950. In *IZIP*, 1951, 20(4), 188–189.

824 ———. Review of W. M. Kranefeldt, *Therapeutische Psychologie: Freud—Adler—Jung.* Berlin: W. de Gruyter, 1950. In *IZIP*, 1951, 20(2), 94.

825 ———. Review of M. Landmann, *Erkenntnis und Erlebnis.* Berlin: W. de Gruyter, 1951. In *IZIP*, 1951, 20(2), 94.

826 ———. Review of H. Leisegang, *Denkformen.* Berlin: W. de Gruyter, 1949. In *IZIP*, 1951, 20(3), 141–142.

827 ———. Review of H. Schwarz, *Ärztliche Weltanschauung.* Wien: W. Maudrich, 1951. In *IZIP*, 1951, 20(2), 95–96.

828 ———. Review of E. B. Strauss, *Quo vadimus?* Innsbruck: Tyrolia, 1948. In *IZIP*, 1950, 19(1), 44.

829 ———. Review of R. Strohal, *Grundfragen der Psychologie.* Innsbruck: Tyrolia, [   ]. In *IZIP*, 1951, 20(1), 43–44.

830 ———. Review of M. Tramer, *Schülernöte.* Basel: B. Schwabe, 1951. In *IZIP*, 1951, 20(4), 191–192.

831 ———. Review of H. Urban, *Über-Bewusstsein.* Innsbruck: Tyrolia, [   ]. In *IZIP*, 1951, 20(2), 89.

832 ———. Review of K. von Sury, *Wörterbuch der Psychologie und ihrer Grenzgebiete.* Basel: B. Schwabe, 1951. In *IZIP*, 1951, 20(4), 191.

833 ———. Review of A. Wellek, *Die Wiederherstellung der Seelenwissenschaft im Lebenswerk Felix Kruegers.* Hamburg: R. Meiner, 1950. In *IZIP*, 1951, 20(3), 142–143.

834 ———. The school and educational guidance (with F. Birnbaum). In

A. Adler & assoc., *Guiding the child.* Pp. 66–83.

835 **Spiel, O.** Schule und Erziehungsberatung. *IZIP*, 1929, 7(3), 184–190 (with F. Birnbaum).

836 ———. Die Schulklasse: Ein Arbeits- und Lebensgemeinschaft. *IZIP*, 1928, 6(3), 236–251 (with F. Scharmer).

837 ———. Schulzucht. In Sofie Lazarsfeld (Ed.), *Technik der Erziehung.*

838 ———. The teacher as psychological observer. *IPB*, 1946, 5, 22–28.

839 ———. Technology of mental hygiene in school. *IPB*, 1951, 9, 4–8.

840 ———. "Unsere Klassengemeinde arbeitet." *IZIP*, 1947, 16(2), 83–91.

841 ———. Verstehende Persönlichkeitserfassung. *IZIP*, 1949, 18(2), 49–74.

842 ———. *Wenn dein Kind mit dem Zeugniss kommt.* Wien: Jungbrunnen, 1952.

843 ———. Zur Psychologie Körperbehinderter. *IZIP*, 1950, 20(2), 79–88.

844 **Spiel, W.** New trends in medical aspects of child care. *World ment. Hlth.*, 1961, 13, 92–100.

845 ———. Portrait. *IPNL*, 1970, 19(4), 79.

846 ———. Review of W. H. Bodamer, *Gesundheit und Technische.* Stuttgart: Vestage & Russell Sage, 1955. In *Int. J. soc. Psychiat.*, 1957, 2(4), 311–312.

847 ———. Review of K. Schneider, *Die psychopathischen Persönlichkeiten.* Wien: Deuticke, 1950. In *IZIP*, 1950, 20(2), 94–95.

848 ———. Review of E. Stern, *Tests in clinical psychology.* Zürich: Rascher, [   ]. In *Int. J. soc. Psychiat.*, 1955, 1(1), 78.

849 ———. Review of R. von Urbantschitsch, *Sexuelle Erziehung von der Kindheit bis zur Ehe.* Wien: R. Cerny, 1951. In *IZIP*, 1951, 20(4), 192.

850 ———. Über Gruppenpsychotherapie. *IZIP*, 1950, 19(4), 161–174.

851 ———. *Zum Problem des Unbewussten vom Standpunkt der Individualpsychologie.* Stuttgart: Klett-Verlag, 1954 (with E. Ringel).

852 ———. Zur Problematik des Unbewussten vom Standpunkt der Individualpsychologie. *Psyche* (Stuttgart), 1952, 6, 378–388 (with E. Ringel).

853 **Spielberger, C. D.** (Ed.). *Anxiety and behavior.* New York: Academic Press, 1966.

854 **Spielman, L.** Wechselwirkung von personaler Finalität und exogenen und endogenen Kräften. *IZIP*, 1935, 13(1), 47-57.

855 **Spier, J.** (Ed.). *Die Schule der Ehe.* München: Mueller, 1919.

856 **Spiro, M. E.** Ghosts, Ifaluk and teleological functionalism. *Amer. Anthropol.*, 1952, 54, 497-503.

857 **Spitzer, Esther P.** Counseling aging persons with self-bounded life styles. *JIP*, 1966, 22, 104-111.

858 ———. Disengagement—Self perservation or self defense. *Voices*, 1970, 5(4), 28-32.

859 ———. Review of R. Ardrey, *The social contract.* New York: Atheneum, 1970. In *JIP*, 1972, 28, 92-93.

860 ———. Review of Dorothy Rabinowitz & Yadida Nielson, *Home life.* New York: Macmillan, 1971. In *Jewish Currents*, May, 1971.

861 ———. Scapegoating an aging parent—An escape from marital conflict. *IP*, 1968, 5(2), 54-58.

862 ———. The self-bound lifestyle. In A. Nikelly (Ed.), *Techniques for behavior change.* Pp. 151-157.

863 **Spreen, O.** Sibling relationship and mental deficiency diagnosis as reflected in Wechsler test patterns. *J. ment. Defic.*, 1966, 71, 406-410 (with W. Anderson).

864 **Squires, H. C.** Individual Psychology and practice (I). *IPMP*, 1932, No. 6 (with E. Wexberg & Olga Knopf).

865 **Sridhara, R. R.** Order of birth and schizophrenia. *Brit. J. Psychiat.*, 1966, 112, 1127-1129 (with N. Sundararaj).

866 **Srirastava, P. K.** The effect of family size, economic condition, and order of birth on adolescent adjustment. *Manas*, 1963, 10, 83-88 (with J. Prakash).

867 **Srole, L.** Anomie, authoritarianism, and prejudice. *Amer. J. Sociol.*, 1956, 62, 63-67.

868 **Stacey, C. L.** *Understanding human motivation.* Cleveland: Howard Allen, 1948 (with M. F. De Martino).

869 **Staffieri, J. R.** Birth order and creativity. *J. clin. Psychol.*, 1970, 26, 65-66.

870 ———. Birth order and perception of facial expressions. *Percep. mot. Skills*, 1970, 30, 606 (with J. E. Bassett).

871 **Stafford, R. E.** Twins: Behavioral differences. *Child Developm.*, 1967, 38, 1055-1064 (with A. M. Brown and S. G. Vandenberg).

872 **Stagner, R.** Personality as related to birth order and family size. *J. appl. Psychol.*, 1936, 20, 340-346 (with E. T. Katzoff).

873 **Stahel, Nelly.** *Das Erkennen seelischer Störungen aus der Zeichnung.* Zürich: Eugen Rentsch, 1969.

874 **Staiman, M.** Thoughts about criminology. *IPB*, 1942, 2(4), 72-73.

875 **Standal, S. W.** *Critical incidents in psychotherapy.* Englewood Cliffs, N. J.: Prentice-Hall, 1959 (with R. J. Corsini).

876 **Stangle, Esther K.** Social gerontology. *IP*, 1968, 5(2), 50-54.

877 **Stanley, F.** See O. Brachfeld.

878 **Staples, F. R.** Anxiety, birth order and susceptibility to social influence. *J. abnorm. soc. Psychol.*, 1961, 62, 716-719 (with R. H. Walters).

879 **Stark, Inez C.** George Meredith: The poet as therapist. *IJIP*, 1937, 3(2), 144-154.

880 ———. Review of L. Danz, *A psychologist looks at art.* New York: Longmans, Green, 1937. In IJIP, 1937, 3(3), 273-274.

881 **Starke, E.** Individualpsychologie und Verbrechenstherapie. *IZIP*, 1927, 6(2), 96-99.

882 ———. Review of F. Kleist, *Im Jugendgefängnis.* In P. Östreich (Ed.), *Die neue Erziehung.* Berlin: Hensel, . In *IZIP*, 1928, 6(3), 265-266.

883 ———. Review of [   ], *Reform des Strafvollzuges.* Berlin: Walter de Gruyter, 1927. In *IZIP*, 1928, 6(5), 419-420.

884 **Starr, Adaline.** Conjunctive use of psychodrama and group psychotherapy in a group living program with schizophrenic patients. *Grp. Psychother.*, 1965, 18(3), 127-135 (with T. P. McGee, Joanne Powers, Frances A. Racusen & A. Thornton).

885 ———. Portrait. *IPNL*, 1972, 21(6), 108.

886 ———. Psychodrama (with A. G. Nikelly). In A. G. Nikelly (Ed.), *Techniques for behavior change.* Pp. 135-139.

887 ———. Psychodrama in the child guidance centers. In R. Dreikurs, R. Corsini, R. Lowe & M. Sonstegard (Eds.), *Adlerian family counseling.* Pp. 75-82.

888 ———. Psychodrama with a child's social atom. *Grp. Psychother.*, 1953, 5(4), 222-225.

889 ———. Psychodrama with a family. *Grp. Psychother.*, 1959, 12(1), 27-31.

890 Starr, Adaline. The role of psychodrama in a child guidance center. *IPB*, 1951, 9(1), 18–24.

891 ———. Role playing: An efficient technique at a business conference. *Grp. Psychother.*, 1959, 12(2), 166–168.

892 ———. Training state hospital personnel through psychodrama and sociometry. *Grp. Psychother.*, 1961, 14, 55–61 (with E. Fogel).

893 Statton, Vicki Soltz. See Soltz, Vicki

894 Statton, W. O. Lay mental health action in a community. *JIP*, 1968, 24, 94–96.

895 Steed, S. P. The influence of Adlerian counseling on familial adjustment. Ph.D. Diss., Univ. of Arizona, 1971.

896 Steffic, E. C. The complementarity of personality needs in friendship choice. *J. abnorm. soc. Psychol.*, 1960, 61, 292–294 (with Mary Reilly & W. D. Commins).

897 Steiger, W. Liesel im Irrgarten der Angst. *IZIP*, 1928, 6(4), 337–338.

898 Stein, L. Beitrag zur Psychologie des Pferdes. *IZIP*, 1928, 6(1), 39–55.

899 ———. Ein Fall von psychogener Aphonie. *IZIP*, 1927, 5(1), 48–50.

900 ———. Review of M. Nadoleczny, *Die Sprach-und Stimmstörungen im Kindesalter.* Leipzig: F. C. W. Vogel, 1926. In *IZIP*, 1927, 5(4), 311.

901 ———. Die Sprache des Kindes und ihre Fehler. In Sofie Lazarsfeld (Ed.), *Richtige Lebensführung.*

902 ———. Über die psychologische Auffassung von organisch bedingten Funktionsstörungen. *IZIP*, 1924, 3(1), 11–17.

903 Stein, M. I. (Ed.). *Contemporary psychotherapies.* New York: Free Press of Glencoe, 1961.

904 Stein, R. S. The effects of ordinal position and identification on the development of philosophical attitudes. *J. genet. Psychol.*, 1970, 117, 13–24 (with A. B. Stein and J. Kagan).

905 Steinboch, Sophia. Review of R. Dreikurs, *The challenge of marriage* and *The challenge of parenthood.* In *IPB*, 1949, 7, 140.

906 Steiner, Gloria. The significance of some Adlerian concepts for the treatment of emotional disorders of childhood. In K. Adler & Danica Deutsch (Eds.), *Essays in Individual Psychology.* Pp. 235–241.

907 Steiner, K. Sinn der Jugendbewegung. *IZIP*, 1924, 2(4), 26–29.

908 Steiner, Lee. *A practical guide for troubled people.* New York: Greenberg, 1952.

909 ———. *Romantic marriage, the twentieth-century illusion.* Phila.: Chilton Books, 1963.

910 ———. *Where do people take their troubles?* Boston: Houghton Mifflin, 1945.

911 Steisel, I. An analysis of manifest content of the earliest memories of children. *J. genet. Psychol.*, 1958, 92, 41–52 (with H. Weiland).

912 Stekel, W. Active psychotherapy in wartime. *IPP*, 1943, No. 23. Pp. 21–27.

913 ———. *The autobiography of Wilhelm Stekel.* New York: Liveright, 1950.

914 ———. *Auto-erotism: A psychiatric study of onanism and neurosis.* New York: Liveright, 1950; London: Nevill, 1951; New York: Evergreen, 1961. Paper.

915 ———. *Bi-sexual love.* New York: Emerson 1944; Boston: R. G. Badger, 1922.

916 ———. *Compulsion and doubt.* 2 vols. New York: Liveright, 1949; London: Nevill, 1950; New York: Universal Libr., 1962; New York: Washington Sq. Press, 1967. Paper.

917 ———. *Conditions of nervous anxiety and their treatment.* New York: Liveright, 1950; London: Routledge & Kegan Paul, 1950.

918 ———. *La educacion de los padres.* Bueno Aires: 1947.

919 ———. *Estados nerviosos de angustia.* Buenos Aires: 1947.

920 ———. *Les états d'angoisse nerveux et leur traitement.* Paris: Payot,

921 ———. *Frigidity in woman in relation to her love life.* 2 vols. New York: Boni & Liveright, 1943; New York: Liveright, 1955; London: Vision, 1952; New York: Evergreen, 1962. Paper.

922 ———. *Homosexual neurosis.* New York: Emerson, 1922, 1944, 1949.

923 ———. *Impotence in the male.* 2 vols. New York: Liveright, 1927; London: Lane 1940; London: Vision, 1952; New York: Evergreen, 1965. Paper.

924 ———. *The interpretation of dreams, new developments and technique.* 2 vols. New York: Liveright, 1943; New York: Evergreen, 1962. Paper.

925 **Stekel, W.** *Life story of a pioneer psycho-analyst.* New York: Liveright, 1950.

926 ———. *Nervöse Angstzustände und ihre Behandlung.* Wien: Urban & Schwarzenberg, 1912.

927 ———. *Patterns of psychosexual infantilism.* New York: Liveright, 1952; London: Nevill, 1954; New York: Evergreen, 1959. Paper.

928 ———. *Peculiarities of behavior.* 2 vols. New York: Liveright, 1924; New York: Grove Press, 1964.

929 ———. *Primer for mothers.* New York: Emerson, 1937; Toronto: McLeod, 1937.

930 ———. *Sadism and masochism: The psychology of hatred and cruelty.* 2 vols. New York: Liveright, 1929, 1955; London: Lane, 1935; London: Vision, 1953; New York: Evergreen, 1964. Paper.

931 ———. *Schülerselbstmord.* In *Disk. Wien psychoanal. Ver.* Wiesbaden: J. F. Bergmann, 1912.

932 ———. *Sexual aberrations.* 2 vols. New York: Liveright, 1952; London: Vision, 1953; New York: Evergreen, 1964. Paper.

933 ———. *Die Technik der analytischen Psychotherapie.* Zurich: Huber, 1938.

934 ———. *Technique of analytical psychotherapy.* New York: Liveright, 1950; Toronto: McLeod, 1939; London: Lane, 1939, 1950.

935 ——— [Suicide]. In P. Friedman, *On suicide: With particular reference to suicide among young students.* (Discussions of the Vienna Psychoanalytic Society, 1910). Pp. 81–109.

936 **Sten, Anna.** A case of identical twins: Personality variation. *IP*, 1968, 5(3), 3–5.

937 ———. Contact. *IP*, 1968, 5(2), 48–49.

938 ———. Recreational therapy. *22nd Cong. Int. d'Histoire de la Médicine* (Bucharest), Sept. 1970. Pp. 499–500.

939 **Stendler, C. B.** Possible causes of overdependency in young children. *Child Developm.*, 1954, 25, 125–147.

940 **Stengel, E.** Review of P. Friedman, *On suicide: Discussions of the Vienna Psychoanalytic Society–1910.* In *Brit. J. Psychiat.*, 1968, 114, 912.

941 **Stenning, W. F.** The relationship of birth order to affiliation and achievement in children of 2 cultures: Mexico and the United States. *Diss. Abstr.*, 1968, 28, 4287.

942 **Stephan, E.** (Ed.). *Die Wirklichkeit und das Böse.* Hamburg: Hans Christian Verlag, 1970 (with V. Derbolowsky).

943 **Stephens, M. W.** Self-acceptance and self-evaluative behavior: A critique of methodology. *Psychol. Bull.*, 1961, 58, 104–121 (with D. P. Crowne).

944 **Stern, A.** Comment [on Barnes' "Adler & Sartre"]. *JIP*, 1965, 21, 202–203.

945 ———. Existential psychoanalysis and Individual Psychology. *JIP*, 1958, 14, 38–50.

946 ———. Further considerations on Alfred Adler and Ortega y Gasset. *JIP*, 1971, 27(2), 139–143.

947 ———. La Psychologie Individuelle d'Alfred Adler et la philosophie. *Rev. Phil. de la France et de l'étranger*, 1960, No. 3. Pp. 313–326.

948 **Stern, E.** Diagnostic value of children's early memories. *Arch. Int. Neurol.*, 1935, 54, 1–11.

949 ———. *Die Emigration als psychologisches Problem.* Paris: Author, 1937.

950 ———. Minderwertigkeitskomplex und Kompensationen in den Geschichten zu Murray's "Thematic Apperception Test." *IZIP*, 1950, 19(3), 109–121.

951 ——— (Ed.). *Die Psychotherapie in der Gegenwart.* Zürich: Rascher, 1958.

952 ———. Review of H. Damage, *Psychiatrie et civilisation.* Paris: Felix Alcan, 1934. In *IZIP*, 1937, 15(2), 92.

953 ———. Review of H. M. Fay, *L'intelligence et le caractère, leurs anomalies chez l'enfant.* Paris: Au foyer central d'hygiene, 1934. In *IZIP*, 1937, 15(2), 92.

954 ———. Review of Gilbert-Robin, *Les troubles nerveux et psychiques de l'enfant.* Paris: Fernand Nathan, 1935. In *IZIP*, 1937, 15(2), 92–93.

955 ———. Review of E. Huguenin, *Les enfants moralement abandonnés.* Paris: Ed. Cerf, 1936. In *IZIP*, 1937, 15(2), 91.

956 ———. Die Schule in der Erinnerung erwachsener Neurotiker. *IZIP*, 1935, 3(3), 176–184.

957 ———. Zur Psychopathologie des Erziehers. *IZIP*, 1934, 12(2), 105–112.

958 **Stern, W.** *Personalistik der Erinnerung.* Leipzig: Joh. Ambrosius Barth, 1931.

959 **Sternberg, E.** Review of I. Svero, *Zeno Cosini.* Basel: Rheinverlag, [   ]. In *IZIP*, 1930, 8.

960 **Sternberg, E.** Zur Theorie der Individual-psychologie. *IZIP*, 1927, 5(3), 187–193.

961 **Sternberg, H.** Review of A. Brauchle, *Psychoanalyse und Individualpsychologie*. In *IZIP*, 1931, 9(1), 72–73.

962 ———. Review of C. Burt, *The subnormal mind*. London: Oxford Univ. Press, 1935. In *IZIP*, 1936, 14(2), 124–125.

963 ———. Review of J. Cocteau, *Enfants terrible*. Berlin: Gustav Kiepenheuer, 1930. In *IZIP*, 1931, 9(1), 79–80.

964 ———. Review of T. Dreiser, *Jennie Gerhart & Schwester Carrie*. In *IZIP*, 1929, 7(6), 481.

965 ———. Review of E. Ebermayer, *Kampf um Odilienberg*. Wien: P. Zsolnay, 1929. In *IZIP*, 1930, 8(2), 277.

966 ———. Review of E. Heun, *Selbsterkenntnis und Selbstentwicklung*. Freiburg: Niels Kampmann, 1930. In *IZIP*, 1931, 9(1), 73.

967 ———. Review of R. Hughes, *High wind in Jamaica* [Sturmwind von Jamaica]. Berlin: Erich Reiss, 1931. In *IZIP*, 1932, 10(1), 79–80.

968 ———. Review of L. Lewisohn, *Das Erbe im Blut*. Leipzig: Paul List, 1929. In *IZIP*, 1931, 9(5), 416.

969 ———. Review of A. Maurois, *Wandlungen der Liebe*, München: R. Piper, 1929. In *IZIP*, 1930, 8(2), 278–279.

970 ———. Review of R. Neumann, *Sintflut*. Stuttgart: I. Engelhorns, 1929. In *IZIP*, 1929, 7(4), 323.

971 ———. Review of L. Paneth, *Gesunde und kranke Nerven*. Berlin: Max Hesses, 1930. In *IZIP*, 1931, 9(2), 158.

972 ———. Review of Agnes Smedley, *Eine Frau allein*. Frankfurt: Frankfurter Societäts-Druckerei, 1929. In *IZIP*, 1930, 8(4), 439–440.

973 ———. Review of I. Svevo, *Zeno Cosini*. Basel: Roman Rheinverlag, [   ]. In *IZIP*, 1930, 8(2), 277–278.

974 ———. Review of F. A. Theilhaber, *Goethe Sexus und Eros*. Leipzig: Horenverlag, 1929. In *IZIP*, 1931, 9(5), 412–414.

975 ———. Review of L. Trotzki, *Mein Leben*. Berlin: S. Fischer, 1930. In *IZIP*, 1931, 9(6), 483–484.

976 ———. Review of K. Tschuppik, *Ludendorff: Die Tragödie des Fachmanns*. Wien: Hans Epstein, 1931. In *IZIP*, 1931, 9(2), 158–159.

977 **Sternberg, H.** Review of H. Unger, *Die Klasse*. Berlin: E. Rowohlt, 1928. In *IZIP*, 1929, 7(4), 321–323.

978 ———. Review of E. Wickenberg, *Farben zu einer Kinderlandschaft*. Berlin: Bruno Cassirer, 1932. In *IZIP*, 1933, 11(2), 158.

979 **Sternberg, Olga.** Das Wesen des romantischen Menschen im Lichte der Individualpsychologie. In *IZIP*, 1932, 10(6), 446–452.

980 **S[tewart], C. W.** A journal whose identity is care. *J. past. Care*, 1971, 25(1), 1–2.

981 **Stewart, L.** The politics of birth order. *Proc. Ann. Conv. Amer. Psychol. Assn.*, 1970, 5, 365–366.

982 **Stewart, L. H.** Where are siblings? A reevaluation of the relationship between birth order and college attendance. *Sociom.*, 1968, 31, 294–303 (with W. T. Smelser).

983 **Stewart, R. H.** Birth order and dependency. *J. Pers. soc. Psychol.*, 1967, 6, 192–194.

984 **Stiggins, R. J.** Double-aspect perception and social interest. *Percep. mot. Skills*, 1970, 30, 387–392 (with R. J. Huber).

985 **Stites, R. S.** Alfred Adler on Leonardo da Vinci. *JIP*, 1971, 27(2), 208–212.

986 **Stock, Dorothy.** An investigation into the interrelations between the self concept and feelings directed toward other persons and groups. *J. consult. Psychol.*, 1949, 13, 176–180.

987 **Stockert, A.** August Forel. *IZIP*, 1923, 2(2), 25–28.

988 **Stockert, F. G.** Sprache und Geistesstörung. *Klin. Wchnschr.*, 1926, No. 45.

989 ———. Über Auskultationsphänomine am Brustkorb. *Arch. klin. Med.*, 1923, 6, 427–436 (with E. Froeschels).

990 ———. Über ein Fall von Sadismus. *IZIP*, 1926, 4(4), 216–227.

991 ———. Zur Ätiologie und Therapie des Sadismus. *IZIP*, 1927, 5(5), 327–335.

992 **Stockert, Marianne.** Family dynamics as an encumbrance for enuretics. *IP*, 1970, 8(1), 21–25.

993 **Stockhammer, M.** Max Steiner's nervöser Charakter. *IZIP*, 1933, 11(4), 316–329.

994 **Stoeckel, J.** *A team approach: Pre-disposition report: An innovative delivery perspective*. Minneapolis, Minn.: Hennepin County Court Services, 1972 (with W. L. Pew & Ira Schwartz).

995 **Stokes, K.** Mommy's mad. *Old Oregon*, Aug.-Sept., 1959.

996 **Stoller, R. J.** Passing and the continuum of gender and identity. In J. Marmor (Ed.), *Sexual inversion.* New York: Basic Books, 1965. Pp. 190–210.

997 ———. The sense of maleness. *Psychoanal. Quart.,* 1965, 34, 207–218.

998 **Stone, Frankie.** Let us remember [About Lydia Sicher]. *IPNL,* 1972, 21(5), 83–84.

999 **Stone, L. A.** Birth order and curricular choice. *Voc. Guid. Quart.,* 1963, 11, 209–211.

1000 ———. Family structure and pain reactivity. *J. clin. Psychol.,* 1966, 22, 33 (with L. G. Collins).

1001 **Stone, Patricia A.** Social interest and performance on the Goodenough Draw-A-Man Test. *JIP,* 1965, 21, 178–186 (with H. L. Ansbacher).

1002 **Stormer, E. G.** Adlerian group counseling in the elementary school: Report of a program. *JIP,* 1969, 25, 155–163 (with J. H. Kirby).

1003 ———. Dimensions of the intellect unmeasured by the Stanford-Binet. *IP,* 1967, 5(1), 13–14.

1004 ———. Milieu group counseling in elementary school guidance. *Elem. Sch. Guid. Counsel.,* 1967, 1(3), 240–254.

1005 **Storr, A.** *Human aggression.* New York: Atheneum, 1968.

1006 **Storrs, C.** Birth order of recovered and nonrecovered schizophrenics. *Arch. gen. Psychiat.,* 1963, 9, 224–228 (with A. Farina, H. Barry & N. Garmezy).

1007 **Stotland, E.** Birth order and an experimental study of empathy. *J. abnorm. soc. Psychol.,* 1963, 66, 610–614 (with J. A. Walsh).

1008 ———. Empathy, self-esteem, and birth order. *J. abnorm. soc. Psychol.,* 1963, 66, 532–540 (with R. E. Dunn).

1009 ———. Identification, "oppositeness", authoritarianism, self-esteem and birth order. *Psychol. Monogr.,* 1962, 76 (9, Whole No. 528) (with R. E. Dunn).

1010 ———. Peer groups and reactions to power figures. Ph.D. Diss, Univ. Michigan, 1954.

1011 **Stout, A. M.** Parent behavior toward children of differing ordinal position and sibling rank. Unpubl. Doctoral Diss., Univ. Cal. (Berkeley), 1960.

1012 **Strachstein, Harriet W.** A search for agreement as to the effectiveness of two methods of psychotherapy: Individual and group. In K. A. Adler & Danica Deutsch (Eds.), *Essays in Individual Psychology.* Pp. 289–294.

1013 **Stransky, E.** Ernährung und durchschnittliche Entwicklung bei Säugling und Kleinkind. In Sofie Lazarsfeld (Ed.), *Technik der Erziehung.*

1014 ———. Zur Gruppenpsychotherapie. *Wien. klin. Wchnschr.,* 1949, 61, 733–734.

1015 **Strasser, Charlot.** Nervöser Charakter, Disposition zur Trunksucht und Erziehung (with Vera Strasser). In A. Adler & C. Furtmüller (Eds.), *Heilen und Bilden* (1914). Pp. 390–398.

1016 ———. Portrait. *IPNL,* 1970, 19(4), 80.

1017 ———. Über Unfall-und Militarneurosen. *ZIP,* 1914, 1(6–9), 185–207.

1018 ———. Zum Geleit des ersten Kriegsheftes unseren Zeitschrift. *ZIP,* 1914, 1(6–9), 145 (with Vera Strasser).

1019 ———. Zur forensischen Begutachtung des Exhibitionismus. *ZIP,* 1914, 1(2), 33–44.

1020 **Strasser, I.** Review of Margarete Rada, *Das reifende Proletariermädchen.* Wien: Verlag f. Jugend u. Volk, 1931. In *IZIP,*

1021 **Strasser, Vera.** Geschlecht und Persönlichkeit. *ZIP,* 1914, 1(6–9), 227–231.

1022 ———. Massenpsychologie und Individualpsychologie. *ZIP,* 1914, 1(6–9), 156–174.

1023 ———. Der psychischen Mechanismus der Dementia praecox. *ZIP,* 1914, 1(4–5), 97–104.

1024 ———. Self-review of *Zur Psychologie des Alkoholismus. ZIP,* 1914, 1(2), 60–61.

1025 ———. Zum Geleit des ersten Kriegsheftes unseren Zeitschrift. *ZIP,* 1914, 1(6–9), 145 (with Charlot Strasser).

1026 ———. *Zur Psychologie des Alkoholismus.* München: E. Reinhardt, 1914.

1027 **Strasser-Eppelbaum, Vera.** See Strasser, Vera.

1028 **Stratton, G. M.** Anger and fear: Their probable relation to each other, to intellectual work and to primogeniture. *Amer. J. Psychol.,* 1927, 39, 125–140.

1029 ———. The relation of emotion to sex, primogeniture and disease. *Amer. J. Psychol.,* 1934, 4, 590–595.

1030 **Straus, E. W.** *Phenomenological psychology.* New York: Basic Books, 1966.

1031 **Strauss, M.** The future progress of Individual Psychology. *IPB,* 1942, 2(3), 57–58.

1032 Streeter, B. H. Psychology and religion. *IZIP*, 1924, 2(6), 22–26.

1033 Stricker, G. (Ed.). *The study of abnormal behavior: Selected readings.* New York: Macmillan, 1969 (with M. Zax).

1034 Strodtbeck, F. L. Family interaction, values and achievement. In D. McClelland (Ed.), *Talent and society.* New York: Van Nostrand, 1958.

1035 Strong, D. J. Measurement of self concept: A critique of the literature. *J. consult. Psychol.*, 1961, 8, 170–178 (with D. D. Feder).

1036 Stroup, A. L. Sibling position in the family and personality of offspring. *J. Marr. Family*, 1965, 27, 65–68 (with Katherine J. Hunter).

1037 Strumpfer, D. J. W. Correlates of the communication organ score on the Harris-Goodenough Drawing Test. *JIP*, 1968, 24, 60–62 (with G. K. Huysamen).

1038 Strunk, O., Jr. Attitudes toward one's name and one's self. *JIP*, 1958, 14, 64–67.

1039 Stuart, J. C. Data on the alleged psychopathology of the only child. *J. abnorm. soc. Psychol.*, 1926, 20, 441.

1040 Stumpf, J. C. Cues influencing judgment of personality characteristics. *J. consult. Psychol.*, 1959, 23, 219–225 (with E. G. Baier).

1041 ———. Day hospital and night hospital programs: An interpretative review of literature. Psychiat. Eval. Proj. Paper 61-3, VA Hospital, Washington, D. C. (with W. R. Dobson & W. H. Clayton).

1042 ———. Dimensions of psychiatric patient ward behavior. Psychiat. Eval. Proj. Rep. 63-1, VA Hospital, Washington, D. C. (with L. Gurel & J. E. Davis, Jr.).

1043 ———. Dimensions of psychiatric symptom ratings. Psychiat. Eval. Proj. Rep. 63-4, VA Hospital, Washington, D. C. (with L. Gurel & J. E. Davis, Jr.).

1044 ———. Dimensions of psychiatric symptom ratings determined at thirteen time-points from hospital admission. *J. consult. Psychol.*, 1966, 30(1), 39–44 (with J. Cohen & L. Gurel).

1045 ———. Interruption of schizophrenic deterioration by VA NP hospitals. Psychiat. Eval. Proj. Rep. 63-2, VA Hospital, Washington, D. C. (with L. Gurel and J. E. Davis, Jr.).

1046 Stumpf, J. C. Release and community stay criteria in evaluating psychiatric treatment. Psychiat. Eval. Proj. Rep. 63-2, VA Hospital, Washington, D. C. (with L. Gurel & J. E. Davis, Jr.).

1047 ———. Release and community stay in chronic schizophrenia. Psychiat. Eval. Proj., VA Hospital, Washington, D. C. (with L. Gurel & J. E. Davis, Jr.).

1048 ———. A survey of the self-care-dependen in selected VA hospitals. Psychiat. Eval. Proj., VA Hospital, Washington, D. C. (with L. Gurel and J. E. Davis, Jr.).

1049 Stungo, E. Analysis under hypnotics. *IPP*, 1943, No. 23. Pp. 59–71.

1050 Strupp, H. Towards a specification of teaching and learning in psychotherapy. *Arch. gen. Psychiat.*, 1969, 21, 203–212.

1051 Suedfeld, P. Anticipated and experienced stress in sensory deprivation as a function of orientation and ordinal position. *J. Pers. soc. Psychol.*, 1968, 76, 259–263.

1052 ———. Birth order of volunteers for sensory deprivation. *J. abnorm. soc. Psychol.*, 1964, 68, 195–196.

1053 ———. Sensory deprivation stress: Birth order and instructional set as interacting variables. *J. Pers. soc. Psychol.*, 1969, 11, 70–74.

1054 Sulzer, K. Arbeitsunterricht und Individualpsychologie. *IZIP*, 1928, 6(2), 164–172.

1055 ———. Portrait. *IPNL*, 1971, 20(6), 112.

1056 Sulzer, M. Portrait. *IPNL*, 1971, 20(6), 112

1057 Sumner, F. C. Measurement of neurotic tendency in women with uncommon names. *J. gen. Psychol.*, 1948, 39, 289–296 (with T. J. Houston).

1058 Sumpf, Else. Die Kunst und der Alltag. In J. Neumann (Ed.), *Du und der Alltag.*

1059 ———. Methodik und Erkenntnisquellen der Menschenkenntnis. In E. Wexberg (Ed.), *Handbuch der Individualpsychologie.* Pp. 47–82.

1060 ———. On the psychic capacity for keeping incidents in true-relation—In the case of healthy persons and of neurotics. *ZIP*, 1924, 3(1), 17–24.

1061 ———. Review of G. Aschaffenburg, *Das Verbrechen und seine Bekämpfung.* Heidelberg: Carl Winters, 1923. In *IZIP*, 1924, 2(3), 57–60.

1062 ———. Das Schicksal der Elisabeth Barrett-Browning. *IZIP*, 1925, 3(3), 110–119.

1063 **Sumpf, Else.** Selbsthauptung und Selbstverleugnung. *IZIP*, 1930, 8(1), 107-115.

1064 ————. Selbstwertgefühl und seelisches Gleichgewicht. *IZIP*, 1928, 6(1), 36-38.

1065 ————. "Störung des Persönlichkeitsgefühls" in der Neurose. In A. Adler & C. Furtmüller (Eds.), *Heilen und Bilden* (1928). Pp. 255-264.

1066 ————. Über psychische Beziehungsfähigkeit bei Gesunden und Nervösen. *IZIP*, 1924, 3(1), 17-24.

1067 ————. Wesen und Wege der ältern und Geschwistern oder anderen Vergleichspartnern. *IZIP*, 1930, 8(5), 486-498.

1068 ————. Zur Bedeutung des Verantwortlichkeitsgefühls in der Menschenkenntnis. In E. Wexberg (Ed.), *Handbuch der Individualpsychologie.* Pp. 47-82.

1069 **Sun, L.** Ordinal position and the behavior of visiting the child guidance clinic. *Acta psychol. Taiwanica*, 1965, 7, 10-16 (with Y. Ko).

1070 ————. Ordinal position and the behavior of visiting the child guidance clinic. II. *Acta psychol. Taiwanica*, 1966, 8, 92-95 (with Y. Ko).

1071 **Sundaraj. N.** Order of birth and schizophrenia. *Brit. J. Psychiat.*, 1966, 112, 1127-1129 (with R. R. Sridhara).

1072 **Sundberg, N. D.** Adler's technique with children: A special review. *JIP*, 1963, 19, 226-231.

1073 ————. *Clinical psychology.* New York: Appelton-Century-Crofts, 1962 (with Leona Tyler).

1074 ————. Review of G. W. Allport (Ed.), *Letters from Jenny.* New York: Harcourt, Brace & World, 1965. In *JIP*, 1965, 21(2), 210-211.

1075 **Sutton, W. M.** A case of delinquency as revenge on the mother. *IJIP*, 1935, 1(4), 60-66.

1076 **Sutton-Smith, B.** The dramatic sibling. *Percep. mot. Skills*, 1966, 22, 993-994 (with B. G. Rosenberg).

1077 ————. The relationship of ordinal position and sibling sex status to cognitive abilities. *Psychonom. Sci.*, 1964, 1, 81-82 (with B. G. Rosenberg).

1078 ————. *The sibling.* New York: Holt, Rinehart & Winston, 1970 (with B. G. Rosenberg).

1079 **Sutton-Smith, B.** Sibling association, family size and cognitive abilities. *J. genet. Psychol.*, 1966, 109, 271-279 (with B. G. Rosenberg).

1080 **Suzuki, H.** The significance of birth order and age difference between siblings as observed in drawings of pre-kindergarten children. *Folia psychiat. neurol. Japonica*, 1964, 17, 315-325 (with K. Abe & K. Tsiji).

1081 **Swanson, B.** Note on the relationship of ordinal position, dogmatism, and personal sexual attitudes. *J. Psychol.*, 1971, 77, 213-215.

1082 **Sward, K.** Review of Karen Horney, *Our inner conflicts.* In *J. abnorm. soc. Psychol.*, 1946, 41, 496-499. [Excerpted in *IPB*, 1946, 5, 125].

1083 **Swartz, M.** Interview and test data in a diagnostic problem: A case report. *J. clin. Psychol.*, 1959, 15, 124-127 (with Eva Ferguson).

1084 **Swartz, P.** Adler and the beginning student. *JIP*, 1964, 20, 101-102.

1085 ————. *Psychology: The study of behavior.* Princeton, N. J.: Van Nostrand, 1963.

1086 ————. Review of A. Adler, *Social interest.* In *JIP*, 1965, 21, 89-90.

1087 ————. Review of A. Angyal, *Neurosis and treatment.* In *JIP*, 1965, 21, 215-216.

1088 ————. Review of R. Arnheim, *Toward a psychology of art.* Berkeley, Cal.: Univ. Cal. Press, 1966. In *JIP*, 1966, 22, 247-248.

1089 ————. Review of J. A. M. Meerloo, *Creativity and eternization.* New York: Humanities Press, 1968. In *JIP*, 1969, 25, 119.

1090 **Sweeney, D. R.** Note on pain reactivity and family size. *Percep. mot. Skills*, 1970, 31, 25-26 (with B. J. Fine).

1091 **Swenson, C. H. Jr.** Factor analysis of self-report statements of love relationships. *JIP*, 1964, 20, 186-188 (with F. Gilner).

1092 ————. Love: A self-report analysis with college students. *JIP*, 1961, 17, 167-171.

1093 **Swenson, S. S.** Changing expressed parental attitudes toward child rearing practices and its effect on social adaptation and level of adjustment perceived by parents. Ed. D. Diss., Boston Univ., 1969.

1094 ————. Dr. Marcelle Robinson—Regarding group process. *OSIPNL*, 1970, 11(3), 3-4.

1095 Swenson, S. S. The life style. *OSIPNL*, 1972, 13(3), 15.

1096 Sykes, W. R. Theory for present-day social events. [Tribute to Alfred Adler on his 100th birthday]. *JIP*, 1970, 26(2), 16.

1097 Sylvus, N. *Herkologische Graphologie.* Vorwort von F. Künkel. Stuttgart: Fr. Frommans Verlag, 1931.

1098 Symonds, P. M. *The psychology of parent-child relationships.* New York: Appleton-Century, 1939.

1099 Szasz, T. S. Freud as a leader. *Antioch Rev.*, 1963 (Summer), 133–144.

1100 ———. The myth of mental illness. *Amer. Psychologist*, 1960, 15, 113–118.

1101 ———. *The myth of mental illness: Foundations of a theory of personal conduct.* New York: Hoeber, 1961.

1102 ———. Open doors or civil rights for mental patients? *JIP*, 1962, 18, 168–171.

1103 ———. The uses of naming and the origin of the myth of mental illness. *Amer. Psychologist*, 1961, 16, 59–65.

1104 Szekely, B. *El psicoanalsis: Teoria y aplicacion.* Buenos Aires: Colegio Libre Estudios Superiores, 1940.

1105 Székely, S. Beiträge zur individualpsychologischen Traumtheorie. *IZIP*, 1934, 12(4), 223–232.

1106 Szent-Gyoergyi, A. Drive in living matter to perfect itself. *JIP*, 1966, 22, 153–162.

1107 Szidon, K. G. Hebbels Jugend. *ZIP*, 1914, 1(4–5), 115–130.

T

1 T. R. Individualpsychologie und Strafgesetz. *IZIP*, 1933, 11(1), 69–74.

2 T. T. Dr. Alfred Adler. (1870–1970). *Morley Mag.*, 1970, 75 (with M. E.).

3 Taft, R. A cluster analysis for Hall and Lindzey. *Contemp. Psychol.*, 1958, 3, 143–144.

4 ———. Selective recall and memory distortion of favorable and unfavorable material. *J. abnorm. soc. Psychol.*, 1954, 49, 23–28.

5 Tagiuri, C. K. The family constellation and overt incestuous relations between father and daughter. *Amer. J. Orthopsychiat.*, 1954, 24, 266–279 (with I. Kaufman & Alice L. Peck).

6 Tagiuri, R. The perception of people (with J. S. Bruner). In G. Lindzey (Ed.), *Handbook of social psychology.* Vol. 2. Pp. 634–654.

7 Taglicht, F. Review of [ ] von Pezold, Betrachtungen über das Reichsgesetz zur Bekämpfung von Geschlechtskrankheiten. *Z. ärztl. Fortbild.*, 1930, No. 14. In *IZIP*, 1931, 9(2), 160.

8 ———. Review of [ ] von Pezold, Ist die Onanie ein therapeutisches Problem? *Fortschr. der Ther.* Vol. 6. In *IZIP*, 1931, 9(2), 160.

9 Tahmisian, J. Birth order student characteristics: A replication. *J. consult. Psychol.*, 1967, 31, 219 (with E. C. Walker).

10 Taintor, Z. Birth order and psychiatric problems in boot camp. *Amer. J. Psychiat.*, 1970, 126, 1604–1610.

11 Takats, J. Kriminologie und Individualpsychologie. *IZIP*, 1936, 14(3), 137–155.

12 ———. Review of F. Gorphe, *La critique du Te'moignage.* Paris: Dalloz, 1927. In *IZIP*, 1929, 7(2), 155–158.

13 ———. The "soul" of a murderer. *IJIP*, 1937, 3(2), 155–170.

14 Talwar, P. P. Forms of age-specific birth rates by orders of birth in an Indian community. *Eugen. Quart.*, 1968, 15, 264–271 (with C. Chandrasekaran).

15 Tanner, Amy. Adler's theory of Minderwertigkeit. *Ped. Sem.*, 1915, 22, 204–217.

16 Tarwater, J. W. Self-understanding and the ability to predict another's response. *Marr. Fam. Living*, 1953, 15, 126–128.

17 Tauber, Esther. Gemeinschaftsgefühl. *IPNL*, 1966, 16(11–12, Whole No. 184–185). P. 43.

18 ———. *Molding society to man* (Israel's new adventure in co-operation). New York: Bloch, 1955.

19 ———. Our generation at the crossroads. *Urim Lahorim* (Tel Aviv), Sept., 1962.

20 Tauber, S. Individualpsychologische Gedankengänge in der medizinische Klinik. *IZIP*, 1933, 11(1), 8–19.

21 Taylor, C. Self-acceptance and adjustment. *J. consult. Psychol.*, 1952, 16, 89–91 (with A. W. Combs).

22 Taylor, D. Encounter groups. *IPNL*, 1972, 21(1), 8–9.

23 Taylor, D. H. Consistency of the self concept. Unpubl. Ph.D. Diss., Vanderbilt Univ., 1953.

24 **Taylor, E. A.** *Meeting the increasing stresses of life: A multiple therapy approach in education.* Springfield, Ill.: C. C. Thomas, 1963.

25 **Taylor, E. L.** Review of A. Adler, *Understanding human nature.* In *IZIP*, 1928, 6(5), 426.

26 **Taylor, J.** Helpful guidelines for eliminating classroom misbehavior. *OSIPNL*, 1972, 13(2), insert.

27 **Taylor, R. E.** Birth order and MMPI patterns. *JIP*, 1966, 22, 208–211 (with R. Eisenman).

28 ———. Birth order and sex differences in complexity-simplicity, color-form preference and personality. *J. proj. Tech. Pers. Assess.*, 1968, 32, 383–387 (with R. Eisenman).

29 ———. Homesickness, future time perspective, and the self concept. *JIP*, 1967, 23, 94–97 (with J. J. Platt).

30 **Taylor, W. S.** Hypnoanalysis of a fetishism. *Psychiat. Quart.*, 1962, 36, 83–95.

31 ———. Morton Princes Anschauungen über die moderne Psychopathologie. *IZIP*, 1928, 6(1), 5–22.

32 **Teichman, M.** Antithetical apperception of family members by neurotics. *JIP*, 1971, 27(1), 73–75.

33 ———. Depreciation and accusation tendencies: Empirical support. *JIP*, 1972, 28, 45–50 (with U. G. Foa).

34 **Teirich, H. R.** Gruppentherapie und dynamische Gruppenpsychotherapie in Deutschland. *Heilkunst*, 1957, 10, 8.

35 ——— (Ed.). *Musik in der Medizin.* Stuttgart: G. Fischer, 1959.

36 ———. Theorie und Praxis der Gruppenpsychotherapie. *Wien. med. Wissensch.*, 1949, 99, 617–618.

37 **Teler, J.** Über die Verwertung unbemerkter eindrücke bei Assoziationen. *Z. gesam. Neurol. Psychiat.*, 1924, 89, 1398 (with R. Allers).

38 **Tellegen, A.** Review of H. L. and Rowena Ansbacher (Eds.), *Superiority and social interest.* In *Contemp. Psychol.*, 1967, 12, 39–40.

39 **Temerlin, M. K.** The belief in psychic determinism and the behavior of the psychotherapist. *Rev. exist. Psychol. Psychiat.*, 1965, 5, 16–33 (with Vera M. Gatch).

40 ———. On choice and responsibility in a humanistic psychotherapy. *J. humanist. Psychol.*, 1963, 3, 35–48.

41 **Terner, Janet R.** LC acquires Dreikurs papers. *Library of Congress, Information Bull.*, 1972, 31(22).

42 **Terris, W.** "Altruistic" behavior in rhesus monkeys. *Amer. J. Psychiat.*, 1964, 121, 584–585 (with J. H. Masserman & S. Wechkin).

43 **Tesarek, A.** Im Kindergarten. In Sofie Lazarsfeld (Ed.), *Technik der Erziehung.*

44 **Thalberg, F.** Zur Berufswahl. In A. Adler & C. Furtmüller (Eds.), *Heilen und Bilden* (1914). Pp. 316–320.

45 **Tharp, R. G.** Psychological patterning in marriage. *Psychol. Bull.*, 1963, 60, 97–117.

46 **Thatcher, P.** Early recollection in a case of juvenile delinquency. *IPB*, 1944–45, 4, 59–60.

47 **Thelen, M. H.** The relationship of selected variables to intrafamily similarity of defense preferences. *J. proj. Tech. Pers. Assess.*, 1967, 31, 23–27.

48 **Thoma, Elizabeth.** Group psychotherapy with underachieving girls in a public high school. *JIP*, 1964, 20, 96–100.

49 ———. Treatment of an adolescent neurotic in a public school setting. In K. A. Adler & Danica Deutsch (Eds.), *Essays in Individual Psychology.* Pp. 423–434.

50 **Thomas, A.** Purpose vs. consequence in the analysis of behavior. *Amer. J. Psychother.*, 1970, 24, 49–64.

51 **Thomas, E. J.** The relationship of goal structure to motivation under extreme conditions. *JIP*, 1959, 15, 121–127 (with A. Zander).

52 **Thomas, G. E.** The influence of selected family background factors on reading readiness, reading achievement and teachers' ratings of pupils in grade one. *Diss. Abstr. Int.*, 1971, 31, 4048–4049.

53 **Thomas, Yvonne.** Review of N. G. Haring & E. L. Phillips, *Educating emotionally disturbed children.* New York: McGraw-Hill, 1962. In *OSIPNL*, 1965, 6(1), 11.

54 **Thompson, Clara.** *Psychoanalysis: Evolution and development.* New York: Hermitage House, 1950; New York: Grove Press, 1950 (with P. Mullahy).

55 **Thorn, Emily F.** *Understanding and helping children's behavior: A primer according to the principles of*

Individual Psychology for use in parents' and teachers' study groups. Wilmington, Del.: Family Educ. Ctr. of Delaware, 1972.

56 **Thorn, P.** Interpersonal conflicts in elementary school classes. *IP*, 1970, 7(2), 38–46.

57 **Thorne, F. C.** Adler's broad-spectrum concept of man, self-consistency and unification. *JIP*, 1970, 26(2), 135–143.

58 ———. [Autobiography]. *Psychol. Today*, 1972, 6(4), 58–62.

59 ———. *Personality: A clinical eclectic viewpoint.* Brandon, Vt.: J. clin. Psychol., 1961.

60 **Thornton, A.** Conjunctive use of psychodrama and group psychotherapy in a group living program with schizophrenic patients (with T. P. McGee, Adaline Starr, Joanne Powers and Frances A. Racusen).

61 **Thorpe, L. P.** *Child psychology and child development.* New York: Ronald Press, 1946.

62 ———. *What I like to do: An inventory of children's interests.* Chicago: Science Research Assoc., 1954 (with C. E. Meyers & M. R. Bonsall).

63 **Thune, N.** *Religion und Minderwertigkeitsgefühl. Eine Untersuchung der Auseinandersetzung der Adler's Individualpsychologie mit der Religion.* Leipzig: Verlag Otto Harassowitz, 1950; Upsala, Sweden: A.-B. Lundequistka Bokhandeln, 1950.

64 **Thurston, J. R.** Infant feeding gratification and adult personality. *J. Pers.*, 1951, 19, 449–458 (with P. H. Mussen).

65 **Thurstone, L. L.** Birth order and intelligence. *J. educ. Psychol.*, 1929, 20, 641–651 (with R. L. Jenkins).

66 **Tidrow, J. W.** Change: A result, not a target. *Texas Outlook*, July, 1970 (with E. J. Chambliss & L. J. Lambert).

67 ———. Reinforcing and changing student motivation. *Publ. Sch. Forum*, 1968, 4, 20–23.

68 ———. Research in classroom learning. *Psychiat. Spectator*, 1968, 6(11).

69 **Tillich, P.** The significance of Kurt Goldstein for philosophy of religion. *JIP*, 1959, 15, 20–23.

70 **Titchener, E. B.** Early memories. *Amer. J. Psychol.*, 1900, 11, 435–436.

71 **Tobin, S. S.** Childhood reminiscence and institutionalization in the aged. *Proc. 7th Int. Congr. Geront.*, Vienna,

Austria, June 26–July 2, 1966. Separatum.

72 **Tobin, S. S.** Effect of stress on earliest memory. *Arch. gen. Psychiat.*, 1968, 19, 435–444 (with Elizabeth Etigson).

73 **Todd, F. J.** Selective perception in the interpretation of symbols. *J. abnorm. soc. Psychol.*, 1952, 47, 255–256 (with H. H. Mosak).

74 **Tolman, R. S.** A note on family position of certain delinquent boys. *Amer. J. Orthopsychiat.*, 1939, 9, 635.

75 **Toman, W.** Choices of marriage partners by men coming from monosexual sibling configurations. *Brit. J. med. Psychol.*, 1964, 37, 43–46.

76 ———. Comment [on Levinger & Sonnheim, "Complementarity in marital adjustment. . . ."]. *JIP*, 1965, 21, 145–146.

77 ———. Die Familienkonstellation und ihre psychologische Bedeutung. *Psychol. Rundsch.*, 1959, 10, 1–15.

78 ———. *Familienkonstellationen: Ihr Einfluss auf den Menschen und seine Handlungen.* München: C. H. Beck, 1965.

79 ———. *Family constellation: Theory and practice of a psychological game.* New York: Springer, 1961.

80 ———. Family constellation as a basic personality determinant. *JIP*, 1959, 15, 199–211.

81 ———. Family constellation as a character and marriage determinant. *Int. J. Psycho-Anal.*, 1959, 40, 316–319.

82 ———. Family constellations of "normal" and "disturbed" marriages: An empirical study. *JIP*, 1961, 17, 93–95 (with B. Gray).

83 ———. Family constellations of the partners in divorced and married couples. *JIP*, 1962, 18, 48–51.

84 ———. Haupttypen der Familienkonstellationen. *Psychol. Rundsch.*, 1960, 11, 273–284.

85 ———. Large age differences among spouses and their family constellations. *Psychol. Rep.*, 1963, 13, 386.

86 ———. Never mind your horoscope: Birth order rules all. *Psychol. Today*, 1970, 4(7), 45–49, 68–69.

87 ———. Sibling positions of a sample of distinguished persons. *Percep. mot. Skills*, 1970, 31, 825–826 (with E. Toman).

88 **Tomeh, A. K.** Birth order and friendship associations. *J. Marr. Fam.*, 1970, 32, 360–369.

89 ——. Birth order and kinship affiliation. *J. Marr. Fam.*, 1969, 31, 19–26.

90 **Tompkins, S. S.** Early recollections as predictors of the Tompkins-Horn Picture Arrangement Test performance. *JIP*, 1961, 17, 177–180 (with R. E. McCarter & H. M. Schiffman).

91 **Torberg, F.** Review of M. Sperber, *Alfred Adler oder das Elend der Psychologie*. In *Die Welt der Literatur* (Hamburg), 1970, 7(6), 3.

92 **Towns, Toni.** Dr. Alfred Adler (1870–1971). *Morley Mag.* (London), 1970, 75, 60 (with Maude Ehrenstien).

93 ——. Teacher found the psychology of Alfred Adler invaluable. *Guernsey Eve. Press & Star*, Feb. 13, 1970.

94 **Trentzsch, P. J.** Detection of early symptoms of psychoses. *IZIP*, 1928, 6(3), 251–257.

95 **Triandaphyllidis, M.** Über Geheimsprachen. *IZIP*, 1925, 3(2), 91–93.

96 **Tsiji, K.** The significance of birth order and age difference between siblings as observed in drawings of pre-kindergarten children. *Folia psychiat. neurol. Japonica*, 1964, 17, 315–325 (with K. Abe & H. Suzuki).

97 **Tsuang, M-T.** Birth order and maternal age of psychiatric in-patients. *Brit. J. Psychiat.*, 1966, 112, 1131–1141.

98 **Tuckman, J.** Ordinal position and behavior problems in children. *J. Hlth. & soc. Behav.*, 1967, 8(1), 32–39 (with R. A. Regan).

99 **Tuites, Ann.** The reeducation of a pampered prince. *IP*, 1969, 6(2), 29–33 (with Jean H. Cripps & Nancy Blockinger).

100 **Tulkin, S. R.** Mother-child interaction: Social class differences in the first year of life. *Proc. ann. Conv. Amer. Psychol. Assn.*, 1970, 5, 261–262 (with J. Kagan).

101 **Tunney, T.** The separation capacity of the Rorschach. *J. consult. Psychol.*, 1955, 19, 194–196 (with W. Severson, H. Uehling, & R. J. Corsini).

102 **Türkinger, H.** Der Alfred Adler Kongress in New York ein grosser Erfolg. *Staats Zeit.*, May 23, 1959.

103 **Tyler, Leona.** *Clinical Psychology.* New York: Appleton-Century-Crofts, 1962 (with N. D. Sundberg).

104 **Tyler, Leona.** Research explorations in the realm of choice. *J. couns. Psychol.*, 1961, 8, 195–201.

U

1 **Uehling, H.** The separation capacity of the Rorschach. *J. consult. Psychol.*, 1955, 19, 194–196 (with W. Severson, T. Tunney, & R. J. Corsini).

2 **Uglmann, Ruth.** Alfred Adler—oder das Elend der Psychologie. *Zürich Tages—Anzeiger*, June 11, 1970.

3 **Ullman, A. D.** Time as a determinant in integrative learning. *Psychol. Rev.*, 1945, 52, 61–90 (with O. H. Mowrer).

4 **Ullman, M.** Dreaming, life style and physiology: A comment on Adler's view of the dream. *JIP*, 1962, 18, 18–25.

5 **Unger, Martha.** Ein Fall von Sprechhemmung. *IZIP*, 1930, 8(6), 582–586.

6 ——. Käufer und Verkäufer. *IZIP*, 1929, 7(6), 459–462.

7 **Updike, J.** Minority report. *IPNL*, 1969, 19(2), 38.

8 **Urban, H. B.** The Individual Psychology of Alfred Adler: A review. *JIP*, 1965, 21, 85–88 (with D. H. Ford).

9 ——. *Systems of psychotherapy: A comparative study.* New York: Wiley, 1963 (with D. H. Ford).

10 **Uytman, J. D.** Adler, Alfred. *Encyclopedia of philosophy.* New York: Macmillan, 1967.

V

1 **V. A.** Review of Mathilde Kelchner, *Kummer und Trost jugendlicher Arbeiterinnen.* Leipzig: C. L. Hirschfeld, 1929. In *IZIP*, 1931, 9(2), 155–157.

2 **Vaihinger, H.** *Philosophie des Als Ob.* Leipzig: Felix Meiner, 1928.

3 ——. *The philosophy of "as if": A system of the theoretical, practical and religious fictions of mankind.* Translated by C. K. Ogden. New York: Harcourt, Brace, 1925; London: Routledge & Kegan Paul, 1965.

4 **Valentiner, T.** Seelische Dynamik im Schülerleben. *IZIP*, 1931, 9(3), 207–213.

5 **van Asperen, G. H.** Afscheid van de Heer H. W. de Ridder. *MNWIP*, 1970, 19(2), 20.

6 ———. In memoriam de Heer J. Vinkenborg. *MNWIP*, 1970, 19(2), 1.

7 ———. In memoriam Mevrou G. J. Winter-de Graaf. *MNWIP*, 1970, 19(2), 2.

8 ———. In memoriam Mevrou J. Ronge-Haslinghuis. *MNWIP*, 1970, 19(2), 2.

9 ———. Een Mogelijkheid Om Beter Te Leren Helpen. *MNWIP*, 1972, 21(2), (with H. M. van Praag).

10 ———. [Obituary of J. A. Delhez]. *MNWIP*, 1971, 21(1).

11 ———. De Oorsprong van de Emoties. *MNWIP*, 1972, 21(2).

12 ———. Pieter H. Ronge (1885–1969). *JIP*, 1969, 25, 261–262.

13 ———. Portrait. *IPNL*, 1970, 19(4), 80.

14 ———. *Psychotherapie—Concentrische Methode.* Utrecht: Spectrum, 1969.

15 ———. Psychotherapie—Concentrische Methode. *MNWIP*, 1970, 19(2), 3–4.

16 **Vanderford, Margaret.** Review of Camilla M. Anderson, *Jan, my brain-damaged daughter.* Portland, Ore.: Durham Press, 1963. In *OSIPNL*, 1964, 4(5), 9–10.

17 ———. Review of R. Dreikurs, *Adult-child relations.* In *OSIPNL*, 1964, 4(4), 11.

18 ———. Review of V. Frankl, *Man's search for meaning.* In *OSIPNL*, 1964, 5(1), 8–9.

19 **VanderHorst, L.** On the conception of space and time. *JIP*, 1959, 15, 89–92.

20 **Vandette, JoAnn.** Application of Adlerian principles to speech therapy. *JIP*, 1964, 20, 213–218.

21 **van Dijk, L. C.** Portrait. *IPNL*, 1971, 20 (6), 110.

22 **Van Dusen, W.** Adler and Binswanger on schizophrenia. *JIP*, 1960, 16, 77–80 (with H. L. Ansbacher).

23 ———. Adler and existence analysis. *JIP*, 1959, 15, 100–111.

24 ———. Invoking the actual in psychotherapy. *JIP*, 1965, 21, 66–76.

25 ———. The ontology of Adlerian psychodynamics. *JIP*, 1959, 15, 143–156.

26 ———. The phenomenology of a schizophrenic existence. *JIP*, 1961, 17, 80–92.

27 ———. Review of W. Barrett, *Irrational man.* Garden City, N. Y.: Doubleday, 1958. In *JIP*, 1959, 15, 237–238.

28 **Van Dusen, W.** Review of L. Binswanger, *Being-in-the-world.* New York: Basic Book 1963. In *JIP*, 1964, 20, 107–108.

29 ———. Review of M. Boss, *The analysis of dreams.* In *JIP*, 1960, 16, 104–105.

30 ———. Review of K. G. Dutt, *Existentialism and Indian thought.* New York: Phil. Libr., 1960. In *JIP*, 1960, 16, 215.

31 ———. Review of G. F. Kneller, *Existentialism and education.* New York: Phil. Libr., 1958. In *JIP*, 1959, 15, 133–134.

32 ———. Review of R. May, C. Angel & H. Ellenberger (Eds.), *Existence.* In *JIP*, 1958, 14, 188–189.

33 ———. Review of M. Merleau-Ponty, *The primacy of perception and other essays on phenomenological psychology, the philosophy of art, history and politics.* Evanston, Ill.: Northwestern Univ. Press, 1964. In *JIP*, 1965, 21(2), 220–221.

34 ———. Review of I. Progoff, *The death and re-birth of psychology.* In *JIP*, 1960, 16, 216–217.

35 ———. Review of K. Sato (Ed.), *Psychologia, an International Journal of Psychology the Orient.* Vol. 1. No. 4. In *JIP*, 1959, 15, 132–133.

36 **Van Enckevert, P. Th.** Vertaald to Sidonie Reiss, *Levenskoers en Levensvernieuwing.*

37 **Van Hine, Nancy P.** Effects of birth order upon personality development of twins. *J. genet. Psychol.*, 1969, 114, 93–95 (with P. S. Very).

38 **van Kaam, A. L.** Assumptions in psychology. *JIP*, 1958, 14, 22–28.

39 ———. *The demon and the dove: Personality growth through literature.* Pittsburgh: Duquesne Univ. Press, 1967 (with Kathleer Healy).

40 ———. The nurse in the patient's world. *Amer. J. Nurs.*, Dec., 1959.

41 ———. Phenomenal analysis: Exemplified by a study of the experience of "really feeling understood". *JIP*, 1959, 15, 66–72.

42 ———. *Religion and personality.* Englewood Cliffs, N. J.: Prentice-Hall, 1964.

43 ———. Review of A. H. Maslow (Ed.), *New knowledge in human values.* New York: Harper, 1959. In *JIP*, 1960, 16, 96–97.

44 **van Lun, W.** Seelsorge und Neurose. *IZIP*, 1951, 20(3), 97–110 (with E. Ringel).

45 van Lun, W. *Die Tiefenpsychologie hilft dem Seelsorger*. Wien: Herder-Verlag, 1953 (with E. Ringel).

46 van Praag, H. M. Een Moglijkheid om Beter Te Leren Helpen. *MNWIP*, 1972, 21(2), (with G. H. van Asperen).

47 van Raalte, F. Kleine und hässlicher Männer. *IZIP*, 1926, 4(3), 150–152.

48 ———. "La loi Adler" et l'exercise. *IZIP*, 1926, 4(1), 30–33.

49 van Schilfgaarde, P. Translator of A. Adler, *Mensenkenntnis*.

50 ———. Translator of A. Adler, *De psychologie van het individueele op school on in het gezin*.

51 van Weerden, Hermine. The Individual Psychologist. *IPNL*, 1969, 19(1), 23–24.

52 ———. Letter to the editor. *IP*, 1968, 5, 39.

53 ———. Mijn ervaring in de Alfred Adler Mental Health Clinic te New York. *MNWIP*, 1970, 19(2), 9–12.

54 Varela, J. A. A cross-cultural replication of an experiment involving birth order. *J. abnorm. soc. Psychol.*, 1964, 69, 456–457.

55 Various. *Articles of supplementary reading for parents*. Chicago: Alfred Adler Inst., 1970.

56 Various. *Articles of supplementary reading for teachers and counselors*. Chicago: Alfred Adler Inst., 1970.

57 Vaughan, R. Translator, with J. Linton, of A. Adler, *Social interest: A challenge to mankind*.

58 Vaughan, W. F. *The lure of superiority*. New York: H. Holt, 1928.

59 ———. *Personal and social adjustment*. New York: Odyssey Press, 1952.

60 ———. The psychology of Alfred Adler. *J. abnorm. soc. Psychol.*, 1926–27, 21, 358.

61 ———. The psychology of compensation. *Psychol. Rev.*, 1926, 33, 467–479.

62 Veit, V. Review of Reichskuratorium für Wirtschaftlichkeit, *Der Mensch und die Rationalisierung*. Jena: Gustav Fischer, 1931. In *IZIP*, 1933, 12(4), 331–332.

63 ———. Zur Psychologie des einzigen Bruders. *IZIP*, 1932, 10(1), 53–59.

64 Vercruysse, G. *Onderzoek naar de evolutie van Alfred Adlers Opvatting over de "Levensstijl": Geschriften uit de Jaren 1898–1917*. Louvain, Belgium: Cath. Univ., 1961.

65 Vercruysse, G. Review of R. Depelchin, *De Opvattingen van Alfred Adler over de Droom*. In *JIP*, 1965, 21(1), 98–99.

66 ———. Self-review of *Onderzoek naar de evolutie van Alfred Adlers Opvatting over de "Levensstijl"*. In *JIP*, 1963, 19, 97–98.

67 Verger, D. Birth order and sibling differences in interest. *JIP*, 1968, 24, 56–59.

68 ———. Early recollections (with A. G. Nikelly). In A. G. Nikelly (Ed.), *Techniques for behavior change*. Pp. 55–60.

69 ———. Early recollections; Reflections of the present. *J. couns. Psychol.*, 1970, 17, 510–515 (with W. L. Camp).

70 ———. A study of the relationships of birth order to the development of interests. Doctoral Diss., Univ. Oregon, 1965; *Diss. Abstr.*, 1966, 26, 5544.

71 Verhaeren, J. Der Eintritt ins Berufsleben. *IZIP*, 1930, 8(6), 576–581.

72 ———. Entrance into vocational life. *IJIP*, 1937, 3(1), 24–29.

73 Vernon, D. T. Effect of mother-child separation and birth order on young children's responses to two potentially stressful experiences. *J. Pers. soc. Psychol.*, 1967, 5, 162–174 (with Jeanne M. Foley & J. L. Schulman).

74 Vernon, J. (Ed.). *Introduction to general psychology*. Dubuque, Ia.: Brown, 1966.

75 Veroff, J. *Motivation: A study of action*. Belmont, Cal.: Brooks-Cole, 1966 (with D. Birch). Paper.

76 Verploegh–Chassé, J. Das nervöse Kind. *IZIP*, 1923, 2(1), 33–40.

77 Vértes, T. A case of speech disturbance (with A. Müller). In A. Adler & assoc., *Guiding the child*. Pp. 241–246.

78 ———. Ein Fall von Organminderwertigkeit. *IZIP*, 1929, 7(3), 238–239 (with A. Müller).

79 ———. Der Weg zum Verbrechen. *IZIP*, 1931, 9(5), 403–406.

80 Very, P. S. Birth order, personality development, and the choice of law as a profession. *J. genet. Psychol.*, 1970, 116, 219–221 (with R. W. Prull).

81 ———. Effects of birth order upon personality development of twins. *J. genet. Psychol.*, 1969, 114, 93–95 (with Nancy P. Van Hine).

82 ———. Relation between birth order and being a beautician. *J. appl. Psychol.*, 1969, 53, 149–151 (with J. A. Zannini).

83 **Vetter, G. E.** The measurement of social and political attitudes and the related personality factors. *J. abnorm. soc. Psychol.*, 1930, 25, 149-189.

84 ———. Personality and group factors in the making of atheists. *J. abnorm. soc. Psychol.*, 1932, 27, 179-194 (with M. Green).

85 **Vetter, H. J.** (Ed.), *Personality theory: A source book*. New York: Appleton-Century-Crofts, 1971.

86 **Vidal, R. A.** *Los consultorios pedagogicos*. Madrid: Gerona, 1935.

87 **Viek, P.** An experimental analogue of fear from a sense of helplessness. *J. abnorm. soc. Psychol.*, 1948, 43, 193-200 (with O. H. Mowrer).

88 **Vinkenborg, J.** Portrait. *IPNL*, 1970, 19 (4), 80.

89 **Vinski-Hollinger, Maria.** Ein psychologisch-pädagogisch Betrachtung des Kindermärchens. *IZIP*, 1933, 11(1), 64-69.

90 **Vislick-Young, Pauline.** Urbanisation—ein Faktor der jugendlichen Kriminalität. *IZIP*, 1931, 9(5), 376-381.

91 **Vlach, M.** Alfred Adler, der Heilpädagoge. *Heilpäd.* (Wien), 1970, 13(2), 18-23.

92 ———. Alfred Adler, ein Helfer der Menschheit. *VOX Nachrichten* (Wien), 1970, 57(2), 1-4.

93 ———. Alfred Adler und die Volksbildung. *Oesterr. Volkshochschule*, 1963, No. 48. Pp. 20-21.

94 ———. Alfred Adlers Lehre von der richtigen Erziehung und Lebensführung. *Erziehung und Unterricht* (Wien), 1962, No. 7. Pp. 398-399.

95 ———. Individualpsychologie als Weltanschauung. *Oesterr. Volkshochschule*, 1970, No. 78. Pp. 16-18.

96 **Vockell, E. L.** Self-classification by subjects using Toman's birth-order categories. *Psychol. Rep.*, 1971, 29, 1010 (with D. W. Felker).

97 **Vocos, N.** Translator of A. Adler, *Anthropinio charactires*.

98 **Vogel, W.** Relationships between memories of their parents' behavior and psychodiagnosis in psychiatrically disturbed soldiers. *J. consult. Psychol.*, 1964, 28, 126-132 (with C. G. Lauterbach, M. Livingston & H. Holloway).

99 ———. Sibling patterns and social adjustment among normal and psychiat-rically disturbed soldiers. *J. consult. Psychol.*, 1963, 27, 236-242 (with C. G. Lauterbach).

100 **Vogt, W.** Zur Frage der mathematischen Begabung. *IZIP*, 1933, 11(1), 28-33.

101 ———. Zur Frage des Trainings. *IZIP*, 1932, 10(2), 146-151.

102 **Voigt, G.** Der Internationale Kongress für Individualpsychologie. *IZIP*, 1930, 8 (6), 537-550 (with A. Kronfeld).

103 **Voight, Martha.** Birth order and achievement in eighteenth century Scotland. *JIP*, 1971, 27(1), 80 (with V. L. Bullough, Bonnie Bullough & Lucy Kluckhohn).

104 **Voisi, H.** Welche Handhaben pietet die Individualpsychologie dem Berufsrater? *IZIP*, 1949, 18(1), 33-41.

105 **Volksdorf, N. R.** The relationship of ego-strength to ordinal position and sex. *Diss. Abstr. Int.*, 1970, 31, 403.

106 **Von Andics, Margarethe.** *Suicide and the meaning of life*. London: William Hodge, 1947.

107 **von Bracken, [   ].** Körperliche Züchtigung. In Sofie Lazarsfeld (Ed.), *Technik der Erziehung*.

108 **von Gebsattel, V. E.** (Ed.), *Handbuch der Neurosenlehre und Psychotherapie*. München: Urban & Schwarzenberg, 1958 (with V. E. Frankl & J. H. Schultz).

109 **von Ihering, R.** Individualpsychologische Gedankengänge in Vergangenheit und Gegenwart. *IZIP*, 1926, 4(5), 307-309.

110 **von Maday, S.** Psychologie der Berufswahl. In A. Adler & C. Furtmüller (Eds.), *Heilen und Bilden* (1914). Pp. 306-315.

111 ———. Review of S. Freud, *Das Ich und das Es*. Wien: Int. Psychoanal. Verlag, 1923. In *IZIP*, 1923, 2(1), 42-44.

112 ———. Review of J. Frobes, *Lehrbuch der experimentellen Psychologie*. Freiburg: Herder, 1923. In *IZIP*, 1926, 4(6), 397-398.

113 ———. Zur Psychologie der Lebensmüden. *IZIP*, 1929, 7(2), 88-94.

114 **von Register, M.** *Indien ist anderns*. Düsseldorf: Dörnersche Verlagsanstalt, 1964.

115 **von Ritterhaus, R.** Gleanings from the English Diary (1939-1941). *IPNL*, 1952, Whole No. 18-19. Pp. 5-6.

116 **von Sassen, G.** Causality versus indeterminism. *IPB*, 1951, 9, 125-126.

117 **von Sassen, H. W.** Adler's and Freud's concept of man: A phenomenological comparison. *JIP*, 1967, 23, 3-10.

118 **von Sassen, H. W.** Causality versus indeterminism. *IPB*, 1951, 9, 122–124.

119 **Vorbrodt, R. G.** Religiöse Eupsychie im Lichte der Individualpsychologie. *IZIP*, 1927, 5(6), 438–450.

120 **Vroegh, K.** The relationship of birth order and sex of siblings to gender–role identity. *Developm. Psychol.*, 1971, 4, 407–411.

121 **Vrolijk, A.** Latente Communicatie. *MNWIP*, 1970, 19(2), 16–20.

122 **Vuyk, Rita.** Eltern vergleichen ihre beiden Kinder zum zweiten Mal. *Schweiz. Z. psychol. Anwend.*, 1963, 22, 220–231.

123 ———. *Das Kind in der Zweikinderfamilie.* Bern: Huber, 1959. Paper.

W

1 **Waelder, R.** *Basic theory of psychoanalysis.* New York: Schocken, 1964.

2 ———. Freud und Naturwissenschaft. *Contemp. Psychol.*, 1964, 9, 332.

3 **Wagenheim, Lillian.** First memories of "accidents" and reading difficulties. *Amer. J. Orthopsychiat.*, 1960, 30, 191–195.

4 **Wagner, N. N.** Birth order of volunteers: Cross-cultural data. *J. soc. Psychol.*, 1968, 74, 133–134.

5 **Wahl, C. W.** Some antecedent factors in the family histories of 392 schizophrenics. *Amer. J. Psychiat.*, 1954, 110, 668–676.

6 **Wahler, H. F.** Response styles in clinical and non-clinical groups. *J. consult. Psychol.*, 1961, 25, 533.

7 **Wahler, H. J.** Hostility and aversion for expressing hostility in neurotics and controls. *J. abnorm. soc. Psychol.*, 1959, 59, 193–198.

8 **Wainwright, Letitia.** The development of a power contest. *AJIP*, 1954, 11, 172–177 (with Eleanore Redwin).

9 **Waldfogel, S.** The frequency and affective character of childhood memories. *Psychol. Monogr.*, 1948, 62(4, Whole No. 291).

10 **Waldman, R. D.** Convergence of concepts of Adler and Ortega y Gasset. *JIP*, 1971, 27(2), 135–138.

11 ———. *Humanistic psychiatry: From oppression to choice.* New Brunswick, N. J.: Rutgers Univ. Press, 1971.

12 ———. The modern age: A dilemma for psychiatry. *Amer. J. Orthopsychiat.*, 1969, 39, 569–577.

13 **Waldman, R. D.** Pain as fiction: A perspective on psychotherapy and responsibility. *Amer. J. Psychother.*, 1968, 22, 481–490.

14 ———. Review of E. Becker, *Beyond alienation: A philosophy of education for the crisis of democracy.* New York: Braziller, 1967. In *JIP*, 1970, 26, 84–85.

15 ———. Review of A. L. Heschel, *Who is man?* Stanford, Cal.: Stanford Univ. Press, 1965. In *JIP*, 1969, 25, 239–241.

16 ———. A theory and practice of humanistic psychotherapy. *JIP*, 1969, 25, 19–31.

17 **Waldrop, Mary F.** Effects of family size and density on newborn characteristics. *Amer. J. Orthopsychiat.*, 1965, 35, 342–343 (Abstract).

18 **Walker, C. E.** Birth order and student characteristics: A replication. *J. consult. Psychol.*, 1967, 31, 219 (with H. Tahmisian).

19 **Walker, G. H.** Birth order and need for achievement. *Psychol. Rep.*, 1965, 16, 73–74 (with G. Levinger).

20 **Walker, K. M.** Discussion of J. C. Young & F. G. Crookshank, The treatment of sexual incompetence by the methods of Individual Psychology. *IPMP*, 1932, No. 3. P. 53.

21 **Walkey, F. H.** Birth order and conservatism: An Adlerian myth? *Psychol. Rep.*, 1971, 29, 392–394 (with R. Boshien).

22 **Waller, W.** *The family: A dynamic interpretation.* New York: Dryden Press, 1938.

23 **Walsh, A. M.** *Self concepts of bright boys with learning difficulties.* New York: Columbia Univ., 1956.

24 **Walsh, J. A.** Birth order and an experimental study of empathy. *J. abnorm. soc. Psychol.*, 1963, 66, 610–614 (with E. Stotland).

25 **Walters, R. H.** Anxiety, birth order and susceptibility to social influence. *J. abnorm. soc. Psychol.*, 1961, 62, 716–719 (with F. R. Staples).

26 **Walton, Florence.** Review of W. & Marguerite Beecher, *Beyond success and failure.* In *OSIPNL*, 1967, 7(3), 13.

27 **Wandeler, J.** *Die Individualpsychologie Adlers in ihrer Beziehung zur Philosophie des Als Ob Hans Vaihingers.* Zurich: "Gutenberg", 1932.

28 **Ward, A.** A study of one hundred only children referred to a child guidance clinic. *Smith Coll. Stud. Soc. Work*, 1930, 1, 41–86.

29 **Ward, C. D.** A further examination of birth order as a selective factor among volunteer subjects. *J. abnorm. soc. Psychol.*, 1964, 69, 311–313.

30 **Ward, G. E. S.** Heart and mind. *IPMP*, 1936, No. 15. Pp. 43–59.

31 ———. Individual Psychology: Theory and practice. *IPMP*, 1936, No. 15 (with C. M. Bevan-Brown & F. G. Crookshank).

32 **Warner, J.** Clark's "peace pill" proposal— A year later. *APA Monitor*, 1972, 3(9-10), 1, 6.

33 **Warner, S. J.** *Self-realization and self-defeat.* New York: Grove Press, 1966.

34 **Warren, J. R.** Birth order and social behavior. *Psychol. Bull.*, 1966, 65, 38–49.

35 ———. The effects of certain selection procedures in forming a group of honors students. Spec. Rep. No. 8, Univ. Nebr. Agricul. Exp. Sta., 1963.

36 ———. Student characteristics associated with farm and non-farm backgrounds. Unpublished report to the Research Council, Univ. Nebr., 1964.

37 **Warren-Steams, A.** Morton Prince. *IZIP*, 1928, 6(1), 1–2.

68 **Washburne, C.** Die Volkschulen von Winnetka. *IZIP*, 1931, 9(4), 282–296.

39 **Wasserman, I.** Ist eine differenzielle Psychotherapie möglich? *Z. Psychother. med. Psychol.*, 1959, 9, 187–193.

40 ———. Letter to the editor. *Amer. J. Psychother.*, 1958, 12, 623–627.

41 **Wastl, J.** Über die Bedingtheit der Haufung gewerblicher Unfälle. *Arch. Gewerbpathol. Gewerbehyg.*, 1931, 2, 359–384 (with Alexandra Adler & E. Brezina).

42 **Waterman, Gerhild M.** Other-orientation versus self-orientation in psychotherapy. *JIP*, 1964, 20, 79–83.

43 **Waters, L. K.** Birth order and PPS affiliation. *J. Psychol.*, 1967, 67, 241–243 (with W. E. Kirk).

44 ———. Characteristics of volunteers and non-volunteers for psychological experiments. *J. Psychol.*, 1969, 73, 133–136.

45 **Watne, D.** The challenge of the Peace Corps in Venezuela. *OSIPNL*, 1972, 13(3), 11–12 (with Pat Watne).

46 **Watne, Pat.** The challenge of the Peace Corps in Venezuela. *OSIPNL*, 1972, 13(3), 11–12 (with D. Watne).

47 **Watson, Catherine.** Centers offer aid to families with problems. *Minneapolis Tribune*, Feb. 27, 1972.

48 **Watson, Catherine.** Family finds democracy hard—but worth effort: Parental tyranny was failing so they tried Adler's ideas. *Minneapolis Tribune*, Feb. 27, 1972.

49 **Watson, G.** Happiness among adult students of education. *J. educ. Psychol.*, 1930, 21, 79–109.

50 **Watson, R. I.** Early recollections and vocational choice. *J. consult. Psychol.*, 1965, 29, 486–488 (with D. S. Holmes).

51 ———. *The great psychologists.* 2nd ed. Philadelphia: Lippincott, 1968.

52 **Watson, W. S.** The rigidity of a basic attitudinal frame. *J. abnorm. soc. Psychol.*, 1939, 34, 314–335 (with G. W. Hartmann).

53 **Way, L.** Adler as man and thinker. *IPNL*, 1970, 19(6), 104–105.

54 ———. *Adler's place in psychology: An exposition of Individual Psychology.* London: Allen & Unwin, 1950; New York: Macmillan, 1950; New York: Collier Books, 1962. Paper.

55 ———. *Adler's Psychologie en Philosophie.* Vertaald door P. H. Ronge. Utrecht: Bijleveld, 1951; Amsterdam: Vitgererij Nieuwe Wieken N. V., n.d.

56 ———. Again "Gemeinschaftsgefühl". *IPNL*, 1966, 16(7-8, Whole No. 180–181). P. 31.

57 ———. *Alfred Adler: An introduction to his psychology.* Baltimore: Penguin Books, 1956; Hammondsworth, Middlesex: Penguin Books, 1956; London: Pelican Books, 1956.

58 ———. Ambition. In *Mind and body, an encyclopedia of medical knowledge.* Vol. 1, Part 6. London: Orbis, 1971. Pp. 121–128.

59 ———. Editor of O. Spiel, *Discipline without punishment.*

60 ———. Friedrich Wilhelm Nietzsche (1841-1900). *IPNL*, 1967, 17(9-10, Whole No. 194–195). Pp. 65–67.

61 ———. Introduction to O. Spiel, *Discipline without punishment.*

62 ———. *Introduzione ad Alfred Adler.* Florence: Univ. Press, 1962.

63 ———. *Man's quest for significance.* London: Allen & Unwin, 1948.

64 ———. Not incest but power. *IPNL*, 1971, 20(1), 3.

65 Way, L. Once more homosexuality. *IPNL*, 1969, 19(1), 4-5.

66 ———. Phyllis Bottome (1882-1963). *JIP*, 1963, 19, 223-225.

67 ———. Portrait. *IPNL*, 1970, 19(4), 79.

68 ———. Reply to J. Hemming's, Sex-phobic pseudo-moralists. *IPNL*, 1972, 21(2), 28.

69 ———. Review of Marguerite & W. Beecher, *The mark of Cain*. In *IPNL*, 1970, 20(3), 52-53.

70 ———. Review of Daphne du Maurier (Ed.), *Best short stories of Phyllis Bottome*. In *IPNL*, 1963-64, 14(3-5, Whole No. 152-154). P 16.

71 ———. What is talent? (Excerpt from *Alfred Adler: An introduction to his psychology*). *IPNL*, 1972, 21(2), 30.

72 Weale, B. Whatever happened to the parlor? *J. Home Econ.*, 1972 (with M. J. Weale & J. W. Croake).

73 Weale, M. J. Whatever happened to the parlor? *J. Home Econ.*, 1972 (with B. Weale & J. W. Croake).

74 Webb, W. B. Self-evaluation compared with group evaluation. *J. consult. Psychol.*, 1952, 16, 305-307.

75 Weber, Hilda. Individual Psychology and the chIld (II). *IPP*, 1933, No. 8 (with Laura Hutton & W. B. Wolfe).

76 ———. Mental disorders of the postmenopausal period. *IPMP*, 1936, No. 14. Pp. 31-

77 ———. Parental influences in the formation of the neurotic character. (2) Parental discord. *IPMP*, 1933, No. 8. Pp. 20-33.

78 Wechkin, D. "Altruistic" behavior in rhesus monkeys. *Amer. J. Psychiat.*, 1964, 121, 584-585 (with J. H. Masserman & W. Terris).

79 Wegener, W. Zur Frage der Wurzeln völkischen gesehens. *IZIP*, 1931, 9(6), 438-447.

80 Wegner, K. W. *Guidance: Theory and practice*. New York: American Book Co., 1964 (with F. N. Zeran & J. F. Lallus).

81 Weicker, H. Der Alkoholismus im Lichte der Individualpsychologie Alfred Adlers. *IZIP*, 1926, 4(5), 295-300.

82 Weigert, Edith V. Dissent in the early history of psychoanalysis. *Psychiat.*, 1942, 5, 349-359.

83 Weigl, E. Ist die Strafe eine Erziehungsmittel? *IZIP*, 1926, 4(6), 348-354.

84 Weigl, E. Review of C. G. Jung, *Analytische Psychologie und Erziehung*. Heidelberg: Niels Kampmann, 1926. In *IZIP*, 1927, 5(5), 391-392.

85 Weigl, Trude. Self-education and education of children. *IJIP*, 1937, 3(1), 38-45.

86 ———. Wechselwirkungen zwischen Selbsterziehung und Kleinkindererziehung. *IZIP*, 1930, 8(1), 171-176.

87 Weiland, H. An analysis of manifest content of the earliest memories of children. *J. genet. Psychol.*, 1958, 92, 41-52 (with I. Steisel).

88 Weiland, I. The value of early memories in psychotherapy. *Psychiat. Quart.*, 1953, 27, 73-82 (with R. Kahana, B. Snyder & M. Rosenbaum).

89 Weill, Blanche C. *Through children's eyes: True stories out of the practice of a consultant psychologist*. New York: Island Workshop Press, 1940.

90 ———. Translator, with Irma Weill, of A. Lichtenberger, *Trott and his little sister*.

91 Weill, Irma. Translator, with Blanche Weill, of A. Lichtenberger, *Trott and his little sister*.

92 Weindl, T. Über die vom Kranken vorgestellte Insuffizienz psychischer Partialvermögen als Grundlegung bei der Systematik psychiatrischer Zustandbilder. *IZIP*, 1928, 6(4), 290-298.

93 Weinmann, K. Criticising other people (Summary). *IPNL*, 1955, 4(9-10, Whole No. 49-50). P. 7.

94 ———. Manish-depressives Irresein. In E. Wexberg (Ed.), *Handbuch der Individualpsychologie*. Pp. 618-645.

95 ———. Das Neurosenproblem in der deutschen Neurologie und Psychiatrie der Gegenwart. *IZIP*, 1926, 4(2), 53-56.

96 ———. Portrait. *IPNL*, 1970, 19(4), 79; 1972, 21(6), 111.

97 ———. Review of A. Homburger, *Vorlesungen über Psychopathologie des Kindesalters*. In *IZIP*, 1928, 6(1), 71-72.

98 ———. Über das seelische Gleichgewicht une seine Erhaltung. *IZIP*, 1926, 4(5), 271-276.

99 ———. Über das Selbstwertgefühl und seine Störungen. *IZIP*, 1926, 4(2), 69-76.

100 ———. Der Weg des Leidens und der Selbsterkenntnis. *IZIP*, 1930, 8(1), 84-87.

101 ———. Wege, Irrwege und Abwege der Persönlichkeitsentwicklung. *IZIP*, 1950, 19(3), 97-109.

102 **Weinmann, K.** Zur Problematik des Gemeinschaftsbegriffen. In Int. Verein Indivpsy., *Alfred Adler zum Gedenken.* Pp. 151–163.

103 ———. Zur Psychogenese und Psychotherapie endokriner Störungen. *IZIP*, 1931, 9(2), 108–112.

104 ———. Zur Psychologie nervöser und cyklothymer Stimmungsschwankungen. *IZIP*, 1923, 2(1), 14–26.

105 **Weinstein, H. M.** The co-therapist method: Special problems and advantages. *Grp. Psychother.*, 1954, 6, 189–192 (with F. J. Loeffler).

106 **Weinstein, Laura.** Social experience and social schemata. *J. Pers. soc. Psychol.*, 1967, 6, 429–434.

107 **Weiskopf, H.** *Das faule Kind.* Dresden: Verlag am andern Ufer, 1926.

108 **Weiss, J. H.** Birth order and asthma in children. *J. psychosom. Res.*, 1968, 12, 137–140.

109 ———. Birth order, recruitment conditions, and preferences for participation in group versus non-group experiments. *Amer. Psychologist*, 1963, 18, 356 (with A. Wolf & R. G. Wiltsey). Abstract.

110 ———. Birth order, recruitment conditions, and volunteering preference. *J. Pers. soc. Psychol.*, 1965, 2, 269–273 (with A. Wolf).

111 **Weiss, Lillie.** Relationships of oral imagery to yielding behavior and birth order. *J. consult. clin. Psychol.*, 1968, 32, 89–91 (with J. Masling & B. Rothschild).

112 **Weiss, R. L.** Acquiescence response set and birth order (extended report). *J. consult. Psychol.*, 1966, 30, 365.

113 ———. Some determinants of emitted reinforcing behavior: Listener reinforcement and birth order. *J. Pers. soc. Psychol.*, 1966, 3, 489–492.

114 **Weisskopf-Joelson, Edith.** Some comments on the psychology of misunderstandings. *JIP*, 1966, 22, 201–203.

115 **Weissman, E.** Portrait. *IPNL*, 1970, 19(4), 79, 80; 1971, 20(6), 110, 112.

116 ———. Review of H. Freund, Zur Organisation der Schwererziehbaren Fürsorge im Freistaate Sachsen. In *IZIP*, 1929, 7(1), 69.

117 **Weissman, S. L.** (Ed.). *Acting out: Theoretical and clinical aspects.* New York: Grune & Stratton, 1965 (with L. E. Abt).

118 **Weiss-Rosmarin, Trude.** Adler's psychology and the Jewish tradition. *JIP*, 1958, 14, 142–152. Condensed in *Jew. Digest*, June, 1959.

119 **Weithorn, H. B.** The functional aspects of Adlerian constructs in understanding and assisting disadvantaged children. Unpubl. Ph.D. Diss., Univ. So. Cal., 1969; *Diss. Abstr.*, 1970, 30(IV), 4786A.

120 **Weitz, I.** Psychische Komponenten bei Haut- und Geschlechtskrankheiten. *IZIP*, 1936, 14(3), 156–166.

121 **Welch, R.** Das schöpferische Schreiben des Kindes. *IZIP*, 1931, 9(3), 238–242.

122 **Welkowitz, J.** Perceived parent attitudes as determinants of ego structure. *Child Developm.*, 1955, 25, 173–183.

123 **Weller, G. M.** Arousal effects on the newborn infant of being first or later born. *Amer. J. Orthopsychiat.*, 1965, 35, 341–342 (Abstract).

124 **Weller, L.** The relationship of birth order to cohesiveness. *J. soc. Psychol.*, 1964, 63, 249–254.

125 **Wellman, B.** The school child's choice of companions. *J. educ. Res.*, 1926, 14, 126–13

126 **Wells, C. H.** Birth order and expressed interest in being a college professor. *J. couns. Psychol.*, 1968, 15, 111–116 (with E. H. Fischer and S. L. Cohen).

127 **Wells, F. L.** A note on singularity in given names. *J. soc. Psychol.*, 1948, 27, 271–272 (with B. M. Savage).

128 **Wells, H. G.** Toward a universal social life. *IJIP*, 1936, 2(2), 51–53.

129 **Wenger, P.** Review of F. Asnaourow, Las defensas psiquicas su mecanismo y aplicacion en la vida. In *IZIP*, 1927, 5(4), 312.

130 ———. Review of F. Chvostek, Gibt es Organneurosen? *Wien. med. Wchnschr.*, 1927, 77. In *IZIP*, 1927, 5(6), 477–478.

131 ———. Review of M. Hirschfeld & E. Bohn, *Sexualerziehung.* Berlin: Deutsche Verlags, A–G, 1929. In *IZIP*, 1930, 8(3), 357.

132 ———. Review of O. Kauders. *Keimdrüse, Sexualität und Zentralnervensystem.* Berlin: S. Karger, 1927. In *IZIP*, 1928, 6(1), 74.

133 ———. Review of L. Klages, *Einführung in die Psychologie der Handschrift.* Heidelberg: Kampmann, 1928. In *IZIP*, 1929, 7(a), 315–316.

134 ———. Review of T. Van de Velde, *Die vollkommende Ehe.* Leipzig: Benno Konegen, 1926. In *IZIP*, 1927, 5(5), 398.

135 **Wenger, P.** Review of G. Venzmer, *Sieh dir die Menschen an!* Stuttgart: Frank'sche Verlagshandl., 1931. In *IZIP*, 1933, 12(4), 334.

136 ———. Review of G. v. Bergmann, Zum Abbau der "Organneurosen" als Folge interner Diagnostik. *Deutsche med. Wchnschr.*, 1923, No. 49.

137 ———. Über Erfolge der Psychotherapie im Rahmen einer Poliklinik für intern Kranke. *Klin. Wchnschr.*, 1930, No. 49.

138 **Wenger-Hornik, Josefine.** Review of M. Picard, *Das Menschengesicht.* Munchen: Delphinverlag, 1929. In *IZIP*, 1933, 12 (4), 336.

139 **Wepman, J. M.** *Concepts of personality.* Chicago: Aldine, 1963 (with R. W. Heine).

140 **Werner, H. D.** Adler, Freud and American social work. *JIP*, 1967, 23, 11–18.

141 ——— (Ed.). *New understandings of human behavior: Non-Freudian readings from professional journals, 1960–1968.* New York: Association Press, 1970.

142 ———. Psychotherapy and consciousness: A preliminary statement. *Int. J. soc. Psychiat.*, 1963, 9(1), 45–50.

143 ———. *A rational approach to social casework.* New York: Association Press, 1965.

144 ———. Review of A. G. Nikelly (Ed.), *Techniques for behavior change.* In *JIP*, 1971, 27(1), 99–101.

145 **West, S. S.** Sibling configuration of scientists. *Amer. J. Sociol.*, 1960, 66, 268–274.

146 **Wexberg, E.** A. Adlers Individualpsychologie. *Z. Kinderforsch.*, 1925, No. 30.

147 ———. Alexander Neuer. *IPN*, 1941, 1(8-9), 9–10.

148 ———. Alfred Adler, der Arzt. *IZIP*, 1930, 8(2), 234–236.

149 ———. Die Angst als Kernproblem der Neurose. *Deutsche Z. Nervenheilkunde*, 1925, 88, 271.

150 ———. *Das ängstliche Kind.* Dresden: Am andern Ufer, 1926.

151 ———. Ängstliche Kinder. In A. Adler & C. Furtmüller (Eds.), *Heilen und Bilden* (1914). Pp. 267–277; (1928). Pp. 160–167.

152 ———. *Arbeit und Gemeinschaft.* Leipzig: S. Hirzel, 1932.

153 **Wexberg, E.** Die Arbeitsunfähigkeit des Nervosen. *ZIP*, 1914, 1(4–5), 105–110.

154 ———. Arzt und Erziehungsberatung. *IZIP*, 1929, 7(3), 170–176 (with Olga Knopf).

155 ———. *Ausdrucksformen des Seelenlebens.* Celle, Germany: Niels Kampmann, 1928.

156 ———. Bibliographie der Individualpsychologie. In *Handbuch der Individualpsychologie.* Pp. 180–190.

157 ———. Concerning laziness. *IJIP*, 1936, 2(1), 104–113.

158 ———. Ein Fall Dementia Paranoides. *IZIP*, 1924, 2(6), 10–22.

159 ———. *Einführung in die Psychologie des Geschlechtslebens.* Leipzig: S. Hirzel, 1930.

160 ———. Die Einwände gegen die Individualpsychologie. *IZIP*, 1928, 6(6), 433–442.

161 ———. *Ergasia kai Koinonia* [Work and society]. Translated by S. G. Marketou. Thessaloniki: Typographeion Odys, 1934.

162 ———. Erziehung der Erzieher. *IZIP*, 1924, 2(3), 41–45.

163 ———. The future progress of Individual Psychology. *IPB*, 1942, 2(3), 58–59.

164 ———. Geleitwort zur zweiten Auflage. In A. Adler, C. Furtmüller & E. Wexberg (Eds.), *Heilen und Bilden.* Pp. v–vi.

165 ———. Die Grundstörung der Zwangsneurose. *Z. gesam. Neurol. Psychiat.*, 1929, 121, 236–

166 ———. *Handbuch der Individualpsychologie.* München: Bergmann, 1926; Amsterdam: Bonset, 1966.

167 ——— (Ed.). *Heilen und Bilden: Ein Buch der Erziehungskunst für Ärzte und Pädagogen.* München: Bergmann, 1928 (with A. Adler & C. Furtmüller).

168 ——— (Ed.). *Heilen und Bilden: Grundlagen der Erziehungskunst für Ärzte und Pädagogen.* 2nd ed. München: Bergmann, 1922 (with A. Adler & C. Furtmüller).

169 ———. *Index of Individual Psychology—A collection of Adlerian writings containing 6 volumes including A. Adler, *The pattern of life;* A. Adler, *Problems of neurosis;* A. Adler, *What life should mean to you;* E. Wexberg, *Individual Psychology;* W. B. Wolfe, *How to be happy though human.* Also index on general topics, child behavior, development, education, etc. New York: T. O. Warfield, 1922; New York: Dodd, Mead, 1926.

170 **Wexberg, E.** *Individual Psychological treatment.* Translated by A. Eiloart. London: C. W. Daniel, 1929; Revised and annotated by B. H. Shulman. Chicago: Alfred Adler Inst., 1970. Paper.

171 ———. Individualpsychologie als Religion und als Wissenschaft. *IZIP*, 1928, 6(3), 228–236.

172 ———. *Individualpsychologie: Eine systematische Darstellung.* Leipzig: S. Hirzel, 1928, 1931, 1938. Pp. 297–360.

173 ———. Die Individualpsychologische Behandlung. In K. Birnbaum (Ed.), *Die psychischen Heilmethoden.* Leipzig: Georg Thieme, 1927.

174 ———. *Individual Psychology.* Translated by W. B. Wolfe. New York: Cosmopolitan, 1929; London: Allen & Unwin, 1929; New York: Rinehart, 1929.

175 ———. Individual Psychology and practice (I). *IPMP*, 1932, No. 6 (with Olga Knopf & H. C. Squires).

176 ———. Individual Psychology and psychoanalysis in practice. *IPMP*, 1932, No. 6. Pp. 7–21.

177 ———. *Individual Psychology and sex.* Translated by W. B. Wolfe. Introduction by F. G. Crookshank. London: Jonathan Cape, 1931. Also appeared as *The psychology of sex.*

178 ———. Individual Psychology and sexual difficulties (I). *IPMP*, 1932, No. 3 (with A. Adler, R. Dreikurs, Adele Hervat, J. C. Young, F. G. Crookshank, Mary C. Luff & others).

179 ———. Individual Psychology and vocational guidance. *IJIP*, 1936, 2(3), 73–82.

180 ———. Insomnia as related to anxiety and ambition. *J. clin. Psychopathol.*, 1949, 4, 373–375.

181 ———. *Introduction to medical psychology.* New York: Grune & Stratton, 1947; London: W. Heinemann, 1948.

182 ———. Lebensstufen der Erotik. *IZIP*, 1933, 11(5), 377–394.

183 ———. Der Mensch in der Krise. *IZIP*, 1933, 11(2), 124–137.

184 ———. Naturwissenschaft und Individualpsychologie. *IZIP*, 1932, 10(3), 230.

185 ———. *Das nervöse Kind: Ein Leitfaden für Eltern und Erzeiher.* Wien-Leipzig: M. Perles, 1926.

186 ———. Neurosenwahl. *IZIP*, 1931, 9(2), 88–105.

187 **Wexberg, E.** *Nevrika Paidia* [Your nervous child]. Translated by S. G. Marketou. Athens: Typographeion Estias, 1930.

188 ———. Organminderwertigkeit, Angst, Minderwertigkeitsgefühl. *IZIP*, 1926, 4(4), 174–182.

189 ———. *Our children in a changing world: An outline of practical guidance.* New York: Macmillan, 1937 (with H. E. Fritsch).

190 ———. The physician and educational guidance (with Olga Knopf). In A. Adler & assoc., *Guiding the child.* Pp. 28–46.

191 ———. Portrait. *IPNL*, 1971, 20(6), 109.

192 ———. Problems of adolescence. *Ment. Hyg.*, 1939, 23(4), 594–600.

193 ———. Die psychologische Struktur der Neurose. In *Handbuch der Individualpsychologie.* Pp. 419–459.

194 ———. *The psychology of sex.* Translated by W. B. Wolfe. New York: Farrar & Rinehart, 1931; New York: Blue Ribbon Books, 1931. Also appeared as *Individual Psychology and sex.*

195 ———. The relationship between neurosis and virginity. *IPMP*, 1932, No. 3. Pp. 19–21.

196 ———. Review of *Allgemeine ärztliche Zeitschrift für Psychotherapie und psychische Hygiene*, 1928, 1. In *IZIP*, 1928, 6(3), 263–264.

197 ———. Review of F. Bonheim, *Wunder der Drüse.* Stuttgart: Hippokrates Verlag, 1927. In *IZIP*, 1927, 5(6), 478.

198 ———. Review of A. Eulenberg, Zur Behandlung der sexualen Neurasthenie. *Z. Sexualwissensch.*, 1914, 1, [   ]. In *ZIP*, 1914, 1(3), 93.

199 ———. Review of H. Hartmann, *Die Grundlagen der Psychoanalyse.* Leipzig: Georg Thieme, 1927. In *IZIP*, 1927, 5(3), 233–234.

200 ———. Review of H. Hoffmann, *Das Problem des Charakteraufbaues.* Berlin: J. Springer, 1926. In *IZIP*, 1927, 5(4), 318–319.

201 ———. Review of J. E. Nicole, *Psychopathology.* In *IZIP*, 1932, 10(5), 392.

202 ———. Review of M. Prince, *Die Psychopathologie eines Falles* von Phobie. *Int. Z. ärztl. Psychoanal.*, 1913, 6, [   ]. In *IZIP*, 1913, 1(1), 26–27.

203 ———. Review of H. Prinzhorn, *Gespräch über Psychoanalyse zwischen*

Frau, Dichter und Arzt. Heidelberg: Niels Kampmann, 1926. In *IZIP*, 1927, 5(3), 234–235.

204 **Wexberg, E.** Review of G. Roffenstein, *Das Problem des psychologischen Verstehens.* Stuttgart: F. Enke, 1926. In *IZIP*, 1926, 4(5), 313–314.

205 ———. Review of O. Rühle, *Karl Marx, Leben und Werk.* In *IZIP*, 1928, 6(5), 420–421.

206 ———. Review of B. Sperk, Über das schwache Kind. *Wiener klin. Wchnschr.*, 1914, No. 8. In *ZIP*, 1914, 1(3), 93–94.

207 ———. Review of Stoltenhoff, *Kurzes Lehrbuch der Psychoanalyse.* Stuttgart: F. Enke, 1926. In *IZIP*, 1926, 4(5), 313.

208 ———. Review of G. Wanke, *Psychoanalyse, Geschichte, Aufgaben und Wirkung.* Halle: C. Marhold, 1926. In *IZIP*, 1927, 5(4), 319.

209 ———. Die Rezeption der Individualpsychologie durch die Psychoanalyse. *IZIP*, 1926, 4(3), 153–156.

210 ———. Rousseau und die Ethik. In A. Adler & C. Furtmüller (Eds.), *Heilen und Bilden* (1914). Pp. 187–206; (1928). Pp. 283–298.

211 ———. Seelische Entwicklungshemmungen. In Sofie Lazarsfeld (Ed.), *Richtige Lebensführung.*

212 ———. Sexuelles und erotisches Problem. In Sofie Lazarsfeld (Ed.), *Technik der Erziehung.* Pp. 237–269.

213 ———. *Sorgenkinder.* Leipzig: S. Hirzel, 1931.

214 ———. La théorie du "caractère nerveux" selon Alfred Adler. *L'Encéphale*, 1926, No. 5.

215 ———. Toldot hitpatchuta shel ha-ishiut regesh hanchitut, tahukat-ha-Oedipus haregesh chevroti. [Historical development of the personality, inferiority feeling, oedipal feeling, social feeling]. In Anon., *Kovets Individual-Psikhologie.* Pp. 5–33.

216 ———. Toxic psychoses associated with administration of quinacrine. *Arch. Neurol. Psychiat.*, 1946, 55, 489–510 (with M. L. Sheppeck).

217 ———. Über die Faulheit. *IZIP*, 1930, 8(1), 132–141.

218 ———. Über Hypnose und Suggestion. *IZIP*, 1927, 5(2), 81–93.

219 ———. Über Pflichtgefühl. *IZIP*, 1929, 7(5), 329–343.

220 **Wexberg, E.** Verzogene Kinder. In A. Adler & C. Furtmüller (Eds.), *Heilen und Bilden* (1928), Pp. 150–154.

221 ———. Vorwort zur dritten Auflage. In A. Adler & C. Furtmuller (Eds.), *Heilen und Bilden* (1928). Pp. v–vi.

222 ———. Was ist wirklich eine Neurose? *IZIP*, 1933, 11(3), 185–192.

223 ———. *Your nervous child.* Translated by W. B. Wolfe. New York: A. & C. Boni, 1927.

224 ———. Zur Beurteilung der Individualpsychologie in der psychiatrischen Literatur. *IZIP*, 1926, 4(3), 156–157.

225 ———. Zur Biologie und Psychologie der Affekte. *IZIP*, 1926, 4(4), 227–235.

226 ———. Zur Entwicklung der Individualpsychologie (with C. Furtmüller). In A. Adler & C. Furtmüller (Eds.), *Heilen und Bilden* (1928). Pp. 1–15.

227 ———. Zur Frage der Psychosen. *IZIP*, 1928, 6(4), 280–289.

228 ———. Zur Frage nach dem Sinn des Lebens. *IZIP*, 1925, 3(3), 106–110.

229 ———. Zur Psychogenese des Asthma nervosum. *IZIP*, 1924, 2(4), 7–15.

230 ———. Zur Verwertung der Traumdeutung der Psychotherapie. *ZIP*, 1914, 1(1), 16–20.

231 **Wexberg, L. E.** See Wexberg, E.

232 **Weyl, N.** Some possible genetic implications of Carthaginian child sacrifice. *Perspec. Biol. Med.*, 1968, 12, 69–78.

233 **Weyr, Helene.** Grosse Männer. *IZIP*, 1932, 10(3), 216–223.

234 ———. Review of *Polnisches psychologisches Archiv*, 1927–28, 2(2, 3, 4). In *IZIP*, 1931, 9(6), 483.

235 **Wheelis, A. B.** How people change. *Commentary*, May, 1969. Pp. 57–66.

236 **White, E.** Review of Karen Horney, *New ways in psychoanalysis.* New York: Norton, 1939. In *IPN*, 1940, 1(1), 2.

237 ———. Review of Hertha Orgler, *Alfred Adler: The man and his work.* In *IPN*, 1940, 1(1), 1.

238 **White, R. K.** Patterns of aggressive behavior in experimentally created "social climates". *J. soc. Psychol.*, 1939, 10, 271–299 (with K. Lewin & Rosemary Lippitt).

239 **White, R. W.** Adler and the future of ego psychology. *JIP*, 1957, 13, 112–124. Also in K. A. Adler & Danica Deutsch (Eds.), *Essays in*

Individual Psychology. Pp. 437–454. Also in I. G. Sarason (Ed.), *Science and theory in psychoanalysis.* Princeton, N. J.: Van Nostrand, 1965. Pp. 67–82.

240 **White, R. W.** Is Alfred Adler alive today? [Review of A. Adler, *The Individual Psychology of Alfred Adler*]. *Contemp. Psychol.*, 1957, 2, 1–4.

241 ———. Motivation reconsidered: The concept of competence. *Psychol. Rev.*, 1959, 66, 287–333.

242 ———. Review of P. Rieff, *Freud: The mind of the moralist.* New York: Viking Press, 1959. In *JIP*, 1960, 16, 102.

243 **White, W. A.** The Adlerian concept of the neuroses. *J. abnorm. Psychol.*, 1917–18, 12, 168–173.

244 **Whiteley, J. M.** In collaboration with Norman A. Sprinthal, Ralph L. Mosher, & Rolla T. Donaghy. *Dimensions of effective counseling: Cognitive flexibility and psychological openness in counselor selection.* Columbus, Ohio: Merrill, 1968 (with T. W. Allen).

245 ——— (Ed.). *Research problems in counseling.* Columbus, Ohio: Charles E. Merrill, 1968.

246 ———. Suggested modifications in scientific inquiry and reporting of counseling research. *The couns. Psychologist*, 1969, 1(2), 84–88 (with T. W. Allen).

247 **Whitman, W.** [The Gemeinschaftsgefühl of Walt Whitman]. *IPNL*, 1967, 17, (7–8, Whole No. 192–193). P. 50.

248 **Whyte, A. H.** The ordinal position of problem children. *Amer. J. Orthopsychiat.*, 1931, 1, 430–434 (with C. Rosenow).

249 **Wiener Arbeitsgemeinschaft der Erzieherinnen, Fürsorgerinnen und Kindergärtnerinnen.** Genügen die bishergeltenden Erziehungsmassnahmen zur Ertüchligung der jungen Generation. *IZIP*, 1931, 9(6), 469–473.

250 **Wiggins, G.** Some basic concepts in human relations training for psychiatric patients. *Hosp. Commun. Psychiat.*, 1970, 21, 137–143 (with W. E. O'Connell, P. Hanson & P. Rothaus).

251 ———. Training patients for effective participation in back-home groups. *Amer. J. Psychiat.*, 1969, 126, 857–862 (with W. E. O'Connell, P. Hanson & P. Rothaus).

252 **Wilder, J.** Alfred Adler in historical perspective. *Amer. J. Psychother.*, 1970, 24(3), 450–460.

253 **Wilder, J.** Introduction to K. A. Adler & Danica Deutsch (Eds.), *Essays in Individual Psychology.* Pp. xv–xvii.

254 **Wile, I. S.** A study of birth order and behavior. *J. soc. Psychol.*, 1931, 2, 52–71 (with Elinor Noetzel).

255 **Wiley, R. E.** Father identification as a function of mother-father relationship. *JIP*, 1964, 20, 167–171 (with J. C. Baxter & D. L. Horton).

256 **Wilheim, Ilka.** Review of R. N. Coudenhove-Kalergi, *Pan-Europa.* Wien: Pan Europa-Verlag, 1923. In *IZIP*, 1924, 3(1), 44.

257 ———. Review of K. Falke, *Machtville und Menschenwürde.* Zurich: Orell Füssli, 1927. In *IZIP*, 1928, 6(4), 339–340.

258 ———. Review of D. L. Forel, *La psychologie des névroses.* Genf: Libr. Kundig, 1925. In *IZIP*, 1925, 3(2), 134–138.

259 ———. Review of M. Isserlin, *Psychotherapie.* Berlin: J. Springer, 1926. In *IZIP*, 1927, 5(5), 399.

260 ———. Review of H. Kogerer, Psychotherapie der Psychosen. *Z gesam. Neurol. Psychiat.*, Vol. 96. In *IZIP*, 1926, 4(2), 105–106.

261 ———. Review of K. K. Kortsen, Die Psychologie der menschlichen Gerfühle und Instinkte in der sogennanten Psychoanalyse. *Eos* (Copenhagen), 1918, 3–4. In *IZIP*, 1924, 2(6), 41–42.

262 ———. Review of R. Laforgue & R. Allendy, *La psychoanalyse et les névroses.* Paris: Payot, 1924. In *IZIP*, 1927, 5(5), 400.

263 ———. Review of I. Marcinowski, *Der Mut zu sich selbst.* Berlin: O. Salle, 1925. In *IZIP*, 1928, 6(4), 345–346.

264 ———. Review of L. Stein, Entwicklungsgeschichtliche Deutung der Entstehung des Silbenwiederholens. *Arch. Psychiat. Nervenkrankheiten*, 1924, 70, [   ]. In *IZIP*, 1925, 3(3), 141–142.

265 ———. Die Schizophrenie im Lichte der Individualpsychologie. In E. Wexberg (Ed.), *Handbuch der Individualpsychologie.* Pp. 583–617.

266 ———. Zum Bedeutungswandel der Worte. *IZIP*, 1924, 3(1), 38–43.

267 ———. Zur individualpsychologischen Deutung des Stotterns. *Wien. med. Wchnschr.*, 1924,

268 **Wilheim, Ilka.** Zur Psychologie des Aberglaubens. *IZIP*, 1924, 2(4), 23-26.

269 **Wilken, F.** Individualpsychologische Betrachtungen zum modernen Wirtschaftsbetrieb. *IZIP*, 1924, 2(3), 1-9; 1924, 2(4), 18-23.

270 ———. Die Jugendbewegung als neurotisches Phänomenon. In A. Adler, C. Furtmüller, & E. Wexberg, (Eds.), *Heilen und Bilden*. (1928). Pp. 265-282.

271 ———. Die nervöse Erkrankung als sinnvolle Erscheinung unseres gegenwärtigen Kulturzeittraumes: Eine Unterschung über die Störung des heutigen Sozialleben. In A. Adler, L. Seif, & O. Kaus (Eds.), *Individuum und Gemeinschaft*.

272 ———. Staats-und Sozialwissenschaften. In E. Wexberg (Ed.), *Handbuch der Individualpsychologie*. Vol. 2.

273 ———. Wesen und Wege der Arbeit des Menschen an sich selbst. *IZIP*, 1930, 8(1), 18-36.

274 **Williams, A. G.** The combined treatment area. *Practice Admin.*, 1969, 6(2), 5-8.

275 ———. Dental "communication"—Not just words, but performance. *Dent. Survey*, June, 1968.

276 ———. Technique for provisional splint with attachment. *J. prosth. Dent.*, 1969, 21, 555-559.

277 **Williams, Barbara.** The comparative effectiveness of two contrasting alcoholic treatment programs. *Nwsltr. Res. Psychol.*, 1972, 14(4), 21-23 (with M. Gallen, W. E. O'Connell & P. M. Sands).

278 **Williams, C.** The influence of experimentally induced inadequacy feelings upon the appreciation of humor. *J. soc. Psychol.*, 1964, 64, 113-117 (with D. L. Cole).

279 **Williams, R. H.** A concept of style of life induced from a study of aging. *JIP*, 1966, 22, 100-103.

280 ———. *Lives through the years: Styles of life and successful aging.* New York: Atherton Press, 1965 (with Claudine C. Wirths).

281 **Williams, W. C.** The PALS tests: A technique for children to evaluate both parents. *J. consult. Psychol.*, 1958, 22, 487-495.

282 **Wilson, A. T. M.** Psychological factors in organic disease. *IPP*, 1938, No. 20. Pp. 23-41.

283 **Wilson, C.** *Religion and the rebel.* Boston: Houghton Mifflin, 1957.

284 **Wilson, Joy D.** A proposed eight week in-service program in Dreikurian principles of child psychology for parents of junior high students. Unpubl. master's thesis, Seattle Pacific Call., 1970.

285 **Wilson, P. R.** Sex, birth order and volunteering behavior. *Austral. J. Psychol.*, 1966, 18, 158-159 (with J. R. Patterson & A. M. Lyssons).

286 **Wiltsey, R. G.** Birth order, recruitment conditions, and preferences for participation in group versus non-group experiments (Abstract). *Amer. Psychologist*, 1963, 18, 356 (with J. H. Weiss & A. Wolf).

287 **Winch, R. F.** Empirical elaboration of the theory of complementary needs in mate selection. *J. abnorm. soc. Psychol.*, 1955, 51, 508-514 (with T. Ktsanes & Virginia Ktsanes).

288 ———. *Mate selection: A study of complementary needs.* New York: Harper, 1958.

289 ———. The study of personality in the family setting. *Soc. Forces*, 1950, 28, 310-316.

290 ———. The theory of complementary needs in mate selection. *Amer. sociol. Rev.*, 1954, 19, 241-249 (with T. Ktsanes & Virginia Ktsanes).

291 ———. The theory of complementary needs in mate selection: Final results on the test of the general hypothesis. *Amer. sociol. Rev.*, 1955, 20, 552-565.

292 **Winer, D.** Participation in psychological research: Relation to birth order and demographic factors. *J. consult. clin. Psychol.*, 1969, 33, 610-613 (with E. H. Fischer).

293 **Winetrout, K.** Adlerian psychology and pragmatism. *JIP*, 1968, 24, 5-24.

294 ———. Review of H. Linschoten, *On the way toward a phenomenological psychology: The psychology of William James*. Pittsburgh: Duquesne Univ. Press, 1968. In *JIP*, 1968, 24, 196-197.

295 **Winick, C. W.** Fees in group therapy. *Amer. J. Psychother.*, 1968, 22, 60-67 (with Asya Kadis).

296 ———. *Group psychotherapy today: Selected papers presented at the scientific meetings of the Eastern Group Psychotherapy Society, 1960-1963.* Basel: Karger, 1965 (with Asya Kadis).

297 **Winick, C. W.** *Guide du psychothérapie de groupe.* Translated by M. Dreyfus. Paris: Ed. Epi, 1971 (with S. H. Foulkes, Asya Kadis & J. D. Krasner).

298 ———. *A practicum of group psychotherapy.* New York: Hoeber, 1963 (with Asya Kadis, J. D. Krasner & S. H. Foulkes).

299 ———. The role of the deviant in the therapy group. *Int. J. soc. Psychiat.,* 1960, 6, 277–287 (with Asya Kadis).

300 **Winkler, F.** Die Individualpsychologie und die Wurzeln der Religion. *IZIP,* 1930, 8(4), 417–421.

301 ———. Review of E. Atzler (Ed.), *Körper und Arbeit.* Leipzig: Geo. Thieme, 1927. In *IZIP,* 1929, 7(1), 74–75.

302 ———. Review of Sofie Lazarsfeld, *Technique der Erziehung.* In *IZIP,* 1930, 8(2), 277.

303 ———. Review of P. Plaut, *Die Psychologie der produktiven Persönlichkeit.* Stuttgart: Ferdinand Enke, 1929. In *IZIP,* 1931, 9 (1), 74.

304 **Winslow, Yvonne.** The autobiography of G. Stanley Hall. *IZIP,* 1924, 2(5), 2–5.

305 ———. Childhood influences. *IZIP,* 1924, 2(3), 36–40.

306 ———. Holding the interest of the patient. *IZIP,* 1926, 4(3), 152–153.

307 ———. The relation of psychology to education. *IZIP,* 1923, 2(1), 11–14.

308 **Winterbottom, M. R.** The relation of childhood training in independence to achievement motivation. Ph.D. Diss., Univ. Michigan, 1953.

309 **Winthrop, H.** Review of V. Packard, *The status seekers.* New York: David McKay, 1959. In *JIP,* 1959, 15, 240–241.

310 ———. Scientism in psychology. *JIP,* 1959, 15, 112–120.

311 ———. Self-sacrifice as autonomy, ego-transcendence and social interest. *J. humanist. Psychol.,* 1962, 2(2), 31–37.

312 ———. Written descriptions of earliest memories: Repeat reliability and other findings. *Psychol. Rep.,* 1958, 4, 320.

313 **Wirths, Claudine G.** *Lives through the years: Styles of life and successful aging.* New York: Atherton Press, 1965 (with R. H. Williams).

314 **Wisinger, Vera.** Portrait. *IPNL,* 1972, 21 (6), 111.

315 **Wisinger, Z.** Portrait. *IPNL,* 1970, 19(4), 79; 1972, 21(6), 111.

316 **Wisinger, Z.** Review of P. Rom, *Alfred Adler und die wissenschaftliche Menschenkenntnis.* In *IPNL,* 1966, 17(1–2, Whole No. 186–187). P. 8.

317 **Witkin, H. A.** Some implications of research on cognitive style for problems of education. *Arch. Psichol. Neurol. Psichiat.,* 1965, 26(1), 27–55.

318 **Wittels, F.** The neo-Adlerians. *Amer. J. Sociol.,* 1939, 45, 433–445.

319 ———. *Sigmund Freud: His personality, his teachings, and his school.* New York: Dodd, Mead, 1924; London: Allen & Unwin, 1924.

320 **Wittgenstein, G.** *Psychotherapie und Theologie.* Stuttgart: Hippokrates Verlag, 1958.

321 **Wittman, R.** Ein entmutigtes Kind. *IZIP,* 1929, 7(2), 148–150.

322 ———. Ein verzärteltes Kind und eine Stiefmutter. *IZIP,* 1930, 8(3), 315–325.

323 ———. Einiges aus einer Klasse schwer erziehbarer Kinder. *IZIP,* 1926, 4(3), 143–149.

324 ———. Mutlosigkeit. *IZIP,* 1929, 7(5), 391–394.

325 ———. A pampered child and his stepmother. *IJIP,* 1936, 2(4), 79–90.

326 ———. Review of I. Jezower, *Das Buch der Träume.* Berlin: E. Rowohlt, 1928. In *IZIP,* 1928, 6(4), 339.

327 **Wittson, C. L.** Ambulatory insulin treatment for chronic schizophrenics. *Psychiat. Quart.,* 1950, 24, 153–159 (with O. Pelzman).

328 **Witty, P. A.** "Only" and "intermediate" children of high school ages. *Psychol. Bull.,* 1934, 31, 734.

329 **Woellner, R. C.** Review of H. W. Hepner, *Finding yourself in your work.* New York: Appleton-Century, 1937. In *IJIP,* 1937, 3(2), 203.

330 **Wohl, J.** The gap between religion and psychiatry. *Insight,* 1963, 19, 69–76 (with W. O'Connell, J. Frizelle, C. Harris, & J. Jernigan).

331 **Wohlfarth, P.** Die psychologische Entwicklung von Dostojewskis Jüngling. *IZIP,* 1935, 13(2), 104–115.

332 **Wohlford, P. E.** Ordinal position, age, anxiety, and defensiveness in unwed mothers. *Proc. 75th Ann. Conv. Amer. Psychol. Assn.,* 1967, 2, 177–178 (with M. R. Jones).

333 **Wolberg, L. R.** Community mental health and family therapy. [Tribute to Alfred Adler on his 100th birthday]. *JIP*, 1970, 26(2), 16.

334 ———. *The techniques of psychotherapy.* 2nd ed. New York: Grune & Stratton, 1967.

335 **Wolf, A.** Birth order, recruitment conditions, and volunteering preference. *J. Pers. soc. Psychol.*, 1965, 2, 269–273 (with J. H. Weiss).

336 ——— (Ed.). *Sources of conflict in contemporary group therapy.* Basel: Karger, 1960 (with W. C. Hulse, Asya L. Kadis, & H. S. Leopold).

337 ———. First born and last born: A critique. *JIP*, 1965, 21, 159 (with Grace Eva Wolf).

338 **Wolf, D. M.** Power and authority in the family. In D. Cartwright (Ed.), *Studies in social power.* Ann Arbor: Univ. Mich., 1959.

339 **Wolf, Grace Eva.** First born and last born: A critique. *JIP*, 1965, 21, 159 (with A. Wolf).

340 **Wolf, H. F.** Die Frau als Erzieheren. *Arch. für Frauenkunde*, 1916.

341 ———. Foreword to R. Dreikurs, *An introduction to Individual Psychology.*

342 ———. *Liebesbeziehungen und deren Störungen.* Wien: M. Perles, 1926.

343 ———. *Das problem der Homosexualität.* München: , 1917.

344 ———. *Strategie der männlichen Annäherung.* Wien: Ilos-Verlag, 1926.

345 ———. *Vorrede zu R. Dreikurs, Einführung in die Individualpsychologie.*

346 **Wolf, K. M.** A comparison of sibling position and academic achievement in the elementary school. *Diss. Abstr.*, 1967, 28(4A), 1222.

347 **Wolf, W.** Review of K. A. Adler & Danica, Deutsch (Eds.), *Essays in Individual Psychology.* In *Amer. J. Psychiat.*, 1960, 117, 384.

348 **Wolfe, Florence T.** Editor of W. B. Wolfe, *Successful living.*

349 **Wolfe, H. E.** The attitude of industrial employees toward hiring of former state mental hospital patients. *J. clin. Psychol.*, 1960, 16, 256–259 (with V. J. Bieliauskas).

350 **Wolfe, W. B.** Adler and the neurotic world: An introductory essay to A. Adler, *The pattern of life.* Pp. 3–46.

351 **Wolfe, W. B.** *Calm your nerves.* London: Routledge & Kegan Paul, 1948; New York: Garden City Publ. Co., 1948. Also published as *Nervous breakdown.*

352 ———. Editor of A. Adler, *The pattern of life.*

353 ———. *How to be happy though human.* New York: Farrar & Rinehart, 1931; London: Routledge & Kegan Paul, 1932, 1934, 1953.

354 ———. *Index of Individual Psychology* [A collection of Adlerian writings containing 6 volumes including: A. Adler, *The pattern of life, Problems of neurosis,* and *What life should mean to you;* E. Wexberg, *Individual Psychology;* and W. B. Wolfe, *How to be happy though human*]. New York: T. O. Warfield, 1922; New York: Dodd, Mead, 1926. Also an index on general topics, child behavior, development, education, etc. (with A. Adler & E. Wexberg).

355 ———. Individual Psychology and the child (II). *IPP*, 1933, No. 8 (with Laura Hutton & Hilda Weber).

356 ———. Individual Psychology and social problems (I). *IPMP*, 1932, No. 5 (with A. Adler, C. L. C. Burns, & J. C. Young).

357 ———. Mental hygiene. *Med. Econ.*, March, 1932.

358 ———. *Nervous breakdown.* New York: Farrar & Rinehart, 1933; London: Routledge & Kegan Paul, 1934. Also published as *Calm your nerves.*

359 ———. The nervous child. *IPMP*, 1933, No. 8. Pp. 34–50.

360 ———. The paradoxic Jew. *IPMP*, 1932, No. 5. Pp. 23–29.

361 ———. The philosophy of Individual Psychology. *IZIP*, 1927, 5(2), 112–124.

362 ———. Psycho-analyzing the depression. *Forum & Century*, April, 1932.

363 ———. The psychopathology of the juvenile delinquent. *IZIP*, 1928, 6(2), 121–130.

364 ———. Review of D. J. Herrick, *Introduction to neurology.* Philadelphia: W. B. Saunders, 1915. In *IZIP*, 1930, 8(3), 358.

365 ———. Review of D. B. Leary, *That mind of yours.* London: Lippincott, 1927. In *IZIP*, 1929, 7(2), 157–158.

366 ———. Review of A. Myerson, *The psychology of mental disorders.* New

York: Macmillan, 1927. In *IZIP*, 1928, 6(6), 508–509.

367 **Wolfe, W. B.** The riddle of homosexuality. *The Modern Thinker*, April, 1932.

368 ———. Studies in contemporary genius. *IZIP*, 1926, 4(5), 291–295.

369 ———. *Successful living*. Edited by Florence T. Wolfe. London: Routledge & Kegan Paul, 1937.

370 ———. Translator of A. Adler, *Understanding human nature*.

371 ———. Translator of E. Wexberg, *Individual Psychology*.

372 ———. Translator of E. Wexberg, *The psychology of sex*.

373 ———. Translator of E. Wexberg, *Your nervous child*.

374 ———. *A woman's best years*. New York: Long & Smith, 1934; London: Routledge & Kegan Paul, 1935, 1946; New York: Emerson Books, 1935; New York: Garden City Publ. Co., 1939, 1946.

375 **Wolfenberger-Hässig, C.** Lächeln und Weinen des Säugling als sociopsychische Instinktphänomene. *Helvet. Pädiat. Acts*, 1966, 21, 197–223.

376 **Wolff, W.** *Contemporary psychotherapists examine themselves*. Springfield, Ill.: C. C. Thomas, 1956.

377 ———. Facts and value in psychotherapy. *Amer. J. Psychother.*, 1954, 8, 466–486.

378 ———. (Ed.) *Success in psychotherapy*. New York: Grune & Stratton, 1962 (with J. A. Precker).

379 **Wolman, G. H.** Birth order and desire for and participation in psychiatric post-hospital services. *J. consult. clin. Psychol.*, 1968, 32(1), 42–46.

380 ———. Birth order and need for achievement. *Psychol. Rep.*, 1965, 16, 73–74 (with G. Levinger).

381 ———. *Contemporary theories and systems in psychology*. New York: Harper, 1960.

382 ———. (Ed.). *Handbook of child psychoanalysis*. New York: Van Nostrand Reinhold, 1972.

383 ———. (Ed.). *Handbook of clinical psychology*. New York: McGraw-Hill, 1965.

384 ———. (Ed.). *Psychoanalytic techniques: A handbook for the practicing psychoanalyst*. New York: Basic Books, 1967.

385 ———. (Ed.). *Scientific psychology: Principles and approaches*. New York:

Basic Books, 1965 (with E. Nagel).

386 **Wolman, R. N.** Early recollections and the perception of others: A study of delinquent adolescents. *J. genet. Psychol.*, 1970, 116, 157–163.

387 **Wolowitz, H. M.** Power motivation in male paranoid children. *Psychiat.*, 1969, 32, 459–466 (with C. Shorkey).

388 **Wolstein, S.** Conjoint psychotherapy of married couples: A clinical report. *Int. J. soc. Psychiat.*, 1966, 12(3), 209–216 (with A. Hoek).

389 **Woodbridge, F. J. E.** Natural teleology. In C. A. Briggs (Ed.), *Essays in modern theology and related subjects*. New York: Scribner's, 1911.

390 **Woodcock, O. H.** Foreword to first edition of Hertha Orgler, *Alfred Adler: The man and his work*.

391 ———. The history of the Medical Society of Individual Psychology of London. *IPP*, 1943, No. 23. Pp. 11–16.

392 ———. Individual Psychology and practice (II). *IPMP*, 1934, No. 12 (with C. H. Bevan-Brown, F. G. Layton, & F. Margery Edwards).

393 ———. Individual Psychology and psychosomatic disorders (I). *IPMP*, 1932, No. 4 (with F. G. Crookshank, W. Langdon-Brown, S. V. Pearson, M. B. Ray, M. Robb, & J. C. Young).

394 ———. The relations between organic disease and the affective life. *IPMP*, 1932, No. 4. Pp. 40–49.

395 ———. The tyranny of the invalid. *IPMP*, 1934, No. 12. Pp. 25–35.

396 **Woodworth, R. S.** *Contemporary schools of psychology*. New York: Ronald Press, 1931, 1964 (with Mary R. Sheehan).

397 **Worcester, D. A.** A comparative study of the only and non-only children. *J. genet. Psychol.*, 1930, 38, 411–426 (with R. B. Guilford).

398 **Worchel, P.** The effects of need-achievement and self-ideal discrepancy on performance under stress. *J. Pers.*, 1956, 25, 176–189 (with K. S. Miller).

399 ———. Ideological change in psychiatric hospital personnel following human relations training. *JIP*, 1967, 23, 98–102.

400 ———. Self concept and defensive behavior in the maladjusted. *J. consult. Psychol.*, 1957, 21, 83–88 (with J. S. Hillson).

401 Worchel, P. The self-concept in the criminal: An exploration of Adlerian theory. *JIP*, 1958, 14, 173–181 (with J. S. Hillson).

402 ———. A test of the psychoanalytical theory of identification. *JIP*, 1960, 16, 56–63 (with Margery H. Krieger).

403 Worsley, A. The approach to the patient. *IPP*, 1943, No. 23. Pp. 28–33.

404 Worthen, R. Social interest and humor. *J. soc. Psychol.*, 1969, 79, 179–188 (with W. E. O'Connell).

405 Wortis, J. *Fragments of an analysis with Freud.* New York: Simon and Schuster, 1954.

406 Wrenn, C. G. Review of J. A. Peterson, *Counseling and values: A philosophical examination.* Scranton, Pa.: Int. Textbook Co., 1970, In *JIP*, 1971, 27(1), 104–106.

407 ———. *Studying effectively.* Stanford, Cal.: Stanford Univ. Press, 1941, 1955, 1956 (with R. P. Larsen).

408 Wright, P. H. Personality and interpersonal attraction. *JIP*, 1965, 21, 127–136.

409 ———. Social interest and interpersonal attraction: Further evidence. *JIP*, 1966, 22, 196–200 (with Carol S. Bidon).

410 Wright, T. Religion and Adlerian psychology. *OSIPNL*, 1972, 13(4), 7–10.

411 Wuebeen, P. L. Honesty of subjects and birth order. *J. Pers. soc. Psychol.*, 1967, 5, 305–352.

412 Wulman, L. (Ed.). *In fight for the health of the Jewish people: 50 years of OSE.* New York: World Liaison OSE & Amer. Com. OSE, 1968.

413 Wurmtöter, H. See Rom, P.

414 Wykert, J. Alfred Adler: A commemorative view of his teachings and impact today. *Psychiat. News*, 1970, 5(11), 8–9.

415 Wylie, Ruth C. *The self concept.* Lincoln, Nebr.: Univ. Nebr. Press, 1961.

416 ———. Some relationships between defensiveness and self-concept discrepancies. *J. Pers.*, 1957, 25, 600–616.

417 Wynne, R. D. A technique for the analysis of affect in early memories. *Psychol. Rep.*, 1965, 17, 933–934 (with B. Schaffzin).

418 Wyss, D. *Depth psychology: A critical history.* Translated by G. Onn. New York: Norton, 1966.

419 ———. *Die tiefenpsychologischen Schulen von den Anfängen bis zur Gegenwart: Entwicklung, Probleme, Krisen.* Göttingen: Vandenhoeck & Ruprecht, 1962.

Y

1 Yamashita, H. Translator of Japanese edition of A. Adler, *Understanding human nature.*

2 Yarnell, T. D. Purpose-in-Life Test: Further correlates. *JIP*, 1971, 27(1), 76–79.

3 Young, J. C. Anorexia nervosa. *IPP*, 1931, No. 2 (with W. Langdon-Brown, F. G. Crookshank, G. Gordon & C. M. Bevan-Brown).

4 ———. Anorexia nervosa. *IPP*, 1931, No. 2. Pp. 41–43.

5 ———. Individual Psychology and holistic medicine. *IPMP*, 1934, No. 11. Pp. 31–62. Also in *IJIP*, 1935, 1(2), 13–28.

6 ———. Individual Psychology and sexual difficulties. (I). *IPP*, 1932, No. 3 (with A. Adler, R. Dreikurs, E. Wexberg, Adele Hervat, F. G. Crookshank, Mary C. Luff, & others).

7 ———. Individual Psychology and social problems (I). *IPMP*, 1932, No. 5 (with A. Adler, W. B. Wolfe, & C. L. C. Burns).

8 ———. Individual Psychology, psychiatry and holistic medicine. *IPP*, 1934, No. 11.

9 ———. Individual Psychology and psychosomatic disorders (I). *IPMP*, 1932, No. 4 (with F. G. Crookshank, W. Langdon-Brown, S. V. Pearson, M. B. Ray, M. Robb, & O. H. Woodcock).

10 ———. The relations between organic disease and the affective life. *IPMP*, 1932, No. 4. Pp. 40–49.

11 ———. The sterility of modern psychiatry. *IPMP*, 1934, No. 11. Pp. 9–30.

12 ———. The treatment of sexual incompetence by the methods of Individual Psychology. *IPMP*, 1932, No. 3. Pp. 29–49 (with F. G. Crookshank).

Z

1 Z. Review of J. Landquist, *Knut Hamsun.* Tübingen: A. Fischer, 1927. In *IZIP*, 1928, 6(1), 80.

2 Z. Review of O. Lipmann & P. Plaut, *Die Lüge*. Leipzig: J. A. Barth, 1927. In *IZIP*, 1928, 6(1), 79-80.

3 Z. Review of L. Mes, *Het voorkomen van Sprackgebreken door oproedkundige maatregeln*. Utrecht: N. V. Cohens, 1927. In *IZIP*, 1928, 6(1), 79.

4 Z. Review of E. Wexberg (Ed.), *Handbuch der Individualpsychologie*. In *IZIP*, 1927, 5(6), 479.

5 Zagona, S. V. Contemporary ratings of psychological theorists. *Psychol. Rec.*, 1962, 12, 315-322 (with R. W. Coan).

6 Zander, A. The relationship of goal structure to motivation under extreme conditions. *JIP*, 1959, 15, 121-127 (with E. J. Thomas).

7 Zanker, A. Ein Bettnässer. *IZIP*, 1937, 15(1), 29-34 (with Martha Holub).

8 ———. Das gehasste Kind. *IZIP*, 1929, 7(3), 230-235 (with Martha Holub).

9 ———. The hated child. *IJIP*, 1936, 2(2), 97-104 (with Martha Holub).

10 ———. The hated child (with Martha Holub). In A. Adler & assoc., *Guiding the child*. Pp. 210-231.

11 ———. Kinderheilkunde und Individualpsychologie. *IZIP*, 1930, 8(5), 502-518.

12 ———. Pediatrics and Individual Psychology. *IJIP*, 1935, 1(2), 70-85.

13 ———. Richtlinien und indikationen für die Zuweisung an eine individualpsychologische Erziehungsberatungsstelle. *IZIP*, 1929, 7(3), 177-178 (with Martha Holub).

14 ———. Trotzphase und Entwicklungshemme im Lichte der Individualpsychologie. *IZIP*, 1933, 11(2), 108-119.

15 ———. Über die Verhandlungen der deutschen Gesellschaft für Kinderheilkunde (zu Hamberg 1929). *IZIP*, 1929, 7(5), 384-388.

16 ———. When to refer children to guidance clinics (with Martha Holub). In A. Adler & assoc., *Guiding the child*. Pp. 47-52.

17 Zannini, J. A. Relation between birth order and being a beautician. *J. appl. Psychol.*, 1969, 53, 149-151 (with P. S. Very).

18 Zavalloni, R. *Self-determination: The psychology of personal freedom*. Chicago: Forum Books, 1962.

19 Zax, M. (Ed.). *The study of abnormal behavior: Selected readings*. New York: Macmillan, 1969 (with G. Stricker).

20 Zax, M. S. Couple multi-couple therapy for marriages in crisis. *Psychother.*, 1972, 9(4), 332-336 (with Esther Kagan).

21 Zeichner, A. M. Alcoholism as a defense against social isolation. *Case Rep. clin. Psychol.*, 1951, 2(2), 51-59.

22 Zeidman, Shoshana. Arelah [Mikre shel tipul ba-yeled be'emtsaut mischak]. [Arelah (Case of child treated with play therapy)]. In *Kovets Individualpsikhologie*. Pp. 128-141.

23 ———. Kavim le-psikhologie shel ha-yaldut [Outlines of child psychology]. In *Kovets Individualpsikhologie*. Pp. 104-127.

24 Zelen, S. L. Acceptance and acceptability: An examination of social reciprocity. *J. consult. Psychol.*, 1954, 18, 316.

25 Zeller, A. F. An experimental analogue of repression. I. Historical summary. *Psychol. Bull.*, 1950, 47, 39-51.

26 Zeller, H. Das Strafrecht in seinen Beziehungen zur Individualpsychologie. *ZIP*, 1914, 1(6-9), 145-156.

27 Zentralausschuss für Erziehung und Unterricht. *Individualpsychologie und Pädagogik*. Berlin: E. S. Mittler u. Sohn, 1927.

28 Zeran, F. N. *Guidance: Theory and practice*. New York: American Book Co., 1964 (with J. F. Lallus & K. W. Wegner).

29 Zerner, T. Die Einfluss der Individualpsychologie auf die Elternvereine. *IZIP*, 1929, 7(3), 190-192.

30 ———. The influence of Individual Psychology upon parents' associations. In A. Adler & assoc., *Guiding the child*. Pp. 84-88.

31 Zilahi, Agnes. The education of the infant. *IPMP*, 1933, No. 7. Pp. 29.

32 ———. Individualpsychologie und Relativitätsprinzip. *IZIP*, 1924, 2(6), 1-10.

33 ———. Individual Psychology and the child. *IPMP*, 1933, No. 7 (with Doris Rayner & L. Seif).

34 ———. Kindlicher Mut und Gemeinschaftsgefühl im Park. *IZIP*, 1930, 8(2), 265-267.

35 ———. Review of Dorothea Hofer-Dernburg, *Babys Welt als Wille und Vorstellung*. Berlin: Paul Neff, 1930. In *IZIP*, 1931, 9(2), 157-158.

36 ———. Review of Maria Montessori, *Selbstätige Erziehung im frühen Kindesalter*. Stuttgart: Julius Hoffman, [ ]. In

37 **Zilahi, Agnes.** Zur Erziehung des Säuglings. *IZIP*, 1929, 7(4), 287–296.

38 ———. Zusammenhänge zwischen Kunst- und Charakterentwicklung. *IZIP*, 1931, 9 (1), 51–60.

39 **Zilahi, L.** Alfred Adler über Amerika. *IZIP*, 1927, 5(3), 225–227.

40 ———. *Alfred Adler zum 60 Geburtstage gewidmet von seinen Schülern und Mitarbeitern der Individualpsychologie.* Leipzig: S. Hirzel, 1930 (with L. Seif).

41 ———. Das Geltungsstreben in Amerika. *IZIP*, 1927, 5(3), 227–228.

42 ———. Die individualpsychologischen Erziehungsberatungsstellen im Wien. *IZIP*, 1929, 7(3), 161–170 (with Regine Seidler).

43 ———. Review of A. Adler, *Liebesbeziehungen und deren* Störungen. In *IZIP*, 1926, 4(6), 393–394.

44 ———. Review of A. Adler, *Menschenkenntnis.* In *IZIP*, 1927, 5(2), 154–155.

45 ———. Review of A. Adler, *Der Sinn des Lebens.* In *IZIP*, 1934, 12(1), 49–50.

46 ———. Review of A. Adler, *Die Technik der Individualpsychologie.* In *IZIP*, 1928, 6(6), 502–503.

47 ———. Review of A. Adler & C. Furtmüller (Eds.), *Heilen und Bilden* (1928). In *IZIP*, 1928, 6(6), 505.

48 ———. Review of F. P. Crozier, *Im Sturm ums Niemandsland.* Berlin: Paul Zsolnay, 1930. In *IZIP*, 1931, 9(1), 75–77.

49 ———. Review of J. G. Frazer, *Der goldene Zweig.* Leipzig: C. L. Hirschfeld, 1928. In *IZIP*, 1929, 7(2), 153–154.

50 ———. Review of E. Jahn & A. Adler, *Religion und Individualpsychologie.* In *IZIP*, 1933, 12(5), 401.

51 ———. Review of H. Keller, *Ärztliche Pädagogik.* Wien: Verlag f. Jugend u. Volk, [ ]. In *IZIP*, 1932, 10(1), 78.

52 ———. Review of [ ], *Kindermisshandlungen.* Berlin: 40, Moltkestrasse, 1928. In *IZIP*, 1928, 6(1), 73–74.

53 ———. Review of F. Kleist, *Jugend am Gesetz.* In *IZIP*, 1929, 7(2), 151–152.

54 ———. Review of F. Kleist, *Jugend hinter Gittern.* In *IZIP*, 1932, 10(1), 78–79.

55 ———. Review of R. Langer, *Totenmasken.* Leipzig: Georg Thieme, 1927, & E. Muller, *Cäsaren-Porträts.* Berlin: W. de Gruyter, 1927. In *IZIP*, 1928, 6(3), 264–265.

56 **Zilahi, L.** Review of Sofie Lazarsfeld, *Zehn Jahre Wiener Beratungsarbeit.* In *IZIP*, 1932, 10(1), 78.

57 ———. Review of E. Ludwig, *Wilhelm der Zweite.* Berlin: E. Rowohlt, 1926. In *IZIP*, 1927, 5(3), 239–240.

58 ———. Review of N. Sylvus, *Lehrbuch der wissenschaftlichen Graphologie.* Leipzig: P. Reclam, 1929. In *IZIP*, 1929, 7(4), 316–319.

59 ———. *Selbsterziehung des Charakters: Alfred Adler zum 60 Geburtstag.* Leipzig: S. Hirzel, 1930 (with L. Seif).

60 ———. Über Gewissenserforschung. *IZIP*, 1930, 8(3), 298–315.

61 ———. The Vienna child guidance clinics (with Regine Seidler). In A. Adler & assoc., *Guiding the child.* Pp. 9–27.

62 **Zilahi-Beke, Agnes.** See Zilahi, Agnes.

63 **Zilboorg, G.** *A history of medical psychology.* New York: Norton, 1941 (with G. W. Henry).

64 **Zimbardo, P.** Emotional comparison and self-esteem as determinants of affiliation. *J. Pers.*, 1963, 31, 141–162 (with R. Formica).

65 **Zimmer H.** Self-acceptance and its relation to conflict. *J. consult. Psychol.*, 1954, 18, 447–449.

66 **Zubin, J.** (Ed.), *Psychopathology of schizophrenia.* New York: Grune & Stratton, 1966 (with P. H. Hoch).

67 **Zucker, R. A.** Birth order, anxiety, and affiliation during a crisis. *J. Pers. soc. Psychol.*, 1968, 8, 354–359 (with M. Manosevitz, & R. I. Lanyon).

68 **Zuckerman, M.** Acceptance of self, parents and people in patients and normals. *J. clin. Psychol.*, 1956, 12, 327–332 (with M. Baer & I. Monashkin).

69 ———. Expectancy and birth order as determinants of affective responses to isolation. *Percep. mot. Skills*, 1968, 27, 279–286 (with K. E. Link).

70 **Zurukzoglu, S.** *Die Bedeutung des Minderwertigkeitsgefühle für den Alkoholismus.* Schwarzenburg, Switzerland: Verlag Gerber-Buchdruck, 1954 (with P. Nussbaum).

71 ———. Unähnlichkeit Quelle von Minderwertigkeitsgefühlen. *Der Psychologe*, 1963, 14.

72 **Zweibel, A.** A technique in group psychotherapy. *IPB*, 1947, 6, 69–70.

73 **Zweibel, A.** Toward the future. *IPB*, 1947, 6, 4.

74 **Zweibel, A. D.** Re-educating parents and teachers. *IPB*, 1947, 6, 54–57.

Addenda

1 **Adams, B. N.** Birth order and college attendance: A re-evaluation of a re-evaluation. *Sociom.*, 1969, 32, 503–504.

2 ———. Economics, family structure, and college attendance. *Amer. J. Sociol.*, 1968, 74, 230–239 (with M. T. Meidan).

3 **Adams, R. L.** Personality and behavioral differences among children of various birth positions. *Diss. Abstr.*, 1967, 28, 1697.

4 **Adler, A.** Preface to P. Friedman (Ed.), *On suicide: With particular reference to suicide among young students* (Discussions of the Vienna Psychoanalytic Society). Pp. 29–32.

5 ———. Zur Massenpsychologie. *IZIP*, 1934, 12, 133–141.

6 **Adler, K. A.** Alfred Adler's contribution to psychology. *POCA*, 1970, 6(2), 4, 14.

7 ———. Discussion [The Adlerian theory of dreams]. In M. Kramer *et al.*, *Dream psychology and the new biology of dreaming.* Pp. 138–140.

8 **Aikins, H. A.** Woman and the masculine protest. *J. abnorm. soc. Psychol.*, 1927, 22, 259–272.

9 **Allers, R.** *Über Schädelschüsse: Probleme der Klinik und der Fürsorge.* Berlin: J. Springer, 1916.

10 **Altman, S.** A didactic approach to structure in short-term group therapy. *Amer. J. Orthopsychiat.*, 1969, 39, 493–497 (with T. A. Leventhal & W. K. Shrader).

11 **Amir, R.** A study of the relationship between mental illness and some socio-demographic characteristics. *Pakistan J. Psychol.*, 1970, 3, 41–51.

12 **Amir, Y.** Birth order, family structure, and avoidance behavior. *J. Pers. soc. Psychol.*, 1968, 10, 271–278 (with Y. Kovarsky & S. Sharan).

13 **Anonymous.** The centennial in journals. *JIP*, 1970, 26(2), 171–177.

14 **Apsler, R. G.** Self attributions and the performance of consonant behavior. *Diss. Abstr. Int.*, 1970, 30, 5062.

15 **Bagby, E.** The inferiority reaction. *J. abnorm. soc. Psychol.*, 1923, 18, 269–273.

16 **Baker, F.** Birth order and fraternity affiliation. *J. soc. Psychol.*, 1969, 78, 41–43 (with G. M. O'Brien).

17 **Barry, H.** Birth order, family size, and schizophrenia. *Arch. gen. Psychiat.*, 1967, 17, 435–440 (with H. Barry, Jr.).

18 **Barry, H., Jr.** Birth order, family size, and schizophrenia. *Arch. gen. Psychiat.*, 1967, 17, 435–440 (with H. Barry).

19 **Barthell, C. N.** Affiliation, birth order and extroversion-introversion. *Diss. Abstr. Int.*, 1971, 31, 4324–4325.

20 **Baudouin, C.** *The mind of the child: A psycho study.* Translated by E. & C. Paul. London: Allen & Unwin, 1933.

21 ———. *Psycho-analysis and aesthetics.* Translated by E. & C. Paul. New York: Dodd, Mead, 1924.

22 **Beattie, N. R.** Community mental health: The preventive aspects. *Comm. Hlth.*, 1972, 4(1),

23 **Becker, G.** Ability to differentiate message from source, and birth-order and subject-sex interaction. *Psychol. Rep.*, 1968, 23, 658.

24 ———. Situational discrimination in repressor-type and sensitizer-type approval seekers, and their birth-order by subject-sex interaction. *J. soc. Psychol.*, 1970, 82, 81–97.

25 **Bedrosian, H.** Birth order, conformity, and managerial achievement. *Personnel Psychol.*, 1969, 22, 269–279 (with P. Dubno & R. Freedman).

26 **Benech, A.** Stages pubertaires, tension artérielle et pouls chez les garçons de 13 ans. (Pubertal stages, arterial pressure and pulse rate in 13 year old boys.) *Biométrie hum.*, 1968, 3, 53–68.

27 **Berkowitz, B.** *How to be your own best friend.* New York: Random House, 1971 (with Mildred Newman).

28 **Bespal'ko, I. G.** [On the significance of birth order in the development of mental deseases]. *Zhrunal nevropatol. psikhiat.*, 1970. 70, 1837–1841.

29 **Bigner, J. J.** The effects of sibling influence on sex-role development in young children. *Diss. Abstr. Int.*, 1971, 31, 6093–6094.

30 ———. Sibling position and definition of self. *J. soc. Psychol.*, 1971, 84, 307–308.

31 Birtchnell, J. Sibship size and mental illness. *Brit. J. Psychiat.*, 1970, 117, 303–308.

32 Bohannon, E. W. A study of peculiar and exceptional children. *Ped. Sem.*, 1896, 7, 43–61.

33 Bornstein, R. Male psychosexual development: Role of sibling sex and ordinal position. *Proc. ann. Conv. Amer. Psychol. Assn.*, 1970, 5, 267–268 (with M. H. Kahn & A. R. Mahrer).

34 Boshien, R. Birth order and conservatism: An Adlerian myth? *Psychol. Rep.*, 1971, 29, 392–394 (with F. H. Walkey).

35 Brachfeld, O. La Psicologia Adleriana et la sociologia. *Revista Int. Sociol.* (Madrid), 1949, 6(24),

36 Bradley, R. W. Birth order and school-related behavior: A heuristic review. *Psychol. Bull.*, 1968, 70, 45–51.

37 ———. Ordinal position of high school students identified by teachers as superior. *J. educ. Psychol.*, 1969, 60, 41–45 (with M. P. Sanborn).

38 Bragg, B. W. Ordinal position and conformity: A role-theory analysis. *Sociom.*, 1970, 33, 371–381 (with V. L. Allen).

39 ———. A role theory interpretation of the effects of birth order on conformity. *Diss. Abstr.*, 1969, 29, 4553.

40 Breslin, P. P. Maternal age and birth order in mental illness. *Diss. Abstr.*, 1968, 28, 4182–4183.

41 Brophy, J. E. Sex x birth-order interaction in measures of sex typing and affiliation in kindergarten children. *Proc. ann. Conv. Amer. Psychol. Assn.*, 1970, 5, 363–364 (with L. M. Laosa).

42 Brown, A. M. The behavior of twins: Effects of birth weight and birth sequence. *Child Developm.*, 1971, 42, 251–257 (with A. P. Mathemy).

43 ———. Twins: Behavioral differences *Child Developm.*, 1967, 38, 1055–1064 (with R. E. Stafford & S. G. Vandenberg).

44 Burtt, H. E. An experimental study of early childhood memory. *J. genet. Psychol.*, 1932, 40, 287–295.

45 ———. An experimental study of early childhood memory: Final report. *J. genet. Psychol.*, 1941, 58, 435–439.

46 Burrow, T. Notes with reference to Freud, Jung, and Adler. *J. abnorm. soc. Psychol.*, 1917, 12, 161–167.

47 Burton, D. Birth order and intelligence. *J. soc. Psychol.*, 1968, 76, 199–206.

48 Carlson, N. L. Occupational choice and achievement of women graduate students in psychology as a function of early parent-child interactions and achievement, as related to birth-order and family size. *Diss. Abstr. Int.*, 1970, 31, 2679.

49 Cartwright, L. K. Women in medical school. *Diss. Abstr. Int.*, 1971, 31, 6237.

50 Cavadas, Juliet. Atomiki psichologia: Mia sintomi axiologissi [Individual Psychology]. *Nea Politia*, 1969.

51 ———. Efthini: I xechasmeni lexi [Responsibility: The forgotten word]. *Tachydromos*, July 10, 1964.

52 ———. I adleriani theoria sti scholike praxi [Adlerian theory and school practice]. *Paidea & Life*, 1967.

53 ———. I gnossis tis psichologias den ine politelia gia to daskalo [Psychological knowledge is not a luxury for teachers]. *Tachydromos*, July 25, 1964.

54 ———. Ine kai diki mas i efthini [It is our responsibility]. *Tachydromos*, Aug. 14, 1964.

55 ———. Introduction to R. Dreikurs, *To pedi.*

56 ———. Min kanis pote gia ena pedi oti bori na kani monacho to [Never do for your child what he can do for himself]. *Tachydromos*, June 30, 1964.

57 ———. O singrafeas ke to ergo tou [The author and his work]. In R. Dreikurs, *Pos tha zissoume irinika me ton eafto mas.*

58 ———. Omades aftognossias [Know thyself groups—A group approach in the Greek tradition]. *Tachydromos*, Aug. 25, 1964.

59 ———. To pedi: Mia antimetopissi [Your child: A new approach]. *Tachydromos*, June 16, 1964.

60 Chandrasekaran, C. Forms of age-specific birth rates by orders of birth in an Indian community. *Eugen. Quart.*, 1968, 15, 264–271 (with P. P. Talwar).

61 Chemers, M. M. The relationship between birth order and leadership style. *J. soc. Psychol.*, 1970, 80, 243–244.

62 Cherry, H. O. Creativity, authoritarianism, and birth order. *J. soc. Psychol.*, 1970, 80, 233–235 (with R. Eisenman).

63 **Chittenden, E. A.** School achievement of first- and second-born siblings. *Child Developm.*, 1968, 39, 1223-1228 (with M. Foan, J. R. Smith, & D. M. Zweil).

64 **Clark, A. H.** Free-play in nursery school children. *J. Child Psychol. Psychiat. allied Discipl.*, 1969, 10 205, 216 (with M. P. Richards & S. M. Wyon).

65 **Clark, J. R.** Adler's theory of birth order. *Psychol. Rep.*, 1970, 26, 387-390 (with R. L. Greene).

66 ———. Birth order and college attendance in a cross-cultural setting. *J. soc. Psychol.*, 1968, 75, 289-290 (with R. L. Greene).

67 **Clark, K. B.** Alternative public school systems. In Beatrice Gross & R. Gross, *Radical school reform.* New York: Simon & Schuster, 1969. Pp. 116-125.

68 ———. Any kind of racism is a constriction of the mind. *Long Island Press, This Week Mag.*, June 8, 1969. P. 2.

69 ———. As old as human cruelty. *New York Times Book Review*, Sept. 22, 1968. P. 3.

70 ———. Beyond the dilemma. In L. Thonssen (Ed.), *Representative American speeches: 1969-1970.* New York: H. W. Wilson, 1970. Pp. 168-178.

71 ———. Black power and basic power: An examination of the futility of black nationalism, and a program for Negro and Jewish relationships. *Cong. Bi-Weekly,* Jan. 8, 1968. Pp. 6-10.

72 ———. Business—The last hope. Bell System *and the City,* June, 1968. Pp. 10-11.

73 ———. Changing spheres of minority influence. In Institute of Collective Bargaining and Group Relations, *Collective bargaining today: Proceedings of collective bargaining forum, 1969.* Washington: Bureau of National Affairs, 1970. Pp. 223-227.

74 ———. A charade of power: Black students at white colleges. *Antioch Rev.*, 1969, 29, 145-148.

75 ———. Comments on significance of first manned landing by U. S. astronauts and Col. Aldrin. *New York Times,* July 21, 1969. P. 7.

76 ———. Contemporary educational emergency in America. *J. Assn. Deans & Administrators of Student Affairs,* 1967, 5, 111-115.

77 **Clark, K. B.** A conversation with Kenneth B. Clark. *Psychol. Today,* 1968, 2, 19-25.

78 ———. The crisis: Attitudes and behavior. In E. Ginzberg (Ed.), *Business leadership and the Negro crisis.* New York: McGraw-Hill, 1968. Pp. 21-32.

79 ———. The dangerous inefficiency of racially separated schools. In S. Goldman & P. L. Clark (Eds)), *Integration and separation in education.* Syracuse, N. Y.: Syracuse University, 1970. Pp. 9-18.

80 ———. The divided city: There are so many solutions—but only one will work. *New York Sunday News, Coloroto Mag.,* Sept. 7, 1969. Pp. 10-14.

81 ———. Efficiency as a prod to social action. *Monthly Labor Rev.*, 1969, 92, 54-56.

82 ———. Equality and opportunity. *Playboy,* Jan., 1969. Pp. 273-275.

83 ———. Explosion in the ghetto. *Psychol. Today,* 1967, 1(5), Pp. 34-38, 62-64.

84 ———. The failure: Three experts discuss it, and what could be done. *South Today,* Dec., 1970. Pp. 4-10.

85 ———. Fifteen years of deliberate speed. In J. H. Johansen *et al.,* (Eds.), *American education: The task and the teacher.* Dubuque, Ia.: William C. Brown, 1971. Pp. 25-30.

86 ———. Ghetto education. *Center Mag.,* Nov., 1968. Pp. 45-60.

87 ———. Higher education for Negroes: Challenges and prospects. *J. Negro Educ.*, 1967, 36, 196-203.

88 ———. Improving the quality of education. In *Teaching in America: Proceedings of the 5th annual conference, National Committee for Support of the Public Schools, April 2-4, 1967. Washington, D. C.* Pp. 94-102.

89 ———. Interaction. *APA Monitor,* Jan., 1971. P. 2.

90 ———. Kenneth B. Clark meets press on high school issue. *Integrated Educ.*, May-June, 1969. Pp. 51-55.

91 ———. Learning from students. *Antioch Notes,* Nov., 1968. Pp. 1-7.

92 ———. Learning obstacles among children. In A. Roaden (Ed.), *Problems of school men in depressed urban centers.* Columbus, Ohio: Ohio St. Univ. Press, 1969. Pp. 27-37.

93 **Clark, K. B.** Letter of resignation from Board of Directors of Antioch College. In *Black studies: Myths and realities.* New York: A. Philip Randolph Educational Fund, 1969. Pp. 32–34.

94 ———. MARC chief sees major role for Joint Center. *JCPS Nwsltr.*, Dec., 1970. P. 2.

95 ———. Minority youth motivation, jobs and technology. In W. L. Hodges & M. A. Kelly (Eds.), *Technological change and human development.* Ithaca, N. Y.: New York St. Sch. Industrial & Labor Relat., Cornell Univ., 1970. Pp. 154–169.

96 ———. A Negro looks at "black power." *New York Post*, Nov. 11, 1967. P. 30.

97 ———. The Negro elected official in the changing American scene. *Black Politician*, July, 1969. Pp. 8–12.

98 ———. The Negro and the urban crisis. In K. Gordon (Ed.), *Agenda for the nation.* Washington, D. C.: Brookings Institution, 1968. Pp. 117–140.

99 ———. Newsreport interview. *Reading Newsreport*, Oct., 1970. Pp. 4–9.

100 ———. No gimmicks, please, whitey. In Urban Research Corp., *Training the hardcore.* Vol. 1. Chicago: Urban Research Corp., 1969. Pp. 102–111.

101 ———. No-nonsense approach to slum schools. *Wall St. J.*, Dec. 26, 1969.

102 ———. Our ghettos are concentration camps. *New York Sunday News, Coloroto Mag.*, Dec. 29, 1968. Pp. 4–6.

103 ———. *A possible reality: A design for the attainment of high academic achievement for the students of the public elementary and junior high schools of Washington, D. C.* New York: MARC, 1970.

104 ———. The present dilemma of the Negro. *Message Mag.*, July, 1968. Pp. 12–13, 32–33.

105 ———. The present dilemma and challenges of Negro elected officials. In K. B. Clark, J. Bond & R. G. Hatcher, *The black man in American politics: Three views.* New York: MARC, 1969. Pp. 7–18.

106 ———. Psychotherapy, social pathology and social change. In F. Zubin (Ed.), *The psychopathology of adolescence.* New York: Grune & Stratton, 1970. Pp. 203–211.

107 ———. Racism for the UUA? *Register-Leader*, May, 1968. Pp. 11–12.

108 **Clark, K. B.** *A relevant war against poverty: A study of community action programs and observable social change.* New York: MARC, 1968 (with Jeannette Hopkins).

109 ———. The search for identity. *Ebony*, Aug., 1967. Pp. 39–42.

110 ———. Sex, status and underemployment of the Negro male. In A. M. Ross & H. Hill (Eds.), *Employment, race and poverty.* New York: Harcourt, Brace & World, 1967. Pp. 138–148.

111 ———. Social conflict and problems of mental health. *J. Relig. & Hlth*, 1969, 8, 217–225.

112 ———. [Statement for *Manhattan Tribune* commemorative issue on the anniversary of Dr. Martin Luther King's death]. March 31, 1969.

113 ———. Toward a defense of "non-relevant" education. *Amherst Alumni News*, July, 1969. Pp. 10–13.

114 ———. Unstructuring education. In *New relationships in instructional television.* Washington, D. C.: Education Media Council, n.d.

115 ———. What business can do for the Negro. *Nation's Business*, Oct., 1967. Pp. 67–70.

116 ———. What's happening to America? *Urban Crisis Monitor*, Aug. 5, 1968. Pp. 12–13.

117 ———. Where it's at: Civil rights. *Vogue*, Apr. 1, 1968. Pp. 178–179, 250.

118 **Cleland, C. C.** Birth order and mental deficiency in institutionalized retardates. *Rev. Interamer. Psicol.*, 1968, 2, 121–133 (with B. N. Phillips).

119 ———. Birth-order and ruralism as potential determinants of attendent tenure. *Amer. J. ment. Defic.*, 1967, 72, 428–434 (with S. Seitz & W. E. Patton).

120 **Clum, G. A.** Sibling position as a factor in psychiatric illness and prognosis in a military population. *J. clin. Psychol.*, 1970, 26, 271–274 (with M. J. Clum).

121 **Clum, M. J.** Sibling position on as a factor in psychiatric illness and prognosis in a military population. *J. clin. Psychol.*, 1970, 26, 271–274 (with G. A. Clum).

122 **Collard, R. R.** Social and play responses of first-born and later-born infants in an unfamiliar situation. *Child Developm.*, 1968, 39, 325–334.

123 Costiloe, T. M. Ordinal position in sibship and mother's R. H. status among psychological clinic patients. *Amer. J. ment. Defic.*, 1969, 74, 10–16.

124 Culver, C. M. Birth order and spatial-perceptual ability: Negative note. *Percep. mot. Skills*, 1969, 28, 301–302 (with F. Dunham).

125 Datta, L. Birth order and potential scientific creativity. *Sociom.*, 1968, 31, 76–88.

126 De Avila, B. E. Birth order differences: An attempt to isolate conditions under which they occur. *Diss. Abstr. Int.*, 1970, 30, 4547.

127 De Fee, J. F. Children's fear in a dental situation as a function of birth order. *J. gen. Psychol.*, 1969, 115, 253–255 (with P. Himelstein).

128 Denham, B. The problem of birth order and schizophrenia: A negative conclusion. *Brit. J. Psychiat.*, 1969, 115, 659–678 (with L. Erlenmeyer-Kimling & E. Van Den Bosch).

129 Dickson, R. M. A descriptive study of the relationship between specific personality factors and ordinal position in the family. *Diss. Abstr.*, 1969, 29, 4278–4279.

130 Dimond, R. E. Race, sex, ordinal position of birth, and self-disclosure in high school students. *Psychol. Rep.*, 1969, 25, 235–238 (with D. T. Heilkamp).

131 Dreikars, R. Perspectives of delinquency prevention. *J. correc. Psychol.*, 1957, 2, 1–9. Also in *Child guidance and education.* Pp. 59–63.

132 ———. *Pos tha zissoume irinike me tom eafto mas* [How to get along with yourself]. Athens: Kedros, 1972.

133 Dubno, P. Birth order, conformity, and managerial achievement. *Personnel Psychol.*, 1969, 22, 269–279 (with H. Bedrosian & R. Freedman).

134 ———. Birth order, educational achievement, and managerial attainment. *Personnel Psychol.*, 1971, 24 63–70 (with R. Freedman).

135 Dunham, F. Birth order and spatial-perceptual ability: Negative note. *Percep. mot. Skills*, 1969, 28, 301–302 (with C. M. Culver).

136 Eisenman, R. Creativity, authoritarianism, and birth order. *J. soc. Psychol.*, 1970, 80, 233–235 (with H. O. Cherry).

137 ———. Birth order, insolence, socialization, intelligence, and complexity-simplicity preferences. *J. gen. Psychol.*, 1968, 78, 61–64.

138 Eisenman, R. Birth order, sex, perception and production of complexity. *J. soc. Psychol.*, 1969, 79, 113–119 (with P. Johnson).

139 ———. Birth order, sex, self-esteem, and prejudice against the physically disabled. *J. Psychol.*, 1970, 75, 147–155.

140 ———. Creativity, birth order and preference for symmetry. *J. consult. clin. Psychol.*, 1970, 34, 275–280 (with N. R. Schussell).

141 ———. Personality and demography in complexity-simplicity. *J. consult. clin. Psychol.*, 1968, 32, 140–143.

142 ———. Teaching about the authoritarian personality: Effects on moral judgment. *Psychol. Rec.*, 1970, 20, 33–40.

143 Elliott, D. H. Effects of birth order and age on aspiration level. *Proc. ann. Conv. Amer. Psychol. Assn.*, 1970, 5, 369–370 (with J. L. Elliott).

144 Elliott, J. L. Effects of birth order and age on aspiration level. *Proc. ann. Conv. Amer. Psychol. Assn.*, 1970, 5, 369–370 (with D. H. Elliott).

145 Emerson, R. W. Compensation. In *Essays.* New York: Crowell, 1961.

146 Erlenmeyer-Kimling, L. The problem of birth order and schizophrenia: A negative conclusion. *Brit. J. Psychiat.*, 1969, 115, 659–678 (with B. Denham & E. Van Den Bosch).

147 Farley, F. H. Birth order and expressed fear. *Proc. Ann. Conv. Amer. Psychol. Assn.*, 1971, 6, 239–240 (with W. L. Mealiea).

148 Farnsworth, P. R. Further data on the Adlerian theory of artistry. *J. gen. Psychol.*, 1941, 24, 447–450.

149 Faterson, H. F. Organic inferiority and the inferiority attitude. *J. soc. Psychol.*, 1931, 2, 87–101.

150 Fentiman, J. R. Population of the 1967 Youth Research Congress. *Charac. Potential*, 1969, 4, 46–51.

151 Finneran, J. A. Birth order in relation to affiliation in male psychiatric patients. *Diss. Abstr.*, 1969, 29, 3910–3911.

152 Flores, L. Sibling position of Phillipine psychiatric patients. *J. soc. Psychol.*, 1969, 77, 135–137 (with L. Sechrest).

153 Foan, M. School achievement of first- and second-born siblings. *Child Developm.*, 1968, 39, 1223–1228 (with E. A.

Chittenden, J. R. Smith, & D. M. Zweil).

154 Forbes, G. B. Fraternity or sorority membership and birth order: Sex differences and problems of reliability. *J. soc. Psychol.*, 1970, 82, 277–278.

155 ———. Smoking behavior and birth order. *Psychol. Rep.*, 1970, 26, 766.

156 Frankel, J. J. The relation of a specific family constellation and some personality characteristics of children. *Diss. Abstr.*, 1967, 28, 2506.

157 Frankl, V. E. Über Laienpsychotherapie. *Oester. Ärztztschr.*, 1949, 10, 3.

158 Frauenfelder, K. J. Ordinal position, sex of sibling, sex, and personal preferences in a group of eighteen-year-olds. *J. consult. clin. Psychol.*, 1970, 35, 122–125 (with H. Heath & M. I. Oberlander).

159 ———. The relationship of ordinal position and sex to interest patterns. *J. genet. Psychol.*, 1971, 119, 29–36 (with H. Heath & M. I. Oberlander).

160 Freedman, R. Birth order, conformity, and achievement. *Personnel Psychol.*, 1969, 22, 269–279 (with H. Bedrosian & P. Dubno).

161 ———. Birth order, educational achievement, and managerial attainment. *Personnel Psychol.*, 1971, 24, 63–70 (with P. Dubno).

162 Freudenberg, Sophie. Aufpassung. *IZIP*, 1930, 8(1), 93–97.

163 Friedman, Alice R. [Alfred Adler Centennial]. *J. clin. Issues in Psychol.*, Mar., 1970.

164 ———. Wie macht man Mut? *Psychol. Menschenkenntnis*, 1964.

165 Geis, H. J. Guilt feelings and inferiority feelings: An experimental comparison. *Diss. Abstr.*, 1966, 13, 8515.

166 Gibson, W. Double speak. *IPNL*, 1972, 21 (6), 106–107.

167 Goldstein, [   ]. Moderne Methoden in de Psychotherapie. *MNWIP*, 1971, 22(1),

168 Gordon, K. K. Birth order, achievement, and blood chemistry levels among college nursing students. *Nurs. Res.*, 1967, 16, 234–236 (with R. E. Gordon).

169 Gordon, R. E. Birth order, achievement, and blood chemistry levels among college nursing students. *Nurs. Res.*, 1967, 16, 234–236 (with K. K. Gordon).

170 Gordon, T. J. Environmental correlates of certain conceptual and social developments in preschool children. *Diss. Abstr. Int.*, 1971, 31, 4993–4994.

171 Gormly, R. Birth order, family size and psychological masculinity-femininity. *Proc. ann. Conv. Amer. Psychol. Assn.*, 1968, 3, 165–166.

172 Greenberg, M. S. Role playing: An alternative to deception? *J. Pers. soc. Psychol.*, 1967, 7(2, Part 1), 152–157.

173 Greenberg, R. A. The sexes of consecutive sibs in human sibships. *Hum. Biol.*, 1967, 39, 374–404 (with C. White).

174 Greenberger, E. Assessment of curiosity in children: A new procedure and some preliminary findings. *Proc. ann. Conv. Amer. Psychol. Assn.*, 1969, 4, 389–390.

175 Greene, R. L. Adler's theory of birth order. *Psychol. Rep.*, 1970, 26, 387–390 (with J. R. Clark).

176 Gross, O. *Über psychopathologische Minderwertigkeiten.*   , 1909.

177 Grosz, H. J. The depression-prone and the depression-resistant sibling: A follow-up note on marital state. *Brit, J. Psychiat.*, 1968, 114, 1559–1560.

178 ———. The depression-prone and the depression-resistant sibling: A study of 650 three-sibling families. *Brit. J. Psychiat.*, 1968, 114, 1555–1558.

179 Hall, G. S. Anger as a primary emotion. *J. abnorm. soc. Psychol.*, 1915, 10, 81–87.

180 ———. A synthetic genetic study of fear. *Amer. J. Psychol.*, 1914, 25, 149–200, 321–392.

181 Hamid, P. N. Birth order and family schemata. *Percep. mot. Skills*, 1970, 31, 807–810.

182 Hancock, F. T. An empirical investigation of the relationships of ordinal position, sex, and sex of sibling to socialization personality and choice behavior among adolescents in one- and two-child families. *Diss. Abstr.*, 1967, 28, 781–782.

183 Hare, A. P. Social correlates of autonomy for Nigerian university students. *J. soc. Psychol.*, 1968, 76, 163–168 (with R. T. Hare).

184 Hare, E. H. Birth order and family size: Bias caused by changes in birth rate. *Brit. J. Psychiat.*, 1969, 115, 647–657 (with J. S. Price).

185 ———. Birth rank in schizophrenia: With a consideration of the bias due to changes in birth rate. *Brit. J. Psychiat.*, 1970, 116, 409–420 (with J. S. Price).

186 **Hare, R. T.** Social correlates of autonomy for Nigerian university students. *J. soc. Psychol.*, 1968, 76, 163–168 (with A. P. Hare).

187 **Harris, I. D.** Birth order and responsibility. *J. Marr. Fam.*, 1968, 30, 427–432 (with K. I. Howard).

188 **Hartnett, J. J.** Some neglected aspects of group risk taking, *Diss. Abstr. Int.*, 1971, 32(1–A), 535–536.

189 **Harwood, B. T.** Expressed preferences for information seeking behavior and their relationship to birth order. *Diss. Abstr. Int.*, 1971, 31, 4313.

190 **Havassy-de Avila, B.** A critical review of the approach to birth order research. *Canad. Psychologist*, 1971, 12, 262–305.

191 **Haywood, C. H., Jr.,** Individual differences in reaction to psychological stress. *Diss. Abstr.*, 1969, 29, 3912.

192 **Heath, H.** Ordinal position, sex of sibling, sex, and personal preferences in a group of eighteen-year olds. *J. consult. clin. Psychol.*, 1970, 35, 122–125 (with K. J. Frauenfelder & M. I. Oberlander).

193 ———. The relationship of ordinal position and sex to interest patterns. *J. genet. Psychol.*, 1971, 119, 29–36 (with K. J. Frauenfelder & M. I. Oberlander).

194 **Hellkamp, D. T.** Race, sex, ordinal position of birth, and self-disclosure in high school students. *Psychol. Rep.*, 1969, 25, 235–238 (with R. E. Dimond).

195 **Himelstein, P.** Children's fear in a dental situation as a function of birth order. *J. gen. Psychol.*, 1969, 115, 253–255 (with J. F. De Fee).

196 **Hinscelwood, R. D.** Schizophrenic birth order: The last but one position. *Nature*, 1968, 220, 490.

197 ———. The evidence for a birth order factor in schizophrenia. *Brit. J. Psychiat.*, 1970, 117, 293–301.

198 **Hopkins, Jeanette.** *A relevant war against poverty: A study of community action programs and observable social change.* New York: MARC, 1958 (with K. B. Clark).

199 **Houlihan, K.** Family size and birth order as determinants of scholastic aptitude and achievement in a sample of eighth graders. *J. consult. clin. Psychol.*, 1970, 34, 19–21 (with J. Jackson, N. Jenkin & M. I. Oberlander).

200 **Howard, K. I.** Dimensions of the family concept in relation to emotional disorder and family position. *Proc. ann. Conv. Amer. Psychol. Assn.*, 1971, 6, 451–452 (with M. T. O'Mahoney & F. Van der Veen).

201 ———. Birth order and responsibility. *J. Marr. Fam.*, 1968, 30, 427–432 (with I. D. Harris).

202 **Innes, J. M.** Paired-associate learning as influenced by birth order and the presence of others. *Psychonom. Sci.*, 1969, 16, 109–110 (with J. E. Sambrooks).

203 **Jackson, J.** Family size and birth order as determinants of scholastic aptitudes and achievement in a sample of eighth graders. *J. consult. clin. Psychol.*, 1970, 34, 19–21 (with K. Houlihan, N. Jenkin & M. I. Oberlander).

204 **Jacoby, H.** Preface to O. Rühle, *Baupläne für eine neue Gesellschaft.*

205 **Jacoby, J.** Birth rank and pre-experimental anxiety. *J. soc. Psychol.*, 1968, 76, 9–11.

206 ———. Situational anxiety and birth order as determinants of dogmatism and authoritarianism. *Diss. Abstr.*, 1967, 27, 4338–4339.

207 **James, W. H.** Central nervous system malformation, still births, maternal age and birth order. *Ann. human. Genet.*, 1969, 32, 223–236.

208 **Jamieson, B. D.** The influences of birth order, family size, and sex differences on risk-taking behavior. *Brit. J. soc. clin. Psychol.*, 1969, 8, 1–8.

209 **Jenkin, N.** Family size and birth order as determinants of scholastic aptitudes and achievement in a sample of eighth graders. *J. consult. clin. Psychol.*, 1970, 34, 19–21 (with K. Houlihan, J. Jackson & M. I. Oberlander).

210 **Jordan, Elizabeth.** His inferiority complex. *Boston Herald*, July 10, 1927.

211 **Juhasz, A. M.** Background factors, extent of sex knowledge and source of sex information. *J. Sch. Hlth.*, 1969, 39(1), 32–39.

212 **Kahn, M. H.** Male psychosexual development: Role of sibling sex and ordinal position. *Proc. ann. Conv. Amer. Psychol. Assn.*, 1970, 5, 267–268 (with R. Bornstein & A. R. Mahrer).

213 **Katz, D.** *Gespräche mit Kindern.* Berlin: J. Springer, 1928 (with Rosa Katz).

214 **Katz, Rosa.** *Gespräche mit Kindern*. Berlin: J. Springer, 1928 (with D. Katz).

215 **Kling, L.** Adler comme je le vois. *BISFPA*, 1970, No. 7. Pp. 12–14.

216 **Knopf, Olga.** Preliminary report on personality studies in 36 Migraine Patients. *J. Nerv. Ment. Dis.*, 1935, 82, 270–286, 400–415.

217 **Koller, K. M.** Parental deprivation, family background and female delinquency. *Brit. J. Psychiat.*, 1971, 118, 319–327.

218 **Kovarsky, Y.** Birth order, family structure, and avoidance behavior. *J. Pers. soc. Psychol.*, 1968, 10, 271–278 (with Y. Amir & S. Sharan).

219 **Kramer, Hilda C.** Orthogenesis of anxiety. *Nerv. Child.*, 1946, 5(1), 25–36.

220 **Lally, J. R.** A study of the scores of trained and untrained twelve-month old environmentally deprived infants on the "Griffiths Mental Developmental Scale." *Diss. Abstr. Int.*, 1969, 30, 587.

221 **Landers, D. M.** Sibling-sex-status and ordinal position effects on females' sport participation and interests. *J. soc. Psychol.*, 1970, 80, 247–248.

222 **Landy, F.** Father-absence effects in families of different sibling compositons. *Child Developm.*, 1968, 39, 1213–1221 (with B. G. Rosenberg & B. Sutton-Smith).

223 **Laosa, L. M.** Sex x birth-order interaction in measures of sex typing and affiliation in kindergarten children. *Proc. ann. Conv. Amer. Psychol. Assn.*, 1970, 5, 363–364 (with J. E. Brophy).

224 **Leanza, V. F.** Tension in the adjustment of normal siblings of mildly retarded children. *Diss. Abstr. Int.*, 1970, 31, 2739.

225 **Le May, M. L.** Birth order and scholastic aptitude and achievement. *J. consult. clin. Psychol.*, 1970, 34, 287.

226 **Levanthal, G. S.** Influence of brothers and sisters on sex-role behavior. *J. Pers. soc. Psychol.*, 1970, 16, 452–465.

227 **Leventhal, T. A.** A didactic approach to structure in short-term group therapy. *Amer. J. Orthopsychiat.*, 1969, 39, 493–497 (with S. Altman & W. K. Shrader).

228 **MacDonald, A. P.** Birth-order effects in marriage and parenthood: Affiliation and socialization. *J. Marr. Fam.*, 1967, 29, 656–661.

229 ———. Anxiety, affiliation, and social isolation. *Developm. Psychol.*, 1970, 3, 242-254.

230 **MacDonald, A. P.** Anxiety, affiliation, and social isolation: Manifestation of differential levels of socialization by birth order. *Diss. Abstr.*, 1968, 29, 1955.

231 ———. Birth order and personality. *J. consult. clin. Psychol.*, 1971, 36, 171–176.

232 ———. Manifestations of differential levels of socialization by birth order. *Developm. Psychol.*, 1969, 1, 485–492.

233 ———. Relation of birth order to morality types and attitudes toward the poor. *Psychol. Rep.*, 1971, 29 (3, Part 1), 732.

234 **Mahrer, A. R.** Male psychosexual development: Role of sibling sex and ordinal position. *Proc. ann. Conv. Amer. Psychol. Assn.*, 1970, 5, 267–268 (with R. Bornstein & M. H. Kahn).

235 **Manaster, A.** Empathy [A poem]. *Voices*, 1967, 3(2), 130.

236 ———. Therapy with the senile geriatric patient. *Int. J. grp. Psychother.*, 1972, 22 (2), 250–258.

237 **Mathemy, A. P.** The behavior of twins: Effects of birth weight and birth sequence. *Child Developm,*, 1971, 42, 251–257 (with A. M. Brown).

238 **McDaniel, E. A.** Relationships between self-concept and specific variables in a low income culturally different population. *Diss. Abstr.*, 1968, 28, 4005.

239 **McDonagh, J. M.** The relationship between familial characteristics and two measures of dependency. *Diss. Abstr. Int.*, 1971, 32, 542.

240 **Mealiea, W. L.** Birth order and expressed fear. *Proc. ann. Conv. Amer. Psychol. Assn.*, 1971, 6, 239–240 (with F. H. Farley).

241 **Melden, A. I.** *Free actions*. New York: Humanities Press, 1961.

242 **Menninger, K. A.** The mental effects of deafness. *Psychoanal. Rev.*, 1924, 11, 144–156.

243 **Molitor, K.** [Suicide]. In P. Friedman (Ed.), *On suicide: With particular reference to suicide among young students*. (Discussions of the Vienna Psychoanalytic Society, 1910). Pp. 121–140.

244 **Mowrer, O. H.** Integrity therapy. *couns. Psychologist*, 1971, 3(2).

245 **Müller, A.** Der Heilweg der Individualpsychologie Alfred Adlers. In L. Szondi, *Heilwege der Tiefenpsychologie*. Bern: Hans Huber, 1956.

246 Nash, J. C. The relationship of ordinal status to sex-role identity, father identification, and self-esteem among university males. *Diss. Abstr. Int.*, 1970, 31(4-A), 1916.

247 Newman, Mildred. *How to be your own best friend.* New York: Random House, 1971 (with B. Berkowitz).

248 Nichols, R. C. Heredity, environment and school achievement. *Meas. Eval. Guid.*, 1968, 1, 122-129.

249 Nowicki, S. Birth order and personality: Some unexpected findings. *Psychol. Rep.*, 1967, 21, 265-267.

250 ———. Ordinal position, approval, motivation, and interpersonal attraction. *J. consult. clin. Psychol.*, 1971, 36, 265-267.

251 Nuttal, E. V. The effect of size of family on parent child relationships. *Proc. ann. Conv. Amer. Psychol. Assn.*, 1971, 6, 267-268 (with R. L. Nuttal).

252 Nuttal, R. L. The effect of size of family on parent child relationships. *Proc. ann. Conv. Amer. Psychol. Assn.*, 1971, 6, 267-268 (with E. V. Nuttal).

253 Oberlander, M. Developmental study of ordinal position and personality adjustment of the child as evaluated by The California Test of Personality. *J. Pers.*, 1967, 35, 487-497 (with E. E. Lessing).

254 Oberlander, M. I. Family size and birth order as determinants of scholastic aptitudes and achievement in a sample of eighth graders. *J. consult. clin. Psychol.*, 1970, 34, 19-21 (with K. Houlihan, J. Jackson & N. Jenkin).

255 ———. Ordinal position, sex of sibling, sex, and personal preferences in a group of eighteen-year-olds. *J. consult. clin. Psychol.*, 1970, 35, 122-125 (with K. J. Frauenfelder & H. Heath).

256 ———. The relationship of ordinal position and sex to interest patterns. *J. genet. Psychol.*, 1971, 119, 29-36 (with K. J. Frauenfelder & H. Heath).

257 O'Brien, G. M. Birth order and fraternity affiliation. *J. soc. Psychol.*, 1969, 78, 41-43 (with F. Baker).

258 Ogara, C. R. [Characteristics and modes of interaction of the family group of schizophrenics]. *Rev. Psiquiat. Psicol. méd.*, 1967, 8, 18-26.

259 Ohlson, E. L. The effects of the female-based family and birth order on the ability to self-disclose. *Diss. Abstr. Int.*, 1970, 31, 2742.

260 O'Mahoney, M. T. Dimensions of the family concept in relation to emotional disorder and family position. *Proc. ann. Conv. Amer. Psychol. Assn.*, 1971, 6, 451-452 (with K. I. Howard & F. Van der Veen).

261 Orgler, Hertha. *Alfred Adler e la sua opera.* Rome: Astralabio,

262 Owens, A. G. Some biographical correlates of assessed performance in some antarctic groups. *Austral. mil. Forces Res. Rep.*, 1968, No. 12-68.

263 Owyang, W. M. Ordinal position, frustration and the expression of aggression. *Diss. Abstr. Int.*, 1971, 31, 6243.

264 Pagani, P. L. *Manuale per l'esame psicologico del bambini e dell adolescente.* Milano: Hoepli, 1971 (with F. Parenti).

265 Parenti, F. *Manuale per l'esame psicologico del bambini e dell adolescente.* Milano: Hoepli, 1971 (with P. L. Pagani).

266 Pearson, S. V. Individual Psychology of phtisis. *IPMP*, 1932, No. 4. Pp. 50-57.

267 Perrin, F. A. C. Physical attractiveness and repulsiveness. *J. exp. Psychol.*, 1921, 4, 203-217.

268 Perrine, M. W. Review of H. Cantril, *The pattern of human concerns.* New Brunswick, N. J.: Rutgers Univ. Press, 1965. In *JIP*, 1966, 22, 128-130.

269 Phillips, B. N. Birth order and mental deficiency in institutionalized retardates. *Rev. Interamer. Psicol.*, 1968, 2, 121-133 (with C. C. Cleland).

270 Prece, G. [Family structure and mental disorders.] *Acta psiquiát. psicol. Amér. Latina*, 1969, 15, 55-65 (with M. Smulever & G. Vidal).

271 Pruette, Lorine. Some applications of the inferiority complex to pluralistic behavior. *Psychoanal. Rev.*, 1922, 9, 32-33.

272 Putnam, J. J. The work of Alfred Adler, considered with especial reference to that of Freud. *Psychoanal. Rev.*, 1916, 3, 121-140.

273 Rao, B. S. Family size, birth order and schizophrenia. *Trans. all-Indian Inst. ment. Hlth.*, 1966, 6, 54-59 (with N. Sundararaj).

274 Richards, M. P. Free-play in nursery school children. *J. Child Psychol. Psychiat. allied Discipl.*, 1969, 10, 205, 216 (with A. H. Clark & S. M. Wyon).

275 **Roback, A. A.** Have the Jews an inferiority complex? *B'nai Brith*, 1925, 39,

276 **Rom, P.** Are you left-sided? *Psychol. Mag.*, (London), Aug., 1965. Pp. 12–13.

277 **Rosenberg, B. G.** Father-absence effects in families of different sibling compositions. *Child Developm.*, 1968, 39, 1213–1221 (with F. Landy & B. Sutton-Smith).

278 **Rühle, O.** *Baupläne für eine neue Gesellschaft.* Hamburg: Rowohlt, 1971.

279 **Schaffer, H.** *A psychologia das profundidas.* Coimbra, Portugal: Atcondida 1963 (with A. Farau).

280 **Sears, R. R.** Relation of early socialization experiences to self-concepts and gender role in middle childhood. *Child Developm.*, 1970, 41, 267–289.

281 **Sechrest, L.** Sibling position of Phillipine psychiatric patients. *J. soc. Psychol.*, 1969, 77, 135–137 (with L. Flores).

282 **Seidman, Rosa.** Review of Martha Holub, *Geschwisterkampf.* In *IZIP*, 1928, 6(5), 419.

283 **Sharan, S.** Birth order, family structure, and avoidance behavior. *J. Pers. soc. Psychol.*, 1968, 10, 271–278 (with Y. Amir & Y. Kovarsky).

284 **Shrader, W. K.** A didactic approach to structure in short-term group therapy. *Amer. J. Orthopsychiat.*, 1969, 39, 493–497 (with S. Altman & T. A. Leventhal).

285 **Smith, J. R.** School achievement of first- and second-born siblings. *Child Developm.*, 1968, 39, 1223–1228 (with E. A. Chittenden, M. Foan & D. M. Zweil).

286 **Smith, S. L.** School refusal with anxiety: A review of sixty-three cases. *Canad. Psychiat. Assn. J.*, 1970, 15, 257–264.

287 **Smulever, M.** [Family structure and mental disorders]. *Acta psiquiát. psicol. Amér. Latina*, 1969, 15, 55–65 (with G. Prece & G. Vidal).

288 **Spiel, O.** Willi. *IZIP*, 1947, 16(4), 186–189.

289 **Stekel, W.** *The depths of the soul.* London: Kegan Paul, Trench, Trubner, 1921.

290 ———. *Dichtung und Neurose.* Wiesbaden: Bergmann, 1909.

291 ———. *Die Geschlechtskälte der Frau.* Berlin: Urban & Schwarzenberg, 1927.

292 ———. *Die Sprache des Traumes.* Wiesbaden: J. F. Bergmann, 1911.

293 ———. *Störungen des Trieb und Affektlebens* (Die parapathischen Erkrankungen). Berlin: Urban & Schwarzenberg, 1912–1928.

294 **Stekel, W.** *Die Träume der Dichter.* Wiesbaden: J. F. Bergmann, 1912.

295 ———. *Twelve essays in sex and psychoanalysis.* New York: Critic and Guide Co., 1922.

296 ———. *Der Wille zum Schlaf! Altes und Neues über Schlaf und Schlaflosigkeit.* Wiesbaden: J. F. Bergmann, 1915.

297 **Sundararaj, N.** Family size, birth order and schizophrenia. *Trans. all-India Inst. ment. Hlth.*, 1966, 6, 54–59 (with B. S. Rao).

298 **Sutton-Smith, B.** Father-absence effects in families of different sibling compositions. *Child Developm.*, 1968, 39, 1213–1221 (with F. Landy & B. G. Rosenberg).

299 ———. Modeling and reactive components of sibling interaction. In J. P. Hill (Ed.), *Minnesota Symposia on Child Psychology*, 1969, 31, 131–152 (with B. G. Rosenberg).

300 ———. Sibling consensus on power tactics. *J. genet. Psychol.*, 1968, 112, 63–72 (with B. G. Rosenberg).

301 **Toman, E.** Sibling positions of a sample of distinguished persons. *Percep. mot. Skills*, 1970, 31, 825–826 (with W. Toman).

302 **Toman, W.** Sibling positions of a sample of distinguished persons. *Percep. mot. Skills*, 1970, 31, 825–826 (with E. Toman).

303 **Touhey, J. C.** Birth order and mate selection. *Psychol. Rep.*, 1971, 29, 618.

304 ———. Birth order and virginity. *Psychol. Rep.*, 1971, 28, 894.

305 **Valdes, P. F.** Translator, with A. von Ritter-Zohóny, of A. Adler, *El caracter neurotico.*

306 **Vandenberg, S. G.** Twins: Behavioral differences. *Child Developm.*, 1967, 38, 1055–1064 (with A. M. Brown & R. E. Stafford).

307 **Van Den Bosch, E.** The problem of birth order and schizophrenia: A negative conclusion. *Brit. J. Psychiat.*, 1969, 115, 659–678 (with B. Denham & L. Erlenmeyer-Kimling).

308 **Van der Veen, F.** Dimensions of the family concept in relation to emotional disorder and family position. *Proc. ann. Conv. Amer. Psychol. Assn.*, 1971, 6, 451–452 (with K. I. Howard & M. I. O'Mahoney).

309 **Vidal, G.** [Family structure and mental disorders]. *Acta psiquiát. Amér. Latina*, 1969, 15, 55–65 (with G. Prece & M. Smulever).

310 **von Ritter-Zohóny, A.** Translator, with P. F. Valdes, of A. Adler, *El caracter neurotico.*

311 von Xylander, E. *Umgang mit schwierigen Menschen*. München: , 1968.

312 Weiss, J. H. Birth order and physiological stress response. *Child Developm.*, 1970, 41, 461–470.

313 White, C. The sexes of consecutive sibs in human sibships. *Hum. Biol.*, 1967, 39, 374–404 (with R. A. Greenberg).

314 White, L. F. Relationship between ordinal position and mental disorders. *Diss. Abstr.*, 1969, 29, 2643.

315 White, W. F. Birth order categories as predictors of select personality characteris-tics. *Psychol. Rep.*, 1968, 22, 857–860 (with T. S. Allman).

316 Woodcock, O. H. The development of In-dividual Psychology in the twentieth century. *IPMP*, 1932, No. 4. Pp. 28–39.

317 Wyon, S. M. Free-play in nursery school children. *J. Child Psychol. Psychiat. allied Discipl.*, 1969, 10, 205, 216 (with A. H. Clark & M. P. Richards).

318 Zweil, D. M. School achievement of first- and second-born siblings. *Child Developm.*, 1968, 39, 1223–1228 (with E. A. Chitten-den, M. Foan & J. R. Smith).

INDEX

Adler, Alfred (*continued*)
   and Mead, G. H., M401
   and Mead, M., D72
   and Nietzsche, F., A885
   and Ortega y Gasset, J., A892, B574, S946, W10
   and Rotter, J., M444
   and Sartre, J. P., B43
   and Straus, E., B647
   and Sullivan, H. S., A1155
Adler, K. A., A781, A842, A869
Adler, M., A168, A799, B205
Adler, R., A842, B17, B524, B536, R418, R424, R476
Adlerian, definition, A1179, B105, D214
Adlerian psychology (*see* Individual Psychology)
Adlerians, European, S409
Adlerian training, M400
"Adlerisms," R254
Adolescence, A297, A434, A529, A534, A535, B230,
   B662, B679, C20, C40, C283, C284, C295, C310,
   D180, D211, E397, E399, H185, M279, M389, N156,
   P9, P47, P48, P327, P340, R108, S274, S441, T49,
   W192, Ad265
   Puerto Rican, M64
Adolescent counseling, D255, G73
Adult education, K113
Adultery, E75, E76, E296
Advice, L233
Aesthetic preference, E39, E42
Aesthetics, Ad21
Affection, A493, A533
Affects, Ad293
Affiliation, F199, G34, S79, Ad228, Ad229, Ad230
Age differences and sibling attitudes, S661
Aggression, A480, A712, B87, E274, E382, L216, M377,
   M406, R230, S28, S80, S1005, W54
   and sex, S421
   children's A635
   drive, A115
Agnosia, visual, A41, A44
Aha-experience, S789
Alcohol, H396, K159, R306, R355
   and sex, K160
Alcoholism, A59, B129, B453, D40, D299, G3, G124,
   G126, K161, K162, K163, N214, R535, S1015, W81,
   W353, Z21
Alexius-song, A116
Alfred Adler Consultation Center (New York), A611,
   A612, D79, D80, D83, D89, D106, P106
Alfred Adler Institute for Individual Psychology (New
   York), L194
Alfred Adler Mental Hygiene Clinic (New York), D73, D79,
   D80, D83, D85, D102, D104, D105, D106, V53
Alienation, A901, E477, N40, S275, S276, S277
   (*See also* Anomie)
Allers, R., A850
Allowance, S711
Allport, G. W., C12, L293
Altruism, M135
   in the rat, G2, G156
Ambition, A30, A121, A146, A155, A156, A157, A307,
   A308, A309, A360, A511, A512, A536, M454, W54,
   W58, W180, W353

Ambivalence, H412, K347, L71
America, Z39, Z41
American Academy of Psychotherapists, E78
American Society of Adlerian Psychology, A671, A672
   A673, A674, A709, A755, A767, A828, A830,
   A831, A834, A835, A836, A837, B547, N23,
   S458
Analysis, M51, M116
Anamnesis, M185
Anarchism, R275
Anger, D47, H118, S1028, Ad179
Angers, W. P., A749
Animals, M268, O111
Anomie, A902, B157, B693, D28, H209, K100, R113,
   R114, S867
   (*See also* Alienation)
Anorexia nervosa, A713, B197, B712, C322, C323, G1
   G118, M198, Y4
Ansbacher, H. L., A907, B809
Anthropology, A22, A23, B87, B88, B647, B765, M53
   W54
Anti-social behavior, K269
Anti-social personality (*see* Psychopathy)
Antithesis, W54
Anxiety, A190, A330, A469, A476, A477, A729, B207,
   C36, C286, D19, D292, E43, F326, G155, J66,
   M152, M455, M456, M500, M513, N111, N135,
   P118, R138, S853, S878, S897, S917, S919, S920,
   S926, W54, W149, W150, W151, W180, W188,
   Ad219, Ad229, Ad230, Ad286
Anxiety neurosis, K359
Aphasia, F425
Apperception, biased, R295, R622
Approach to patient, W403
Aptitudes, L251
Arnstein, E., A793
Art, A1172, B62, G99, G237, H272, K314, L31, P267,
   R14, R449, R469, S22, S1059, Z38
   Lithuanian, B258
   and mental disturbances, S873
   and sex E90
Artists, L169
Art therapy, D533, G90, G91, G94, G103, H122
Ascendance–submission, B166
As If, V2, V3, W27, W54
Aspiration behavior, D539
Assassination, C58, E297, E298, K74, O64, P352, S184
Assertiveness, A686
Assessment, M294
   (*See also* Diagnosis)
Associations, A650, H73
Assumptions, psychological, V38
Asthma, H279, H280, H291, L276, M94, W108, W229
Atheism, G151
Attention, W54
Attitude change, S784
Attitudes, B767, E198, H106, L284
   toward authority figures, C287
   death, C16, C257
   homosexual male, D144
   toward life, R821
   toward Negroes, L281

toward non-parental figures, C136
toward others, P265, S987
parent, B31, B459, J69
toward parental figures, C136, G9, K56,
Parent-child, D140
toward peers, K227
toward premarital behavior, C288, C289, C290
primitive spiritual, B439
prisoners, B48, B49
self-regarding, B499, B500, P265
superior, D12
toward therapists, K56
Authoritarianism, D140, D577, K70, L267, M55, M200,
    S867
Authority, C85, C287, L265, M322, M554, R283, R812,
    S39, S306, W174, W338
Autocracy, D563
Autoeroticism, B643, S914
    (See also Masturbation)
Autonomy, W311, Ad183
Awareness, B202

Babies, R290, R456
Babysitters, S25
Bajor, M., A794
Balloting, C221
Balzac, H., R288
Barrett-Browning, E., S1062
Barrie, J. M., R444
Baudouin, C., R310
Beards, R203, R261
Beauty culture, L256
Becoming, A654, R292, S368
Behavior, S853, W141
Behavior change, N180
Behavior disturbances, S928
Behaviorism, B212, W54
Behavior problems, children, W174
Behavior therapy, E11, M460
Behind-the-back technique, C168
Being, M120, M132, R292
Bekh-Widmanstetter, M., E71
Bellow, S., R332
Berger, A., A257, A260, A324, A486
Bergson, H., S205
Bhagavad Gita, N2
Bible, K356, S493
Bibliographies, A637, S66
    Adler, A., A132, A133
    Dreikurs, R., A851
    friendship, C124
    Goldstein, K., M208, M219, M220
    Group therapy, C170
    Individual Psychology, A787, A940, D223, R296,
        S406, W156
    love, E108, E109, E110
    marriage and family life, E92, E97, E108, E109,
        E110, E258
    military psychology, A929
    sex, E108, E109, E110, E257
Bibliotherapy, G141
Binswanger, L., A872

Biological expansion, F196
Biology, J17, S644, S645
Biosocial theory, G51
Biotypology, B173
Birnbaum, F., D307, S285, S489, S799
Birth control, H224
Birth order, A3, A5, A6, A28, A147, A293, A653, D141,
    G110, G154, H90, H348, L295, M332, P207, P344,
    P345, P346, S52, S202, T86, V54, Ad65, Ad126,
    Ad173, Ad184, Ad190, Ad301
    and academic achievement, C77, F37, H229, J40,
        W346
    and academic primogeniture, A662
    and achievement, B53, B813, F37, K54, L204,
        L360, M531, R578, S50, S641, S941,
        Ad199, Ad225
    and acquiescence, W112
    and adolescent adjustment, P340, R82
    and affiliation, C155, D46, G194, M118, M566,
        R758, S641, S941, T88, Ad19, Ad44
    and aggression, Ad263
    and alcoholism, B46, B453, D40, S664
    and anger, S1028
    and anxiety, B622, G194, S60, Ad205, Ad206
    and approval, B175, M393, Ad37, Ad250
    and aptitude, A667, H27, H198, K344, L360
    and arousal, W123
    and artistic creativity, E40
    and asthma, W108
    and attendant tenure, Ad119
    and attitudes to poor, Ad233
    and attraction, S376
    and authoritarianism, D577, Ad62, Ad206
    and avoidance behavior, Ad12
    beauticians, V82
    and behavior, N195
    and CNS malformation, Ad207
    and child development, J64
    and child guidance, K223, K224
    and children's problems, L197, R106, R760
    and choice behavior, Ad182
    and cognitive abilities, R745
    and cohesiveness, W124
    college professors, F111
    and college students, A663, B71, L163, S666, Ad1,
        Ad2, Ad66
    and complexity-simplicity, E42, E45, Ad137, Ad138,
        Ad141
    and conformity, A634, B93, B94, C26, C27, C28,
        H49, P363, R146, R147, R148, S50, S191, Ad25,
        Ad38, Ad39
    and conservatism, Ad34
    and cooperativeness, R738
    creative writers, B457
    and creativity, H89, L224, S869, Ad62
    and curricular choice, S999
    and delinquency, A1173, L149, N143, S659, T74
    and dependency, S983
    and depression, Ad177, Ad178
    and diabetes, P234
    and dogmatism, K123, S1081, Ad206
    and education, S76, S631

ody defect, H287
  (*See also* Organ inferiority)
ody development, G230, K75
olivar, S., B553
olshevism, A134, V58
orgia, L., R198
oston Coconut Grove disaster, A72
ottome, P., F343, R467, R527, W66
oys, H42
rachfeld, F. O., M302, R490, R511
rain, K174
randes, G., H112
reathing exercises, R833
rentano, F., K281, R19
rodsky, P., B810, G180, R491
rothers, V63
rown, P., R25
üchner, G., R301
ureaucracy, J18
usiness, Ad72, Ad115
usiness psychology, S136, S137, S138, S139, S140,
  S145, S146, S148, S149, S150
uyers, U6
yron, Lord G., H415

C" group, D153
amp, B696
amus, A., R264, R485, R716, S9
antril, H., K124
are, mentally ill, D218, D504, D516
areer patterns, R23
aring, M157
arrel, A., R708
ases, A137, A138, A139, A140, A147, A190, A191,
  A192, A193, A293, A330, A353, A446, A451, A462,
  A469, A473, A474, A476, A492, A629, A640, A692,
  A693, A879, A1203, B30, B104, B131, B730, C279,
  D107, D242, D243, D253, E104, E105, E159, E275,
  E276, E440, H351, H391, H446, J11, L112, L113,
  L115, L235, L236, L270, M67, M72, O120, P115,
  R17, R140, R307, R446, R628, R802, R803, S248,
  S284, S484, S654, S745, S749, S804, S806, Z22,
  Ad288
ase study, E106, F77, F192, H95, H116, H119, H120,
  H123
ausality, A391, A887, A910, A911, B99, D109, D125,
  D227, N79, R162, R732, V116, V118, W54,
  W174
hange, C53, E336, E430, W235
haracter, A446, A451, A462, A496, A558, A638, A646,
  B609, B328, C358, D64, D142, F344, G31, K346,
  K348, K349, K350, K351, K352, K353, K354, K360,
  K362, K369, K372, K373, K385, L301, M270, S147,
  W54, W174, W353
  child, L191
  development, A121, A146, A155, A156, A157, A307,
    A308, A309, A360, A511, A512, A536, Z38
  disturbances, S108
  education, D233
  government, A978

Mexican, B58
  neurotic, A136, A316, A317, A330, A469, A476,
    A477, A497, A498, C355, W214
  study, K282
  talent, A143
  traits, A121, A146, A155, A156, A157, A307, A308,
    A309, A360, A511, A512, A536
Chardin, T. de, H166
Chess, A840
Child(ren), F345, F346, L335, P210, R31, R160, R847,
  Ad59, Ad213
  abandoned, A27
  anxious, C65, C282, D19, J70, K361, S263, S266,
    V76, W150, W151, W185, W187, W213, W223,
    W359
  defiant, B151
  delinquent, A1173, N8
  dependent, O153
  difficult, A233, A297, A312, A374, A393, A400,
    A430, A431, A434, A474, A529, A534, A535,
    A627, B5, B64, B120, B160, B661, B674, B741,
    F395, G40, G72, G75, H129, I10, R820, R827,
    S266, W89, W323
  disadvantaged, J16, W119
  discouraged, A166, W321
  dramatic, R742
  East African, M558
  eldest, A144, A335, A380, A668, B497, C55, C126,
    C376, F112, G108, G233, H97, H440, K130,
    L52, M4, M161, M183, M558, N30, R759, S262,
    S811, S812, W54, W123, W337, Ad63, Ad122
  enlightened, B719
  exceptional, D511, Ad32
  fantastic, K264
  female, C114, D2
  friendless, R30
  German, A934
  gifted, G182
  handicapped, H157, H284, H403, K260
  hated, H355, H359, H360
  homeless, P71
  independent, O153
  Israeli, M30
  jealous, F202
  Jewish, M30, O112, P62
  last but one, Ad196
  later born, W123, W328, Ad122
  male, C113, D2
  Mexican, M31, M32, S941
  middle, H353, N137
    (*See also* Child[ren], second)
  mismanaged, C279
  model, S315
  neglected, A517, B84, B164, R848
  only, A78, B461, B477, C7, C377, D61, F68,
    G228, H400, K88, K130, R778, S1039, W28,
    W54
  pampered, A514, B4, B460, B733, F317, K178, S160,
    W322, W325
  precocious, S119
  problem prevention, B419

Child(ren) (*continued*)
proletarian, K51, R841, R845
refugee, P36, P38, P51
retarded, W220
school age, D175
second, A144, B622, C127, L52, M4, M161, R776, Ad63
sick, L33, R118
stupid, K358
successful, H155
third, A144
troubled, L247
United States, S941
youngest, C376, F112, M586, S262, W54, W337
Child behavior, A280, G113, L162, T55
Child care, F297, F298, P50
Child care center, F355
Child development, A196, D154, D155, D266, D548, G7, G8, H223, K390, M279, P12, R28, R79, R182, T61, W174
Child guidance, A47, A100, A204, A227, A228, A659, B496, B655, D88, D196, D234, D238, D320, D392, D437, D448, E115, E117, E456, F332, F394, G36, G72, G85, H78, K185, K190, K191, K192, K255, L112, L113, L115, L333, L340, L344, R87, R289, S310, S619, S746
Jamaica, W. I., S735
role of parents, A21
school, S834, S835
Vienna, D304
Child Guidance Centers, A311, A603, A604, A743, B266, B734, F296, G35, H59, H60, H387, H393, L133, L327, M102, R80, S61, S718, S887, S890, W54
Vienna, A263, L126, L127, S282, S287, S299, S301, S303
Childhood, A298, A434, A529, A534, A536
Childhood disease, L308
Childhood impressions, S748
Childhood influences, W305
Childhouse, S488
Child life, F434
Child psychiatry, H225
Child psychoanalysis, W382
Child psychology, A283, B29, C23, F210, F379, F380, H167, H408, H463, M256, M396, M564, N21, R84, R810, T61, W284, Z23, Ad265
Child psychotherapy, C128, D381, G103, K48, K71, M449, M551, S906, Z11
Child rearing, A504, A513, A701, A1176, A1195, B53, D219, D229, D231, D236, D252, D262, D336, D339, D348, D499, D525, D532, H85, L326, P158, P163, R182, S250, S261, S272, S273, S1093, Ad56
Soviet Union, A585
Children's compositions, B7
community, R85
conversation, D73, D77
dreams, B6, B8
fantasies, B6, B7, B8
fears, C297, C298, C299
feelings, B59
interests, T62

mental life, A284
misbehavior, E476
needs, A735, D342
personality, E480
play, B6, B7, B8
power, D407
sense of community, A284
symptom selection, A238
Child sacrifice, W232
Child sexuality, S261
China, E19
Chinese, K403
Choice, B213, M162, S617, T40, T104, W11, W54
Christ, S207
Christensen, O., B811
Christian attitudes, S39
Christianity, O72, R193
Chrysostomus, J., L69
Churchill, W., R324
Cialix, R., S90
Civil rights, C98, Ad117
mental patients, S1102
Civil war, O48
Clark, K. B., A732, H32, W32, Ad77, Ad90
Class community, S840
Class council, L228, L229
Class discussion, P172, P301
Classicism, B458
Classroom democracy, S697
Classroom psychology, B799, D251, D273, D274, G213, G214, G215, G217, G218, G219, G220, G222, G223, T26
Client-centered therapy, A630, B827, E128
and Individual Psychology, D247, D289, D290, M410, M411
Clinical inference, H43
Clinical psychology, B706, P96, P126, P205, R123, R798, S1073, W383
Clinics, Adlerian, A611, A612, D73, D79, D80, D83, D85, D89, D102, D104, D105, D106, P106, V53
Clothes, K118, L37
Cognition, O150, R783, S133
Cognitive attitudes, H443
Cognitive change, H65, K119
Cognitive consistency, A4
Cognitive development, P7
Cognitive futurity, K69
Cognitive grouping, R155
Cognitive innovation, A11, M196
Cognitive rigidity, F56, P19
Cognitive structure, H43, R751
Cognitive style, B465, D195, F106, G43, G134, K136, L239, M184, M532, S186, W317
children's, R780
schizophrenia, R755
Coitus, E114, E150, E178, E343
College attendance, C306
College students, G167, G184, S1092
Collingwood, R. G., R277
Color, M349
Color vision, S5, S6, S7, S11, S20

Group psychotherapy (*continued*)
    didactic, K139, K140, K143, K146, K150, K152, K158
    married couples, D86
    military, S442
    war neuroses, B450
    work, D284, D535, D536, J65, K113, P75
Growth, K348, K354, K388
Growth motivation, M121
Grunwald, B., B768, P223
Guessing, B180, D3, R398
Guidance, A310, A556, A557, C122, D162, D170,
    D172, D173, D174, D286, L8, M541, M543,
    P226, Q2
      (*See also* Counseling)
    education, A101, B417, B418
    elementary school, H61
    secondary school, H186
Guidance counseling, A1170, M342
Guilt, A119, A335, A380, E162, E244, M500, S195,
    S495, S501
Guilt feelings, B118, B232, B253, B718, D334, E190,
    F48, R653, S495, Ad165
Gutheil, E., A798
Gymnastics, K76
Gynecology, B264, E21, E22, F4, K313

Habit, B229
Habits, J63
Halacha, K53
Hall, G. S., A892, W304
    and Adler, A893
Hallucination, A159, A160, A548, L330
Hamlet, M47, M48, R401
Hamsen, K., S764
Handedness, A1078, B455, D74, F321, F334, L231,
    P150, R673, R674, W353
    (*See also* Sidedness)
Handicap, physical (*see* Physical disability)
Handicaps, N77, S502, W353
Happiness, S211, W49, W353
Headache, A330, A469, A476, A477, C353, S455, Ad216
Healing, K319, K352
    spiritual, C324
Health, tailors, A225
Health education, A643
Health insurance, L300, L311
Hearing, F419, F423, F424
Hebbel, F., S1107
Hefner, H., E280
Helpfulness, R293, R406, R478
Heredity, K374, L132, W54, Ad248
    (*See also* Genetics)
Hermaphroditism, E377
    (*See also* Psychic hermaphroditism)
Hermits, S802
Heroin, D178, F328
Herostratus, R278
Heurigen, S480
High school equivalency program, S68
Hildebrand, R., A1056
Hinrichsen, O., D39

Historical investigation, M254
History
    psychiatry, A608
    psychoanalysis, A609
    psychology, D554, L260
    world, S776
Hitler, A., R531
Hobbies, W353
Hoff, H., A55
Hoffman, H., R672
Hofrat Eysenhardt, A257, A260, A324, A486
Holism, A658, A971, B835, C139, D340, K329, M106,
    M124, R664, S350, S477, S682, W54
Holistic medicine, G88, N75, Y5, Y8
Holistic-organismic theory, C139, C143, C144
Holland, V., R688
Home education, H96
Homesickness, D137, P302
Homosexuality, A149, A234, A235, A236, A237, A377,
    A379, A501, A569, E85, E86, E119, E126, E139,
    E160, E167, E168, E169, E170, E171, E172, E195,
    E231, E251, E266, E415, F313, G232, H399, K286,
    K287, R515, S922, W54, W65, W343, W353, W367
Honors students, W35
Hope, B444
Horney, K., F268, J35
Horses, S898
Hospitalization, H14, H63, H66, H67, H68, H263, H401,
    H402, J65, K103, K138, K151, L33
Hospital patients, O47
Hospital psychiatry, D151, E454, E455
Hospital psychotherapy, O32, O105
Hospitals, L152
Hospitals, day, B269, B270, B271, B272, B273, B274,
    B275, B283, B293, B294, B304
Hospitals, mental B287
Hospitals, night, B278, B284
Hospital stay, D487
Hostility, B128, P104, W7
H-T-P Test, A1207, B214, B219, B220, B222, B223,
    B226, B227, B228, B243, B250, B257, H142
Huch, R., S219
Humanism, D346, D347, D425, D498, H172, H173,
    M104, M538, M542, W11
Humanistic identification (*see* Social interest)
Humanistic psychology, A894
Humanistic psychotherapy, W16
Humanity, progress of, A282, A382
Human nature, A120, A121, A146, A155, A156, A157,
    A247, A307, A308, A309, A360, A511, A512, A536
    D115, F320, M371, M576, O129, R48, R297, S1059,
    S1068
Humanness, psychotherapy, D540, D541, D542, D543
Human race, S499
Human relations, B554, D501
Human relations training, H62, H65, H66, H68, O68, O7
    W398
Humor, C132, C257, C260, D341, G185, H233, K68,
    L145, L168, L184, O10, O20, O43, O44, O45, O46,
    O50, O52, O54, O57, O59, O65, O80, O92, O93,
    O108, R415, R450, R547, V58, W353

Literature, A560, A771, A772, A1208, B65, B476, B512,
B513, B514, B515, B516, B518, B519, B520, B525,
B526, B527, B529, B532, B533, B534, B538, B542,
B543, B544, B551, B555, B559, B617, B824, C25,
F277, F444, H137, H448, K94, L214, L226, L364,
N188, O123, O125, O126, O128, O151, R245, R246,
R247, R248, R249, R250, R251, R252, R341, R429,
R430, R433, R444, R455, R459, R477, R537, R623,
R624, R670, R672, S9, S174, S213, S220, S223,
S270, S879
Liver disease, A292
Lobotomy, K262
Löewy, I., M142, S163, S498
Logic, C205, S387
Logical consequences, D389, D416, G178, G183,
S43
Logotherapy, F224, F225, F226, F228, F233, F239,
F245
Loneliness, S387
Longfield, B. A., R495
Love, A147, A293, A295, A297, A298, A434, A529,
A534, A535, A962, B235, B238, B530, E89, E267,
E309, E329, E383, E384, E388, E389, G55, H190,
K84, K353, L110, M152, N107, O28, O144, R35,
R304, R717, R828, S216, S239, S387, S1092, W174,
W182, W212, W342, W353
"Lover of life," B143
Lowe, R. N., B811
Lying, K95, L94, S756

McClelland, A. R., A728
McDougall, W., R105, W54
Maimonides, K53
Maladjustment, A64, K271, K280, N163
Malingering, S237
Man, F222, F232, F251, F402, N102, O126, R678, S613,
W183
authentic, E94
models of, D397
social nature, D66
Man-woman relations, K364
Mandell, S., A97
Manic-depressive reactions, A1191, B182, R1, S447,
S485, S610, W94
Manipulation, J68, S633
Mann, T., R71, R72
Marat, J. P., A164
Marathons, A13, A17, A18, E184
Marital adjustment, L205, L206, P331, T76
Marital choice, D26, D237, D506, D513, K114, K116,
K117, K331, K332, T76, W288, W291
Marital conflict, S861
Marital fidelity, L84
Marital resemblance, R156
Marital satisfaction, K114
Marital therapy, P109, P111, P112, P113
(See also Marriage counseling)
Marlowe, C., B555
Marriage, A147, A184, A185, A293, A297, A335, A380,
A434, A529, A534, A535, B549, C212, D103, D230,

D264, D291, D409, D426, D478, E123, E238, E379,
K120, K353, L83, L85, L208, L348, M524, M525,
N47, R828, S855, S909, T45, W54, W174, W353
broken, D343
complementarity, M580
group, E158
sex adjustment, A105
sick, A148
Marriage counseling, A147, A293, A605, C204, C205, C26
C261, C262, E122, E125, E133, E235, E236, E237,
E311, H82, H245, J33, K15, K25, L119, M357, P242,
P244
(See also Marital therapy)
Marx, K., K311, R382, R835, R836, R837
Masculine approach, W344
Masculine inadequacy, H476
Masculine protest, A2, A121, A146, A155, A156, A157,
A300, A307, A308, A309, A358, A360, A386, A506,
A511, A512, A516, A536, A594, A1075, B568,
F319, G204, K101, K323, R362, R470, V58, W54,
Ad8
Masculine superiority, W174
Masculinity, A915, B208, B235, B236, B247, E286, S997
Masculinity-femininity, B241, B242, B708, L43, M330
Maslow, A. H., H31
Masochism, A426, A1192, A1193, B648, S45, S930
Masturbation, E239, E240, E253, F308, W54, W353
(See also Autoeroticism)
Materialism, W54
Maternal behavior, F430
Maternal deprivation, C31
Maternal rejection, N140, N167
Mathematics, A179, A525, A975, B154, L32, R458,
V100
Maturity, K370, M258, R204
Maugham, W. S., B824
May, R., A733, H35, H92
Mead, G. H., A677, M402
Meaning, B88, B89, C371, S135
life, A297, A302, A434, A435 A436, A446, A447,
A451, A462, A529, A534, A535, B723, F236,
F253, F254, P238, V106, W228
world, B420
Medical clinic, T20
Medical curriculum, L29
psychology in, C360
Medical psychology, H204, L26
Medical Society of Individual Psychology (London),
A844, W391
Medicine, C332, C367, K175, K185, K190, M87, S59
and history, C362
and philosophy, C362
psychological, B38
and psychology, A398, G144
and psychotherapy, B687, C255
Meetings, psychological, E93
Meignant, P., S91
Melancholia (see Depression)
Memories, screen (see Early recollections)
Memory, A121, A146, A155, A156, A157, A307, A308,
A309, A360, A511, A512, A536, A661, A884, A987,

B44, B54, B210, B642, C72, C135, D13, D25, D579,
E18, E452, F183, G111, G186, J67, K55, K228, L84,
M35, M255, M572, O133, P335, P362, R22, R110,
S75, S677, S958, Ad44, Ad45
in the aged, B831
early spouse, C261, C262
and feeling, G50
selective, C32, D538, K47, T4

Men
great, W233
primitive, A555
psychosexual attitude, A402
small, V47
Menopause, K4, S486, W76
Mental activity, A213, A214
Mental development, W211
Mental difficulties, A43, P308
Mental health, B676, B710, C51, N165, N168, N181,
O55, P119, R626, R627
Mental hospitals, O32, O33
Mental hygiene, B632, D431, D507, F50, H430, R128,
S265, S271, S650, S908, W357
in school, S839
Mental illness, K234, R627, S1100, S1101, S1103
(See also Psychosis)
Mental life, W155
Mental retardation, A135, A290, A685, B11, B204,
E116, G102, L240, M244, P214, S264, W220,
Ad224
Meredith, G., S879
Metaphysics, P359
Method, B635
Metric system, R395
Mexican-Americans, K30, K128, R107
Mexicans, K30
Milieu therapy, P125, P325
Millon, J., G164
Milton, J., M583, M584
Mind, B260, W54
children's, S270, Ad20
Mind-body problem, A538, C350, K87
Minor, M., A802
Minor psychotherapy, D396
Minorities, Ad73, Ad95
Mirror images, F377
Misunderstandings, W114
MMPI, C248, I16
Modern age, W12
Modesty, bodily, V107
Molière, J. B., L364
Monks, W104
Monogamy, N183
Monroe, M., A897
Mood, W54
Mood fluctuations, W104
Moon landing, Ad75
Moore, G. E., N186

Moore, M., A803
Morality, A652, H174, H175, H177, H178, H179, K292,
K293, M494, N97, N186
and religion, E138
sexual, E144, E255, E305, E318, E322, E420
and therapy, E241, F220
Moral meaning, D52
Moral opinions, R26
Moral responsibility, B578
More, T., O62
Moreno, J. L., A954, C186, C211
Mosak, H. H., A604
Moses, R680
Mother(s), A297, A434, A529, A534, A535, B145, B147,
B689, P80, S795, S929, S995, W54, W174
attitudes toward, S279
function, A221
psychopathology, H454
Mother-child relationship, M288
Mothers' school, L189, L190
Mothers' therapy groups, R93
Motivation, B90, B316, D45, D398, E25, H180, H227,
L147, M127, M131, P161, P229, V75, W241
deficiency, M121
growth, M121
patient, W306
student, T67
Movement, A446, A451, A462, S611
Movements, expressive, A147, A293, A335, A380
Movies, O58, P46
Mowrer, O. H., A734, E243, M453, M457, M461, O22
Muehlman, W., A23
Müller, A., G136, R487
Multiple psychotherapy, A1183, D418, D419, D493, H10,
K106, L274, M222, M348, M425, M426, N169, T24
Munroe, R. L., A852
Murder, O39, S501, T13
Music, A712, B663, B677, B684, D124, D439, D440,
P354, R267, R477, R648, R675
Jewish, R762
in medicine, T35
Music therapy, C21, C22, D239, D240, D275, D276,
D351, D399, D400, D401, D402, D403, D429, D430
with psychotic children, C317
with schizophrenic adolescents, C20
Musical talent, L161
Mussolini, B., A347
Mutism, S448
deaf-mutism, H281, H283
Mysticism, B732, B815
Myth, A1196, L70, M154, S228
Mythology, F444, H448, J21

Names, proper, A968, E143, H434, R313, R482, R512,
R539, R542, R549, R706, R715, R786, S64, S247,
S1038, Ad24
and emotional disturbances, B142, B499
Narcissism, S333, W54
Narcotics (see Drugs)
Nash, E. M., A804
Nationalism, M261

Socialism, R49, S188, S189
Social isolation, C152, Z21, Ad229, Ad230
Socialization, Ad137, Ad228, Ad280
    sensitivity to, A6
Social learning, B2, S275
Social life, W128, W271
Social norms, A969
Social obligation, S817
Social participation, D184
Social pathology, Ad196
Social perception, C244, N141
Social philosophy, public schools, B720
Social problems, A272, D580, W54
Social process, S677
Social psychiatry, F304
Social psychology, L36, M571
Social responsibility, C104
Social science, W272
Social service, B165
Social studies, H195
Social task, A120, A145, A154, A155, A156, A307,
    A308, A309, A360, A511, A512, A536
Social values, D447
Social welfare, D485
Social work, N26, P28, R193, W140, W143
Societies, Adlerian, A671, A672, A673, A674, A709,
    A738, A750, A755, A767, A779, A780, A818,
    A820, A822, A828, A829, A830, A831, A832, A834,
    A835, A836, A837, A844, A854, A855, A859, A860,
    B291, B547, B770, B780, F295, J9, N23, N38, S458,
    W391
Society, B25, C328, F30, H165, S87, S100, S313, S329,
    S496, S497, S807, W54, W161, Ad278
    (See also Community)
Sociology, B55, B563, B577, N101
    psychiatric, E66
Sociometry, C35
    classroom, S417
Socrates, R237
Solidarity, R640, R716, S176
Somatotherapy, O42, S341
Sorge-Boehmke, E., A811, R419
Sorokin, P. A., A826
Soul, A121, A146, A155, A156, A307, A308, A309,
    A360, A482, A511, A512, A536, B251, D18, J24,
    K83, Ad289
    masculine, B152
Space, V19
Spanking, K169
    (See also Punishment; Reward)
Spann, O., B626
Speakers, R711
Speech, F397, F398, F403, F411, F415, F421, K230,
    S988
    children's, E74, S901
Speech disturbances, A1160, A1161, A1163, A1164,
    A1165, A1166, A1167, A1168, F406, F407, M69,
    M536, R140, S901, U5
    (See also Stuttering)
Speech therapy, F404, F405, F407, F411, F416, F418,
    F421, J39, V21

Sperber, H., S164
Spiel, O., B812, R423, S504
Spiritual disturbances, S988
Spirituality, O35
Spiritual life, R806
Sport, D220, D314
Spranger, E., S257
Stagefright, H413, H428
Standal, S., J54
Stanford-Binet Test, S1003
State opinion, R145, R158
Steiner, M., S993
Stekel, W., R644, S913
Stendhal, B65
Stepchild, R829
Stepmothers, W322, W325
Stoicism, S34, S629
Straus, E. W., B647
Stress, D186, H149, M337, R12, S1051, S1053, T51
    and attitudes, K344
    reactions, Ad191
    social, K271
Strindberg, A., F277, S223
Striving, A347
    feminine, M374
    power, A885
    (See also Power; Power contest; Power drive)
    recognition, A207
    significance, A117, S816, W63, W174
    success, A1198
    superiority, A347, A429, A500
Stubbornness, A479, A490
Student activism, A6, A580
Student protest, N159, N173
Study group leaders, S704
Study groups, B745, B794, B797, G116, K62, P179,
    P181, P182, P183, P184, P191, P245, P246
Studying, L50
Study manuals, S74
Stupidity, L336, L345
Stuttering, A1160, A1164, A1165, A1166, A1167, A1168
    B34, C79, F330, F399, F400, F401, F407, F412,
    F416, H238, K288, M75, R705, S24, S121, S484,
    W267
Styles
    cognitive, B465, B702, B703, B704, B705
    life (see Life style)
    neurotic, S361
    presidential, B34
    response, A1197, C254, C318, C319, W6
Suburbs, B158
Success, A1198, B97, B204, D149, D544, E470, G226,
    H115, L217, M195, W369
Suffering, K352, L301, W100
Suggestion, W218
Suicide, A147, A178, A293, A297, A349, A433, A434,
    A464, A499, A529, A534, A535, A864, A874, A875,
    A963, A1064, A1065, D61, D530, E272, F34, F383,
    F384, G46, K65, K66, L199, L201, P223, R171,
    R646, S166, S167, S172, S196, S248, S255, S931,
    S935, V106, W353, Ad4, Ad243